OXFORD EC LAW LIBRARY

General Editor: F. G. Jacobs
Advocate General, The Court of Justice
of the European Communities

INTELLECTUAL PROPERTY RIGHTS IN EU LAW

Volume I

OXFORD EC LAW LIBRARY

The aim of this series is to publish important and original studies of the various branches of EC Law. Each work provides a clear, concise, and original critical exposition of the law in its social, economic, and political context, at a level which will interest the advanced student, the practitioner, the academic, and government and Community officials.

Other Titles in the Library

Intellectual Property Rights in EU Law

Volume I

Free Movement and Competition Law

DAVID T. KEELING

OXFORD

UNIVERSITY PRESS

This book has been printed digitally and produced in a standard specification
in order to ensure its continuing availability

OXFORD
UNIVERSITY PRESS

Great Clarendon Street, Oxford OX2 6DP

Oxford University Press is a department of the University of Oxford.
It furthers the University's objective of excellence in research, scholarship,
and education by publishing worldwide in

Oxford New York

Auckland Cape Town Dar es Salaam Hong Kong Karachi
Kuala Lumpur Madrid Melbourne Mexico City Nairobi
New Delhi Shanghai Taipei Toronto
With offices in
Argentina Austria Brazil Chile Czech Republic France Greece
Guatemala Hungary Italy Japan South Korea Poland Portugal
Singapore Switzerland Thailand Turkey Ukraine Vietnam

Oxford is a registered trade mark of Oxford University Press
in the UK and in certain other countries

Published in the United States
by Oxford University Press Inc., New York

ISBN 978-0-19-825918-3

Printed and bound in Great Britain by CPI Antony Rowe,
Chippenham and Eastbourne

General Editor's Foreword

In some respects perhaps the most fundamental provision in the Treaty of Rome of 1957, which laid the foundations for the common market and for today's European Union, was, and remains, the prohibition between Member States of restrictions on the free movement of goods. That provision (formerly Article 30, now Article 28 of the EC Treaty), has enabled the Court of Justice, over the years, to strike down innumerable barriers to trade, unless found to be 'justified', and to flesh out the grounds of justification mentioned in the Treaty.

One of the most significant exceptions recognized by the Treaty was for restrictions 'justified on grounds of . . . the protection of industrial and commercial property'. The language has not changed with successive amendments to the Treaty—although the term 'intellectual property' is now more widely used.

The exception made for intellectual property was essential, if only because intellectual property rights were still regulated by Member States on the basis of national law; and because such rights—in the field of patents, trade marks, copyright, etc.—were almost universally recognized as being of great importance, not only to their owners but also in the public interest.

Yet to allow the unfettered exercise of those rights could unduly restrict free trade between Member States—the most fundamental of the fundamental freedoms of the Treaty.

In what circumstances then could restrictions on free trade be 'justified' for the protection of those rights? This issue was left—as were so many great issues raised by the Treaty—to the Court of Justice to grapple with. It gave rise to one of the most challenging and controversial range of questions the Court has had to resolve. Moreover, the Court has also had to deal with the relationship between intellectual property and the freedom to provide services, and with the substantial impact on intellectual property of competition law.

The story of how the Court has responded to these challenges is essentially the main subject of this book: in this first volume the author deals primarily with the case-law, which is both explained in some detail and analysed in depth. The second volume will deal both with the legislation harmonizing intellectual property rights throughout the European Union—notably the Trade Marks Directive—and with the legislation creating unified European rights—notably the Community Trade Mark (under the Trade Mark Regulation) and the Community Patent (under the impending Patent Regulation), as well as unitary rights in other sectors of intellectual property.

While that legislation, and its interpretation by the Court and by the Court of First Instance, will be of increasing significance in the future, the case-law of the Court under the Treaty still provides the foundations of today's European intellectual property law. This book provides not only a full and rigorous analysis of that case-law, but also an exceptionally lucid, readable and even entertaining account of its development. The author shows how the Court has developed a complex set of principles—after what he clearly sees as an occasionally shaky start—in an attempt to balance the competing interests.

Notwithstanding the author's robust and penetrating critique, it may be thought that those principles—some of which, notably that of Community exhaustion, have been adopted by the Community legislature—now form a reasonably coherent system. In any event, this book is likely to provide essential reading for all those wishing to have a fuller understanding of European intellectual property law.

July 2003   FRANCIS G. JACOBS

Preface

There are plenty of books on EC law and no shortage of books on the law of intellectual property. There are not so many that deal with the relationship between those two fields of law. That is what this book attempts to do.

Intellectual property is everywhere. There is no escaping it. It would be difficult to poach an egg nowadays without encountering at least half a dozen intellectual property rights. Your stove may incorporate patented technology. It will bear a distinctive sign or logo which will be registered as a trade mark. The saucepan may be protected by design rights and may even have been registered as a three-dimensional trade mark. The hen that laid your egg may have been fed a new variety of corn protected by plant breeders' rights. If you are a true gourmet you will poach your egg according to a recipe by Auguste Escoffier, whose cookery books will be protected by copyright until 2005, seventy years after his death. And if you add a little butter or olive oil, you will surely use one that is protected as a designation of origin.

EC law (or EU law) is likewise omnipresent. An English judge once spoke of it creeping up our estuaries. That was an understatement. It has by now washed all over Shakespeare's sceptred isle and over the other countries belonging to the European Union. Another ten eagerly await its beneficial influence. It brings great advantages: among them, the right to work, travel, and shop all over Europe and the right to engage in trade without let or hindrance in the world's biggest market-place, which is regulated by laws designed to ensure vigorous and fair competition.

Sometimes intellectual property rights come into conflict with the rules and principles that govern this great European market, in particular the free movement of goods and services and competition law. The main task of this book is to examine the way in which that conflict has been handled by the Community's judicial and legislative authorities. In particular, I have attempted to analyse the contribution of the Court of Justice of the European Communities, which I served as an official from 1979 to 1996.

I plan a second volume in which I will look more closely at the work of the European Union's legislative organs. There I intend to describe and comment on the numerous Directives that harmonize the laws of the Member States in the field of intellectual property. I shall also deal with the Regulations establishing unitary intellectual property rights valid throughout the European Union.

I have done most of the work on this book as an extra-curricular activity while serving as a member of the Boards of Appeal of the Office for Harmonization in the Internal Market (Trade Marks and Designs), widely known by the acronym 'OHIM'. Without the back-up of OHIM resources (in particular secretaries, computers and library facilities) it would not have been possible to complete the book. My thanks go to all concerned, particular Udo Henn, Joëlle de Bruyne and Jasmina Hrapovic, who have done the bulk of the typing. My thanks go also to the staff of Oxford University Press, whose patience and tolerance in the face of numerous missed deadlines have been extraordinary.

It goes without saying that the book is my sole responsibility and that the opinions expressed in it are entirely my own.

DAVID T. KEELING

Alicante 26 May 2003

Contents

Table of Cases

EC Legislation

International and National Legislation

International Treaties, Conventions and Agreements

National Legislation

Benelux Countries

Germany

Italy

Poland

Spain

United Kingdom

Table of Abbreviations

Note on the renumbering of the EC Treaty articles

The original numbering of the articles of the EC Treaty was changed by the 1997 Amsterdam Treaty, which entered into force on 1 May 1999. The title of the Treaty had itself been changed by the 1992 Maastricht Treaty, which entered into force on 1 November 1993. This causes problems for authors who attempt to describe the historical development of the law. For example, the judgment in *Deutsche Grammophon v Metro* refers to Article 36 of the EEC Treaty. This has now become Article 30 of the EC Treaty. What is the best way to refer to that provision when commenting on a judgment delivered in 1971? Here, as in other areas, I have found inspiration in Jones and Sufrin's book *EC Competition Law: Text, Cases and Materials*. I have followed their example and used the new numbering systematically, resorting to square brackets when a Treaty article is mentioned in a direct quotation from a judgment of the European Court of Justice. I have done the same when a Treaty article is mentioned in the title of a legislative act.

David T. Keeling

1

The scope of the undertaking

The purpose of this book is to examine the relationship between intellectual property rights and the law of the European Community ('EC Law').[1] The term 'intellectual property' is used here in the wide sense that it has acquired in common law countries. It embraces all exclusive rights which the law grants to certain individuals in order to reward creative effort or to protect commercial reputation.[2] We are concerned in particular with patents, trade marks, copyright and related rights, design rights, designations of origin, plant breeders' rights and certain aspects of the law of unfair competition.

The use of the term 'intellectual property' to cover something as mundane as a trade mark or as arcane as the exclusive right to develop a new plant variety is open to criticism. Lawyers from some countries in continental Europe would reserve the term for the exclusive rights of authors and artists, though none would deny that the inventor who advances scientific progress expends intellectual effort, as does the creative designer. For exclusive rights such as those granted to trade mark owners the term 'industrial and commercial property' would be considered preferable in some countries. While that terminology is undoubtedly more logical, the need for a compendious, all-embracing term justifies the use of 'intellectual property' in the broad sense and explains why it has achieved a degree of international acceptance. As Cornish points out, the expression is used in the

---

[1] The term 'EC law' refers to the law created as a result of the Treaty establishing the European Community ('the EC Treaty') (OJ 2002 C 325, p. 53; consolidated version). The original version of the Treaty (known as 'the Treaty of Rome' or 'the EEC Treaty', since the organization established by it was called 'the European Economic Community') was signed in Rome on 25 March 1957. The word 'economic' was deleted from the title of the organization by the Treaty on European Union, signed in Maastricht on 7 February 1992 (OJ 2002 C 325; consolidated version); as a result the EEC Treaty became the EC Treaty. The Treaty on European Union, which has since been amended by the Treaties of Amsterdam (OJ 1997 C 340, p. 1) and Nice (OJ 2001 C 80, p. 1), created a wider political organization known as the European Union ('the EU'). The terms 'European Community' and 'European Union' may both be used to refer to the geographical and political entity which at the time of writing (May 2003) comprises Belgium, Denmark, Germany, Greece, Spain, France, Ireland, Italy, Luxembourg, the Netherlands, Austria, Portugal, Finland, Sweden, and the United Kingdom. It is envisaged that on 1 May 2004 the following countries will accede to the organization: Cyprus, the Czech Republic, Estonia, Hungary, Latvia, Lithuania, Malta, Poland, Slovakia, and Slovenia.

[2] 'Intellectual property law is that area of law which concerns legal rights associated with creative effort or commercial reputation and goodwill', D. I. Bainbridge, *Intellectual Property*, 4th edn, Financial Times/Pitman Publishing, 1999, p. 3.

title of the UN organ 'World Intellectual Property Organization (WIPO)',[3] which deals, *inter alia*, with trade marks.

Virtually every country in the world recognizes certain exclusive rights: the right of an inventor, for example, to exploit his invention commercially; the right of an author to have copies of his book printed and offered for sale to the public; the right of a singer to authorize the sale of recordings of his performance; the right of a film-maker to show his work in cinemas; or the right of a business to protect the reputation of its goods by preventing others from using its trade mark.

Why do such exclusive rights exist? Before we attempt to answer that question, it is worth emphasizing that there must always be a good reason for the State (or the European Community) to grant an exclusive right— some overriding consideration pertaining to the general interest which justifies interfering with the ordinary commercial freedom of everyone except the exclusive right-holder. Suppose, for example, that the government of Ruritania granted Company X the exclusive right to import, manufacture and sell playing cards or the exclusive right to publish Homer's *Odyssey*. That would be arbitrary and indefensible: there would be no good reason for granting preferential treatment to Company X and for restricting the rights of others.

The fundamental reason for protecting intellectual property is a moral and ethical one: if someone expends time and energy, including of course intellectual energy, in developing a new invention capable of industrial application, it is right that he alone should be allowed to make money out of the invention, at least for a limited period; it would be unfair if some other person were allowed to steal the fruits of the inventor's work. Exactly the same argument applies to literary, cinematographic, and artistic works, and to designs and computer programs. Trade marks may be justified in the same way—if a trader builds up a reputation by producing goods of high quality (and also perhaps by spending a fortune on advertising), other traders should not be allowed to steal his goodwill by selling goods under the same name.

In addition to this moral or ethical justification, other arguments are sometimes advanced in favour of certain exclusive rights. Thus, patents are said to stimulate scientific research by offering the possibility of an economic reward to the inventor (or to his employer); also they encourage the inventor (or his employer) to divulge the invention to the whole scientific community instead of attempting to protect it in the form of secret know-how. Trade marks not only enable businesses to protect their goodwill, they also enable consumers to make rational decisions about how to spend their

---

[3] W. R. Cornish, *Intellectual Property: Patents, Copyright, Trade Marks and Allied Rights*, 4th edn, Sweet and Maxwell, London, 1999, p. 3.

money, on the assumption that if a firm's products have been outstandingly good (or outstandingly bad) in the past they are likely to be just as good (or just as bad) in the future. We all make these assumptions and they are the foundation of effective competition in a market economy.[4]

So intellectual property is a very fine thing. Without it the world would be a much less civilized place. The interests protected by the law of intellectual property are noble and worthy ones. But intellectual property does sometimes have harmful effects, especially if a proper balance is not struck between the particular interests of the intellectual property owner and the general interests of society. In the field of EC law intellectual property rights sometimes come into conflict with two of the fundamental principles enshrined in the EC Treaty:

(1) the principle that trade in goods and services between Member States should not be impeded without proper justification (Arts 28–30 and 49–55); and
(2) the principle that competition should not be distorted by agreements in restraint of trade (Art. 81) or by abusive practices on the part of dominant undertakings (Art. 82).

Chapters 2 to 10 examine the relationship between intellectual property rights and the free movement provisions of the Treaty. Here it is sufficient to observe that most of the problems that arise in this area are due to the *territoriality* of intellectual property rights. There is an obvious tension between exclusive rights valid for the territory of a single Member State and the concept of a common (or internal) market. The task of 'managing' that tension in such a way as to ensure that it destroys neither the common market nor the intellectual property rights of those who trade on the common market has fallen largely to the European Court of Justice. Thus this part of the book will be concerned mainly with analysing the Court's abundant case law. Chapters 2 to 7 examine the general principles established by the Court. Chapters 8 to 10 deal respectively with the application of those principles to trade marks, patents, and copyright.

The Community legislature has also had a part to play in meeting the challenge posed by exclusive rights defined by reference to the territory of individual Member States. It has been active on two fronts. First, by means of harmonization directives, it has sought to reduce the discrepancies in national laws relating to intellectual property, in particular in the fields of trade mark law, designs, copyright, and the protection of computer programs. Secondly, the legislative organs have pursued the more ambitious aim of creating unitary rights of intellectual property, valid throughout the

---

[4] 'Trade marks and names have become nothing more nor less than the fundament of most market-place competition.' Cornish, op. cit. (n. 3), p. 599.

common market, as an alternative to national rights limited to the territory of each Member State. These initiatives will be mentioned in passing in several chapters, together with the various attempts to harmonize and unify intellectual property law that have taken place on the wider, international stage. A more complete analysis of EC legislation in the field of intellectual property will have to await a second volume.

As well as posing a threat to the unity of the common market, intellectual property rights might, if not kept within proper limits, provide their proprietors with a highly effective instrument for undermining the fundamental aims of EC competition policy. Agreements licensing or assigning patents, know-how and trade marks could restrict competition within the common market, in breach of Article 81 of the Treaty, for example by sharing out markets along the lines of national frontiers. By virtue of their exclusivity, intellectual property rights might also make it easier for an undertaking to achieve market dominance; moreover, they might be exercised in such a way as to amount to an abuse of a dominant position, in breach of Article 82 of the Treaty. These various aspects of competition law will be considered in Chapter 11.

In all these areas it will be argued that the fundamental concern of the various authorities—legislative, judicial, and administrative—that are responsible for making and applying the law must be to strike a balance between the legitimate interests of intellectual property owners and the sometimes conflicting interests of other market participants and the general public. The need to strike such a balance is perhaps so obvious that it should hardly be necessary to state it. The fact remains, nonetheless, that the Commission and the European Court have not always found the task easy. Over the years, both institutions have sometimes appeared to display open hostility towards certain forms of intellectual property; and both institutions have occasionally treated certain categories of intellectual property owner with an indulgence that is scarcely compatible with the public interest. It cannot be emphasised too strongly therefore that, however difficult the task may be, the search for the proper balance must never be abandoned.

2

The free movement of goods and services: an overview of the basic principles

1. THE GOAL OF MARKET INTEGRATION

The fundamental aim of the EC Treaty is to fuse together the economies of the Member States and to create an integrated market in which the factors of production, as well as the fruits of production, can move freely, without let or hindrance, thus achieving, over a period of time, a better allocation of resources and greater all-round prosperity.

To that end, the Treaty lays down four fundamental freedoms: free movement of goods (Arts 23–31), persons (Arts 39–48), services (Arts 49–55), and capital (Arts 56–60). Although the Treaty deals separately with these various freedoms, it is important to stress at the outset that they are not hard-and-fast categories and that the distinction between them is sometimes blurred.

There is, for example, an obvious overlap between the movement of persons and services:

(1) A plumber from Member State A who crosses a frontier to unblock a U-bend in Member State B is providing a service within the meaning of Article 49.
(2) If he sets up business in Member State B permanently, he is exercising his right of establishment under Article 43.
(3) If he takes up paid employment with a plumbing firm in Member State B, he is a worker within the meaning of Article 39.

In the second and third examples the Treaty considers that a movement of persons is taking place, while the phenomenon occurring in the first example is treated as a movement of services. Obviously there are cases in which these distinctions are not clear-cut.

Nor it is easy sometimes to distinguish between trade in goods and trade in services.[1] A company which provides correspondence courses may send its students a teaching manual, audio tapes, video-cassettes, and CD-roms by mail. It may allow them to download information from the internet. It may also communicate with them by telephone, fax and e-mail. Is it

[1] See, e.g., Case C-2/90 *Commission v Belgium* [1992] ECR I-4431 (as regards the classification of non-recyclable waste) and Case C-275/92 *Schindler v H.M. Customs and Excise* [1994] ECR I-1039 (as regards the classification of German lottery tickets impounded by the British customs authorities).

providing goods or services? A guitarist from Member State A may give a concert in Member State B, after which he sells compact discs of his performances to members of the audience. Or he may allow the concert to be filmed and broadcast live in Member State C or distributed in Member State D in video form. Gramophone records made in Member State A may be sold in Member State B, where they are bought by a discotheque owner, who plays them in his discotheque, paying a royalty to a copyright management society which distributes the income among the various right-holders.[2]

It is important therefore to treat the provisions governing the various freedoms as forming a coherent whole and to interpret them accordingly. Together they lay down the principle of an open, integrated market in which goods, services, persons, and capital may circulate freely unless some overriding interest justifies the restriction of free movement. Some of those overriding interests are expressly identified in the wording of the Treaty. Thus, Article 30 permits restrictions on inter-State trade in goods on grounds of, *inter alia*, the protection of public morality, public security, health, artistic treasures or industrial and commercial property, provided that they do not amount to arbitrary discrimination or a disguised restriction on trade between Member States. Sometimes the overriding interest has been implied into the Treaty by the creative jurisprudence of the Court of Justice. Thus the Court has held that the cross-frontier provision of services may be restricted on grounds of the protection of intellectual property in spite of the silence of the relevant Treaty provisions.[3] Of more general interest is the 'Cassis de Dijon' judgment[4] in which the Court held that restrictions applying without distinction to domestic and imported goods may be justified on grounds of, *inter alia*, consumer protection and fair trading, even though such matters are not mentioned in Article 30 of the Treaty. That case law has since been extended to trade in services.[5]

Before concluding this brief overview of the fundamental principles governing the integration of national markets under the scheme created by the Treaty of Rome in 1957, it is necessary to mention two changes that have taken place either as a result of the amendment of the original Treaty or as a result of the conclusion of an international treaty by the European Community and its Member States.

---

[2] Some of these issues were discussed in Joined Cases C-92/92 and C-326/92 *Phil Collins v Imtrat and others* [1993] ECR I-5145 at paras 20–28 of the judgment; see also paras 14–18 of the opinion of Advocate General Jacobs.

[3] Case 62/79 *Coditel v Ciné Vog Films* ('*Coditel I*') [1980] ECR 881.

[4] Case 120/78 *REWE v Bundesmonopolverwaltung für Branntwein* [1979] ECR 649.

[5] Case C-288/89 *Collectieve Antennevoorziening Gouda* [1991] ECR I-4007 at paras 12–14; Case C-76/90 *Säger v Dennemeyer* [1991] ECR I-4221 at paras 12–15; and Case C-384/93 *Alpine Investments* [1995] ECR I-1141.

The Single European Act, which came into force on 1 July 1987, added an Article 8a to the EEC Treaty (which subsequently became Article 7a of the EC Treaty as a result of the Treaty on European Union signed in Maastricht and was then renumbered as Article 14 by the Treaty of Amsterdam). The new article required the establishment of an 'internal market' by the end of 1992, comprising 'an area without internal frontiers in which the free movement of goods, persons, services and capital is ensured in accordance with this Treaty'.

Although there is room for argument about the extent to which such an internal market differs from the common market established by the Treaty in its original version of 1957,[6] it may be noted here that the abolition of internal frontiers has one significant effect as regards the application of trade restrictions justified on grounds of the protection of intellectual property rights. Suppose, for example, that goods lawfully on the market in Member State A would, if marketed in Member State B, infringe a patent or a trade mark in that State. On the assumption that the enforcement of the patent or trade mark is compatible with Article 30 of the Treaty, one highly effective way of keeping the infringing goods off the market in Member State B would be to secure the co-operation of the customs authorities in that country and have the goods seized at the frontier. Obviously that remedy is no longer available after the abolition of customs controls. Instead the intellectual property owner is forced to rely on alternative remedies that operate within Member State B, in particular court injunctions prohibiting the sale of infringing goods and seizure orders that will take effect internally (i.e. not at the point of entry).

If the Single European Act was meant to deepen economic integration between the Member States, the Agreement on the European Economic Area (the EEA)[7] was meant to extend the effect of that integration to the States belonging to the European Free Trade Association (EFTA). The purpose of the EEA Agreement is 'to promote a continuous and balanced strengthening of trade and economic relations between the Contracting Parties with equal conditions of competition, and the respect of the same rules, with a view to creating a homogeneous European Economic Area'.[8]

The parties to the EEA Agreement, which came into force on 1 January 1994, were the European Community and its Member States, on the one hand, and the EFTA States—Austria, Finland, Iceland, Liechtenstein, Norway, Sweden, and Switzerland—on the other. Of the latter, Austria, Finland and Sweden have since acceded to the European Community, while

---

[6] See. e.g., P. Pescatore, 'Die einheitliche Europäische Akte. Eine ernste Gefahr für den Gemeinsamen Markt' (1986) 21 EuR 153, and 'Some critical remarks on the Single European Act' (1987) 24 CML Rev. 9.

[7] OJ 1994 L 1, p. 3.   [8] EEA Agreement, Art. 1.

Switzerland decided after a referendum not to join the EEA.[9] Thus, the 'economic area' created by the EEA Treaty consists of the territory of the EC Member States and that of Iceland, Liechtenstein, and Norway.

The EEA Agreement extends to the new economic area the principles of the free movement of goods, persons, services, and capital, in terms drawn verbatim from the corresponding articles of the EC Treaty. The main differences are that the EEA rules generally apply only to products originating in the contracting States[10] and do not apply to agricultural products except those that are expressly named.[11]

A protocol to the Agreement (Protocol No. 28)[12] deals specifically with intellectual property rights.

2. THE EC TREATY PROVISIONS ON THE FREE MOVEMENT OF GOODS AND SERVICES

2.1 *Goods*

Title I of Part Three of the EC Treaty is devoted in its entirety to the free movement of goods. Title I is divided into two chapters (in addition to the introductory Arts 23 and 24). Chapter 1 (Arts 25–27) is entitled 'The Customs Union' and provides for the elimination of customs duties between Member States and the establishment of a common customs tariff applicable to goods imported from non-member countries. Chapter 2 (Arts 28–31) provides for the elimination of quantitative restrictions on trade between Member States.

Little need be said here about the Customs Union. It is sufficient to note that under Article 25 no customs duties, or charges having equivalent effect, may be levied on imports or exports of goods in trade between Member States.

The term 'customs duties' does not in practice give rise to difficulties. The concept of charges having equivalent effect to customs duties has often been the subject of litigation. The European Court of Justice has always opted for a broad definition of that concept. In *Sociaal Fonds voor de Diamantarbeiders v Brachfeld*[13] the Court said that:

. . . any pecuniary charge, however small and whatever its designation and mode of application, which is imposed unilaterally on domestic or foreign goods by reason

---

[9] See the Protocol of 17 March 1993 adjusting the Agreement on the European Economic Area; OJ 1994 L 1, p. 572.
[10] EEA Agreement, Art. 8(2).
[11] EEA Agreement, Art. 8(3)(b), and Protocol No. 3 to the Agreement.
[12] OJ 1994 L 1, p. 194.
[13] Joined Cases 2 and 3/69 [1969] ECR 211.

of the fact that they cross a frontier, and which is not a customs duty in the strict sense, constitutes a charge having equivalent effect within the meaning of Articles [23] and [25] of the Treaty, even if it is not imposed for the benefit of the State, is not discriminatory or protective in effect or if the product on which the charge is imposed is not in competition with any domestic product.

Of much greater importance to the present subject are the Treaty articles governing the elimination of quantitative restrictions in trade between Member States. The key provisions are Articles 28, 29, and 30, which provide as follows:

- Article 28: 'Quantitative restrictions on imports and all measures having equivalent effect shall be prohibited between Member States.'
- Article 29: 'Quantitative restrictions on exports, and all measures having equivalent effect, shall be prohibited between Member States.'
- Article 30: 'The provisions of Articles 28 and 29 shall not preclude prohibitions or restrictions on imports, exports or goods in transit justified on grounds of public morality, public policy or public security; the protection of health and life of humans, animals or plants; the protection of national treasures possessing artistic, historic or archaeological value; or the protection of industrial and commercial property. Such prohibitions or restrictions shall not, however, constitute a means of arbitrary discrimination or a disguised restriction on trade between Member States.'

It is important to note that the above provisions apply not only to goods produced within the territory of a Member State but also to goods originating in third countries once they are in free circulation in a Member State.[14] Products coming from a third country are considered to be in free circulation in a Member State 'if the import formalities have been complied with and any customs duties or charges having equivalent effect which are payable have been levied in that Member State, and if they have not benefited from a total or partial drawback of such duties or charges'.[15]

The net effect of Articles 28 to 30 is that quantitative restrictions on imports or exports, and measures having equivalent effect, are prohibited in trade between Member States, unless they are justified on one of the grounds listed in Article 30.

2.2 Services

The Treaty provisions on the provision of services are to be found in Chapter 3 of Title III of Part Three (Arts 49–55). Chapters 1, 2, and 4 of Title III deal

---

[14] Art. 23(2) of the EC Treaty.   [15] Art. 24 of the EC Treaty.

respectively with the free movement of workers, the right of establishment and the free movement of capital.

The most important provision, as regards services, is Article 49, which states:

Within the framework of the provisions set out below, restrictions on freedom to provide services within the Community shall be prohibited in respect of nationals of Member States who are established in a State of the Community other than that of the person for whom the services are intended.

The Council may, acting by a qualified majority on a proposal from the Commission, extend the provisions of the Chapter to nationals of a third country who provide services and who are established within the Community.

Article 50 provides as follows:

Services shall be considered to be 'services' within the meaning of this Treaty where they are normally provided for remuneration, in so far as they are not governed by the provisions relating to freedom of movement for goods, capital and persons. 'Services' shall in particular include:

(a) activities of an industrial character;
(b) activities of a commercial character;
(c) activities of craftsmen;
(d) activities of the professions.

Without prejudice to the provisions of the Chapter relating to the right of establishment, the person providing a service may, in order to do so, temporarily pursue his activity in the State where the service is provided, under the same conditions as are imposed by that State on its own nationals.

Derogations from the principle of free movement are contained in Articles 45 and 46. Although contained in the chapter on the right of establishment, these provisions apply to services by virtue of Article 55. The first paragraph of Article 45 provides: 'The provisions of this Chapter shall not apply, so far as any given Member State is concerned, to activities which in that State are connected, even occasionally, with the exercise of official authority.' Article 46(1) provides: 'The provisions of this Chapter and measures taken in pursuance thereof shall not prejudice the applicability of provisions laid down by law, regulation or administrative action providing for special treatment for foreign nationals on grounds of public policy, public security or public health.'

3. THE SCOPE OF ARTICLE 28:
FROM *DASSONVILLE* TO *KECK* AND BEYOND

The expression 'quantitative restrictions' is not difficult to grasp; it means quotas and prohibitions. It was once argued before the Court that the expression could not embrace an outright prohibition, as opposed to a mere restriction. That argument was rejected by the Court in *Regina v Henn and Darby*,[16] where it was held that the expression used in Article 28 must be read as equivalent to the expression 'prohibitions or restrictions on imports' used in Article 30. In *Geddo v Ente Nazionale Risi*[17] the Court stated that: 'The prohibition on quantitative restrictions covers measures which amount to a total or partial restraint of, according to the circumstances, imports, exports or goods in transit.'

It is the concept of measures having equivalent effect to quantitative restrictions that has given rise to the greatest difficulties in this field. There is now a substantial body of case law on the subject, but there still remain many unresolved problems—partly, it must be admitted, because the Court has not always been consistent in its approach to the concept of 'measures having equivalent effect'.

One brief point should be made before embarking on a review of that case-law. Although the language of Articles 28 and 29 is virtually identical, the Court has always taken a less rigorous attitude towards restrictions on exports than towards restrictions on imports, presumably on the ground that Member States are less likely to wish to impede exports. The Court considers that Article 29 of the Treaty applies only to measures which have as their specific object or effect the restriction of exports and thus establish a difference in treatment between a Member State's domestic trade and its export trade: *Groenveld v Produktschap voor Vee en Vlees*.[18] In that case the Court held that Article 29 was not infringed by a Dutch law which prohibited sausage manufacturers in the Netherlands from having in stock or processing horsemeat. Obviously the law affected exports in a sense, since it prevented Dutch sausage-makers from manufacturing horsemeat sausages for export to other Member States. However, the non-discriminatory nature of the law meant that it was not contrary to Article 29.

In relation to measures restricting imports, the Court has been more stringent. It has opted for a wide definition of the concept of measures having equivalent effect to a quantitative restriction on imports. The leading case is *Procureur du Roi v Dassonville*,[19] in which the Court held that: 'All trading rules enacted by Member States which are capable of hindering, directly or indirectly, actually or potentially, intra-Community trade are to be considered as measures having an effect equivalent to quantitative restrictions.'

The breadth of that definition of measures having equivalent effect was amplified by a ruling to the effect that even a slight hindrance to imports is

---

[16] Case 34/79 [1979] ECR 3795. [17] Case 2/73 [1973] ECR 865.
[18] Case 15/79 [1979] ECR 3409. [19] Case 8/74 [1974] ECR 837.

sufficient to bring Article 28 into play: *Van de Haar and Kaveka de Meern*.[20] Thus it follows that, at least in theory, even a measure which causes a slight, indirect, potential hindrance to trade between Member States offends against Article 28.

Perhaps the greatest obstacles to trade between Member States are due to disparities between national legislation regarding, for example, technical standards, the composition of foodstuffs, sizes, packaging, labelling and so forth. Obviously the best solution to such obstacles to trade is to strike at the root of the problem by eliminating the disparities in national legislation. To that end, Articles 94 and 95 of the EC Treaty empower the Council of Ministers to adopt directives and other measures harmonizing legislation that directly affects the establishment or functioning of the common market. Many such directives have been issued.

But harmonization is a slow process and may not even be perceived as desirable by everyone. It follows that obstacles resulting from disparities in national legislation will continue to hamper trade between Member States for a long time to come. Initially, it was thought by many that, provided a Member State applied its legislation without distinction to domestic goods and to goods produced in other Member States, there was no breach of Article 28. In other words, it was believed that Article 28 only prohibited discriminatory measures. That myth was shattered in 1979 by the Court's judgment in *REWE-Zentral v Bundesmonopolverwaltung für Branntwein* ('Cassis de Dijon').[21] In that case the German authorities refused to authorize the marketing in Germany of a French liqueur known as Cassis de Dijon on the ground that it did not comply with a German provision under which such beverages must have a minimum alcohol content of 25 per cent. It was argued that since the German provision applied without distinction to domestic and imported products it was not caught by the prohibition laid down in Article 28. The Court rejected that argument and held that obstacles to trade caused by disparities in national laws were caught by the prohibition laid down in Article 28 unless the provisions in question were necessary in order to satisfy mandatory requirements relating, in particular, to the effectiveness of fiscal supervision, the protection of public health, fair trading, and consumer protection. The Court indicated that the measure in question was not justified on such grounds.

Since 1979 the Court has delivered many judgments confirming the principle that goods manufactured and marketed in a Member State in accordance with the local legislation may be imported into any other Member State unless some mandatory requirement justifies their exclusion. The Court has, for instance, condemned a Belgian law requiring margarine

---

[20] Joined Cases 177 and 178/82 [1984] ECR 1797.   [21] Case 120/78 [1979] ECR 649.

to be sold only in square packets,[22] a German law prohibiting the use of additives in beer,[23] and an Italian law permitting only durum wheat to be used for the manufacture of pasta.[24] The Court has, on the other hand, upheld a Danish law prohibiting the use of non-returnable bottles—thus recognizing a further mandatory requirement, namely, protection of the environment.[25]

The cases cited above had one thing in common: the Member State concerned prohibited the sale of goods not manufactured in accordance with certain rules governing the physical characteristics of goods. The obstacles to trade resulting from such rules are obvious. Disparities in laws regulating the composition and presentation of goods, or prescribing technical standards for goods, have an obvious capacity to impede trade between Member States.

In the 1980s and early 1990s the Court was faced with a number of cases in which Article 28 and the 'Cassis de Dijon' principle were invoked, not in relation to legislation governing the physical characteristics of goods, but in relation to legislation governing the circumstances in which goods may be marketed—rules as to where, when, by whom, how, or at what price goods may be sold or rules on the advertising of goods.[26]

Although it is not impossible for such legislation to impede trade between Member States, the obstacles to trade are much less obvious than in the case of an outright prohibition on, for example, the sale of margarine in round tubs. As a result the Court has had great difficulty when confronted with rules governing the circumstances in which goods may be marketed. It has not always been consistent and has veered between a narrow construction and a broad construction of the concept of measures having equivalent effect to a quantitative restriction.

An example of the narrow view is *Blesgen v Belgium*,[27] in which the Court held that a Belgian law prohibiting the sale of strong alcoholic beverages in bars and restaurants (as opposed to shops) lay entirely outside the scope of Article 28 because it had no connection with the importation of goods and therefore was not of such a nature as to impede trade between Member States. In *Quietlynn v Southend Borough Council*[28] the Court took the same attitude towards a British law prohibiting the sale of pornographic material, except in licensed 'sex shops'.

---

[22] Case 133/85 *Rau v De Smedt* [1982] ECR 3961.
[23] Case 178/84 *Commission v Germany* [1987] ECR 1227.
[24] Case 407/85 *3 Glocken v USL Centro-Sud* [1988] ECR 4233.
[25] Case 302/86 *Commission v Denmark* [1988] ECR 4607.
[26] This formula has been taken from E. L. White, 'In search of the limits to Article 30 of the EEC Treaty' (1989) CML Rev. 235, 259.
[27] Case 75/81 [1982] ECR 1211.
[28] Case C-23/89 [1990] ECR I-3059.

Those cases must be contrasted with *Buet*,[29] in which the Court was faced with a French law which prohibited the door-to-door selling of educational material. Mr Buet was prosecuted for using that sales method to market a language course that happened to have been manufactured in Belgium. The Court held that such a law might impede imports and proceeded to enquire, as in the 'Cassis de Dijon' case, whether the obstacle to free movement was justified in order to satisfy mandatory requirements such as consumer protection or fair trading. A similarly broad view of the prohibition laid down in Article 28 was taken in the judgment in *Aragonesa de Publicidad Exterior v Departamento de Sanidad y Seguridad Social de la Generalitat*.[30] There the Court held that a law prohibiting the advertising of strong alcoholic beverages in cinemas, on public transport, and along roads and streets was equivalent in effect to a quantitative restriction on imports in so far as it was applied to goods imported from other Member States. In *Yves Rocher*[31] the Court held that Article 28 applied to German legislation prohibiting eye-catching publicity with price comparisons; such legislation was not justified by the mandatory requirements of consumer protection.

To add to the confusion, the Court gave several conflicting rulings, between 1989 and 1992, about the compatibility with Article 28 of restrictions on Sunday trading.[32]

Aware of the contradictions in the case law, the Court made a conscious attempt to redefine the scope of Article 28 in *Keck and Mithouard*.[33] It held that a law prohibiting the resale of goods at a loss lay outside the scope of Article 28, observing that:

> . . . contrary to what has previously been decided, the application to products from other Member States of national provisions restricting or prohibiting certain selling arrangements is not such as to hinder directly or indirectly, actually or potentially, trade between Member States within the meaning of the *Dassonville* judgment, provided that those provisions apply to all affected traders operating within the national territory and provided that they affect in the same manner, in law and in fact, the marketing of domestic products and of those from other Member States.

The *Keck* judgment made a rigid distinction between rules relating to the physical characteristics of goods (rules on composition, presentation, labelling, and packaging) and rules that restrict certain 'selling arrangements' (*modalités de vente* in French). The former automatically fell within the scope

---

[29] Case 382/89 |1989| ECR 1235.
[30] Joined Cases C-1/90 and C-176/90 |1991| ECR I-4151.
[31] Case C-126/91 |1993| ECR I-2361.
[32] Case C-145/88 *Torfaen Borough Council v B & Q* |1989| ECR 765; Case C-312/89 *CGT v Conforama* |1991| ECR I-997; Case C-332/89 *Marchandise* |1991| ECR I-1027; and Case C-169/91 *Stoke on Trent Council v B & Q* |1992| ECR I-6635.
[33] Joined Cases C-267/91 and C-268/91 |1993| ECR I-6097.

of Article 28, whereas the latter did so only if they produced some discriminatory effect to the detriment of imported goods. This rigid distinction is debatable: there are many examples of measures restricting selling arrangements which have a very substantial effect on imports (e.g. a restriction on the type of establishment that may sell a particular type of product). For that reason, Advocate General Jacobs suggested, in his opinion in *Leclerc-Siplec*,[34] that a *de minimis* test, rather than a discrimination test, should be used to determine whether such measures were caught by Article 28. The Court did not adopt that suggestion and has clung tenaciously to the *Keck* formula in its subsequent rulings.

In *Hünermund*[35] the Court ruled that Article 28 did not apply to a rule of professional conduct which prohibited pharmacists from advertising, outside their pharmacies, parapharmaceutical products which they were authorized to sell. In *Leclerc-Siplec* a measure prohibiting the entire distribution sector from advertising on television was held to fall outside the scope of Article 28. Restrictions on the opening hours of shops have, since *Keck*, been dealt with as rules relating to *modalités de vente*.[36] In *Commission v Greece*[37] the Court held that a rule reserving the sale of processed milk for infants to pharmacies lay outside the scope of Article 28.

On the other hand, the Court has held that Article 28 is broad enough to catch a rule which prevents the sale of an imported product under the trade mark 'Clinique' on the ground that it is likely to mislead consumers into believing that the product has medicinal properties.[38] The same applies as regards a measure which prevents the sale of an imported product, the quantity of which is increased during a short publicity campaign and the wrapping of which is marked '+ 10%'.[39]

The Court's reluctance, in *Leclerc-Siplec*, to admit that restrictions on advertising can impede imports is difficult to understand. Without effective advertising—which in many cases means advertising on television—new markets may be impossible to penetrate. Fortunately, in *Konsumentenombudsmannen v De Agostini and TV-Shop*,[40] the Court did indeed recognize that a ban on television advertising might affect imported products more than domestic products and thus fall within the scope of Article 28 under the *Keck* formula. De Agostini published a children's magazine about dinosaurs

---

[34] Case C-412/93 [1995] ECR I-179.   [35] Case C-292/92 [1993] ECR I-6787.

[36] Joined Cases C-401/92 and C-402/92 *Tankstation 't Heukske and Boermans* [1994] ECR I-2199 and Joined Cases C-69/93 and C-258/93 *Punto Casa* [1994] ECR I-2355.

[37] Case C-391/92 [1995] ECR I-1621.

[38] Case C-315/92 *Verband Sozialer Wettbewerb v Clinique Laboratoires and Estée Lauder* [1994] ECR I-1923.

[39] Case C-470/93 *Verein gegen Unwesen in Handel und Gewerbe Köln e.V. v Mars GmbH* [1995] ECR I-1923.

[40] Joined Cases C-34/95, C-35/95 and C-36/95 [1997] ECR I-3843.

and was prevented from advertising it on television in Sweden by a law which prohibited television advertising directed at children.

In *Konsumentenombudsmannen v Gourmet International Products*[41] a Swedish law banning the advertising of alcohol in the press, on television, or radio, by posters on the roadside, or by direct mailing was likewise held by the Court to be discriminatory in fact. Those two judgments suggest that the Court has, without admitting it, belatedly decided to adopt the approach recommended by Advocate General Jacobs in *Leclerc-Siplec*. That impression is reinforced by the judgment in *Schutzverband gegen unlauteren Wettbewerb v TK-Heimdienst Sass*,[42] in which the Court held that an Austrian law banning bakers, butchers, and grocers from selling door-to-door outside their own administrative district was likely to affect imported goods more severely than domestic produce.

4. THE SCOPE OF ARTICLE 49

The case law on the scope of Article 49 has developed along the same lines as the case law on the scope of Article 28. Thus the early cases emphasize that Article 49 prohibits discriminatory restrictions that place on out-of-State providers of services burdens not applying to domestic traders.[43] Later cases establish that Article 49 also prohibits restrictions which do not discriminate, either in substance or in form, on the basis of the country of origin of the service.[44]

The Court has, however, wisely refrained from extending the *Keck and Mithouard* ruling to the field of services.[45] The distinction between rules based on the physical characteristics of goods and rules restricting 'certain selling arrangements' is difficult enough to apply in relation to goods. It would make no sense at all to attempt to transpose it to the field of services.

5. DEROGATIONS FROM THE PRINCIPLE OF FREE MOVEMENT

5.1 *Goods*

Article 30, it will be recalled, expressly excludes from the prohibitions laid down in Articles 28 and 29 measures that are justified on certain grounds, namely:

---

[41] Case C-405/98 [2001] ECR I-1795.   [42] Case C-254/98 [2000] ECR I-151.
[43] See, e.g., Case 33/74 *Van Binsbergen v Bestuur van de Bedrijfsvereniging voor de Metaalnijverheid* [1974] ECR 1299.
[44] See, e.g., *Collectieve Antennevoorziening Gouda* and *Säger v Dennemeyer*, cited in n. 5.
[45] *Alpine Investment*, cited in n. 5.

(1) public morality, public policy, or public security;
(2) the protection of health and life of humans, animals, or plants;
(3) the protection of national treasures possessing artistic, historic, or archaeological value; or
(4) the protection of industrial and commercial property.

Until 'Cassis de Dijon' in 1979, it appeared that the matters listed in Article 30 were the only grounds on which measures restricting trade could be justified. The Court had in fact held on several occasions that, since Article 30 derogates from a fundamental principle of the Treaty, it must be construed narrowly, with the result that its list of grounds justifying restrictions on free movement is exhaustive (see e.g. *Bauhuis v Netherlands*).[46]

Although 'Cassis de Dijon' was a landmark judgment, in the sense that it swept aside many obstacles to free movement which it was previously thought could only be removed by means of the harmonization of national laws, it was at the same time a backward step, from the point of view of economic integration, because the Court recognized a new catalogue of exceptions to the principle of free movement, additional to those expressly stated in Article 30. The result is that there are now two lists of grounds on which a measure restricting imports may be justified: there is the one set out in Article 30 and there are the 'mandatory requirements' referred to in 'Cassis de Dijon' and subsequent judgments (i.e. consumer protection, fair trading, the effectiveness of fiscal supervision, the protection of public health, and the protection of the environment). It will be noted that public health is included in both lists.

The precise relationship between the interests protected by Article 30 and the mandatory requirements recognized in 'Cassis de Dijon' has been the subject of much academic debate. The most important point to remember is that the mandatory requirements recognized in 'Cassis de Dijon' can only be invoked in favour of measures that apply without distinction to domestic and imported goods,[47] whereas Article 30 may save measures that do not satisfy that test provided that they do not constitute arbitrary discrimination or a disguised restriction on trade as laid down in the second sentence of Article 30 (see, in particular, para. 13 of the judgment in *Aragonesa de Publicidad Exterior*).[48]

The expressions 'arbitrary discrimination' and 'disguised restriction' require explanation. Discrimination would be arbitrary if a difference in treatment were not objectively justified. If, for example, a Member State applied severe controls to imports of poultry meat from a country where a

---

[46] Case 46/76 [1977] ECR 5.

[47] In one notorious judgment the Court appears to misunderstand this requirement: see Case C-2/90 *Commission v Belgium*, cited in n. 1.

[48] Cited in n. 30.

dangerous disease affecting poultry were rampant, but did not apply the same controls to domestic poultry meat, that difference in treatment might be justified if the disease in question had not infected domestic poultry. Such discrimination would not be arbitrary (cf. *REWE-Zentralfinanz v Land-wirtschaftskammer*).[49] The expression 'disguised restriction' is rather vague. The Court appears to interpret it as referring to measures which, though ostensibly covered by Article 30, lose the benefit of that provision because they are protectionist in intent (see *Commission v United Kingdom*).[50]

If, for example, a trade mark owner were allowed to rely on his trade mark to block parallel imports of goods which he had marketed under the trade mark in another Member State where statutory price controls were in force, that would amount to a disguised restriction. The importation and sale of those goods would not prevent the trade mark from performing its essential function of distinguishing between the goods of different traders. To block such imports would amount to using the trade mark as a means of cancelling out the effects of discrepancies in national legislation on price controls.[51]

In most cases, the reason for derogating from the principle of free movement is that differing standards and values apply in the different Member States. Europe is large and diverse and each Member State has its own ideas and traditions relating to matters such as morality, fair trading, and consumer protection. Moreover, standards of health and hygiene are not uniform. Article 30 recognizes that Member States remain competent to legislate on such matters and to apply their legislation, within limits, to goods imported from other Member States. The same point was recognized by the Court in the 'Cassis de Dijon' judgment. Article 30 and the 'Cassis de Dijon' case law seek to strike a balance between the needs of free trade and the Member States' right to apply their own standards and values in certain fundamental areas. The reason for including intellectual property rights in the catalogue of overriding interests in Article 30 is, of course, rather different. It is simply a recognition that intellectual property rights have historically been linked to the territory of individual Member States.

Over the years a substantial body of case law has developed with regard to the various grounds on which exceptions to the principle of free movement may be justified. The main task in the following chapters will be to analyse the cases concerning intellectual property rights. Before we embark on that task, two points of general interest must be emphasized.

First, whatever ground is invoked as justification for a measure restricting free movement, whether it be an interest mentioned in Article 30 or a

---

[49] Case 4/75 |1975| ECR 843.   [50] Case 40/82 |1982| ECR 2793.

[51] See the opinion of Advocate General Jacobs in Joined Cases C-427, C-429 and C-436/93 *Bristol-Myers, Squibb v Paranova* |1996| ECR 3457; see also Case 16/74 *Centrafarm v Winthrop* |1974| ECR 1183.

mandatory requirement under 'Cassis de Dijon', the measure in question will be tested against the principle of proportionality. That means that the measure will only be upheld if (a) it is an appropriate means of attaining the objective in question (e.g. the protection of public health or fair trading) and (b) the objective could not be attained by other means less restrictive of trade between Member States. The proportionality test is a strict one and it considerably limits the scope of the permitted derogations from the principle of free movement. The Court has frequently emphasized that Article 30, as an exception to a fundamental principle of the Treaty, must be interpreted strictly. It does not give Member States *carte blanche* to exclude imports simply because to do so would contribute to one of the interests mentioned therein. The restrictive measure must be necessary. *A fortiori*, the same is true of the mandatory requirements recognized in the 'Cassis de Dijon' judgment.

Secondly, the justification for restricting imports will often be removed as a result of the harmonization of national laws. Thus, for example, once national legislation on the use of additives in the production of animal feeding-stuffs has been harmonized, by means of a directive adopted under Article 94 or 95 of the Treaty, a product manufactured in a Member State in accordance with the harmonized legislation may be traded throughout the Community; another Member State could not invoke Article 30 to exclude such a product on grounds of the protection of health and life of humans or animals (*Tedeschi v Denkavit*).[52]

In the field of intellectual property rights, however, the extent to which the justification for import restrictions can be removed by mere harmonization of national laws is much more limited. In that field most of the obstacles to free movement are caused, not by discrepancies in national laws, but by the territoriality of intellectual property rights. Thus, harmonization alone would not be an effective way to strike at the root of such barriers to trade.[53] The only definitive solution would be to replace national intellectual property rights by unitary rights, valid throughout the Community.

5.2 Services

The parallelism between the cases on goods and those on services is again in evidence as regards the derogations from the basic prohibitions laid down by the Treaty. Thus, the Court has held that national rules restricting the cross-border provision of services which are not applicable without

---

[52] Case 5/77 [1977] ECR 1555.
[53] See the opinion of Advocate General Jacobs in Case C-10/89 CNL *Sucal v HAG GF ('HAG II')* [1990] ECR I-3711 at para. 55. See also I. Govaere, 'Intellectual Property Protection and Commercial Policy', in *The European Community's Commercial Policy after 1992: The Legal Dimension* (ed. M. Maresceau) Nijhoff, 1993. pp. 197, 216 *et seq.*

distinction as regards the country of origin of the service, are compatible with Community law only if they can be brought within the scope of an express derogation in the Treaty, such as that contained in Article 46(1).[54]

Unfortunately, the drafting of Article 46(1) is somewhat deficient. The draftsman had in mind the *locus classicus* of an individual who physically crosses a border in order to perform a service in another Member State. That is why it speaks of rules providing for 'special treatment for foreign nationals on grounds of public policy, public security or public health'. Such an approach takes no account of the complexity of a highly developed economy, in which 'the provision of services covers a vast spectrum of different types of activity'.[55]

Services may, for example, be provided by post, telephone, fax, e-mail, or by means of satellite broadcasting. The inadequacy of Article 46(1), as a means of authorizing legitimate restrictions on services in the age of telecommunications, is evident. For that reason it was necessary for the Court to develop, in the field of services, a doctrine of mandatory requirements analogous to the 'Cassis de Dijon' doctrine which had been so successful in relation to trade in goods. The effect of the judgments by which that purpose was achieved was summarized in *Collectieve Antennevoorziening Gouda*, where the Court held that restrictions caused by the application to service-providers established in another Member State of the national legislation of the State in which the service is received are contrary to Article 49 unless they are justified by 'overriding reasons relating to the public interest'.[56] The Court went on to list the overriding reasons thus far recognized, which included:

- professional rules intended to protect recipients of services;
- protection of intellectual property;
- protection of workers;
- consumer protection; and
- conservation and protection of the national historic and artistic heritage.[57]

As in the case of goods, there are thus two lists of requirements which can justify restrictions on the provision of services—there are the requirements mentioned in Article 46(1) of the Treaty, which can justify special

---

[54] *Collectieve Antennevoorziening Gouda* (cited in n. 5) at para. 11.

[55] As stated by Advocate General Jacobs in his opinion in *Säger v Dennemeyer* (cited in n. 5) at para. 25.

[56] At para. 13 of the judgment. The French version speaks of 'raisons impérieuses d'intérêt général', clearly echoing the language used in the 'Cassis de Dijon' case, which speaks of 'exigences impératives'. The words 'impérieuses' and 'impératives' seem to be synonymous in this context and could both be translated by 'overriding' or 'imperative'. The use of the word 'mandatory' in the English version of 'Cassis de Dijon' is rather unfortunate.

[57] At para. 13 of the judgment, where further cases are cited.

(i.e. discriminatory) treatment of service-providers from other Member States, on condition that the discrimination is not arbitrary;[58] and there are the overriding reasons relating to the public interest recognized in *Collectieve Antennevoorziening Gouda* and other cases. As in the case of the mandatory requirements recognized in 'Cassis de Dijon', these overriding reasons may in principle only be invoked to justify restrictions which apply without distinction to all service-providers, regardless of their Member State of origin.

However, in the case of restrictions on the provision of services based on the protection of intellectual property rights, the position is slightly different because the Court has in effect applied Article 30 by analogy. Thus in *Coditel I*[59] the Court held that such restrictions may be justified (and are hence compatible with Art. 49), provided that they do not constitute arbitrary discrimination or a disguised restriction on trade between Member States.

Finally, it is important to stress that whatever ground is invoked as justification for restrictions on the cross-border provision of services, whether it is a ground mentioned in Article 46(1) or an overriding reason recognized in the Court's case law, the principle of proportionality applies. The restriction must therefore be an appropriate means of attaining the objective in question and must not burden trade between Member States more than necessary.[60]

---

[58] Arbitrary discrimination is invariably contrary to Community law. It is the Community law equivalent of mortal sin. Although there appears to be no case establishing that rule in relation to Art. 46(1), the similarly worded derogation relating to the free movement of workers in Art. 39(3) has been interpreted as not permitting arbitrary discrimination: Joined Cases 115 and 116/81 *Adoui and Cornuaille v Belgium* [1982] ECR 1665. Arts 39(3) and 46(1) are to be interpreted in the same way: see D. Wyatt and A. Dashwood, *European Community Law*, 3rd edn. 1993, p. 293.

[59] Cited in n. 3.

[60] Case 352/85 *Bond van Adverteerders v Netherlands* [1988] ECR 2085, at para. 36; *Collectieve Antennevoorziening Gouda* (cited in n. 5) at para. 15; and *Säger v Dennemeyer* (cited in n. 5) at para. 15.

3

The conflict between intellectual property rights and the principle of free movement

1. THE ESSENCE OF THE PROBLEM

Intellectual property rights have an obvious propensity to interfere with the principle of free movement. There is an inevitable conflict—German lawyers would speak of a *Spannungsverhältnis* (relationship of tension)—between that principle and the protection of exclusive rights which are limited to the territory of a Member State.

It is easy to see what kind of problems may arise. X has a patent in Germany but has not sought patent protection in Italy (or perhaps could not obtain it because the substantive law of patents was different in Italy). Y makes products incorporating the patented invention in Italy and markets them there. Z buys the products and exports them to W in Germany. W, who may know nothing about X's patent, is sued by X for patent infringement. If X's action succeeds and W is prevented from importing the goods into Germany, that will amount to restricting the free movement of goods between Member States. But if X is unable to obtain an injunction against infringing goods imported from Italy, the value of his patent will be seriously undermined. Thus, there is a conflict between an intellectual property right and the free movement of goods. And it is of course easy to imagine similar conflicts in relation to trade marks, design rights, copyright and so forth. Any exclusive right limited to the territory a Member State has the potential to come into conflict with the principle of free movement.

To take an example from the field of trade marks, suppose that Company A manufactures margarine in the United Kingdom and markets it under the registered trade mark BINGO. In Ireland Company B (which is unrelated to Company A) sells butter under the trade mark BONGO, which is registered in Ireland. The goods are similar and the trade marks are similar, so there is a possibility that consumers would be confused if the two products were both on the market in the same territory. A consumer might buy BONGO thinking that it was made by the same people as BINGO, a product which he has tasted and found to his liking. Such a situation would be unsatisfactory for all concerned. Consumers would be misled as to the commercial origin of goods and neither manufacturer would be able to defend its goodwill and commercial reputation. But if each manufacturer is allowed to exclude from its own territory goods manufactured by the other, a barrier to trade between Member States will have been erected.

Moving to the field of copyright, let us suppose that the duration of the author's exclusive right ('the term of protection') varies from one Member State to another. As a result, a work may be in copyright in Member State A, but belong to the public domain in Member State B. Can the owner of the copyright in Member State A prevent the importation of goods lawfully marketed in Member State B?

In the field of design rights, problems may arise because the scope of protection varies. In Member State A, car makers may enjoy an exclusive right to manufacture bodywork parts for their models, while in Member State B the design right covers only the car as a whole and does not extend to individual parts. Suppose that an independent manufacturer in Member State B makes spare body panels for a Ford Mondeo and exports them to Member State A. Can Ford sue for infringement of its design right?

This is just a selection of some of the more obvious examples of conflicts between intellectual property rights and the free movement of goods. In all of these examples, if the owner of the right were allowed to invoke it in order to oppose the importation and sale of goods which were lawfully on the market in another Member State, that would amount to a measure equivalent in effect to a quantitative restriction on imports within the meaning of Article 28 of the Treaty. The compatibility of the measure with EC law would depend on whether it could be justified under Article 30 of the Treaty.

Here we have taken for granted that reliance on the right comes within the scope of Article 28. There is ample case law to justify such an approach. Theorists none the less point out that Article 28 is concerned with state measures, not with the actions of private individuals.[1] How then can reliance on a patent, trade mark, copyright, or design right, by an individual right-holder, in order to prevent the importation and sale of infringing goods, be a measure within the compass of Article 28?[2] The answer is simple. The right-holder can only prevent such infringements by using the machinery of the State. He will need injunctions, seizure orders, and other judicial remedies which will be granted in accordance with some provision of national law. Whether the measure, within the meaning of Article 28, is the individual injunction or the legislative provision on which it is based need not be debated.[3] On either view there is a state measure which impedes imports

---

[1] See, e.g., P. Van Ommeslaghe, 'Les droits de propriété industrielle et commerciale et les dispositions des articles 30, 36, 59, 60, 85 et 86 du Traité de Rome' in *Liber amicorum Frédéric Dumon*, Kluwer, Antwerp, 1983, p. 1247, at p. 1250.

[2] For an extreme version of this view, which would remove individual attemps to exercise intellectual property rights from the scope of Art. 28 altogether, see F. A. Mann, 'Industrial Property and the EEC Treaty' (1975) 24 ICLQ 31.

[3] According to W. Alexander, the legislative provision is the measure within the meaning of Art. 28: see 'L'établissement du marché commun et le problème des brevets parallèles', (1968) RTDE 513, 527. The same view was taken by Advocate General Warner in Joined Cases 55 and

and that is sufficient to bring Article 28 into play.[4] It is in any event clear from the wording of Article 30 that the authors of the Treaty assumed that the exercise of industrial property rights fell within the scope of Article 28.[5]

All the examples given above involved conflicts between intellectual property rights and the free movement of goods. Intellectual property rights can also come into conflict with the freedom to provide services. Suppose, for example, that the exclusive right to show a film on television and in cinemas is assigned to different persons in Member States A and B. The film is shown on television in Member State B and the signal is picked up in Member State A and transmitted to viewers in that country by a cable television company; the owner of the rights in the film in Member State A attempts to stop the cable broadcast, on the ground that it infringes his exclusive right. Those were the facts of the *Coditel* cases.[6] Other such conflicts could be imagined, though surprisingly few have arisen in practice.

2. RADICAL SOLUTIONS TO THE CONFLICT: HARMONIZATION OF NATIONAL LAW AND THE CREATION OF UNITARY INTELLECTUAL PROPERTY RIGHTS

Before examining the voluminous case law on the interpretation of Article 30, in which the European Court of Justice has come face to face with the conflict between free movement and the protection of intellectual property rights, we must first say something about two methods of resolving that conflict which are much more radical:

(1) the harmonization of national laws on intellectual property; and
(2) the creation of unitary intellectual property rights.

It goes without saying that those methods lie in the hands, not of the Court of Justice, but of the Community legislature and the Member States in their capacity as treaty-makers.

57/80 *Musik-Vertrieb Membran v GEMA* [1981] ECR 147, at 175. See also the opinion of Advocate General Trabucchi in Cases 15 and 16/74 *Centrafarm v Sterling Drug* [1974] ECR 1147, at 1178. Advocate General Mayras stated in his opinion in Case 119/75 *Terrapin v Terranova* [1976] ECR 1039, at 1069, that the judicial decision prohibiting imports was the relevant measure.

[4] See R. Joliet, 'Patented Articles and the Free Movement of Goods within the EEC' (1975) 28 *Current Legal Problems* 15, 25. For a full discussion of this issue, see M. Waelbroeck, 'Les rapports entre les règles sur la libre circulation des marchandises et les règles de concurrence applicables aux entreprises dans la CEE', in *Du droit international au droit de l'intégration. Liber amicorum Pierre Pescatore*, Nomos Verlagsgesellschaft, Baden-Baden, 1989, p. 781.

[5] V. Korah, *An Introductory Guide to EC Competition Law and Practice*, 5th edn, Sweet and Maxwell, London, 1994, p. 191.

[6] Case 62/79 *Coditel v Ciné Vog Films (Coditel I)* [1980] ECR 881; Case 262/81 *Coditel v Ciné Vog Films (Coditel II)* [1982] ECR 3381.

In some of the examples given above of conflicts between the free movement of goods and the protection of intellectual property rights, it is clear that a radical solution (i.e. a solution that strikes at the root of the problem) can be found in the harmonization of national laws. Thus, the problems that arise when a literary work is still in copyright in one Member State but belongs to the public domain in another Member State would not exist if the national copyright laws all provided for the same term of protection. And indeed such a solution has now been adopted by Council Directive 93/98/EEC of 29 October 1993 harmonizing the term of protection of copyright and certain related rights.[7]

Similarly, harmonization could prevent the conflict that arises when automobile spare parts, made by an independent manufacturer in a country where the exclusive design right does not extend to spare parts, are exported to a country where such protection does exist.[8] Any discrepancy in the national laws governing the scope of protection of intellectual property rights may lead to a situation in which a product which is lawful in one country (where the scope of protection is relatively narrow) would become an infringing product when exported to another country (where the scope of protection is wider). Such a situation would obviously not occur if the laws defining the scope of protection were the same in all the countries concerned. If, for example, all Member States granted car makers the exclusive right to manufacture spare parts for their models during a period of ten years after the launch of a model anywhere in the Community, there would be no legitimate trade in unauthorized parts in any Member State during that period. By the same token, if all the Member States confined design protection to the model as a whole and denied protection

---

[7] OJ 1993 L 290, p. 9.

[8] In fact Directive 98/71/EC of the European Parliament and the Council of 13 October 1998 on the legal protection of designs (OJ 1998 L 289, p. 28) fails to harmonize completely the Member States' laws on spare parts. The issue was so controversial that agreement on a common solution could not be reached. Art. 14 of the Directive requires Member States to retain, for the time being, 'their existing legal provisions relating to the use of the design of a component part used for the purpose of the repair of a complex product so as to restore its original appearance' and to 'introduce changes to those provisions only if the purpose is to liberalize the market for such parts'. Under Art. 18 of the Directive, the Commission is to submit a report on this issue by 28 October 2004 and is to propose legislation within the following 12 months. A component part of a complex product may be registered as a design if, after being incorporated into the complex product, it remains visible during normal use of the latter (Art. 3(3)). However, under Art. 7(2) no design right may subsist 'in features of appearance of a product which must necessarily be reproduced in their exact form and dimensions in order to permit the product in which the design is incorporated or to which it is applied to be mechanically connected to or placed in, around or against another product so that either product may perform its function' (the 'must fit' exception). The effect of these provisions is that visible spare parts are protectable unless they are caught by the 'must fit' exception, which is concerned with functional, rather than aesthetic necessity. As regards Community design rights, corresponding provisions are contained in Arts 4(2) and 8(2) of Council Reg. (EC) No. 6/2002 of 12 December 2001 on Community Design (OJ 2002 L 3, p. 1).

to parts of the model, unauthorized parts made in one Member State would not infringe any exclusive right when exported to another Member State.

From the point of view of eliminating obstacles to free movement, it does not matter which choice the harmonizing authority makes. Uniform protection can be granted at the narrow end of the range, at the wide end, or somewhere between. The choice as to where to set the level of protection raises delicate policy issues, about which there is often great scope for divergent views. For that reason, progress on harmonization has been slow and laborious.[9]

There are, moreover, limits to what can be achieved by the harmonization of national laws. Harmonization can solve problems caused by discrepancies in national laws but it can do nothing to attenuate certain problems due to the territoriality of intellectual property rights. Where, for example, identical or confusingly similar trade marks belong to different, unrelated persons in different Member States, the confusion that would be engendered for consumers if each proprietor could use his trade mark in the territory of the other would not be diminished by the harmonization of substantive trade mark law. Such confusion is not caused by discrepancies in national law; it is caused by the fact that in one country a particular trade mark has acquired, through registration and use, an association in the minds of consumers with the products of its proprietor, while in another country a similar or identical trade mark has become associated with someone else's products. In other words, the problem is due to the territoriality of trade mark rights.

The long-term solution to problems of that nature lies, not in the harmonization of laws, but in the replacement (or at any rate, partial replacement) of national intellectual property rights with a unitary right valid throughout the territory of the Community. Some authorities regard the eventual replacement of national intellectual property rights by Community rights as a necessary element of a genuine internal market. Thus Beier observes:[10] 'A genuine internal market, which constitutes a uniform economic zone, must not only be a uniform customs and monetary zone, but also a uniform industrial property territory, in which there would no longer be German, French, British and Italian patents, utility models, designs or trademarks, but only European industrial property rights valid for the entire territory.'

To that end, Council Regulation (EC) No. 40/94 of 20 December 1993 on the Community trade mark[11] established a Community trade mark office, the seat of which is in Alicante (Spain). Thus, by means of a single proced-

---

[9] For an account of the progress made up to 1990, see F.-K. Beier, 'Industrial Property and the Free Movement of Goods in the Internal European Market' (1990) 21 IIC 131.

[10] Op. cit. (n. 9), at 132.   [11] OJ 1994 L 12, p. 1.

ure, traders will be able to obtain the exclusive right to use a trade mark in all the Member States. The Community trade mark does not completely replace national trade marks—it constitutes an alternative, available to those who wish to obtain Community-wide protection by means of a single procedure. Traders who only need protection in specific Member States may continue to register trade marks nationally. The establishment of a Community trade mark office may help to prevent future conflicts between national trade marks from arising but it cannot do anything to solve the problem of existing conflicts, of which there are more than might be supposed.[12] Thus, no matter how successful the Community trade mark may be, Article 30 of the Treaty will continue to be relevant in this field for a long time to come.

Patent law is another area in which harmonization clearly cannot remove all the obstacles to free movement caused by the territoriality of the exclusive right. Suppose, for example, that an inventor obtains patents in a number of Member States, but does not bother to seek protection in Luxembourg, thinking perhaps that the Luxembourg market is of no significance. Can the inventor oppose the importation, into the countries where his invention is protected, of infringing goods lawfully manufactured in Luxembourg? And if he assigns the German patent to someone else, can he oppose the sale of that person's products in the countries in which he has retained the patent?

The answers to such questions are locked away in the vague wording of Article 30. But to prevent such questions from arising in the first place, it would surely be preferable to create a single, unitary patent which is valid for the whole of the common market. To that end, a Community Patent Convention was signed in Luxembourg in 1975.[13] Unfortunately, the Convention never came into force. The Commission has now put forward a proposal for a Council Regulation on the Community Patent.[14] There is, however, an alternative—less perfect from the point of view of the inventor and of the common market—namely, to seek a bundle of national patents from the European Patent Office in Munich under the European Patent Convention signed in Munich in 1973.

The unification of intellectual property territories is clearly an arduous task. It would be little short of utopian to imagine that national intellectual property rights will in the foreseeable future be entirely replaced by unitary rights obtained by a single procedure and producing identical effects

---

[12] According to one author there were 300,000 in the mid-1970s: F. K. Beier, 'Trade Mark Conflicts in the Common Market: Can they be Solved by Means of Distinguishing Additions?' (1978) IIC 221.

[13] OJ 1976 L 17, p. 1. The Convention was amended by the Council Agreement relating to Community Patents in 1989 (OJ 1989 L 401, p. 1).

[14] OJ C 337 E, p. 278.

throughout the Community. Thus, Article 30 of the Treaty is not destined for early redundancy in this field and the case law of the European Court of Justice on the conflict between intellectual property rights and the free movement of goods will lose none of its relevance. The following chapters attempt to analyse that case law, first describing the main principles established by the Court of Justice and then examining some of the specific issues that arise in relation to the various types of intellectual property right.

3. THE MAIN PRINCIPLES ESTABLISHED BY THE EUROPEAN COURT OF JUSTICE

Article 30 recognizes the existence of a conflict between intellectual property rights and the free movement of goods. It resolves that conflict by giving priority to intellectual property rights. But it confers only a qualified priority on such rights. It does not grant Member States *carte blanche* to erect barriers to trade between Member States in the name of intellectual property. The restriction on trade must be 'justified' and it must not constitute 'arbitrary discrimination' or a 'disguised restriction on trade between Member States'.

And that is all the Treaty says on the subject of intellectual property rights. A striking feature of the Treaty is that it does not confer any role on the legislative organs of the Community—the Council, the European Parliament, and the Commission—in establishing the proper balance between the free movement of goods and the protection of intellectual property rights. The legislature's work in harmonizing national legislation on intellectual property and in creating unitary intellectual property rights is indirectly relevant. But the legislature has no power to define what restrictions are saved by Article 30, just as it has no power to define what measures are caught by Article 28. Thus, the task of establishing the proper balance between the requirements of free movement and the protection of intellectual property (or of the other overriding interests mentioned in Art. 30) falls to the Court of Justice.

Even the most ardent admirers of the European Court would not claim that coherence and consistency are its strong points. Inevitably the Court's approach to the difficult issues raised as a result of the uncomfortable relationship between intellectual property rights and the principle of free movement has varied over the years. While the Court cannot escape criticism, it is important to remember the sparseness of the texts which it has to interpret. A code with a hundred articles would still leave unanswered many of the questions that arise in this field. All that the Court of Justice had to start out with were the two elliptical sentences of Article 30, which contain vague concepts such as 'justified', 'arbitrary discrimination' and 'disguised restriction'.

A number of principles can be extracted from the Court's case law:

(1) In the absence of harmonization it is for national law to determine the conditions and procedures under which intellectual property rights are protected.
(2) The Treaty does not affect the existence of intellectual property rights protected under national law, but may limit the exercise of those rights.
(3) Article 30 safeguards only the rights that constitute the 'specific subject-matter' of an intellectual property right.
(4) Article 30 protects the legitimate exercise of intellectual property rights but does not protect any improper use thereof.
(5) Whenever the proprietor of an intellectual property right allows products to be placed on the market anywhere in the Community, he exhausts his intellectual property rights in relation to those products.
(6) The prohibition of discrimination on grounds of nationality applies to rules governing the existence and exercise of intellectual property rights.

These principles will be examined in the following chapters.

4

The applicability of national laws governing the creation of intellectual property rights, in the absence of harmonization

1. A QUESTIONABLE PRINCIPLE

The European Court of Justice has consistently held that, in the absence of harmonization by the Community institutions, it is for national law to determine the procedures and conditions governing the grant of intellectual property rights. On the face of it, that might appear to be nothing more than a harmless statement of the obvious. Clearly, if there is no Community legislation on a particular matter, the relevant rules must be sought in national law, subject of course to compliance with the Treaty rules on the free movement of goods and with the general principles of Community law, such as the principle of non-discrimination. In that respect, intellectual property is no different from any other area regulated by law, such as technical standards applied in the production of lawnmowers or rules on the composition of animal feeding-stuff.

If we are talking about purely procedural rules, such as a rule that trade mark applications must be filed in triplicate between 9 a.m. and 5 p.m. from Monday to Friday, there can be no objection to the unlimited application of national law. Once such a principle is extended beyond the area of procedural rules into the area of the substantive conditions governing the creation of exclusive rights, it becomes rather dangerous. To say that Member States are free to create exclusive rights, characterized in national law as intellectual property rights, on whatever conditions they judge appropriate, would be to endow them with the power to erect barriers to inter-State trade for which there may be no objective justification.

2. *KEURKOOP V NANCY KEAN GIFTS*: THE COURT GIVES *CARTE BLANCHE* TO NATIONAL LAW AS REGARDS DESIGN RIGHTS

The point just made is well illustrated by the facts of the first case in which the Court established the principle that national law prevails in the absence of harmonization. That case was *Keurkoop v Nancy Kean Gifts*.[1] In 1977,

---

[1] Case 144/81 [1982] ECR 2853.

Nancy Kean Gifts, a Dutch trading company, had registered a design for a ladies handbag in the Benelux register of designs, thus acquiring the exclusive right to sell handbags of that design in Belgium, the Netherlands, and Luxembourg. Nancy Kean Gifts was not the author of the design and it had not filed the design with the consent of the author. It had, as appears from the report on the case,[2] simply copied the design from the United States register of designs. That was no obstacle to obtaining in Benelux a valid design right enforceable against everyone except the author himself (who does not seem to have been in any way involved in the proceedings between Nancy Kean Gifts and Keurkoop). Under the Benelux Uniform Design Law, it was not necessary for the person filing the design to show that he was the author of the design or that he had acquired the right to the design from the author. It was sufficient to be the first person to file the design in the Benelux register of designs. It was thus possible to copy someone else's design and obtain, by registration, the exclusive right to use the design. That exclusive right was valid against all persons except the author of the design (or the person who employed or commissioned the author).

Nancy Kean Gifts obtained supplies of handbags, made in accordance with the registered design, from a Swiss undertaking. The handbags were manufactured in Taiwan, whence they were dispatched directly to the Netherlands. At the beginning of 1980, Nancy Kean Gifts discovered that another Dutch company, Keurkoop, was selling in the Netherlands a ladies handbag identical in appearance to the design which Nancy Kean Gifts had registered. Keurkoop also obtained its supplies from Taiwan and imported them directly into the Netherlands. Nancy Kean Gifts applied to the competent Dutch court for an injunction restraining Keurkoop from infringing its design right. Keurkoop argued in its defence that the granting of an injunction would be an unjustified restriction on trade between Member States, contrary to Article 28 of the Treaty. Keurkoop's contention was that Nancy Kean Gifts was a mere copyist and that, as such, it was not entitled to invoke Article 30 of the Treaty in favour of an exclusive design right that could hardly be considered intellectual property.

The Dutch court referred two questions to the Court of Justice for a preliminary ruling. Essentially it asked whether it was compatible with Articles 28 and 30 to enforce an exclusive design right against goods imported from another Member State, when the exclusive right had been granted to the person who was first to file the design and no person other than the author of the design or the person commissioning or employing the author was entitled to challenge the exclusive right on the ground that the person who filed the design was not the author or the person

---

[2] See para. 10 of the judgment; see also the detailed account in the 'facts and issues' part of the report.

commissioning or employing the author. In other words did Article 30 protect an exclusive right granted to a mere copyist?

An unusual feature of the case is that at first sight it appears, on the facts, to have little to do with the free movement of goods between Member States: both of the parties were importing the goods in question directly into the Netherlands from a non-member country. Indeed the Commission argued, in its observations to the Court, that intra-Community trade could not be concerned in so far as the goods at issue were imported directly from outside the common market.[3] However, as Advocate General Reischl pointed out, the questions would have arisen squarely if the goods, though originating outside the common market, had been imported via another Member State.[4] It was doubtless on that basis that the Court chose to reply to the questions. While the Court was undoubtedly right to do so, one cannot help feeling that the Court's approach might have been different if it had been confronted with a factual situation which demonstrated the implications for trade between Member States more clearly.

The Court was, in fact, extremely generous in the latitude which it granted to national legislatures. In spite of seeming to be aware of the unsatisfactory nature of an exclusive right granted to a copyist, it ruled that: 'In the present state of Community law and in the absence of Community standardization or of a harmonization of laws the determination of the conditions and procedures under which protection of designs is granted is a matter for national rules.'[5]

The Court was, not surprisingly, reluctant to engage in a comparative-law exercise to ascertain the minimum characteristics of an exclusive design right worthy of the name 'intellectual property'. It is submitted none the less that just such an exercise must be undertaken whenever the protection of Article 30 is invoked on behalf of exclusive rights of such a dubious nature. If Member States were allowed to grant exclusive rights, valid against goods imported from other Member States, on whatever conditions they thought fit, they would be able to erect wholly unjustified barriers to trade between Member States. If the formula used by the Court were taken literally, it would be broad enough to cover, for example, an exclusive right to import ordinary playing cards granted on the most

---

[3] See 2860 of the report on the case.

[4] See the opinion of Advocate General Reischl at p. 2878.

[5] At para. 18 of the judgment. The law governing design rights has now been harmonized by Directive 98/71/EC of the European Parliament and the Council of 13 October 1998 on the legal protection of designs (OJ 1998 L 289, p. 28). A design is only protected if it is 'new' and has 'individual character' (Art. 3(2)). A design is considered new if no identical design has been made available to the public before the filing of the application for registration (Art. 4). As regards Community design rights, similar provisions are contained in Arts 4 and 5 of Council Reg. (EC) No 6/2002 of 12 December 2001 on Community designs (OJ 2002 L 3, p. 1).

arbitrary of grounds, provided only that the right was characterized under national law as an intellectual property right.

It is submitted, therefore, that the Court did not really mean what it said in paragraph 18 of its judgment in *Keurkoop v Nancy Kean Gifts*. A condition of reasonableness must be read into the Court's formulation of the freedom granted to Member States. What the Court meant (or at least what it should have said) is that the conditions and procedures under which intellectual property rights are granted are a matter for national law, *provided that such conditions and procedures are not unreasonable or arbitrary and provided that they do not lead to the grant of intellectual property rights for which there is no objective justification*. There are some indications in subsequent judgments to indicate that that is indeed the appropriate test.

But does the design right granted to Nancy Kean Gifts satisfy that test? The answer must, it is submitted, be in the negative. The starting point for any discussion on this subject must be the simple, uncontestable observation (which was made in Chapter 1 of this book) that there must always be a good reason for the State to grant an exclusive right; there must be some over-riding consideration, pertaining to the general interest, which justifies interfering with the ordinary commercial freedom of everyone except the exclusive right-holder. In relation to design rights the justification for granting exclusivity is the need to reward and stimulate creativity, and also the moral and ethical consideration that someone who uses his skill, labour, and original thought in the creation of a new design should be allowed to prevent others from depriving him of the fruits of his success. If, on the other hand, someone simply copies the work of another person without authorization, it is difficult to see any justification for granting him an exclusive right.

3. THE CONCEPT OF RELATIVE NOVELTY

At the heart of the debate is the issue of novelty. How novel must a design or an invention be in order to qualify for protection? Must novelty be *absolute*, in the sense that the design or invention has not been anticipated by another person's work even in some remote part of the globe or at a distant point in the past? Or is *relative* novelty sufficient, meaning that the design or invention need only be new within a specific geographical area (e.g. the territory for which the exclusive right is granted) or that anticipations which occurred outside a specific time span may be disregarded?

Historically, intellectual property laws have often been satisfied with relative novelty in the geographical sense. Thus, to obtain a patent, it was sufficient in some countries to show that the invention was new within the territory of the granting State.[6] Indeed, that is how patents started out: in the fourteenth century, patents were used as a device to encourage the introduction of foreign technologies. There was no need 'to ascertain that the grantee had originated anything, only that at the time of the grant the practice was not being carried out, and hence could be presumed to be unknown, within the sovereign's domains'.[7] Such 'importation patents' survived for a very long time. They were available in Spain as recently as 1986.[8]

With the growing internationalization of patent law, and of trade in general, it was inevitable that such a concept of relative novelty would have to be abandoned. Modern patent laws have thus incorporated the concept of absolute novelty.[9] Design law does not seem to have been internationalized to the same extent, as is evidenced by the Benelux provision at issue in *Keurkoop v Nancy Kean Gifts* and a not dissimilar provision in the United Kingdom legislation.[10]

It is unfortunate that in *Keurkoop v Nancy Kean Gifts* the design was copied from a third country and that both the proprietor and the alleged infringer were importing goods directly from a third country. The potential damage to competition and free movement in the common market was perhaps not sufficiently obvious. If the design had been copied from the design register of another Member State and if the infringing goods had been manufactured in another Member State, it is difficult to believe that the Court would have been so indulgent. It would be a very strange common market if unscrupulous traders were allowed to copy designs from the registers existing in other Member States and thus not only secure a monopoly against competing suppliers in their own country but also wall off their national market against goods produced in other Member States, even goods produced by or with the consent of the author of the design.[11]

---

[6] That used to be the position in the United Kingdom: see ss. 14(1)(d) and 32(1)(e) of the Patents Act 1949.

[7] P. A. David, 'Intellectual Property Institutions and the Panda's Thumb: Patents, Copyrights, and Trade Secrets in Economic Theory and History', in *Global Dimensions of Intellectual Property Rights in Science and Technology* (eds. M. B. Wallerstein, M. E. Mogee and R. A. Schoen), National Academy Press, Washington, D.C., 1993, pp. 19–61, at p. 45.

[8] One author suggests that these 'outdated Spanish peculiarities' may have been justified when the country was at a low level of technological advancement: Luis Gimeno, 'Politics, Patents and Copyright in Twentieth Century Spain', in *The Prehistory and Development of Intellectual Property Systems* (ed. Alison Firth), Sweet and Maxwell, London, 1997, pp. 166 and 168.

[9] See, e.g., Art. 4 of the 1963 Strasbourg Convention on the Unification of Certain Points of Substantive Law on Patents for Invention and Art. 54 of the European Patent Convention. As regards the law of the United Kingdom, see s. 2(1) of the Patents Act 1977.

[10] See s. 1(4) of the Registered Designs Act 1949. The concept of absolute novelty has, however, now been adopted in the Community legislation: see the provisions cited in n. 5.

[11] The validity of the exclusive right granted to Nancy Kean Gifts could have been contested, under the Benelux Uniform Design Law, by the author of the design, by the author's employer, or by the person who commissioned the design. But it does not seem that an independent importer who traded in goods produced by the author or with the author's consent would have been able to contest the validity of the exclusive right.

But that is the absurd situation that could occur if the disputed Benelux provision and similar provisions in other Member States were deemed immune to challenge under Article 28.

It is interesting to note that Spain's importation patents were considered incompatible with the common market at the time when Spain's accession to the Community was negotiated. Protocol No. 8 to the Act of Accession of Spain and Portugal required their abolition and Spain complied with that obligation by Law No. 11/1986 of 20 March 1986.[12] It is difficult to discern any difference of substance between an importation patent and the design right granted to Nancy Kean Gifts. In both cases an exclusive right to deal in a particular type of product is granted to someone for no better reason than that he has introduced into the national territory a product that was not previously available in that territory.

At no point in its judgment did the Court make any attempt to state what justification there could be for granting an exclusive right to a mere copyist. The Advocate General was equally remiss. An attempt at justification was made by the United Kingdom, which submitted written observations (and which may have been anxious to protect its own legislation from attack). The case report reads as follows:

According to the United Kingdom the object of the Uniform Benelux Law is not the exclusive protection of the author of the design. It is also intended to protect anyone who, desirous of introducing a new design, has made a substantial investment (both of money and of skill) in launching and popularizing the design and, if he is a manufacturer, in the actual manufacture. It is right that the law should give him a limited monopoly so that someone else cannot take advantage of his investment by marketing a substantially identical product.

That argument is unconvincing. The same sort of logic could be used to justify an exclusive right granted to someone who, noticing that, say, electric toothbrushes are for some reason unobtainable in a particular Member State, invests money in manufacturing facilities, a distribution network and advertising, and then fills the gap in the market. If he has invented a new type of electric toothbrush, there is every reason to allow him to protect his invention by means of a patent; if he has devised an attractive new styling for the electric toothbrush, there is ample justification for conferring on him a design right to protect him against imitators; and if he sells his toothbrushes under a distinctive sign no one would dispute his right to sue infringers of his trade mark. But there is absolutely no justification, in a common market based on the principles of free trade and free

---

[12] *Boletín Oficial del Estado 1986*, No. 73 of 26 March 1986. De las Heras Lorenzo states that importation patents were abolished because they were considered anachronistic, not conducive to technological progress in Spain, and totally incompatible with European patent law: *Leyes de la Propiedad Industrial* (ed. T. de las Heras), 2nd edn, Aranzadi, 2002.

competition, for granting him an exclusive right to sell perfectly ordinary electric toothbrushes.

4. *INDUSTRIE DIENSTEN GROEP V BEELE*:[13]
THE COURT REQUIRES JUSTIFICATION FOR
A NATIONAL RULE AGAINST 'SLAVISH IMITATION'

Beele, a Dutch undertaking, was the sole importer for the Netherlands of certain cable ducts manufactured in Sweden. The ducts had been covered by patents in the Netherlands, Germany, and elsewhere but the patents had expired. Beele sought an injunction to prevent Industrie Diensten Groep from importing and selling in the Netherlands cable ducts made in Germany on the ground that these were a 'slavish imitation' of the products sold by Beele. The Dutch court took the view that, under Dutch law, the claimant was entitled to an injunction on the grounds that the German manufacturer could have designed a cable duct different from the Swedish product without impairing the quality of its products economically or technically and that by not doing so it had caused its products to be confused with those of the Swedish manufacturer. The Dutch court, entertaining doubts about the compatibility of such rules with Articles 28 and 30 of the Treaty, referred the matter to the Court of Justice.

The Court of Justice ruled as follows:

The rules of the [EC] Treaty on the free movement of goods do not prevent a rule of national law which applies to domestic and imported products alike, from allowing a trader, who for some considerable time in the Member State concerned has marketed a product which differs from similar products, to obtain an injunction against another trader restraining him from continuing to market in that Member State a product coming from another Member State in which it is lawfully marketed but which for no compelling reason is almost identical to the first-mentioned product and thereby needlessly causes confusion between the two products.

The Court does not seem to have regarded the right invoked by Beele as an intellectual property right as such. The case was therefore dealt with, not under Article 30, but under the 'Cassis de Dijon' case law developed in relation to Article 28. It will be recalled that the 'mandatory requirements' doctrine was devised in the 'Cassis de Dijon' case as a means of testing the legality of trading obstacles caused, in particular, by national rules on fair trading and consumer protection.[14] The Court's refusal to examine fair trading and consumer protection in the light of Article 30 is hardly

---

[13] Case 6/81 [1982] ECR 707.
[14] Case 120/78 *REWE-Zentrale v Bundesmonopolverwaltung für Branntwein* [1979] ECR 649; see section 3 of Chap. 2.

logical since they often raise issues that are closely related to the law of trade marks and passing-off. The Court was clearly aware of this in *Industrie Diensten Groep v Beele* because it pointed out that Article 10 *bis* of the Paris Convention for the Protection of Industrial Property prohibits, *inter alia*, all acts of such a nature as to create confusion with the goods of a competitor.[15] That suggests that if Beele had a right that was worthy of protection—and capable of prevailing over the free movement of goods—it should have been classified as an intellectual property right.

One consequence of applying the 'Cassis de Dijon' doctrine to the case was that the Court could not do what an identically composed Court was to do just six months later in *Keurkoop v Nancy Kean Gifts*: it could not say that in the absence of harmonization it was for national law to determine the conditions governing the grant of an exclusive right. In a 'Cassis de Dijon' analysis, the Court always enquires whether the import restriction is justified as being necessary to satisfy 'mandatory requirements' relating, for example, to consumer protection and fair trading. Thus, in *Industrie Diensten Groep v Beele* the Court solemnly declared that 'the protection against imitation provided in the way described in the judgment making the reference for a preliminary ruling must be examined to determine whether it meets those conditions'.[16]

The Court decided—a little generously perhaps—that the Dutch courts were justified in granting protection against slavish imitation in the type of situation under consideration. The Court noted that protection did not appear to be granted in a discriminatory fashion: it did not 'depend on country of origin of the product imitated and country of origin of the imitation'.[17] Moreover, the Dutch practice appeared to be consistent with Article 10 *bis* of the Paris Convention.[18] Crucially, the Court noted that, according to the findings of the Dutch court, the imported product was for no compelling reason practically identical to the products imitated and that Industrie Diensten Groep was needlessly causing confusion.

The Court was doubtless influenced by the comparative law study submitted by the Commission which showed that all the Member States (of whom there were ten at the time) granted some sort of protection against 'slavish imitation'.[19] The position was summed up by Advocate General VerLoren van Themaat in the following terms:

Only Italy expressly prohibits precise imitation by statute, namely in Article 2598 of its Civil Code. All other Member States infer such a prohibition either from specific legislation on unfair competition in general or from general principles of tortious

---

[15] At para. 9 of the judgment. For further discussion of the law of unfair competition, see section 5 of Chap. 8.
[16] At para. 7 of the judgment.
[17] At para. 8 of the judgment.
[18] At para. 9 of the judgment.
[19] At 712 of the report.

liability. The concept of 'precise imitation' prevailing in academic writing appears, admittedly not without some confusion, to be this: (1) even the exact imitation of someone else's product is not caught *per se* by the prohibition and (2) all the legal systems of the Member States are based on the principle that in the absence of a specific industrial property right like a patent anyone may freely draw inspiration in his industrial or trading activities from what others have done. In principle that freedom also comprises the right to imitate a competitor's product. Only if such imitation may create confusion in the mind of purchasers as to the identity or origin of the product do all the legal systems of the Member States regard imitation as prohibited.[20]

In the light of that comparative study, the Court could hardly hold that the practice of the Dutch courts was unjustified, even though it is difficult to feel any enthusiasm for the idea that trade between Member States should be restricted in the particular circumstances of *Industrie Diensten Groep v Beele*. What is significant, and praiseworthy, for present purposes is that the Court carefully scrutinized the national rule that impeded imports and examined whether it was justified. Unfortunately the Court appears to have been willing to do that only because the exclusive right in issue was not formally characterized as an intellectual property right. The design right in *Keurkoop v Nancy Kean Gifts* was not scrutinized as to its justification because it wore the mantle of intellectual property. The right against slavish imitation in *Industrie Diensten Groep v Beele* was subjected to scrutiny because it was presented as a rule of fair trading and consumer protection. There is no logic in this distinction.

5. *THETFORD V FIAMMA*: THE COURT ENQUIRES WHETHER A RULE OF NATIONAL PATENT LAW IS JUSTIFIED

Since *Keurkoop v Nancy Kean Gifts*, the Court has given a number of judgments confirming the principle that the conditions governing the grant of intellectual property rights are determined solely by national law.[21] The case

---

[20] At 721 of the report. As far as English law is concerned, the Commission and the Advocate General were obviously referring to the law of passing-off. It is doubtful whether the English courts would find in favour of the claimant in such a case as *Industrie Diensten Groep v Beele*, since the likely customers for the goods would be technically well-informed individuals in business who would readily distinguish between the goods of different suppliers. The 'Jif Lemon' case is an example of an English case in which an action for passing-off succeeded on the basis of the external appearance of the product: *Reckitt & Colman v Borden* [1990] RPC 340. That was, however, a case about ordinary consumer goods.

[21] See, in particular: Case 35/87 *Thetford v Fiamma* [1988] ECR 3585 at para. 12; Case 53/87 *CICRA v Renault* [1988] ECR 6039 at para. 10; Case 238/87 *Volvo v Veng* [1988] ECR 6211 at para. 7; Case 341/87 *EMI Electrola v Patricia Im-und Export* [1989] ECR 79 at para. 11; Case C-317/91 *Deutsche Renault v AUDI* [1993] ECR I-6227 at paras 20 and 31, and Joined Cases C-241/91P and C-242/91P *RTE and ITV v Commission* ('*Magill*') [1995] ECR I-743 at para. 49.

of *Thetford v Fiamma* is of particular interest because, in spite of reaffirming that principle, the Court showed a certain willingness to enquire into the justification for an intellectual property right used as a barrier to imports. Thetford was the proprietor of two United Kingdom patents relating to portable toilets. It appears that the invention in question could not have been patented in any other Member State.[22] It was patentable in the United Kingdom only by virtue of a provision in the Patents Act 1949,[23] according to which an invention was deemed not to have been anticipated only by reason of the fact that it was published in the United Kingdom either in a specification filed in pursuance of an application for a patent made in the United Kingdom more than 50 years earlier or in a specification describing the invention for the purposes of an application for protection in any country outside the United Kingdom made more than 50 years earlier. The invention patented by Thetford had been anticipated in such a specification.

Fiamma manufactured portable toilets in Italy and exported them to the United Kingdom through its British subsidiary. Considering that the imported toilets infringed its patents, Thetford sued Fiamma and sought an injunction to restrain the imports. Fiamma argued that the use of patents granted in such circumstances to prevent imports from another Member State could not be justified under Article 30, on the ground that the invention lacked novelty. Fiamma contended that, even if the patents could be relied on under Article 30, the principle of proportionality limited the type of relief that could be sought by Thetford and that only a claim for reasonable royalties, as opposed to an injunction, should be allowed.

The Court of Appeal referred two questions to the Court of Justice, asking essentially:

(1) whether a patent granted in such circumstances constituted 'industrial and commercial property' within the meaning of Article 30; and
(2) whether, if such a patent was entitled to the benefit of Article 30, the only relief that could be granted was an order to pay reasonable royalties.

Fiamma argued that the precedent established in *Keurkoop v Nancy Kean Gifts* in relation to the protection of designs could not be transposed to the field of patent law 'in view of the higher degree of harmonization of national legislation achieved in that field and the existence of international conventions based on the principle of absolute novelty'.

The Court rejected that argument on the grounds that no harmonization of national patent law had yet been achieved by measures of Community

---

[22] Except possibly Ireland: see the opinion of Advocate General Mischo at 3594, para. 2.
[23] S. 50(1).

law and that none of the international patent conventions in force was capable of supporting the argument.[24] The 1973 Munich Convention on the Granting of European Patents (the European Patent Convention or EPC), which was indeed based on the principle of absolute novelty, did not affect the existence of national legislation on the granting of patents. The 1963 Strasbourg Convention on the Unification of Certain Points of Substantive Law on Patents for Invention entered into force after the patent in question had been granted and could not therefore serve as a determining factor for the interpretation of Community law, and the 1975 Luxembourg Convention on the European Patent for the Common Market (the Community Patent Convention or CPC)[25] had not entered into force.[26] The Court held that the existence of patent rights was therefore a matter solely for national law.[27]

There was, in fact, some truth in Fiamma's assertion that national law had undergone a process of *de facto* harmonization and that relative novelty (both in the temporal and the geographical sense) had been swept away (even in the United Kingdom). The decisive point, however, was surely that the legislation of the Member States had not been harmonized at the time when the contested patent was granted; it would be wrong in principle to assume that such harmonization as had taken place destroyed the acquired rights of existing patent-holders, especially since none of the instruments invoked by Fiamma purported to have that effect.

The most interesting aspect of the *Thetford* judgment, however, is that the Court did not content itself with the observation that in the absence of relevant harmonization measures it was for national law alone to determine the conditions governing the grant of patents. The Court went on to consider whether the contested rule of United Kingdom patent law (the so-called '50-year rule') might constitute a means of arbitrary discrimination or a disguised restriction on trade between Member States, within the meaning of the second sentence of Article 30.

The Court found that the 50-year rule was not tainted with arbitrary discrimination: on the one hand, the rule prevented consideration being given to a specification disclosing an invention whether it was filed in the United Kingdom or in another State; secondly, there was no discrimination based on the nationality of applicants for patents, since foreign nationals had the same rights as United Kingdom nationals.[28]

The Court also found that the application of the 50-year rule did not give rise to a disguised restriction on trade between Member States. The Court

---

[24] At para. 14 of the judgment.

[25] Erroneously referred to in the Court's judgment as the European Patent Convention.

[26] It has still not entered into force and may never do so. The Commission is now proposing to create the Community patent by means of a Council Regulation.

[27] At para. 15 of the judgment.   [28] At para. 17 of the judgment.

considered that the rule was justified because it enabled a reward to be given, in the form of patent protection, to an inventor who rediscovered an old invention that had been forgotten.[29]

It is submitted that the Court's conclusion was correct. An invention that is gathering dust in the archives of a patent office can hardly be said to belong to the state of the art if the entire scientific community has forgotten about its existence. A researcher who unearths the lost technology, or an inventor who independently reinvents it, may make a significant contribution to scientific progress. Moreover, this is not such an unlikely hypothesis as might be thought. According to one author,[30] a patent specification filed in 1867 described an invention remarkably similarly to the jet engine patented in 1935 by Sir Frank Whittle.

It is interesting to speculate as to what results the Court would have reached in *Keurkoop v Nancy Kean Gifts* if it had considered the implications of the second sentence of Article 30. It is difficult to see what justification it could have found for granting an exclusive right to a person who simply copied, without authorization, a design belonging to another person. Thus the Court would have been required to conclude that reliance on the design right to block imports would have amounted to a disguised restriction on trade between Member States. Although the term 'disguised restriction' is seldom given much definition in the Court's judgments, it seems to be used in *Thetford* to mean simply a restriction designed to protect an exclusive right which purports to be a genuine intellectual property right but which, regardless of its characterization under national law, cannot be considered intellectual property at all. Of course that amounts to an important—and, it is submitted, wholly desirable—qualification of the principle that in the absence of harmonization Community law does not interfere with the Member States' freedom to lay down the conditions governing the grant of intellectual property rights. Typically, the Court gave the impression in *Thetford* of confirming *Keurkoop v Nancy Kean Gifts*, whereas in reality it was modifying its case law significantly. It is not easy to tell whether the change in the Court's stance was deliberate or unconscious. One thing, however, is clear: after *Thetford* it can no longer be said that the Court is unwilling to enquire whether there is any justification for the grant of an intellectual property right recognized by national law. In that case the Court demonstrated its readiness, at least from a hypothetical standpoint, to deny the benefit of Article 30 to an exclusive right that does not display the essential minimum features of intellectual property, regardless of the right's classification under national law.

---

[29] At para. 19 of the judgment. See also para. 26 of the opinion of Advocate General Mischo at 3598.

[30] P. Meinhardt, *Inventions, Patents and Monopolies*, 1950, p 73.

6. *CICRA V RENAULT*: THE COURT STILL REFUSES
TO SCRUTINIZE NATIONAL DESIGN LAWS

In *Thetford* the Court was doubtless influenced by a typically lucid opinion by Advocate General Mischo. The same Advocate General also delivered the opinion in *CICRA v Renault*.[31] Curiously, in a judgment given only three months after *Thetford*,[32] an almost identically composed full Court[33] was much less disposed to follow Advocate General Mischo's line of argument about the need to consider whether there was any real justification for an intellectual property right invoked under Article 30. The case was concerned with the exclusive design rights of car manufacturers. CICRA, an Italian association representing the interests of independent manufacturers of spare parts, challenged Renault's exclusive right to manufacture bodywork spare parts for Renault cars. CICRA argued that a design right covering the whole model was sufficient to ensure a fair return for car manufacturers and that there was no justification for extending the design right to separate bodywork parts. Since CICRA's members presumably manufactured spare parts in Italy and the contested design right was Italian, it is not immediately apparent how the free movement of goods was affected. Obviously it would not have been difficult to envisage a scenario in which an issue of free movement was raised directly, and that was presumably sufficient to persuade a court in Milan to request a preliminary ruling from the Court of Justice on the question whether a design right extending to bodywork spare parts was compatible with Articles 28 and 30 of the Treaty.

Advocate General Mischo thought it clear that the Court was entitled to enquire whether the legislation in question could be justified on grounds of the protection of industrial and commercial property.[34] The Advocate General concluded that such legislation was not objectionable in principle. He rejected the argument that it led to a 'double return' for car manufacturers, considering that the national legislature was not exceeding the limits of the protection of industrial and commercial property if it allowed the car manufacturer to apportion the amortization of the sums invested in creating new designs between the price of the vehicle as a whole and the price of spare parts.[35]

It is submitted that the Advocate General's approach was entirely correct. He was right to consider the issue of justification and right to conclude that national legislation recognizing a design right for spare parts was not

---

[31] Cited in n. 21.

[32] The dates of the two judgments were 30 June 1988 and 5 October 1988.

[33] Ten of the 11 judges were the same. The two cases were not, however, assigned to the same judge-rapporteur.

[34] See para. 21 of the opinion.   [35] See para. 31 of the opinion.

so unreasonable as to be denied protection under Article 30. The extension of design rights to spare parts is a highly controversial issue.[36] It is an issue on which there is room for differing opinions. When considering whether an exclusive right is capable of justifying restrictions on trade under Article 30 in the name of intellectual property, the Court should allow the Member States a wide margin of appraisal.

The judgment of the Court in *CICRA v Renault* does not, however, follow the approach of the Advocate General or, more surprisingly, the approach which the Court had itself taken three months earlier in *Thetford*. The Court cited *Keurkoop v Nancy Kean Gifts* as authority for the proposition that in the absence of harmonization the conditions under which designs are protected fall to be determined by national law.[37] It noted that the right to oppose the manufacture, sale, export, or import of products infringing the design was part of the substance of the exclusive right, the existence of which would be jeopardized if the proprietor of the right was not allowed to oppose such activities.[38] As regards the second sentence of Article 30, the Court simply noted that the exclusive right granted to car manufacturers by the legislation in issue could be enforced without distinction, against domestic and imported products and that the legislation was not intended to favour national products at the expense of products originating in other Member States.[39]

The difference between the Court's approach to the second sentence of Article 30 in *CICRA v Renault*, on the one hand, and in *Thetford*, on the other hand, is striking. In *Thetford* the Court used that provision as a basis for enquiring whether there was any objective justification for a patent granted under the 50-year rule. In *CICRA v Renault* the Court seemed to assume that the second sentence of Article 30 was concerned solely with the issue of discrimination between domestic and imported goods and saw no reason to examine the issue of objective justification for a design right extending to spare parts.

7. DESIGNATIONS OF ORIGIN: THE COURT REQUIRES JUSTIFICATION

It is interesting to contrast the Court's attitude towards the Benelux design law in *Keurkoop v Nancy Kean Gifts* with the attitude that it had taken some years earlier towards the German legislation reserving the terms 'Sekt' and 'Weinbrand' to products made in Germany or other German-speaking countries. In *Commission v Germany*[40] the German government argued

---

[36] For an exhaustive discussion of the issue, see I. Govaere, *The Use and Abuse of Intellectual Property Rights in EEC Law*, Part 3, Sweet and Maxwell, London, 1996.
[37] At para. 10 of the judgment.   [38] At para. 11 of the judgment.
[39] At para. 12 of the judgment.   [40] Case 12/74 [1975] ECR 181.

that such a rule was justified on grounds of protection of intellectual property, since the terms 'Sekt' and 'Weinbrand' functioned as indirect indications of origin and were therefore a form of industrial and commercial property. The Court rejected the argument and held that an appellation of origin or indication of origin may only justify restrictions on the free movement of goods in so far as the product which it describes possesses 'qualities and characteristics which are due to the fact that it originated in a specific geographical area'.[41]

The legislation on appellations (or 'designations') of origin had not been harmonized at the time.[42] The Court did not, however, say that in view of that circumstance it was for national law alone to determine the conditions under which appellations of origin were to be protected. On the contrary, the Court expressly ruled that 'Sekt' and 'Weinbrand' were not indications of origin but merely generic terms denoting sparkling wine and brandy respectively, and were therefore not eligible for protection as industrial property rights. Why then could the Court not say that the design right invoked by Nancy Kean Gifts was not an industrial property right?

In *Exportur v Lor and Confiserie du Tech* the Court again showed a willingness to inquire whether there was any justification for a trade restriction caused by a geographical indication of origin. That case concerned the terms 'turrón de Alicante' and 'turrón de Jijona'. 'Turrón' is a type of Spanish dessert which is made in particular in Jijona, a town in the province of Alicante. Under Spanish legislation the terms 'turrón de Alicante' and 'turrón de Jijona' may be used only by producers from that region. By means of a bilateral Convention, France and Spain had agreed to protect each other's designations of origin. The Court decided that a trade restriction caused by such a Convention might be justified under Article 30 of the Treaty, provided that the designation in question was not generic in the country of origin at the time when the Convention came into force. The judgment is of particular interest, in the present context, because the Court expressly referred to a comparative study of the national laws governing designations of origin.[43] That is exactly the kind of step that the Court avoided taking in *Keurkoop v Nancy Kean Gifts*. The Court did not explain why designations of origin should be treated differently from designs.

---

[41] At para. 7 of the judgment.

[42] This subject is now covered by Community legislation: see Council Regulation (EEC) No. 2081/92 of 14 July 1992 on the protection of geographical indications and designations of origin for agricultural products and foodstuffs (OJ 1992 L 208, p. 1) and, as regards wine and sparkling wine, Council Regulation (EC) No. 1493/1999 of 17 May 1999 on the common organization of the market in wine (OJ 1999 L 179, p. 1). Geographical indications for spirits are covered by Council Regulation (EEC) No. 1976/89 of 29 May 1989 laying down the general rules on the definition, description and presentation of spirit drinks (OJ 1989 L 160, p. 1).

[43] At para. 11 of the judgment.

8. *WARNER BROTHERS AND METRONOME V CHRISTIANSEN*: THE COURT REQUIRES JUSTIFICATION FOR A NATIONAL RULE ON VIDEO RENTAL RIGHTS

In his opinion in *CICRA v Renault*, Advocate General Mischo based his view that the Court was entitled to consider whether the national legislation in question was justified on the judgment delivered one month earlier in *Warner Brothers and Metronome v Christiansen*.[44] The national legislation in issue in that case was a Danish law on the rental of video-cassettes incorporating cinematographic works. Under that law the owner of the copyright in such a work was entitled to prohibit the renting of video-cassettes which had been sold with his authorization. Warner Brothers owned the copyright in a James Bond film and assigned the management of the video rights in Denmark to Metronome.

Mr Christiansen, the owner of a video shop in Copenhagen, bought a copy of the film in the United Kingdom, where it had been marketed with the consent of Warner Brothers. Mr Christiansen advertised the film as being available for hire in Denmark. Warner Brothers and Metronome sought an injunction to prohibit Mr Christiansen from hiring out the video without their consent. The Danish *Østre Landsret* (Eastern Division of the High Court) requested a preliminary ruling from the Court of Justice on the question, essentially, whether it was compatible with Articles 28 and 30 to allow the owner of the copyright in a film to prohibit the hiring-out of copies of the film which had been marketed in another Member State with his consent.

After an unusually detailed scrutiny of the economic justification for a law which allowed the copyright owner to control the rental of video-cassettes, the Court concluded that such legislation was compatible with the Treaty provisions on the free movement of goods, even where the video-cassettes had been marketed in another Member State with the consent of the copyright owner. The judgment is of particular interest, for present purposes, because of what it does not say. The problem in *Warner Brothers* was due essentially to discrepancies in national laws. In some countries (notably Denmark and France)[45] a separate right to control the rental of videos existed. In other countries no such right was recognized. The ideal solution to problems caused by such discrepancies would, of course, be to harmonize the national laws and ensure either that a rental right exists in all the Member States[46] or in none of them. One might have expected the

---

[44] Case 158/86 [1988] ECR 2605.

[45] For a comparative survey of the laws of the Member States, see the opinion of Advocate General Mancini in *Warner Brothers* at 2619, para. 3.

[46] Such a solution was subsequently adopted in Council Directive 92/100/EEC of 19 November 1992 on rental right and lending right and on certain rights related to copyright in the field and intellectual property (OJ 1992 L 346, p. 61).

Court to state that in the absence of harmonization it is for national law to determine whether the owners of copyright (in books, films, gramophone records, etc.) should enjoy a separate right to control rentals. That would seem to follow from the general principle that in the absence of harmonization the conditions governing the grant of intellectual property rights are determined by national law.

Strangely, there is no mention of that principle either in the Court's judgment or in the advocate general's opinion. The Court seems to have assumed implicitly that the principle applies only to the basic rights conferred on the copyright owner, namely the exclusive right to perform the work in public and the exclusive right to reproduce the work.[47] The Court seems not to have accepted that the exclusive rental right, in those Member States which recognized the existence of such a right, was a distinct intellectual property right.

If the Court had recognized the distinctness of the rental right, it would presumably have ruled that in the absence of harmonization the conditions governing the creation of the right were to be determined by national law. It seems therefore that Advocate General Mischo was overestimating the significance of the *Warner Brothers* precedent when he assumed that it heralded a general willingness on the part of the Court to enquire into the justification for national legislation granting intellectual property rights which are capable of impeding trade between Member States.[48]

9. THE PRINCIPLE OF NON-DISCRIMINATION: THE *PHIL COLLINS* CASE

The Court of Justice has expressly recognized one important qualification with regard to the Member States' sovereign power to lay down the conditions governing the grant of intellectual property rights—those conditions must not discriminate against the nationals of other Member States.

The unlawfulness of such discrimination is apparent from Article 12 of the Treaty, which proclaims: 'Within the scope of application of this Treaty, and without prejudice to any special provisions contained therein, any discrimination on grounds of nationality shall be prohibited.'

The need to eliminate discriminatory conditions affecting the grant of intellectual property rights was recognized by the Council of Ministers as early as 1961, in the General Programme for the Abolition of Restrictions

---

[47] See para. 13 of the judgment.

[48] For further consideration of the significance of *Warner Brothers* as a precedent, see G. Friden, 'Recent Developments in EEC Intellectual Property Law: The Distinction between Existence and Exercise Revisited' (1989) CML Rev. 192.

on Freedom to Provide Services[49] and in the General Programme for the Abolition of Restrictions on Freedom of Establishment.[50] Both of those programmes called for the abolition of 'provisions and practices which, in respect of foreign nationals only, exclude, limit or impose conditions on the power to exercise rights normally attaching to the provision of services [or to an activity as a self-employed person] and in particular the power . . . to acquire, use or dispose of intellectual property and all rights deriving therefrom'.

The Court observed in 1976 in *Thieffry v Conseil de l'Ordre des Avocats à la Cour de Paris* that the General Programmes provide 'useful guidance for the implementation of the relevant provisions of the Treaty'.[51]

We have already seen that in *Thetford* the Court attached some importance to the non-discriminatory nature of the United Kingdom's 50-year rule. It is clear that if the rule had treated nationals of other Member States differently from United Kingdom nationals, an import restriction caused by a patent granted under that rule might have lost the benefit of Article 30. The importance of the principle of non-discrimination, in the field of intellectual property, was spelled out in two joined cases decided in 1993.[52] The facts of the cases, in which two aging British rocks stars were able to make a surprising contribution to the development of Community law, were as follows.

Phil Collins gave a concert in California in 1983. It was recorded without his consent and compact discs reproducing it were sold in Germany. Mr Collins sought an injunction from the German courts to prevent the sale of such recordings and an order for the seizure of the infringing copies. He was denied protection under German law because the concert had taken place in a State that was not a party to the 1961 Rome Convention for the Protection of Performers, Producers of Phonograms and Broadcasting Organizations.[53] Under Article 4 of that Convention, each Contracting State is required to grant 'national treatment' to performers in respect of performances that take place in another Contracting State. Germany and the United Kingdom were parties to the Rome Convention but the United States was not. Hence Mr Collins could not claim protection under Article 4 of the Convention. He would, however, have been able to object to the distribution of the unauthorized recordings if he had been a German national. By virtue of paragraph 125(1) of the *Urheberrechtsgesetz* (German Copyright Law), German nationals enjoyed protection for all their performances regardless of the place of performance.

---

[49] OJ (English Special Edition, Second Series IX), p. 3.
[50] OJ (English Special Edition, Second Series IX), p. 7.
[51] Case 71/76 [1977] ECR 765 at para. 14.
[52] Joined Cases C-92/92 and C-326/92 [1993] ECR I-5145.
[53] This Convention is dealt with in section 9.3 of Chap. 10.

The other case concerned recordings of certain works performed by Cliff Richard. The recordings were first published in the United Kingdom in 1958 and 1959. The copyright had been assigned to a company called EMI Electrola, which attempted to prevent the sale of unauthorized copies in Germany. EMI Electrola was denied protection under German law, apparently because the performance had taken place before the date on which the Rome Convention came into force in Germany. Once again that would not have been a problem if the performer had been a German national. A German performer and his assignees would have enjoyed protection under the *Urheberrechtsgesetz*. Foreign nationals had to have recourse to the Rome Convention and could derive no benefit from it as regards performances that took place before its entry into force in Germany.

There was, then, blatant discrimination in both cases. United Kingdom nationals (or their assignees) were unable to prevent the distribution of unauthorized recordings of their performances, whereas German nationals (or their assignees) enjoyed such a right. The only issue that needed to be clarified was whether the discrimination fell 'within the scope of application of [the] Treaty', as required in order for Article 12 to apply. The Court had no difficulty in holding that it did:

Like the other industrial and commercial property rights, the exclusive rights conferred by literary and artistic property are by their nature such as to affect trade in goods and services and also competitive relationships within the Community. For that reason, and as the Court has consistently held, those rights, although governed by national legislation, are subject to the requirements of the Treaty and therefore fall within its scope of application.[54]

The Court held that Article 12 requires each Member State to ensure that nationals of other Member States in a situation governed by Community law are placed on a completely equal footing with its own nationals.[55] The legislation of a Member State could not, therefore, deny authors and performers from other Member States, and those claiming under them, the right, accorded by that legislation to nationals of that Member State, to prohibit the marketing of a phonogram manufactured without their consent, where the performance was given outside its national territory.[56]

The Court also confirmed that Article 12 produces direct effect, meaning that 'the principle of non-discrimination . . . may be directly relied upon before a national court by an author or performer from another Member State, or by those claiming under them, in order to claim the benefit of protection reserved to national authors and performers'.[57]

Dire predictions were made by the defendants in *Phil Collins* that application of the principle of non-discrimination in the field of copyright would

[54] At para. 22 of the judgment.   [55] At para. 32 of the judgment.
[56] At para. 33 of the judgment.   [57] At para. 34 of the judgment.

upset the delicate balance established by various international Conventions. In particular, authors from other Member States would be able to claim the long term of protection (seventy years after the death of the author) provided for in German law, whereas under Article 7(8) of the Berne Convention[58] Germany was not required to grant them a longer term of protection than the term fixed in the country of origin of the work.[59] As Advocate General Jacobs pointed out, that is indeed what Article 12 requires.

The Advocate General's view was confirmed nine years later in *Land Hessen v Ricordi*.[60] That case arose out performances of Puccini's opera *La Bohème* which took place in a German theatre between 1993 and 1995 without the authorization of the copyright owner (Ricordi). Puccini died in 1924. Under Italian law prior to harmonization, copyright expired fifty-six years after the death of the author. Under German law the term of protection was seventy years *post mortem auctoris*. Since Italy was the country of origin of *La Bohème*, the work was protected under the German Copyright Law, in conjunction with Article 7(8) of the Berne Convention, until 1980. Had Puccini been a German national, it would have been protected until the end of 1994 and Ricordi's authorization would have been required for at least some of the performances. The Court had no difficulty in holding that this sort of discrimination was contrary to Article 12 of the Treaty. The Court pointed out that the Berne Convention did not prevent Germany from granting foreign authors the same term of protection as German authors.[61] The granting of the shorter term of protection available in the country of origin was merely an option. Given that situation and the requirement of a 'completely equal footing', it was clear that the works of authors who had the nationality of another Member State must benefit from 'national treatment', i.e. the same treatment as works by German authors.

There is nothing shocking in this. There are various international Conventions, especially in the field of copyright, that require or permit the contracting parties to grant a minimum standard of protection to the nationals of other countries rather than national treatment. In so far as an EC Member State grants its own nationals something above the minimum standard, all that Article 12 requires is that such a Member State should grant the same treatment to nationals of other Member States. This is hardly likely to jeopardize the whole system of international copyright protection. Moreover, under Community law it is a perfectly normal

---

[58] This Convention is dealt with in section 9.1 of Chap. 10.

[59] See para. 27 of the Advocate General's opinion. It appears that Italian furniture is now protected by copyright in the Netherlands (in the same way as Dutch furniture) as a result of the *Phil Collins* judgment, even though in Italy it is protected only under the law of designs: Herman Cohen Jehoram, 'European Copyright Law—Ever More Horizontal', (2001) 32 IIC 532, 535.

[60] Case C-360/00 [2002] ECR I-5089.   [61] At para. 33 of the judgment.

phenomenon for someone to receive better treatment in another Member State than in his own country.

A more difficult issue raised by *Land Hessen v Ricordi* is whether the principle of non-discrimination can be invoked on behalf of someone who was never in fact a Community national for the simple reason that he died before the European Community came into existence. The Court answered that question in the affirmative.[62] It did so on the ground that copyright may be relied on not only by an author but also by those claiming under him. It pointed out that the copyright in issue was still producing its effect as regards the persons claiming under Puccini when the Treaty entered into force in 1958.

The Court's reasoning on this point is not entirely convincing.[63] The fact that Puccini's successors in title still possessed exclusive rights in his works in Italy and Germany when the Treaty entered into force is not a reason for saying that the duration of their rights in Germany had to be the same as they would have been if Puccini had died a citizen of the Weimar Republic. Perhaps a more convincing reason is that the persons who claim under deceased authors tend to have the same nationality as the author. Thus a German rule that discriminates against deceased Italian authors will also discriminate against their successors in title, who are likely to have Italian nationality.[64] There must, however, be doubts about how to apply the principle of non-discrimination in relation to authors who, at the time of their death, had the nationality of a State that has since ceased to exist as such. Theoretically this problem could arise in connection with some of the countries that are due to accede to the European Union in May 2004, namely Estonia, Latvia, Lithuania, and Slovenia.[65]

---

[62] At para. 25 of the judgment.

[63] Advocate General Ruiz-Jarabo Colomer argued (at paras 42–50 of his opinion) that Art. 12 should apply in the circumstances of the case because its application is not dependent on the existence of an individual with the capacity to invoke it. This reasoning seems equally unconvincing. Art. 12 cannot apply in a vacuum. Its application is dependent on the existence of an individual or group of individuals who are treated differently on the basis of their nationality.

[64] Advocate General Ruiz-Jarabo Colomer mentioned this possibility (at para. 47 of his opinion) but considered it unnecessary to have recourse to the concept of indirect discrimination.

[65] In practice the point is unlikely to arise because the term of protection has now been harmonized, at 70 years after the death of the author, by Art. 1 of Council Directive 93/98/EEC of 29 October 1993 harmonizing the term of protection of copyright and certain related rights (OJ 1993 L 290, p. 9).

5

The dichotomy between the existence of the right and its exercise

1. THE SEARCH FOR THE APPROPRIATE TEST

It is clear from Article 30 that a balance must be struck between the principle of free movement and the protection of intellectual property rights. Since the mid-1960s the European Court of Justice has been in search of the correct balance. It has not always found the task easy. In order to determine what restrictions on free movement are 'justified' under Article 30, the Court has developed a number of tests. None of those tests has proved entirely satisfactory, mainly because of the extreme vagueness of some of the terms used in them. The Court's approach has fluctuated over the years and it has not always shown great fidelity to the various tests that it has elaborated. The overall impression one has is that the Court is still searching for wisdom in this difficult area.

2. THE ORIGIN OF THE DISTINCTION BETWEEN EXISTENCE AND EXERCISE IN COMPETITION LAW

The oldest principle established by the Court is based on a rather puzzling dichotomy between the existence of an intellectual property right and the exercise of the right. According to that principle, the Treaty guarantees the existence of the right, but the exercise of the right may be limited by the prohibitions laid down in the Treaty. The existence/exercise dichotomy dates back to the *Consten and Grundig*[1] case decided in 1966.

The facts of *Consten and Grundig* were as follows. Grundig, the German company, granted the exclusive right to distribute its products in France to a French company called Consten. Grundig also allowed Consten to register in France the trade mark GINT (a contraction of Grundig International). Another French company (UNEF) obtained products marketed by Grundig in Germany under the GINT trade mark and started to sell them in France. Consten commenced trade mark infringement proceedings against UNEF before a French court. UNEF complained to the European Commission, which adopted a decision, in the exercise of its powers in the field of competition law, declaring, *inter alia*, that the agreement between Grundig

---

[1] Joined Cases 56 and 58/64 [1966] ECR 299.

and Consten on the registration and use of the GINT trade mark was contrary to Article 81 of the Treaty. The decision required Grundig and Consten to refrain from any action designed to prevent other persons from acquiring Grundig products with a view to their resale in France. Consten and Grundig applied to the Court of Justice for the annulment of the Commission's decision.

One of the arguments advanced by Consten and Grundig was based on Articles 30 and 295 of the Treaty which, according to the applicants, guaranteed industrial property rights. Article 295 provides that: 'This Treaty shall in no way prejudice the rules in the Member States governing the system of property ownership.'

According to the applicants, the GINT trade mark, registered in France as the property of Consten, was an industrial property right granted in accordance with the system of property ownership in force in France and could not be prejudiced by Article 81 or by any other provision of the Treaty.

The Court was not impressed by that argument. As regards Article 30, it held that that provision, belonging to the section of the Treaty dealing with the free movement of goods, could not limit the field of application of the competition rules of the Treaty. As regards Article 295, the Court simply observed that the injunction contained in the contested decision to refrain from using rights under national trade mark law in order to set an obstacle in the way of parallel imports 'does not affect the grant of those rights but only limits their exercise to the extent necessary to give effect to the prohibition under Article [81(1)]'.[2]

Thus was born the dichotomy between the existence of intellectual property rights and their exercise. The existence of the right is guaranteed by the Treaty, whether by Article 30 or by Article 295; but the exercise of the right may be limited by other provisions of the Treaty. Although the origin of the distinction between existence and exercise is habitually traced back to *Consten and Grundig*, the Court did not in fact use the term 'existence' in that judgment; instead it used the less colourful expression 'grant'.[3] It was not until the *Parke, Davies*[4] judgment in 1968 that the Court first spoke of the existence of the right.

3. THE EXTENSION OF THE DISTINCTION TO THE FREE MOVEMENT OF GOODS

As we have seen, the existence/exercise dichotomy was born in the context of a case which focused on the competition rules of the Treaty. Its applic-

---

[2] At 345.   [3] The word used in the French version was *attribution*.
[4] Case 24/67 *Parke, Davies v Centrafarm* [1968] ECR 55.

ability in the context of the rules on the free movement of goods was confirmed five years later in *Deutsche Grammophon v Metro*.[5] That too was a case about parallel imports.

Deutsche Grammophon manufactured and marketed gramophone records. In Germany it attempted to control the prices charged by retailers of its products. Metro owned a chain of stores in Germany in which it sold records produced by Deutsche Grammophon. As a result of Metro's failure to respect the prices fixed by the manufacturer, Deutsche Grammophon refused to supply its products to Metro. Metro then acquired from a wholesaler records which Deutsche Grammophon had marketed in France through its French subsidiary. Metro placed those records on sale in Germany, once again undercutting Deutsche Grammophon's official prices. Deutsche Grammophon obtained an injunction from a German court prohibiting Metro from selling its products. The German court based its decision on the German Copyright Law, which granted the manufacturer of gramophone records an exclusive right of distribution. Under that law, the manufacturer could not prevent the sale and resale of products which had been marketed in Germany by the manufacturer or with his consent, but it was not clear whether the manufacturer could oppose the resale of products which he had marketed outside Germany.

The case reached the *Hanseatisches Oberlandesgericht*, which referred two questions to the Court of Justice for a preliminary ruling on the competition rules of the Treaty. The Court of Justice did not confine itself to answering those questions but went on to examine the situation in the light of Articles 28 and 30 of the Treaty. The real significance of the judgment is that it established what is now known as the principle of the exhaustion of rights. According to that principle (which is dealt with in Chapter 7), the owner of an intellectual property right cannot rely on that right in order to prevent the further marketing of goods which he has placed on the market anywhere in the European Community. In the course of establishing that principle, the Court observed that it was clear from Article 30 that 'although the Treaty does not affect the existence of rights recognized by the legislation of a Member State with regard to industrial and commercial property, the exercise of such rights may nevertheless fall within the prohibitions laid down by the Treaty'.[6]

Marenco and Banks argue that the extension of the existence/exercise dichotomy beyond the field of competition law to the field of free movement is illogical. They maintain that while the prohibitions laid down in Articles 81 and 82 tend to affect only a given use of an intellectual property right,

---

[5] Case 78/70 [1971] ECR 487.
[6] At para. 11 of the judgment.

and not the right as such, the prohibitions resulting from Article 28 have a far more incisive effect.[7]

4. THE DUBIOUS MERITS OF THE DISTINCTION

Altogether the Court has invoked the distinction between the existence of a right and its exercise in approximately a dozen judgments,[8] in relation to both competition law and the free movement of goods. The Court has also held that the distinction applies in the context of the free movement of services.[9]

The distinction has been criticized by many authors on the ground that it is vague, artificial, unhelpful and unworkable.[10] The criticism seems to

---

[7] G. Marenco and K. Banks, 'Intellectual Property and Community Rules on Free Movement: Discrimination Unearthed' (1990) EL Rev. 224, 226. The first part of Marenco and Banks' assumption is questionable in the light of the *Magill* case (see below). The second part is not always well founded: the application of the exhaustion principle in a straightforward case of parallel national rights of equal scope does not impose an intolerable burden on the right-holder.

[8] *Consten and Grundig* (cited in n. 1); *Parke, Davies* (cited in n. 4); Case 40/70 *Sirena v Eda* |1971| ECR 69; Case 192/73 *Van Zuylen v HAG ('HAG I')* |1974| ECR 731 at para. 8; Case 15/74 *Centrafarm v Sterling Drug* |1974| ECR 1147 at para. 7; Case 16/74 *Centrafarm v Winthrop* |1974| ECR 1183 at para. 6; Case 119/75 *Terrapin v Terranova* |1976| ECR 1039 at para. 5; Case 102/77 *Hoffmann-La Roche v Centrafarm* |1978| ECR 1139 at para. 6; Case 3/78 *Centrafarm v American Home Products Corporation* |1978| ECR 1823 at para. 9; Case 58/80 *Dansk Supermarked v Imerco* |1981| ECR 181 at para. 11; Case 1/81 *Pfizer v Eurim-Pharm* |1981| ECR 2913 at para. 6; Case 262/81 *Coditel v Ciné-Vog Films ('Coditel II')* |1982| ECR 3381 at para. 13. The distinction between existence and exercise was, in addition, implicitly recognized in Case 158/86 *Warner Brothers and Metronome v Christiansen* |1988| ECR 2605 at para. 18 (where the Court spoke of the right being rendered worthless if its exercise were limited in a particular way). Case 238/87 *Volvo v Veng* |1988| ECR 6211 at paras 8 and 9, and Case 53/87 *CICRA v Renault* |1988| ECR 6039 at paras 11 and 16. In para. 11 of *CICRA v Renault* the Court stated that to prevent the application of the national legislation allowing the owner of a design right over car body panels to oppose the manufacture of such panels by third parties would be tantamount to 'challenging the very existence of that right'. In para. 16 the Court held that exercise of the exclusive right could be prohibited under Art. 82 if it gave rise to certain forms of abusive conduct on the part of a dominant undertaking.

[9] *Coditel II* (cited in n. 8) at para. 13.

[10] See, e.g., V. Korah, 'Dividing the Common Market through National Industrial Property Rights' (1972) 35 MLR 634, 636; R. Joliet, 'Patented Articles and the Free Movement of Goods within the EEC' (1975) 28 *Current Legal Problems* 15, 23; R. Casati, 'The "Exhaustion" of Industrial Property Rights in the EEC: Exclusive Manufacturing and Sales Provisions in Patent and Know-how Licensing Agreements' (1978) 17 *Columbia Journal of Transnational Law* 313, 322; F.-K. Beier, 'Industrial Property and the Free Movement of Goods in the Internal European Market' (1990) 21 IIC 131, 147; R. Joliet, in collaboration with D. T. Keeling, 'Trade Mark Law and the Free Movement of Goods: The Overruling of the Judgment in *HAG I*' (1991) 22 IIC 303, 314; P. Van Ommeslaghe, 'Les droits de propriété industrielle et commerciale et les dispositions des articles 30, 36, 59, 60, 85 et 86 du Traité de Rome', in *Liber amicorum Frédéric Dumon*, Kluwer, Antwerp, 1983, pp. 247, 1256; D. Wyatt and A. Dashwood, *The Law of the European Community*, 3rd edn, Sweet and Maxwell, London, 1994, p 574; V. Korah, *An Introductory Guide to EC Competition Law and Practice*, 5th edn. Sweet and Maxwell, London, 1994, p. 190; J. Massaguer, *Mercado Común y Patente Nacional*, Bosch, Barcelona, 1989, pp. 138 *et seq.*; G. Tritton, 'Articles 30 to 36 and

have been taken to heart. Whereas the distinction was referred to, almost ritualistically, in virtually every judgment in this field between 1971 and 1982, the formula first used in paragraph 11 of *Deutsche Grammophon* does not occur in any judgment after *Coditel II*.[11] The distinction is hinted at in some later judgments but it is no longer treated as providing the key to the problem. Some authors[12] have concluded that the distinction has quietly been abandoned by the Court. In a note on the *HAG II* case, Rothnie speaks of the 'apparent demise of the dichotomy between existence and exercise'.[13] Tritton, in a note on the *Ideal Standard*[14] judgment, suggests tentatively that the doctrine 'has now become only of historical and academic interest'. Advocate General Fennelly rallied to this position in his opinion in *Merck v Primecrown*,[15] where he stated that the distinction is at times 'quite unreal' and 'may now at least in so far as the interpretation of the Articles 28 to 30 is concerned, be discarded'. None of those distinguished authorities seems to lament the passing of the much-derided distinction.

The obvious difficulty with the distinction between existence and exercise is that it does not have any clear meaning in relation to something as intangible as an intellectual property right. If we say that a person's ownership of land cannot be called in question but that the law may limit his use of the land, we are making a reasonably clear statement about legal rights in terms that will readily be understood by anyone who is remotely familiar with planning law. We would mean, for example, that the authorities may not confiscate the land or burn down a house situated on the land, but that they may prevent the owner from running a brothel or building a multi-storey car park on his land.

The same statement, made in relation to intellectual property as opposed to land, conveys much less meaning. Intellectual property has no tangible existence and merely denotes a bundle of rights recognised in law. As Wyatt and Dashwood observe, 'if Community law prevents any right in the bundle from being exercised, the property is to that extent diminished'.[16] That raises the question how much diminution can an intellectual property right withstand before its existence can be said to be threatened.

Intellectual Property: Is the Jurisprudence of the ECJ Now of an Ideal Standard?' [1994] 10 EIPR 422, 423; W. A. Rothnie, '*HAG II*: Putting the Common Origin Doctrine to Sleep' [1991] 1 EIPR 24, 28. The distinction between existence and exercise was defended by J. Mertens de Wilmars (then a judge at the European Court, subsequently its President) in 'Aspects communautaires du droit des marques' (1972) 87 *Journal des Tribunaux*, No. 4806.

[11] Cited in n. 8.

[12] Note, however, Marenco and Banks, who mantained in 1990 that the distintion had not become obsolete: op. cit. (n. 7), at p. 226.

[13] Op. cit. (n. 10), at 29.

[14] Op. cit. (n. 10), at 423.

[15] Joined Cases C-267/95 and C-268/95 [1996] ECR I-6285 at para. 93 of the opinion.

[16] D. Wyatt and A. Dashwood, loc. cit. (n. 10).

Perhaps the one useful element in the existence/exercise dichotomy is that it serves as a reminder that, whatever limitations Community law imposes on the exercise of an intellectual property right, it must not destroy the substance of the right. The nucleus of the exclusive right recognized by national law must remain intact. The judicial and legislative organs of the Community must not curtail the exercise of the right to such an extent as to produce a confiscatory effect.

5. ARTICLE 295 AS A GUARANTEE OF PROPERTY RIGHTS

The relevance of Article 295 of the Treaty, as a constitutional guarantee of property rights, is debatable.[17] Tritton observes that that provision was derived from Article 85 of the ECSC Treaty, which was intended only to ensure that Member States would be free to determine whether enterprises subject to the ECSC Treaty were publicly or privately owned.[18] A similar view was canvassed by the Commission in the *Parke, Davies* case,[19] but was firmly rejected by Advocate General Roemer, who thought that Article 295 should be interpreted 'as meaning that all the basic elements of the national system of property ownership must remain unchanged', including the basic elements of industrial property rights.[20] The Court of Justice has generally avoided making clear statements as to the relevance of Article 295 in relation to the safeguarding of such rights.[21]

Regardless of the role of Article 295, it is in any event clear that an act amounting to a confiscation of property rights recognized under the national law of a Member State would, in principle, be incompatible with the Community legal order. Such an act would constitute a breach of a fundamental right which the Court is required to uphold in accordance with its general duty under Article 220 of the Treaty to ensure that the law is

[17] See the opinion of Advocate General Jacobs in Case C-10/89 *CNL Sucal v HAG GF* (*'HAG II'*) [1990] ECR I-3711 at para. 14. See also J. Díaz Herranz, 'Las limitaciones a la actuación legislativa comunitaria respecto de la propiedad industrial' (1991) *Gaceta Jurídica de la CEE* B-64, 3, 5.

[18] Op. cit. (n. 10), at 423. ECSC stands for 'European Coal and Steel Community'.

[19] Cited in n. 4, at 63, where the Commission's observations are summarized as follows: 'It may be doubted whether this provision really applies to the system of commercial and industrial property ownership. It is mainly intended to state that the Treaty leaves to Member States the freedom to decide, so far as regards observance of the obligations imposed on them by the Treaty, between a system of private property and a system of public property.'

[20] Cited in n. 4, at 77.

[21] The President of the Court of First Instance referred to Art. 295 in relation to a trade mark in Case T-151/01 R *Der Grüne Punkt–DSD v Commission* [2001] ECR II-3295 at para. 181. He relied on Art. 295 to support the view that the proprietor of a trade mark could not be held to have abused its dominant position by including certain provisions in a licensing agreement unless those provisions went beyond what was necessary to preserve the essential function of the trade mark.

observed in the application and interpretation of the Treaty. In *Hauer v Land Rheinland-Pfalz*,[22] a case in which the owner of land challenged a Council Regulation which prohibited her from planting new vines on her land, the Court stated:[23] 'The right to property is guaranteed in the Community legal order in accordance with the ideas common to the constitutions of the Member States, which are also reflected in the first Protocol to the European Convention for the Protection of Human Rights.' The same principle must, logically, apply to intangible property rights, including rights of intellectual property.

Thus it is clear that there is a basis in Community law, without recourse to Article 295 and even regardless of the terms of Article 30, for the proposition that the Treaty should not be construed as calling in question the existence of a properly constituted intellectual property right. There is, however, an obvious danger in this analysis. Driven to its logical conclusion, it would lead, in conjunction with the principle that in the absence of harmonization the existence of intellectual property rights is determined solely by national law, to the unfortunate result that Community law safeguards the existence of exclusive rights for which there may be no objective justification. It would be regrettable if an analysis based on fundamental rights meant that Community law could not affect the existence of an exclusive right granted to a design copyist or to an 'inventor' who was allowed to patent technology already available to the scientific community. The only way to avoid such a result is to recognize that, however broadly the fundamental right to property is construed, it cannot be invoked in favour of a spurious intellectual property right or any other exclusive right granted arbitrarily (such as the hypothetical exclusive right to market electric toothbrushes discussed in Chapter 4). Fundamental rights should not be used as a means of defending the indefensible. There is no such thing as a fundamental right for a copyist to go on being the only person entitled to exploit the copied work.

6. THE OUTER LIMITS OF THE PRINCIPLE THAT COMMUNITY LAW DOES NOT AFFECT THE EXISTENCE OF INTELLECTUAL PROPERTY RIGHTS

By this stage it will be abundantly clear that the existence/exercise dichotomy is closely related to the principle, discussed in the previous chapter, that in the absence of harmonization the conditions governing the grant of intellectual property rights are solely a matter for national law. Indeed, some authors treat that principle as being nothing more than a

---

[22] Case 44/79 [1979] ECR 3727.   [23] At para. 17 of the judgment.

reformulation of the old doctrine that the Treaty cannot affect the existence of intellectual property rights recognized in national law.[24] Taken together, those two aspects of the European Court's case law appear to represent a truly remarkable act of self-denial on the part of the Court. The Court grants national law unlimited freedom to create exclusive rights in the name of intellectual property—rights which are inherently capable of impeding the free movement of goods—and then says that the existence of those rights is guaranteed by the Treaty. Friden perceptively points out the drawback in this approach:

If the distinction is to have content and dictate the limits of the respective scopes of national and Community law in this matter, Member States must remain unfettered in deciding which conditions are to be fulfilled when an intellectual property right is granted. They could however use this freedom granted to them by the Court, to jeopardise the free movement of goods and competition, for instance, by granting patents for 'inventions' which are not novel. This is an unsatisfactory consequence inherent to the logic of the distinction itself.[25]

It would be unfortunate if an excessive respect for the prerogatives of the national legislatures were to lead to the maintenance of barriers to trade between Member States for which there were no objective justification. The Court does not, however, always pursue the logic of its stated principles to the ultimate limit. Friden points out that in *Warner Brothers and Metronome v Christiansen* and in *Thetford v Fiamma* the Court showed an unusual willingness to scrutinize the merits of an intellectual property right granted under national law. There are, moreover, at least two cases in which the Court has gone very close to destroying the existence of an intellectual property right recognized in national law. The two cases are *HAG I*[26] and *Magill*.[27]

The facts of *HAG I* were as follows. The original owner of the trade mark HAG, registered for coffee in various countries, was a German company whose assets in Belgium and Luxembourg, including the trade mark HAG, were sequestrated as enemy property at the end of the Second World War. The Belgian and Luxembourg marks were subsequently bought by a company called Van Zuylen. When the original German owner, who retained

---

[24] G. Friden, 'Recent Developments in EEC Intellectual Property Law: The Distinction between Existence and Exercise Revisited' (1989) 26 CML Rev. 193, 194; G. Bonet, (1990) *Revue Trimestrielle de Droit Européen* 713, 723; and J. J. Burst and R. Kovar, who state in 'Les licences imposées et le droit communautaire' (1990) CDE 251, 263: 'Le sens de la notion d'existence n'a pas toujours été évident. On peut toutefois estimer qu'elle signifie que tout ce qui a trait aux conditions d'obtention et au contenu d'un droit de propriété industrielle, relève du seul droit national, au moins, tant qu'il n'existe pas, en la matière, soit une harmonisation ou un droit unique.'

[25] G. Friden, loc. cit. (n. 24).   [26] Cited in n. 8.

[27] Joined Cases C-241/91 P and C-242/91 P *RTE and ITV v Commission* ('*Magill*') [1995] ECR I-743.

the German registration, started selling coffee in Luxembourg under the trade mark HAG, Van Zuylen sued for infringement of its trade mark. It failed to prevent the imports as a result of a preliminary ruling in which the Court of Justice held that: 'To prohibit the marketing in one Member State of a product legally bearing a trade mark in another Member State for the sole reason that an identical trade mark, having the same origin, exists in the first State, is incompatible with the provisions for the free movement of goods within the Common Market.'

The effect of the decision, which was overruled 16 years later in *HAG II*, was to destroy the trade mark rights of Van Zuylen. A trade mark which has to be shared with another person in the same territory and in relation to identical goods may rapidly become worthless because neither of the persons entitled to use it will be in a position to defend the reputation of the mark by consistently producing goods of high quality.[28] It is difficult to avoid the conclusion that the very existence of Van Zuylen's industrial property right was threatened.[29] And yet, astonishingly, the Court solemnly affirmed in *HAG I* that 'the Treaty does not affect the existence of rights recognized by the legislation of a Member State in matters of industrial and commercial property'.[30] The truth of the matter is that the Court simply did not, at that stage, have an adequate understanding of the role of trade marks in a market economy. The Court destroyed Van Zuylen's industrial property rights by accident.

The *Magill* case was concerned with the application of the competition rules of the Treaty. It arose out of the unusually wide scope of copyright in common law countries. Magill attempted to publish a weekly television guide but was prevented from doing so by television companies in Ireland and the United Kingdom, which, anxious to protect the market for their own programme guides, obtained injunctions prohibiting the publication of weekly listings of their programmes. The television companies were able to obtain such injunctions on the ground that their programme listings were covered by copyright. Such material would not be protected by copyright in Member States other than Ireland, the United Kingdom[31] and, surprisingly, the Netherlands.[32] Magill complained to the Commission, which adopted a decision finding that the television companies had abused their dominant position, in breach of Article 82 of the Treaty, and ordering them to put an

---

[28] See the opinion of Advocate General Jacobs in *HAG II* at paras 18, 19 and 24.

[29] Rothnie describes the judgment as a 'nuclear strike' on the very existence of the right: op. cit. (n. 10), at 29.

[30] At para. 8 of the judgment.

[31] The law has since been changed in the United Kingdom. Under s. 176 of the Broadcasting Act 1990 broadcasting organizations are obliged to license the reproduction of their programme listings.

[32] As regards the Dutch copyright law, see D. W. Feer Verkade (1996) IIC 78, 97.

end to the breach by supplying third parties on request and on a non-discriminatory basis with their individual advance weekly programme listings and by permitting reproduction of those listings; any royalties requested were to be 'reasonable'.

The television companies sought the annulment of that decision. They failed both before the Court of First Instance[33] and before the Court of Justice.[34] The judgments are analysed more fully in the Chapter 11 on competition law.[35] Here it is sufficient to note that, although the Court of Justice confirmed that in the absence of harmonization it was for national law to determine the conditions governing the grant of intellectual property rights, the judgment seems to have destroyed the substance of an exclusive right, classified as intellectual property, which the television companies enjoyed under national law. It is true that under the Commission's decision the television companies were to receive 'reasonable' royalties. But a right to royalties is very different from the exclusive right to publish certain information in a magazine. Under national law each television company had a monopoly right to publish a magazine giving information about its programmes. As a result of the Court's judgment that monopoly right has been lost and, if the television companies wish to remain in the publishing business, all they can do is license each other to publish information about their programmes and produce comprehensive television guides in competition with the Magills of the world. That is no doubt very good for the consumer and one can of course question whether programme listings merit copyright protection. But it would be useless to pretend that the substance of the exclusive right granted under national law has not been destroyed.

---

[33] Case T-69/89 *RTE v Commission* [1991] ECR II-485 and Case T-76/89 *ITP v Commission* [1991] ECR II-575.

[34] Cited in n. 27.

[35] Chap. 11, section 4.3.3.2.

6

The specific subject-matter of the right

The greatest defect in the existence/exercise distinction is that it is too vague to be of much use by itself.[1] It provides no guidance as to when the exercise of the right will fall foul of Articles 28 and 30. Those who criticize the European Court of Justice on this ground are perhaps being a little harsh. They are ascribing to the distinction ambitions which it never pretended to have. It was never meant to solve, by itself, all the problems that arise as a result of the conflict between intellectual property rights and the free movement of goods. In fact, it is doubtful whether it was meant to solve any specific problem. It is merely a starting point. The statement that the Treaty safeguards the existence of intellectual property rights, but may limit their exercise, is, like the statement that in the absence of harmonization the creation of such rights is governed by national law, little more than a truism. In order to determine when the exercise of an intellectual property right is contrary to the Treaty provisions on the free movement of goods, it is clearly necessary to develop supplementary criteria. One such criterion involves the esoteric concept known as the 'specific subject-matter' of the right, which made its first appearance on the stage of Community law in *Deutsche Grammophon v Metro*[2] in 1971. Paragraph 11 of that judgment merits citation in full:

Amongst the prohibitions or restrictions on the free movement of goods which it concedes Article 30 refers to industrial and commercial property. On the assumption that those provisions may be relevant to a right related to copyright, it is nevertheless clear from that article that, although the Treaty does not affect the existence of rights recognised by the legislation of a Member State with regard to industrial and commercial property, the exercise of such rights may nevertheless fall within the prohibitions laid down by the Treaty. Although it permits prohibitions or restrictions on the free movement of products,[3] which are justified for the purpose of protecting industrial and commercial property. Article [30] only admits derogations from that freedom to the extent to which they are justified for the purpose of safeguarding rights which constitute the specific subject-matter of such property.

---

[1] *Contra*, G. Friden, 'Recent Developments in EEC Intellectual Property Law: The Distinction between Existence and Exercise Revisited' (1989) 26 CML Rev. 193. Friden maintains that the 'distinction can be given an exploitable theoretical content' and that 'both the concept of existence and that of exercise have relatively clear meanings'.

[2] Case 78/70 [1971] ECR 487.

[3] The meaning of this sentence would be clearer without the comma before the word 'which'.

The second sentence of that paragraph contains the classic formulation of the existence/exercise dichotomy. *Deutsche Grammophon* appears to have been the first judgment to use that formulation of the dichotomy, which had merely been adumbrated in earlier judgments. The classic formulation was repeated verbatim in virtually all the relevant judgments from *Deutsche Grammophon* until 1982. The final sentence of the paragraph quoted above was entirely novel: the Court had never before referred to the specific subject-matter of an intellectual property right. The most striking feature of the *Deutsche Grammophon* judgment is that the Court made no attempt to define the specific subject-matter of the intellectual property right in issue (a right related to copyright) or even to explain what was meant by this new concept of Community law. It simply went on to establish, in the following paragraph, the principle of exhaustion (which is discussed in Chapter 7). The concept of specific subject-matter seems entirely superfluous to the process of reasoning by which the Court reached the view, in *Deutsche Grammophon*, that the copyright owner could not oppose the further marketing in Germany of goods which it had placed on the market in France.

It was not until 1974 that the Court explained, in *Centrafarm v Sterling Drug*[4] and *Centrafarm v Winthrop*[5] precisely what it meant by 'specific subject-matter'. Both cases concerned parallel imports into the Netherlands of a pharmaceutical product which had been placed on the market in the United Kingdom by a subsidiary (Sterling Winthrop) of an American corporation (Sterling Drug). The product was protected by patents in the Netherlands and the United Kingdom. It was marketed in both countries by Sterling Drug or its subsidiaries under a registered trade mark. Sterling Drug was able to sell the product at a much higher price in the Netherlands than in the United Kingdom, where the price was restricted by government measures. That price difference made it economically worthwhile for Centrafarm, the parallel importer, to sell in the Netherlands products marketed by Sterling Drug's subsidiary in the United Kingdom. In an attempt to prevent the parallel imports, Sterling Drug and its Dutch subsidiary, Winthrop, brought two separate actions before a Dutch Court, one based on patent rights and the other on trade mark rights. The *Hoge Raad* (the Dutch Supreme Court) sought preliminary rulings from the Court of Justice on the compatibility with Article 28 of national legislation allowing the owner of a patent or trade mark to oppose imports of goods marketed with his consent in another Member State.

The two cases gave the Court an opportunity to develop further the doctrine of exhaustion established in *Deutsche Grammophon*. This time the Court underpinned the doctrine with elaborate definitions of the specific

---

[4] Case 15/74 [1974] ECR 1147.   [5] Case 16/74 [1974] ECR 1183.

subject-matter of patent and trade mark rights. In *Centrafarm v Sterling Drug* the Court stated:

> Inasmuch as it provides an exception to one of the fundamental principles of the Common Market, Article [30] in fact only admits of derogations from the free movement of goods where such derogations are justified for the purpose of safe-guarding rights which constitute the specific subject matter of this property.
> In relation to patents, the specific subject matter of the industrial property is the guarantee that the patentee, to reward the creative effort of the inventor, has the exclusive right to use an invention with a view to manufacturing industrial products and putting them into circulation for the first time, either directly or by the grant of licences to third parties, as well as the right to oppose infringements.[6]

The first of those two paragraphs also appears in *Centrafarm v Winthrop*. The second is replaced by the following text:

> In relation to trade marks, the specific subject-matter of the industrial property is the guarantee that the owner of the trade mark has the exclusive right to use that trade mark, for the purpose of putting products protected by the trade mark into circulation for the first time, and is therefore intended to protect him against competitors wishing to take advantage of the status and reputation of the trade mark by selling products illegally bearing that trade mark.[7]

Before examining more closely those remarkably complex definitions of the specific subject-matter of patent and trade mark rights, it might be useful to reflect upon the meaning of the expression 'specific subject-matter', which sounds, at least in English, arcane and esoteric. It must be borne in mind that the Court of Justice has, for better or worse, since its inception, adhered to the practice of drafting all its judgments in French. The words 'specific subject-matter' are intended to translate the French *objet spécifique*. In this context the word *objet* in French appears to have a double meaning. On the one hand, it has a purely descriptive meaning: it describes the core of essential rights granted to the proprietor of a patent, trade mark or some other form of intellectual property. But it also has a meaning akin to the English word 'objective' or 'purpose': it refers to the policy aims pursued by the legislation which created the intellectual property right. Thus the expression *objet spécifique* describes what rights are granted to the owner of intellectual property and it indicates why those rights are granted. In the English translation only the first meaning survives; the second meaning is entirely lost.

The confusion caused by the sheer obscurity of the term 'specific subject-matter' is compounded by the Court's inconsistency in its choice of terminology. Occasionally the Court uses the expression 'substance of the right',

---

[6] At paras 8 and 9 of the judgment.   [7] At para. 8 of the judgment.

apparently as a synonym of 'specific subject-matter of the right'.[8] Advocate General Fennelly remarked in his opinion in *Merck v Primecrown* that the Court appears to use the terms 'specific subject-matter', 'object' or 'substance' of the right interchangeably. In fact, much of the inconsistency detected by the Advocate General is evident only in the English version of the Court's judgments. The translators have an impossible task because there is no English term capable of rendering the ambiguity inherent in the French *objet spécifique*. As a result we sometimes find in the English version of a judgment 'specific purpose'[9] or 'specific objective'.[10]

The double meaning[11] is apparent in the definitions, given in the *Sterling Drug* and *Winthrop* judgments, of the specific subject-matter of patent and trade mark rights respectively. In paragraph 9 of *Sterling Drug* the Court describes the core of essential rights granted to the proprietor of a patent in the following terms: 'the exclusive right to use an invention with a view to manufacturing industrial products and putting them into circulation for the first time, either directly or by the grant of licences to third parties, as well as the right to oppose infringements'. In the same sentence the Court refers to the underlying purpose of granting patent protection, i.e. 'to reward the creative effort of the inventor'. (One can of course object that that is only one of the reasons for protecting patents and that the Court should not have singled out one of the competing theories about the justification for patents without a more profound analysis.)

In paragraph 8 of the *Winthrop* judgment the Court describes the essential rights of the trade mark owner in the following terms: 'the exclusive right to use [the] trade mark, for the purpose of putting products protected by the trade mark into circulation for the first time'. At the end of the sentence the Court tags on a reference to the underlying purpose of trade mark protection: the exclusive right granted to the proprietor of the trade mark is 'intended to protect him against competitors wishing to take advantage of the status and reputation of the trade mark by selling products illegally bearing that trade mark'. Once again one can criticize the Court for singling out one aspect of the purpose of trade mark protection

[8] See, e.g., Case 35/87 *Thetford v Fiamma* [1988] ECR 35 at para. 24, and Case 53/87 *CICRA v Renault* [1988] ECR 6039 at para. 11. Cf. para. 11 of *CICRA v Renault* with para. 8 of the judgment in Case 238/87 *Volvo v Veng* [1988] ECR 6211, where the expression 'the very subject-matter' is used in a sentence clearly intended to convey the same idea.

[9] See, e.g., Case 12/74 *Commission v Germany* [1975] ECR 181 at para. 7, where the French text says *fonction spécifique*, and Case 187/80 *Merck v Stephar* [1981] ECR 2063 at para. 9.

[10] See, e.g., Case 119/75 *Terrapin v Terranova* [1976] ECR 1039 at para. 7; in that judgment the translator hedged his bets by using 'specific subject-matter' in para. 5.

[11] Korah is one of the few authors to have noted the double meaning of 'specific subject-matter'. She states: 'Is the specific subject-matter of the right its function—the policy reason for granting an exclusive right to the innovator—or its essence—the nature of the protection granted? The Court refers to both.' V. Korah 'National Patents and the Free Movement of Goods within the Common Market' (1975) 38 MLR 333, 335.

and for neglecting other aspects, such as the trade mark's role in preventing the deception of consumers.

There are in fact many criticisms that can be levelled against the Court's definitions in *Sterling Drug* and *Winthrop* of the specific subject-matter of patent and trade mark rights. It is, for example, strange that the Court referred to the possibility of exploiting a patent by means of licensing but made no mention of trade mark licensing. Nor is it clear why the Court referred expressly to the right to oppose infringements as being part of the specific subject-matter of a patent, but made no reference to a similar right in its definition of the specific subject-matter of a trade mark.

However, the most serious criticism of the specific subject-matter criterion—and one that is made by numerous authors—is that it operates what Cornish describes as a 'definitional stop'; that is to say, the Court purports to establish a general test but defines it arbitrarily in such a way as to determine *a priori* the result which it wishes to reach, thus excluding any further debate.[12] Korah, commenting on the *Sterling Drug* judgment, makes the same point:

The Court may have been right to give priority to the rules for the free movement of goods over the national patent laws, but by defining their specific subject-matter as the right to one bite of the cherry, to a licence fee, or monopoly price on first sale, without considering the amount of protection required to achieve its purpose, the Court foreclosed rational discussion.[13]

This criticism is formulated in scathing terms by Macfarlane, Wardle, and Wilkinson:

The ECJ invented the doctrine of specific subject-matter which allows the ECJ to define arbitrarily what the specific subject-matter of a patent is. The ECJ defines the specific subject-matter so as to exclude the restrictions the ECJ wishes to exclude. The ECJ can then conclude that as these restrictions are not part of the specific subject-matter they are not saved by Article [30].[14]

Marenco and Banks express the same idea in more poetic language:

. . . the definition of the specific subject-matter of a given right has had to be modified with every new case in order to fit the particular problem under consideration and to justify the solution to be given to it. Thus, one could have the impression that the notion of specific subject-matter, instead of being a steady beam of light giving guidance as to the likely solution of problems by the Court, is in fact only the wavering reflection of such solutions.[15]

---

[12] W. R. Cornish, 'The Definitional Stop Aids the Flow of Patented Goods' (1975) JBL 50.

[13] Op. cit. (n. 11), at 339.

[14] N. MacFarlane, C. Wardle and J. Wilkinson, 'The Tension between National Intellectual Property Rights and Certain Provisions of EC Law' [1994] 12 EIPR 525, 527.

[15] G. Marenco and K. Banks, 'Intellectual Property and the Community Rules on Free Movement: Discrimination Unearthed' (1990) ELR 224, 230.

There is undeniably a great deal of truth in these criticisms. A criterion that is so fluid and hazy that it does not permit useful predictions to be made about the probable outcome of specific cases that arise in practice is of little use to lawyers and can hardly be said to serve the interests of legal certainty. There is nonetheless something to be said for flexibility, and some authorities have defended the specific subject-matter test on that very ground. Advocate General Jacobs observed in his opinion in *HAG II* that the concept of specific subject-matter was an essential concomitant of the existence/exercise dichotomy because it made it possible to determine, in relation to each type of intellectual property, the circumstances in which the exercise of the right would be permissible under Community law.[16]

In fact, the Court has made surprisingly little use of that possibility. For many years it eschewed any attempt to formulate a definition of the specific subject-matter of copyright and related rights. That failure dates back, as we have seen, to *Deutsche Grammophon* and has not been fully rectified in the subsequent case law. The judgments of the Court of First Instance and of the Court of Justice in the *Magill* cases are equally remiss. The former simply state that 'in principle the protection of the specific subject-matter of a copyright entitles the copyright-holder to reserve the exclusive right to reproduce the protected work'.[17] The latter states, even more laconically, that 'the exclusive right of reproduction forms part of the author's rights'.[18] The Court came closer to an adequate definition of the specific subject-matter of copyright in *Warner Brothers and Metronome v Christiansen*,[19] where it stated, without using the concept 'specific subject-matter', that the 'two essential rights of the author, namely the exclusive right of performance and the exclusive right of reproduction, are not called in question by the rules of the Treaty'.[20]

For a more complete definition of the specific subject-matter of copyright we have to turn to the *Phil Collins* judgment, delivered in 1993. There the Court said:

The specific subject-matter of those rights, as governed by national legislation, is to ensure the protection of the moral and economic rights of their holders. The protection of moral rights enables authors and performers, in particular, to object to any distortion, mutilation or other modification of a work which would be prejudicial to their honour or reputation. Copyright and related rights are also

---

[16] Case C-10/89 *CNL Sucal v HAG GF ('HAG II')* [1990] ECR I-3711 at para. 14 of the Advocate General's opinion.

[17] Case T-69/89 *RTE v Commission* [1991] ECR II-485 at para. 70; Case T-70/89 *BBC v Commission* [1991] ECR II-535 at para. 57; and Case T-76/89 *ITP v Commission* [1991] ECR II-575 at para. 55. These cases and the one cited in n. 18 are known collectively as the *Magill* cases.

[18] Joined Cases C-241/91 P and C-242/91 P *RTE and ITP v Commission* [1995] ECR I-743 at para. 49.

[19] Case 158/86 [1988] ECR 2605.   [20] At para. 13 of the judgment.

economic in nature, in that they confer the right to exploit commercially the marketing of the protected work, particularly in the form of licences granted in return for payment of royalties.[21]

The Court has not fared any better in the field of design law. In *Keurkoop v Nancy Kean Gifts*,[22] the first case on design law, the Court did not even have recourse to the concept of specific subject-matter. In *CICRA v Renault and Volvo v Veng* the Court said that the right of the proprietor of a design to prevent third parties from manufacturing, selling, or importing products incorporating the design was part of the 'very subject-matter' or 'substance' of the right.

It is striking that in relation to both copyright and design rights the Court has, in so far as it has relied on the concept of specific subject-matter, used the expression in the purely descriptive sense. In other words, it has treated the concept as a means of identifying the core of essential rights granted to the intellectual property owner. It has not attempted to build into the definition of specific subject-matter any reference to the policy reasons underlying the grant of an exclusive right. In relation to copyright the Court has, however, developed an additional criterion—described as the 'essential function' of copyright—which focuses, at least in *Magill*, on the *raison d'être* of the exclusive right.[23] In *Magill* the Court of First Instance said that the essential function of copyright 'is to protect the moral rights in the work and to ensure a reward for the creative effort'.[24] That definition was cited approvingly by the Court of Justice in the judgment on appeal.[25]

The question that must be asked is whether, in the light of more than twenty years of experience, the specific subject-matter test serves any useful purpose. Before we can answer that question we must first ask what purpose the test was intended to serve. Clearly it was devised as a way of limiting the circumstances in which intellectual property rights can be relied on to justify restrictions on the free movement of goods. The theoretical basis for the test, ever since the *Sterling Drug* and *Winthrop* judgments, is that Article 30, as an exception to one of the fundamental principles of the common market, must be construed narrowly. The wisdom of that sort of abstract, formalistic approach to Article 30 is questionable.[26] When a conflict arises between two such important interests as the free movement

---

[21] Joined Cases C-92/92 and C-326/92 *Phil Collins* [1993] ECR I-5145 at para. 20.

[22] Case 144/81 [1982] ECR 2853.

[23] Case 62/79 *Coditel v Ciné Vog Films* ('*Coditel I*') [1980] ECR 881 at para. 14; *RTE and ITP v Commission* (cited in n. 18) at para. 28.

[24] At para. 71 of the judgment in the *RTE* case and para. 56 of the judgment in the *BBC* case (cited in n. 17).

[25] At para. 28 of the judgment in *RTE and ITP v Commission*.

[26] See J. Mertens de Wilmar, 'Aspects communautaires du droit des marques' (1972) 87 *Journal des Tribunaux* No. 4806.

of goods and the protection of intellectual property, it hardly seems appropriate to assume *a priori* that one of those interests is more fundamental than the other. It would surely be more satisfactory to seek to balance the specific interests that are at stake in each case, to ask what is the intrinsic value of each and to determine on that basis whether a restriction on the free movement of goods is justified on grounds of the protection of intellectual property.

Does the specific subject-matter test have anything to contribute to that balancing exercise? It depends on the sense in which the term is used. We have already seen that 'specific subject-matter' (or, rather, *objet spécifique*) has two meanings—one descriptive and one purposive. The descriptive use of the term can be broken down into two sub-meanings, depending on how the core of essential rights is defined. There are two possibilities. Those rights may be defined purely by reference to the national law of the State which grants the intellectual property right in issue; or they may be defined on the basis of a comparative-law analysis which seeks to identify either the common minimum content of the type of intellectual property right in issue or the essential prerogatives generally granted to the holder of such a right in the Member States.

It is not entirely clear which approach the Court adopts. In the *Sterling Drug* and *Winthrop* cases the Court appears to have defined the specific subject-matter of a patent and a trade mark, respectively, on the basis of an implicit understanding of the level of protection generally enjoyed by patent and trade mark proprietors in the Member States. No one would claim that the definitions are the fruit of a thorough comparative-law survey; at most, they seem to have been inspired by a casual browse through one or two patent and trade mark manuals. Certainly there is nothing to suggest that the Court was focusing on specific features of Dutch patent and trade mark law; on the contrary, it assumed that it was making statements of more or less universal validity about patent and trade mark laws in general.

Beier,[27] who considered specific subject-matter an 'unsuitable criterion', rejected that approach on the ground that there was no legal basis in the Treaty or in Community legislation for the Court to define a common minimum standard of protection for intellectual property. Beier contended that in the absence of harmonization it was for national law to determine not only the conditions governing the creation of intellectual property rights but also the 'exclusive rights characteristic of such property'. He pointed out, correctly, that the more recent case law supported that proposition.

---

[27] F.-K. Beier, 'Industrial Property and the Free Movement of Goods' (1990) 21 IIC 131, 148.

Advocate General Gulmann clearly assumed, in his opinion in *Magill*, that the specific subject-matter of an intellectual property right was to be identified on the basis of the national law in issue: 'The application of the concept of the specific subject-matter is an expression of the reasoning that for each intellectual property right it is possible to identify a number of core rights which the owner of that right enjoys under national law and whose exercise is not affected by the Treaty rules.'[28] The Advocate General went on to make some interesting remarks about the relationship between the specific subject-matter test and the existence/exercise dichotomy:

> . . . the concept of the specific subject-matter was developed for the purposes of applying that distinction [i.e. the distinction between the existence of a right and its exercise]. An exercise of rights that falls within the specific subject-matter of an intellectual property right will relate to its existence. In other words the distinction between the existence and the exercise of rights and the application of the concept of the specific subject-matter are basically expressions of the same conceptual approach. Accordingly I consider that the distinction between the existence and exercise of rights has no independent significance for resolving specific questions of delimitation.[29]

The problem with this analysis is that it does not advance the debate very far. It does not tell us which rights may be curtailed and which may not. The truth of the matter is that the specific subject-matter test can only perform a useful function if it is applied in the manner objected to by Beier or if it is construed in its purposive sense: that is to say, if the emphasis is placed on the policy reasons for granting an exclusive right. That is of course how the test was applied and construed in *Sterling Drug* and *Winthrop*. If the test had been understood in the manner suggested by Advocate General Gulmann in *Magill*, it is difficult to see how the Court could have extracted from it a principle of Community-wide exhaustion. Suppose that under Dutch patent law non-exhaustion by a first sale outside the Netherlands were regarded as belonging to the core of essential rights conferred by a patent. That would have formed part of the specific subject-matter of the right and would have been safeguarded by Article 30.

The Court was able to arrive at a doctrine of Community-wide exhaustion through a first sale with the consent of the right-holder mainly because it included in its definition of the specific subject-matter of patents and trade marks a reference to the purpose of such rights. If the purpose of a patent is to reward the inventor by allowing him a first sale in monopoly conditions, there is no justification for allowing the patent-holder to oppose further

---

[28] [1995] ECR I-756 at para. 28 of the opinion.

[29] At para. 31 of the opinion. Advocate General Fennelly agreed with this view in his opinion in Joined Cases C-267/95 and C-268/95 *Merck v Primecrown* [1996] ECR I-6285 at footnote 98 of the opinion.

dealing in goods that he has placed on the market in a country where he enjoys patent protection.[30] If the purpose of a trade mark is to enable the proprietor to protect his goodwill by preventing unauthorised persons from using the trade mark, there is no justification for allowing the proprietor to oppose further dealing in goods that he has placed on the market under the trade mark.

There must always be a good reason for granting exclusive rights which interfere with the free movement of goods. One is reluctant therefore to counsel complete abandonment of the one test developed by the Court which contains at least a passing reference to the *raison d'être* of intellectual property rights, even though one deplores the mystic obscurity of a test which Marenco and Banks describe, in a memorable understatement, as 'an arguably awkward tool of analysis'.[31]

The usefulness of a test that focuses on the purpose of, and justification for, an intellectual property right is demonstrated best of all by a judgment in which no such test was used: namely *Keurkoop v Nancy Kean Gifts*,[32] the facts of which are set out in Chapter 4. It will be recalled that Nancy Kean Gifts registered a copied design in Benelux, without the permission of the author, and invoked the exclusive right thus obtained to prevent Keurkoop from importing goods covered by the design.

That was the first case on design rights to come before the Court of Justice. In at least ten previous judgments the Court had stated that Article 30 only admits of derogations from the free movement of goods where such derogations are justified for the purpose of safeguarding rights which constitute the specific subject-matter of industrial and commercial property. One might therefore have expected the Court to repeat that statement in *Keurkoop v Nancy Kean Gifts*, since it appears to embody a principle of general validity not limited to the patent and trade mark fields. Anxious to build up a body of coherent case law, the Court would then have seized the opportunity to define the specific subject-matter of a design right. A simpler task would be difficult to imagine. With a few minor adjustments the definition of the specific subject-matter of a patent could have been borrowed from *Sterling Drug*. The Court would thus have stated:

'In relation to design rights, the specific subject-matter of the industrial property is the guarantee that the proprietor of the right, to reward the creative effort of the designer, has the exclusive right to use a design with a view to manufacturing industrial products and putting them into circulation for the first time, either

---

[30] See section 5 of Chap. 7 for discussion of the question whether the existence of price controls or the total absence of patent protection in the country of the first sale prevents the patent from achieving its purpose.

[31] Marenco and Banks, op. cit. (n. 15), at 232.   [32] Cited in n. 22.

directly or by the grant of licences to third parties. as well as the right to oppose infringements.'

The Court would then have been compelled to observe that the creative effort of the designer would not be rewarded by conferring an exclusive right on someone who had copied the design (as opposed to someone who had acquired the design from its author) and that there was no justification for allowing such a person to impede imports from other Member States on the basis of the design right.

None of that happened of course. The Court said nothing whatsoever about the specific subject-matter of the right, thus ignoring what had for a decade been treated as the key criterion by the Court. Seldom can silence have been so eloquent. The Court must surely have realised that if it had embarked upon a definition of the specific subject-matter of a design right it would have been forced to recognise that the right in question was unworthy of the protection of Article 30. Reluctant to take the bold step of declaring that an industrial property right granted under national law could not be relied on against imports from other Member States, the Court sought refuge in the principle that in the absence of harmonization the creation of industrial property rights is governed solely by national law.

Keurkoop v Nancy Kean Gifts exposed the limitations of specific subject-matter analysis. The test is of no use unless the Court is willing to question certain policy choices made by national legislatures when those choices lead to restrictions on the free movement of goods. Marenco and Banks observe perceptively 'the essential difficulty with the specific subject-matter test, i.e. the risk of having to assess the wisdom of the national legislator, came into the open with *Keurkoop v Nancy Kean*, the case which constituted the moment of truth for this test and from which it has never fully recovered'.[33]

The approach taken by Advocate General Reischl in *Keurkoop v Nancy Kean Gifts* is of particular interest in this regard. Unlike the Court, he did not feign amnesia as regards the specific subject-matter test. Instead, he examined the important question whether:

. . . the specific subject-matter of a right in a design is determined by reference to a uniform, as it were ideal, model of this property right or whether . . . it is necessary, in determining the specific subject-matter of the right in a design within the meaning of Article [30] of the [EC] Treaty, to take as a basis each time the relevant national legislation governing rights in a design. regard being had to the specific structure and content of that legislation.[34]

The Advocate General considered that in the light of the purpose of the exception provided for by Article 30 the answer to that question could only be that, as long as the national provisions of the individual Member States

---

[33] Op. cit. (n. 15), at 232.   [34] [1982] ECR 2853 at 2880.

on the protection of industrial property had not been harmonized, only the legislatures of the Member States could determine whether industrial property rights exist. He thus concluded that the specific subject-matter of a design right under the Benelux law could be defined as 'the exclusive right of the proprietor, in practice the person filing the design, to market a product of a given industrial design for the first time'.

Strangely the Advocate General thought that that definition corresponded to the description of the specific subject-matter of patent and trade mark rights previously applied by the Court. That is clearly not the case because, as we have seen, the definitions given in *Sterling Drug* and *Winthrop* were, though not the fruit of a rigorous comparativist analysis, based on assumptions about what is normally protected under the industrial property laws of the Member States. The Advocate General's definition is a pale shadow of the definitions of the specific subject-matter of patents and trade marks in *Sterling Drug* and *Winthrop*, above all because it contains no reference to the *raison d'être* of design protection. It is nothing more than a rather comical way of formulating a first-sale doctrine, otherwise known as an exhaustion principle.

The truth is that the only useful contribution made by the specific subject-matter test is that it helped the Court to reason its way towards a principle of Community-wide exhaustion. Having played the role of midwife to the exhaustion principle, it was led off to early retirement in spite of its obvious potential for performing more challenging roles. Since then it has been allowed back on stage in a few cameo parts where it was unlikely to cause embarrassment, and it has of course continued to go through its familiar routine in the exhaustion cases. That is not, however, sufficient to prevent the conclusion that its active career came to an abrupt end in 1982.

If the concept of specific subject-matter is not going to provide a general test for determining when the exercise of an intellectual property right is compatible with the free movement of goods, an alternative criterion must be sought. The *Keurkoop v Nancy Kean Gifts* judgment itself proposed one such alternative:

Article [30] is . . . intended to emphasise that the reconciliation between the requirements of the free movement of goods and the respect to which industrial and commercial property rights are entitled must be achieved in such a way that protection is ensured for the legitimate exercise, in the form of prohibitions on imports which are 'justified' within the meaning of that article, of the rights conferred by national legislation, but is refused, on the other hand, in respect of any improper exercise of the same rights which is of such a nature as to maintain or establish artificial partitions within the common market. The exercise of industrial and commercial property rights conferred by national legislation must consequently be restricted as far as is necessary for that reconciliation.[35]

---

[35] At para. 24 of the judgment.

That passage was based largely on one that appeared in *Terrapin v Terranova*,[36] in which the Court held that the proprietor of a trade mark may oppose the importation and sale of goods bearing a confusingly similar trade mark which belongs to an entirely separate undertaking in another Member State.[37]

The same passage was quoted approvingly by the Court of First Instance in the *Magill* judgments.[38] The opposition between legitimate exercise of a right and improper (or abusive)[39] exercise also appears in *EMI Electrola v Patricia Im-und Export*,[40] in which the Court held that a copyright owner could oppose the importation and sale of infringing goods produced without his consent in another Member State where the term of protection had expired. A similar approach was taken in *Basset v SACEM*, where the Court held that the charging of an additional royalty on the public performance of a recorded work under French legislation did not constitute a measure having equivalent effect under Article 28 even if it were capable of restricting imports 'inasmuch as it must be regarded as a *normal exploitation* of copyright and does not constitute a means of arbitrary discrimination or a disguised restriction on trade between Member States' (emphasis added).[41]

Beier, who rejected the existence/exercise dichotomy and the specific subject-matter test as ambiguous and unsuitable respectively, considered the opposition between legitimate and improper exercise to be 'a more appropriate solution'. In his opinion, 'it allows a clear demarcation line to be drawn and, at the same time, a balanced judgment of the conflict between the justified interest in adequate protection of industrial property recognised by the EEC Treaty and the principles of the free movement of goods and freedom of competition under Community law'.

Beier's enthusiasm for this 'test' is difficult to understand. Of all the formulas used in the sometimes desperate search for the appropriate balance between the protection of intellectual property and the free movement of goods, this is surely the vaguest and least helpful. Joliet described its inadequacy in characteristically pungent style. In a note on the *HAG II* case, he stated:

. . . the distinction between legitimate use and abuse, which was found in the *Keurkoop* judgment in 1982, does not appear in the *Hag II* judgment. It is just as

---

[36] Cited in n. 10, at para. 7 of the judgment.

[37] The judgment also emphasized the absence of a common origin of the two trade marks, but that factor is no longer relevant in the light of the judgment in Case C-10/89 *CNL Sucal v HAG GF* ('*HAG II*') [1990] ECR I-3711.

[38] *RTE v Commission* at para. 67; *BBC v Commission* at para. 54; and *ITP v Commission* at para. 52 (all cited in n. 17). The passage was cited, apparently with approval, by the Court of Justice in its judgment on appeal (*RTE and ITP v Commission* (cited in n. 18) at para. 25).

[39] The French versions of the judgments speak of *exercice abusif*, which is usually translated as 'improper exercise' but occasionally as 'abusive exercise'.

[40] Case 341/87 [1989] ECR 79 at para. 8.   [41] At para. 16 of the judgment.

well that it has not been used, because it does not in itself provide any objective criterion for determining what is legitimate or abusive. Classification of some use of the trade mark as abusive or legitimate may be the result of an analysis but it cannot be the instrument of the analysis.[42]

The unhelpful nature of the distinction is particularly apparent from the definition given in *Keurkoop v Nancy Kean Gifts* of what constitutes legitimate exercise of an intellectual property right conferred by national legislation. According to that definition, there is legitimate exercise in the case of 'prohibitions on imports which are "justified" within the meaning of [Article 30]'. That amounts to saying that under Article 30 measures are justified when they are justified. It is purely circular reasoning.

It has been suggested above that there is a strong case for abandoning the existence/exercise dichotomy and the specific subject-matter test on the grounds that they are vague in their conception and arbitrary in their results. There would, however, be little point in dropping those concepts from the Court's vocabulary if they were to be replaced by nothing more than a statement of the obvious. There is clearly a pressing need for new thinking in this field.

---

[42] R. Joliet, in collaboration with D. T. Keeling, 'Trade Mark Law and the Free Movement of Goods: The Overruling of the Judgment in *HAG I*' (1991) 22 IIC 303, 315.

7

The exhaustion of rights

1. THE CONCEPT OF EXHAUSTION

If the proprietor of a patent and a trade mark manufactures goods incorporating the patented technology and markets them under the trade mark, it would be logical (at least to the layman) to assume that the purchasers of those goods may do what they like with the goods—use them, consume them, sell or rent them, destroy them etc.—just as any other property owner may exercise all the prerogatives of legal ownership over his property. It would be strange if the proprietor of the patent could complain that the purchaser of the goods was infringing the patent simply by using the goods for their intended purpose or by reselling them. It would be stranger still if he could argue that the resale of the goods amounted to a trade mark infringement. Similar considerations apply to copyright and to other exclusive rights: one would not, for example, expect a publisher to be able to sue a bookseller for selling copies of books that he had bought from the publisher or from an intermediate supplier.

If the owners of intellectual property rights could rely on those rights in order to prevent further dealing in goods which they had marketed, those owners would have a magnificent tool for dividing up markets, practising differential pricing, stifling intra-brand competition and generally engaging in anti-competitive behaviour.

Various theories have been developed to ensure that intellectual property owners do not acquire the sort of exorbitant rights described above. One of them is the theory of exhaustion, which is generally considered to be a creature of German law. The paternity of the exhaustion theory is ascribed to the German jurist Joseph Kohler.[1] The word 'exhaustion' (*Erschöpfung* in German) seems, however, to have been first used by the German *Reichsgericht* in a number of judgments in the early years of the twentieth century. In a judgment of 26 March 1902 the *Reichsgericht* held, for example, that the effect of the protection conferred by a patent (i.e. the exclusive right to manufacture products covered by the patent and to put them on the market) was exhausted by the first sale.[2] In other words, once

---

[1] T. de las Heras Lorenzo, *El agotamiento del derecho de marca*, Editorial Montecorvo, Madrid, 1994, p. 47; F.-K. Beier, 'Grenzen der Erschöpfungslehre im Markenrecht: zur Beurteilung des Vertriebs umgepackter und neu gekennzeichneter Originalwaren in den Ländern der Europäischen Wirtschaftsgemeinschaft.'

[2] *Guajakol-Karbonat* RGZ 51. 139.

the patent-holder had transferred legal ownership of goods made in accordance with the patent, by selling them to another person, he lost the power to control the further destiny of those goods and could not restrict the commercial freedom of persons who acquired the goods subsequently.

The theory of exhaustion, in relation to patents, was based on the idea that the basic objective of the patent (namely, to reward the creative effort of the inventor and thus stimulate scientific progress) could be achieved by granting the patentee the right to make the first sale of the goods in monopoly conditions. The patentee takes his profit on the first sale and cannot expect further profits to accrue to him, after that point, from goods which he has had the advantage of selling in monopoly conditions. There is no justification, inherent in the logic of patent law, for allowing the patentee to interfere with the ordinary commercial freedom of subsequent acquirers of such goods.

Similar considerations apply to other types of exclusive right. The copyright owner obtains an appropriate reward for the creative effort of the author by selling copies of the protected work in monopoly conditions. There is no reason why he should be allowed to control further sales of those copies. The question whether he should be allowed to control the rental of copies that he has sold is, as we shall see, a rather different matter.

The essential functions of a trade mark are to enable consumers to distinguish between the products of different manufacturers and to prevent unscrupulous traders from misappropriating commercial goodwill belonging to other traders. Those functions are not undermined if 'genuine' goods (i.e. goods which have been marketed under the trade mark by, or with the consent of, the proprietor of the mark) are resold, hired out, or otherwise used in commerce.

It is important to stress that the exhaustion principle only applies to specific products marketed by, or with the consent of, the right-owner.[3] Exhaustion does not, of course, mean that the purchaser of a patented product may take it to pieces, find out how it works and then manufacture further examples of the product; or that one may buy a work protected by copyright, run it through the photocopier, and sell copies on the corner of the street. Exhaustion means simply that the lawful owner of specific products that have been placed on the market by, or with the consent of, the right-owner may use, sell, or otherwise dispose of those products.[4]

---

[3] Case C-173/98 *Sebago v GB-Unic* [1999] ECR I-4103.

[4] 'The principle of "exhaustion" of industrial property rights and copyrights, which has been applied by German courts since the beginning of this century, adopted by the ECJ, and often misunderstood abroad, is nothing but the descriptive expression of the simple legal notion that further distribution and use of genuine goods according to their very purpose should not be controlled after the owner, a licensee or a related company has put the genuine goods on the market.' F.-K. Beier. 'Industrial Property and the Free Movement of Goods in the Internal European Market' (1990) 21 IIC 131, 152.

Something resembling the exhaustion principle has been developed in most legal systems, though different terminology may be used. In the United States, for example, similar results are achieved by the 'first sale doctrine', also known, at least in the field of patents, as 'the *Adams v Burke*[5] doctrine'. In trade mark law the doctrine dates back to *Appolinaris Co v Scherer*, decided in 1886.[6]

In the United Kingdom the situation was more complex (at least before the impact of EC law). Britain and Ireland were the only EC countries whose patent laws did not recognize a rule of national exhaustion.[7] In principle a purchaser of a patented product, even a genuine product marketed by the patentee, required the latter's licence in order to use or resell the product. A result similar—but by no means identical—to exhaustion was achieved by means of the implied licence doctrine, under which the purchaser of patented products was deemed to possess an implied licence to use or sell them freely.[8] The weakness in that doctrine was that the patentee could avoid the effect of the implied licence by the simple expedient of imposing express contractual restrictions on the use or resale of the product at the time of the first sale.[9] Such restrictions were binding on subsequent purchasers who had notice of them.[10]

The English courts also used the implied licence doctrine in trade mark cases. If a trade mark proprietor allowed goods to be marketed abroad bearing the trade mark, he was deemed to have consented to further transactions in the goods, including export to and resale in the United Kingdom.[11] But if the goods were sold abroad subject to an export restriction and were of markedly different quality, the proprietor of the trade mark could object to their resale in the United Kingdom.[12]

---

[5]   84 US (17 Wall.) 453 (1873). For a review of American case law on exhaustion of patents, see W. A. Birdwell, 'Exhaustion of Rights and Patent Licensing Market Restrictions' (1978) JPOS 203.

[6]   T. H. Hiebert, 'Foundations of the Law of Parallel Importation: Duality and Universality in 19th-Century Trademark Law' (1990) 80 TMR 497.

[7]   W. R. Cornish, *Intellectual Property: Patents, Copyright, Trade Marks and Allied Rights*, 2nd edn, Sweet and Maxwell, London, 1989, p. 200.

[8]   A. Benyamini, *Patent Infringement in the European Community*, VCH, Weinheim and New York, 1993, p. 290.

[9]   According to de las Heras Lorenzo, the implied licence doctrine dates back to an English judgment of 1871 and was introduced into Germany by Kohler, but was found to be inadequate because the patentee could easily frustrate its effect by means of express restrictions: de las Heras Lorenzo, op. cit. (n. 1), at p. 44. The English judgment referred to is *Betts v Willmott* (1871) LR 6 Ch 239.

[10]   *National Phonograph Company of Australia Ltd v Menck* [1911] 28 RPC 229, 248 (P. C. of Australia) and *British Mutoscope and Biograph Ltd v Homer* [1901] 18 RPC 177, 179 (both cases cited by Benyamini, op. cit. (n. 8), at p. 290).

[11]   *Revlon v Cripps & Lee* [1980] FSR 85.

[12]   *Colgate Palmolive Ltd v Markwell Finance Ltd* [1989] RPC 497.

2. DIFFERENT TYPES OF EXHAUSTION: NATIONAL, INTERNATIONAL, AND COMMUNITY-WIDE

The fundamental purpose of an exhaustion rule is to prevent intellectual property owners from using their exclusive rights in order to partition the market. To determine the precise consequences of such a rule it is first necessary to define the geographical market whose unitary character we wish to safeguard. Much will depend on the viewpoint of the authority (legislative, regulatory, or judicial) which is laying down the rule. A national authority will be primarily concerned about the competitive structure of the national market and—unless it takes an 'enlightened' view about the need to expose domestic traders to the stimulus of foreign competition and about the advantages accruing to consumers through easy access to imported goods— such an authority may not be unduly perturbed by the partitioning of foreign markets or by barriers between the national market and the world beyond.

To take a concrete example, the United Kingdom authorities would, one assumes, be deeply concerned if the manufacturers of light bulbs were partitioning the British market, charging much higher prices in south-east England than in Scotland and taking steps to prevent goods marketed in Glasgow from being resold in London. It comes as no surprise therefore that patent and trade mark rights cannot generally be used to achieve that sort of effect. On the other hand, if British manufacturers of light bulbs were flooding the German and Indonesian markets with cheap exports, we would hardly be shocked if the United Kingdom authorities were indifferent to attempts by the manufacturers to prevent such goods from returning to the British market or being shipped on to Poland or Australia.

It follows from the above that the place of first marketing is a crucial element in the characterization of an exhaustion rule. If, in the hypothetical example given above, the United Kingdom authorities decided that patent and trade mark rights could not be invoked to prevent the resale in London of goods marketed with the consent of the right-owners in Glasgow, they would be applying a rule of national exhaustion (although they might not of course describe it thus). If those authorities also decided that patent and trade mark rights could not be invoked to prevent the importation of goods marketed in Germany and Indonesia with the consent of the right-owners, they would be applying a rule of international exhaustion.

National exhaustion can be regarded as an essential minimum. No country has any reason to permit the partitioning of its own domestic market on the basis of intellectual property rights. Not surpisingly, most advanced legal systems have attained that essential minimum.[13] The

---

[13] For comparative surveys, see Benyamini, op. cit. (n. 8), at pp. 287–93, and de las Heras Lorenzo, op. cit. (n. 1), at pp. 41–135.

exceptions in recent times have been rare, the most notable (apart from the peculiar features of British and Irish patent law mentioned earlier) being the French case law in the 1960s which, on the basis of the so-called *droit de suite*, allowed the proprietor of a trade mark to control the use and distribution of a trade-marked product until it reached the end-user. It was thus possible for manufacturers who established selective distribution systems to invoke their trade mark rights against unauthorized parallel distributors. De las Heras Lorenzo points out that the judges who permitted such extraordinarily anti-competitive practices in the name of trade mark law, and rejected exhaustion as a German construction, were oblivious to the nineteenth-century case law which had established exhaustion (without using that expression) as part of French law.[14] Fortunately, the *Cour de Cassation* held, in a series of judgments in 1987 and 1988, that the proprietor of a trade mark cannot invoke it to prevent the resale of genuine goods which he has placed on the market.[15] Exhaustion has, in any event, now been formally recognized by French statute law as a result of EC harmonization.

Some legal systems have gone beyond national exhaustion and introduced a rule of international exhaustion. In the field of trade marks, international exhaustion could even be regarded as the norm,[16] whereas in the field of patents it appears to be the exception.[17] It is not immediately obvious why such a marked difference exists.[18] The explanation may be that in trade mark cases the courts focus on the role of trade marks in

[14] Ibid., at p. 75.

[15] Ibid., at p. 76. See also the note by J. Pagenberg in (1988) 19 IIC 707. For a review of the French case law in the 1980s, see C. Lebel and S. Aicardi, 'Legal Aspects of Selective Distribution of Luxury Products in France' [1990] 7 EIPR 246.

[16] De las Heras Lorenzo, op. cit. (n. 1), at p. 70. That conclusion is confirmed by the comparative survey conducted by F.-K. Beier and A. von Mühlendahl, 'Der Grundsatz der internationalen Erschöpfung des Markenrechts in den Mitgliedstaaten der EG und ausgewählten Drittstaaten', (1980) 71 *Mitteilungen der Deutschen Patentanwälter*, Heft 6, 101–8.

[17] That conclusion is confirmed by Benyamini's comparative survey: Benyamini, op. cit. (n. 8), at pp. 287–93. It seems, however, that the Japanese and Swiss courts have recently favoured the international exhaustion of patents: see A. van der Merwe, 'The Exhaustion of Rights in Patent Law with Specific Emphasis on the Issue of Parallel Importation' [2000] IPQ 286, 292, and T. Hays, '*BBS Kraftfahrzeugtechnik AG v Racimex Japan KK*; Jap Auto Products KK—Japan Opens the Door to Parallel Imports of Patented Goods' (2001) *Melbourne Journal of International Law* 191.

[18] For a rather unconvincing attempt to justify the different treatment of patents and trade marks as regards international exhaustion, see S. Ladas, 'Exclusive Territorial Licences under Parallel Patents' (1972) 3 IIC 335, 345. Ladas states: 'the grant by a State of the advantages inherent in a patent calls for the recognition, reconciliation and satisfaction of interests, claims and demands of an individual and of the social order. This fashioning of the scope of the rights and limitations of a patent is a task made independently by each State. Such independent determination would be falsified and seriously encroached upon if the exclusive rights granted by a State to the patentee, and through him to a licensee, should be interfered with, and their scope affected by importation of products from another State without the authority or consent of the patentee or licensee.' The underlying protectionism of these sentiments is revealed by the following sentence, where Ladas says that the interests of the State may be adversely affected 'if the local licensee's investment should be imperiled by the inundation of its market by foreign-made products'.

preventing the deception of consumers and find it difficult to accept that consumers are misled when they buy 'genuine goods' which the trade mark owner has marketed abroad. In patent cases, on the other hand, the courts are possibly more willing to think of the patent as a property right whose obvious territoriality means that the respective rights of assignors, assignees, and exclusive licensees are readily taken into account. Arguments based on the absence of a parallel patent in the country of first marketing or on differences in the scope of protection in the various territories concerned have also had an influence.

It was pointed out above that national authorities, whose chief preoccupation is the unity of the national market, will automatically tend to elaborate some rule that amounts to a principle of (at least) national exhaustion. By virtue of the same logic it is equally certain that the EC authorities, whose aim—as the Court of Justice has recognized—is to 'merge the national markets into a single market bringing about conditions as close as possible to those of a genuine internal market',[19] will insist on a principle of Community-wide exhaustion. In the following sections we shall see how the Court of Justice has established—and tenaciously defended—such a principle.

3. THE EARLY CASES: *CONSTEN AND GRUNDIG* AND *DEUTSCHE GRAMMOPHON*

The principle of Community-wide exhaustion was implicit in the *Consten and Grundig* judgment,[20] the facts of which are summarized above.[21] It will be recalled that the Court upheld the Commission's decision finding that Article 81(1) of the Treaty had been infringed by an agreement under which Grundig allowed Consten to register Grundig's trade mark in France in Consten's name, so that Consten could use the trade mark to block parallel imports of Grundig products from Germany. The case was dealt with under the competition rules of the Treaty, although it clearly concerned the free movement of goods as much as competition law. In fact, it was not until the early 1970s that parallel importers began to invoke the provisions of Articles 28 *et seq*. The explanation for that may be that the prohibition of measures equivalent in effect to quantitative restrictions did not become effective until the end of the transitional period on 31 December 1969.[22] If the case were to arise now, the parallel importer would invoke Article 28 before the national court in which the proprietor of the trade mark brought infringement proceedings against him and that court would

---

[19] Case 15/81 *Schul v Inspecteur der Invoerrechte en Accijnzen* [1982] ECR 1409 at para. 33.

[20] Joined Cases 56 and 58/64 [1966] ECR 299.   [21] See Chap. 5.

[22] See P. Oliver, *Free Movement of Goods in the European Community*, 3rd edn, Sweet and Maxwell, London, p. 71.

have to apply the exhaustion doctrine established by the Court of Justice. A firm in the situation of Consten would be unable to invoke the trade mark to oppose the importation and sale of goods marketed by Grundig in another Member State. The marketing would be deemed to have taken place with Consten's consent in view of the close economic links between Grundig and Consten. (The latter was the former's exclusive distributor.) The essential reason given by the Court for judging the agreement to be contrary to Article 81 was identical to the reasoning on which the exhaustion principle is based: 'Since the agreement . . . aims at isolating the French market for Grundig products and maintaining artificially, for products of a very well-known brand, separate national markets within the Community, it is therefore such as to distort competition in the Common Market.'[23]

Five years after *Consten and Grundig* the Court expressly established a principle of Community-wide exhaustion on the basis of the Treaty provisions on the free movement of goods. It did so in *Deutsche Grammophon v Metro*,[24] the facts of which are described in Chapter 5. It will be recalled that Deutsche Grammophon attempted to prevent the resale in Germany of records which its French subsidiary had marketed in France. To do so, it invoked its exclusive distribution right as a producer of phonograms[25] (a right akin to copyright under German law).

Although the questions referred to the Court of Justice by the German court were confined to the field of competition law, the Court of Justice decided of its own motion to consider whether the exercise of the right in question was compatible with the Treaty provisions on the free movement of goods. The Court answered that question in the negative.

The reasoning followed by the Court is interesting. After reciting the (by then familiar) formula about the existence and exercise of the right and mentioning in passing the concept of specific subject-matter (without, however, defining it), the Court proceeded to base the exhaustion principle on far less abstract, and consequently much more solid, foundations. It is clear from paragraph 12 of the judgment that the principle is firmly anchored in the logic of market integration. There the Court stated:

If a right related to copyright is relied upon to prevent the marketing in a Member State of products distributed by the holder of the right or with his consent on the territory of another Member State on the sole ground that such distribution did not take place on the national territory, such a prohibition, which would legitimize the isolation of national markets, would be repugnant to the essential purpose of the Treaty, which is to unite national markets into a single market. That purpose could

---

[23] At 343.   [24] Case 78/70 [1971] ECR 487.
[25] 'Phonogram' is the technical term for gramophone records, recorded cassettes, compact discs and the like. It is defined by Art. 3(b) of the 1961 Rome Convention for the Protection of Performers, Producers of Phonograms and Broadcasting Organizations as meaning 'any exclusively aural fixation of sounds of a performance or of other sounds'.

not be attained if, under the various legal systems of the Member States, nationals of those States were able to partition the market and bring about arbitrary discrimination or disguised restrictions on trade between Member States.

Recognizing that territorially limited intellectual property rights have an inherent tendency to isolate markets, the Court was anxious to keep such partitioning within strict limits. One obvious limitation was to deny market-splitting capacity to traders who owned parallel intellectual property rights in several Member States. Although the Court did not refer expressly to the existence of parallel rights, it doubtless assumed that Deutsche Grammophon or its subsidiaries held exclusive distribution rights in France and other Member States in respect of the recordings in question. That is implicit in the reference to individuals partitioning the market 'under the various legal systems of the Member States'. The Court's fundamental concern was to ensure that an intellectual property owner who held parallel rights in a number of Member States could not use those separate rights to partition the common market and create artificial barriers to trade between Member States.

It is sometimes suggested that Deutsche Grammophon would not have been entitled at the material time to prevent the distribution of infringing copies of its records in France.[26] It is true that record producers did not then enjoy a primary right in France corresponding exactly to the right which existed in Germany. It would, however, be misleading to suggest that record piracy was lawful in France in 1971. The correct position seems to have been stated by Advocate General Roemer in his opinion in *Deutsche Grammophon v Metro*. Mr Roemer noted that Italian law granted phonogram producers a specific right similar to the one that existed in Germany and that in the other Member States (i.e. Belgium, France, Luxembourg, and the Netherlands as the Community was then constituted) corresponding protection was ensured 'by the laws on unfair competition or by the acquisition by the record manufacturer of the primary right of the author or of the performer'.[27]

4. SALES BY RELATED UNDERTAKINGS

4.1 *The nature of the problem*

It is clear from *Deutsche Grammophon* that the exhaustion principle applies to goods placed on the market in a Member State by the holder of the right

---

[26] See the opinion of Advocate General Reischl in Case 187/80 *Merck v Stephar* [1981] ECR 2063 at 2087, and the opinion of Advocate General Fennelly in Joined Cases C-267/95 and C-268/95 *Merck v Primecrown* [1996] ECR I-6285 at para. 98. See also R. Joliet, 'Patented Articles and Free Movement of Goods within the EEC' (1975) *Current Legal Problems* 15, 19.

[27] [1971] ECR 487 at 504.

or with his consent. The meaning of this key concept of consent is not always as clear as may appear at first sight. A number of relationships must be considered. The first sale may be effected by a subsidiary of the right-holder (as in *Deutsche Grammophon*), by the parent company of the right-holder, by a licensee, assignee, exclusive distributor, or agent of the right-holder. The owner of parallel patents or parallel trade mark registrations in Member States A, B, and C may retain the right in Member State A but assign it to company X in Member State B and Company Y in Member State C. Or the owner may grant exclusive licences to Companies X and Y for those territories. An assignment may be a clear-cut transaction in which the right-holder parts with the right definitively in return for a single payment and retains no special relationship with the assignee. It may, on the other hand, take the form of an assignment but resemble in substance a licence, for example where the assignor receives a royalty based on the number of units sold, retains the power to control the quality of goods produced by the assignee, limits the quantity of such goods, and is entitled to have the right assigned back to him after a certain period.

The treatment of these multifarious situations from the point of view of the free movement of goods is far from straightforward. It must not be assumed that uniform rules will apply to all forms of intellectual property. The differing functions of patent and trade mark rights may, for example, command different solutions to apparently identical problems. A further complication is that the implications of competition law cannot be disregarded in this context. A practice may be deemed compatible with Articles 28 and 30 and yet still offend against Article 81 or 82. The converse may also be true. These two sets of provisions complement each other and must be interpreted coherently. Here, as elsewhere, a holistic approach to the Treaty is required.

4.2 Sales by members of the same economic group

The exhaustion principle undoubtedly applies to goods placed on the market by undertakings which belong to the same economic group. This is in accordance with the general rule, long established in EC competition law, that subsidiaries which have no freedom to determine their own course of action are treated as forming, along with their parent company, a single legal entity.[28] It will be recalled that in *Deutsche Grammophon v Metro* the recordings in question had been placed on the market in France by a subsidiary of Deutsche Grammophon. It was held that Deutsche Grammophon could not oppose the resale of the recordings in Germany. It is clear

---

[28] Case 15/74 *Centrafarm v Sterling Drug* [1974] ECR 1147 at para. 41. See also D. G. Goyder, *EC Competition Law*, 2nd edn, Oxford, 1993, pp. 87–91.

that the exhaustion principle would likewise have been upheld in the reverse situation. Thus, if Deutsche Grammophon had transferred whatever exclusive rights it held under French law to its French subsidiary, the latter could not have opposed the resale in France of recordings marketed by the parent company in Germany.

4.3 *Sales by an agent or distributor*

Exhaustion will also occur when goods are placed on the market by an agent or distributor (exclusive or otherwise) acting on behalf of the right-holder. In *Consten and Grundig v Commission* a German manufacturer had allowed its trade mark to be registered in France by its exclusive distributor for that country. Although the case was decided under Article 81 of the Treaty, there cannot be any doubt that if the case arose today it would be resolved (with exactly the same result) under the exhaustion rule. It is not, of course, strictly accurate to say that the exclusive distributor consents to goods being marketed by the manufacturer. But that would be to miss the point. The economic links between a manufacturer and a distributor of goods (especially an exclusive one) are so strong that, where the former assigns his trade mark or patent rights to the latter, the two are clearly involved in a joint enterprise to exploit intellectual property rights. Responsibility for the acts of one must be imputed to the other.

4.4 *Sales by licensees*

Similar considerations apply to licensees. Where an intellectual property owner grants a licence authorizing another person to exploit his rights in a given territory, he exhausts his rights as regards goods marketed by the licensee and cannot complain if those goods are resold in another part of the common market. A clearer case of consent would be difficult to imagine. If an exclusive licensee is authorized to sue for infringements, either in his own name or on behalf of the right-holder, he cannot claim that an infringement takes place when goods placed on the market by another exclusive licensee in another Member State are exported to his territory. Such goods were placed on the market with the consent of the right-holder, so exhaustion applies.

4.5 *Compulsory licences*

There is one category of licensee whose activities do not entail the exhaustion of the licensed right. In *Pharmon v Hoechst*[29] the Court of Justice held

---

[29] Case 19/84 [1985] ECR 2281.

that the proprietor of parallel patents (Hoechst) in the Netherlands and the United Kingdom could oppose the importation into the Netherlands of goods manufactured in the United Kingdom by an undertaking which had obtained a compulsory licence to work the patent in the United Kingdom. The licence had been issued to a firm called DDSA by the United Kingdom Patent Office under section 41 of the Patents Act 1949, which made special provision for patents in respect of foodstuffs, medicines, and surgical instruments. In connection with such patents, the Comptroller General of Patents was required to grant a compulsory licence to any person who applied for one, on such terms as he thought fit, unless it appeared to him that there were good reasons for refusing the application. The licence granted to DDSA contained a prohibition on exportation outside the United Kingdom. Notwithstanding that prohibition, DDSA sold a consignment of tablets which it had produced under the compulsory licence to Pharmon, a Dutch pharmaceutical company. Hoechst applied to a Rotterdam court for an injunction restraining Pharmon from infringing Hoechst's patent by selling in the Netherlands products manufactured by the compulsory licensee in the United Kingdom.

When the case was referred to the Court of Justice for a preliminary ruling, no fewer than six Member States (out of a total of ten) made use of their right to submit observations. All contended, like the Commission, that a patent-holder in one Member State could oppose the importation of products manufactured under a compulsory licence in another Member State. The Court of Justice agreed with that view. It ruled that:[30] 'Articles [28] and [30] of the [EC] Treaty do not preclude the application of legal provisions of a Member State which give a patent proprietor the right to prevent the marketing in that State of a product which has been manufactured in another Member State by the holder of a compulsory licence granted in respect of a parallel patent held by the same proprietor.'

The Court based its decision on the absence of consent by the patent-holder. The compulsory licence deprived the patent-holder of the right to determine freely the conditions under which he marketed his products.[31] Rather less convincingly the Court maintained that the specific subject-matter of the patent (referred to here as the 'substance' of the patent) would be impaired if the patentee could not oppose the importation of products manufactured by a compulsory licensee. The substance of the patent was defined as the patentee's exclusive right of first placing a product on the market 'so as to allow him to obtain the reward for his creative effort'.[32] It could be argued that the substance of a patent, thus defined, is not impaired by applying the principle of free movement to products made

---

[30] At para. 27 of the judgment. [31] At para. 25 of the judgment.
[32] At para. 26 of the judgment.

by a compulsory licensee, if the compulsory licence fixes a reasonable royalty. The problem with that argument is that there is no universal standard for deciding what constitutes a reasonable royalty. The patentee is normally entitled to whatever royalty he can negotiate from his advantageous position as a monopoly supplier of the patented product. The Court, in any event, held that the payment of royalties under a compulsory licence was irrelevant.

The Court's ruling was certainly consistent with the general thrust of its case law on exhaustion, and the basic proposition that a compulsory licensee's products do not benefit from the principle of free movement is sound. It is, however, regrettable that the Court did not introduce into its ruling a qualification proposed by Advocate General Mancini to the effect that the exhaustion principle should apply where the national court finds in an individual case that the patent proprietor contributed by his own voluntary act to the granting of a compulsory licence.[33] It is, for example, conceivable that the patentee might indicate to an applicant for a licence that rather than grant a voluntary licence he would prefer that person to set in motion the procedure for obtaining a compulsory licence. Benyamini states that 'any voluntary act of the patentee leading to a compulsory licence' will result in exhaustion.[34] Such a test may, of course, involve difficult issues of fact. It is in any event clear that the distinction between voluntary and compulsory licences is not as simple and straightforward as the Court appears to believe.[35] Certainly, it cannot be doubted that, if there exist between the patent proprietor and the compulsory licensee the legal or economic links which normally bring the exhaustion rule into play, the rule cannot be ousted simply because the licence is, from a formal point of view, compulsory.

An unusual feature of *Pharmon v Hoechst* is that the compulsory licensee exported the goods directly to the Netherlands (notwithstanding an export prohibition in the compulsory licence). Ullrich suggests that the case might have been decided differently if the goods had first been placed on the market in the United Kingdom by the compulsory licensee and then exported to the Netherlands by a third party (i.e. a parallel importer).[36] There is nothing in the language of the judgment to support that suggestion. Indeed, Ullrich seems to have misunderstood the basis of the judgment. He states that the inapplicability of the exhaustion principle to goods produced by a compulsory licensee is not due to the absence of consent by the patentee, since the compulsory licence substitutes that consent; instead exhaustion is excluded 'because admitting such imports would preempt a

---

[33] At 2289.   [34] Op. cit. (n. 8), at p. 308.

[35] See G. Tritton, *Intellectual Property in Europe*, Sweet and Maxwell, London, 1996, p. 301.

[36] H. Ullrich, 'Patents and Know-how, Free Trade, Interenterprise Cooperation and Competition within the Internal European Market' (1992) 23 IIC 582, 593 (footnote 44).

public-policy decision which the importing State must be free to take by its own sovereign judgment'.[37] But the argument that the decision of the national authorities to grant a compulsory licence may be deemed to replace the consent of the patent proprietor was pleaded by Pharmon and expressly rejected by the Court.[38] In fact, it would be difficult to find a judgment which emphasized so strongly the importance of the right-holder's consent for the operation of the exhaustion principle.

It is submitted therefore that nothing turns on whether the compulsory licensee's products are exported directly by the compulsory licensee or by a third party after being released on the home market by the compulsory licensee. In neither case will the right be exhausted if the patent proprietor did not consent to the sale of the goods by the compulsory licensee in a Member State.

4.6 Assignments

The case law on exhaustion through sales by related undertakings was summarized in *Ideal Standard*,[39] which is the leading case on trade mark assignments. There the Court of Justice stated:

> . . . application of a national law which would give the trade-mark owner in the importing State the right to oppose the marketing of products which have been put into circulation in the exporting State by him or with his consent is precluded as contrary to Articles [28] and [30]. This principle, known as the exhaustion of rights, applies where the owner of the trade mark in the importing State and the owner of the trade mark in the exporting State are the same or where, even if they are separate persons, they are economically linked. A number of situations are covered: products put into circulation by the same undertaking, by a licensee, by a parent company, by a subsidiary of the same group, or by an exclusive distributor.

In the *Ideal Standard* case an undertaking which owned a trade mark in France and Germany assigned the French registration to another undertaking with which it had no legal or economic links. The assignee began marketing products bearing the trade mark in Germany, where it had remained in the hands of the original proprietor. Infringement proceedings commenced by the latter led to a preliminary ruling in which the Court held that the exhaustion principle did not apply in such a situation. The basis for the judgment was that the trade mark's function as an indicator of the commercial origin of goods would be compromised if a trade mark could be used in the same territory by unconnected undertakings, neither of which was in a position to control the quality of the goods produced by the other.

---

[37] Ibid.   [38] At paras 16 and 25 of the judgment.

[39] Case C-2/93 *IHT Internationale Heiztechnik v Ideal Standard* [1994] ECR I-2789 at para. 34. The case is dealt with more fully in Chap. 8.

The result reached in *Ideal Standard* appears correct, since any other outcome would be incompatible with the trade mark's essential function. It would, however, surely have been preferable if the Court had recognized expressly that in certain situations the function (or specific subject-matter) of an intellectual property right must prevail over an abstract theory based purely on consent to a first sale anywhere in the common market. Instead the Court clung to the theory that consent is the sole criterion and attempted to square the theory with the result by adopting a definition of 'consent' which has rightly been described as idiosyncratic.[40] The Court stated that: 'The consent implicit in any assignment is not the consent required for application of the doctrine of exhaustion of rights.'[41]

The main outstanding question is whether the solution adopted in *Ideal Standard* also applies to patent assignments. The first point to note is that, regardless of the position when the assignment is a clear-cut, once-and-for-all transaction, and there are no legal or economic links between the assignor and assignee (apart from the contract of assignment), exhaustion must occur when such links do exist. In particular, when the assignment is in substance more in the nature of a licence (as would be the case if the assignor received a royalty based on the number of units sold by the assignee), the exhaustion principle must apply. In such a situation there is simply no room for any argument, based on the function or specific subject-matter of the patent, for denying that the consent implicit in the assignment is sufficient to bring the exhaustion principle into play. It is also interesting to note that for the purposes of Community competition law an assignment is treated as a licence when the consideration for the assignment consists of the payment of royalties.[42]

The question whether exhaustion also applies when no such links exist between the assignor and assignee or assignees is more controversial. Some authors[43] affirm that exhaustion should not apply in that situation on the ground that the assignor and assignees cannot be regarded as having consented to the marketing of each other's products or as having obtained a reward in respect of such products. They also point out that Article 76(2) of the Community Patent Convention implies that exhaustion does not apply in such circumstances because it expressly provides for exhaustion only when 'economic connections' exist between the various patent

---

[40] P. Oliver, op. cit. (n. 22), at p. 283.   [41] [1994] ECR I-2789 at para. 43.

[42] Art. 6(2) of Commission Reg. No. 240/96 on the application of Art. [81(3)] of the Treaty to certain categories of technology transfer agreements, OJ 1996 L 31, p. 2. The Court of Justice is also willing to treat an assignment as a licence in the light of the economic context in which it takes place: see Case 258/78 *Nungesser v Commission* [1982] ECR 2015 at para. 47.

[43] E.g. Benyamini, op. cit. (n. 8), at pp. 326–7, and the authors cited by him in note 19 on p. 326. Benyamini admits that the matter is not free from doubt.

owners.[44] Other authors argue that, since the owner of parallel patents cannot use them to partition the common market, he should not be allowed to obtain such a result by assigning the patents to different entities, regardless of whether they are economically linked.[45] The latter view appears correct, especially in the light of *Ideal Standard*. The rationale of that judgment, though theoretically based on the idea of consent, was that a trade mark cannot perform its essential function unless it is under the control of a single undertaking in a specific territory. That rationale simply does not apply to patents. There is no reason therefore why exhaustion should not apply.

For the same reasons exhaustion should apply to goods covered by copyright, where the ownership of the copyright has been split up as a result of assignments.[46]

4.7 *Sales made in breach of a contractual agreement with the right-holder*

Consent, in the sense in which it is used above, is normally granted by means of a contractual agreement between the proprietor of the intellectual property right and the person who acquires the right (in the case of an assignment) or is authorized to use the right (in the case of a licence). The above discussion has assumed that that other person acts in accordance with the contract when he places products on the market. It is now necessary to consider what consequences ensue when that is not the case. A number of hypotheses must be envisaged:

- a trade mark licensee may infringe the quality standards prescribed by the trade mark owner;
- a patent licensee may infringe field-of-use or quantity restrictions; or
- the licensee may sell products outside his allocated territory.

The basic question that arises is whether the right-holder may oppose the importation of products that have been manufactured or marketed by a licensee or assignee in breach of a contractual stipulation. The Court of Justice has yet to rule on that issue, which must therefore be approached with a degree of circumspection. It is submitted that the starting-point must be to recognize that the provisions on the free movement of goods must be interpreted in harmony with the competition rules of the Treaty.[47] The first

---

[44] This argument must now be discounted since the Community Patent Convention never came into force. The current intention is to introduce the Community Patent by means of a Council regulation. The Commission proposal for a regulation (OJ 2000 C 337 E, p. 278) does not contain any provision resembling Art. 76(2) of the Convention.

[45] See the authors cited by Benyamini, op. cit. (n. 8), in note 14 on p. 325 of his book.

[46] Different considerations apply to the performance right and analogous rights, such as rental right: see Chap. 10.

[47] See Goyder, op. cit. (n. 28), at p. 338.

question therefore must be whether the contractual provision is valid under Article 81 of the Treaty. If it is contrary to Article 81(1) and not exempted under Article 81(3), it is automatically void under Article 81(2) and cannot, at least in theory, produce any effect. The right-holder cannot therefore rely on the provision to claim that its non-observance nullifies the right-holder's consent. Article 30 should not be used to enforce a contractual stipulation that is contrary to Article 81.[48] Thus, if P, the proprietor of patents in Member States A, B, and C, grants an exclusive licence to undertaking L for Member State B and prohibits L from responding to unsolicited orders from Member State C (where another exclusive licensee has been appointed) for fifteen years, such a restriction would not qualify for the group exemption available under Commission Regulation (EC) No. 240/96 on the application of Article 81(3) of the Treaty to certain categories of technology transfer agreements,[49] because a prohibition on responding to unsolicited orders from territories licensed to other licensees within the common market may not exceed five years.[50] Such a restriction seems to have no hope of qualifying for individual exemption and must be regarded as automatically void. If L supplies patented products to X in Member State C, in response to an unsolicited order, and X sells the goods to Y in Member State A, then P cannot invoke his patent in Member State A to prevent Y from using or selling the goods. Nor could P prevent X from using or selling the patented products in Member State C. P must be deemed to have consented to L's sale of the goods to X. His consent cannot be nullified by an unlawful clause in the licence agreement with L. Therefore the right is exhausted.

If, on the other hand, the licence agreement contained a clause prohibiting L, throughout the period of validity of the patent, from exploiting the patent in Member State A, which P has reserved for himself, such a clause would qualify for group exemption under Article 1(1), point 3, of Regulation No. 240/96. For these purposes, 'exploitation' of the patent means 'any use of the licensed technology in the production, active or passive sales in a territory even if not coupled with manufacture in that territory, or leasing of the licensed products'.[51] So if L exports patented products to a buyer (Z) in Member State A, whether in pursuance of an active sales policy or in response to an unsolicited order, P may sue Z for patent infringement if Z uses or resells the products.[52] The goods were not placed on the market

---

[48] Benyamini, op. cit. (n. 8), p. 321. See also U. Schatz, 'The Exhaustion of Patent Rights in the Common Market' (1971) 2 IIC 1, 13.

[49] OJ 1996 L 31, p. 2.

[50] Art. 1(1), point 6, in conjunction with Art. 1(2) and (4), second subparagraph, of Regulation No. 240/96.

[51] Art. 10, point 10, of Reg. No. 240/96.

[52] P may also sue L for breach of the licensing agreement.

with the consent of P and so the right is not exhausted. The clause in the licensing agreement withholding P's consent to the sale of the goods by L to Z is not in principle contrary to the competition rules of the Treaty, so there is no objection to allowing P to enforce the clause by means of infringement proceedings in which P may plead Article 30 in response to any argument by Z that the infringement proceedings are a measure having equivalent effect under Article 28.

Such an outcome may, of course, seem harsh upon Z, who may have acted innocently, in the sense that he may have known nothing of P's patent or of the terms of the licence agreement between P and L. The innocent infringer is a well-known figure in the national patent law of numerous Member States.[53] Benyamini points out that some legal systems afford him a degree of protection,[54] but Articles 28 and 30 of the Treaty do not seem to contain any principle according to which the innocent infringer cannot be sued whenever his activity involves a cross-border movement of goods within the Community.

The above remarks about patent licences apply *mutatis mutandis* to trade mark licences, the main difference being that the Commission has never adopted a group exemption regulation in relation to that category of licensing agreement.[55] One interesting question is whether the exhaustion principle applies to a licensee's goods which do not comply with the quality norms stipulated in the licence agreement. In principle, a negative answer is called for—at least if the failure to comply is substantial—on two grounds. In the first place, the trade mark owner cannot be deemed to have consented to the marketing of inferior goods that would be likely to damage his own goodwill. Secondly, the interests of the consumer would be adversely affected if goods of markedly inferior quality were in circulation under a trade mark which had generated certain expectations as to quality. Using the terminology of the European Court of Justice, one may say that the specific subject-matter and the essential function of the trade mark would be impaired.

In one of several *obiter dicta* in *Ideal Standard* the Court stated that:

. . . the decisive factor is the possibility of control over the quality of goods, not the actual exercise of that control. Accordingly, a national law allowing the licensor to oppose importation of the licensee's products on grounds of poor quality would be

---

[53] As regards the United Kingdom, see D. Young, A. Watson, S. Thorley and R. Miller, *Terrell on the Law of Patents*, 14th edn, Sweet and Maxwell London, 1994, p. 175; as regards other countries, see Benyamini, op. cit. (n. 8), at p. 319, and the literature cited in note 3 of that work.

[54] Ibid., at p. 320.

[55] Regulation No. 240/96 may apply to trade mark licensing provisions included in patent or know-how licensing agreements, provided those provisions are ancillary: Art. 1(1), opening sentence. The concept of ancillary provisions is construed restrictively by the Commission: see Commission Decision 90/186/EEC of 23 March 1990 (*Moosehead*), OJ 1990 L 100, p. 32.

precluded as contrary to Articles [28] and [30]: if the licensor tolerates the manufacture of poor quality products, despite having contractual means of preventing it, he must bear the responsibility.[56]

It is never easy to interpret a loosely worded *obiter dictum*. The passage cited clearly establishes that the exhaustion principle applies to the licensee's inferior goods if the licensor fails to take the necessary steps to enforce contractual stipulations as to quality, thus acquiescing in the licensee's breach. The question left unanswered is whether a licensor who takes all possible steps to ensure the licensee's compliance with quality stipulations must accept that inferior goods released on to the market by a rogue licensee, in spite of all the licensor's precautions, may circulate throughout the Community. It is submitted that there are circumstances in which the proprietor of the trade mark must be allowed to oppose parallel imports of a licensee's shoddy goods (or, rather, oppose the use of the trade mark on such goods). In particular, that must be so where use of the trade mark might give rise to product liability under Council Directive 85/374/EEC of 25 July 1985 on the approximation of the laws, regulations, and administrative provisions of the Member States concerning liability for defective products.[57] Articles 1 and 3(1) of the Directive impose liability for defective products on 'any person, who, by putting his name, trade mark or other distinguishing feature on the product presents himself as its producer'.[58]

The question of quality control under trade mark licensing agreements is the subject of express provisions in Council Directive 89/104/EEC to approximate the law of the Member States relating to trade marks[59] and Council Regulation (EC) No. 40/94 on the Community trade mark.[60] Article 8 of the former and Article 22 of the latter authorize the trade mark proprietor to invoke the rights conferred by the trade mark 'against a licensee who contravenes any provisions in the licensing contract with regard to . . . the quality of the goods manufactured or of the services provided by the licensee'. Those provisions are not decisive on the issue of exhaustion because they do not state whether the trade mark may be invoked against third parties who acquire defective goods manufactured by a licensee. Taken literally, they appear to confer the right to bring infringement proceedings against a specific class of infringer, namely a licensee who fails to comply with the quality norms stipulated in the licence. The utility of the provisions is questionable, since the trade mark proprietor

---

[56] At para. 38 of the judgment.

[57] OJ 1985 L 210, p. 29. The Directive was implemented in the United Kingdom by the Consumer Protection Act 1987.

[58] On the subject of product liability in relation to licensing, see D. Good and C. Easter, 'Product Liability and Product Safety: The Implications for Licensing' [1993] EIPR 10, and N. J. Wilkof, *Trade Mark Licensing*, Sweet and Maxwell, London, 1995, sections 14–14–14–32.

[59] OJ 1989 L 40, p. 1.   [60] OJ 1994 L 11, p. 1.

would in any case have a contractual claim against such a licensee. It is submitted that the question whether infringement proceedings may be brought against a third party (e.g. a parallel importer) who deals in the licensee's defective goods must be resolved, in the manner suggested above, on the basis of the relevant Treaty provisions.

4.8 *The distinction between direct sales and parallel imports*

It is clear from the above discussion that a distinction must sometimes be made between direct sales and parallel imports. 'Direct sales' take place, for example, when a licensee or assignee effects sales directly into the territory reserved to the licensor or assignor (or into the territory reserved to another licensee or assignee).[61] Parallel imports take place when the licensee or assignee first places goods on the market in the territory allocated to him and a third party ('the parallel importer') buys the goods and exports them to a territory reserved to another person.

According to Benyamini, it is the prevailing view among legal writers that the exhaustion doctrine developed by the Court of Justice does not extend to direct sales in view of the requirement that the goods must first be placed on the market in a Member State with the consent of the right-holder.[62] The Commission, on the other hand, has on occasions defended the view that a licensee who has been authorized to manufacture products under a patent licence should be allowed to sell the products anywhere in the EC, regardless of any territorial restriction in the licence agreement.[63] In his opinion in *Pharmon v Hoechst*, Advocate General Mancini suggested that there was some support for that view in the case law.[64] Such a view has also been defended by legal writers.[65]

---

[61] According to Benyamini, the phrase 'direct sales' means that 'the products are exported for the purpose of sale by a licensor, licensee, assignor, or assignee who holds the right in one Member State, directly to a person in another Member State, where their importation is opposed by the person holding a parallel right there, without being marketed first in the State of exportation.' Op. cit. (n. 8), at p. 329.

[62] Ibid., at p. 331. See also R. Casati, 'The Exhaustion of Industrial Property Rights in the EEC: Exclusive Manufacturing and Sales Provisions in Patent and Know-how Licensing Agreements' (1978) 17 *Columbia Journal of Transnational Law* 313, 330, note 92; G. Tritton, op. cit. (n. 35), at p. 304; Y. Jeanrenaud, 'Exclusive Licences of Patent Rights and Territorial Restraints in the EEC: Certainty v Flexibility' (1986) 26 *Swiss Review of International Competition Law* 21, 33; and I. Roudart, *Droit européen des licences exclusives des brevets*, 1989, at pp. 154 *et seq.*

[63] Fourth Report on Competition Policy (1975), points 22–27, Fifth Report on Competition Policy (1976), point 11.

[64] [1985] ECR 2281 at 2285.

[65] Including, perhaps rather surprisingly, R. Joliet, 'Patented Articles and the Free Movement of Goods within the EEC' (1975) *Current Legal Problems* 15, 38. See also M. Waelbroeck, 'The Effect of the Rome Treaty on the Exercise of National Industrial Property Rights' (1976) *The Antitrust Bulletin* 99, 130. Waelbroeck argues that the licensee should be allowed to sell directly into the territory of other licensees but that the licensor should be authorized to protect himself against direct sales by his licensee. Such a distinction seems difficult to justify.

It is submitted that neither the Commission's view nor the 'prevailing view' described by Benyamini can be wholly correct. Indeed the Commission's view is hardly consistent with its approach to the exemption of licensing agreements from the prohibition laid down by Article 81(1) of the Treaty. The group exemption regulations on patent licensing and know-how licensing, and the regulation which replaced them, all allow the licensor to prohibit the licensee from making direct sales into territory reserved to the licensor.[66] The effect of the exemption is that, where it is applicable, the licensor may sue, for breach of contract, a licensee who infringes the terms of the licensing agreement by selling directly into the licensor's territory. There would be little point in holding that the licensor is barred from suing the licensee for infringing the licensor's patent or trade mark in such circumstances. The issue of exhaustion is of limited relevance if the proprietor of the intellectual property right can prevent the infringing sales by means of a contractual action. Nor does it make sense to say that, if an infringing sale takes place, the buyer of the goods may resell them anywhere in the Community on the ground that the right has been exhausted. As we have seen, the right will not be exhausted if the infringing sale took place in breach of a valid territorial restriction in the licence agreement: the licensor will not have consented to the placing of the goods on the market.

On the other hand, the view that exhaustion can never take place as a result of direct sales outside the licensee's territory is equally untenable, for the reasons given earlier. If the clause prohibiting direct sales is contrary to Article 81, it is void and there is no legal basis for denying that the licensor consented to the direct sale. Consent cannot be withheld by a contractual term that is null and void. The principle governing this type of problem is simple: whenever the owner of an intellectual property right attempts to exercise the right as a means of preventing a transaction on the ground that it constitutes a breach of contract, the right cannot be invoked if the contractual provision in question is contrary to the competition rules of the Treaty. The legality of trade restrictions arising out of a contractual agreement is to be appraised under Article 81.

None of this should be taken as implying that the distinction between direct sales and parallel imports is irrelevant. All that is meant is that the

---

[66] See Commission Reg. (EEC) No. 2349/84 on the application of Art. |81(3)| of the EEC Treaty to categories of patent licensing agreements (OJ 1984 L 219, p. 15), Art. 1(1), point 3; Commission Reg. (EEC) No. 556/89 on the application of Art. |81(3)| of the Treaty to categories of know-how licensing agreement (OJ 1989 L 61, p. 1), Art. 1(1), point 3; and Commission Reg. (EC) No. 240/96 on the application of Art. |81(3)| of the Treaty to certain categories of technology transfer agreements (OJ 1996 L 31, p. 2), Art. 1(1), point 3. It should, however, be noted that point 11 in the preamble to Reg. No. 240/96 states that the exemption of export prohibitions on the licensor and on licensees does not prejudice any developments in the jurisprudence of the Court in relation to these agreements, notably with respect to Arts 28–30 and Art. 81(1) of the Treaty.

issue of exhaustion as a result of direct sales is of limited importance because, if the competition rules and the rules on free movement are interpreted coherently, the right-holder's contractual claim against an infringing licensee will normally be coextensive with his right to bring infringement proceedings where the right is held not to be exhausted. The distinction between direct sales and parallel imports is, however, important because of the unique status of parallel imports, which are regarded as almost sacrosanct in Community law.

The role of parallel imports has been recognized since the earliest days (*Consten and Grundig* and *Deutsche Grammophon*) and was confirmed in *Nungesser*, where the Court observed that it had 'consistenly held that absolute territorial protection granted to a licensee in order to enable parallel imports to be controlled and prevented results in the artificial maintenance of separate national markets, contrary to the Treaty'.[67] The group exemption regulations adopted by the Commission blacklist measures designed to impede parallel imports.[68] What this means in practical terms is that, once a licensee has placed goods on the market in accordance with the terms of his licence, a third party may export them to another Member State, even though the licensee himself could have been enjoined from doing so. This can lead to some curious results. For example, a licensee (L) who is prevented from meeting an unsolicited order directly may ensure that the potential customer (C) knows the identity of a willing parallel importer (P) established in L's Member State. C may then ask P to order the goods from L, and P may resell them to C. Obviously a ban on passive sales outside the licensee's territory will not be watertight as long as parallel imports are possible.

The economic function of parallel imports is to promote intra-brand competition by making it more difficult for traders to wall off national markets. Competition between the goods of a licensor and his licensees will normally prevent significant price discrepancies from being practised for identical products within the common market. While sound in the case of consumer goods, the theory breaks down in the case of goods in which there is no intermediate trade (such as large industrial products). If the manufacturer sells directly to the end-user, there is obviously not much scope for parallel importers. It is in that context that particular relevance attaches to the question whether the licensor may prevent a licensee from exporting directly outside his allotted territory, either by means of infringement proceedings or by an action for breach of contract.

---

[67] Case 258/78 *Nungesser v Commission* [1982] ECR 2015 at para. 61.

[68] See, e.g., Art. 3, point 11, of Reg. No. 2349/84; Art. 3, point 12, of Reg. No. 556/89; and Art. 3, point 3, of Reg. No. 240/96. However, the Commission adopted a more lenient attitude in *Comasso* (OJ 1990 C 6, p. 3); see W. A. Rothnie, *Parallel Imports*, Sweet and Maxwell, 1993, at pp. 440 and 450.

5. IS CONSENT THE ONLY RELEVANT FACTOR?

5.1 *Introduction*

It is clear from *Pharmon v Hoechst* that consent to the first marketing is a necessary condition for the application of the exhaustion principle. The question that remains to be resolved is whether consent is the only condition. In other words: even though the right-holder consented to the sale of the goods within the Community, can the application of the exhaustion principle be excluded on some other ground, e.g. because the right-holder was prevented, by some feature of the law of the country in which the first sale took place, from securing the reward that an intellectual property owner is entitled to expect?

Pharmon v Hoechst establishes that the positive obtaining of a reward is irrelevant. In that case the patentee was entitled to royalties from the compulsory licensee in respect of the goods manufactured by the latter in the United Kingdom and exported to the Netherlands. The *Hoge Raad* asked the Court of Justice whether the availability or the actual receipt of royalties affected the applicability of the exhaustion principle to goods sold by a compulsory licensee. The Court declared the issue of royalties to be irrelevant. Its failure to state any reasons for that finding suggests that as far as the Court was concerned the application of the exhaustion principle was so obviously dependent on consent to the first sale by the right-holder that in the absence of consent it was unnecessary to consider the possible relevance of other factors, such as whether the right-holder had obtained an adequate reward.

The crucial importance attached to consent in *Pharmon v Hoechst* was entirely consistent with a number of judgments delivered in 1974 and 1981, in which the reverse situation obtained; that is to say, the right-holder consented to the first sale but was unable to a secure a full reward because of some peculiarity of the law in the country of the first sale. The issue that arose in those cases was whether, notwithstanding the right-holder's consent to the first sale, the exhaustion principle should be excluded on the ground that the first sale had taken place in circumstances which prevented the right-holder from obtaining the reward which the exclusive right was intended to secure for him.

5.2 *The* Sterling Drug *and* Winthrop *cases*

The first cases in which that issue arose were *Centrafarm v Sterling Drug*[69] and *Centrafarm v Winthrop*,[70] the facts of which were described in Chapter

---

[69] Case 15/74 [1974] ECR 1147.   [70] Case 16/74 [1974] ECR 1183.

6. It will be recalled that a pharmaceutical company invoked its patent and trade mark rights in order to block parallel imports into the Netherlands of products which it had placed on the market in the United Kingdom. Of course, parallel imports only take place if there is a significant difference in the prices at which identical products are on the market in the Member States concerned. The products marketed by Sterling Drug and Winthrop were significantly cheaper in the United Kingdom than in the Netherlands, mainly as a result of governmental measures restricting the price of pharmaceutical products in the United Kingdom. Currency fluctuations were also cited as a contributory factor. The *Hoge Raad* asked the Court of Justice whether the proprietor of a patent or a trade mark should be allowed to block parallel imports when the first sale had taken place in a Member State in which governmental measures restricted the price at which the goods could be sold.

It is obvious that where price differences are due to a conscious decision of the opponent of parallel imports he has no ground to complain about the application of the exhaustion principle. On the contrary, one of the main objects of that principle is to prevent traders from practising differential pricing within the common market. It is equally certain that differences due to currency fluctuations are irrelevant. To hold otherwise would be to postpone the realization of the common market until the day when full monetary union is achieved. Pending that day, currency fluctuations are a phenomenon which traders in the common market have to anticipate and make allowance for, and which can benefit as well as injure them.

Price differences due to direct government intervention in the mechanism of price formation raise more difficult issues, at least as regards goods protected by a patent. As far as trade marks are concerned, it seems reasonably clear that the existence of statutory price controls is not a ground for allowing the proprietor of a trade mark to oppose parallel imports. The function of a trade mark as a guarantee of origin is not impaired simply because trade-marked goods which are sold at a restricted price in Member State A are resold by a parallel importer in Member State B, where the price is uncontrolled. As Advocate General Jacobs remarked in his opinion in the *Paranova* cases, it is not the function of trade marks to correct discrepancies caused by legislation on prices.[71] It is true that one of the economic functions of a trade mark is to enable the proprietor to maintain prices at a higher level than would be possible in the case of unbranded goods. Such price levels can be achieved by advertising and by consistently producing goods of high quality, neither method being effective without trade mark protection. In legal terms, however, that function is

---

[71] Joined Cases C-427/93, C-429/93 and C-436/93 *Bristol-Myers Squibb and others v Paranova* [1996] ECR I-3457 at para. 74 of the opinion.

purely ancillary; or, to use the language of the Court of Justice, it is not part of the specific subject-matter of the trade mark right. It cannot therefore justify derogating from the principle of free movement.

As regards patents, however, different considerations may apply. The purpose of a patent is to stimulate scientific progress by rewarding the creative effort of the inventor. The reward takes the form of a right to sell the patented product (or products made in accordance with the patented process) in monopoly conditions. The effect of the monopoly is to enable the patentee to sell at a higher price than that which would be obtainable if he had to face competition from other manufacturers of the patented product. How, then, can he obtain the monopoly reward that should be his by right if he is prevented from fixing his own selling price in the country in which he first places the goods on the market? How can the specific subject-matter of the patent be achieved if the first sale takes place at a controlled price?

The Court of Justice did not address those issues satisfactorily in *Centrafarm v Sterling Drug*. In fact, its answer to the question whether exhaustion should apply when the first sale took place at a controlled price is wholly unconvincing. The Court stated:

It is part of the Community authorities' task to eliminate factors likely to distort competition between Member States, in particular by the harmonization of national measures for the control of prices and by the prohibition of aids which are incompatible with the Common Market, in addition to the exercise of their powers in the field of competition.

The existence of factors such as these in a Member State, however, cannot justify the maintenance or introduction by another Member State of measures which are incompatible with the rules concerning the free movement of goods, in particular in the field of industrial and commercial property.[72]

On that basis, the Court ruled that the exhaustion of patent rights was not affected by government price controls in the State of the first sale. The Court stated that it was 'a matter of no significance that there exist, as between the exporting and importing Member States, price differences resulting from governmental measures adopted in the exporting State with a view to controlling the price of the product'. In *Centrafarm v Winthrop* the Court made similar statements regarding the irrelevance of government price controls to the exhaustion of trade mark rights.[73]

For the reasons given above, there cannot be any serious objection to such a ruling in relation to trade mark rights. The application of the exhaustion principle to patent rights after a first sale at controlled prices merited a more penetrating analysis and a more convincing statement of reasons. The Court was right to identify divergent national legislation on

[72] At paras 23 and 24 of the judgment.
[73] At paras 16 and 17 and point 2 of the operative part of the judgment.

prices as the root of the problem. Indeed, such divergencies distort competition in the common market and interfere with the free movement of goods to such an extent that one may regret the Court's long-standing reluctance to classify government price controls as measures equivalent in effect to import restrictions under Article 28 of the Treaty.[74]

The Court was also right to chide the Community's legislative authorities for failing to take any action to harmonize national measures on price controls. But the Court was surely wrong to assume that discrepancies which remain between national laws as a result of the Community authorities' failure to act cannot justify derogations from the principle of free movement. On the contrary, Article 30 and the Court's case law on mandatory requirements are to a large extent founded on the opposite assumption: namely, that exceptions to the principle of free movement must be permitted precisely because discrepancies between national laws have not been removed by means of harmonization. The most serious defect in the logic of the *Sterling Drug* judgment is that the Court blamed the Community institutions for failing to harmonize measures on price controls but held that the negative consequences of that failure must be borne by the individuals whose patents were exhausted by a first sale in a country where price controls limited the economic reward accruing to the patentee. No reason was given by the Court to explain why private individuals should suffer the consequences of an omission perpetrated by the public authorities.

5.3 *The* GEMA *case*

Seven years later the Court was invited to give preliminary rulings in two more cases in which intellectual property owners who opposed parallel imports argued that the exhaustion principle should not apply because some peculiarity in the law of the country in which the first sale took place prevented them from obtaining a proper reward. The cases were *Musik Vertrieb Membran v GEMA*[75] and *Merck v Stephar*.

In the first of those two cases (referred to hereafter as the *GEMA* case) a German copyright management society (GEMA) brought infringement actions against two importers and distributors (Musik-Vertrieb Membran and K-Tel International) who had imported into Germany consignments of gramophone records and musical cassettes which had been placed on the market in various other countries, including EC Member States, with the consent of the copyright owners. GEMA did not seek to prevent the importations altogether; it merely claimed from the importers a sum equal to the

---

[74] For a review of the case law on price controls see P. Oliver, op. cit. (n. 22), at paras 7.63–7.81. See also the literature cited in note 53 on p. 161 of that work.
[75] Joined Cases 55 and 57/80 [1981] ECR 147.

difference between the royalties paid to the copyright owners in the country of first sale and the higher royalties normally payable in Germany. In the case of some of the goods the first sale had taken place in the United Kingdom, where a statutory provision had the effect of limiting the amount that could be obtained by way of royalties. Section 8 of the Copyright Act 1956 provided for a statutory licence scheme: once a recording of a musical work had been made, with a view to sale, by—or with the licence of—the copyright owner, anyone was entitled to manufacture sound recordings of the work, on condition that he notified the copyright owner of his intention to make a recording of the work for the purpose of sale and paid him a royalty of 6.25 per cent of the retail selling price of the sound recordings. The practical result of that provision was that the royalty fixed in licensing contracts was invariably 6.25 per cent of the retail selling price, since no prospective licensee was willing to agree to pay a higher rate. Thus the statutory licence scheme (which has since been abolished)[76] had the effect of placing a ceiling on the remuneration of the copyright owner.

GEMA argued that it should be allowed to recover the difference between the 8 per cent royalty which copyright owners had been able to negotiate freely in Germany and the 6.25 per cent royalty which was in effect imposed by statute in the United Kingdom. GEMA contended moreover that account should be taken of the higher retail prices obtaining in Germany. Thus, even if the copyright owner had received 8 per cent of the retail price in the United Kingdom, he would still, according to GEMA, have been entitled to receive an additional amount representing the difference between 8 per cent of the German retail price and 8 per cent of the (lower) United Kingdom retail price. The latter part of GEMA's argument was clearly misconceived. As Advocate General Warner pointed out,[77] differences in price levels between different parts of the common market are not a ground for seeking to isolate those parts from each other (at least, one might add, where such differences are due to purely commercial factors rather than to legislative and regulatory interventions).

The Advocate General was, however, more sympathetic to GEMA's basic argument that the copyright owner was prevented from obtaining his proper reward by the *de facto* statutory ceiling imposed in the United Kingdom and should therefore be able to claim an additional amount on imports into Germany in order to counteract the limiting effect of the British legislation. The Advocate General did not think that GEMA should be allowed to claim the difference between 6.25 per cent of the United Kingdom retail price and 8 per cent of the German retail price, since that would amount to taking into account the difference in prices in the two countries as well as the limitation imposed by the statutory licensing scheme. Instead

[76] Copyright, Designs and Patents Act 1988.   [77] At 177.

the Advocate General proposed that GEMA should be entitled to the difference between the royalty actually paid in the United Kingdom and the royalty that could have been negotiated in the United Kingdom in the absence of the statutory licensing scheme and on the footing that records in respect of which that royalty had been paid could be freely marketed anywhere in the Community.[78]

The Court of Justice, however, did not need to agonize about the correct method of calculating the additional revenue due to the copyright owners. As far as the Court was concerned, the matter was clear. GEMA was not entitled to collect any additional royalty on the importation into Germany of records which had been marketed in the United Kingdom with the consent of the copyright owner. To hold otherwise would be to allow a private undertaking to impose a charge on the importation of goods which were in free circulation in the common market 'on account of their crossing a national frontier'.[79] The language used seems to imply that the Court regarded the levying of an additional royalty as a charge equivalent in effect to a customs duty within the meaning of Article 23 of the Treaty.[80] As Advocate General Warner pointed out,[81] such a classification would have meant that the levying of an additional royalty was absolutely prohibited, regardless of whether it was justified for the protection of intellectual property, since Article 30 could not be invoked in relation to a customs duty or charge having equivalent effect.

The Court was not sympathetic to the argument that the statutory licensing scheme in the United Kingdom prevented copyright owners from obtaining a fair reward for the exploitation of their works. It observed that GEMA was 'in fact seeking to neutralize the price differences arising from the conditions existing in the United Kingdom and thereby eliminate the economic advantage accruing to the importers of the sound recordings from the establishment of the Common Market'.[82] Citing *Centrafarm v Sterling Drug*, the Court stated that: 'the existence of a disparity between national laws which is capable of distorting competition between Member States cannot justify a Member State's giving legal protection to practices of a private body which are incompatible with the rules concerning free movement of goods'.[83]

The Court did not, however, repeat the tendentious remark made in the *Sterling Drug* case, to the effect that it was for the Community authorities to eliminate such disparities by means of harmonization. This time the Court gave less unsatisfactory reasons for refusing to allow an intellectual

---

[78] At 179.   [79] At para. 18 of the judgment.

[80] See the definition of a charge equivalent in effect to a customs duty given by the Court in Joined Cases 2 and 3/69 *Sociaal Fonds voor de Diamantarbeiders v Brachfeld* [1969] ECR 211 at paras 15–18.

[81] At 173. [82] At para. 23 of the judgment. [83] At para. 24 of the judgment.

property owner to invoke competition-distorting factors in the country of first sale as a ground for opposing parallel imports. It observed that:

> . . . in a common market distinguished by free movement of goods and freedom to provide services an author, acting directly or through his publisher, is free to choose the place, in any of the Member States, in which to put his work into circulation. He may make that choice according to his best interests, which involve not only the level of remuneration provided in the Member State in question but other factors such as, for example, the opportunities for distributing his work and the marketing facilities which are further enhanced by virtue of the free movement of goods within the Community. In those circumstances, a copyright management society may not be permitted to claim, on the importation of sound recordings into another Member State, payment of additional fees based on the difference in the rates of remuneration existing in the various Member States.[84]

The Court thus established that consent to the first sale is the key to the problem. The intellectual property owner is free to decide where to release goods on to the common market. Once he makes his choice, he must accept that those goods can be resold in any other part of the common market. The argument that some feature of the legal environment in which the first sale took place prevented him from obtaining a just reward will fall on deaf ears. In so far as that appears to result in unfairness, the Court's attitude is that the intellectual property owner must take the rough with the smooth. The principle of free movement confers on him the inestimable benefit of access to the whole of the common market, but entails the drawback that he cannot act as though the common market consisted of a series of partitionable national markets.

5.4 Merck v Stephar

Six months after the *GEMA* case the Court gave judgment in *Merck v Stephar*,[85] which demonstrates even more clearly the Court's extreme reluctance to allow any inroads into the principle that an intellectual property right cannot be relied on to oppose parallel imports of goods which have been placed on the market in a Member State by or with the consent of the right-holder, regardless of whether he has had an opportunity to obtain a just reward in the country of the first sale.

Merck was the proprietor of two Netherlands patents protecting a pharmaceutical product and the process by which it was manufactured. Merck was unable to obtain patent protection in Italy because the Italian Law on Patents prohibited the grant of patents for pharmaceutical products and their manufacturing processes.[86] Notwithstanding the absence of

---

[84] At para. 25 of the judgment.   [85] Case 187/80 [1981] ECR 2063.

[86] By the time the case reached the Court of Justice, that law had been declared unconstitutional as regards process patents by the Italian Constitutional Court. That did not help Merck because the process was no longer patentable for lack of novelty.

patent protection, Merck marketed the product in Italy, though at a much lower price than in the Netherlands. Stephar imported the product into the Netherlands and marketed it there in competition with Merck. It was not disputed that the goods in question had been placed on the market in Italy by Merck. Merck applied to the President of the *Arrondissementsrechtbank* (district court), Rotterdam, for an injunction restraining Stephar and its managing director from infringing Merck's patents. The Dutch judge referred the case to the Court of Justice for a preliminary ruling on the question whether the Treaty rules on free movement prevented the proprietor of the patents from opposing parallel imports in such a situation.

Merck undoubtedly had a strong case. In fact, it would be difficult to imagine a stronger case on which to base a challenge to the unlimited application of the principle of exhaustion by a first sale in the Community with the consent of the right-holder. Merck's argument, in which it was supported by France and the United Kingdom, was founded on the purpose (or specific subject-matter) of a patent, which had been defined in *Centrafarm v Sterling Drug* as the guarantee that the patentee, in order to reward the creative effort of the inventor, had the exclusive right to use an invention with a view to manufacturing industrial products and putting them into circulation for the first time. In *Centrafarm v Sterling Drug* there was room for argument about whether the specific subject-matter of a patent, thus defined, could be achieved when government measures restricted the prices at which the patented products could be sold. It is, however, difficult to see how the specific subject-matter of a patent, thus defined, can be achieved when the products in question have been sold in a country in which no patent could be obtained. Merck had no exclusive right in Italy and was doubtless compelled to sell at a lower price than that which it could have obtained if it had been able to sell in monopoly conditions. It presumably made a profit on sales in Italy but it cannot have made a higher profit than a competitor with an equally efficient manufacturing operation. The whole philosophy underlying the grant of a patent is that the patentee will obtain an additional profit, as a result of his monopoly, which constitutes a reward for the inventor's creative effort and an incentive for him to invest in research. Merck did not receive that additional profit in respect of sales in Italy.

That Merck should not receive any reward corresponding to the purpose of its patents in respect of sales in Italy is hardly surprising. It was an inevitable consequence of the non-patentability of its product and process in Italy. Merck could console itself with the knowledge that it had valid patents in other countries, including the Netherlands. It could sell in each of the markets concerned, making an ordinary commercial profit in Italy, where it had to face direct competition from other manufacturers, and a higher 'patentee's reward' profit in the Netherlands (and in any other country in which it held a patent). Merck would no doubt feel annoyance at having to face competition from competitors who were, from Merck's point of view, infringers taking a free ride on the coat-tails of Merck's research and development department. But that annoyance would be mitigated by the knowledge that the damage could be confined to Italy. Products manufactured by free-riding competitors could be excluded from the Netherlands on the basis of the Dutch patent. That was clear from paragraph 11 of the judgment in *Centrafarm v Sterling Drug*. And—Merck might have supposed[87]—products which Merck itself had placed on the market in Italy could be excluded from the Netherlands.

If such products could not be excluded from the Dutch market, the effect would be to undermine the value of the Dutch patent. Merck would be forced to sell at a relatively low price in Italy on account of the presence of direct competitors. Parallel importers would ship those goods to the Netherlands and undercut Merck's prices in the Netherlands. Merck would be forced to reduce its prices in the Netherlands in order to compete with parallel imports of its own products. It would thus forego the additional profit which it would normally obtain from selling in monopoly conditions and which constitutes the patentee's reward.

The calamitous effect of permitting parallel imports in such a situation becomes clearer if a specific example with figures is considered. Suppose that a pharmaceutical company (P) develops a new drug and patents it in the Netherlands but is unable to obtain patent protection in Italy. In Italy there is market for 1,000,000 units of the product at a price of €12. P, whose manufacturing costs are €6 per unit, sells to wholesalers at €8 per unit and captures 20 per cent of that market, thus making a profit of €400,000. The other 80 per cent of the market is taken by P's competitors, who are also entitled to manufacture the product in the absence of patent protection. In the Netherlands there is a market for 300,000 units at a retail price of €20 per unit. As a result of patent protection, P has the whole of that market. It sells to wholesalers at €14 per unit and makes a profit of €8 per unit, i.e. a total profit of €2,400,000. Without patent protection it would have had to sell at a lower price and, even then, might not have been able to capture the whole of the market. Let us suppose that without patent protection in the Netherlands it would have been able to sell 100,000 units at a retail price of €13 per unit and a wholesale price of €9 per unit, making a profit of €300,000. The difference between that profit and the profit which we assumed to be obtainable with patent protection is €2,100,000. We may describe that additional profit as the patentee's reward.

What happens if parallel imports are allowed? The 200,000 units placed on the market by P in Italy will not all reach retail pharmacies in Italy.

---

[87] Advocate General Warner certainly made such an assumption in his opinion in the *GEMA* case (at 178). See also the article by M. Waelbroek which the Advocate General cites.

A large proportion (let us say 50 per cent) will find their way on to the Dutch market, where they will sell at, say, €18 per unit. The parallel importer, who may well be a Dutch wholesaler, will buy from an Italian wholesaler at €10 per unit and sell direct to Dutch pharmacies at €15 per unit. The parallel importer will in effect be helping himself to a large slice of the patentee's reward due to P. But worse consequences ensue. P will make up the shortfall on the Italian market caused by the export to the Netherlands of half the goods which it intended for the Italian market. A similar percentage of the extra goods placed on the Italian market will again find their way to the Netherlands. The process will go on indefinitely until a stage is reached when the Dutch market is supplied largely with goods which P placed on the market in Italy, and on which it enjoyed no monopoly profit and hence no patentee's reward.

If P maintains its high prices on the Dutch market, virtually the whole of that market will be supplied by parallel imports of products that it has put on the market in Italy at a much lower price. To prevent that, P will perhaps lower its price on the Dutch market from €20 to €18 per unit, in which case the parallel importer may again undercut P's price. If P and the parallel importer go on responding to each other's price cuts, a point will, of course, be reached at which parallel imports are no longer worthwhile. The parallel importer will then withdraw from the market and P will in due course attempt to raise its prices on the Dutch market. Its freedom of action will, however, be circumscribed by the knowledge that the parallel importer, whose start-up costs are low, will be ready to return, as soon as it becomes profitable for him to do so.

The net result of all this is that P will end up having to reduce its prices on the Dutch market so drastically that its patentee's reward will virtually be wiped out. The only remaining options for P would be to withdraw from the Italian market altogether or to raise its prices on that market to a level that would make the parallel importer's activities uneconomic. In view of the presence of competitors on the Italian market, the second option may be little different from the first in reality. That is all very well, but why should P, which after all invented the patented product and process, abandon the whole of an important market to the free riders who take advantage of its research and development?

It is clear that if the 'exhaustion'[88] principle is applied to a first sale that takes place in a Member State where no patent exists, the value of a patent in another Member State will be severely undermined. In fact, it is difficult to avoid the conclusion that its substance, specific subject-matter (as defined

---

[88] The inverted commas are used because it is obviously inappropriate to speak of the exhaustion of a right that does not exist. Advocate General Warner said in his opinion in the *GEMA* case (at 178): 'There can be no exhaustion of rights where no rights exist.'

by the Court of Justice), and very existence will be destroyed. None of those considerations deterred the Court from ruling in *Merck v Stephar* that the proprietor of a patent in one Member State who markets products covered by the patent in another Member State where no patent protection exists cannot rely on his patent in the first Member State to prevent the importation and resale of the products in that Member State.

As in *GEMA*, the Court stressed the importance of the right-holder's freedom of choice in deciding where to market his product. If he decides to market the product in a country in which patent protection is not available, he must accept the consequences of his choice as regards the free movement of goods within the common market.[89] As has been demonstrated above, that reasoning is inadequate because the patentee's freedom of choice is illusory. If he markets the products in a country in which no patent protection exists, he will not be able to maintain significantly higher prices in other Member States in which he holds patents. His choice is between (a) allowing the value of patent protection to be whittled away by parallel imports in those Member States in which it exists, or (b) withdrawing from the market in those Member States in which patent protection is unavailable and leaving the market in those countries to the free-riders.

In addition to stressing the patent-holder's alleged freedom of choice, the Court made some rather puzzling remarks about the specific subject-matter of a patent:

... in accordance with the definition of the specific purpose of the patent, ... the substance of a patent right lies essentially in according the inventor an exclusive right of first placing the product on the market.

That right of first placing a product on the market enables the inventor, by allowing him a monopoly in exploiting his product, to obtain the reward for his creative effort without, however, guaranteeing that he will obtain such a reward in all circumstances.[90]

That is of course true, but it is nothing more than a statement of the obvious. No patent law theorist would ever suggest that the exclusive right granted to the patentee guarantees that he will obtain a reward for his creative effort in all circumstances. The vicissitudes of commerce make such a notion unthinkable. There are thousands of patented widgets that have failed to make a fortune for their inventors. What the patent should, however, guarantee is that its proprietor will have an *opportunity* to obtain a reward for his creative effort as a result of the exclusive right to sell the

---

[89] At para. 11 of the judgment.

[90] At paras 9 and 10 of the judgment. The use of the expression 'specific purpose' is just another example of the translator hedging his bets. In para. 4 we find the more usual (but not necessarily more correct) translation 'specific subject-matter'. In both passages the French text has *objet spécifique*.

patented product. As we have seen, he will be denied such an opportunity if, in the territory where he enjoys patent protection, he has to face competition from parallel imports of products which he has placed on the market in a country where he has no patent protection.

The Court seems to have been influenced by certain remarks of Advocate General Reischl, who, after stressing that a patent merely provides a possibility of a reward, drew attention to the absence of any causal relationship between patentability and price levels. The Advocate General pointed out that the market in pharmaceuticals is extensively influenced by interventions in the process of price formation by various public authorities.[91] The weakness in that argument is that it posits the infallibility of judicial precedent, for it assumes that *Centrafarm v Sterling Drug* was correctly decided and that the intellectual property owner should never be allowed to oppose parallel imports on the ground that statutory price controls prevented him from earning an adequate profit in the country where the first sale took place. That assumption is questionable. The arguments used above to show that exhaustion should not apply to goods sold by the patentee in a country where no patent protection exists also suggest that the patentee should be allowed to oppose parallel imports of goods which he has placed on the market in a country where statutory price controls severely restrict his profit margin. Such measures may deprive him of the normal patentee's reward in the country in which they are applied. If goods which he sells in that country can be exported to other countries where price formation is theoretically unrestricted, he will be forced to reduce his prices in those countries to a level at which parallel imports are no longer economically worthwhile. As a result he will lose his patentee's reward in those countries too.

From the above analysis we may extract a general principle, i.e. whenever significant differences exist in the level of protection granted for intellectual property rights in a number of countries, the application of the exhaustion principle as between those countries will make it impossible to obtain in any of those countries effective protection of a significantly higher level than that available in the country which grants the lowest level of protection (unless of course the owner of the right withdraws from the market in that country altogether). Whatever peculiar feature of national legislation keeps the level of protection relatively low in one country will, in effect, be exported to the other countries. In *Centrafarm v Sterling Drug* the effects of the United Kingdom price controls were exported to the Netherlands. In the *GEMA* case the effects of the United Kingdom statutory licensing scheme were exported to Germany. And in *Merck v Stephar* the non-patentability of pharmaceutical products in Italy meant, as a result of

---

[91] At 2091.

exhaustion, that pharmaceutical products might just as well not be patentable in the Netherlands.

There is clearly a strong case for limiting the application of the exhaustion principle when the first sale takes place in a Member State whose legislation grants a significantly lower level of protection for an intellectual property right than that which exists in the Member State into which parallel imports are effected.[92] The case becomes unanswerable when the first sale takes place in a Member States which grants no protection at all. To speak of an intellectual property right being 'exhausted' by a first sale in a country where no such right exists is little short of perverse.

5.5 Merck v Primecrown[93]

5.5.1 *The background*

In 1995 the Court of Justice was invited to reconsider its judgment in *Merck v Stephar*. The Merck company was once again involved. Merck and another pharmaceuticals producer (the Beecham Group) held United Kingdom patents for various pharmaceutical products. They also marketed those products in Spain and Portugal, where patent protection was, until recently, not available for pharmaceutical products. Primecrown imported into the United Kingdom products which Merck had placed on the market in Spain and Portugal. A company called 'Europharm of Worthing' imported into the United Kingdom products which Beecham had placed on the market in Spain. Merck and Beecham brought infringement proceedings against Primecrown and Europharm of Worthing. The Patents Court of the Chancery Division of the English High Court referred three questions to the European Court of Justice, the last of which amounted in effect to an invitation to reconsider the judgment in *Merck v Stephar*. The Patents Court alluded to several factors which might negate the central assumption on which that judgment was founded, namely that the pharmaceuticals manufacturer was free to choose whether to market products in Spain (or, as the case might be, Portugal). The Patents Court pointed out that the manufacturer might have a legal or ethical obligation to market a pharmaceutical product in Spain and Portugal and that the national or EC legislation might require that once a pharmaceutical product was on the market in those countries the patent owner supplied sufficient quantities to satisfy the needs of domestic patients. The Patents Court also alluded to the existence of legislation in Spain and Portugal under which the authorities fixed mandatory selling prices for the products in question at

---

[92] This is well argued by P. Demaret in *Patents, Territorial Restrictions and EEC Law: A Legal and Economic Analysis*, IIC Studies, Weinheim, 1978, pp. 87–89.

[93] Cited in n. 26.

a level at which substantial exports to the country in which patent protection existed might be anticipated.

The background to the cases was complicated by certain provisions in the Act of Accession of Spain and Portugal (i.e. the Act governing the conditions under which those two countries acceded to the European Community). Protocols attached to the Act of Accession required Spain and Portugal to adjust their patent laws so as to make them compatible with the principle of the free movement of goods and with the level of protection attained in the Community.[94] To that end, Spain and Portugal undertook to accede to the European Patent Convention,[95] which would have the effect of making pharmaceutical products patentable in those countries. Article 47 (referring to Spain) and Article 209 (referring to Portugal) of the Act of Accession postponed the effect of the judgment in *Merck v Stephar* for a three-year period as regards products marketed in Spain and Portugal at a time when patent protection was not available. Article 47(1) states that, notwithstanding the provisions in the Act of Accession which required the abolition on 1 January 1986 of quantitative restrictions on exports and imports and measures having equivalent effect in trade between the existing Member States and Spain, 'the holder, or his beneficiary, of a patent for a chemical or pharmaceutical product or a product relating to plant health, filed in a Member State, at a time when a product patent could not be obtained in Spain for that product may rely upon the rights granted by that patent in order to prevent the import and marketing of that product in the present Member State or States where the product enjoys patent protection even if that product was put on the market in Spain for the first time by him or with his consent'. According to Article 47(2), the rights conferred by Article 47(1) could be invoked 'until the end of the third year after Spain has made these products patentable'. Article 209 contains identical provisions regarding Portugal.

The first two questions referred to the European Court by the Patents Court were concerned with establishing when the three-year period mentioned in paragraph (2) of Articles 47 and 209 ended. Since those questions are now of purely historical interest, we need not devote further attention to them here. It is, however, worth noting:

(1) that the above-mentioned provisions in the Act of Accession demonstrate that the Member States were aware of the injustice that *Merck v Stephar* was capable of causing;

(2) that they rightly attacked the root of the problem by requiring Spain and Portugal to modernize their patent laws so as to make pharmaceutical products patentable; and

---

[94] Para. 1 of Protocols No. 8 and No. 19.   [95] Para. 3 of Protocols No. 8 and No. 19.

(3) that it is perhaps surprising that the transitional provisions contained in Articles 47 and 209 of the Act of Accession were not more generous to the patent-holders concerned. To postpone the *Merck v Stephar* injustice for three years hardly seems sufficient when set against the normal 20-year duration of a patent.

It should also be noted that the first two questions raised by the Patents Court (concerning the expiry of the three-year transitional period) would cease to be relevant if in replying to the third question the Court were to overrule *Merck v Stephar*.[96]

5.5.2 *The opinion of Advocate General Fennelly*

Advocate General Fennelly argued cogently that *Merck v Stephar* should be overruled. Referring to the flawed basis of the judgment, he stated that:

Merck v Stephar went too far in ensuring that industrial property rights are not used to compartmentalize national markets to the detriment of the common market and thus undermined what should have been recognized as the fundamental core of a patent, namely the right of a patentee to market each particular unit of its patented product for the first time in a Member State with the benefit of the absence of competition from unauthorized copies for the duration of the patent.[97]

According to the Advocate General, the effect of *Merck v Stephar* was 'to export not merely the product but also the commercial consequences of the legislative choice made by the exporting State to the importing State because the patentee has made a commercial choice to sell the product even in a less protected environment'.[98]

The result would, in Advocate General Fennelly's opinion, be that the patentee would be encouraged to partition the common market in a different way, i.e. through refusing to supply the product in Member States where the patent was not recognized. In other words, *Merck v Stephar* encouraged 'commercially irrational decisions to withhold products from the market in such States, even though sales of the product would hold out some prospect of profit'.[99]

The Advocate General criticized the Court's excessive reliance on the notion of free consent:

In my view the reliance on the notion of free consent to marketing in *Merck v Stephar* unacceptably glosses over the logical fallacy that a patentee can be said to have exhausted his rights by choosing to market units of the protected product in Member States where no patent protection exists. Accepting, as I do, the Court's definition of the specific subject-matter of a patent, I do not consider that commercially rational

---

[96] See para. 73 of Advocate General Fennelly's opinion.
[98] At para. 108 of the opinion.
[97] At para. 106 of the opinion.
[99] Ibid.

marketing of a protected product in a Member State where no protection exists is accompanied by the crucial element guaranteed by that specific subject-matter.[100]

The Advocate General pointed out that the judgment in *Merck v Stephar* was inconsistent with the Court's own definition of the specific subject-matter (or substance) of a patent, which lay essentially in enabling the inventor, by allowing him a monopoly in exploiting his product, to obtain the reward for his creative effort.[101] The judgment effectively imposed on patentees the discipline of the common market where it did not in fact exist.[102]

The Advocate General also considered that the judgment in *Merck v Stephar* was inconsistent with the Court's subsequent case law, in particular the judgment in *Warner Brothers and Metronome v Christiansen*.[103] In that case the Court had held that the sale in one Member State of a video-cassette with the consent of the exclusive right-holder did not exhaust his exclusive rental right in another Member State. Logically, therefore, the sale of a product in a Member State which granted no patent protection should not exhaust a patent right in another Member State which did grant patent protection. The Advocate General approved Joliet's explanation[104] as to why the rationale of *Warner Brothers and Metronome v Christiansen* should be preferred to that of *Merck v Stephar*:

'The exhaustion doctrine is based on the availability of parallel prerogatives in both the country of exportation and that of importation; a decision applying the doctrine in the absence of such parallelism would be tantamount to lowering the protection available in the country of importation to the level of the less protective legislation of the country of exportation, thus operating a choice of legislative policy which must be left to the Member States.'[105]

The Advocate General proposed, however, that if the Court were to overrule *Merck v Stephar* it should do so prospectively, in the sense that the ruling should apply only from the date of the judgment in *Merck v Primecrown*. The justification for limiting the temporal effect of the judgment was that the parallel importers had relied on the binding nature of *Merck v Stephar* and that it would be wrong to transform them into wrongdoers for past acts which were considered lawful when they were carried out.[106] The effect of such a limitation would be that *Merck v Stephar* would continue to apply to parallel trade between Spain and Portugal and the rest of the Community for the period between the expiry of the three-year transitional period introduced by the Act of Accession and the judgment in *Merck v Primecrown*.[107]

---

[100] At para. 110 of the opinion.
[101] Ibid.
[102] At para. 111 of the opinion.
[103] Case 158/86 [1988] ECR 2605.
[104] R. Joliet, ' Geistiges Eigentum und Freier Warenverkehr' (1989) GRUR Int. 177, 179.
[105] At para. 135 of the opinion.
[106] At para. 169 of the opinion.
[107] At para. 170 of the opinion.

The Advocate General also gave consideration to the question whether, should the Court decide not to overrule *Merck v Stephar*, the broad principle established thereby should be qualified in the sense that exhaustion would be excluded on account of certain special factors, namely the existence of a legal or ethical obligation for the patentee to market the product and the presence of government price controls in the country where the product was marketed. Although the Advocate General proposed a negative answer to that question, it is clear from his arguments that he accepted that consent would be vitiated (and that exhaustion would not therefore apply) if the patentee was under a genuine legal obligation to place the product on the market.[108] Even if the initial marketing took place voluntarily, consent would be vitiated if later batches of the product were marketed under compulsion.[109] The existence of an ethical obligation to market could not, however, be relevant to the operation of the exhaustion principle, according to the Advocate General, mainly because it would create legal uncertainty, which would be unacceptable for parallel importers and manufacturers alike.[110]

5.5.3 *The judgment of the Court*

In spite of Advocate General Fennelly's eloquent and convincing critique of *Merck v Stephar*, the Court declined to overrule its previous judgment. The Court accepted that the patentability of pharmaceutical products had now become the norm and took notice of the fact that the Community legislature had recognized the need to give enhanced protection to the holders of patents for pharmaceutical products.[111] But the Court denied that such developments meant that the reasoning underlying the rule in *Merck v Stephar* was superseded. The Court recalled the nature of that underlying reasoning, i.e. that if patentees could oppose parallel imports of goods which they had themselves placed on the market in a Member State they would be able to partition the common market.[112] Strictly speaking, the Court was right to observe that the underlying reasoning of *Merck v Stephar* had not been superseded. The pertinent question was whether that reasoning was valid in the first place. The Court was, however, in no mood for recanting:

The arguments put forward in the present cases have not shown that the Court was wrong in its assessment of the balance between the principle of free movement of goods in the Community and the principle of protection of patentees' rights, albeit that, as a result of striking that balance, the right to oppose importation of a

---

[108] At para. 150 of the opinion.   [109] At para. 152 of the opinion.

[110] At paras 157 and 158 of the opinion.

[111] At paras 34 and 35 of the judgment. Here the Court was referring to Council Reg. (EEC) No. 1768/92 of 18 June 1992 concerning the creation of a supplementary protection certificate for medicinal products (OJ 1992 L 182, p. 1).

[112] At para. 36 of the judgment.

product may be exhausted by its being marketed in a Member State where it is not patentable.[113]

That is a very dubious statement. The Court's terminology is, to say the least, a little wayward. It is inappropriate to speak of the right to oppose importation of a product being exhausted by its being marketed in another Member State. The relevant question is whether the patent has been exhausted, i.e. whether its substance (or specific subject-matter) has been achieved, in other words whether its proprietor has had a chance to earn a reward for his creativity and a contribution to his investment by being able to sell the patented product in monopoly conditions. Obviously the answer to that question could only be in the negative if no patent could be obtained in the country where the first sale took place. By its careless use of terminology the Court side-stepped the real issue and once again glossed over the logical fallacy, as Advocate General Fennelly put it, that a patent cannot be exhausted if no patent exists.

The Court also rejected the argument that its later judgments in *Pharmon v Hoechst* and *Warner Brothers and Metronome v Christiansen* were inconsistent with *Merck v Stephar*.[114] As regards the former, the Court was undoubtedly correct: no judgment underlines more clearly the importance of the right-holder's consent in the application of the exhaustion principle. The Court's attempts to distinguish between *Warner Brothers* and *Merck v Stephar* were less convincing. The Court simply pointed out that *Warner Brothers* concerned legislation which granted copyright-holders a specific right to control rentals as well as the initial sale. The essential point was, however, that where the importing State grants more extensive rights than the exporting State those rights will be undermined if the right-holder is unable to control further marketing in the importing State of goods which he has placed on the market in the exporting State.

Reading the judgment in *Merck v Primecrown*, it is difficult to avoid the conclusion that the Court was to a considerable extent persuaded by Advocate General Fennelly's critique of *Merck v Stephar* and was aware of the injustice perpetrated by that judgment. It was thus faced with a dilemma that plagues all supreme courts from time to time—whether to overrule a previous decision that appears unsound but is perhaps not so obviously wrong as to justify the damage that is invariably done to the principle of legal certainty and to the prestige of the judiciary when a precedent is cast aside.[115] The following passage from the judgment in *Merck v Primecrown* suggests that those considerations were uppermost in the judges' minds:

---

[113] At para. 37 of the judgment.   [114] At paras 41 and 42 of the judgment.
[115] Advocate General Fennelly made some interesting comments on the implications of overruling a previous decision in paras 138–147 of his opinion.

'It is important to remember . . . that the transitional measures provided for by Articles 47 and 209 of the Act of Accession were adopted in the light of the ruling in *Merck* [*v Stephar*]. Although the Member States considered it necessary to postpone the effects of that ruling for a long period, they provided that, upon expiry of the transitional arrangements, Articles [28] and [30] of the Treaty, as interpreted in *Merck* [*v Stephar*], should apply in full to trade between Spain and Portugal, on the one hand, and the existing Member States, on the other.

Furthermore, the situations addressed by the ruling in *Merck* [*v Stephar*] are set to disappear since pharmaceutical products are now patentable in all the Member States. If, upon accession of new States to the Community, such situations were to recur, the Member States could adopt the measures considered necessary, as was the case when the Kingdom of Spain and the Portuguese Republic acceded to the Community.[116]

The Court apparently felt that if the Member States, as masters of the Treaty, had thought that the ruling in *Merck v Stephar* was indefensible they would have abrogated it completely instead of merely postponing its effects for three years.[117] The Court was also noting, in the passage quoted above, that in so far as injustice was perpetrated by the ruling in *Merck v Stephar* the Act of Accession had solved the problem in the long term by ensuring that pharmaceutical products would be patentable in all Member States. Thus it could be argued that from a practical point of view there was no compelling need to overrule *Merck v Stephar* and that in the absence of such a need the considerations that generally militate in favour of adhering to precedent should prevail over the desire to achieve total justice in the specific case.

6. GEOGRAPHICAL SCOPE OF THE EXHAUSTION PRINCIPLE IN EC LAW

6.1 *The basic rule: Community-wide exhaustion*

Deutsche Grammophon established the principle of Community-wide exhaustion of intellectual property rights: whenever the proprietor of the right consents to the marketing of goods in any Member State, he is precluded from invoking the right to prevent importation of the goods into any other Member State.

Arguably, the proprietor of the right is also prevented from invoking it to prevent further dealing in the goods within the same Member State, in those

---

[116] Paras 38 and 39 of the judgment.

[117] Advocate General Fennelly rejected the argument that the Member States had implicitly accepted the ruling in *Merck v Stephar* by not abrogating it in the Act of Accession: see para. 114 of the opinion. The argument is, however, accepted by P. L. C. Torremans and I. A. Stamatoudi ('*Merck v Stephar* Survives the Test' (1997) 22 EL Rev. 248, 253). They defend the two *Merck* judgments but, like the Court, seem to give excessive importance to the notion of consent.

instances when national law does not impose a principle of national exhaustion. Thus, it could be argued that Article 28 of the Treaty was infringed by the French case law in the 1960s which allowed a trade mark owner to invoke his trade mark rights against unauthorised distributors who resold within France goods which the trade mark owner had placed on the market in France.

At first sight such a conclusion may be surprising, since trade between Member States does not appear to be affected by a restriction on trade within a Member State. It is submitted nonetheless that the principle of Community-wide exhaustion must include a principle of national exhaustion. There are several reasons for taking that view.

It would be illogical, and contrary to the whole principle of a single market, to abolish restrictions on trade between Member States and yet permit direct impediments to trade within a Member State. Moreover, the granting of such a *droit de suite* to trade mark owners would affect imported goods as well as domestic goods. In an integrated market, no rigid distinctions can be made between inter-State and intra-State trade. The unity of the single market is undermined by any form of partitioning based on intellectual property rights, regardless of whether the partitioning is confined within the frontiers of a single Member State.

Such a view is supported by the Court of Justice's case law on customs duties and charges having equivalent effect. In *Lancry v Direction Générale des Douanes*[118] the Court held that a charge levied on goods as a result of crossing a frontier within a single Member State (*in casu*, the frontier between metropolitan France and the French overseas departments) was contrary to Article 23 of the Treaty. The basis of the judgment was that the unity of the Community customs territory would be undermined by the establishment of a regional customs frontier, regardless of whether the charge was levied on domestic goods or on goods imported from other Member States, and that 'since the very principle of a customs union covers all trade in goods . . . it requires the free movement of goods generally, as opposed to inter-State trade alone'.[119] Oliver points out, rightly, that such reasoning also applies to Articles 28 and 29 of the Treaty.[120]

6.2 *Exhaustion under the EEA Agreement*

The geographical scope of the exhaustion principle was extended as a result of the entry into force, on 1 January 1994, of the Agreement on the European Economic Area (the EEA).[121] Articles 11, 12, and 13 of the EEA

---

[118] Joined Cases C-363/93 and C-407/93 to C-411/93 [1994] ECR I-3957.
[119] Paras 27–29 of the judgment.
[120] P. Oliver, op. cit. (n. 22), at p. 127. Oliver is, however, critical of the *Lancry* judgment.
[121] OJ 1994 L 1, p. 3.

Agreement reproduce the terms of Articles 28, 29, and 30 respectively of the EC Treaty, except that the term 'Contracting Parties' is used instead of 'Member States'. The significance of the virtual identity of the two sets of provisions is clear from Article 6 of the EEA Agreement, which states:

Without prejudice to future developments of case law, the provisions of this Agreement, is so far as they are identical in substance to corresponding rules of the Treaty establishing the European Economic Community and the Treaty establishing the European Coal and Steel Community and to acts adopted in application of these two Treaties, shall, in their implementation and application, be interpreted in conformity with the relevant rulings of the Court of Justice of the European Communities given prior to the date of signature of this Agreement.

Thus the intention of the Contracting Parties was that identical provisions in the EC Treaty and the EEA Agreement should be interpreted in the same way. The difficulty facing them was that the EC Treaty created a living system of law which was capable of evolving as a result of supervening judgments of the Court of Justice. Since the EFTA States participating in the EEA are not in any way 'represented' at the European Court of Justice, it would not have been politically acceptable to require them to be absolutely bound by judgments of the Court delivered after the signing of the EEA Agreement (on 1 May 1992). It is nonetheless eminently desirable that the interpretation of identical provisions should not diverge. As a result, an EFTA Court was created for the purpose of ensuring that the EEA Agreement is correctly applied in the EFTA countries belonging to the EEA. The EFTA Court is required to 'pay due account' to the principles laid down by the European Court of Justice after the signing of the EEA Agreement.[122]

As regards the exhaustion of rights, it is clear that Articles 11 and 13 of the EEA Agreement, interpreted in the light of Article 6 thereof, would in themselves be sufficient to establish that the exhaustion principle applies to goods sold with the consent of the right-holder anywhere in the EEA. In other words, the effect of Article 6 is to ensure that the Court's ruling in *Polydor v Harlequin Record Shops*[123] does not apply to the interpretation of the EEA Agreement. While falling short of a full customs union, the EEA is clearly meant to be something more than a conventional free trade area.

Lest there should be any doubt about the applicability of the exhaustion principle in the EEA, an express provision on the subject was included in Protocol No. 28 on intellectual property (which is one of many protocols and annexes to the EEA Agreement). Article 2 of Protocol No. 28 states:

---

[122] Art. 3(2) of the EFTA Surveillance Agreement.
[123] Case 270/80 [1982] ECR 329. See section 6.3.1 below.

Exhaustion of rights

1. To the extent that exhaustion is dealt with in Community measures or jurisprudence, the Contracting Parties shall provide for such exhaustion of intellectual property rights as laid down in Community law. Without prejudice to future developments of case law, this provision shall be interpreted in accordance with the meaning established in the relevant rulings of the Court of Justice of the European Communities given prior to the signature of the Agreement.

2. As regards patent rights, this provision shall take effect at the latest one year after the entry into force of the Agreement.

Protocol No. 28 applies to trade in all products and services unless otherwise specified.[124] While it is conceivable that the EFTA Court or the national courts in the EFTA countries might not wish to subscribe to some future development in the case law of the European Court of Justice on the exhaustion of rights, they are unlikely in practice to depart from the Court's interpretation of the law.[125]

The EEA Agreement also provided for the incorporation, and extension to the EFTA countries, of 1,700 legislative Acts adopted before 31 July 1991. These are set out in 22 annexes, with appropriate modifications. Legislation adopted after the cut-off date may be incorporated by decision of the EEA Joint Committee. Annex XVII sets out the intellectual property legislative Acts incorporated into EEA law. These include:

- Directive 87/54/EEC on the legal protection of topographies of semi-conductor products;[126]
- Council Directive 89/104/EEC[127] to approximate the laws of the Member States relating to trade marks;
- Council Directive 91/250/EEC on the legal protection of computer programs;
- Council Directive 92/100/EEC[128] on rental right and lending right and on certain rights related to copyright in the field of intellectual property;[129]
- Directive 96/9/EC of the European Parliament and the Council on the legal protection of databases;[130] and
- Directive 98/71/EC of the European Parliament and the Council on the legal protection of designs.[131]

---

[124] Art. 65(2) of the EEA Agreement.   [125] G. Tritton, op. cit. (n. 35), at p. 30.

[126] OJ 1987 L 24, p. 36.   [127] OJ 1989 L 40, p. 1.   [128] OJ 1991 L 122, p. 42.

[129] OJ 1992 L 346, p. 61. This was added to Annex XVII by Decision No. 7/94 of the EEA Joint Committee.

[130] OJ 1996 L 77, p. 20. This was added to Annex XVII by Decision No. 59/96 of the EEA Joint Committee.

[131] OJ 1998 L 289, p. 28. This was added to Annex XVII by Decision No. 21/2000 of the EEA Joint Committee.

Annex XVII amends the exhaustion provisions of those directives[132] so as to provide for a principle of EEA-wide exhaustion.

Although the Community trade mark has not been extended to the EFTA countries, there cannot be any doubt that, as a result of Article 2 of Protocol No 28 (and also of Articles 11 and 13 of the EEA Agreement), the proprietor of a Community trade mark exhausts his right throughout the EEA whenever he consents to the marketing of goods bearing the trade mark in any State belonging to the EEA.[133]

A final point to be noted is that there may be a significant difference in the scope of the exhaustion principle under EC law and EEA law respectively. Under EC law the principle applies not only to goods originating in a Member State but also to goods originating in third countries once they have been placed on the market in the territory of a Member State with the consent of the right-holder. That is clear from the general rule set out in Article 23(2) of the Treaty, that the common market applies to products originating in Member States and to products coming from third countries which are in free circulation in Member States.

The EEA Agreement, unlike the EC Treaty, does not create a customs union and the Contracting Parties are free to fix their own customs duties. The arrangements governing trade between the EC and the EFTA countries do, to that extent, resemble a classical free trade area, as is recognised by Article 8(2) of the EEA Agreement, which provides that, unless otherwise specified, the articles on the free movement of goods apply only to products originating in the territory of the Contracting Parties.

At first sight, that seems to imply that under EEA law exhaustion does not apply to goods originating in a third country. On that view, if a patented product made in Taiwan is placed on the market with the patent-holder's consent in Denmark, he may invoke his Norwegian patent to prevent the importation of the product into Norway, if that is allowed by Norwegian law. (He may not, of course, on any view, invoke a patent in another EC Member State to oppose the importation of the product, since trade within the Community continues to be governed by ordinary EC law.)

Such a position is defended by Abbey,[134] who points out that Article 2 of Protocol No. 28 to the EEA Agreement requires the Contracting Parties to provide for 'such exhaustion of intellectual property rights as laid down in Community Law' and that under Article 1(1) of the Protocol 'the term "intellectual property" shall include the protection of industrial and

---

[132] With the exception of Directive 96/9/EC. Art. 5(c) of which does not seem to have been adapted.

[133] A. M. Tobio Rivas, in *Comentarios a los reglamentos sobre la marca comunitaria*, Vol. I (eds. A. Casado Cerviño and M. L. Llobregat Hurtado), Alicante, 1996, commentary on Art. 13, p. 179.

[134] M. Abbey, 'Exhaustion of IP Rights under the EEA Agreement Does Not Apply to Third-country Goods' (1992) 6 ECLR 231.

commercial property as covered by Article 13 of the Agreement'. Article 8(2) expressly states that Article 13 applies only to products originating in the Contracting States.

Abbey's view has been challenged by Prändl,[135] who argues that the scope of Article 2 of Protocol No. 28 is not limited in the manner suggested by Abbey. Prändl points out that Protocol No. 28 is not referred to in Part II of the EEA Agreement (i.e. the part dealing with the free movement of goods) but in Part IV, entitled 'Competition and other rules'. Prändl also points out that the adjustments made by Annex XVII to specific legislative measures in relation to exhaustion do not limit the scope of the exhaustion principle to goods originating in Contracting States. He argues that 'for coherency reasons' intellectual property rights which are not subject to one of the directives listed in Annex XVII must be treated in the same way.

It is impossible to state with certainty which view is correct. Although the textual arguments favour Abbey, teleological considerations suggest that Prändl's may be the better view. The main reason for not extending free movement to third-country goods under EEA law is that the Contracting States are free to fix their own customs duties. That freedom could be subverted by routing goods through low-tariff countries if third-country goods benefited from free movement. The existence of different customs duties is not, however, a valid reason for excluding the application of the exhaustion principle to third-country goods.

6.3 Exhaustion under free trade agreements

6.3.1 The old Agreements with the EFTA countries

Before the signing of the EEA Agreement the EC was already linked to the EFTA countries by a series of bilateral free trade agreements.[136] The purpose of those agreements was to establish a free trade area within the sense of Article XXIV of GATT between the EFTA countries and the EC.[137] The free trade agreements contained provisions which were in substance identical to Articles 28 and 30 of the EC Treaty.

---

[135] F. Prändl, 'Exhaustion of IP Rights in the EEA Applies to Third-country Goods Placed on the EEA Market' (1993) 2 ECLR 43. A similar view is defended by Jeremy Brown, 'Parallel Importing in the United Kingdom and the EEC', in *International Intellectual Property Law and Policy*, Vol. I (ed. Hugh C. Hansen, Fordham University School of Law), Juris Publishing, Inc., Sweet and Maxwell, 1996, p. 344.

[136] Agreeements were concluded with the following countries: Austria (OJ 1972 L 300, p. 2); Finland (OJ 1973 L 328, p. 2); Iceland (OJ 1972 L 301, p. 2); Norway (OJ 1973 L 171, p. 2); Portugal (OJ 1972 L 301, p. 165); Sweden (OJ 1972 L 300, p. 97); and Switzerland (OJ 1972 L 300, p. 189).

[137] J.-F. Bellis, 'The Interpretation of the Free Trade Agreements between the EFTA Countries and the European Community' (1985) No. 23 *Swiss Review of International Competition Law* 21.

For example, Article 14(2) of the Agreement with Portugal stated: 'Quantitative restrictions on imports shall be abolished on 1 January 1973 and any measures having an effect equivalent to quantitative restrictions on imports shall be abolished not later than 1 January 1975.'

Article 23 of the Agreement stated: 'The Agreement shall not preclude prohibitions or restrictions on imports . . . justified on grounds of . . . the protection of industrial and commercial property . . . Such prohibitions or restrictions must not, however, constitute a means of arbitrary discrimination or a disguised restriction on trade between the Contracting Parties.'

It would be tempting to assume that those provisions should be interpreted in the same way as Articles 28 and 30 of the Treaty. The Court was invited to adopt such an approach in *Polydor v Harlequin Record Shops.*[138] A company called RSO owned the copyright in certain recordings of musical performances. In the United Kingdom it granted an exclusive licence to manufacture and distribute those recordings to Polydor. In Portugal it granted a similar licence to Phonogram and Polygram Discos. RSO, Polydor, Phonogram, and Polygram Discos all belonged to the same group of companies. Records placed on the market in Portugal (which was not yet an EC Member State) by the Portuguese licensee were purchased by Simons Records Limited and resold to Harlequin Record Shops, for the purpose of retail sale in the United Kingdom. Polydor and RSO sued Simons Records Limited and Harlequin Record Shops for copyright infringement. The Court of Appeal established that under English law the claimants were entitled to succeed even though the infringing goods had been manufactured and marketed by their licensees in a foreign country. The defendants argued that, if the copyright owners were allowed to oppose the importation and sale of goods which had been marketed with their consent in Portugal, that would amount to a measure equivalent in effect to a quantitative restriction on imports under Article 14(2) of the Free Trade Agreement between the EC and Portugal and that such a measure could not be justified on grounds of the protection of industrial and commercial property within the meaning of Article 23 of the Agreement.

The Court of Appeal sought a preliminary ruling on whether there was a measure having equivalent effect in such circumstances and, if so, whether the measure was justified. It also asked whether Article 14(2) of the Agreement with Portugal had direct effect.

On the issue of direct effect, the Court made no ruling in *Polydor v Harlequin Record Shops.* In a subsequent case, however, the Court held that provisions in the Agreement with Portugal may produce direct effect if they are unconditional and sufficiently precise.[139]

---

[138] Cited in n. 123.
[139] Case 104/82 *Hauptzollamt Mainz v Kupferberg* [1982] ECR 3641.

In view of the similarity between Articles 14(2) and 23 of the Agreement with Portugal and Articles 28 and 30 of the EC Treaty there was a strong argument for saying that the copyright owners had exhausted their exclusive rights by consenting to the marketing of the goods in Portugal. Several authors had suggested that provisions of a free trade agreement that were similar to provisions of the EC Treaty should be construed in the same way.[140]

The Court of Justice chose a different approach. It observed that the similarity in the terms of the Agreement and of the Treaty was not a sufficient reason for transposing to the provisions of the Agreement the case law on the exhaustion of rights.[141] The scope of that case law must be determined in the light of the Community's objectives as defined in Articles 2 and 3 of the Treaty. By establishing a common market and progressively approximating the economic policies of the Member States, the Treaty sought to unite the national markets into a single market having the characteristics of a domestic market.[142] The considerations which led the Court to infer the exhaustion principle from Articles 28 and 30 of the Treaty did not apply in the context of the relations between the Community and Portugal as defined by the Agreement. The Agreement did not seek to create a single market reproducing as closely as possible the conditions of a domestic market.[143] It followed that, in the context of the Agreement, restrictions on trade in goods might be considered to be justified in a situation in which their justification would not be possible in the Community.[144] The Court then stated, in what is perhaps the key passage, that:

In the present case such a distinction is all the more necessary inasmuch as the instruments which the Community has at its disposal in order to achieve the uniform application of Community law and the progressive abolition of legislative disparities within the common market have no equivalent in the context of the relations between the Community and Portugal.[145]

On that basis the Court held that the copyright owner was entitled to invoke his exclusive right against the importation and sale, in the Community, of goods which his licensee had placed on the market in Portugal. Such a measure was justified on grounds of protection of industrial and commercial property under Article 23 of the Agreement and did not constitute a means of arbitrary discrimination or a disguised restriction on trade between the Community and Portugal.[146]

---

[140] M. Waelbroeck, 'The Effect of the Rome Treaty on the Exercise of National Industrial Property Rights' (1976) 21 *Antitrust Bulletin* 99; W. Alexander, 'Droit communautaire et droit national des marques' (1976) 12 *Cahiers de Droit Européen* 431, 433; N. March Hunnings, 'Enforceability of the EC-EFTA Free Trade Agreements' (1977) 2 EL Rev. 163.
[141] At para. 15 of the judgment.   [142] At para. 16 of the judgment.
[143] At para. 18 of the judgment.   [144] At para. 19 of the judgment.
[145] At para. 20 of the judgment.   [146] At paras 21 and 22 of the judgment.

The conclusion reached by the Court has received the approval of some commentators.[147] The Court's reasoning is, however, far from convincing. While the Court gave adequate reasons for not automatically transposing the case law on the EC Treaty to the relationship defined by the Free Trade Agreement, it made no serious attempt to explain why a provision in the Free Trade Agreement which was practically identical to Article 30 of the Treaty should be interpreted in the diametrically opposite manner. The Court did not say what justification there was for allowing the copyright owner to oppose the importation of goods which had been placed on the market with its consent in Portugal.[148]

It is clear that the Court was deeply concerned with the issue of reciprocity.[149] When it commented on the absence of any instruments to achieve uniform application of the Free Trade Agreement in the Community and Portugal, the Court was implicitly acknowledging the possibility that the Portuguese courts might, following the example set by the Austrian Supreme Court[150] and the Swiss Federal Court[151] in judgments cited in Advocate General Rozès' opinion, refuse to read an exhaustion principle into the Free Trade Agreement.

At first sight, the possible absence of reciprocity seems to be a serious problem. A free trade agreement that brings about free movement in one direction only is obviously less than ideal. The Court's approach to free trade agreements has not, however, been entirely coherent. If the impossibility of ensuring uniform application of an international agreement (due to the absence of a single judicial organ empowered to issue binding interpretations applicable in all the countries concerned) is a major concern, the logical response would be to exclude *a priori* all possibility of giving direct

---

[147] See J.-F. Bellis, 'After Polydor—the Territoriality of the Community Doctrine of Exhaustion of Industrial Property Rights' (1982) 16 *Swiss Review of International Competition Law* 17; by the same author, 'The Interpretation of the Free Trade Agreements between the EFTA Countries and the European Community' (1985) 23 *Swiss Review of International Competition Law* 21; G. Bonet (1982) *Revue Trimestrielle de Droit Europeén* 300. A more critical view is expressed by N. Ruiz, 'Os acordos de comércio livre e a ordem jurídica comunitária: o caso 'Polydor' e o acordo Portugal-CEE 1972' (1982) *Assuntos Europeus* 267. See also the cogent criticism of S. Soltysinski, 'International Exhaustion of Intellectual Property Rights under the TRIPS, the EC Law and the Europe Agreements' (1996) GRUR Int. 316.

[148] Soltysinski (cited in n. 147) expresses this criticism eloquently: 'The ECJ failed to answer the basic question, namely, why acts of exercising intellectual property rights in the Community trade characterized by the same Court as measures entailing the insulation of national markets and of leading to an artificial partitioning of the market turn into full legitimate practices when applied to trade relations between the Community market and Portugal.'

[149] 'It seems fair to say that the Court's judgment was inspired to some extent by the increasingly controversial notion of reciprocity.' M. Bronckers (1982) 76 *American Journal of International Law* 857, 861.

[150] Judgment of 10 July 1979, *Austro-Mechana v Gramola Winter & Co.* (1980) Rev. Int. Dr. Aut. No. 104.

[151] Judgment of 25 January 1979, *Sunlight AG v Bosshard Partners Intertrading* (1980) 3 CMLR 664 (the 'Omo' case).

effect to the agreement. Divergent interpretations of an agreement only acquire practical relevance if the courts of some Contracting Parties allow individuals to invoke the agreement. However, the Court accepted, in a subsequent decision,[152] that certain provisions of free trade agreements might have direct effect. In *Pabst & Richarz* the Court held that an article in an Association Agreement with Greece which prohibited discriminatory taxation (i.e. the equivalent to Art. 90 of the Treaty) had direct effect, without appearing concerned as to whether the Greek courts would allow the provision to be invoked in Greece. As one commentator observed, the Court may have been carried away by 'accession euphoria' on that occasion.[153]

It should not be assumed, without further analysis, that non-reciprocity is necessarily harmful to the Community's interests.[154] Two types of interest are at stake: one public, the other private. As to the public interest, it may at first sight seem that one-way exhaustion will adversely affect the Member States' balance of payments: after all, goods produced in a third country (Portugal before 1986) would be free to enter a Member State (the United Kingdom), whereas if the situation were reversed goods produced in the United Kingdom might not be free to enter Portugal.

On closer inspection, the apparent damage to the Community economy is not so evident. Parallel imports only take place when identical (or nearly identical) goods are offered in two markets at significantly different prices. That may happen, for example, if production costs in Portugal are lower than in the United Kingdom (assuming that the cost advantage is passed on to the consumer) or if the competitive structure of the two markets allows a higher price to be charged in the United Kingdom than in Portugal. If both of those conditions are fulfilled, the copyright owner is likely to have his records manufactured in Portugal and supply both the Portuguese and United Kingdom markets from Portugal, charging a higher price in the United Kingdom. The price difference will attract the interest of parallel importers. If the copyright owner is allowed to block parallel imports into the United Kingdom, that will not reduce the total volume of imports from Portugal to the United Kingdom because the copyright owner will himself continue to supply the United Kingdom market with goods which he has produced in Portugal. The only difference is that the copyright owner will extract higher profits from the United Kingdom market and consumers in the United Kingdom will not benefit from the price reduction that the parallel importer would normally bring about.

---

[152] *Kupferberg* (see n. 139) and Case 17/81 *Pabst & Richarz v Hauptzollamt Oldenburg* [1982] ECR 1331.

[153] Bronckers, op. cit. (n. 149), at 862.

[154] On the evils of 'reciprocalism' in general, see W. R. Cornish, 'The Cancer of Reciprocity' [1988] 4 EIPR 99.

Exactly the same considerations apply if the situation is reversed and we assume that production costs and retail prices are higher in Portugal than in the United Kingdom. The copyright owner will supply the Portuguese and United Kingdom markets with goods made in the United Kingdom. Once again the underlying pattern of trade between the two countries will remain the same, regardless of whether the copyright owner can block parallel imports from the United Kingdom to Portugal. If he can block parallel imports, he will supply all the requirements of the Portuguese market directly. If he cannot block parallel imports, he will still supply all the copies of his own copyright goods that the Portuguese market can absorb but a percentage of the trade will be routed through a parallel importer. It is an illusion to imagine that a one-way principle of exhaustion would have a major impact on the balance of payments, to the detriment of the country which admits parallel imports.

The question that remains is whether, after balancing the private interests that are at stake (i.e. the interest of copyright owners in stopping parallel imports and the interest of parallel importers in ensuring that such imports are not stopped), it can be said that a refusal to admit exhaustion in the absence of reciprocity is justified. Exhaustion is never in the interests of intellectual property owners: the narrower its scope, the greater are the opportunities for them to divide up the markets. Conversely, parallel importers are favoured by any widening of the exhaustion principle, because it limits the extent to which intellectual property owners may prevent parallel imports. Before the Community institutions decide that exhaustion should be accepted only if reciprocity is guaranteed, they should not idly assume that the persons who are adversely affected by one-way exhaustion are mainly Community nationals or businesses established in the Community and that the beneficiaries of one-way exhaustion are mainly persons or businesses from outside the Community. Such assumptions are far from the truth. The intellectual property owners who are adversely affected by one-way exhaustion and the parallel importers who benefit from it may be Community nationals or nationals of third countries. The consumers who benefit will, of course, be consumers in the Member States.

Thus, if we look at the problem from a purely protectionist point of view and ask ourselves whether the unilateral acceptance of exhaustion with no guarantee of reciprocity is likely to damage Community interests, it is far from obvious that the Court took the correct approach in *Polydor v Harlequin Record Shops*. Neither the macro-economic interests of the Member States, in the form of concern about the balance of payments, nor the micro-economic interests of individual traders command such an approach. The interests of consumers in the Community certainly do not.

It is submitted, therefore, that the correct starting-point would have been to ask whether a measure which allows imports to be blocked at the request of a copyright owner is 'justified' when the goods in question have been placed on the market by the copyright owner in a third country linked to the Community by a free trade agreement and when the copyright owner enjoys a parallel exclusive right in that third country. It is difficult to see how the justification for such a measure can be any greater in the case of trade between such a third country and a Member State than it is in the case of trade between two Member States. It is also difficult to understand what the Court had in mind when it stated in paragraph 21 of the judgment in *Polydor v Harlequin Record Shops* that:

> The findings of the national court do not disclose any factor which would permit the conclusion that the enforcement of copyright in a case such as the present constitutes a means of arbitrary discrimination or a disguised restriction on trade within the meaning of the second sentence of [Article 23 of the Free Trade Agreement with Portugal].

It is settled beyond doubt that arbitrary discrimination and a disguised restriction on trade occur when an intellectual property owner is allowed to use parallel rights in various Member States to block imports of his own goods in circumstances in which the substance of the right is not jeopardised.[155] No additional factor is required. The simple desire to partition markets and extract additional monopoly profits from each market is enough, by any standard, to establish the existence of arbitrary discrimination and a disguised restriction on trade. It is not easy to see why an additional factor should be required, or indeed what sort of additional factor might be relevant, when an attempt is made to block parallel imports from a country that is linked to the Community by a free trade agreement.

The judgment in *Polydor v Harlequin Record Shops* is an example of the judicial self-restraint that is often practised by the Court of Justice. There are many such examples, though they are frequently overlooked by the polemicists who spread the myth about the agenda-pursuing, activist Court.[156] In *Polydor*, no fewer than five Member States (out of a total of ten) submitted written observations. All argued, along with the Commission, that the Free Trade Agreement with Portugal should not be construed as entailing an exhaustion principle. In such circumstances it would not have been easy for

---

[155] See, e.g., *Deutsche Grammophon* at para. 12; Case 102/77 *Hoffmann-La Roche v Centrafarm* [1978] ECR 1139 at para. 14; and Case 3/78 *Centrafarm v American Home Products Corporation* [1978] ECR 1823 at para. 22.

[156] See, e.g., Sir Patrick Neill, 'The European Court of Justice: A Case Study in Judicial Activism,' published by European Policy Forum, August 1995, and T. C. Hartley, 'The European Court, Judicial Objectivity and the Constitution of the European Union' (1996) 112 LQR 95. See also the reply to Hartley's article by A. Arnull, 'The European Court and Judicial Objectivity: A Reply to Professor Hartley' (1996) 112 LQR 411, and D. T. Keeling, 'In Praise of Judicial Activism. But What Does It Mean? And Has the European Court of Justice Ever Practised It?' in *Scritti in onore di G. Federico Mancini*, Giuffrè, 1998, Vol. II, pp. 505–36.

the Court to hold otherwise. Moreover, the knowledge that the courts in Austria and Switzerland had already refused to read an exhaustion principle into parallel free trade agreements cannot have helped. Things might have turned out very differently, as Ruiz has remarked,[157] if the Court of Justice had been first to rule on the issue. The Court's concern about a possible lack of reciprocity is understandable, even though on the view taken above it is misconceived, but the result is a minimalist approach on all sides, since the judicial authorities in all the countries concerned are reluctant to advance at a pace which they imagine may not be matched by their colleagues in the other countries. As Bellis remarks, the 'institutional set-up of the Free Trade Agreements contains a built-in bias in favour of cautious judicial interpretations'.[158]

6.3.2 *Free trade agreements with countries in Eastern Europe*

The free trade agreements between the EC and the EFTA countries (with the exception of Switzerland) have become obsolete because the EFTA countries have acceded either to the EC or to the EEA. It might be thought, therefore, that the judgment in *Polydor v Harlequin Record Shops* is now of limited interest. Its relevance has, however, been enhanced as a result of the conclusion of a series of free trade agreements with countries in Central and Eastern Europe which formerly belonged to the Soviet bloc.[159] These Agreements resemble the old agreements with the EFTA countries but pursue, in some important respects, an even closer degree of integration.[160]

The history of these agreements is described in detail by von Lewinski,[161] who distinguishes three phases:

(1) A first generation of Trade and Cooperation Agreements with Hungary,[162] Poland,[163] the USSR,[164] Czechoslovakia,[165] Bulgaria,[166] and Romania[167] came into being between 1988 and 1990. The last four of

---

[157] Ruiz, op. cit. (n. 147), at 303.

[158] J.-F. Bellis, 'The Interpretation of . . . ', cited in n. 147, at 30.

[159] For further information on the agreements, see, in addition to Soltysinski's article (cited in n. 147), D. Horowitz, 'The Impending "Second Generation" Agreements between the European Community and Eastern Europe—Some Practical Considerations' (1991) 25 *Journal of World Trade Law* 56; I. Govaere, 'The Impact of Intellectual Property Protection on Technology Transfer between the EC and Central and Eastern European Countries' (1991) *Journal of World Trade* 58; S. von Lewinski, 'Europäische Integration jenseits der Union—geistiges Eigentum im Netzwerk intereuropäischer Beziehungen', in *Aktuelle Herausforderungen des geistigen Eigentums, Festgabe von Freunden und Mitarbeitern für Friedrich-Karl Beier zum 70. Geburtstag* (ed. J. Straus), Carl Heymanns Verlag KG, p. 607; and M. Franzone, 'Les relations entre la Communauté et les pays d'Europe centrale et orientale: vers une voie européenne des droits de propriété intellectuelle?' (1993) Dir. Aut. 245.

[160] See Soltysinski, op. cit. (n. 147), at pp. 323 *et seq.* [161] Op. cit. (n. 159).

[162] OJ 1988 L 327, p. 1. [163] OJ 1989 L 339, p. 1.

[164] OJ 1990 L 68, p. 3. [165] OJ 1990 L 291, p. 28.

[166] OJ 1990 L 291, p. 9. [167] OJ 1991 L 79, p. 13.

these contained provisions requiring the Contracting Parties to ensure an adequate level of protection of intellectual property and adequate enforcement of intellectual property rights.

(2) A second generation of Trade and Cooperation Agreements was concluded in 1992: the countries concerned were Estonia,[168] Latvia,[169] Lithuania,[170] Albania,[171] and Slovenia.[172] These agreements went slightly farther inasmuch as they required the countries concerned to ensure a level of protection of intellectual property rights comparable with that obtaining in the European Community and to accede to (unspecified) international conventions on the protection of intellectual property.

(3) Most of the above agreements have been replaced by Association Agreements based on Article 310 of the EC Treaty. These are known as 'Europe Agreements'[173] and are supposed to constitute the last step on the road to accession to the EC. In addition to the free movement of goods, they deal with the free movement of workers, services and capital, the right of establishment, competition rules, approximation of legislation and economic, financial, and cultural co-operation.

In the field of intellectual property, the Europe Agreements require the Contracting States, within a period of five years, to ensure an effective and appropriate level of protection comparable to that existing in the Community, to provide for comparable means of enforcement and to accede to specified international conventions.

In 1995 the Commission published a White Paper on the preparation of the countries of Central and Eastern Europe for integration in the internal market.[174] The White Paper proposed that the associated countries should adapt their legislation in accordance with the principal harmonisation directives in the field of intellectual property.

As regards the free movement of goods in general, the new Europe Agreements, like the old agreements with the EFTA countries, contain provisions copied almost verbatim from Articles 28 and 30 of the Treaty. Soltysinski, who is critical of *Polydor v Harlequin Record Shops*, argues that that judgment should not be transposed to the context of the Europe

---

[168] OJ 1992 L 403, p. 2.   [169] OJ 1992 L 403, p. 11.   [170] OJ 1992 L 403, p. 19.
[171] OJ 1992 L 343, p. 2.   [172] OJ 1993 L 189, p. 1.
[173] Agreement with Poland (OJ 1993 L 348, p. 2); Agreement with Hungary (OJ 1993 L 347, p. 2); Agreement with Romania (OJ 1994 L 357, p. 2); Agreement with Bulgaria (OJ 1994 L 358, p. 3); Agreement with Slovakia (OJ 1994 L 359, p. 2); Agreement with the Czech Republic (OJ 1994 L 360, p. 2); Agreement with Latvia (OJ 1998 L 26, p. 3); Agreement with Lithuania (OJ 1998 L 51, p. 3); Agreement with Estonia (OJ 1998 L 68, p. 3); Agreement with Slovenia (OJ 1999 L 51, p. 3). Soltysinski lumps together von Lewinski's first and second generations and classifies the 'Europe Agreements' as the second generation.
[174] COM(95)163 def. of 3 May 1995.

Agreements.[175] He maintains, on the contrary, that the Court's case law on Articles 28 and 30 should be applied.[176] He points out that the agreements with Central and Eastern European countries provide for a deeper and more comprehensive degree of integration than the earlier free trade agreements; in particular, the Central and Eastern European countries are obliged to approximate their laws with those of the Community, including their intellectual property legislation, which is to be harmonised within three to five years.[177] The author also observes that Poland has set an example by incorporating in its 1994 Law on Copyright and Neighbouring Rights an exhaustion principle extending to countries with which Poland is linked by free trade agreements.[178]

The latter development is encouraging in view of the Court's obvious concerns about reciprocity in *Polydor v Harlequin Record Shops*. In that case the negative precedents set by the Swiss and Austrian courts left the Court of Justice little scope for a bold initiative on extra-Community exhaustion. Only time will tell whether Poland's positive precedent will prove equally influential, but with the opposite result. The really significant development, however, is that the Europe Agreements provide for harmonisation of the substantive law governing intellectual property rights. As we have seen, the exhaustion principle cannot operate satisfactorily if the scope of protection of intellectual property rights varies substantially under the laws of the countries concerned. Freedom of movement drags the effective level of protection in each country down to the lowest common denominator. If intellectual property rights in the associated countries enjoy the same level of protection as in the Community, there should be no fundamental objection to allowing parallel imports into the Community of goods which have been placed on the market in an associated country with the consent of the right-holder. That, it is submitted, is a far more important consideration than reciprocity. On that basis the Europe Agreements can be distinguished from the Free Trade Agreement with Portugal and should be construed as laying down an exhaustion of rights principle.

---

[175] Op. cit. (n. 147), at 323 *et seq.*

[176] This would correspond to the position requested by the Polish delegation during the negotiations on the Europe Agreement with Poland: I. Wiszniewska, 'Approximation of the Polish Law on Trade Marks to European Standards' (1998) 28 IIC 152, 165.

[177] 'While the objectives of the Europe Agreements differ from the purposes of the EC Treaty one cannot dispute that they seek to achieve full economic integration and substantially the same level of elimination of trade barriers as that existing within the Community before the adoption of the Maastricht Treaty when the exhaustion concept was adopted as a necessary precondition of abolishing non-tariff barriers'. Sołtysiński, op. cit. (n. 147), at 324.

[178] At p. 325 (see n. 73 and the accompanying text). The author also points out that in 1995 Poland's Anti-monopoly Office required Sony to remove a ban on parallel imports of genuine trade-marked goods from its selective distribution agreements with Polish distributors.

6.4 *International exhaustion under EC law*

6.4.1 *The position under the Treaty*

Articles 28 and 30 establish, as we have seen, a principle of Community-wide exhaustion: sale anywhere in the Community with the consent of the right-holder exhausts the right throughout the Community. We have also noted that the EEA Agreement widened that principle into one of EEA-wide exhaustion. Articles 28 and 30 do not, of course, impose a principle of international (i.e. world-wide) exhaustion. If the owner of an intellectual property right in a Member State relies on that right in order to oppose the importation of goods which he has placed on the market in a third country, Articles 28 and 30 are not relevant. Trade between Member States is not affected by such a measure, so Article 28 does not come into play.[179]

The Treaty provisions on the free movement of goods do not, however, preclude a Member State from applying a principle of international exhaustion as part of its domestic law. What this means in practice is that, if a right-holder places goods on the market in a third country and a parallel importer, acting without the right-holder's consent, imports those goods into a Member State which recognises international exhaustion, the goods may be excluded from other Member States which do not apply such a principle. As Bellis points out, the essential condition to which the application of the Community-wide exhaustion principle is subject is that the product concerned must have been put on the market in a Member State by the owner of the right or with his consent.[180]

Surprisingly, Beier suggested that once goods have entered into free circulation in a Member State which applies international exhaustion, even without the consent of the right-holder, they may 'move freely and be sold in every other Member State of the EC'.[181] While one hesitates to disagree with such a distinguished author, Beier was surely wrong if by that he meant that the right-holder cannot keep the goods out of other Member States which do not recognize international exhaustion. Such a view would mean that, if a single Member State adopts the principle of international exhaustion, the principle will be indirectly imposed on the other Member

---

[179] See Case 51/75 *EMI Records v CBS United Kingdom* [1976] ECR 871 at para. 10 (and the corresponding passages in two related judgments delivered on the same day). *Polydor v Harlequin Record Shops* also establishes implicitly that the Treaty does not impose a principle of international exhaustion.

[180] J.-F. Bellis, 'After Polydor . . .', op. cit. (n. 147), at 27. The same point is made by Wiszniewska, op. cit. (n. 176), at 167. The decision of the English High Court cited by Bellis (*The Who Group Limited and Polydor Limited v Stage One (Records) Limited* [1980] CMLR 429) is clearly wrong, for the reasons given by Bellis.

[181] F.-K. Beier, op. cit. (n. 4), at 158. *Contra:* J. Rasmussen, 'The Principle of Exhaustion of Trade Mark Rights pursuant to Directive 89/104 (and Regulation 40/94)' [1995] 4 EIPR 174, 178.

States, since the parallel importer could always route goods through the first Member State. It cannot, of course, be denied that there is a barrier to trade between Member States when goods that are in free circulation in some of them (those that recognise international exhaustion) can be excluded from others (those that do not recognise international exhaustion). Such a barrier is not, however, caused by the action of the right-holder—who would doubtless prefer to preserve the unity of the common market by keeping parallel imports of his goods out of all the Member States—but solely by the discrepancies in the laws of the Member States with regard to international exhaustion. There is no reason to deny the right-holder the benefit of Article 30 in such circumstances.

6.4.2 *Intervention of the Community legislature*

6.4.2.1 *Relevant provisions*

It is now necessary to consider whether and to what extent the position described above has been affected by legislative developments. The following provisions are relevant:

- **Article 7(1) of Council Directive 89/104/EEC** ('the Trade Mark Directive')[182] of 21 December 1988 to approximate the laws of the Member States relating to trade marks: 'The trade mark shall not entitle the proprietor to prohibit its use in relation to goods which have been put on the market in the Community under that trade mark by the proprietor or with his consent.'
- **Article 13(1) of Council Regulation (EC) No. 40/94** ('the Community Trade Mark Regulation')[183] of 20 December 1993 on the Community trade mark: 'A Community trade mark shall not entitle the proprietor to prohibit its use in relation to goods which have been put on the market in the Community under that trade mark by the proprietor or with his consent.'
- **Article 15 of Directive 98/71/EC of the European Parliament and the Council** ('the Designs Directive')[184] of 13 October 1998 on the legal protection of designs: 'The rights conferred by a design right upon registration shall not extend to acts relating to a product in which a design included within the scope of protection of the design right is incorporated or to which it is applied, when the product has been put on the market in the Community by the holder of the design right or with his consent.'
- **Article 21 of Council Regulation (EC) No. 6/2002** ('the Community Design Regulation')[185] of 12 December 2001 on Community Designs:

---

[182] OJ 1989 L 40, p. 1.   [183] OJ 1994 L 11, p. 1.
[184] OJ 1998 L 289, p. 28.   [185] OJ 2002 L 3, p. 1.

'The rights conferred by a Community design shall not extend to acts relating to a product in which a design included within the scope of protection of the Community design is incorporated or to which it is applied, when the product has been put on the market in the Community by the holder of the Community design or with his consent.'

- **Article 9(1) and (2) of Council Directive 92/100/EEC** ('the Rental Right Directive')[186] of 9 November 1992 on rental right and lending right and on certain rights related to copyright in the field of intellectual property:

'1. Member States shall provide

—for performers, in respect of fixations of their performances,

—for phonogram producers, in respect of their phonograms,

—for producers of their first fixations of films, in respect of the original copies of their films,

—for broadcasting organisations, in respect of fixations of their broadcast as set out in Article 6(2)

the exclusive right to make available these objects, including copies thereof, to the public by sale or otherwise, hereafter referred to as the 'distribution right'.

2. The distribution right shall not be exhausted within the Community in respect of an object as referred to in paragraph 1, except where the first sale in the Community of that object is made by the right-holder or with his consent.'

- **Article 4 of Directive 2001/29/EC of the European Parliament and the Council** ('the Copyright Directive')[187] of 22 May 2001 on the harmonization of certain aspects of copyright and related rights in the information society:

'1. Member States shall provide for authors, in respect of the original of their works or of copies thereof, the exclusive right to authorise or prohibit any form of distribution to the public by sale or otherwise.

2. The distribution right shall not be exhausted within the Community in respect of the original or copies of the work, except where the first sale or other transfer of ownership in the Community of that object is made by the right-holder or with his consent.'

- **Article 4(c) of Council Directive 91/250/EEC** ('the Software Directive')[188] of 14 May 1991 on the legal protection of computer programs:

'The first sale in the Community of a copy of a program by the

---

[186] OJ 1992 L 346, p. 61. The 'credit' for this bizarre title belongs to the European Parliament, which suggested that a reference to 'intellectual property' should be added to the title proposed by the Commission: J. Reinbothe and S. von Lewinski, *The EC Directive on Rental Right and Lending Rights and on Privacy*, Sweet and Maxwell, London, 1993, p. 21.

[187] OJ 2001 L 167, p. 10.　　　　　　　　　　[188] OJ 1991 L 122, p. 42.

right-holder or with his consent shall exhaust the distribution right within the Community of that copy, with the exception of the right to control further rental of the program or a copy thereof.'

- **Article 5(c) of Directive 96/9/EC of the European Parliament and the Council** ('the Databases Directive')[189] of 11 March 1996 on the legal protection of databases: 'The first sale in the Community of a copy of the database by the right-holder or with his consent shall exhaust the right to control resale of that copy within the Community.'
- **Article 5(1) and (5) of Council Directive 87/54/EEC** of 16 December 1986 on the legal protection of topographies of semiconductor products:[190]

  '1. The exclusive rights [conferred on creators of topographies of semi-conductor products] shall include the rights to authorise or prohibit any of the following acts:

     (a) . . .

     (b) commercial exploitation or the importation for that purpose of a topography or of a semiconductor product manufactured by using the topography.

  . . .

  5. The exclusive rights to authorise or prohibit the acts specified in paragraph 1(b) shall not apply to any such act committed after the topography or the semiconductor product has been put on the market in a Member State by the person entitled to authorise its marketing or with his consent.'

- **Article 16 of Council Regulation (EC) No 2100/94** ('the Plant Varieties Regulation')[191] of 27 July 1994 on Community plant variety rights: 'The Community plant variety right shall not extend to acts concerning any material of the protected variety, or of a variety covered by the provisions of Article 13(5), which has been disposed of to others by the holder or with his consent, in any part of the Community, or any material derived from the said material, unless such acts:

  (a) involve further propagation of the variety in question, except where such propagation was intended when the material was disposed of; or

  (b) involve an export of variety constituents into a third country which does not protect varieties of the plant genus or species to which the variety belongs, except where the exported material is for final consumption purposes.'

- **Article 10 of the Proposal for a Council Regulation on the Community patent:**[192] 'The rights conferred by a Community patent

---

[189] OJ 1996 L 77, p. 20.   [190] OJ 1987 L 24, p. 36.
[191] OJ 1994 L 227, p. 1.   [192] OJ 2001 C 337 E, p. 278.

shall not extend to acts concerning the product covered by that patent which are carried out within the territories of the Member States after that product has been put on the market in the Community by the proprietor of the patent or with his consent, unless there are legitimate grounds for the proprietor to oppose further commercialisation of the product.'

What consequences flow from those provisions as regards the international exhaustion of intellectual property rights? It is appropriate to begin by examining the position in relation to trade marks, noting at the outset that trade marks are the one form of intellectual property for which international exhaustion has tended to be the norm rather than the exception under national law.

6.4.2.2 *Trade marks*

Silhouette v Hartlauer: *the demise of international exhaustion* The language used by Article 7(1) of the Trade Mark Directive and Article 13(1) of the Community Trade Mark Regulation is identical (except of course that the latter refers to a 'Community trade mark' and the former to a 'trade mark' *tout court*, by which is meant a national trade mark or a Benelux trade mark).

The Court of Justice was invited to interpret Article 7(1) of the Trade Mark Directive in *Silhouette v Hartlauer*.[193] The facts of the case were as follows. Silhouette, an Austrian company, sold a large consignment of sunglasses, bearing the trade mark 'Silhouette', to a Bulgarian trading company, with instructions to market them only in Bulgaria and countries of the former Soviet Union. The sunglasses were an outdated model which Silhouette considered to be no longer appropriate for the European market. Hartlauer managed to acquire the entire consignment and started to sell the sunglasses in shops in Austria. Silhouette commenced proceedings against Hartlauer for infringing the 'Silhouette' trade mark.

The infringement action would have failed under the old, pre-Directive Austrian trade mark law because the Austrian *Oberster Gerichtshof* (Supreme Court) had adopted the principle of international exhaustion in the *Agfa* case in 1970.[194] The *Silhouette* litigation ended up before that same court, which sought guidance from the Court of Justice on the interpretation of Article 7(1) of the Directive. Essentially, the *Oberster Gerichtshof* asked whether Article 7(1) precluded Member States from applying international exhaustion.

---

[193] Case C-355/96 [1998] ECR I-6.   [194] (1971) 2 IIC 220.

Theoretically the legislation left open three possibilities:

(1) All Member States were required to apply international exhaustion.[195]
(2) No Member State was allowed to apply international exhaustion.[196]
(3) Each Member State was free to apply international exhaustion if it so wished.[197]

The first option is certainly the most attractive from the point of view of the consumer. *De lege ferenda* the arguments in favour of it—moral, legal, and economic—are overwhelming. Morally, the whole idea of allowing a trade mark proprietor to bring infringement proceedings against an honest trader who sells genuine goods which the trade mark proprietor has himself placed on the market is distasteful, to say the least. Legally, the origin function of the trade mark is not jeopardized by the resale in the Community of genuine goods which the trade mark proprietor has marketed in a third country. Economically, it is absurd to pretend that European industry would be handicapped if Europe applied international exhaustion without a guarantee of 'reciprocity' from other countries. If international exhaustion really did impose an undue burden on domestic industry, it would never have been accepted in so many industrialized countries.[198]

---

[195] Before *Silhouette* this interpretation was defended by de las Heras, op. cit. (n. 1), at pp. 356 *et seq*. The author bases his view in part on an erroneous interpretation of Council Reg. (EEC) No. 3842/86 of 1 December 1986 laying down measures to prohibit the release for free circulation of counterfeit goods (OJ 1986 L 357, p. 1), which has since been replaced by Council Reg. (EC) No. 3295/94 of 22 December 1994 laying down measures to prohibit the release for free circulation, export, re-export, or entry for a suspensive procedure of counterfeit and pirated goods (OJ 1994 L 341, p. 8). Reg. No. 3842/86, like its successor, prohibited the release for free circulation of counterfeit goods and required the customs authorities of the Member States to confiscate such goods. Under Art. 1(2) of Reg. No. 3842/86 (cf. Art. 1(4) of Reg. No. 3295/94) the provisions of the Regulation do not apply to goods which bear a trade mark with the consent of its proprietor but which have been declared for release into free circulation without his consent. De las Heras Lorenzo argues that that provision introduces international exhaustion. In fact, it merely establishes the rather obvious rule that genuine goods which are imported without the consent of the trade mark owner are not to be treated as counterfeit goods. Thus the trade mark owner cannot, under the Regulation, ask the customs authorities of the Member States to assist him in excluding parallel imports. That does not mean that he cannot apply to the courts for an injunction preventing further dealing in the goods. That is clear from the 10th recital in the preamble to Reg. No. 3295/94, which states that 'Member States' provisions on the competence of the judicial authorities and procedures are not affected by this Regulation'.

[196] This interpretation was defended by Rasmussen, op. cit. (n. 181) and by other commentators cited in note 11 of Rasmussen's article.

[197] This interpretation was defended by: N. Shea, 'Does the First Trade Marks Directive allow International Exhaustion of Rights?' [1995] 10 EIPR 463; F.-K. Beier, op. cit. (n. 4), at 160; von Gamm, 'Zur Warenzeichenrechtsreform' (1993) *Wettbewerb in Recht and Praxis* 793, 795; U. Loewenheim, 'Nationale und internationale Erschöpfung von Schutzrechten im Wandel der Zeiten' (1996) GRUR Int. 307, 313; and by Wiszniewska, op. cit. (n. 176), at 164 *et seq*. The Swedish legislature retained international exhaustion and the Austrian implementing legislation left the question to be decided by the courts: see A. Kur, 'Harmonization of Trade Mark Laws in Europe: Results and Open Questions' (1996) *Rivista di Diritto Industriale* 227, 241.

[198] Even Japan, whose predilection for non-tariff barriers is well known, has opted for international exhaustion: see S. K. Verma, 'Exhaustion of Intellectual Property Rights and Free

Unfortunately the wording of Article 7(1) of the Directive did not support the first option. There is nothing in the text of that provision (or of Art. 13(1) of the Community Trade Mark Regulation) to justify the view that the Council intended to introduce a wider principle of exhaustion than the one expressly provided for. If the Council had such an intention, the draftsman chose exceedingly inappropriate language to express it.

In fact, we know from the legislative history of the Regulation and of the Directive that the Council deliberately refrained from adopting inter-national exhaustion, contrary to the original wishes of the Commission. The first version of the Regulation proposed by the Commission,[199] like the original proposal for the Directive,[200] provided that a trade mark would not entitle its proprietor to prohibit its use in relation to goods which had been 'put on the market' under the trade mark by the proprietor or with his consent. The expression 'put on the market', without any geographical limitation, was intended to introduce a principle of international exhaus-tion.[201] That proposal encountered vigorous opposition from 'almost all Member States, all interested circles, the Economic and Social Committee and the European Parliament'.[202] As a result, the Commission's amended proposals[203] added the words 'in the Community' after the words 'put on the market'. That is the wording used in the definitive versions of the Regulation and Directive.

Although the historical method of interpretation occupies a relatively minor role in the work of the Court of Justice,[204] this appears to be one case in which the Court could hardly disregard the legislative history of the texts that it has to interpret.[205] The *travaux préparatoires* cited above demonstrate that the legislative organs of the Community had no intention of introducing anything wider than a principle of Community-wide[206] exhaustion.

Trade—Article 6 of the TRIPS Agreement' (1998) 29 IIC 534, 540, and the articles by van der Merwe and Hays cited in n. 17.

[199] OJ 1980 C 351, p. 1. In the proposal for a regulation, exhaustion was dealt with in Art. 11.

[200] OJ 1980 C 351, p. 1. In the proposal for a directive, exhaustion was dealt with in Art. 6.

[201] H. Cohen Jehoram, 'International Exhaustion Versus Importation Rights: A Murky Area of Intellectual Property Law' (1996) GRUR Int. 280, 281.

[202] I. Schwartz, 'Community Trade Mark Legislation: Changes made in the Proposed Commu-nity Trade Mark Regulation and the Directive on Approximation of National Trade Mark Laws' (1985) 3 EIPR 70, 72. Only Germany opposed the abandonment of international exhaustion.

[203] OJ 1984 C 230, p. 1 (as regards the Regulation) and OJ 1985 C 351, p. 4 (as regards the Directive).

[204] For examples of cases in which the Court has referred to *travaux préparatoires* for the purpose of interpreting legislation, see Rasmussen, op. cit. (n. 181), at 177.

[205] In fact the historical argument was apparently ignored by the Court and mentioned only in passing by the Advocate General (at paras 32 and 59 of the opinion). It must nonetheless have exerted some influence, if only subliminally, on the process of judicial decision-making: see D. T. Keeling (1999) *Revue des Affaires Europénnes/Law & European Affairs* 238 at 241.

[206] EEA-wide exhaustion, since 1 January 1994.

The only way in which it might perhaps have been argued that the Community Trade Mark Regulation and Trade Mark Directive required international exhaustion, notwithstanding the above considerations, would have been to contend that the provisions which define the exclusive rights of the trade mark proprietor cannot in any case authorize infringement proceedings against a dealer in genuine goods. Those provisions are to be found in Article 9 of the Regulation and Article 5 of the Directive. The latter provides:

1. The registered trade mark shall confer on the proprietor exclusive rights therein. The proprietor shall be entitled to prevent all third parties not having his consent from using in the course of trade:
   (a) any sign which is identical with the trade mark in relation to goods or services which are identical with those for which the trade mark is registered;
   (b) any sign where, because of its identity with, or similarity to, the trade mark and the identity or similarity of the goods or services covered by the trade mark and the sign, there exists a likelihood of confusion on the part of the public, which includes the likelihood of association between the sign and the trade mark.

. . .
3. The following, inter alia, may be prohibited under paragraphs 1 and 2:
   (a) affixing the sign to the goods or to the packaging thereof;
   (b) offering the goods, or putting them on the market or stocking them for these purposes under that sign, or offering or supplying services thereunder;
   (c) importing or exporting the goods under the sign;
   (d) using the sign on business papers and in advertising.[207]

It could perhaps have been argued that the type of activity engaged in by *Hartlauer* lay entirely outside the compass of Article 5 of the Directive. That provision is concerned with the activities of trade mark infringers in the normal sense of the term, i.e. persons who place an infringing trade mark on goods that have no connection with the trade mark proprietor. It could have been argued that Article 5 simply did not apply to persons who resold genuine goods on which the trade mark had been placed by its proprietor. The defect in that argument would have been that it rendered Article 7(1) entirely redundant.

In fact no one involved in the *Silhouette* case contended that the Directive should be construed as requiring international exhaustion. Both Hartlauer and the Swedish government, which alone of the Member States defended the cause of international exhaustion, maintained that the Directive left the Member States free to provide for international exhaustion.[208]

---

[207] Art. 9 of the Community Trade Mark Regulation is similarly worded.
[208] See paras 19 and 20 of the judgment.

One strong argument against the option of leaving the matter to the Member States was that it was clearly out of the question for Community trade marks; it would run counter to the basic principle that the Community trade mark has a unitary character and produces the same effect throughout the Community.[209] A Community trade mark would not produce the same effect throughout the Community if in some Member States but not in others its proprietor could rely on it to prevent parallel imports of goods which he had placed on the market outside the Community. Moreover, the whole purpose of the Community trade mark is to enable goods bearing a Community trade mark to circulate throughout the Community free of any impediment due to trade mark law. As we have seen, differing approaches to the issue of international exhaustion can lead to situations in which goods are lawfully on the market in one Member State (one that recognises international exhaustion) but can be excluded from other Member States (those that do not recognise international exhaustion) on trade mark grounds. Such a situation would be incompatible with the Community Trade Mark Regulation.

Theoretically it might have been possible to allow Member States to provide for international exhaustion as regards national trade marks, even though Community trade marks were subject only to EEA-wide exhaustion. It would, however, have made life extremely complicated for all concerned. It would also have been contrary to the logic of the system of trade mark law set up by the Regulation and Directive. Advocate General Jacobs attached some importance to that argument.[210]

A further strong argument against leaving the matter to the Member States is that it would have the effect of creating internal trade barriers. As we have seen, goods would have to be admitted to a Member State that had international exhaustion but the trade mark proprietor would be able to prevent the export of those goods from such a Member State to another Member State that did not have international exhaustion.

That would have frustrated the fundamental purpose of the Directive which was to 'facilitate the free circulation of goods and services, to ensure that henceforth registered trade marks enjoy the same protection under the legal systems of all the Member States'.[211] For that reason the Swedish government was surely wrong to argue that the Council had no competence, by means of a Directive based on Article 95 of the Treaty, to regulate the issue of international exhaustion.[212]

---

[209] Reg. No. 40/94, Art. 1(1).   [210] See paras 60 and 61 of the opinion.
[211] See the ninth recital in the preamble to the Directive. See para. 27 of the Court's judgment in *Silhouette*.
[212] *Contra*: C. T. Ebenroth, *Gewerblicher Rechtsschutz und europäische Warenverkehrsfreiheit: ein Beitrag zur Erschöpfung gewerblicher Schutzrechte*, Schriftenreihe Recht and internationale Wirtschaft, Heidelberg, 1992, Vol. 38, pp. 28 *et seq*. Loewenheim also points out that divergent

Ultimately, then, the second of the three options outlined above was the only one that had a realistic chance of being chosen by the Court. It is hardly surprising therefore that the Court held that national rules providing for international exhaustion are contrary to Article 7(1) of the Directive. It follows that EEA-wide exhaustion is no longer the minimum standard; it is the only standard that Member States are allowed to apply. A trade mark proprietor may not rely on the trade mark in order to oppose further dealing in goods that have been placed on the market with his consent in the EEA; but he must be allowed to oppose further dealing in goods that he has marketed outside the EEA. Although the *Silhouette* case was concerned with a national trade mark, it is clear that the same solution applies to Community trade marks.

The special situation of the EFTA countries in the EEA   On 3 December 1997, just a few months before the Court of Justice gave judgment in the *Silhouette* case, the EFTA Court delivered an advisory opinion in *Mag Instruments Inc. v California Trading Company*.[213] There the EFTA Court held that Article 7(1) of the Directive leaves it to the EFTA countries (i.e. Iceland, Liechtenstein, and Norway) to decide whether to introduce or maintain international exhaustion as regards trade-marked goods originating outside the EEA. As a result of that opinion Mag Instruments Inc. was unable to rely on its trade mark rights in order to prevent a parallel importer from selling in Norway (which had retained the principle of international exhaustion) torches manufactured in the United States and not marketed in the EEA with the consent of the trade mark owner.

The EFTA Court's main line of reasoning was that the EEA Agreement does not create a customs union but merely a free trade area.[214] The Court noted that the principle of free movement applied only to goods originating in the EEA.[215] This suggests that if 'Maglite' torches had been made in the EEA, rather than the United States, and first marketed outside the EEA, the trade mark proprietor would have been able to prevent parallel imports into Norway. It is difficult to see any logic in such a distinction.

Implied consent   We noted earlier that English law arrived at a solution similar to exhaustion by means of the implied licence doctrine. It was not surprising therefore that English lawyers attempted to mitigate the effects of *Silhouette* by arguing that trade mark proprietors who marketed goods outside the EEA implicitly consented to the goods being resold within the

---

rules on international exhaustion lead to distortions of competition: Loewenheim, op. cit. (n. 197), at 313.

[213] (1998) 29 IIC 316.   [214] At para. 25 of the advisory opinion.
[215] At para. 26 of the advisory opinion.

EEA, unless they inserted in the contract of sale a clause expressly prohibiting resale in the EEA.

The question whether consent, within the meaning of Article 7(1) of the Directive, may be implied in certain circumstances was referred to the Court of Justice by the High Court in the *Davidoff and Levi Strauss* cases.[216]

The Court did not rule out the possibility of implied consent completely. However, it placed such emphasis on the need for consent to be unequivocal that it is not easy to imagine circumstances in which a parallel importer would be able to succeed on the basis of implied consent. The Court ruled that:

> . . . the consent of a trade mark proprietor to the marketing within the EEA of products bearing that mark which have previously been placed on the market outside the EEA by that proprietor or with his consent may be implied, where it is to be inferred from facts and circumstances prior to, simultaneous with or subsequent to the placing of the goods on the market outside the EEA which, in the view of the national court, unequivocally demonstrate that the proprietor has renounced his right to oppose placing of the goods on the market within the EEA.[217]

It follows that implied consent cannot be inferred from the trade mark proprietor's silence. The onus is on the parallel importer to prove that the trade mark proprietor has consented to marketing in the EEA.[218] Implied consent cannot be inferred from the facts that:

(1) the proprietor of the trade mark has not communicated to all subsequent purchasers of the goods placed on the market outside the EEA his opposition to marketing within the EEA;
(2) the goods carry no warning of a prohibition on their being placed on the market within the EEA;
(3) the trade mark proprietor has transferred the ownership of the products bearing the trade mark without imposing any contractual reservations and, according to the law governing the contract, the property right transferred includes, in the absence of such reservations, an unlimited right of resale or, at the very least, a right to market the goods subsequently within the EEA.[219]

In *Davidoff and Levi Strauss* the Court seemed unusually sympathetic to trade mark proprietors who wish to divide up the world market as a result of the abandonment of international exhaustion. In order to justify requiring unequivocal proof of consent to marketing in the EEA, the Court referred to the 'serious effect in extinguishing the exclusive rights of the proprietors of the trade marks in issue in the main proceedings (rights which enable them

---

[216] Joined Cases C-414/99 to C-416/99 [2001] ECR I-8691.
[217] At para. 47 of the judgment.   [218] At para. 54 of the judgment.
[219] At para. 60 of the judgment.

to control the initial marketing in the EEA)'. The Court's approach seems unbalanced. The effect on the purchaser of branded goods who is unable to resell them within the EEA is also serious. So too is the effect on competition and on consumers, who have to pay higher prices for branded goods as a result of the Court's judgment.

The burden of proof One of the practical problems engendered by the abandonment of international exhaustion is that the legality of parallel imports now depends on a question of fact that may not be easy to prove: were the goods placed on the market within the EEA by the trade mark proprietor or with his consent, express or implicit?

The troublesome nature of that question became apparent in *Van Doren v Lifestyle*.[220] Stussy, Inc., a United States company, marketed clothing world-wide under the trade mark 'Stüssy'. Van Doren was its exclusive distributor in Germany. Stussy, Inc. authorised Van Doren to bring trade mark infringement proceedings in its own name. Stussy, Inc. had, in each EEA country, only one exclusive distributor and general importer for 'Stüssy' articles and that distributor was contractually bound not to sell goods to intermediaries for resale outside his contractual territory. Lifestyle began to market 'Stüssy' articles in Germany. Lifestyle had not obtained the goods from Van Doren. Van Doren brought trade mark infringement proceedings against Lifestyle. It maintained that the 'Stüssy' articles marketed in Germany by Lifestyle had originally been put on the market in the United States and that their distribution in the EEA had not been authorised by the trade mark owner. Lifestyle maintained that it had purchased the goods in the EEA from an intermediary who, Lifestyle assumed, had acquired them from an authorised distributor.

The German courts decided that everything turned on the burden of proof. According to the *Bundesgerichtshof*, the general rule under German law was that each party to proceedings must prove the existence of the conditions for the application of the rule on which he relied. Hence the parallel importer had the burden of proving that the trade mark proprietor had consented to the marketing of the goods in the EEA. Moreover, according to the *Bundesgerichtshof*, a reversal of the burden of proof could unduly prejudice the trade mark proprietor's exclusive rights. It would 'limit the effect of EEA-wide exhaustion to such an extent as to render it almost redundant, even though the alleged trade mark infringer could easily show the origin of the goods in question'.[221]

The *Bundesgerichtshof* recognised, however, that such rules on the burden of proof might make it impossible for a parallel importer to market trade-marked goods, even though they had been placed on the market in the EEA with the trade mark owner's consent. The *Bundesgerichtshof*

---

[220] Case C-244/00, judgment of 8 April 2003.   [221] At para. 19 of the judgment.

pointed out that, even though the parallel importer could show who he had acquired the goods from, he would not necessarily be able to identify earlier links in the distribution chain. Moreover, even if he could trace the distribution chain back to the trade mark proprietor and thus show that the goods had been put on the market in the EEA with that person's consent, his source of supply would be likely to dry up as soon as he revealed it.[222]

Aware of the obvious danger that the trade mark owner would be able to partition national markets and block parallel imports within the EEA as a result of the rules on the burden of proof, the *Bundesgerichtshof* referred the following question to the Court of Justice:

Are Articles 28 EC and 30 EC to be interpreted as meaning that they permit the application of national legislation under which an infringer against whom proceedings are brought on the basis of a trade mark for marketing original goods, and who claims that the trade mark right has been exhausted within the meaning of Article 7 of Directive 89/104/EEC . . . has to plead and, if necessary, prove that the goods marketed by him have already been put on the market in the European Economic Area for the first time by the trade mark owner himself or with his consent?[223]

As a general rule, the burden of proof is a question of procedural law and as such falls to be determined by national law in the absence of any specific rule of Community law.[224] The principle was perhaps so well established that the Court of Justice did not feel compelled to recall it.

The Court had no difficulty in holding that a rule of national law whereby the parallel importer has the burden of proving that the goods in question were placed on the market within the EEA with the trade mark proprietor's consent is consistent with Community law and, in particular, with Articles 5 and 7 of the Trade Mark Directive.[225]

The Court went on to observe, however, that such a rule of evidence might need to be qualified as a result of requirements deriving from the principle of the free movement of goods, in particular if it allowed the trade mark proprietor to partition national markets.[226] The Court realised that there was a real risk of partitioning markets within the EEA, in particular where the trade mark proprietor marketed his products in the EEA through an exclusive distribution system. In such a situation, if the parallel importer was required to reveal his source of supply within the EEA, the trade mark proprietor would know which member of the exclusive distribution network

---

[222] At para. 21 of the judgment.   [223] At para. 24 of the judgment.
[224] See para. 102 of the opinion of Advocate General Jacobs in Joined Cases C-427/93, C-429/93 and C-436/93 *Bristol-Myers Squibb v Paranova*, together with the case law and literature cited there.
[225] At paras 35 and 36 of the judgment.
[226] At paras 37 and 38 of the judgment.

had supplied the parallel importer and would be able to prevent him from obtaining further supplies.[227] The Court therefore ruled that, where the parallel importer established that there was a real risk of partitioning national markets if he bore the burden of proving that the goods were placed on the market in the EEA by the trade mark proprietor or with his consent, it was for the latter to establish that the products were initially placed on the market outside the EEA by him or with his consent. If such evidence was adduced, it was then for the parallel importer to prove the consent of the trade mark proprietor to subsequent marketing of the products in the EEA.

Conclusion The sad truth is that, however desirable international exhaustion may be from the point of view of promoting free trade and granting consumers access to cheaper goods, and however little justification there may be for allowing trade mark proprietors to use trade marks as a means of dividing up the world market by opposing parallel imports of genuine goods, the cause of international exhaustion has been lost, at least for the time being. While that is presented as a victory for Community industry and as a means of legitimate self-protection against the Community's non-reciprocating trading partners, it is really a victory for trade mark proprietors, regardless of their nationality.[228] As was pointed out above in relation to *Polydor v Harlequin Record Shops*, the merits of the reciprocity argument are questionable. When a country adopts international exhaustion without insisting on reciprocity, it does not handicap its domestic industry;[229] it simply limits the extent to which trade mark proprietors, domestic or foreign, may use trade marks to divide up markets and practise differential pricing to the detriment of consumers.[230] As a result of the globalization of markets, it is perfectly possible that in any particular trade mark territory the majority of trade marks will be owned by foreign undertakings. There is no reason for the authorities in such a territory to confer on trade mark proprietors privileges unnecessary for the protection of the reputation of their trade marks. The fact that trade mark proprietors enjoy such privileges in other countries is irrelevant. It is

---

[227] At paras 39 and 40 of the judgment.

[228] 'Despite a resolute support of the concept |of international exhaustion| by Germany and its eloquent defense by Professor F.-K. Beier, the majority of the Member States yielded to a concerted lobbying of the owners of trademarks.' S. Soltysinski, op. cit. (n. 147), at 320.

[229] Wiszniewska argues, however, that international exhaustion may have detrimental consequences for countries like Poland, where the need for foreign investment exists and selective distribution systems are not yet fully developed: op. cit. (n. 176), at 168 *et seq.*

[230] As Soltysinski observes, intellectual property owners 'take advantage of the territoriality principle and the limited scope of the exhaustion concept to maximize their profits by producing and marketing . . . goods on the basis of exclusivity for each national territory, thus reaping the benefits of international price discrimination and suppressing transnational competition.' S. Soltysinski, op. cit. (n. 147), at 317.

of course deeply ironic that international exhaustion should be abandoned at the very moment when a global economy is supposedly being created.

Before we leave the issue of reciprocity, one final point may be noted. In an Explanatory Memorandum[231] the Commission observed that the Community must be empowered to conclude bilateral or multilateral treaties with important trading partners whereby international exhaustion would be introduced. The Commission also observed that national courts could grant international exhaustion in respect of Community trade marks where, even in the absence of a formal agreement, reciprocity was guaranteed. There can be no objection to the conclusion of treaties on exhaustion (except that they would be unnecessary if an enlightened view on unilateral international exhaustion were taken). It is difficult, though, to see how such treaties could be given effect without amending Article 13(1) of the Community Trade Mark Regulation. There seems little merit, however, in the suggestion that national courts should decide to introduce international exhaustion in specific cases if the imported goods were first placed on the market in a country which offers reciprocity.[232] The main defect in that suggestion is that the national courts might come to different conclusions about the availability of reciprocity. As well as creating great uncertainty, that would impair the unitary character of the Community trade mark, which must, as we have seen, be exhausted in all Member States or in none at all. Rasmussen's suggestion[233] that the issue could be referred to the Court of Justice does not seem to provide a solution. The Court of Justice could not decide, in a preliminary ruling, whether a third country guaranteed reciprocity.

6.4.2.3 *Designs*

Following *Silhouette* it is clear that design rights must, like trade marks, be subject only to EEA-wide exhaustion. All the arguments relied on in that judgment apply with equal force to design rights. Thus Article 15 of the Designs Directive and Article 21 of the Community Design Regulation must be interpreted as meaning that the proprietor of a registered design, whether granted by the competent authorities of a Member State or by the Office for Harmonization in the Internal Market, may bring infringement proceedings against someone who imports into, or resells in, the EEA goods protected by the design right which the proprietor has marketed outside the EEA. The same must apply to the unregistered Community design right provided for in Article 11 of the Community Design Regulation.

---

[231] Cited by Rasmussen, op. cit. (n. 181), at 176.
[232] Rasmussen points out the practical difficulties that this would entail, ibid., at 178.
[233] Ibid.

The Designs Directive does not apply to unregistered designs.[234] Hence Member States may, if they wish, apply the principle of international exhaustion to unregistered design rights governed by national law.

6.4.2.4 *Copyright*

The drafting of the exhaustion provisions in Article 4(c) of the Software Directive, Article 9(2) of the Rental Right Directive, Article 4(2) of the Copyright Directive and Article 5(c) of the Databases Directive is not of a high standard. A first point to note is that all four provisions speak of an intellectual property right being 'exhausted' by a 'first sale' in the Community. This use of jargon in legislation is unfortunate. It is all very well for academic writers to speak of an exhaustion principle and a first-sale doctrine, since they have the space in which to explain what their terms of art mean. There is no place for such language in legislative texts, which should be clear, concise, and readily intelligible to the people who are likely to be affected by them. What computer programmer or film producer will understand terms like 'exhaustion of rights' and 'first sale'? The statement that a right is exhausted by a first sale in the Community is meaningless to the non-specialist. The ordinary language used in the Community's trade mark legislation is infinitely preferable and there is no reason why it could not have been used in the copyright legislation.

A further serious defect in the drafting of this legislation is the inexplicable discrepancy between the wording of the exhaustion provisions in the Rental Right and Copyright Directives, on the one hand, and those in the Software and Databases Directives, on the other. The former state that the 'distribution right *shall not be exhausted* within the Community in respect of [the goods in question], *except* where the first sale . . . in the Community of [the goods in question] is made by the right-holder or with his consent' (emphasis added). The latter state that a first sale in the Community of a copy of the protected work exhausts the right in that copy.

The use of the negative form of the verb 'exhaust' in conjunction with the word 'except', in the Rental Right and Copyright Directives, strongly suggests that the act described (sale within the Community) is the only act that exhausts the right. If that is correct—and on a literal reading no other view seems possible—Member States are not free to provide for exhaustion by a sale outside the Community.[235]

---

[234] Seventh recital in the preamble.

[235] That view is affirmed categorically by the authors of the leading text book on the subject: Reinbothe and von Lewinski, op. cit. (n. 186), at p. 105. It is also the view of the Commission: Cohen Jehoram, op. cit. (n. 201), at 284, citing the Commission's answers to questions in the European Parliament. See also Brown op. cit. (n. 135), at 345.

The language of the Software and Databases Directives, on the other hand, contains the same ambiguity as Article 7(1) of the Trade Mark Directive: those Directives make it clear that a sale within the Community exhausts the right but do not state what consequences ensue from a sale outside the Community. Before *Silhouette* it would certainly have been possible to argue that Member States would not have been implementing the Directives incorrectly if they provided for international exhaustion. However, Loewenheim pointed out, in an article published in 1996, that it would be incongruous if the exclusive rights covered by the Software and Databases Directives were subject to different rules as regards international exhaustion from the one applicable to the rights covered by Article 9 of the Rental Right Directive (i.e. the exclusive distribution rights in relation to phonograms, films, and fixations of performances and of broadcasts).[236] That cannot have been the intention of the Community legislature, according to Loewenheim. He may well be right. All that one can say with certainty is that it is regrettable that legislation which involves the participation of so many institutions, organs, and groups of experts cannot be drafted more clearly.

Following *Silhouette* the above discussion is probably of a largely academic nature. The rationale of *Silhouette* was that a common solution to the question of international exhaustion is needed in order to prevent barriers to the free movement of goods within the common market. That applies equally to trade in products covered by copyright and related rights. The preambles to the Software Directive,[237] the Database Directive,[238] and the Copyright Directive[239] emphasize the need to harmonize legislation in order to safeguard the proper functioning of the internal market. It would be difficult therefore, in the light of *Silhouette*, to argue that international exhaustion is a matter for national law.

6.4.2.5 *Plant variety rights*

The conclusion arrived at in relation to the Community trade mark seems equally valid for the exclusive rights created by the Plant Varieties Regulation. Article 2 of the Regulation provides that: 'Community plant variety rights shall have uniform effect within the territory of the Community and may not be granted, transferred or terminated in respect of the above-mentioned territory otherwise than on a uniform basis.'

It follows that a common rule on exhaustion is required. The only common rule that can logically be deduced from Article 16 of the

---

[236] Loewenheim, op. cit. (n. 197), at 315.
[237] See the fourth and fifth recitals in the preamble.
[238] See the second and third recitals in the preamble.
[239] See the seventh recital in the preamble.

Regulation is that the right in question is exhausted only when the protected material is disposed of to others by the holder or with his consent
within the Community (or, for the reasons given above, within an EEA
Contracting State). Moreover, in the light of *Silhouette* no other solution
seems possible.

6.4.2.6 *Patents*

As in the case of the Community trade mark, it is clear that the Community
patent will be exhausted only by marketing of the patented product in the
EEA by the patent proprietor or with his consent. There is no scope for
Member States to apply a different rule on exhaustion in view of the unitary
effect of the Community patent decreed by Article 2(1) of the proposed
regulation.[240]

Although Article 10 of the draft regulation speaks of putting the patented
product on the market 'in the Community', it is clear from Article 2(2) of
Protocol No. 28 to the EEA Agreement[241] that marketing anywhere in the
EEA will exhaust a Community patent.

---

[240] Benyamini, op. cit. (n. 8), at p. 355.
[241] See above, section 6.2.

8

Trade Marks

1. THE ROLE OF TRADE MARKS IN A MARKET ECONOMY

1.1 *The origin function of trade marks*

Since the dawn of capitalism, honest traders have sought to distinguish their goods from goods produced by other persons by affixing distinguishing signs to them. Equally ancient, no doubt, is the practice, on the part of dishonest traders, of imitating such signs in an attempt to pass off their goods as the goods of a more successful trader with an established reputation. This then is the basic function of trade marks: to indicate the origin of goods (and, in a developed economy, of services also). Thus trade marks are the essential means by which traders protect their commercial reputation and build up an intangible asset known by the evocative term 'goodwill'. 'Goodwill' was pithily defined in 1810 by Lord Eldon as 'the value of that probability, that old customers will resort to the old place'.[1]

It would not be an exaggeration to say that trade marks are the very foundation of competition in a developed market economy.[2] Trade marks are the means by which manufacturers establish direct communication with the ultimate consumers of goods. Without trade marks, manufacturers would have no incentive to produce goods of high quality because consumers would have no way of identifying goods emanating from a particular source and would not be able to reward a supplier of quality produce with their continued patronage.

Before the advent of registration systems in the late nineteenth century, various forms of action were developed by different legal systems as a means of enabling traders to protect the reputation of their products. The English common law invented the tort of passing-off, which requires proof that the defendant's activities cause actual damage to the claimant, normally through the former's goods being mistaken for those of the latter.[3] In continental Europe a general action for unfair competition came to fulfil a similar role. Such actions continue to be relevant, in particular for trade marks which do not meet the requirements for registration. However, a

---

[1] *Crutwell v Lye* (1810) 1 Rose 123; 17 Ves 335; 34 ER 129. The passage is quoted by B. E. Cookson, in 'The Significance of Goodwill' [1991] 7 EIPR 248.

[2] W. R. Cornish, *Intellectual Property: Patents, Copyright, Trade Marks and Allied Rights*, 4th edn, Sweet and Maxwell, London, 1999, p. 599.

[3] See, e.g., *Erven Warnink v Townend* [1979] FSR 397. On the subject of passing-off in general, see C. Wadlow, *The Law of Passing-off*, 2nd edn, Sweet and Maxwell, London, 1995.

registered trade mark presents considerable advantages in terms of legal certainty, enforceability, and the ease with which it can be assigned or licensed.

It is not just manufacturers and traders who have an interest in preserving the origin function of trade marks. Their customers share the same interest in avoiding confusion as to the commercial origin of goods and services. For example, consumers who stroll around a supermarket, wondering which brand of coffee or shampoo to buy, place implicit faith in the origin function of trade marks. They act on the assumption that all the packets of coffee bearing a particular distinguishing sign will emanate from the same source and be of similar quality. If they bought the product once and liked it, they will buy it again. If they disliked it, they will switch to a different brand.

It is interesting to speculate on the precise mental processes through which consumers pass. The more naive may imagine that every tube of shampoo bearing a well known trade mark has been made in the same factory out of the same ingredients by the same workers. The more sophisticated will be aware that large multinationals frequently decentralise production by licensing other firms to make goods and place the licensor's trade mark on them. They may also appreciate that some manufacturers adapt a product in accordance with perceived differences in local taste, or that trade marks are sometimes assigned to different persons in different countries. The implications of this, in the context of a common market and a global economy, are considerable. Two radio batteries may bear the same trade mark and be identical in appearance, yet contain different chemical mixes which radically affect their performance. If a manufacturer of batteries markets inferior products at a lower price in Greece because the Greek market is less demanding as to quality and competition is based essentially on price, a parallel importer may resell the products in Germany, where the manufacturer markets higher-quality products at a higher price. The German consumer who relies on the origin function of the trade mark is likely to be disappointed.

A further problem is that people travel. If a Swiss manufacturer of chocolate thinks that chocolate made of skimmed milk powder will do nicely for Spanish consumers but uses only fresh milk for the more discriminating Belgian market, this may result in disappointment for the Belgian holiday-maker who buys his favourite brand of chocolate in Benidorm.

None of these remarks are intended to call in question the origin function of trade marks. The point that is being made is that the origin function must be understood in the light of the territoriality principle, which says that the trade mark's legal effects are confined to the specific territory in which it enjoys protection, and in the light of the multinationals' passion for compartmentalising markets. Unfortunately the average consumer, whose assumptions and intuitions are fundamental to a proper understanding of the role of trade marks, is unlikely to understand the implications of either the territoriality principle or the market-dividing tendencies of manufacturers. In an imperfect world, trade marks perform their origin function imperfectly.

1.2 *Ancillary functions of trade marks*

The problems alluded to above doubtless help to explain why it has become increasingly common in recent times to downplay the importance of the origin function and to emphasize certain other functions of trade marks. Proponents of this view of trade mark law speak of the guarantee function, goodwill function, quality function, and publicity function of trade marks.[4] Many authors criticize the traditional view that trade marks are meant to do little more than indicate the commercial origin of goods and prevent confusion in the market-place between the goods of different suppliers.[5]

It is certainly important to avoid taking an excessively narrow view of the origin function of trade marks. Nor should we focus exclusively on confusion in the literal sense when deciding whether a trade mark has been infringed or whether a similar or identical mark should be registered. Often, especially if the earlier mark is well known, it is really a question of giving the mark the scope of protection that it merits, even though consumers will not actually be confused as to the origin of goods. It is true nonetheless that the other recognized functions of trade marks are to a large extent ancillary in the sense that they are direct consequences of the origin function. If a trade mark provides the consumer with a certain guarantee that a product will live up to his expectations of quality and encapsulates the manufacturer's goodwill, it does so because the consumer believes that all products bearing the trade mark emanate from the same commercial source, i.e. were produced under the control of the same person, company or group of undertakings.[6] If a trade mark is an effective means of advertising goods, that is because the

---

[4] There seems to be an international consensus on the relevance of these various functions: see, e.g., N. J. Wilkof, *Trade Mark Licensing*, Sweet and Maxwell, London, 1995, pp. 19–36; A. Braun, *Précis des marques: loi uniforme Benelux, droit belge, droit international*, 3rd edn, Maison Larcier, 1995, at pp. 10–19; R. Franceschelli, *Sui marchi di impresa*, 4th edn, Giuffrè PTO editore, Milan, 1988, at pp. 227–237; and C. Fernández-Novoa, *Fundamentos de derecho de marcas*, Editorial Montecorvo, Madrid, 1984, pp. 44–64.

[5] See, e.g., C. D. G. Pickering, *Trade Marks in Theory and Practice*, Hart Publishing, Oxford, 1998, pp. 43–50; T. Martino and P. Groves, 'Trade marks—Deliver us from Days of Old' [1991] 10 EIPR 355; and A. Kamperman Sanders, 'The Wagamama Decision: Back to the Dark Ages of Trade Mark Law' [1996] 1 EIPR 3. For a defence of the traditional viewpoint, see F.-K. Beier, 'Territoriality of Trademark Law and International Trade' (1970) 1 IIC 48, 61 *et seq*.

[6] On the quality function of trade marks, see T. Martino and W. Ullah, 'The Quality Guarantee Function of Trade Marks: an Economic Viewpoint' [1989] 8 EIPR 267.

persons at whom the advertisements are aimed will assume that the goods bearing the advertised mark will have been produced under the control of the advertiser.

There are, however, two respects in which the importance of the origin function—understood in its narrowest, most literal sense—has declined. In the first place, the restrictions that previously applied to the assignment and licensing of trade marks in some countries have gradually been eased.[7] Trade marks may now generally be transferred separately from the undertaking which previously owned and exploited them.[8] The proprietor of a trade mark may license an entirely separate undertaking to use the trade mark.[9] As a result of this liberal attitude towards assignments and licensing, the trade mark offers no guarantee that today's goods will have been made in the same place by the same people as yesterday's. But that does not mean that the trade mark's origin function ceases to operate. The licensor will, if he is rational, ensure that all his licensees comply with his own quality standards. The assignee will, if he is rational, seek to maintain, or improve, the quality standards of the assignor; if he does not, he will reduce the value of his investment. In assessing the role of trade marks it seems reasonable to assume that most market participants (manufacturers, dealers, and consumers) are likely to behave rationally. A packet of 'Marlboro' will, as Martino and Groves concede,[10] go on being a packet of 'Marlboro' even if the mark is assigned or licensed out.

Secondly, as a result of the acceptance of anti-dilution theories, trade marks with a reputation now generally enjoy a degree of protection that transcends the rationale of the origin function.[11] If, for example, a manufacturer of dishwashers were to advertise his products with the slogan 'a Rolls Royce among dishwashers', the owner of the 'Rolls Royce' trade mark, which is known world-wide for motor cars but not for dishwashers, would be able, in many jurisdictions, to take legal action to enjoin such use of its trade mark. Here confusion as to origin would be out of the question. No one would assume that the dishwashers were made by Rolls Royce or by a

[7] For an example of the hostility to 'trafficking' in trade marks that used to characterize the law of the United Kingdom, see *Holly Hobbie Trade Mark* [1984] FSR 199.

[8] As regards Community trade marks, this rule is laid down in Art. 17(1) of Council Reg. (EC) No. 40/94 on the Community trade mark: OJ 1994 L 11, p. 1.

[9] See Art. 22 of Reg. No. 40/94 and Art. 8 of Council Directive 89/104/EEC approximating the laws of the Member States relating to trade marks: OJ 1989 L 40, p. 1.

[10] Op. cit. (n. 5), at 357. The quality function also operates at an emotional level which transcends the purely rational. The vice president of marketing at Starbucks is quoted as saying that 'consumers don't truly believe there's a huge difference between products' and that brands must therefore 'establish emotional ties': see N. Klein, *No Logo*, Flamingo, 2001, p. 20.

[11] On the subject of well-known and famous trade marks, see the articles cited by F.-K. Beier, in 'The Development of Trade Mark Law in the Last Twenty-five Years' (1995) 26 IIC 769, 780 (footnote 47). For an exhaustive study, see F. W. Mostert, *Famous and Well-known Marks: An International Analysis*, Butterworths, 1997.

company connected with Rolls Royce. The basis for the action would be that the manufacturer of dishwashers was taking unfair advantage of the reputation of the 'Rolls Royce' trade mark and diluting its distinctiveness.[12] In the Member States of the European Union such an action could be founded on national provisions adopted pursuant to Article 5(2) of Directive 89/104/EEC ('the Trade Mark Directive'), which allows Member States to provide that the proprietor of a trade mark with a reputation may prevent others from using it where such use 'takes advantage of, or is detrimental to, the distinctive character or the repute of the trade mark'.[13] No test of confusion as to origin applies in that hypothesis.

As regards what has come to be known as the advertising function of trade marks, it must be conceded that that too is capable of broadening the scope of protection of trade marks in a manner that goes beyond the rationale of the origin function. There are situations in which the trade mark owner may be entitled to rely on the trade mark to prevent advertising by unauthorised dealers which might damage the reputation of the mark, without, however, creating any confusion as to the origin of the branded goods. The point is illustrated by two cases that came before the Court of Justice.[14]

There is one further function which certain trade marks have acquired in recent times and which is genuinely different from the origin function. This may be termed the 'merchandising function' or the 'cashing-in function'. A curious practice has developed whereby celebrities, performing artists, football clubs, universities, and companies engaged in the manufacture of glamorous, luxury goods register their names, logos, and distinctive symbols as trade marks in respect of a whole range of goods which have little or no connection with their principal activity.

Not so long ago any enterprising person who wished to cash in on the fame of a pop group or football team could produce souvenir mugs, towels, scarves, pens, lamps, etc., just as anyone could produce busts of Beethoven or bookmarkers with a picture of Shakespeare's head or Anne Hathaway's cottage. Beethoven and Shakespeare are doubtless safely in the public domain but any entrepreneur who attempts to exploit the image of

---

[12] In Germany the owner of the 'Rolls Royce' trade mark was successful, on the basis of unfair competition law, in an action against a whisky manufacturer who incorporated a picture of a Rolls Royce into his advertisements: see K.-H. Fezer, 'Trademark Protection under Unfair Competition Law' (1988) 19 IIC 192, 197.

[13] Although the provisions of Art. 5(2) are optional, all Member States have made use of the option, according to the Commission: see para. 7 of the Advocate General's Opinion in Case C-292/00 *Davidoff v Gofkid*, delivered on 21 March 2002. The corresponding provision in Reg. No. 40/94 is Art. 9(1)(c), which of course applies in all Member States in relation to Community trade marks.

[14] Case C-337/95 *Christian Dior v Evora* [1997] ECR I-6034 and Case C-63/97 *BMW v Deenik* [1998] ECR I-925. The cases are dealt with in section 4 below.

well-known entertainers or football clubs is likely to become the defendant in trade mark infringement proceedings.[15]

If pop groups and football clubs register their names as trade marks for mugs, tee-shirts, and pens, they clearly do not do so for the purpose of protecting their reputation as makers of mugs, tee-shirts, and pens. The function of these trade marks is not to ensure that consumers' expectations as regards the quality of the goods are satisfied. The consumers of such goods are likely to be relatively indifferent to quality and more concerned by the need to make a statement about their emotional attachment to their idols; or they may want to be associated with the aura of luxury and glamour that surrounds them. In this context the origin function of the trade mark is of little relevance, except in so far as the most devoted fan wants souvenirs that have actually been authorised by his favourites and cares whether the latter benefit financially.

The function of trade marks used in this manner is simply to ensure that those who have achieved eminence in a particular field enjoy an exclusive right to exploit lucrative secondary markets. There is room for debate about the rights and wrongs of this. When the exclusive rights are claimed by living persons or companies who seek to exploit their own fame, few would object. The issue becomes less clear when the exclusive rights are claimed by the successors in title to deceased persons (such as Elvis Presley or Diana, Princess of Wales) or by free-riders who have no connection with the deceased celebrity. It is in any event clear that the merchandising function of trade marks is genuinely different from the origin function and that the legal problems raised by this phenomenon cannot easily be resolved by applying the traditional canons of trade mark law.

The developments outlined above tend to suggest, not that the origin function has declined in importance, but simply that the scope of the protection conferred by a registered trade mark has gradually been broadened and that the concept of the trade mark in an advanced market economy has undergone a subtle transformation. Registration of a trade mark may once have been seen as a useful means of supplementing the protection conferred by a passing-off action; the advantages of registration were greater legal certainty and simplified enforcement procedures. A registered trade mark has now evolved into something akin to an ordinary property right—not radically different from the title deeds to a farm. By careful husbandry (consistently producing high-quality products and carefully controlling advertising) the property may be improved and its value

[15] Mr Matthew Reed, who since 1970 has sold football souvenirs and memorabilia outside Highbury Stadium, discovered this to his cost when he was sued for infringing the registered trade marks of Arsenal F.C.; see Case C-206/01 *Arsenal F. C. v Reed*, judgment of 12 November 2002. For a balanced discussion of the justification for using trade marks to protect merchandizing, see Pickering, op. cit. (n. 5), at pp. 67–70.

enhanced. It becomes a capital asset reflected in a company's balance sheet. Like a farm, it may be freely bought and sold, or rented out in return for a tithe, which is known as a 'royalty'. Not surprisingly, these developments may pose new legal challenges, some of which may have profound implications in Community law. It remains to be seen how the Court of Justice will respond to those challenges.

1.3 *The Court of Justice's understanding of the role of trade marks*

In its earliest judgments on trade marks—happily now of purely historical interest—the Court of Justice displayed an alarming lack of comprehension of even the most basic function of a trade mark. Worse still, the Court's attitude towards trade marks was positively disparaging. They were looked down on as second-class industrial property rights. Whereas patents and copyright were thought to advance the cause of humanity because they stimulated and rewarded scientific progress and literary creativity respectively, trade marks were despised as vulgar commercial rights hardly worth of protection. The negative conception of trade marks seems to stem from some curious remarks made by Advocate General Dutheillet de Lamothe in his opinion in *Sirena v Eda* in 1971.[16] The Advocate General observed:

Both from the economic and from the human point of view the interests protected by patent legislation merit greater respect than those protected by trade-marks.
. . .
From the human point of view, the debt which society owes to the 'inventor' of the name 'Prep Good Morning' is certainly not of the same nature, to say the least, as that which humanity owes to the discoverer of penicillin.[17]

On the basis of that outlandish comparison between a trade mark for shaving cream and one of the greatest advances in the history of medicine, the Court stated that 'a trade mark right is distinguishable . . . from other rights of industrial and commercial property, inasmuch as the interests protected by the latter are usually more important, and merit a higher degree of protection, than the interests protected by an ordinary trade-mark'.[18]

That negative conception of trade marks produced disastrous results. In *Sirena v Eda* the Court gave a ruling which meant that, where a trade mark was originally owned in two Member States by the same company and that company assigned one of the registrations to a different, unrelated company long before the entry into force of the EEC Treaty, the assignment was

---

[16] Case 40/70 *Sirena v Eda* [1971] ECR 69.   [17] At 87.
[18] At para. 78 of the judgment.

caught by Article 81 of the Treaty; with the result, apparently, that neither owner of the trade mark could oppose the marketing, in the territory in which it owned the supposedly exclusive rights flowing from the trade mark, of products to which the trade mark had been affixed by the other owner. In *Van Zuylen v HAG*, decided in 1974,[19] the Court arrived at a similar result, on the basis of the Treaty provisions on the free movement of goods, in relation to a trade mark whose unitary ownership had been shattered by an act of expropriation.

Such results were not, of course, compatible with the origin function of trade marks. If identical trade marks may be used in relation to identical goods by unrelated persons in the same territory, neither of those persons will be able to protect the reputation of his products by ensuring that the trade mark is used only on goods of uniform quality. The trade mark no longer guarantees that all products on which it is placed emanate from the same source. That is severely detrimental to the interests not only of the trade mark owners but also of consumers. The latter will continue to rely on the assumption that all products bearing the trade mark, at least in their own familiar market where they make most of their purchases, will be of similar quality. They will be deceived into buying Company X's product in the belief that it has the qualities which they have come to expect from Company Y's products.

The Court would probably have avoided those unfortunate results if it had attempted to develop the specific subject-matter test which, as we have seen, was beginning to play a role in its case law in the first half of the 1970s. However inadequate that test is, it would at least have led the Court to reflect on the fundamental purpose of trade mark protection; and such reflection would surely have made the Court realise that a trade mark cannot be shared by unrelated undertakings in the same territory.[20]

But these were early days. The concept of specific subject-matter first appeared in *Deutsche Grammophon*[21] in 1971, though the Court made no attempt to define the specific subject-matter of the intellectual property right in question. In *Sirena v Eda* the concept was not even mentioned. In *HAG I*, as in *Deutsche Grammophon*, the Court formally declared the specific subject-matter test applicable but made no attempt to define the specific subject-matter of the right in question.[22]

The rehabilitation of trade marks in the eyes of the Court of Justice was a slow process, and was not finally accomplished until the Court expressly

[19] Case 192/73 *Van Zuylen v HAG* ('*HAG I*') [1974] ECR 731.

[20] Interestingly, the judge rapporteur in *HAG I* had a clear understanding of the origin function of trade marks: see Lord Mackenzie Stuart, 'The Function of Trade Marks and the Free Movement of Goods in the European Economic Community' (1976) 7 IIC 27.

[21] Case 78/70 *Deutsche Grammophon v Metro* [1971] ECR 487.

[22] At para. 9 of the judgment.

overruled *HAG I* in 1990 in *CNL Sucal v HAG GF ('HAG II').*[23] Surprisingly, the process of rehabilitation began a mere three months after the judgment in *HAG I*. The occasion for this was presented by the case of *Centrafarm v Winthrop*,[24] in which a trade mark owner attempted to rely on the trade mark to block parallel imports into the Netherlands of products which it had marketed in the United Kingdom. The attempt failed, for the Court insisted, rightly, on applying the exhaustion principle. As in *HAG I*, the Court observed that Article 30 of the Treaty admits of derogations from the free movement of goods only in so far as is necessary for the purpose of safeguarding the rights that constitute the specific subject-matter of an industrial property right.[25] This time, however, the Court went on to define the specific subject-matter of a trade mark. It did so in the following terms:

> In relation to trade marks, the specific subject-matter of the industrial property is the guarantee that the owner of the trade mark has the exclusive right to use that trade mark, for the purpose of putting products protected by the trade mark into circulation for the first time, and is therefore intended to protect him against competitors wishing to take advantage of the status and reputation of the trade mark by selling products illegally bearing that trade mark.[26]

The reference to competitors selling products 'illegally' bearing the trade mark was doubtless intended to cater for the situation that arose in *HAG I*. Obviously the Court was not likely to voice any doubts in October 1974 about the merits of a judgment delivered in July of the same year.

The next step came two years later in *Terrapin v Terranova*,[27] in which the Court resisted the temptation to extend the ultra-integrationist approach of *HAG I* to the type of situation that exists when confusingly similar trade marks belong to different persons in two Member States and the two marks have come into being independently of each other. In *Terrapin v Terranova* the Court made its first reference to the 'basic function' of the trade mark, which was defined thus: 'to guarantee to consumers that the product has the same origin'.[28] From today's perspective we should not worry too much about the fact that the Court used that definition of the basic function of the trade mark in a spurious attempt to justify the judgment in *HAG I*. (The Court stated, unconvincingly, that the basic function was already undermined by the subdivision of the original right.) The truly significant development was that the Court had finally arrived at an understanding of the *raison d'être* of trade mark protection, namely the origin function.

In subsequent judgments a slight change of terminology took place. What was referred to as the 'basic function' in *Terrapin v Terranova* was

---

[23] Case C-10/89 *CNL Sucal v HAG GF ('HAG II')* [1990] ECR I-3711.
[24] Case 16/74 *Centrafarm v Winthrop* [1974] ECR 1183.
[25] At para. 7 of the judgment.   [26] At para. 8 of the judgment.
[27] Case 119/75 *Terrapin v Terranova* [1976] ECR 1039.   [28] At para. 6 of the judgment.

rebaptized the 'essential function'. It was, moreover, defined in more force-ful language. Thus, in *Hoffmann-La Roche v Centrafarm*, the Court said that 'regard must be had to the essential function of the trade mark, which is to guarantee the origin of the trade-marked product to the consumer or ultimate user, by enabling him without any possibility of confusion to distinguish that product from products which have another origin'.[29] On the basis of such a clear understanding of the origin function the Court could not have produced judgments such as *Sirena v Eda* and *HAG I*. That suggests that even as early as 1978 the Court must have had an inkling that those cases were wrongly decided.

Hoffmann-La Roche v Centrafarm set a pattern that has been followed to this day. In any case concerning a conflict between the free movement of goods and a trade mark right the Court starts by emphasising that Article 30 of the Treaty only allows exceptions to the free movement principle if they are justified in order to safeguard the specific subject-matter of an intellectual property right. The specific subject-matter of a trade mark is then defined in the terms first used in *Centrafarm v Winthrop* (i.e. the trade mark owner's right to prevent competitors from stealing his goodwill by selling products on which it has been placed illegally). Finally, the Court adds that regard must be had to the trade mark's essential function, which is to guarantee to consumers that all goods bearing the trade mark have the same origin.

Although the Court seems to regard the specific subject-matter and the essential function of a trade mark as two different concepts, it is obvious from the above definitions that they are simply two sides of the same coin. Both the formulas describe the basic role of the trade mark in a market economy. The definition of specific subject-matter contemplates that role from the viewpoint of the trade mark owner; the definition of the essential function looks at matters through the eyes of the consumer.

Since 1978, then, the Court has had a clear understanding of the origin function of trade marks. That understanding has enabled the Court to avoid the kind of errors that occurred in *Sirena v Eda* and *HAG I*. The last traces of the disparaging attitude which the Court once displayed towards trade

---

[29] Case 102/77 *Hoffmann-La Roche v Centrafarm* [1978] ECR 1139 at para. 7. The words 'without any possibility of confusion' are unfortunate. No trade mark system can hope to eleminate all possibility of confusion. It is sufficient if the risk of confusion is kept within certain well-defined limits. The Court has achieved this in its case law on likelihood of confusion (see section 2.3.2 below). The wording used in *Hoffmann-La Roche v Centrafarm* led Advocate General Léger badly astray in Case C-104/01 *Libertel v Benelux-Merkenbureau* (judgment of 6 May 2003) where he took the view that a colour *per se* or combination of colours lacked the capacity to distinguish the goods or services of a specific undertaking since colours by themselves could not pass the 'no possibility of confusion' test (see paras 93–95 of the opinion). The fact remains that colours are used in the market-place as secondary indicators of origin and deserve to be protected. Fortunately the Court did not follow the Advocate General on this point.

marks were finally eradicated in 1990 when the Court made a particularly emphatic statement about the importance of trade marks in *HAG II*:

'Trade mark rights are, it should be noted, an essential element in the system of undistorted competition which the Treaty seeks to establish and maintain. Under such a system, an undertaking must be in a position to keep its customers by virtue of the quality of its products and services, something which is possible only if there are distinctive marks which enable customers to identify those products and services. For the trade mark to be able to fulfil this role, it must offer a guarantee that all goods bearing it have been produced under the control of a single undertaking which is accountable for their quality.'[30]

Just as the earlier negative view of trade marks was inspired by Advocate General Dutheillet de Lamothe, the new enthusiasm for trade marks bears testimony to the influence of Advocate General Jacobs, who stated in his opinion in *HAG II*:

Like patents, trade marks find their justification in a harmonious dove-tailing between public and private interests. Whereas patents reward the creativity of the inventor and thus stimulate scientific progress, trade marks reward the manufacturer who consistently produces high-quality goods and they thus stimulate economic progress. Without trade mark protection there would be little incentive for manufacturers to develop new products or to maintain the quality of existing ones. Trade marks are able to achieve that effect because they act as a guarantee, to the consumer, that all goods bearing a particular mark have been produced by, or under the control of, the same manufacturer and are therefore likely to be of similar quality. The guarantee of quality offered by a trade mark is not of course absolute, for the manufacturer is at liberty to vary the quality; however, he does so at his own risk and he—not his competitors—will suffer the consequences if he allows the quality to decline. Thus, although trade marks do not provide any form of *legal* guarantee of quality—the absence of which may have misled some to underestimate their significance—they do in economic terms provide such a guarantee, which is acted upon daily by consumers.

While the Court can only be applauded for admitting to past errors and recognising the importance of trade marks in the clearest of terms, its critics would no doubt complain that it is still 20 years behind the times. The gist of the criticism would be that the Court's appreciation of the origin function of trade marks comes at the very moment when that function is said to be in relative decline and the ancillary functions are gaining increasing recognition.[31] Is there a danger that the Court's new enthusiasm for the origin function might lead it to neglect other functions?

---

[30] *HAG II*, cited in n. 23, at para. 13 of the judgment.
[31] In fact few commentators seem to have noticed that the Court is moving in one direction (emphazising the paramount importance of the origin function), while Community legislation and academic opinion are taking the opposite direction (emphasizing the ancillary functions). Vito Mangini makes the point but suggests that both tendencies can be reconciled as part of a

The answer appears to be negative. In two judgments delivered in the late 1990s (*Christian Dior v Evora* and *BMW v Deenik*)[32] the Court showed an awareness of the advertising function of the trade mark, and accepted that the trade mark owner may prevent a parallel importer or dealer from advertising the trade-marked product in a manner detrimental to the image of the trade mark. The Court has also accepted that the trade mark owner may oppose certain repackaging operations by third parties which are capable of damaging the reputation of the trade mark, even though they do not create any confusion about the origin of goods bearing the trade mark.[33] The operations in question involved the repackaging of pharmaceutical products by a parallel importer in order to comply with different national rules or practices as regards, amongst other things, the number of pills per packet. The Court held that, even if the repackaging was done in such a way that the original condition of the goods could not be affected and the parallel importer clearly indicated who was responsible for the repackaging, the trade mark owner could still object to 'an inappropriate presentation of the repackaged product', since 'defective, poor quality or untidy packaging could damage the trade mark's reputation'. Reliance on the trade mark in that situation has nothing to do with preventing confusion about the origin of goods; the rationale of that type of extended protection is that the aura of quality surrounding the trade mark will be impaired if consumers mentally associate it with shoddy presentation. The same rationale underlies the *Christian Dior* and *BMW* cases on the trade mark owner's power to restrict certain forms of advertising.

Together, these cases show that, while the Court continues to proclaim its fidelity to the old tests based on narrow definitions of the specific subject-matter and essential function of trade marks, it is nonetheless aware that the scope of trade mark protection may sometimes be wider than those tests imply.

1.4 *The Community legislature's view of the functions of trade marks*

The two major items of Community legislation on trade marks are the Trade Mark Directive[34] and the Community Trade Mark Regulation.[35] What

---

general trend to strengthen the protection of intellectual property: 'Die Marke: Niedergang der Herkunftsfunktion?' (1996) 4 GRUR Int., 462 at 466.

[32] Cited in n. 14.

[33] Joined Cases C-427/93, C-429/93 and C-436/93 *Bristol-Myers Squibb and others v Paranova* [1996] ECR I-3457, at paras 75 and 76; Joined Cases C-71/94, C-72/94 and C-73/94 *Eurim-Pharm v Beiersdorf and others* [1996] ECR I-3603, at paras 65 and 66; and Case C-232/94 *MPA Pharma v Rhône-Poulenc* [1996] ECR I-3671, at paras 46 and 47.

[34] Council Directive 89/104, cited in n. 9.

[35] Council Reg. No. 40/94, cited in n. 8.

conception of the trade mark's functions has been reflected in the work of the legislature? As in the case of the Court, the conclusion must be that the emphasis is placed on the origin function, but that the ancillary functions are not disregarded. The preamble to both the Directive and the Regulation states that the function of a trade mark is 'in particular to guarantee the trade mark as an indication of origin'.[36] The words 'in particular' suggest that the origin function is not the only relevant function. That is borne out by the provisions, cited above, on the extended protection granted to trade marks with a reputation, on the licensing of trade marks, both national and Community, and on the assignment of Community trade marks.[37] The abandonment of international exhaustion is also difficult to explain or justify on the basis of the origin function.[38]

2. TRADE MARK CONFLICTS IN THE EUROPEAN COMMUNITY

2.1 *The nature of the problem*

A trade mark can only fulfil its function as a guarantee of origin if it is exclusive.[39] The trade mark owner must be able to prevent other undertakings from using, in the territory in which he owns the mark, an identical or confusingly similar trade mark ('a conflicting mark') in relation to identical or similar goods or services. At national level, trade mark conflicts have traditionally been resolved on the basis of seniority: the earlier mark prevails over the more recent one. Registration systems have simplified matters considerably. They have brought transparency and order to the marketplace. Undertakings register their trade marks, whenever possible, and so gain official recognition of their exclusive rights. Registration constitutes universal notice of the existence of the exclusive right, and serves as a basis for preventing other undertakings from using or registering conflicting trade marks. Unregistered trade marks are also protected in many legal systems, though the extent of this protection varies from country to country.

Trade mark law has traditionally operated on the basis of the principle of territoriality. In determining whether an earlier, conflicting right exists,

---

[36] See the tenth recital in the preamble to the Directive and the seventh recital in the preamble to the Regulation.

[37] See nn. 8, 9, and 13 and the related text.   [38] See section 6.4.2.2 of Chap. 7.

[39] See the opinion of Advocate General Jacobs in *HAG II* (cited in n. 23), at para. 19: ' . . . A trade mark can only fulfil that role [i.e. as an indicator of origin] if it is exclusive. Once the proprietor is forced to share the mark with a competitor, he loses control over the goodwill associated with the mark. The reputation of his own goods will be harmed if the competitor sells inferior goods. From the consumer's point of view, equally undesirable consequences will ensue, because the clarity of the signal transmitted by the trade mark will be impaired. The consumer will be confused and misled.'

courts and registries have generally been concerned only with the situation within their own national frontiers. The United Kingdom authorities, for example, will not as a rule refuse to allow someone to register a trade mark on the ground that a confusingly similar mark has been registered by a different person in Germany or the United States.[40] As a result of this territorial approach, it frequently happens that separate, unconnected undertakings own conflicting trade marks in different Member States of the European Community. As long as each undertaking's products remain within national frontiers, no major problem arises. Tourists and cross-border shoppers may be misled as to the origin of goods, but that is unavoidable. The matter becomes more serious when the products of one of the undertakings are shipped to the territory of the other undertaking, either directly or by a parallel importer. Suppose, for example, that Company Z owns the trade mark ZING for cigarette lighters in France and Company Y (which has no connection with Company Z) owns the trade mark YING for matches in Germany. Let us accept for the sake of the argument that cigarette lighters and matches are similar products, that ZING and YING are similar trade marks, and that these similarities are sufficient to give rise to a likelihood of confusion on the part of consumers.[41] Company Z will doubtless bring trade mark infringement proceedings against persons who import and sell YING matches in France. If Company Z succeeds, a barrier to the free movement of goods will exist. If it fails, the specific subject-matter and essential function of its trade mark will be compromised. Consumers will attribute responsibility for YING matches to the makers of ZING lighters.

The scale of this problem should not be underestimated. Beier estimated that 300,000 trade mark conflicts existed in the European Community in 1978. Since then, six more countries have acceded to the European Community and the number of trade mark conflicts has presumably increased. Before we examine how Community law deals with such conflicts, it must be emphasised that the exhaustion principle provides a ready solution in so far as the conflicting trade marks are owned by connected undertakings (e.g. parent and subsidiary, subsidiaries of a common parent, licensor and licensee, manufacturer and distributor, and so forth). These issues are dealt with in Chapter 7 on the exhaustion of rights. In this section we are dealing

---

[40] There is an exception to this rule as regards 'well-known trade marks' within the meaning of Art. 6 *bis* of the Paris Convention for the Protection of Industrial Property: see ss. 6(1)(c), 55 and 56 of the Trade Marks Act 1994, as amended by the Patents and Trade Marks (World Trade Organization) Regs 1999 (SI 1999/1899).

[41] It must be remembered that the similarity of the goods and the similarity of the trade marks are interdependent criteria, in the sense that a lesser degree of similarity of the goods may be offset by a greater degree of similarity of the marks, and vice versa: Case C-39/97 *Canon v Metro-Goldwyn-Meyer* [1998] ECR I-5507, at para. 17.

with the situation that arises when conflicting trade marks are owned by unconnected undertakings.

2.2 The rise and fall of the doctrine of common origin

2.2.1 The concept of common origin

There are two ways in which conflicting trade marks may come to be owned by separate undertakings in different Member States. Either the trade marks may be of common origin or they may have been created independently.

In the first situation, a firm registers a trade mark in a number of Member States and later disposes of one of the registrations by way of an assignment. That may happen when a firm takes a decision, on business grounds, to withdraw from a particular market; rather than abandon whatever goodwill it has built up in that market, it transfers that goodwill to another firm by selling its trade mark rights in that territory. Unity of ownership of a trade mark may also be severed by an act of expropriation (an unusual event which normally happens only after a war) or as a consequence of insolvency.

In the second situation, two firms, quite by chance, hit on similar names for similar products. At first sight, that may seem an unlikely coincidence. In fact, such accidental trade mark conflicts occur rather frequently because many firms tend to choose semi-descriptive names for their products. A fondness for using Latin and Greek roots in the creation of trade marks also results in the invention of similar trade marks for similar products.

In the first type of situation the conflicting trade marks will, as a rule, be identical and be used in relation to identical products. In the second type of situation the conflicting trade marks are more likely to be similar, rather than identical.

2.2.2 The birth of the doctrine of common origin: Sirena v Eda and HAG I

At one time the Court of Justice attributed decisive importance to the common origin of conflicting trade marks. It did so on the basis of a theory known as the doctrine of common origin, which was adopted in *HAG I* in 1974 and abandoned in *HAG II* 16 years later.

The first traces of the doctrine of common origin emerged three years before *HAG I*, in *Sirena v Eda*. That case concerned the trade mark 'Prep', which was originally owned by the American company Mark Allen in Italy and Germany. In 1937 Mark Allen assigned the Italian registration to Sirena. At an unspecified point in time Mark Allen licensed a German company to use the trade mark in Germany. When the German licensee's goods, bearing the trade mark 'Prep', appeared on the Italian market,

Sirena brought trade mark infringement proceedings against the importer and resellers (Eda and others). The Italian court sought a preliminary ruling from the Court of Justice on the interpretation of the competition rules of the Treaty.

The Court ruled in effect that Article 81 of the Treaty applied to an agreement or series of agreements which led to a trade mark being owned by different persons in different Member States. The Court made it clear that the effect of the applicability of Article 81 was that the various persons who had acquired the trade mark, or the right to use it, under such agreements could not oppose parallel imports of each other's trade-marked products. That was so even if the agreements had been concluded before the entry into force of the Treaty, provided that they continued to produce effects after that date.

The Court's ruling was given on the basis that there was no continuing business relationship between Sirena and the German licensee or between Sirena and Mark Allen. Rather, it seems to have been assumed that the owners of the trade mark 'Prep' in Germany and Italy were genuinely separate undertakings and had been so for some time. Thus German 'Prep' and Italian 'Prep' might have been two completely different products, sharing nothing more than the name; in which case Italian consumers expecting to find the qualities they had come to associate with 'Prep' might have been disappointed if they unwittingly bought the imported product. Moreover, the goodwill associated with the trade mark—which in Italy belonged to Sirena—might have been damaged if the German licensee's products were inferior.[42]

Those defects in the Court's judgment were obvious to many commentators at the time and inspired widespread criticism.[43] Particularly objectionable was the manner in which the Court appeared to give retroactive effect to Article 81, by applying it to agreements concluded long before the entry into force of the Treaty. Fortunately, that aspect of the ruling was corrected five years later in the *EMI v CBS* cases,[44] where the Court held that Article 81 did not apply to agreements no longer in force unless the persons concerned continued to engage in some form of concerted practice and coordination; the mere exercise of national trade mark rights by the various owners of the mark was not sufficient to produce that effect.[45]

---

[42] Even if the German licensee's product were of superior quality, it could still damage Sirena's goodwill because the trade mark might lose its reputation for consistent quality. Unpredictable variations in quality tend to create consumer dissatisfaction.

[43] See the list of articles cited by H. Ullrich, in 'The Impact of the *Sirena* Decision on National Trademark Rights' (1972) IIC 193 (footnote 3) and 218. Ullrich himself defends the decision. See also W. Mak, 'Trademarks and the European Common Market' (1975) 6 IIC 29.

[44] Case 51/75 *EMI Records v CBS United Kingdom* [1976] ECR 811. See also two related judgments of the same date involving other CBS subsidiaries.

[45] At paras 31 and 32 of the judgment.

In *HAG I* there was no possibility of applying Article 81 because owner-ship of the trade mark was split up, not by way of a contractual assignment, but as a result of an act of expropriation carried out by governmental authorities.

The trade mark HAG, used for decaffeinated coffee, was originally owned by a German company (HAG Bremen) in Germany and several other countries, including Belgium and Luxembourg. At the end of the Second World War, HAG Bremen's entire assets in Belgium and Luxembourg, including its trade mark rights in those countries, were sequestrated as enemy property. In 1947 the trade marks were sold to a firm called Van Oevelen. In 1971 they were assigned to Van Zuylen. In 1972 HAG Bremen began exporting coffee to Luxembourg under the HAG trade mark. Van Zuylen commenced infringement proceedings before a Luxembourg court, which asked the Court of Justice to give a preliminary ruling on the interpretation of the Treaty rules on competition (Art. 81) and on the free movement of goods. The Court observed that Article 81 was inapplicable, since the trade mark had not been split up as a result of a contractual assignment and there was 'no legal, financial, technical or economic link' between HAG Bremen and Van Zuylen.[46]

As regards the free movement of goods, the Court gave the following ruling: 'To prohibit the marketing in one Member State of a product legally bearing a trade mark in another Member State for the sole reason that an identical trade mark, having the same origin, exists in the first State, is incompatible with the provisions for the free movement of goods within the Common Market.'

The implications of the ruling were alarming. It seemed to mean that, whenever a trade mark had at some point in history belonged to the same person in different Member States and had for some reason become the property of different persons, they were all entitled to use it in any of the countries concerned.

The judgment in *HAG I* was the object of almost unanimous criticism at the time.[47] Like the ruling in *Sirena v Eda*, it was potentially fatal to the

---

[46] At para. 14 of the judgment.

[47] See, e.g., S. P. Ladas, 'The Court of Justice of the European Community and the *HAG* Case' (1974) 3 IIC 302; W. Alexander, 'Some Comments on the *Café HAG* Judgment' (1974) CML Rev. 387; W. R. Cornish, 'Trade Marks, Consumer Confusion and the Common Market' (1975) 38 MLR 329; D. C. Maday, 'The *HAG* and *Negram* Decisions of the European Court of Justice' (1975) 65 TMR 34; K. Lewis, '*Café HAG*: A Critical Comment' (1975) EL Rev. 71; W. Mak, 'Waren-zeichen und der gemeinsame Markt' (1975) GRUR Int. 118; A. Kraft, 'Die Stellung des Europäischen Gerichthofs zum Warenzeichen im Lichte des HAG-Urteils' (1975) GRUR Int. 283; W. Tilmann, 'Das markenrechtliche Importverbot bei "ursprungsgleichen" Auslandsmar-ken' (1975) RIW/AWD 479; J.-J. Burst and R. Kovar, 'Sur une jurisprudence récente de la Cour de justice des Communautés européennes en matière de propriété industrielle' (1975) *La Semaine Juridique, Edition commerce et industries,* No. 18, *Etudes et commentaires,* No. 11728, 225; M. Ridolfi, 'Begrenzung des Warenzeichenschutzes im gemeinsamen Markt:

origin function of trade marks and therefore detrimental to the interests of consumers, who would inevitably confuse goods bearing the same trade mark but emanating from different sources. A suggestion made by the Court[48] that consumers could be informed about the different origin of identical goods bearing identical trade marks by means of a notice on the packaging hardly deserves to be taken seriously.[49]

Although the Court piously asserted that 'the Treaty does not affect the existence of rights recognised by the legislation of a Member State in matters of industrial and commercial property', the ruling effectively destroyed Van Zuylen's property rights. Worse still, *HAG I*, like *Sirena v Eda*, attempted to give certain provisions of the Treaty a retroactive effect that could never have been intended by the authors of the Treaty. Van Oevelen, in 1947, (like Sirena in 1937) paid valuable consideration for the trade mark under a transaction that was undoubtedly valid under Belgian and Luxembourg law at the time. They cannot have anticipated that the EEC Treaty would come along in 1958 and wipe out not just their initial investment but all their subsequent efforts to preserve the reputation of the mark. As for Van Zuylen, if they considered the implications of the Treaty when they purchased the mark in 1971, they were surely entitled to assume that they were acquiring exactly the kind of property rights that Article 30 expressly safeguarded. Moreover, if Van Oevelen held a valid exclusive right in 1971, they were entitled to pass on an equally valid right to a future purchaser. To hold otherwise would have made Van Oevelen's trade mark rights unsaleable, which again was wrong in principle.

2.2.3 Terrapin v Terranova: *free movement denied where the conflicting marks are of independent origin*

In *HAG I* the Court failed to explain why the common origin of trade mark rights should be relevant. The rationale of the judgment was that

---

Kaffee-HAG-Entscheidung des EuGH' (1975) RIW/AWD 153. The judgment was defended by: H. Johannes, 'Zum Kaffee-HAG-Urteil des Gerichtshofes der Europäischen Gemeinschaften' (1975) GRUR Int. 111; H. Johannes and G. Wright, 'In Defence of Café HAG' (1976) EL Rev. 230; B. Schwab, 'Der freie Verkehr von Markenwaren im Lichte der Rechtsprechung des Gerichtshofs der Europäischen Gemeinschaften' (1975) GRUR Int. 73; F. W. Fricke, 'Die Rechtsprechung des Gerichtshofes der Europäischen Gemeinschaften zur Koexistenz von identischen oder verwechslungsfähigen nicht-ursprungsgleichen Warenzeichen innerhalb des gemeinsamen Marktes' (1977) No. 1 *Wettbewerb in Recht und Praxis* 7; H. J. Herrmann, 'Nationales Warenzeichenrecht und freier Warenverkehr in den Europäischen Gemeinschaften' (1976) 40 Rabel Z 272; F. G. Jacobs, 'Industrial Property and the EEC Treaty: A Reply' (1975) 24 ICLQ 643.

[48] At para. 14 of the judgment.

[49] One author thought the suggestion was 'better regarded as naïve than disingenuous': W. R. Cornish, op. cit. (n. 47), at 330. For a detailed study of the subject of additional distinguishing matter, see F.-K. Beier, 'Trade Mark Conflicts in the Common Market: Can They Be Solved by Means of Distinguishing Additions?' (1978) 9 IIC 221.

separately owned conflicting trade marks contributed to the partitioning of markets.[50] That effect does not, of course, depend on whether the conflicting trade marks have a common origin. If market integration was so important and if confusion amongst consumers could be prevented by means of labelling, why not go one step further and apply the logic of *HAG I* to all trade mark conflicts, regardless of whether the marks had a common origin? Some authors feared that such an approach would come.[51] Some even advocated it.[52]

The chance to take such a step came in *Terrapin v Terranova*. A British company trading under the name 'Terrapin (Overseas) Ltd' manufactured prefabricated houses, which it sold under the trade mark 'Terrapin'. A German company trading under the name 'Terranova Industrie C. A. Kapferer & Co' manufactured plaster for facades and other construction materials. It had registered, for those products, the trade marks 'Terra', 'Terra Fabrikate' and 'Terranova' in Germany. The British company's attempt to register the trade mark 'Terrapin' in Germany was opposed, successfully, by the German company, which managed to persuade the *Bundespatentgericht* (Federal Patent Court) that there was a risk of confusion between the two marks. The German company subsequently commenced proceedings to obtain a court order prohibiting the British company from using the trade mark 'Terrapin' in Germany. The case reached the *Bundesgerichtshof* (Federal Supreme Court), which considered the two marks confusingly similar and asked the Court of Justice for a preliminary ruling on the question whether, essentially, an undertaking established in one Member State could rely on its trade mark rights in that country to prevent the importation of goods produced by an undertaking in another Member State with a trade mark which was confusingly similar to the first undertaking's trade mark, where there were no connections between the two undertakings and their trade mark rights had arisen independently of each other.

The Court replied to that question in the affirmative, observing that, if 'in such a case the principle of free movement were to prevail over the protection given by the respective national laws, the specific objective of industrial and commercial property rights would be undermined'.[53] Few commentators would disagree that that was the correct answer to the question put by the *Bundesgerichtshof*.

---

[50] See paras 11 and 13 of the judgment.

[51] Maday, op. cit. (n. 47), at 41; Mak, op. cit. (n. 47), at 123; Kraft, op. cit. (n. 47), at 289 *et seq.*

[52] Notably Johannes (see the articles cited in n. 47); see also Fricke, op. cit. (n. 47).

[53] At para. 7 of the judgment. The expression 'specific objective' is just an alternative translation of 'object spécifique', which is of course normally rendered as 'specific subject-matter' in English.

In other respects, the *Terrapin v Terranova* litigation must provoke misgivings. In the first place, the Court of Justice made a wholly unconvincing attempt to justify *ex post facto* the doctrine of common origin, observing that free movement must prevail 'when the right relied on is the result of subdivision, either by voluntary act or as a result of public constraint, of a trade mark right which originally belonged to one and the same proprietor' because in those cases 'the basic function of the trade mark to guarantee to consumers that the product has the same origin is already undermined by the subdivision of the original right'.[54] The flaw in that argument is that it disregards the territoriality of trade marks; the question whether the origin function of a trade mark is compromised must be considered in relation to each of the territories in which it is protected. As Advocate General Jacobs was to point out in *HAG II*, the HAG trade mark was throughout its history, in each of the territories in which it was used, 'in the exclusive ownership of a single person who had the power either to build up the goodwill associated with it by maintaining the quality of the product or to destroy that goodwill by allowing the quality to deteriorate'.[55] The origin function was only compromised by the Court's judgment in *HAG I*, which allowed the products of two distinct undertakings to be placed on the market in the same territory under identical trade marks. Until that point the only consumers who might be misled as to the origin of coffee bearing the HAG trade mark were transnational consumers, who moved across the border separating Germany from Belgium and Luxembourg. But as Advocate General Jacobs pointed out, such persons are always likely to be confused when conflicting marks are owned by different persons in different countries (and regardless of whether the marks have a common origin). The unavoidable confusion of some is not an argument for inflicting similar confusion on all.[56]

The second unsatisfactory aspect of the *Terrapin* case is that, from a common sense point of view, it is difficult to see why the two marks could not coexist, in view of the modest degree of similarity between the marks and between the products. That aspect will be addressed in a later section.

For fourteen years, then, it seemed that the solution to trade mark conflicts depended on whether the trade marks had a common origin. If at some point in history someone had created a trade mark and registered it in more than one of the countries that eventually became EC Member States and if the two registrations came to be owned by different persons, with or without the consent of the original owner, free movement prevailed.

---

[54] At para. 6 of the judgment.
[55] *HAG II* (cited in n. 23), at para. 24 of the Advocate General's opinion. See also U. Löwenheim, 'Trade Marks and European Community Law' (1978) 9 IIC 422, 426.
[56] At para. 25 of the opinion.

If by chance confusingly similar trade marks were created independently in different Member States, each trade mark proprietor could rely on his trade mark to exclude from his territory goods on which the conflicting trade mark had been placed by the other proprietor. There was no logical reason for such a distinction. Indeed, as the *HAG* and *Terrapin v Terranova* cases show, the arguments against free movement are likely to be stronger in the case of trade marks of common origin (because of the automatic identity or near identity of the trade marks and the goods) than in the case of accidental conflicts between trade marks created independently. In the latter type of case many of the supposed conflicts exist only in the imagination of over-vigilant trade mark owners and of judges who underestimate the intelligence of consumers. *Terrapin v Terranova* may well be an example.

2.2.4 HAG II: *the abandonment of the doctrine of common origin*

In 1990 the Court of Justice had occasion to reconsider the doctrine of common origin when the *HAG* case came back to the Court, this time with the facts neatly reversed. Ownership of the HAG mark in Belgium and Luxembourg had by now passed into the hands of CNL Sucal, a subsidiary of Jacobs-Suchard, which was the market leader in coffee, except of course decaffeinated coffee. In that sector the HAG name still had a unique magic, especially in Germany, which made it extremely difficult for any trader to penetrate the German market in decaffeinated coffee under a different trade mark.

Having acquired ownership of the HAG trade mark in Belgium and Luxembourg, Jacobs-Suchard started to market its own version of HAG decaffeinated coffee in Germany. Not surprisingly, HAG Bremen commenced infringement proceedings in the German courts against the Jacobs-Suchard subsidiary. The case was eventually referred to the Court of Justice. There were basically four options available to the Court.

The first option would have been to confirm the doctrine of common origin and rule that it applied in both directions. That would mean not only that the original owner of the trade mark could use it in the territories in which it had been expropriated but also that the person who had acquired it in those territories could use it in the territories in which it still belonged to the original owner.

The second option would have been to confirm the doctrine but limit its scope by saying that the owner of the mark in the expropriated territories could not use it in the territories belonging to the original owner. The justification (highly dubious) for that approach would have been that, while HAG Bremen had never consented to the subdivision of the rights in the HAG trade mark, all those who had owned the trade mark in Belgium and Luxembourg after the expropriation (i.e. the Belgian government, Van

Oevelen, Van Zuylen and finally CNL Sucal) voluntarily acquired a fragmented right and were, so to speak, willing participants in, or beneficiaries of, the subdivision of the trade mark. That solution would presumably enjoy the support of anyone who regarded *Sirena v Eda* as correctly decided.

The third option was simply to abandon the doctrine of common origin altogether and accept that, while trade barriers due to the divided ownership of a trade mark are regrettable in a common market, realism commands that, once a trade mark has been fragmented, each owner must enjoy exclusive use of the trade mark in his territory—at least when the fragmentation took place as a result of an expropriation carried out by a government before the common market was even dreamt of.

The fourth option, which hardly merited serious consideration, was to overrule *Terrapin v Terranova* and institute a Community-wide doctrine of honest concurrent user, under which anyone with a legitimate right to a trade mark in a Member State might market his products under the trade mark throughout the Community, using additional distinguishing matter in the event of a conflict with a trade mark owned by someone else.

The Court chose the third option. It was surely right to do so, as most commentators have recognised.[57] Indeed, once the essential function of trade marks in a market economy had been correctly analysed, no other solution could be seriously contemplated. If the same trade mark could be used on identical goods in the same territory by two separate and unrelated persons, neither of them would be able to defend the goodwill associated with the trade mark and consumers would be unable to rely on the trade mark as an indicator of the commercial origin of the trade-marked goods.

2.2.5 Ideal Standard: *no free movement where the conflicting trade marks were split up by a contractual assignment*

One important question left open by *HAG II* was whether the same solution should apply when the ownership a trade mark had been split up as a result,

---

[57] See, e.g., P. Oliver, 'Of Split Trade Marks and Common Markets' (1991) 54 MLR 587; G. Metaxas-Marangidis, '*HAG II*: A New Taste from the Old Label' (1991) EL Rev. 128; R. Joliet in collaboration with D. T. Keeling, 'Trade Mark Law and the Free Movement of Goods: The Overruling of the Judgment in *HAG I*' (1991) 22 IIC 303; W. A. Rothnie, '*HAG II*: Putting the Common Origin Doctrine to Sleep' [1991] EIPR 24; C. Shelley, 'Abolition of the Doctrine of Common Origin: Some Reflections on *HAG II* and Its Implications' (1991) *European Business Law Review* 85; M.-A. Hermitte, (1991) *Journal du Droit International* 490; A. Strowel, 'Droit des marques et libre circulation des marchandises; exit de la doctrine de l'origine commune' (1991) 81 *Revue de Droit Intellectuel: L'ingénieur-conseil* 193; R. Kovar, 'Les fonctions des marques selon la Cour de justice des Communautés européennes après l'arrêt *HAG II*' (1991) *Revue de Jurisprudence de Droit des Affaires* 751; D. Martin, 'Erreur avouée est à moitié pardonnée . . . ' (1991) *Revue de jurisprudence de Liège, Mons et Bruxelles* 254; S. Martínez Lage, 'Vuelco jurisprudencial en el Derecho de marcas: de *HAG I* a *HAG II*' (1990) No. 87 B. 58 noviembre 90 *Gaceta Jurídica de la CEE* 1.

not of a governmental act such as expropriation, but of a contractual assignment. The Court answered that question, affirmatively, four years later in *IHT Internationale Heiztechnik v Ideal Standard*.[58] The facts were rather complicated. The trade mark 'Ideal Standard' was previously owned by the American Standard Group, through its subsidiary companies, in France and Germany, for both sanitary fittings and heating equipment. A series of transactions took place, as a result of which American Standard retained control of the French registration of the 'Ideal Standard' mark for sanitary fittings and of the German registrations for both sanitary fittings and heating equipment, while the French registration for heating equipment was assigned to Compagnie Internationale de Chauffage (CICh). CICh began to market in Germany, through its German subsidiary IHT, heating equipment bearing the trade mark 'Ideal Standard' which CICh had manufactured in France. Ideal Standard GmbH (the German subsidiary of American Standard) brought trade mark infringement proceedings against IHT.

Although Ideal Standard GmbH had retained the registration of the trade mark in Germany for both sanitary fittings and heating equipment, it had ceased manufacturing heating equipment in 1976 and its action for infringement was based on its ownership of the mark for sanitary fittings. There was some dispute between the parties as to whether sanitary fittings and heating equipment were similar products. The Court of Justice insisted that that was essentially an issue for the national court to determine on the basis of its own domestic trade mark law, subject to the proviso that it must not carry out the assessment in an arbitrary manner, in view of the terms of the second sentence of Article 30 of the Treaty. The Court also stressed that a restriction on imports of the French products would not be justified if the national court concluded that the products were not similar.[59]

More delicate was the general question whether goods produced by one of the owners of a trade mark that had been split up by a contractual assignment should be allowed to circulate, under the trade mark, in a territory in which the trade mark belonged to the other owner. That question led to much agonising in a long, not always coherent, opinion by Advocate General Gulmann. In the end, the Advocate General came down in favour of free movement. The same view had been taken by the Commission, which based its approach on a straightforward application of the exhaustion principle in which the paramount criterion was consent, by the assignor of the trade mark, to its use by the assignee in part of the common market. Under that theory American Standard had, by allowing

---

[58] Case C-9/93 [1994] ECR I-2789.
[59] At para. 19 of the judgment. Presumably if the trade mark had a reputation in Germany, a restriction on imports might be justified under the German legislation implementing Art. 5(2) of the Trade Mark Directive. The Court seems to have overlooked that point.

CICh to market goods bearing the trade mark in France, exhausted its right throughout the common market and could not prevent the export of the trade-marked goods to other Member States.[60]

The Court did not follow the advice of the Commission and the Advocate General. Instead, it ruled in effect that where an undertaking which originally owned a trade mark in Member States A and B retains control of the trade mark in Member State A but voluntarily assigns it to an unrelated undertaking in Member State B, it may oppose the sale in Member State A of goods bearing the trade mark which have been manufactured in Member State B by the assignee of the trade mark.

The result reached by the Court is, it is submitted, correct. The logic of *HAG II* is surely transposable to the facts of *Ideal Standard*.[61] As already noted, the confusion suffered by consumers when identical trade marks are used in connection with identical or similar products in the same territory by unrelated undertakings does not depend on whether the marks are of common or independent origin. By the same token, if the trade marks are of common origin, consumer confusion does not depend on whether ownership of the marks was split up as a result of an act of expropriation or a contractual assignment.

The real basis of the Court's judgment was the inability of the respective owners of the trade mark to control the quality of each other's products.[62] That part of the Court's reasoning is impeccable. Other aspects of its analysis are open to criticism. In particular, its attempt to deal with the Commission's consent-based approach to the exhaustion principle is unconvincing and verges on the disingenuous. The Court rejected the Commission's argument with these remarks:

'The consent implicit in any assignment is not the consent required for application of the doctrine of exhaustion of rights. For that, the owner of the right in the importing State must, directly or indirectly, be able to determine the products to which the trade mark may be affixed in the exporting State and to control their quality. That power is lost if, by assignment, control over the trade mark is surrendered to a third party having no economic link with the assignor.'[63]

It would be gratifying to believe that all problems in this field could be solved on the basis of the right-holder's consent to marketing in the common market. The illusion that such a simple, easy-to-use criterion can always produce the right result was doubtless encouraged by judgments such as *HAG II* and *Pharmon v Hoechst*,[64] in which the total absence

---

[60] See para. 42 of the judgment.
[61] See G. F. Kunze, 'Waiting for *Sirena II*—Trademark Assignment in the Case Law of the European Court of Justice' (1991) 22 IIC 319.
[62] See paras 41 and 43 of the judgment.   [63] At para. 43 of the judgment.
[64] Case 19/84 [1985] ECR 2281.

of consent, on the part of the right-holder, simply highlighted the injustice that would ensue if the right-holder were prevented from enforcing his right against imported goods. The *Ideal Standard* case demonstrates that consent is not the only relevant criterion and that in certain circumstances the purpose, function or—for those who prefer jargon—specific subject-matter of the intellectual property right is the decisive element. That, it is submitted, is what the Court should have recognised in *Ideal Standard* instead of attempting to square the theory of exhaustion with the facts of the case by means of a definition of consent 'so idiosyncratic that it cannot be regarded as consent in any normal sense'.[65]

Notwithstanding the Court's willingness, in the *Ideal Standard* case, to tolerate obstacles to free movement caused by the contractual splitting of trade mark rights, trade mark owners would be well advised to exercise caution before entering into such arrangements. In the first place, it should be obvious that in an age when more and more consumers regularly travel beyond their national frontiers, damage done to the reputation of a trade mark in one country will have repercussions in other countries; if the assignee of a trade mark markets shoddy goods in Member State A, the reputation of the trade mark in Member State B is likely to suffer even though the assignee's goods never physically leave Member State A. Secondly, the possible implications of Article 81 of the Treaty are not entirely clear. In *Ideal Standard* the Court entered an important caveat regarding the treatment of trade mark assignments under Community competition law. It observed that:

. . . where undertakings independent of each other make trade-mark assignments following a market-sharing agreement, the prohibition of anti-competitive agreements under Article [81] applies and assignments which give effect to that agreement are consequently void. However, ... that rule and the accompanying sanction cannot be applied mechanically to every assignment. Before a trade-mark assignment can be treated as giving effect to an agreement prohibited under Article [81], it is necessary to analyse the context, the commitments underlying the assignment, the intention of the parties and the consideration for the assignment.[66]

It is far from certain what the Court meant by that. It seems safe to venture that the Court implicitly overruled *Sirena v Eda* and that the retroactive application of Article 81 to assignments consummated before the entry into force of the Treaty is now out of the question. The fate of assignments made after that date is less clear.

When X, the owner of a trade mark in Member States A, B, and C assigns the trade mark to Y and Z in Member States A and B respectively and retains

[65] P. Oliver, *The Free Movement of Goods*, 3rd edn, Sweet & Maxwell, London, 1996, p. 283.
[66] At para. 59 of the judgment.

the trade mark in Member State C, it is difficult not to see that as evidence of a market-sharing agreement. The very act of splitting up a trade mark raises a presumption that the parties' aim is to split up markets. There may be circumstances in which the presumption can be rebutted, but they are not easy to imagine. Curiously, the *Ideal Standard* case may provide an example. American Standard had withdrawn from the heating sector in both France and Germany, and had decided to concentrate on the sanitary sector. In an attempt to make the best of a bad situation it sold not just the production plants of its loss-making heating division in France but also the French trade mark rights in the name 'Ideal Standard'. From that moment the trade mark was split up *within* France: for heating equipment it belonged to CICh, while American Standard retained it for sanitary equipment. That splitting of the trade mark within France was risky from American Standard's point of view, because their reputation as manufacturers of sanitary equipment might have suffered if poor-quality heating equipment were produced under the 'Ideal Standard' trade mark by CICh, whose activities could not be controlled by American Standard. (The same risk was, of course, taken by CICh.) Arguably, the splitting of the mark within France was undesirable from the point of view of French consumers, who might be confused as to the origin of the various goods (heating equipment and sanitary fittings) bearing the 'Ideal Standard' trade mark. Be that as it may, the fact remains that French law tolerated such a situation, whereas German law did not.[67] It was perfectly natural therefore that American Standard should attempt to prevent CICh's heating equipment from circulating on the German market. It was simply accepting the consequences of a disparity between French and German trade mark law. German law, unlike French law, did not allow it to sell its goodwill in the heating sector separately from its goodwill in the sanitary sector. Having been prevented from selling that goodwill, it should not be required to give it away, in the name of the free movement of goods or competition law.

The above analysis shows that, whatever American Standard and CICh were attempting to achieve through their transactions in the 'Ideal Standard' trade mark, their aim was not to split up the Community market in heating equipment. The case is thus an example—probably a rare one—of a situation in which a trade mark owner may assign a trade mark in Member

---

[67] See para. 52 of the judgment, where the Court stated: 'French law, which governs the assignment in question here, permits assignment of trade marks confined to certain products, with the result that similar products from different sources may be in circulation on French territory under the same trade mark, whereas German law, by prohibiting assignments of trade marks confined to certain products, seeks to prevent such co-existence. The effect of IHT's argument, if it were accepted, would be to extend to the importing State whose law opposes such co-existence the solution prevailing in the exporting State despite the nature of the rights in question.'

State A to an unrelated undertaking, while retaining it in Member State B, without infringing Article 81 of the Treaty.

When such an assignment does infringe Article 81, the consequences of that breach are no longer, in the light of the *Ideal Standard* judgment, what they appeared to be under the old case law. In *Sirena v Eda* the Court implied that, where a trade mark is split up by contractual assignment, goods on which the trade mark is placed by the various parties to the assignment may circulate in any territory in which the trade mark is owned by one of the other parties, regardless of whether the parties are able to control the quality of each other's goods. The problem with that approach is that it disregarded the essential function of the trade mark and meant that consumers would no longer be able to rely on the trade mark as guaranteeing that all goods bearing the trade mark, at least within a particular Member State, emanate from the same source.

In *Ideal Standard* the logic of the Court's interpretation of Articles 28 and 30 was founded on the assumption that similar goods emanating from different sources but bearing the same trade mark should not be present on the same market since that would expose consumers to unnecessary confusion. If that assumption was so important for the interpretation of Articles 28 and 30, it would have been absurd for the Court to abandon it when interpreting Article 81. The need for a coherent approach to the Treaty provisions on free movement and the competition rules of the Treaty is self-evident. The Court attempted to ensure the necessary coherence by holding that a trade mark assignment designed to give effect to a market-sharing agreement, instead of giving rise to the sort of free-for-all envisaged in *Sirena v Eda*, is simply void.[68]

The Court did not dwell on the consequences of voidness. Perhaps it was not aware of the difficulties raised by its *obiter dictum*. In theory, if an assignment is void, the assigned trade mark remains the property of the assignor and its use by the assignee violates the trade mark rights of the assignor. However, the assignor would presumably be estopped from claiming damages from the assignee for infringements that have already taken place, though arguably he might be able to seek (a) an injunction preventing the assignee from continuing to use the mark and (b) an order for the mark to be reassigned to him. In that case, any consideration paid for the assignment would presumably have to be repaid on grounds of unjust enrichment. However, it would hardly be equitable to order repayment of the whole sum if the assignee had benefited from the use of the mark for a lengthy period. Perhaps, therefore, the assignor would be allowed to retain a proportion of the consideration as a royalty for the use of the trade mark during the period when the assignment was treated as valid.

---

[68] At para. 59 of the judgment.

If the assignor's goods are shipped to the territory of the assignee either by the assignor himself or by a third party, even greater problems ensue. An infringement action commenced by the assignee against the assignor, the importer, or a reseller would presumably fail on the ground that the assignee's title to the trade mark was bad, having been acquired through a void assignment. That would raise the spectre of products emanating from different sources (the assignor and the assignee) circulating on the same market under the same trade mark—the very problem that the Court attempted to avoid in *Ideal Standard*. The national court would therefore have to take the necessary measures to ensure the reassignment of the trade mark to its original owner.

2.3 The likelihood of confusion: who decides and by what criteria?

2.3.1 Before the Trade Mark Directive

Essentially a trade mark entitles its proprietor to prevent others from using an identical mark for identical goods or a mark which, on account of the similarity of the marks and the similarity of the goods for which they are used, is likely to confuse consumers as to the origin of the goods.[69] That is of course an over-simplification and neglects the differences between national laws prior to harmonization.

In *Sirena v Eda* and the *HAG* cases the conflicting trade marks were identical, as were the goods for which they were registered and used. The issue of likelihood of confusion, due to the similarity of the trade marks and the goods, did not therefore arise.

When the trade marks are similar rather than identical (as in *Terranova v Terrapin*) or the goods are similar rather than identical (as in *Ideal Standard*), the following questions arise:

(1) Who is to decide whether there is a likelihood of confusion between the trade marks?
(2) What criteria are to be applied?
(3) Does Article 30 of the Treaty impose any limitations when the defendant's goods have been imported from another Member State?

Few would dispute that the answer to question (1) must in principle be 'the appropriate national court' (normally the court in which infringement proceedings are brought) and that the answer to question (2) was, in principle, prior to the harmonization effected by the Trade Mark Directive, 'the criteria provided by national law'.

---

[69] Cf. Art. 5(1) of the Trade Mark Directive and Art. 9(1) of the Community Trade Mark Regulation. See also Art. 16(1) of the Agreement on Trade-related Aspects of Intellectual Property Rights (TRIPS).

Certainly the Court of Justice could not be expected, either before or after harmonization, to give straightforward yes/no answers—under Article 234 of the Treaty—to questions as to whether there is a likelihood of confusion between specific trade marks. To hold otherwise would be to blur the distinction between the Community Court's role as an *interpreter* of the law, and the national court's role as the organ responsible for *applying* the law to the facts of the case.[70] It is equally clear that the basic criteria for determining whether trade marks and goods are similar could, in the absence of harmonization, only be those existing in national law. Apart from the obvious fact that no other criteria existed before harmonization, it would hardly be realistic to expect the national courts to use wholly different criteria depending on whether the alleged conflict was between two domestic trade marks or a domestic mark and one protected in another Member State.

As to the limits imposed by the Treaty on the national court's freedom in this area, the case law of the Court of Justice suggests that they are few in number; and that such as exist flow directly from the wording of the second sentence of Article 30.

The question was first aired, briefly, in *Terrapin v Terranova*.[71] In that case, the German court had found that there was a likelihood of confusion between the German and British trade marks, and it asked the Court of Justice whether in that event a prohibition on the importation of the British product was justified, having regard to the independent origin of the trade marks. The German court's finding of a likelihood of confusion was none the less questioned in the proceedings before the Court of Justice both by Terrapin and the Commission. The latter argued that German law concluded too readily that trade marks were confusingly similar and that 'the principles defining the risk of confusion must be reduced to the strict minimum necessary to guarantee the protection of national trade-mark rights'.[72]

The Court of Justice noted that the national court had not put any question to it regarding the likelihood of confusion and stressed that its reply to the question actually raised by the national court did not prejudice the question whether 'an allegation by one undertaking as to the similarity of products originating in different Member States and the risk of confusion of trade marks or commercial names legally protected in those States may perhaps involve the application of Community law with regard in particular to the second sentence of Article [30] of the Treaty'.[73] The Court then went on to observe that it was for the national court to enquire whether the

---

[70] On this point, see the eloquent comments of Advocate General Mayras in his opinion in *Terrapin v Terranova* (cited in n. 27), at 1073.
[71] Cited in n. 27.   [72] At 1058.   [73] At para. 4 of the judgment.

exercise of a trade mark might in a particular case constitute a means of arbitrary discrimination or a disguised restriction on trade between Member States; in particular, the national court must ascertain whether the rights in question were being exercised by the proprietor with the same strictness whatever the national origin of any possible infringer.

There is an obvious defect in the Court's approach: in suggesting that trade mark owners are subject to the prohibition of discrimination on grounds of nationality when deciding whether to sue infringers, the Court was forgetting that Articles 28 and 30 of the Treaty are addressed to the Member States, not to individual traders.[74] The measures prohibited by Article 28 are state measures. In the field of intellectual property rights the measure equivalent in effect to a quantitative restriction is the national legislation granting an exclusive right valid as against goods imported from another Member State or the judicial decision enforcing that right as against the imported goods. Thus the ban on arbitrary discrimination, under the second sentence of Article 30, applies to the legislative and judicial authorities of the Member States. The action of the right-holder in commencing infringement proceedings is not caught by Article 28 and is not therefore subject to the strictures of the second sentence of Article 30. The intellectual property owner whose rights are being infringed by 20 persons in five Member States is not obliged to sue them all or to sue an equal number from each Member State. He may pick and choose on the basis of the criteria used by any potential claimant: the chances of success, the resources of the potential defendants, the damage likely to be done by each defendant if unchecked, etc.[75]

Perhaps, the Court's greatest mistake in *Terrapin v Terranova* lay in the reductionist approach to Article 30 which led it to focus on the narrow wording of the second sentence of that provision instead of looking at the article as a whole. The Court seems to have assumed that any obstacle to trade caused by a finding that trade marks are confusingly similar is 'justified', within the meaning of the first sentence, unless it can be challenged as a 'means of arbitrary discrimination' or a 'disguised restriction' within the meaning of the second sentence. It would surely have been better to stress that a measure really must be 'justified' in order to benefit from

---

[74] See W. Alexander 'Droit communautaire et droit national des marques' (1976) 4 *Cahiers de Droit Européen* 431, at 444. See also R. Knöpfle, 'Die gewerblichen Schutzrechte und der gemeinschaftsrechtliche Grundsatz des freien Warenverkehrs' (1977) *Betriebsberater* Heft 22, 1073; this author questions whether Art. 28 should apply to infringement actions brought by individuals at all.

[75] For some interesting comments on the difficulty of applying the prohibition of discrimination in this context, see H. Sprick, 'Die Auswirkungen des EWG-Rechts auf den Schutz des Warenzeichens gegenüber nicht ursprungsgleichen, verwechslungsfähigen Warenzeichen' (1977) GRUR Int. Heft 8/9, 285, at 292; see also the article by Beier cited in footnote 44 of that article.

Article 30. The Court could also have developed its case law on the specific subject-matter and essential function of a trade mark, insisting that a trade-marked product from another Member State cannot be excluded unless there is a genuine risk of its being confused with another trader's product (or at least a risk of damage to the trade mark's reputation or distinctiveness). The Court could also have made use of the proportionality principle, according to which the overriding interests recognised in Article 30 must be pursued by the means least restrictive of intra-Community trade.

The problems encountered by Terrapin in entering the German market demonstrate the need for some input from Community law in the area of trade mark conflicts. More than 100 firms were using trade marks containing the element 'terra' in Germany in the building sector. 'Terra' seems to have been little more than a generic indicator of some kind of connection with the building industry. 'Terranova' was thus a weak trade mark, the first element of which was somewhat lacking in distinctiveness. It is difficult to understand how the German courts could see a risk of confusion between 'Terranova' and 'Terrapin' when the only point of similarity related to an element that possessed so little distinctiveness. To make matters worse, the *Bundesgerichtshof*, after obtaining a preliminary ruling from the Court of Justice, confirmed an injunction granted by a lower court which prohibited Terrapin not only from selling its products under the trade mark 'Terrapin' but also from using its business name ('Terrapin (Overseas) Ltd').[76] Such an extensive prohibition could surely not survive if tested against the principle of proportionality. The British company was totally shut out of the German market and could not even send a business letter to a German firm. It is questionable whether that exclusion is compatible with the Treaty or with Article 8 of the Paris Convention.[77]

Cases such as *Terrapin v Terranova* have led some commentators to suggest that the concept of confusingly similar trade marks is exceptionally broad under German law.[78] Certainly, it would be difficult to find a judgment in another legal system comparable to the one in which the *Bundespatentgericht* held that the English trade mark LUCKY WHIP was confusingly similar to the German trade mark 'Schöller-Nucki'.[79] In his opinion in *HAG II* Advocate General Jacobs described that as a decision which seemed 'to postulate a body of consumers afflicted with an acute form of dyslexia'.[80]

---

[76] For an English translation of the judgment of the *Bundesgerichtshof*, see (1978) 9 IIC 52.

[77] Art. 8 provides: 'A trade name shall be protected in all the countries of the Union without the obligation of filing or registration, whether or not it forms part of a trade mark.'

[78] See, for example, Alexander, op. cit. (n. 74), at 444. This view is disputed by F.-K. Beier, op. cit. (n. 11), at 772.

[79] BPatG, 28.3.1973, GRUR 1975, 74.

[80] *HAG II*, cited in n. 23, at para. 36 of the opinion.

In *Terrapin v Terranova* the *Bundesgerichtshof* had not put to the Court of Justice any question as to whether Articles 28 and 30 of the Treaty might affect the application of the domestic rules on likelihood of confusion where the alleged conflict was between a domestic trade mark and a trade mark lawfully used in another Member State. The few comments which the Court directed to that issue, at the prompting of the Commission, were clearly not intended to be exhaustive. In alerting the German court to the possibility of a discriminatory exercise of trade mark rights, the Court was saying as little as possible, hoping perhaps that it might be formally seized of the issue in a future reference.

If that was indeed the Court's hope, it was not rapidly fulfilled. The issue did not come before the Court until 17 years later in *Deutsche Renault v AUDI*.[81] Once again the referring court was the *Bundesgerichtshof*. The case concerned the similar names adopted by two car makers to designate the four-wheel-drive version of their vehicles. AUDI, a German firm, had been using the term 'quattro' since 1980 and had registered it as a trade mark in Germany. 'Quattro' is the Italian word for the numeral 'four'. In 1988 Renault, a French firm, launched a four-wheel-drive version of the Renault Espace under the name 'Espace Quadra'. At the same time Renault applied to the German trade mark office for the cancellation of AUDI's 'quattro' mark. The trade mark office granted the application on the ground that a numeral, even in a foreign language, could not in principle be registered unless it had acquired distinctiveness through use. AUDI's appeal to the *Bundespatentgericht* failed. In separate proceedings AUDI sought an injunction restraining Renault from using the name 'Quadra', on the ground of risk of confusion with 'quattro'. That action was founded both on AUDI's registered trade mark and on its *Ausstattungsrecht* (right to trade dress) which granted certain protection to unregistered trade marks. The litigation reached the *Bundesgerichtshof*, which decided to seek aid from the Court of Justice. The question referred by the *Bundesgerichtshof* amounted to asking whether a car maker established in Member State A, where it used the trade mark 'Quadra' to designate a four-wheel-drive vehicle, could be prevented from using that trade mark in Member State B, on the ground that another car maker owned the trade mark 'quattro' (or enjoyed an *Ausstattungsrecht* over the term 'quattro') in Member State B.

The Court could not, of course, be expected to answer such a specific question directly, since that would amount to applying—as opposed to interpreting—the law. The case none the less presented the Court with an opportunity to indicate, by way of general criteria, the extent to which Articles 28 and 30 of the Treaty circumscribe the Member States' freedom to allow trade mark owners to impede imports from other Member States on

[81] Case C-317/91 [1993] ECR I-6227.

the ground of alleged trade mark conflicts. The Court could, for example, have said something along the following lines:

In the absence of harmonization it is for national law to determine the conditions governing the grant of trade mark rights. It is also for national law, essentially, to determine the conditions governing the exercise of trade mark rights, including the rules as to when the proprietor of a trade mark may oppose the use by other persons of similar or identical trade marks. However, when the proprietor of a trade mark relies on it to prevent the use, on goods produced in another Member State, of a trade mark belonging to another person in that other Member State, on the ground that the trade marks are confusingly similar, the national court must have regard to the requirements of the free movement of goods; in particular, it must not prohibit the importation and sale of the imported products on trade mark grounds, unless there is a genuine risk of confusion between the two trade marks on the part of the relevant group of consumers.

A ruling along those lines would have been consistent with the Court's case law to the effect that intellectual property rights justify barriers to intra-Community trade only in so far as that is necessary in order to safeguard the specific subject-matter of the right. It would also have been consistent with the Court's case law on the essential function of trade marks.

Such a ruling would, without exceeding the Court's jurisdiction under Article 234, probably have led the German court to conclude that there was no justification for excluding Renault's car from the German market under the name 'Renault Espace Quadra'. It does after all seem unlikely that a potential purchaser of a car might go into a Renault showroom and buy a 'Renault Espace Quadra' in the belief that he was buying an 'AUDI quattro'.

Unfortunately the Court did not follow the approach outlined above in spite of being urged to do so by the Commission. Instead the Court made the following pronouncements:

. . . the specific subject-matter of trade-mark rights consists in protecting the proprietor of the mark against a risk of confusion such as to allow third persons to take unlawful advantage of the reputation of the proprietor's goods . . .

Further, the adoption of criteria for a finding of risk of confusion forms part of the detailed rules for trade-mark protection which . . . are a matter for national law. A trade-mark right as an exclusive right and protection against marks giving rise to risk of confusion are in reality . . . two sides of the same coin: reducing or extending the scope of protection against the risk of confusion simply reduces or extends the scope of the right itself. Both aspects must accordingly be governed by a single, homogeneous source of law—that is, at present, by national law.

Community law does not therefore lay down any strict interpretative criterion for the concept of risk of confusion.'[82]

---

[82] At paras 30–32 of the judgment.

It is difficult to find any thread of logic in that passage. The Court seems to be saying that trade mark law is a terribly technical matter which must be left to the Member States. Exactly the same could be said of public health, and yet the Court has never said that Article 30 gives the Member States *carte blanche* to erect trade mark barriers devoid of objective justification in the name of protecting public health. The Court has never said that every aspect of public health protection must be governed by 'a single, homogeneous source of law'. And the Court has never said that import restrictions imposed with a view to protecting public health do not have to be tested against the principle of proportionality.[83]

The judgment in *Deutsche Renault v AUDI* almost induces nostalgia for the much-derided dichotomy between the existence and the exercise of the right, which is seldom mentioned in the Court's more recent decisions. That distinction might, after all, be useful in the field of trade marks. The Court could have recognised that national law determines the conditions governing the grant of trade mark protection and may permit the registration of trade marks composed of, or containing, semi-descriptive, technically relevant terms (such as 'quattro', 'quadra', 'tetra', '4x4', or '4WD' for cars). However, since the exercise of the right may be limited by Community law, the scope of protection enjoyed by such 'weak' trade marks should not be so extensive as to exclude products made in other Member States, where there is no genuine risk of confusion or of damage to the reputation or distinctiveness of the earlier trade mark, above all where the only points of similarity relate to semi-descriptive elements.

In the passage cited above, the Court seems not merely to have forgotten about the distinction between existence and exercise but to have consciously abandoned any attempt to keep intellectual property rights in check. The Court's 'two sides of the coin' argument is perplexing. One commentator observes aptly: 'Protection of the [specific] subject-matter of industrial property rights and their limitation in the interest of free movement are the two sides of the coin, not the Member State creation of industrial [property] rights and their "protection unlimited" . . . '[84]

2.3.2 *Since the advent of the Trade Mark Directive*

2.3.2.1 *The likelihood of confusion, 'which includes the likelihood of association'*

In his opinion in *HAG II* Advocate General Jacobs observed that the concept of confusingly similar trade marks is now a concept of Community law as a

---

[83] The Court's general reluctance to apply the proportionality principle in trade mark cases is discussed by T. E. Luder, in 'Die Abwägung zwischen nationalem Markenrecht und der Freiheit des Warenverkehrs', EuZW Heft 1/1995, 15.

[84] N. Reich, 'The "November Revolution" of the European Court of Justice: *Keck, Meng* and *AUDI* Revisited' (1994) CML Rev. 459, 476.

result of the adoption of the Trade Mark Directive. The Advocate General noted that the Court of Justice would be competent to interpret the Directive by way of preliminary rulings, thus ensuring a uniform approach to trade mark conflicts and preventing abuses.

In *Deutsche Renault v AUDI* the Court stressed that the Directive was inapplicable *ratione temporis*, presumably because AUDI had commenced proceedings before the expiry (on 31 December 1992) of the period for implementing the Directive.[85]

It would be tempting to believe that discrepancies and abuses due to an excessively broad concept of the likelihood of confusion are a thing of the past and that all such problems can now be solved on the basis of the Directive. Regrettably, that does not seem to be the case. As the Court noted in *Deutsche Renault v AUDI*,[86] the Directive concerns only registered trade marks and not such rights as the *Ausstattungsrecht*. One of the most unsatisfactory aspects of the *Deutsche Renault* judgment is that it grants Member States total freedom to create exclusive rights in the name of protection of get-up, trade dress or unregistered rights when there is no prospect that Community harmonization might exercise a moderating influence in the area.

With that *caveat* in mind, we may now examine the relevant provisions of the Directive.[87] Article 4(1) states:

A trade mark shall not be registered or, if registered, shall be liable to be declared invalid:
(a) if it is identical with an earlier trade mark, and the goods or services for which the trade mark is applied for or is registered are identical with the goods or services for which the earlier trade mark is protected;
(b) if because of its identity with, or similarity to, the earlier trade mark and the identity or similarity of the goods or services covered by the trade marks, there exists a likelihood of confusion on the part of the public, which includes the likelihood of association with the earlier trade mark.

Article 5(1) defines the scope of protection of a registered trade mark in corresponding terms:

The registered trade mark shall confer on the proprietor exclusive rights therein. The proprietor shall be entitled to prevent all third parties not having his consent from using in the course of trade:
(a) any sign which is identical with the trade mark in relation to goods or services which are identical with those for which the trade mark is registered;

---

[85] At para. 14 of the judgment. The Court was surely wrong to treat the Directive as irrelevant, since AUDI had obtained an injunction against Renault which was of course being enforced after 31 December 1992: see the opinion of Advocate General Jacobs in *Paranova* (cited in n. 33), at para. 58.

[86] At para. 14 of the judgment.

[87] In relation to Community trade marks, similar provisions are contained in Arts 8(1) and 9(1) of Council Reg. No. 40/94.

(b) any sign where, because of its identity with, or similarity to, the trade mark and
    the identity or similarity of the goods or services covered by the trade mark
    and the sign, there exists a likelihood of confusion on the part of the public,
    which includes the likelihood of association between the sign and the trade
    mark.

The effect of these provisions is that, where the goods[88] are identical and
the trade marks are also identical, the issue of confusion does not pose any
problem. The owner of the earlier trade mark has an absolute right to
prevent others from using the same mark on the same goods. Confusion
is, in effect, taken for granted in such cases.[89] The need to appraise the
likelihood of confusion arises only when:

(1) the trade marks are identical and the goods are similar; or
(2) the goods are identical and the trade marks are similar; or
(3) the trade marks are similar and the goods are similar.

Although the 10th recital in the preamble to the Directive states that it is
indispensable to give an interpretation of the concept of similarity in relation to the likelihood of confusion, no such definition appears in the text of
the Directive. The only guidance is to be found in the 10th recital, which
goes on to state that appreciation of the likelihood of confusion 'depends on
numerous elements and, in particular, on the recognition of the trade mark
on the market, . . . the association which can be made with the used or
registered sign, . . . the degree of similarity between the trade mark and the
sign and between the goods or services identified'. An earlier version of the
Directive (and of the Community Trade Mark Regulation) required 'a *serious*
risk of confusion', in line with the restrictive approach pursued by the
Commission. The adjective was, however, omitted from the final version.

The authors of the Directive and of the Regulation faced difficulties due to a
fundamental difference of approach between the Benelux countries and the
other Member States.[90] In most of the European Union the scope of protection of a trade mark was determined essentially by the concept of confusion as
to origin: Company X (the proprietor of a trade mark) may prevent Company
Y from using a mark which may lead consumers to believe that Company Y's
goods emanate from the same source as Company X's goods.

In the Benelux countries the scope of protection was based on the looser
concept of 'association': under that concept a trade mark is infringed where
the use of a similar sign calls to mind the trade mark, even though it does
not cause any actual confusion as to the origin of the goods on which it is

---

[88] For the sake of simplicity, reference is made to 'goods' in this context; strictly speaking one
should refer to 'goods and services' or to 'goods or services', depending on the context.

[89] That is exactly what is stated in the second sentence of Art. 16(1) of TRIPS.

[90] The legislative history of the provision is discussed in the judgment of Laddie J., in *Wagamama Ltd v City Center Restaurants PLC* [1995] 32 IPR 613.

used.[91] The Benelux concept is founded on a theory of dilution and it does, of course, widen the scope of protection, at least in theory,[92] as compared with legal systems which adhere to the classical concept of confusion as to origin.

When the draft Community legislation was debated at the level of the Council of Ministers, there was disagreement between the Benelux delegations and the other Member States. The wording of Article 4(1)(b) (and the other provisions cited above) reflects a compromise between the differing points of view. The following statement was included in the Council minutes: 'The Council and the Commission note that "likelihood of association" is a concept which in particular has been developed by Benelux case law.'[93]

Compromises seldom produce good law-making. The formula used in the Directive is vague, ambiguous, and self-contradictory. To say that the likelihood of confusion includes the likelihood of association is meaningless. As we have seen, the latter is wider than the former. How can the wider concept be included within the narrower?[94]

The interpretation of Article 4(1)(b) of the Directive came before the Court for the first time in *SABEL v Puma*.[95] Puma was the proprietor of a figurative trade mark registered in Germany which consisted of a silhouette of a large feline beast in a leaping position. The mark was registered, *inter alia*, for 'leather and imitation leather, goods made therefrom (bags) and articles of clothing'. SABEL applied to register a trade mark incorporating the word SABEL and a picture of a large feline closely resembling the animal in Puma's trade mark. The goods covered by SABEL's application were virtually identical to the goods covered by Puma's registration. Puma opposed the

---

[91] In its judgment of 20 May 1983 in *Jullien v Verschuere* (A 82/5, Jur. 1983, Vol. 4, p. 36) the Benelux Court of Justice stated: 'il y a ressemblance entre une marque et un signe lorsque, compte tenu des particularités de l'espèce, notamment du pouvoir distinctif de la marque, la marque et le signe, considérés en soi et dans leurs rapports mutuels, présentent sur le plan auditif, visuel ou conceptuel, une similitude de nature à établir une association entre le signe et la marque.' The Benelux concept is explained by C. Gielen, in 'Likelihood of Association: What does it Mean?' (February 1996) *Trademark World* 20. For more information about the Benelux case law on dilution, see Sabine Casparie-Kerdel, 'Dilution Disguised: Has the Concept of Trade Mark Dilution made its Way into the Laws of Europe' [2001] EIPR 185, 188 *et seq*.

[92] Braun points out that the risk of confusion, as interpreted by the German courts, is in fact considerably wider than the risk of association under Benelux law: see A. Braun, *Précis des Marques*, 3rd edn, Maison Larcier, Brussels, 1995, p. 321.

[93] For the text of this and other statements included in the Council minutes, and for a discussion of their history and legal status, see C. Gielen, 'European Trade Mark Legislation: The Statements' [1996] EIPR 83. The Court has held that such statements cannot be used to interpret legislative provisions since no reference was made to the content thereof in the wording of the provisions themselves: *Libertel* (cited in n. 29), at para. 25. The same position had already been taken by a Board of Appeal of the Office for Harmonization in the Internal Market in Case R 46/1998-2 *Giacomelli Sport*, at para. 16 (OJ OHIM 6/2000, 731).

[94] A. Wagner, 'Infringing Trade Marks: Function, Association and Confusion of Signs according to the EC Trade Marks Directive' [1999] EIPR 127, 130.

[95] Case C-251/95 [1997] ECR I-6214.

application. The case reached the *Bundesgerichtshof*, which considered that under the old (i.e. pre-Directive) German law there was no likelihood of confusion between the two marks.[96] It wondered, however, whether the position might have changed as a result of the provision in Article 4(1)(b) of the Directive according to which the likelihood of confusion 'includes the likelihood of association'. The question arose whether the mere association which the public might make between the two marks, through the idea of a bounding feline, justified refusing SABEL's application. The *Bundesgerichtshof* referred the following questions to the Court of Justice:

With reference to the interpretation of Article 4(1)(b) of the . . . Directive . . . is it sufficient for a finding that there is a likelihood of confusion between a sign composed of text and picture and a sign consisting merely of a picture, which is registered for identical and similar goods and is not especially well known to the public, that the two signs coincide as to their semantic content (in this case, a bounding feline)?

What is the significance in this connection of the wording of the Directive, in terms of which the likelihood of confusion includes the likelihood that a mark may be associated with an earlier mark?

The governments of Belgium, Luxembourg, and the Netherlands attempted to persuade the Court that the formula used in Article 4(1)(b) was intended to be construed in the same manner as the expression 'likelihood of association' in Article 13a of the Uniform Benelux Law on Trade Marks. On that view, Puma would have been able to oppose the registration of SABEL's mark if there was a likelihood that consumers, when confronted with SABEL's mark, would call to mind Puma's mark, without necessarily assuming that the products all emanated from the same source. In other words, confusion as to origin was not required. Although there was some support for that view in the above-mentioned statement recorded in the Council minutes,[97] that was not sufficient to overcome the obvious textual flaw in the argument: namely, that the likelihood of association is, according to the wording of Article 4(1)(b), described as being included within the likelihood of confusion on the part of the public. The Court therefore had no difficulty in holding that 'the concept of likelihood of association is not an alternative to that of likelihood of confusion, but serves to define its scope. The terms of the provision itself exclude its application where there is no likelihood of confusion on the part of the public'.[98]

---

[96] For an explanation of the reasoning followed by the *Bundesgerichtshof* see E. Ullmann, 'Reconciling Trade Mark Decisions of National Courts and the European Court of Justice' (1996) 27 IIC 791, 794 *et seq.* The author is a judge of the *Bundesgerichtshof*.

[97] See n. 93. A similar result was reached by Laddie, J., in the *Wagamama* case (cited in n. 90). For criticism of that judgment, see the article by Kemperman Sanders cited in n. 5, and, by the same author, 'The Return to *Wagamama*' [1996] 10 EIPR 521. For a defence of *Wagamama*, see P. Prescott, 'Think Before You Waga Finger' [1996] 10 EIPR 317.

[98] At para. 18 of the judgment.

The result is not likely to please some Benelux trade mark lawyers, because it appears to treat the reference to likelihood of association, in the text of the Directive (and of the Community Trade Mark Regulation, by extension), as nothing more than a cosmetic embellishment. On the view taken by the Court, the words 'likelihood of association' appear to add nothing of substance to the Directive. As a result, the general scope of protection is now limited to confusion as to origin,[99] and protection against dilution seems to be confined to marks which enjoy a reputation, by virtue of the special provisions of Article 4(3) and (4)(a) and Article 5(2) of the Directive.[100]

The Court went on to make some general comments about the appraisal of the likelihood of confusion. Referring to the tenth recital in the preamble to the Directive, the Court observed that the 'likelihood of confusion must . . . be appreciated globally, taking into account all factors relevant to the circumstances of the case'.[101] The Court then stated:

That global appreciation of the visual, aural or conceptual similarity of the marks in question, must be based on the overall impression given by the marks, bearing in mind, in particular, their distinctive and dominant components. The wording of Article 4(1)(b) of the Directive—' . . . there exists a likelihood of confusion on the part of the public . . . '—shows that the perception of marks in the mind of the average consumer of the type of goods or services in question plays a decisive role in the global appreciation of the likelihood of confusion. The average consumer normally perceives a mark as a whole and does not proceed to analyse its various details.

In that perspective, the more distinctive the earlier mark, the greater will be the likelihood of confusion. It is therefore not impossible that the conceptual similarity resulting from the fact that two marks use images with analogous semantic content may give rise to a likelihood of confusion where the earlier mark has a particularly distinctive character, either *per se* or because of the reputation it enjoys with the public.[102]

The Court noted that since, according to the national court's order for reference, the earlier mark was not especially well known and consisted of an image with little imaginative content, the mere fact that the two marks were conceptually similar was not sufficient to give rise to a likelihood of confusion.[103] On that basis the Court ruled as follows:

---

[99] Although this means that the Benelux courts may have to reconsider some of their established case law, many of the cases decided on the basis of likelihood of association could probably have been decided in the same way on the basis of a broad construction of likelihood of confusion: G.-J. van de Kamp, 'Protection of Trade Marks: The New Regime—Beyond Origin' [1998] EIPR 364, 366. Pickering points out that the Court adopted a fairly broad concept of confusion in *SABEL v Puma* which will be capable of protecting the 'wider integrity' of the trade mark, including the goodwill and advertising functions: op. cit. (n. 5), at p. 112 *et seq.*

[100] These provisions are dealt with below in section 2.3.2.3.

[101] At para. 22 of the judgment.　　　　[102] At paras 23 and 24 of the judgment.

[103] At para. 25 of the judgment.

The criterion of 'likelihood of confusion which includes the likelihood of association with the earlier mark' contained in Article 4(1)(b) of [the Trade Mark] Directive . . . is to be interpreted as meaning that the mere association which the public might make between two trade marks as a result of their analogous semantic content is not in itself a sufficient ground for concluding that there is a likelihood of confusion within the meaning of that provision.

On the whole, the Court's judgment in *SABEL v Puma* is to be welcomed. Its rejection of the Benelux approach to the likelihood of association is understandable. By insisting that trade mark conflicts must, unless the earlier mark has a reputation, be resolved on the basis of confusion as to origin the Court remained faithful to its long-standing case law on the specific subject-matter and essential function of trade marks.

That said, it is important none the less that the concept of origin confusion should not be construed too narrowly or literally. In order to succeed in an infringement action it should not be necessary to show that consumers will think that the goods were made in the same factory or under the direct control of the same undertaking.[104] Indirect confusion—in the sense that consumers assume that there is some sort of link or connection (such as a licensing agreement) between the producers of the goods—should suffice. The following comments by Wagner are of interest: 'It is not necessary that the consumer worries about the origin of the marked products; it does not even need to enter his thoughts. Any confusion is sufficient which detracts from the function of the mark as distinguishing the product and assigning to it a special image and goodwill and therefore from serving as a means of communication with the consumer.'[105]

The Benelux concept of association, though too broad to be used for resolving all trade mark conflicts, has some merit when the earlier mark has a reputation or possesses great inherent distinctiveness. Confusion in the literal sense will often not occur simply because the earlier mark is so well known or so distinctive that the consumer will readily distinguish between that and a slightly different mark. A fizzy drink sold under the trade mark POPSI is unlikely to be mistaken for PEPSI. But POPSI would certainly call to mind PEPSI. There would be a strong likelihood of association, though no confusion in the narrow sense. Notwithstanding *SABEL v Puma*, the concept of likelihood of association could be used as a basis for upholding an infringement action in that sort of situation. In fact the Court achieved a similar result by emphasizing that 'the more distinctive the earlier mark, the greater will be the likelihood of confusion'. That is, of course, counter-

---

[104] In Case C-39/97 *Canon Kabushiki Kaisha v Metro-Goldwyn-Mayer* [1998] ECR I-5507, at para. 29, the Court held that confusion exists if the public believe that goods come from 'economically-linked undertakings'; to rebut a likelihood of confusion it is not sufficient to show that the public are not confused as to the place of production.

[105] Op. cit. (n. 94), at 132.

intuitive. It is to some extent a legal fiction, albeit a necessary one. Marks that possess exceptional distinctiveness—either inherent or acquired through use—merit a wider scope of protection.

An attempt was made to consolidate that principle in *Marca Mode v Adidas*,[106] where the *Hoge Raad* (the Dutch Supreme Court) invited the Court of Justice to rule that a likelihood of confusion may be presumed where the earlier trade mark is particularly distinctive, either *per se* or because of its reputation, and the later mark so closely resembles it as to give rise to a likelihood of association. Although the Court rejected that possibility, it emphasized once again that highly distinctive marks merit broader protection and that reputation is an important element in assessing distinctiveness.[107]

As for the Court's general comments about the appraisal of the likelihood of confusion, they appear to stem from a comparativist approach and amount to a synthesis of the basic principles recognised in the majority of the Member States. The Court was surely right to emphasise the need for a global appraisal of the 'visual, aural and conceptual similarity of the trade marks in question . . . based on the overall impression given by the marks'. The Court was also right to focus on the 'average consumer of the type of goods or services in question' rather than the abnormally careless or simply dyslexic consumer, or the exceptionally attentive, ultra-brand-conscious consumer.

2.3.2.2 *Similarity of goods and similarity of trade marks: interdependent criteria*

The general rule is that a registered trade mark enjoys protection only in relation to similar or identical goods. The basis for this 'rule of specificity' is that consumers do not assume that totally different goods emanate from the same source simply because they bear the same trade mark. For example, a consumer who is familiar with the trade mark BONGO for tractors will not, if he sees the same mark on a pair of sunglasses, assume that the tractors and sunglasses were manufactured by, or under the control of, the same undertaking. The approach followed in the United Kingdom, at least in *British Sugar plc v James Robertson & Sons*,[108] was to appraise the likelihood of confusion in two stages. The first step was to decide whether there was similarity of goods. If there was, it was then necessary to ask whether the marks were so similar as to engender a likelihood of confusion. The alleged advantage of this approach was that a 'strong' mark would not get protection for a greater range of goods than a 'weak' mark.[109]

---

[106] Case C-425/98 [2000] ECR I-4861. [107] At para. 41 of the judgment.
[108] *British Sugar plc v James Robertson & Sons* [1996] RPC 281. [109] Ibid.

It is perhaps not surprising that such an approach appealed to British judges. Under section 4(1) of the Trade Marks Act 1938 a registered trade mark was only infringed if an identical or deceptively similar mark was used in relation to goods or services in respect of which the mark was registered.

In *Canon Kabushiki Kaisha v Metro-Goldwyn-Mayer*[110] the Court of Justice opted for a very different approach. In 1986 Metro-Goldwyn-Mayer applied to register the trade mark CANNON in Germany for 'films recorded on video tape cassettes (video film cassettes); production, distribution and projection of films for cinemas and television organisations'. The application was opposed by the Japanese company Canon Kabushiki Kaisha (CKK) on the basis of its earlier trade mark 'Canon', which was registered in Germany in respect of, *inter alia*, 'still and motion picture cameras and projectors; television filming and recording devices, television retransmission devices, television receiving and reproduction devices, including tape and disc devices for television recording and reproduction'.

The *Bundespatentgericht* rejected the opposition on the ground that the goods/services were not similar. CKK appealed to the *Bundesgerichtshof*, which referred the following question to the Court of Justice:

'May account be taken, when assessing the similarity of the goods or services covered by the two marks, of the distinctive character, in particular the reputation, of the mark with earlier priority . . . so that, in particular, likelihood of confusion within the meaning of Article 4(1)(b) of [the Directive] . . . must be taken to exist even if the public attributes the goods and/or services to different places of origin (*"Herkunftsstätten"*)?'

At first blush, the German court's question seems surprising. Goods are either similar or they are different. Dissimilar goods do not suddenly start to resemble each other because someone happens to have registered a trade mark for one of the products in question and that trade mark acquires particular distinctiveness through reputation. It seems that what the *Bundesgerichtshof* really wanted to know was whether it must appraise the likelihood of confusion on a step-by-step basis, deciding first whether the goods are similar and only then considering whether the marks are similar and, if so, whether there is a likelihood of confusion, or whether it should make a global appraisal. That, at any rate, is how the Court of Justice understood the question.

The Court of Justice opted, rightly, for a global appraisal, as in *SABEL v Puma*. The Court established the important principle that the similarity of the goods and the similarity of the trade marks are interdependent criteria. This means that 'a lesser degree of similarity between [the] goods . . . may be offset by a greater degree of similarity between the marks, and vice versa.'[111]

---

[110] Cited in n. 104.   [111] At para. 17 of the judgment.

The Court went on to repeat what it had said in *SABEL v Puma*: namely that the likelihood of confusion increases in direct proportion to the distinctiveness of the earlier mark; thus marks with a highly distinctive character, either *per se* or because of the reputation they possess on the market, enjoy broader protection than marks with a less distinctive character.[112] It follows that 'registration of a trade mark may have to be refused, despite a lesser degree of similarity between the goods . . . where the marks are very similar and the earlier mark, in particular [on account of] its reputation, is highly distinctive.'[113]

These principles were further developed in *Lloyd Schuhfabrik Meyer v Klijsen Handel* where the Court laid down guidelines for assessing the distinctiveness of the earlier mark:

In making that assessment, account should be taken, in particular, of the inherent characteristics of the mark, including the fact that it does or does not contain an element descriptive of the goods or services for which it has been registered; the market share held by the mark; how intensive, geographically widespread and long-standing use of the mark has been; the amount invested by the undertaking in promoting the mark; the proportion of the relevant section of the public which, because of the mark, identifies the goods or services as originating from a particular undertaking; and statements from chambers of commerce and industry or other trade and professional associations.[114]

It is submitted that the approach taken by the Court in *SABEL v Puma*, *Canon Kabushiki Kaisha v Metro-Goldwyn-Mayer* and *Lloyd Schuhfabrik Meyer v Klijsen Handel* is, broadly speaking, correct. Similarity of goods and trade marks are elastic concepts. The various elements involved in appraising likelihood of confusion are all interrelated. Strangely the *British Sugar* case, in which Mr Justice Jacob objected to the global approach, provides an excellent illustration of the need for a global approach. The claimant had registered TREAT for 'dessert sauce' and 'syrup'. The defendant was alleged to have infringed by using an identical trade mark on 'toffee-flavoured spread'. The inherent distinctiveness of the trade mark was very low.[115] In the absence of evidence that its distinctiveness had been enhanced through reputation, its scope of protection was obviously narrow; at most, it deserved protection against the use of an identical trade mark in relation to identical or near-identical goods. It would have been reasonable to say that the differences between dessert sauce and syrup, on the one hand, and toffee-flavoured spread, on the other, were sufficient to exclude a likelihood of confusion. Suppose, however, that the earlier trade mark had been a highly distinctive mark, composed of a fanciful word element and an

---

[112] At para. 18 of the judgment.   [113] At para. 19 of the judgment.
[114] Case C-342/97 [1999] ECR I-3819, at para. 23 of the judgment.
[115] In fact Jacob, J., declared it invalid on the ground that it was devoid of any distinctive character.

unusual device, and that its inherent distinctiveness had been enhanced as a result of its reputation. Consumers would surely assume that toffee-flavoured spread bearing such a trade mark had the same origin as the dessert sauce and syrup on which they had seen it previously.

It must be stressed that the goods do have to be similar in order to support a finding of likelihood of confusion under Articles 4(1)(b) and 5(1)(b) of the Directive. If the goods are wholly dissimilar, no amount of similarity of the trade marks can lead to a finding that there is a likelihood of confusion.[116] In that event, an opposition or an infringement action can only succeed if the earlier mark has a reputation and certain other requirements are fulfilled. This possibility is examined in the following section.

2.3.2.3 *Extended protection for trade marks with a reputation*

The reputation of the earlier trade mark, if it has one, is always important. As we have seen, reputation can enhance the distinctiveness of the mark and enlarge its scope of protection: the likelihood of confusion is deemed to be greater if the earlier trade mark is highly distinctive, whether because of its inherent characteristics or its reputation.

Sometimes the reputation of the earlier trade mark can broaden its scope of protection to such an extent that it is protected against the use of an identical or similar mark even in respect of goods that are entirely dissimilar to the goods for which the mark is registered. The example was given above of the use of the trade mark 'Rolls Royce' in relation to dishwashers. It was noted that the basis of protection in such a case would not be likelihood of confusion but dilution: the maker of the dishwashers would be taking advantage of the famous mark's reputation and diluting its distinctiveness.

The need to give this sort of extended protection to marks with a reputation has been recognized in the European trade mark legislation. Under Article 9(1)(c) of the Community Trade Mark Regulation, the proprietor of a Community trade mark may prevent all third parties from using in the course of trade:

' . . . any sign which is identical with or similar to the Community trade mark in relation to goods or services which are not similar to those for which the Community trade mark is registered, where the latter has a reputation in the Community and where use of that sign without due cause takes unfair advantage of, or is

---

[116] This point seems to be misunderstood by some authors. M. Spence ('Section 10 of the Trade Marks Act 1994: Is There Really a Logical Lapse?' [2001] EIPR 423, 424) says that as a result of *Canon* an infringement action under s. 10(2) of the Trade Marks Act 1994 (which implements Art. 5(1)(b) of the Directive) can succeed 'even where the goods in question are dissimilar'. That is plainly wrong, as is clear from para. 22 of *Canon*. A similar mistake is made by R. Montagnon (' "Strong" Marks Make More Goods "Similar" ' [1998] EIPR 401). Strong marks do not make goods similar: they increase the likelihood of confusion.

detrimental to, the distinctive character or the repute of the Community trade mark.'[117]

Article 5(2) of the Trade Mark Directive contains a similar provision applicable to national trade marks, though the Member States, oddly, are not obliged to implement it.[118]

The interpretation of Article 5(2) of the Directive was in issue in *General Motors v Yplon*.[119] General Motors owned the Benelux trade mark 'Chevy', registered in particular for automobiles. Yplon registered an identical trade mark in Benelux, at a later date, for detergents, *inter alia*. General Motors sought an injunction from a Belgian court prohibiting Yplon from using the mark 'Chevy' in relation to detergents on the ground that such use diluted General Motors' trade mark and damaged its advertising function. The Belgian court asked the Court of Justice to define the term 'repute of the trade mark' in Article 5(2) of the Directive.

The Court of Justice inferred from the various language versions that Article 5(2) postulated a 'knowledge threshold'.[120] The trade mark did not, however, need to be known by a given percentage of the relevant public[121] (which might be the public at large or a more specialized public, depending on the product).[122] The necessary degree of knowledge must be deemed to be reached when the mark was known 'by a significant part of the public concerned'.[123] In considering whether that condition was fulfilled the national court must take into consideration 'all the relevant facts of the case, in particular the market share held by the trade mark, the intensity, geographical extent and duration of its use, and the size of the investment made by the undertaking in promoting it'.[124] The trade mark did not need to have a reputation throughout the territory of the Member State concerned; it was sufficient if the reputation existed in a substantial part of the Member State.[125]

The ruling in *General Motors v Yplon* gives rise to an important question concerning the Community trade mark (CTM): if the proprietor of a CTM seeks protection in relation to different goods under Article 8(5) or Article 9(1)(c) of the Community Trade Mark Regulation, in what territory must he show that the trade mark has a reputation? Applying the ruling in *General*

---

[117] Art. 8(5) of the Regulation makes a corresponding provision for opposition proceedings against an application to register a Community trade mark.

[118] Art. 4(4)(a) of the Directive contains a corresponding provision—also optional for the Member States—as regards opposition and invalidation proceedings. Art. 4(3) of the Directive, which deals with the protection of Community trade marks with a reputation in opposition proceedings, is, however, mandatory.

[119] Case C-375/97 [1999] ECR I-5421.   [120] At para. 22 of the judgment.
[121] At para. 25 of the judgment.   [122] At para. 24 of the judgment.
[123] At para. 26 of the judgment.   [124] At para. 27 of the judgment.
[125] At para. 28 of the judgment. For this purpose the Benelux territory must be treated like the territory of a Member State (para. 29).

Motors v Yplon by analogy, one arrives at the conclusion that the mark must have a reputation in a substantial part of the territory of the European Union. An unfortunate side-effect of that conclusion is that it makes the Community trade mark marginally less attractive than it might otherwise be, at least to undertakings which are unlikely to use their marks extensively in a sufficiently large slice of EU territory. An undertaking which, for example, initially intends to use a trade mark on a large scale only in Greece should apply for a CTM if it also plans to be active in other EU countries; but it might be advised to take a Greek registration as well, since it might find it easier to establish that the mark has acquired a reputation in Greece than in the Community as a whole.

In one respect the wording of Article 4(3) and (4)(a) and Article 5(2) of the Directive (and of the corresponding provisions of the Community Trade Mark Regulation) is unfortunate. Those provisions appear to apply only where the owner of the earlier trade mark seeks protection against the registration or use of a conflicting trade mark in relation to goods that are *dissimilar* to the goods for which the earlier trade mark is registered. It would surely be illogical to grant protection in relation to dissimilar goods but not in relation to similar goods. At first sight there might seem to be no danger of that happening, since protection in relation to similar goods is granted by Articles 4(1)(b) and 5(1)(b) of the Directive.[126] The problem is that there may be a gap due to the fact that the legislation uses different criteria depending on whether protection is sought in relation to similar or dissimilar goods. If the goods are similar the issue is likelihood of confusion. If the goods are dissimilar the question to be asked is whether the use of the later trade mark takes unfair advantage of, or is detrimental to, the distinctive character or reputation of the earlier trade mark. There may be situations in which there is no likelihood of confusion between similar marks used in relation to similar goods but the use of the later mark nonetheless takes unfair advantage of the reputation of the earlier mark. Suppose, for example, that cheap watches bearing the trade mark 'Rolox' are offered for sale on a market stall. A reasonably aware consumer is unlikely to think that such goods have any connection with the well-known Swiss watchmaker 'Rolex'. There will be no likelihood of confusion because the consumer is well aware that genuine 'Rolex' watches are not sold on market stalls for €10. The use of such a similar trade mark on watches would none the less be designed to take advantage of the reputation of the famous trade mark 'Rolex'. It would also be detrimental to its distinctive character. Dilution is clearly not confined to the use of a trade mark in relation to dissimilar goods.

---

[126]   And by Arts 8(1)(b) and 9(1)(b) of the Community Trade Mark Regulation.

It cannot seriously be argued that the proprietor of the Rolex trade mark, in the above example, should be allowed to prevent the use of 'Rolox' as a trade mark for sunglasses, raincoats, and sportscars but not for watches. The question that has to be addressed is whether protection in relation to goods that are similar to the goods for which the mark is registered should be granted under the general provisions on likelihood of confusion (Arts 4(1)(b) and 5(1)(b) of the Directive)[127] or under the special provisions that grant extended protection to marks with a reputation (Art. 4(3) and (4)(a) and Art. 5(2) of the Directive).[128] That question was answered by the Court of Justice in *Davidoff v Gofkid*[129] on a reference from the *Bundesgerichtshof*. The trade mark 'Davidoff' (in a special font) was registered for 'gentlemen's cosmetics, cognac, ties, glasses frames, cigars, cigarillos and cigarettes, together with related accessories, and pipes and pipe tobacco together with related accessories, and leather goods'. Gofkid used the trade mark 'Durfee' (written in a font that closely resembled the font used for the 'Davidoff' trade mark), *inter alia*, for 'precious metals and their alloys and also goods made from precious alloys, precious metal alloys and goods plated with precious metals, including handmade and decorative items, tableware (except for flatware), centrepieces, ashtrays, cigar and cigarette cases, cigar holders and cigarette holders, jewellery, silversmith's and goldsmith's items, precious stones, watches and time-measuring instruments'.

The Court of Justice opted for a broad interpretation of Articles 4(3) and (4)(a) and 5(2) of the Directive.[130] The Court considered that those provisions needed to be interpreted, not solely on the basis of their wording, but also in the light of the overall scheme and objectives of the system of which they are a part.[131] The Court observed that the legislation could not be interpreted in a way that would lead to marks with a reputation having less protection in relation to similar goods than in relation to dissimilar goods.[132]

The Court decided that the way to achieve that was to disregard the textual difficulty posed by the clear reference to dissimilar goods in Articles 4(3) and (4)(a) and 5(2) and to apply those provisions even where the goods concerned were similar. An alternative—and possibly more logical solution—would have been to resurrect the concept 'likelihood of association' in Articles 4(1)(b) and 5(1)(b) and to hold that there is a likelihood of association when the later trade mark takes advantage of the earlier trade mark's reputation or distinctiveness. Since the Court has stressed on several

---

[127] Or Arts 8(1)(b) and 9(1)(b) of the Community Trade Mark Regulation.

[128] Or Arts 8(5) and 9(1)(c) of the Community Trade Mark Regulation.

[129] Case C-292/00, judgment of 9 January 2003.

[130] The same interpretation will of course apply to Arts 8(5) and 9(1)(c) of the Community Trade Mark Regulation.

[131] At para. 24 of the judgment.   [132] At para. 25 of the judgment.

occasions that the reputation and distinctiveness of the earlier trade mark are relevant when assessing likelihood of confusion under Articles 4(1)(b) and 5(1)(b), such an approach might have increased the overall coherence of the case law. Unfortunately, the Court felt that, having more or less written likelihood of association out of the legislation in *SABEL v Puma*, it could hardly revive that concept a few years later.

Even though the judgment in *Davidoff v Gofkid* does some violence to the wording of Articles 4(3) and (4)(a) and 5(2), the result is entirely acceptable. The facts of that case demonstrate the point. Some of the goods in question were identical, some were similar and some were dissimilar. Such a situation occurs in many opposition cases and infringement actions. As a result of the Court's ruling it is possible to deal with that type of case— assuming that the earlier trade mark has a reputation—on the basis of a single provision and using uniform criteria. It is thus possible to avoid the artificiality of using one criterion (likelihood of confusion, construed broadly) in so far as the goods are similar and a different criterion (taking advantage of reputation) in so far as the goods are different. It is also possible to avoid the absurdity of holding that there is an infringement when the later trade mark is used on dissimilar goods but not when it is used on similar goods.[133]

3. REPACKAGING AND RELABELLING OF TRADE-MARKED GOODS

3.1 *The nature of the phenomenon*

Why, it may be wondered, would an honest trader want to remove branded goods from their original containers and repackage them, reaffixing the original, authentic trade mark, before reselling them? It appears that such a practice occurs mainly in the pharmaceutical industry and is due to two distorting factors in a market that is anything but common. The first factor is the tendency of governments to interfere to an exceptional degree in the process of price formation, either by directly imposing maximum prices for pharmaceuticals or by limiting the amount that can be reimbursed under social security schemes. Such interference, not being carried out in a uniform manner, leads to large price discrepancies between Member States. The price discrepancies provide an incentive for parallel imports. These, however, are hindered by the second distorting factor, i.e. the existence of different rules on the packaging of pharmaceuticals, in particular rules as to

---

[133] The absurdity of such an interpretation was pointed out by Advocate General Ruiz-Jarabo Colomer in his opinion (at para. 33) in *Arsenal v Reed* (cited in n. 15). The same point is made by A. von Mühlendahl, 'Zum Schutz bekannter Marken im Europäischen Markenrecht', in *Festschrift für Willi Erdmann*, Carl Heymanns Verlag, 2002, at p. 429.

the number of pills per bottle or packet. In order to overcome such rules the parallel importer is sometimes obliged to engage in repackaging. When he reaffixes the trade mark to the repackaged product, that might amount to a trade mark infringement. The proprietor of the trade mark—who has an understandable desire to prevent parallel imports from a market in which he has been forced to sell at a low price to a market in which the regulatory framework allows him to make a higher profit—is not likely to pass over the opportunity to bring infringement proceedings against the parallel importer. The question then arises whether the exhaustion principle applies to such goods, which have after all been placed on the market by, or with the consent of, the trade mark proprietor, or whether the latter is entitled to oppose the further marketing of his goods as a result of the physical manipulation of the goods carried out by the parallel importer.

3.2 *The early cases:* Hoffmann-La Roche *and* Pfizer

The first case on repackaging was *Hoffmann-La Roche v Centrafarm*.[134] The facts were as follows. Hoffmann-La Roche marketed a drug under the trade mark 'Valium' in Germany in packages of 20 or 50 tablets for individual buyers and in batches of five packages containing 100 or 250 tablets for hospitals. Its United Kingdom subsidiary marketed the same product in the United Kingdom in packages of 100 or 500 tablets at considerably lower prices. Centrafarm, a parallel importer, began to sell Valium purchased in the United Kingdom in the original packages which it put up in new packages of 1,000 tablets, to which it affixed the trade mark of Hoffmann-La Roche together with a notice that the product had been marketed by Centrafarm. Centrafarm also gave notice of its intention to repack the tablets into smaller packages intended for sale to individuals. Hoffmann-La Roche attempted to prevent the parallel imports in reliance on its trade mark. The *Landgericht Freiburg* considered that under German law Centrafarm's conduct amounted to an infringement of Hoffmann-La Roche's trade mark. The *Landgericht* sought a preliminary ruling on the question whether a trade mark owner was empowered under Article 30 of the Treaty to invoke the trade mark in order to prevent parallel imports in such circumstances.

The Court of Justice adopted what was at the time (1978) its customary approach. It began with ritual declarations about the existence and exercise of industrial property rights and about derogations from the principle of free movement only being permitted if justified for the purpose of safeguarding the specific subject-matter of the right.[135] It then referred to the essential function of the trade mark, which was to guarantee the identity of origin of

---

[134] Case 102/77 [1978] ECR 1139.   [135] At para. 6 of the judgment.

the trade-marked product to the consumer or ultimate user.[136] That guarantee of origin meant that the consumer or ultimate user could be certain that a trade-marked product sold to him had not been subject at a previous stage of marketing to interference by a third person, without the authorization of the proprietor of the trade mark, such as to affect the original condition of the product.[137]

The Court then examined whether the exercise of such a right might constitute a 'disguised restriction on trade between Member States' within the meaning of the second sentence of Article 30. Such a restriction might arise, *inter alia*, from the proprietor of the trade mark putting on the market in various Member States an identical product in various packages while availing himself of the rights inherent in the trade mark to prevent repackaging by a third party even if it were done in such a way that the identity of the trade-marked product and its original condition could not be affected.[138] That might be the case where, for example, the proprietor of the trade mark had marketed the product in a double packaging and the repackaging affected only the external packaging, leaving the internal packaging intact, or where the repackaging was inspected by a public authority for the purpose of ensuring that the product was not adversely affected. Where the essential function of the trade mark to guarantee the origin of the product was thus protected, the exercise of his rights by the proprietor of the trade mark in order to fetter the free movement of goods between Member States might constitute a disguised restriction within the meaning of the second sentence of Article 30 of the Treaty if it was established that the use of the trade mark right by the proprietor, having regard to the marketing system which he had adopted, could contribute to the artificial partitioning of the markets between Member States.[139] The Court then laid down two further conditions which the parallel importer must satisfy before he could market the repackaged product on which the trade mark had been reaffixed without the authorization of its proprietor: he must give the proprietor prior notice of the marketing[140] and state on the new packaging by whom the product had been repackaged.

Viewed from the perspective of 1978 (a mere four years after *HAG I*), the judgment in *Hoffmann-La Roche v Centrafarm* looks like a jurisprudential masterpiece. Certainly the Court deserves praise for striving to find the right balance between the competing interests of trade mark protection and the free movement of goods.

---

[136] At para. 7 of the judgment.   [137] Ibid.
[138] At para. 9 of the judgment.   [139] At para. 10 of the judgment.
[140] The requirement of prior notification is a remarkable piece of creative jurisprudence. For speculation about its significance, see W. Alexander, 'Droit de marque et droit communautaire' (1975) 15 *Cahiers de Droit Européen* 75, 81.

The judgment is not, however, free of defects. The worst is the reductionist approach to Article 30. It is not generally helpful to analyse a restriction separately in the light of the first sentence of Article 30 and then in the light of the second sentence. As Advocate General Jacobs was to point out years later in the *Paranova* cases (discussed below), either a measure is justified on one of the grounds listed in Article 30 or it is not justified.[141] The two sentences must be read as a whole. The second sentence should not be read as an exception to the first.[142]

A second defect is that the Court did not enhance legal certainty by its reference to 'the artificial partitioning of the markets between Member States', which created the impression that the parallel importer must demonstrate a subjective intention, on the part of the trade mark proprietor, to partition the common market by using different packaging in different Member States. In this respect, the Court's judgment was sufficiently ambiguous to persuade some commentators[143] that an objective test was implied (Did the use of different packaging lead to a partitioning of the market, regardless of the intentions of the trade mark owner?), while others[144] assumed that the test was subjective (Did the trade mark owner deliberately intend to partition the market by using different packaging?). The German courts which had to deal with the case after the preliminary ruling were equally confused.[145]

A further case on the repackaging of pharmaceutical products came before the Court of Justice three years after *Hoffmann-La Roche v Centrafarm*. The facts of *Pfizer v Eurim-Pharm* were as follows. Pfizer marketed an antibiotic under the trade mark 'Vibramycin' through its subsidiary companies in Germany and the United Kingdom. The packaging used by Pfizer in those two countries differed and the prices charged were considerably lower in the United Kingdom. Eurim-Pharm imported and sold in Germany 'Vibramycin' which had been marketed in the United Kingdom by Pfizer in

---

[141] Cited in n. 33, at para. 82 of the opinion. [142] Ibid.

[143] D. Guy, 'Centrafarm—Again!' [1978] EIPR 34, 36; M. Röttger, 'The Hoffmann-La Roche Ruling Repackaged by the National Court' [1979] EIPR 283, 285, and (by the same author) 'AHPC and Centrafarm: The Court's Decision in the Light of its Earlier Rulings' [1980] EIPR 322. By 1982, however, Röttger seems to have persuaded himself that in *Hoffmann-La Roche* the Court established a subjective test: see Röttger, 'Article 36—More Subjective Views on Objectivity' [1982] 8 EIPR 215.

[144] In particular, M. van Empel, 'Centrafarm Revisited: A Few Comments on Cases 102/77 and 3/78' (1979) 16 CML Rev. 251, 257.

[145] The *Oberlandesgericht Karlsruhe* construed the ruling as meaning that Centrafarm's activities must be permitted: Röttger, 'The Hoffmann-La Roche Ruling Repackaged by the National Court' (cited in n. 143), at 285. However, the *Bundesgerichtshof* finally decided that Centrafarm could be prevented from repackaging 'Valium' since Hoffmann-La Roche had not 'artificially' partitioned the market, the use of different packaging being due to special factors applying in the various countries: D. Guy, 'Hoffmann-La Roche v Centrafarm: "Artificial" and "Natural" Restrictions on Interstate Trade' [1985] 4 EIPR 118.

packets containing a number of blister strips. Each blister strip contained five capsules and the words 'Vibramycin Pfizer' appeared on a sheet incorporated in each blister strip. Eurim-Pharm removed the blister strips from the manufacturer's original external packaging and placed each strip in a new box designed by it, without altering the strip or its contents. On the front of the box there was an opening covered with transparent material through which the words 'Vibramycin Pfizer' appearing on the sheet incorporated in the blister strips were visible. The back of the box bore a statement that the goods had been manufactured by the United Kingdom subsidiary of Pfizer and had been imported and repackaged by Eurim-Pharm. Pfizer sought an injunction in the German courts to prevent Eurim-Pharm from marketing the repackaged 'Vibramycin' on the ground that such a practice amounted to an infringement of its trade mark. The *Landgericht Hamburg* requested a preliminary ruling from the Court of Justice.

In its judgment the Court of Justice repeated the observations that it had made in *Hoffmann-La Roche v Centrafarm* about the specific subject-matter and essential function of the trade mark and about its role as a guarantee of origin. It then stated:

No use of the trade mark in a manner liable to impair the guarantee of origin takes place in a case such as the one in point where, according to the findings of the national court and the terms of the question submitted by it, a parallel importer has repackaged a pharmaceutical product merely by replacing the outer wrapping without touching the internal packaging and by making the trade mark affixed by the manufacturer on the internal packaging visible through the new external wrapping.

In such circumstances the repackaging in fact involves no risk of exposing the product to interference or influences which might affect its original condition and the consumer or final user of the product is not liable to be misled as to the origin of the product, above all where, as in this case, the parallel importer has clearly indicated on the external wrapping that the product was manufactured by a subsidiary of the proprietor of the trade mark and has been repackaged by the importer.[146]

3.3 *Two types of repackaging: are they significantly different?*

In *Pfizer v Eurim-Pharm* the Court felt it unnecessary to answer the question—expressly raised by the *Landgericht Hamburg*—whether an artificial partitioning of the market existed only when the trade mark owner used different packaging with the deliberate intention of obstructing parallel imports or whether the test was purely objective. The point was, however, dealt with by Advocate General Capotorti. He took the view that the test laid down in *Hoffmann-La Roche* was objective.[147]

---

[146] At paras 10 and 11 of the judgment.
[147] See point 6 of the Advocate General's opinion, at 293.

There is an obvious difference between Centrafarm's repackaging of 'Valium' and Eurim-Pharm's repackaging of 'Vibramycin'. Centrafarm removed the goods from their original external packaging and, without altering the internal packaging, placed the goods in new external packaging to which it affixed the trade mark. Eurim-Pharm also replaced the external packaging but, instead of affixing the trade mark to the new external packaging, it designed that packaging with a window through which the trade mark affixed to the internal packaging by the proprietor of the mark remained visible.

The Court appeared to attach great significance to the difference between the two types of repackaging. It seemed to imply that the proprietor of the trade mark could object to parallel imports of products repackaged according to Centrafarm's method (by virtue of the first sentence of Art. 30), unless the proprietor's use of different packaging artificially partitioned the common market and thus created a disguised restriction on trade (within the meaning of the second sentence of Art. 30). Eurim-Pharm's method of repackaging, on the other hand, was deemed unobjectionable *per se*, since it could not affect the condition of the goods and could not therefore impair the trade mark's function as a guarantee of origin.[148] There was therefore no justification for allowing the trade mark proprietor to oppose parallel imports of goods repackaged according to Eurim-Pharm's method. In *Pfizer v Eurim-Pharm* the Court appeared to reach that conclusion on the basis of the first sentence of Article 30, without having to consider the issue of a disguised restriction under the second sentence.

As Advocate General Jacobs was to point out in the *Paranova* cases some 15 years later, it was not logical to make a rigid distinction between the two types of repackaging. The Advocate General made the following comments:

Suppose, for example, that Company X buys a large quantity of a well-known carbonated beverage which has been placed in cardboard boxes, each containing 100 cans bearing the trade mark 'Coca Cola', by the Coca Cola Company and marketed in Member State A; Company X removes the external packaging and places 12 cans of the beverage in a cardboard box and writes on the outside of the box '12 cans of Coca Cola manufactured by the Coca Cola Company, Atlanta, USA, and repackaged by Company X'. If Company X then imports the product into Member State B, would there be any justification for allowing the proprietor of the trade mark 'Coca Cola' to block such parallel imports? Would the justification be any greater than if Company X placed 12 cans of Coca Cola in a cardboard box with cellophane windows through which the trade mark on the cans could be seen?

[148] The Court has rightly been criticized for exceeding its competence by deciding that the repackaging carried out by Eurim-Pharm could not impair the condition of the goods. That is really a question of fact for the national court. For example, if the inner wrapping had been of paper, a different finding might have followed: see J. Jandoll. '*Pfizer Inc. v Eurim-Pharm GmbH*: Repackaging of Drugs in Transparent Holders' [1982] 3 EIPR 83, 84. See also K. H. Hendry. 'Repackaging and the Essential Function of Trade Marks' (1982) 7 EL Rev. 403, 407.

In my view, it is difficult to see how there can be grounds for opposing parallel imports in the one case but not in the other. In neither case does Company X misappropriate goodwill belonging to the Coca Cola Company or represent its own goods as being the goods of another. In neither case does the repackaging impair the ability of the trade mark to function as a guarantee of origin. In both cases it is equally clear that the repackaging cannot affect the quality of the goods.

It would of course be a different matter if Company X bought Coca Cola in 100 litre barrels and then transferred the beverage to cans on which it placed the trade mark. In such a case there would be no way of ensuring that the repackaging did not affect the quality of the product. The beverage might be contaminated or adulterated and the trade mark's function as a guarantee of origin would clearly be compromised. This suggests that the crucial factor in determining whether the trade mark proprietor is justified in opposing parallel imports of repackaged goods is, not whether the parallel importer affixes the trade mark to the goods or merely allows the original mark to remain visible, but whether he interferes with the goods in such a way that it is no longer possible to be certain that their original condition has not been affected.[149]

The Advocate General argued that, if the Court's reasoning in *Hoffmann-La Roche* and *Pfizer* were scrutinised more closely, the case law did not in fact establish a rigid distinction between the two methods of repackaging. He maintained that the two judgments, read together, established that the trade mark could not be used to prevent the sale of repackaged goods where the use of different packages in different Member States had led to a partitioning of the market and where it was established that the repackaging could not affect the original condition of the goods.[150]

3.4 *Reappraisal of the case law in* Paranova

The facts of *Paranova* and the related cases were complicated because of the number of different cases. Altogether the litigation involved the following:

- three joined Danish cases which arose from actions brought against a Danish parallel importer (Paranova) by three pharmaceutical companies (Bristol-Myers Squibb, Boehringer, and Bayer);[151]
- three joined cases referred to the Court by the *Bundesgerichtshof* in actions brought against a German parallel importer (Eurim-Pharm) by three pharmaceutical companies (Beiersdorf, Boehringer, and Farmitalia);[152] and

---

[149] At paras 66–68 of the opinion.   [150] At para. 70 of the opinion.
[151] Joined Cases C-427/93, C-429/93 and C-436/93 *Bristol-Myers Squibb and others v Paranova* [1996] ECR I-3457.
[152] Joined Cases C-71 to 73/94 *Eurim-Pharm v Beiersdorf, Boehringer Ingelheim and Farmitalia Carlo Erba* [1996] ECR I-3603.

- one case referred to the Court by the *Oberlandesgericht Köln* as a result of an action against another German parallel importer (MPA Pharma) by the German subsidiary of a French pharmaceutical company (Rhône-Poulenc).[153]

In total, no fewer than 14 different pharmaceutical preparations were involved. The parallel importers used a variety of repackaging methods.[154] Here it is sufficient to note that both of the methods discussed above in relation to the earlier case law were in use. Thus, in some cases the parallel importers reaffixed the trade mark to the new external packaging, while in others they designed the new external packaging with a window so that the trade mark printed on the original packaging remained visible. In some cases the internal packaging consisted of blister packs which had to be cut up so that the repackaged products contained the number of pills required in the country of importation.

The legal situation had of course changed since the *Hoffmann-La Roche* and *Pfizer* judgments, inasmuch as the Trade Mark Directive had been adopted in 1988 and should have been implemented by the end of 1992. The exhaustion of rights is expressly dealt with in Article 7 of the Directive, which provides:

1. The trade mark shall not entitle the proprietor to prohibit its use in relation to goods which have been put on the market in the Community under that trade mark by the proprietor or with his consent.
2. Paragraph 1 shall not apply where there exist legitimate reasons for the proprietor to oppose further commercialisation of the goods, especially where the condition of the goods is changed or impaired after they have been put on the market.

Article 7(2) was obviously inspired by the Court's case law on repackaging, though its terms are sufficiently general to cover other situations (e.g. the resale of trade-marked goods which have passed their 'sell-by' or 'use-by' date or which have deteriorated to such an extent as to be capable of damaging the reputation of the trade mark).

The relationship between Article 7 of the Directive and Articles 28 and 30 of the Treaty was the subject of much debate in *Paranova* and the related cases. The German government argued that the effect of Article 7 was that the parallel importer was only allowed to resell trade-marked products in the form in which the trade mark owner had put them on the market in another Member State.[155] On that view, the parallel importer's limited right to repackage trade-marked goods, under the pre-Directive case law, had been abrogated by the Directive.

---

[153] Case C-232/94 *MPA Pharma v Rhône-Poulenc Pharma* [1996] ECR I-3671.
[154] For further details, see paras 6–36 of the Advocate General's opinion.
[155] See para. 32 of the judgment in *Bristol-Myers Squibb v Paranova*.

The Court rightly rejected that argument on the ground that 'a directive cannot justify obstacles to intra-Community trade save within the bounds set by the Treaty rules'.[156] The Court took the view that the legitimacy of repackaging must in principle be assessed under Article 7 of the Directive, but the Directive must, like any secondary source of law, be interpreted in the light of the Treaty rules.[157] The effect of that is that Article 7 of the Directive is unlikely to have any real bearing on the repackaging issue.

The Court went on to confirm expressly the judgment in *Hoffmann-La Roche v Centrafarm* but added that the existing case law must be clarified further in the light of the arguments raised in the new cases.[158] The principal clarification related to the concept of artificial partitioning of the market. The Court rejected categorically the argument that artificial partitioning took place only when the trade mark proprietor deliberately sought to partition the common market by marketing an identical product in various forms of packaging in different Member States.[159] The Court, concurring with the Advocate General,[160] made it clear that artificial partitioning occurred when the trade mark proprietor relied on his trade mark to oppose the marketing of repackaged products, even though such action was not justified by the need to safeguard the essential function of the trade mark.[161] Basically, that would be the case whenever the repackaging was done in such a way that the original condition of the product could not be affected by the repackaging.[162] What mattered in this respect was the condition of 'the product inside the packaging', not the condition of the packaging.[163] A mere 'hypothetical risk of isolated error' did not suffice to confer on the trade mark owner the right to oppose any repackaging of pharmaceutical products in new external packaging.[164] However, the trade mark owner could legitimately object to the marketing of repackaged goods if it was shown that 'defective, poor quality or untidy packaging could damage the trade mark's reputation'.[165] Here, the Court was taking up a point raised by the Advocate General, i.e. that the repackaging might be done in such a way that the image of the mark could be damaged because of the appearance of the product, even though its technical quality might not be affected.[166] The practices that provoked the Advocate General's concern were the use of severed blister packs and of external packaging with a

---

[156] Ibid., at para. 36 of the judgment. [157] Ibid., at paras 26 and 27 of the judgment.
[158] Ibid., at paras 50 and 51 of the judgment. [159] Ibid., at para. 57 of the judgment.
[160] See paras 82 and 83 of the opinion.
[161] *Bristol-Myers Squibb v Paranova*, at para. 57 of the judgment.
[162] See paras 58–66 of the judgment in *Bristol-Myers Squibb v Paranova* for a detailed discussion of this point.
[163] Ibid., at para. 58 of the judgment.
[164] Ibid., at para. 63 of the judgment.
[165] Ibid., at para. 76 of the judgment.
[166] See paras 116–118 of the Advocate General's opinion.

window through which the trade mark printed on the original internal packaging remained visible.[167] There is a certain irony in this, since the last-mentioned practice is the one used by the parallel importer in *Pfizer v Eurim-Pharm*, which was treated as particularly unobjectionable under the old case law.

Although the judgments in *Paranova* and the related cases are generally regarded as more favourable to the parallel importers than the old, pre-Directive case law, it must be noted that in one important respect they appear to have strengthened the position of the trade mark owners.[168] The Court insisted in *Paranova* and the related cases that parallel importers do not have a general right to repackage trade-marked products. They may only resort to repackaging when that is indispensable in order to be able to market the product in the Member State of importation and when they cannot gain access to that market by means less intrusive upon the rights of the trade mark owners (e.g. by affixing new labels to the original packaging in the appropriate language or by adding a translation of the instructions for the user).[169] Here the Court seems to have effected an ingenious and unconventional application of the proportionality principle.[170]

To sum up, the state of the law on repackaging, after *Paranova*, may be described in the following terms. The trade mark owner may oppose parallel imports of repackaged goods unless the conditions set out below are met. (In the following summary the words in italics indicate qualifications to the earlier case law added by the *Paranova* judgments.)

(1) It is established that the trade mark owner's reliance on his trade mark contributes to the artificial partitioning of the market, *which will be the case if he has put the same product on the market in several Member States in different packaging and the repackaging carried out by the parallel importer is*

---

[167] That is clear from para. 116 of the opinion.

[168] The judgments in *Paranova* and the related cases have nonetheless been criticized by several authors on the ground that they undermine the rights of trade mark owners: see, e.g. J. Calvo, 'Le reconditionnement des produits marqués en droit communautaire' (1997) No. 19 *Les Petites Affiches* 22–7; N. Dwyer Chapman, '*BMS et al v Paranova*: Parallel Importation in Light of the European Court of Justice Decision', November/December 1996, *Trademark World* 14–23; M.-A. Hermitte, 'Reconditionnement des produits marqués' (1997) *Journal du Droit International* 532; V.-L. Benabon, 'Cher nouveau visage pour la marque dans la jurisprudence de la Cour de justice; à propos des arrêts du 11 juillet 1996 sur le reconditionnement des produits marqués', (1996, novembre), *Europe, Chronique*, 1–6. The most critical author is Calvo, who accuses the Court of legalizing the rape of trade mark owners. For a more balanced view, see N. Ghea, 'Parallel importers' Use of Trade Marks: The European Court of Justice Confers Rights But Also Imposes Responsibilities', [1997] 3 EIPR 103.

[169] *Bristol-Myers Squibb v Paranova*, at paras 55 and 56 of the judgment.

[170] The proportionality principle usually means that restrictions on free movement are only permissible if they pursue a legitimate aim which cannot be obtained by less restrictive means. Here the effect of the principle is that restrictions on the rights of trade mark owners are only permissible if they pursue a legitimate aim which cannot be attained by less restrictive means.

necessary in order to be able to market the product in the Member State of importation.

(2) It is shown that the repackaging cannot affect the original condition of the product inside the packaging.

(3) The new packaging clearly states who repackaged the product and indicates the name of the manufacturer.

(4) *The presentation of the repackaged product is not liable to damage the reputation of the trade mark, as would happen if, for example, it was defective, of poor quality, or untidy.*

(5) The importer gives notice to the trade mark owner before the repackaged product is put on sale *and, on demand, supplies him with a specimen of the repackaged product.*

It will be seen, then, that the judgments in *Paranova* and the related cases basically confirmed the judgment in *Hoffmann-La Roche v Centrafarm*, but added several new elements.

3.5 *Further refinements of the* Paranova *principles*

The principles established in the *Paranova* series of cases were refined in a series of judgments delivered in 2002: *Merck, Sharp & Dohme v Paranova*,[171] *Boehringer v Swingward*,[172] and *Aventis Pharma Deutschland v Kohlpharma*.[173] Those cases also concerned repackaging of pharmaceuticals. Various types of repackaging were involved. One of the issues raised in *Merck, Sharp & Dohme v Paranova* and in *Boehringer v Swingward* was whether the parallel importer was allowed to repackage goods, as opposed to merely relabelling them, on the ground that consumers would be reluctant to buy pharmaceuticals that had clearly been packaged for sale in a different country.

The Court stressed that repackaging must be permitted if it was necessary in order for parallel imports to gain effective access to the market concerned. The Court recognized that strong resistance from a significant proportion of consumers to relabelled pharmaceutical products might create a hindrance to effective market access.[174] In such circumstances the parallel importer would be entitled to repackage the goods instead of simply relabelling them or placing stickers over the original labels.

The situation in *Aventis Pharma v Kohlpharma* was unusual. Aventis Pharma manufactured a pharmaceutical in packs of five cartridges and packs of ten cartridges. It marketed the former in France and the latter in

---

[171] Case C-443/99 [2002] ECR I-3703.   [172] Case C-143/00 [2002] ECR I-3759.
[173] Case C-433/00 [2002] ECR I-7761.
[174] At para. 31 of the judgment in *Merck, Sharp & Dohme v Paranova* and para. 52 of the judgment in *Boehringer v Swingward*.

Germany. It held central marketing authorizations for both package sizes, pursuant to Council Regulation (EEC) No. 2309/93.[175] Kohlpharma purchased products placed on the French market by Aventis Pharma and repackaged them in packs of ten cartridges for sale in Germany. Aventis Pharma argued that the repackaging was not necessary since the parallel importer could gain access to the German market by joining two packs of five cartridges and placing a sticker on them. The Court of Justice decided, however, in response to questions put to it by a German court, that that would not be compatible with Regulation No. 2309/93, since each marketing authorization issued in accordance with the Regulation relates to the specific presentation concerned. The Court held that the national court must decide, in the light of that conclusion, whether the circumstances prevailing at the time of marketing in the Member State of importation made the creation of new packaging objectively necessary in order for parallel imports to gain effective access to the market of that State.[176]

In *Boehringer v Swingward* the Court dealt again with the parallel importer's obligation to give notice of the intended repackaging to the trade mark proprietor. The Court held that it was incumbent on the parallel importer itself to give notice to the trade mark proprietor. It was not sufficient for the proprietor to be notified by other sources, such as the authority which issued a parallel import licence to the importer.[177]

As to the period of notice, the Court ruled that a trade mark proprietor must be given a 'reasonable time . . . to react to the intended repackaging' but that 'consideration must be given to the parallel importer's interest in proceeding to market the pharmaceutical product as soon as possible after obtaining the necessary licence from the competent authority'.[178] The Court suggested that, on the basis of the available evidence, fifteen working days might be a reasonable time.[179]

3.6 *Loendersloot: the relabelling of whisky*

The reaffixing of trade marks by a parallel importer was generally thought to be a phenomenon peculiar to the pharmaceutical trade until the *Loendersloot* case came before the Court.[180] In that case a Dutch trader (Mr Loendersloot) dealing in Scotch whisky removed the original labels placed on the bottles by the manufacturers and reaffixed them or replaced them with copies. He then re-exported them to various countries, including several Member States. He relabelled the bottles for the purpose of eliminating certain identification

---

[175] OJ 1993 L 214. p. 1.   [176] At para. 26 of the judgment.
[177] At para. 64 of the judgment.   [178] At para. 66 of the judgment.
[179] At para. 67 of the judgment.
[180] Case C-349/95 *Loendersloot v Ballantine and others* [1997] ECR I-6244.

numbers placed on the original labels by the manufacturers. He claimed that the manufacturers were attempting to partition the market and used the identification numbers to determine which of their dealers were supplying the parallel trade. They could thus cut off supplies to those dealers and prevent parallel imports. Mr Loendersloot argued therefore that without the relabelling parallel imports would be impossible. He also maintained that in some cases he had to remove the word 'pure' from the label and replace the name of the official importer with that of the parallel importer in order to comply with the legislation of the country of importation. Since the labels also bore the manufacturers' trade marks, the latter contended that the relabelling amounted to a trade mark infringement and applied to the competent Dutch court for an injunction to prevent Mr Loendersloot from relabelling their products. Mr Loendersloot argued that parallel imports could not take place without the relabelling, so the Dutch court queried whether an injunction could be granted in view of the Treaty provisions on the free movement of goods. It may be noted that, since Mr Loendersloot was exporting the goods from the Netherlands to other Member States, the relevant provision was Article 29 (not Art. 28) of the Treaty in conjunction with Article 30.

The Court of Justice repeated much of what it had said in *Paranova* and the related cases. On that basis it was easy to reach a provisional conclusion that, if the relabelling was necessary in order for parallel imports to take place, the whisky manufacturers would be artificially partitioning the market and practising a disguised restriction on trade between Member States by taking action to prevent the relabelling, on the assumption that the relabelling could not affect the original condition of the goods and hence could not compromise the specific subject-matter and essential function of the trade mark.

However, the matter was rendered more complex by the terms of Council Directive 89/396/EEC of 14 June 1989 on indications or marks identifying the lot to which a foodstuff belongs.[181] It appeared that the manufacturers might be under a legal obligation, as a result of that Directive, to place identification numbers on their bottles. Obviously, if that was the case, the manufacturers could not be accused of artificially partitioning the market simply because they were complying with a legal obligation.[182] As regards the possibility that the identification numbers, though placed on the bottles for a legitimate purpose, might also be used by the manufacturers as a means of combating parallel imports, the Court observed that the parallel traders should seek protection against that type of action under the Treaty provisions on competition.[183] Presumably that was a suggestion that

---

[181] OJ 1989 L 186, p. 21.   [182] See para. 42 of the judgment.
[183] At para. 43 of the judgment.

Mr Loendersloot should consider complaining to the Commission, which could then use its powers under Council Regulation No. 17 to investigate whether the whisky manufacturers and their official distributors were engaging in agreements or concerted practices of a type prohibited by Article 81 of the Treaty.

As regards the removal of the word 'pure' and the replacement of the official importer's name with that of the parallel importer, the Court adhered closely to the line followed in *Paranova* by holding that reliance on trade mark rights to prevent such relabelling would contribute to artificial partitioning of the market if it were established that the presence of the word 'pure' and the name of the official importer on the original labels would prevent the products from being marketed in the Member State of destination because it was contrary to the rules on labelling in force in that State.[184]

The Court added, however, that the relabelling must 'use means which make parallel trade possible while causing as little prejudice as possible to the specific subject-matter of the trade mark right'. Thus, if the necessary result could be achieved simply by applying to the bottles a sticker with additional information required in the Member State of importation, that method must be used instead of relabelling.[185] Once again, that amounts to an interesting adaptation of the principle of proportionality under which the Court has consistently held that, if certain legal requirements can be satisfied by the application to products of stickers containing additional information, there is no justification for banning the importation and sale of the product. The Court's maxim has always been that stickering is better than an import ban. In *Loendersloot* the Court neatly turned that maxim on its head by ruling that stickering is better than relabelling and reaffixing of trade marks.

3.7 The use of different trade marks for the same product

3.7.1 Reasons for using different trade marks

In normal circumstances, an undertaking that markets its products internationally will want to use the same trade mark for the same product, in the various territories in which it does business. The advantages of using the same trade mark are obvious—the undertaking will be able to organise its publicity on a global scale, advertising at (and sponsoring) international sports events, transmitting commercials on satellite television, and generating 'goodwill' internationally; it will also save on costs by not having to repackage the product for each market.

---

[184] At para. 45 of the judgment.   [185] At para. 46 of the judgment.

Sometimes a manufacturer will be forced to change a trade mark for a particular market. Its normal trade mark may conflict with a mark of greater seniority, owned by someone else. Or there may be an absolute bar to the registration and use of its trade mark in one or more countries; a trade mark chosen in good faith in its country of origin may turn out to be descriptive, misleading, or simply obscene in a foreign language. Again a trade mark, though eligible for registration, may have negative connotations in a particular country. The *Clinique* case[186] provides an example of a trade mark which was deemed acceptable in most of Europe but encountered problems in Germany, where it was considered misleading inasmuch as it induced consumers to believe that the products (cosmetics) possessed therapeutic properties.

When an undertaking uses different trade marks to designate the same products in different countries for no apparent reason, such a practice is likely to arouse the suspicion that its real aim is to use trade marks as a means of reinforcing a partitioning of the markets; the undertaking could then apply differential pricing without stimulating parallel imports, since the parallel importer would have little interest in importing a product that had no established reputation in the country of importation.

3.7.2 American Home Products Corporation: *the subjective intention of the trade mark owner appears decisive*

Until the judgment in *Upjohn v Paranova*[187] in 1999 there had been a dearth of case law on this particular subject (which suggests that the phenomenon may not be common-place). Apart from some *dicta* in the Advocate General's opinion in *Paranova* and the related cases, the only case to have come before the Court of Justice was *Centrafarm v American Home Products Corporation*.[188] The facts were as follows:

American Home Products Corporation sold the same pharmaceutical product under the trade mark 'Serenid' in the United Kingdom and under the trade mark 'Seresta' in the Netherlands. Centrafarm bought 'Serenid' pharmaceuticals which American Home Products Corporation had marketed in the United Kingdom and remarked them as 'Seresta' before marketing them in the Netherlands. Under Dutch law that amounted to a trade mark infringement. Litigation was commenced before a Dutch court, which sought a preliminary ruling on whether reliance on a trade mark in such circumstances was compatible with the Treaty rules on the free movement of goods.

---

[186] Case C-315/92 *Verband Sozialer Wettbewerb v Clinique Laboratoires and Estée Lauder* [1994] ECR I-317.
[187] Case C-379/97 [1999] ECR I-6927.   [188] Case 3/78 [1978] ECR 1823.

The Court gave its ruling less than five months after the judgment in *Hoffmann-La Roche v Centrafarm*. The two judgments followed the same pattern. Accordingly, the Court had no difficulty in holding that the trade mark proprietor who had marketed products in Member State A was entitled, in principle, to prevent them from being marketed in Member State B by a third party who had removed the trade mark used in Member State A and replaced it with the trade mark which the proprietor used in Member State B.[189] That conclusion was reached on the basis of the first sentence of Article 30 of the Treaty. The restriction on parallel imports was justified because the trade mark proprietor's right to prohibit any unauthorised affixing of his trade mark to his product came within the specific subject-matter of the trade mark.[190] Moreover, the essential function of the trade mark, which was to guarantee the origin of the trade-marked product to the consumer, would be jeopardised if a third party were allowed to affix the trade mark to the product, even an original product.[191]

As in *Hoffmann-La Roche v Centrafarm*, the Court went on to consider the implications of the second sentence of Article 30. The Court stated as follows:

> . . . it is necessary to consider whether the exercise of [the trade mark right] may constitute a 'disguised restriction on trade between Member States' within the meaning of the second sentence of Article [30].
>
> In this connection it should be observed that it may be lawful for the manufacturer of a product to use in different Member States different marks for the same product.
>
> Nevertheless it is possible for such a practice to be followed by the proprietor of the marks as part of a system of marketing intended to partition the markets artificially.
>
> In such a case the prohibition by the proprietor of the unauthorised affixing of the mark by a third party constitutes a disguised restriction on intra-Community trade for the purpose of partitioning the markets.[192]

In contradistinction to *Hoffmann-La Roche v Centrafarm*, the Court gave little guidance to the national court on how to identify a disguised restriction effected by the use of different trade marks.[193] Advocate General Capotorti was slightly more helpful. He suggested that an undertaking which used different trade marks in each Member State for a proprietary medicinal product having identical therapeutic properties must be required to provide 'an appropriate objective justification'.[194]

In spite of the parallelism between the judgments in *Hoffmann-La Roche v Centrafarm* and *Centrafarm v American Home Products Corporation* there

---

[189] At para. 18 of the judgment.   [190] At para. 17 of the judgment.
[191] At paras 12–14 of the judgment.   [192] At paras 19–23 of the judgment.
[193] L. Stevenson, 'The European Court Passes the Buck—New Problems in Choosing Trade Marks' [1979] EIPR 61. The title of the article provides an apposite comment on the judgment.
[194] [1978] ECR 1850.

were significant differences as regards the question whether the subjective intentions of the trade mark proprietor were relevant. The language used in *Hoffmann-La Roche v Centrafarm* did not necessarily imply that the concepts 'disguised restriction on trade between Member States' and 'artificial partitioning of the markets between Member States' contained a subjective element. As we have seen above, the Court was later to make it clear in *Paranova* and the related cases that a subjective element was not required. Where, therefore, the parallel importer reaffixes to the repackaged product the trade mark used on the original packaging, he does not have to prove that the trade mark proprietor deliberately sought to partition the markets by using different packaging.[195]

In contrast, the language used in *Centrafarm v American Home Products Corporation* clearly implied that a subjective element must be present. There the Court referred to 'a practice . . . followed by the proprietor of the marks as part of a system of marketing *intended to* partition the markets artificially'[196] (emphasis added). The Court also stated that the national court must ascertain 'whether the proprietor has followed the practice of using different marks for the same product *for the purpose of* partitioning the markets' (emphasis added).[197] It appeared therefore that, where the repackaging operations involved the *substitution* of trade marks, the trade mark proprietor would be entitled to oppose parallel imports, unless it could be shown that his use of different trade marks for the same product was deliberately intended to partition the markets.[198]

3.7.3 *The opinion of Advocate General Jacobs in* Paranova

The last point was highlighted by Advocate General Jacobs in his *Paranova* opinion.[199] The Advocate General noted that 'rather more difficult problems arise when the parallel importer changes the trade mark, as opposed to

---

[195] *Bristol-Myers Squibb v Paranova* at para. 57 of the judgment.

[196] At para. 21 of the judgment.   [197] At para. 23 of the judgment.

[198] It is, of course, debatable whether the different treatment which the Court accorded to the repackaging operations at issue in *Hoffmann-La Roche* and *American Home Products Corporation* is justified. One commentator regards the two judgments as irreconcilable: Röttger, op. cit. (the second article cited in n. 143). The conflict is also highlighted by J. Jandoll, in '*Pfizer Inc. v Eurim-Pharm GmbH*: Repackaging of Goods in Transparent Holders' [1981] 3 EIPR 83, 85. Van Empel suggests that when the Court came to decide *American Home Products Corporation* it already had misgivings about the judgment in *Hoffmann-La Roche*: op. cit. (n. 144, at 257). It could certainly be argued that the substitution of trade marks entails a greater interference with the prerogatives of the trade mark owner than mere repackaging. It might not always be easy to establish that products sold under different trade marks really are the same. In his *Pfizer* opinion Advocate General Capotorti put forward an alternative justification for the different approaches taken by the Court in *Hoffmann-La Roche* and *American Home Products Corporation*: see point 6 of the opinion, at 2394.

[199] At para. 84 of the opinion.

simply changing the packaging, and different solutions may be called for'.[200]

The use of different trade marks for the same product played only a minor role in one of the *Paranova* family of cases. In *Eurim-Pharm v Farmitalia Carlo Erba*[201] the pharmaceutical product in question was marketed in two versions in Germany. The two versions contained 5 mg and 10 mg of the active ingredient respectively. The weaker version was called 'Sermion' and the stronger version 'Sermion forte'. In Portugal the manufacturer marketed only the stronger version and called it simply 'Sermion' without the addition of the word 'forte'. The parallel importer repackaged the product marketed in Portugal and placed it on the market in Germany, having added the word 'forte' to the packaging so that the consumer would know that he was in fact buying the stronger version of the product. In a sense, therefore, the parallel importer's practice resembled that in issue in *Centrafarm v American Home Products Corporation*. Surprisingly, the Court's judgment did not comment on that particular feature of the case. The Advocate General, on the other hand, dealt with the matter at some length. The Court's silence justifies reproducing the Advocate General's comments in full:

124. The addition of the word 'forte' raises more difficult problems. In some ways there is a parallel with *American Home Products Corporation* . . . in so far as slightly different names (Sermion and Sermion forte) are used for the same product (the stronger version of the drug, with 10 mg of the active ingredient) in different Member States (Portugal and Germany). If the ruling in the former case were applied directly, the result might be that Farmitalia could object to the changing of the name by the parallel importer unless it were shown that Farmitalia and its associates had used different names with a view to deliberately partitioning the market.

125. I do not advocate that approach in the present case. It will be recalled that in *American Home Products Corporation* the two trade marks were 'Serenid' and 'Seresta'; one mark could not be turned into the other simply by adding a sticker with an extra word. The present case is therefore not identical. The starting-point in the search for a solution to the problem raised in the present case is the observation that Sermion marketed with Farmitalia's consent in Portugal may in principle be resold in Germany by a parallel importer under the name 'Sermion'; the owner of the trade mark cannot object on the ground that the product which it sells in Portugal under the name 'Sermion' is different from the product which it sells in Germany under the name. The owner of the mark cannot contend that consumers (or pharmacists) will be misled into thinking that the product contains 5 mg of the active ingredient rather than 10 mg. In *IHT Internationale Heiztechnik v Ideal Standard* the Court held that 'if the manufacture of products is decentralised within a group of companies and the subsidiaries in each of the Member States manufacture

---

products whose quality is geared to the particularities of each national market, a national law which enabled one subsidiary of the group to oppose the marketing in the territory of that State of products manufactured by an affiliated company on grounds of those quality differences would . . . be precluded [by Articles 28 and 30]'.

126. It is clear then that Eurim-Pharm may in principle sell in Germany under the mark 'Sermion' a product which the owner of that mark has placed on the market in Portugal under the mark 'Sermion'. But if that would cause confusion, since the product is twice as strong as the product known as 'Sermion' in Germany, it is clearly necessary, from everyone's point of view, that Eurim-Pharm should be allowed to remove the confusion by making it clear that the product corresponds to the product known in Germany as 'Sermion forte'.[202]

What the Advocate General seemed to be saying, in a nutshell, was that if the trade mark owner created a situation in which consumer confusion would inevitably result when his goods were the subject of parallel imports, then the parallel importer was entitled to take reasonable measures to eliminate the confusion.

3.7.4 Upjohn: *the objective need to relabel is decisive*

Following the judgment in *Upjohn v Paranova* it is now clear that the parallel importer who wishes to replace the original trade mark with another trade mark owned by the manufacturer of the product does not have to show that the trade mark proprietor deliberately used different trade marks for the purpose of partitioning the common market. The subjective intentions of the trade mark proprietor are no longer considered relevant. The law governing trade mark 'switching' is the same as the law governing repackaging.

Upjohn marketed an antibiotic, of which the generic name was clindamycin, under three slightly different trade marks: 'Dalacin' in Denmark, Germany and Spain, 'Dalacine' in France, and 'Dalacin C' in the other Member States. It appears that the use of different trade marks was not entirely of Upjohn's own choosing but was due to a trade mark dispute with—coincidentally—American Home Products Corporation. Paranova purchased clindamycin marketed by Upjohn in France under the trade mark 'Dalacine'. Paranova's intention was to re-mark the product as 'Dalacin' so that it could be resold in Denmark. Paranova also purchased 'Dalacin C' in Greece and resold it in Denmark as 'Dalacin'.

Upjohn applied to the Danish courts for an injunction restraining Paranova from marketing those products in Denmark. The *Sø og Handelsret* (Maritime and Commercial Court) sought guidance from the Court of

---

[202] At paras 124–126 of the opinion.

Justice on the interpretation of Article 7 of the Directive and Articles 28 and 30 of the Treaty. Essentially the Danish court wanted to know whether Paranova's right to change the original trade mark depended on the subjective intention of the trade mark proprietor and to what extent it was affected by the fact the trade mark proprietor's use of different trade marks was due to objective circumstances outside its control.

Although the Court did not expressly overrule the judgment in *American Home Products Corporation*, it made it clear in *Upjohn v Paranova* that the subjective intentions of the trade mark proprietor are no longer to be considered relevant. The practice of trade mark 'switching' is to be treated in the same way as repackaging and reaffixing the original trade mark.[203] Thus the parallel importer is allowed to replace the original trade mark with a different one that the manufacturer uses in the country of importation if that is objectively necessary in order that the product in question may be placed on the market in that country by the parallel importer. The Court defined this condition in the following terms:

This condition of necessity is satisfied if, in a specific case, the prohibition imposed on the importer against replacing the trade mark hinders effective access to the markets of the importing Member State. That would be the case if the rules or practices in the importing Member State prevent the product in question from being marketed in that State under its trade mark in the exporting Member State. This is so where a rule for the protection of consumers prohibits the use, in the importing Member State, of the trade mark used in the exporting Member State on the ground that it is liable to mislead consumers.[204]

The Court went on to observe, rather mysteriously, that 'the condition of necessity will not be satisfied if replacement of the trade mark is explicable solely by the parallel importer's attempt to secure a commercial advantage'.[205] It is not clear what the Court meant by this comment, which appears to have been inspired by the observations of the Commission. It is regrettable that the Court did not follow the advice of Advocate General Jacobs, who '[did] not find it helpful to postulate a category of "purely commercial reasons" which can never fall within the concept of necessity'.[206]

4. ADVERTISING AND THE EXHAUSTION OF THE TRADE MARK OWNER'S RIGHT

A distributor of goods will often want to inform potential customers that he stocks particular trade-marked products. He can only do so by means of

---

[203] At paras 37–39 of the judgment.   [204] At para. 43 of the judgment.
[205] At para. 44 of the judgment.   [206] At para. 54 of the opinion.

advertising and in the course of that advertising he will necessarily mention the trade marks under which the goods are sold. A jeweller may, for example, place an advertisement in a local newspaper stating that he offers for sale 'Rolex' watches. A chain of supermarkets may launch a television advertising campaign in which it informs shoppers that it has a special offer on 'Heinz' baked beans, 'Colgate' toothpaste, and 'Whiskas' cat food. It may print leaflets with colour pictures of those and other trade-marked products. A garage may want to tell the world that it repairs BMWs or has a large collection of used Jaguars for sale. The companies which manufacture those products and own the respective trade mark rights may or may not look favourably on such advertising campaigns. Everything depends on their marketing strategies and on the way they would like their brand image to be perceived by the public. On the one hand, a manufacturer of goods might welcome free publicity and view with enthusiasm any attempt by distributors to increase sales of the manufacturer's goods. On the other hand, some manufacturers—in particular those who produce goods with an image of luxury—prefer to exercise tight control over distribution channels, selecting distributors according to specific criteria and determining the place, time, content, and intensity of publicity about their products. If the trade mark is viewed as a vehicle for communicating a unique message to the public, it is not surprising that some trade mark owners wish to control the broadcasting of that message. In a much-quoted passage, H. G. Wells, the novelist, observed the process by which trade marks provided a means of direct communication between the manufacturer and the public: 'even in our childhood there was already a number of vigorous firms reaching their hands over the retail tradesman's shoulder, so to speak, and offering their goods in their own name to the customer'.[207]

The Wellsian metaphor captures the passive role that some trade mark owners would gladly assign to distributors, whom they regard as mute purveyors of their branded goods, denied even the right to tell the public what is for sale on their premises.

Attempts by trade mark owners to control the use of their trade marks in advertising carried out by distributors raise some interesting issues of Community law, above all in relation to exhaustion. Manufacturers who sell their goods through a network of selective distributors do not look kindly on interlopers. If a retailer not belonging to the network obtains branded goods which the owner of the trade mark has marketed in another Member State, and advertises the fact that he is offering those goods for sale,

---

[207] H. G. Wells, *The World of William Clissold*, Vol. I, p. 237, quoted by Martino and Groves, op. cit. n. 5, at 356. The first trade mark specialist to draw attention to this passage from Wells was probably Frank I. Schechter, who quoted it in his memorable article 'The Rational Basis of Trademark Protection' (1926–1927) *Harvard Law Review* 813, 818.

his unauthorised use of the trade mark in that advertising may amount to an infringement under the law of some Member States. If the owner of the trade mark can prevent such advertising by means of trade mark infringment proceedings, the question arises whether that is a restriction of imports contrary to Article 28 of the Treaty and, if so, whether the restriction is justified under Article 30.

Surprisingly, no cases on that point reached the Court of Justice before the entry into force of the Trade Mark Directive. Several provisions of the Directive are relevant. Article 5 defines the exclusive rights conferred on the proprietor of a registered trade mark. Under Article 5(3)(d) he may prohibit the use of the trade mark 'on business papers and in advertising'. Article 6 defines certain limitations on the effects of a trade mark. Under Article 6(1)(c), the proprietor may not prohibit a third party from using, in the course of trade, 'the trade mark where it is necessary to indicate the intended purpose of a product or service, in particular as accessories or spare parts'. Also relevant is Article 7 on the exhaustion of the rights conferred by a trade mark, the terms of which have already been quoted.

The interpretation of those provisions was considered by the Court in *Christian Dior v Evora*,[208] the facts of which were as follows. Christian Dior produced perfumes and other cosmetic goods which it sold at premium prices under an exclusive distribution system. It attached great importance to the luxury image of its goods. It had registered illustrations of the packaging of its perfumes as trade marks and also claimed copyright in the packaging and in the bottles in which its perfumes were sold. Evora, a Dutch company, operated a chain of shops which sold cosmetics and toiletries under the name Kruidvat. Although not appointed as distributors by Christian Dior, the Kruidvat shops sold Dior products which Evora obtained by means of parallel imports. In a Christmas promotion, in 1993, Kruidvat advertised for sale certain Dior products and during the promotion it depicted in advertising leaflets the packaging and bottles of those products. The advertising was carried out 'in a manner customary to retailers in [the market sector in question]'. Christian Dior considered that the advertising did not correspond to the luxurious and prestigious image of its products. It brought trade mark and copyright infringement proceedings in a Dutch court and applied for an injunction prohibiting Evora from reproducing pictures of its products in catalogues, brochures, advertisements, or otherwise. The litigation reached the *Hoge Raad der Nederlanden*, which referred a number of questions to the Court of Justice on the interpretation of Articles 5 and 7 of the Trade Mark Directive and Articles 28 and 30 of the Treaty. Basically the Dutch court wanted to know:

---

[208] Cited in n. 14.

(1) whether, on a proper interpretation of Articles 5 to 7 of the Directive, when trade-marked goods have been marketed within the Community by, or with the consent of the trade mark owner, the reseller, besides being free to resell those goods, is also free to make use of the trade mark in order to bring to the public's attention the fact that he is offering the goods for sale;

(2) whether, in the event of an affirmative answer to that question, there are exceptions to the ensuing rule where the advertising function of the trade mark is endangered inasmuch as the reseller's advertising damages the luxurious and prestigious image of the mark; and

(3) whether, under Articles 28 and 30 of the Treaty, the owner of a trade mark or holder of copyright in the bottles or packaging in which his goods are presented may invoke the trade mark or copyright in order to prevent a reseller from advertising the goods in a manner customary to retailers in the relevant sector, in particular when the advertising is done in such a way as to damage the luxurious and prestigious image of the trade mark.

The Court had no difficulty in giving an affirmative answer to the first question as summarised above. It ruled that if the right to prohibit the use of the trade mark in relation to goods, conferred on the trade mark proprietor by Article 5 of the Directive, is exhausted once the goods have been placed on the market with the consent of the proprietor, in accordance with Article 7(1) of the Directive, the same must apply to the right to use the trade mark for the purpose of attracting customers for the goods.[209]

As regards the second question (as reformulated above), the Court's reply was more nuanced. It recognised that the danger of damage to the reputation of the trade mark might be a legitimate reason, within the meaning of Article 7(2) of the Directive, for allowing the proprietor of the trade mark to oppose its use in relation to goods placed on the market with his consent.[210] The Court then observed that a balance must be struck between the legitimate interest of the trade mark owner and the reseller's legitimate interest in being able to resell the goods in question by using advertising methods which were customary in his sector of trade.[211] The reseller must not act unfairly in relation to the legitimate interest of the trade mark owner and must endeavour to prevent his advertising from affecting the value of the trade mark by detracting from the allure and prestigious image of the goods and from their aura of luxury.[212] However, where the reseller used for the trade-marked goods the modes of advertising which were customary in his trade sector, even if they were not the same as those used by the trade

---

[209] At paras 36 and 37 of the judgment.   [210] At paras 42 and 43 of the judgment.
[211] At para. 44 of the judgment.   [212] At para. 45 of the judgment.

mark owner himself or by his approved retailers, that was not a legitimate reason for allowing the trade mark owner to oppose the advertising, unless it was established that, given the specific circumstances of the case, the use of the trade mark in the reseller's advertising seriously damaged the reputation of the trade mark.[213] Such damage might occur if, in an advertising leaflet, the reseller put the trade mark in a context which might seriously detract from the image of the trade mark.[214]

Finally, as regards the third question (as reformulated above), the Court held, as in *Paranova*, that Article 30 of the Treaty and Article 7 of the Directive must be interpreted in the same way. That merely left the issue of copyright, which the Court disposed of neatly by observing that in circumstances such as those of the *Christian Dior* case the protection conferred by copyright as regards the reproduction of protected works in a reseller's advertising could not in any event be broader than the protection conferred by a trade mark in the same circumstances.[215]

The overall effect of the *Christian Dior* judgment may be summarised as follows. A manufacturer who markets goods in the common market cannot invoke trade mark rights and copyright in relation to those goods to prevent a reseller of the goods from advertising them, unless he can point to some specific circumstance which shows that the advertising will seriously damage his commercial reputation. For an example of such a circumstance, reference may be made to the opinion of Advocate General Jacobs, who suggested that the owner of a trade mark for luxury perfumes might be entitled to oppose an advertisement which depicted his perfumes in a cut-price 'sale-bin' along with rolls of toilet paper and toothbrushes.[216]

Bearing in mind that the *Christian Dior* case was the first in which the Court was expressly invited to examine the advertising function of trade marks, the judgment is worthy of the highest praise. The Court performed an admirable balancing exercise as it sought to weigh the competing interest of the trade mark owner in protecting the advertising function of his trade mark[217] and the interest of the unauthorised dealer in effectively marketing trade-marked goods obtained from parallel sources. The Court also deserves commendation for its robust refusal to allow copyright to be abused as a means of erecting barriers to the free movement of trade-marked goods.

---

[213] At para. 46 of the judgment.   [214] At para. 47 of the judgment.
[215] At para. 58 of the judgment.   [216] At para. 51 of the Advocate General's opinion.
[217] The judgment can also be regarded as recognizing 'the interests of the proprietor in the trade mark itself as a vehicle for creating goodwill, as well as . . . the interests of consumers in not being misled about the nature or quality of the goods': H. Norman, 'Perfume, Whisky and Leaping Cats of Prey: A U.K. Perspective on Three Recent Trade Mark Cases before the European Court of Justice' [1998] EIPR 306, 307.

The advertising function of trade marks was again in issue in *BMW v Deenik*.[218] In that case a Dutch garage owner (Mr Deenik), who specialised in selling second-hand BMWs and in repairing cars of that make, was sued by BMW for allegedly infringing its trade marks. Mr Deenik, who did not belong to BMW's network of authorised dealers, used those trade marks in his advertisements to indicate his field of specialisation. The first-instance court granted an injunction prohibiting Mr Deenik from using BMW's trade marks in such a way as to create the impression that he was an authorised BMW dealer but considered that he was entitled to describe himself in his advertisements as a 'BMW specialist' and to offer the service of 'repairing and maintaining BMWs'. BMW appealed to the *Hoge Raad der Nederlanden*, which referred a number of questions to the Court of Justice on the interpretation of Articles 5 and 7 of the Directive. The basic issue was similar to that raised in *Christian Dior*, i.e. to what extent might an unauthorised reseller of branded goods use the trade mark in his advertising? Also raised was the issue to what extent an unauthorised repairer of such goods might use the trade mark in his advertising to indicate that he repaired the products of a specific manufacturer.

The Court ruled that, under Article 7 of the Directive, an unauthorised dealer is allowed to use the trade mark to advertise the fact that he specialises in the sale of cars of a particular mark, provided that the advertising concerns cars that have been placed on the market in the Community by the proprietor of the trade mark or with his consent and provided that the way in which the trade mark is used in the advertising does not constitute a 'legitimate reason' within the meaning of Article 7(2) of the Directive for the proprietor to oppose further marketing of the goods.[219] As an example of such a legitimate reason, the Court referred to advertising which gave rise to the impression that there was a commercial connection between the dealer and the trade mark proprietor, and in particular that the dealer was affiliated to the trade mark proprietor's distribution network.[220]

As regards the garage owner's use of the trade mark in advertising designed to inform the public that he specialises in the repair and maintenance of cars of a particular mark, the Court reached exactly the same conclusion on the basis of Article 6(1)(c) of the Directive.[221] According to that provision, the trade mark proprietor is not entitled to prohibit another person from using the trade mark in the course of trade where its use is necessary in order to indicate the intended purpose of a product or service, in particular as accessories or as spare parts, provided that he uses the trade

---

[218] Cited in n. 14.   [219] At para. 50 of the judgment.
[220] At para. 51 of the judgment.   [221] At paras 58–63 of the judgment.

mark 'in accordance with honest practices in industrial or commercial matters'.[222]

5. UNFAIR COMPETITION, CONSUMER PROTECTION, AND TRADE MARKS

5.1 *Introduction*

The concept of unfair competition (*concurrence déloyale*), as a catch-all category of judicially restrainable unlawful business practices, began in France around 1850.[223] The French approach spread to other countries in continental Europe, in particular Germany, where paragraph 1 of the 1909 Law against Unfair Competition (*das Gesetz gegen den unlauteren Wettbewerb*)[224] provided: 'Any person who in the course of trade and for purposes of competition commits acts contrary to honest practices may be enjoined from these acts and held liable in damages.'

The principal concern of unfair competition law is thus to prevent dishonest business practices such as:

- the misuse of distinguishing signs to create confusion about the origin of goods;
- the misuse of geographical designations;
- the 'slavish' imitation of a competitor's goods;
- the use of disparaging or negative advertising (including, to some extent, comparative advertising); and
- the misappropriation of business secrets (know-how).

It is clear, then, that unfair competition law intersects with various categories of intellectual property rights, in particular trade marks. The affinity between unfair competition law and the protection of intellectual property rights is demonstrated by the existence of Article 10 *bis* of the Paris Convention for the Protection of Industrial Property, which states:

Unfair Competition

(1) The countries of the Union are bound to assure to nationals of such countries effective protection against unfair competition.

---

[222] The language of the proviso to Art. 6(1) is borrowed from Art. 10 *bis* (2) of the Paris Convention for the Protection of Industrial Property (see the section 5.1 of this chapter).

[223] For historical surveys, see G. Schricker, 'Unfair Competition and Consumer Protection in Western Europe' (1970) 1 IIC 415, and F.-K. Beier, 'The Development and Present Status of Unfair Competition Law in Germany—An Outline' (1973) 4 IIC 77.

[224] The Law is still in force, though it has been amended on numerous occasions. The current version is available, in German, at http://transpatent.com. An English translation is available on the website of the World Intellectual Property Organization (WIPO) at http://clea.wipo.int.

(2) Any act of competition contrary to honest practices in industrial or commercial matters constitutes an act of unfair competition.

(3) The following in particular shall be prohibited:

1. all acts of such a nature as to create confusion by any means whatever with the establishment, the goods, or the industrial or commercial activities, of a competitor;

2. false allegations in the course of trade of such a nature as to discredit the establishment, the goods, or the industrial or commercial activities, of a competitor;

3. indications or allegations the use of which in the course of trade is liable to mislead the public as to the nature, the manufacturing process, the characteristics, the suitability for their purpose, or the quantity, of the goods.

Despite the United Kingdom's membership of the Paris Union, the common law has traditionally been distrustful of the continental method of attacking unfair competition by means of a general clause such as the German provision cited above. Comparativists regard the tort of passing-off as the common law's nearest equivalent to a law of unfair competition. Attempts to develop a more general concept of unfair competition were resisted on grounds of judicial self-restraint, of which the classic example is Lord Fry's dictum in the *Mogul* case that 'to draw a line between fair and unfair competition, between what is reasonable and unreasonable, passes the power of the Courts'.[225]

A common feature of the nineteenth-century approach, both in England and in continental jurisdictions, was that the law focused on the interest of honest traders in preventing unscrupulous competitors from gaining an unfair advantage. The interest of the consumer was only incidentally protected. Later statutory developments on both sides of the English Channel, particularly in the second half of the twentieth century, have stressed the importance of the consumer as the ultimate beneficiary of fair competition in a properly regulated market-place. Thus the concepts of fair trading and consumer protection have come to be bracketed together, not least in the case law of the Court of Justice.[226]

Disparities in the laws of the Member States on fair trading and consumer protection have an obvious capacity to result in barriers to trade between Member States. For that reason attempts have been made to harmonize the national laws.[227] Success has been limited. The main achievement has been

---

[225] *Mogul Steamship Co. v McGregor* (1889) 23 QBD 598, 626.

[226] Above all in the 'Cassis de Dijon' line of cases starting with Case 120/78 *REWE-Zentrale v Bundesmonopolverwaltung für Branntwein* [1979] ECR 649.

[227] For an account of these attempts, see G. Schricker, 'European Harmonization of Unfair Competition Law—A Futile Venture?' (1991) 22 IIC 788. See also G. Schricker, 'Twenty-five Years of Protection against Unfair Competition' (1995) 26 IIC 782; and F.-K. Beier, 'The Law of Unfair Competition in the European Community—Its Development and Present Status' [1985] 10 EIPR 284.

a Council Directive on misleading advertising,[228] adopted in 1984, and since amended so as to deal with comparative advertising.[229] In addition, there have been numerous directives harmonizing laws on matters such as the composition and labelling of foodstuffs and other products.

5.2 *The Court's general approach to unfair competition and consumer protection*

Barriers to trade caused by disparate national legislation on unfair competition and consumer protection will be around for a long time to come. The Court of Justice has frequently had occasion to address such problems in its decisions, a number of which have concerned the relationship between unfair competition, consumer protection and trade marks. Before examining those cases, we must briefly recall the general principles developed by the Court. First, Article 30, as an exception to a fundamental rule cannot be interpreted extensively, so fair trading and consumer protection cannot simply be added to the list of overriding interests which are capable of justifying trade restrictions under Article 30.[230] However, a trade barrier due to disparate national laws lies outside the scope of Article 28 if the measure in question applies without distinction to domestic and imported goods and if it is necessary in order to safeguard certain 'mandatory requirements' such as fair trading or consumer protection.[231]

The logic of excluding unfair competition and consumer protection from Article 30 has never been evident, especially in view of the terms of Article 10 *bis* of the Paris Convention. That provision suggests that the expression 'industrial and commercial property' in Article 30 of the Treaty is broad enough to include rights flowing from the law of unfair competition. As a result of the 'Cassis de Dijon' case law, the exclusion is rarely of any consequence. It simply means that a trading rule designed to promote fair competition and consumer protection must apply without distinction to domestic and imported goods (otherwise any import restriction caused by the rule will automatically infringe the Treaty), whereas a rule which benefits from Article 30 may differentiate between domestic and imported goods provided that the difference in treatment does not amount to arbitrary discrimination or a disguised restriction on trade. In both cases the trading rule must, if it results in import restrictions, be justified; that will only be the case if it is an appropriate means of pursuing an objective recognised in Community law (e.g. the protection of intellectual property

---

[228] Council Directive 84/450/EEC of 10 September 1984 (OJ 1984 L 250, p. 7).
[229] Council Directive 97/55/EC of the European Parliament and the Council of 6 October 1997 (OJ 1997 L 290, p. 18).
[230] See, e.g., Case 113/80 *Commission v Ireland* ('Irish souvenirs' case) [1981] ECR 1625.
[231] See, e.g., 'Cassis de Dijon', cited in n. 226.

rights, fair trading or consumer protection) and if the objective cannot be attained by means less restrictive of the free movement of goods.

5.3 *A potpourri of cases*

5.3.1 Dansk Supermarked v Imerco

The first case to be considered in this context is *Dansk Supermarked v Imerco*,[232] the facts of which were highly unusual. Imerco, a Danish company whose shareholders were hardware merchants, operated as a wholesale hardware merchant. The shareholders were the customers of the company. In celebration of its fiftieth anniversary, Imerco commissioned from a British manufacturer a number of china services decorated with Danish castles and bearing on the reverse an inscription with the words 'Imerco Fiftieth Anniversary'. It intended the services to be marketed in Denmark solely by its shareholders and publicised the operation 'on a very large scale'.[233] As a result of the stringent quality standards, approximately 1,000 lots were rejected as substandard. Imerco authorised the manufacturer to sell the substandard services itself, but not in the Scandinavian countries. Dansk Supermarked obtained through dealers a number of the substandard services marketed in the United Kingdom. Dansk Supermarked offered those services for sale in its shops in Denmark at prices appreciably lower than those of the services sold by Imerco's members. Imerco sought an injunction restraining Dansk Supermarked from selling the substandard services. Imerco invoked Danish provisions on unfair competition[234] and also contended that the sale infringed its trade mark and its copyright.

The Danish Supreme Court submitted a preliminary question to the Court of Justice, asking simply whether the Treaty or measures implementing it precluded the application to the case of the Danish laws on copyright, trade marks and marketing. The question was, of course, badly formulated. The Danish court made no attempt to identify the relevant provisions of Community law and asked the Court of Justice to decide the case on its behalf rather than give an interpretative ruling. None of that can excuse the confusing manner in which the Court dealt with the case.

The Court decided that Articles 28 and 30 of the Treaty were the relevant provisions of Community law and stated, astonishingly, that Article 81 had no bearing on the case.[235] In the very next paragraph the Court stated that the question referred to it must be understood as asking whether

---

[232] Case 58/80 [1981] ECR 181.　　　　　　　　[233] At 183 of the report.

[234] The provision in question was a general clause not unlike the German provision cited earlier. It prohibited 'all actions contrary to fair marketing practices'.

[235] At para. 8 of the judgment.

'goods which have been lawfully marketed in one Member State with the consent of the undertaking which is entitled to sell them may be prohibited, *under an agreement concluded between that undertaking and the manufacturer*, from being marketed in another Member State either on the basis of national provisions on the protection of copyright or trade marks or under legislation on marketing'[236] (emphasis added). In view of the words in italics, one may well ask how Article 81 could be irrelevant.[237]

The Court had no difficulty in disposing of the trade mark and copyright issues by stating correctly that such rights were exhausted once the proprietor had consented to the marketing of the products in question in another Member State.[238] Since Imerco had consented to the sale of the substandard sets in the United Kingdom, there could be no question of allowing it to oppose their resale in Denmark on the basis of a trade mark or copyright.

On the issue of unfair competition the Court seems to have had no clear idea of what it wanted to say. Its treatment of the issue was hopelessly confusing. It analysed the Danish court's question as seeking to establish whether 'it is possible to consider as contrary to approved marketing usage the sale in Denmark of goods marketed in another Member State with the agreement of a Danish undertaking but subject to the condition that the goods must not be exported to Denmark so as to compete there with the goods marketed exclusively by the undertaking concerned'.[239]

Presumably the Court thought that such a question must be answered in the negative. It contrived nonetheless to give an answer which allowed the Danish Court, when it came to apply the preliminary ruling, to grant the injunction sought by Imerco.[240] The Court of Justice achieved that remarkable result by means of some unusually turgid prose. It stated that Community law does not in principle prevent the application in a Member State to goods imported from other Member States of the provisions on marketing in the State of importation. It followed that the marketing of imported goods might be prohibited if the conditions on which they were sold constituted an infringement of the marketing usages considered proper and fair in the Member State of importation.[241] Citing an old judgment (*Béguelin*),[242]

---

[236] At para. 9 of the judgment.

[237] Advocate General Capotorti, to his credit, proposed a ruling to the effect that an agreement of the kind in issue was incompatible with Art. 81 if it affected trade between Member States and the free play of competition within the common market to an appreciable extent; see the report at 203.

[238] At paras 11 and 12 of the judgment. This is one of the rare cases, in that period, in which the Court actually used the expression 'exhaustion'.

[239] At para. 14 of the judgment.

[240] Decision of the Højesteret of 2 December 1981 (1983) 14 IIC 280. See also the case note by K. Dyekjaer-Hansen, 'A/S Imerco v Dansk Supermarked A/S: Parallel Import of Branded Seconds' [1982] 3 EIPR 85.

[241] At para. 15 of the judgment.

[242] Case 22/71 [1971] ECR 949.

the Court stated that 'the actual fact of the importation of goods which have been lawfully marketed in another Member State cannot be considered as an improper or unfair act since that description may be attached only to offer or exposure for sale on the basis of circumstances distinct from the importation itself.'[243] In the context of *Imerco v Dansk Supermarked* that statement is virtually incomprehensible.

Finally, the Court emphasised that agreements between individuals could not in any circumstances derogate from the Treaty provisions on the free movement of goods; it followed that an agreement involving a prohibition on the importation into a Member State of goods lawfully marketed in another Member State could not be relied on or taken into consideration in order to classify the marketing of such goods as an improper or unfair commercial practice.[244]

The Court's ruling was sufficiently vague to allow the Danish Supreme Court to rule (by a majority of five to two) that Dansk Supermarked should be enjoined from selling the services without expressly marking them as substandard.

Surprisingly, two authors[245] criticise the Court's judgment on the ground that it was too harsh on firms which, like Imerco, attempt to dispose of substandard goods on part of the common market while taking measures to ensure that their reputation is not affected when the goods resurface in other parts of the common market. The gist of the criticism is that if Imerco could not prevent the parallel imports it would have an incentive to have the goods manufactured in Denmark.[246] The criticism is surely misplaced. It denies the logic of the common market. Firms cannot take the benefits of the common market (access to supplies in other Member States, possibilities of marketing products in various Member States) and refuse the disadvantages (parallel imports). Above all, the criticism neglects the need for a coherent approach to intellectual property rights and to concepts such as unfair competition and consumer protection. In *Ideal Standard*[247] the Court categorically insisted that undertakings which adapt the quality of their products to the perceived requirements of the market in different Member States, but sell them under the same trade mark, cannot rely on their trade mark rights to oppose parallel imports. The Court was not unduly con-

---

[243] At para. 16 of the judgment.   [244] At para. 17 of the judgment.

[245] Dyekjaer-Hansen, op. cit. (n. 240), and V. Korah, *An Introductory Guide to EC Competition Law and Practice*, 5th edn, Sweet and Maxwell, London, 1994, para. 9.4.3.

[246] In fact the place of manufacture is irrelevant. If Imerco had had the goods manufactured in Denmark and then disposed of the substandard services in the United Kingdom (without an indication that they were substandard), it should not have been allowed to prevent the importation and resale in Denmark of the substandard services (without such an indication). Thus, if the law is properly applied there is no incentive for a firm in Imerco's situation to have the goods manufactured in any particular Member State.

[247] Cited in n. 58, at para. 38 of the judgment.

cerned about consumer confusion caused by such practices in *Ideal Stand-ard*. Why then should a different approach commend itself when the argu-ment is presented in terms of unfair competition and consumer protection? Undertakings and consumers should be encouraged to adapt to the reality of the common market. The former should not attempt to subvert that reality by specious arguments about unfair competition; and the latter might find that access to cheap imports benefits them more than a host of measures adopted in the name of consumer protection.

5.3.2 Kohl v Ringelhan & Rennett

Different problems arose in *Kohl v Ringelhan & Rennett*,[248] but once again the issue of alleged consumer confusion about the quality of goods was at the forefront. The defendant was a French company founded in 1971 as the subsidiary of the German company 'Ringelhan & Rennett', which was at the time a leading manufacturer of pharmaceutical equipment. The German parent company was wound up in 1982. The French subsidiary was sold to a third party. With the authorisation of the German liquidator it continued to use the symbol 'r + r' in white letters on a contrasting background. The symbol had previously been used by both the German parent company and the French subsidiary. It is not clear from the report whether, after the liquidation of the German parent company, the French company registered the symbol as a trade mark in its own name or in the name of the newly created German company 'Ringelhan Einrichtungs GmbH', which acted as its commercial representative in Germany. Nor does the report reveal whether Ringelhan Einrichtungs GmbH was a sub-sidiary of the French company. It is, however, clear that no other person had any special claim to the use of the symbol in Germany after the liquidation of the original German owner. The claimant (Kohl), which also manufactured pharmaceutical equipment, certainly did not claim any right of its own to the symbol in question. It simply argued that the French company's use of the symbol amounted to a 'misleading statement regarding the origin of goods', contrary to paragraph 3 of the German Law on Unfair Competition.[249] Kohl's claim was that the defendant's use of the symbol, without indicating that there was no longer any legal or economic connection with the old Ringelhan & Rennett, which had a considerable

---

[248] Case 177/83 [1984] ECR 3651.

[249] Paragraph 3 states: 'Any person who, in the course of trade and for the purpose of competition, makes misleading statements about business matters, in particular about the nature, the origin, the manner of manufacture or the pricing of individual goods or commercial services or of the offer as a whole, about price lists, the manner or the source of acquisition of goods, the possession of awards, the occasion or purpose of the sale or the size of the available stock, may be enjoined from making such statements.'

reputation, misled the German public. Kohl sought an injunction prohibiting the French company from using the symbol without such an indication. The German court asked the Court of Justice, in effect, whether such a prohibition would be contrary to Article 28 of the Treaty.

The case is a marvellous illustration of how unfair competition law, if not applied with restraint, can make a nonsense of trade mark law. Trade marks, along with the goodwill which they embody, frequently change hands as a result of assignments, mergers, demergers, company restructuring, insolvency, etc. The argument that the person who acquires the right to use a trade mark through such operations, or through a licence, may be prevented from doing so on the ground that consumers might associate the trade mark with its former owner or with a licensor would, if accepted, place a wholly unjustified restriction on commercial freedom. It would also destroy one of the supposed advantages of a trade mark registration system, i.e. the ease with which registered trade marks can be assigned and licensed. The argument becomes particularly absurd when the former owner of the trade mark no longer exists. It would mean, in effect, that moribund companies would be unable to dispose of their goodwill by selling their trade marks; the victims would be the shareholders and creditors of the insolvent company, since the liquidator would be prevented from realising a part of the company's assets. Once again we are in the face of an argument that denies the logic of the common market. German companies are allowed to set up companies in other Member States (Art. 43, second para. of the Treaty) and to assign trade marks to their subsidiaries. There is no reason why such a subsidiary should become disinherited because the original parent ceases to exist. Kohl would presumably not have dared to raise such an argument if the 'r + r' had been acquired by a German company which had bought a German subsidiary of the original Ringelhan & Rennett. Kohl's argument was in any case manifestly unfounded in the light of the legal and economic links that existed between the original, now defunct German owner of the 'r + r' symbol and the French undertaking which had acquired the right to use it. The German and French companies had, until recently, been part of the same group and carried on an integrated business with the same managing director:[250] there was every reason to suppose that the French company now using the 'r + r' symbol had inherited the technical expertise and know-how that had helped to create the reputation of the symbol.

Fortunately the Court of Justice gave a ruling which left no doubt that the prohibition sought by Kohl would be contrary to Article 28. The Court's reasoning was, however, thoroughly unsatisfactory. Instead of addressing the important points of substance outlined above, the Court followed a

---

[250] See the opinion of Advocate General Lenz, at 3666.

purely formalistic approach. It observed that the German legislation on unfair competition, as interpreted by the national court, did not apply without distinction to domestic and imported goods and could not therefore benefit from the 'Cassis de Dijon' case law on mandatory requirements relating to consumer protection and fair trading.[251] The reason for that finding was that the German legislation, although ostensibly non-discriminatory, was being interpreted in such a way that it became possible 'to prohibit the use of a distinctive symbol for the sole reason that the public may be misled as to the domestic or foreign origin of the goods, without its being necessary to adduce evidence of other specific factors establishing the existence of unfair competition'.[252] That finding was questionable. Although there may well have been an underlying element of protectionism—xenophobia even—in Kohl's case and in the German court's treatment of it, it was not presented in such terms and it is difficult to see what justification the Court had for drawing such conclusions. Kohl's argument was not that consumers would be misled into believing that the French goods were of German origin, but that consumers would associate the goods with a specific (now defunct) German company. That is not quite the same thing. Thus the formalistic basis for refusing to examine whether the prohibition sought by Kohl was justified under the 'mandatory requirements' doctrine was lacking. If formalistic tools of analysis are to be used, they should at least be applied accurately. It would in fact have been far better if the Court had treated the German legislation as non-discriminatory in form and then gone on to consider whether the prohibition sought by Kohl was necessary on grounds of unfair competition and consumer protection. For the reasons of policy given above, the answer would clearly have been negative.

The Court indulged in further formalism with regard to an alternative argument put forward by the German government to the effect that the measure could be justified under Article 30 of the Treaty if the term 'public policy' in that article were interpreted broadly so as to embrace considerations of consumer protection. On that point, the Court adhered to its settled case law, according to which Article 30 must be interpreted restrictively and cannot include matters such as consumer protection, which must therefore be addressed exclusively under the 'mandatory requirements doctrine' with its essential precondition of application without distinction to domestic and imported goods.[253] In that respect the Court's formalism is too well established to be open to challenge. Even there, though, one cannot help observing that the law would be much simpler and clearer if the Court were willing to bring unfair competition and consumer protection (not to

---

[251] At paras 14–17 of the judgment.   [252] At para. 15 of the judgment.
[253] At paras 18 and 19 of the judgment.

mention protection of the environment and other recognised 'mandatory requirements') under the umbrella of Article 30. The law would certainly be healthier if the Court could be persuaded to drop formalism and apply a policy-orientated approach to import barriers caused by legislation on unfair trading. In few areas can there be a greater need for an examination of policy considerations and a balancing of competing interests.

5.3.3 *Prantl*

Policy considerations were certainly not absent from the Court's judgment in *Prantl*,[254] which was decided a few months before *Kohl v Ringelhan & Rennett*. Nor may it be said that in *Prantl* the Court did not strive to balance the competing interests.

Prantl was yet another case about the alleged susceptibility of German consumers to confusion. This time the perceived source of confusion lay in the shape of a particular type of wine bottle. The 'Bocksbeutel' bottle, which has a characteristic bulbous shape, is traditionally used by wine-growers in Franconia (Germany). Under the relevant German wine legislation only wine-growers in certain parts of Franconia are entitled to use the Bocksbeutel bottle. A bottle of similarly bulbous shape is traditionally used by wine-growers in the Italian province of Bolzano. Mr Prantl, a dealer in beverages, was prosecuted in Germany for importing and selling wine from Bolzano in Bocksbeutel bottles. He was initially acquitted, on the basis of Articles 28 and 30 of the Treaty, but the public prosecutor appealed. The appellate court sought guidance from the Court of Justice on the compatibility of the German legislation with the Treaty provisions on the free movement of goods.

Although trade mark law was hardly mentioned in the judgment of the Court of Justice, it is appropriate to deal with the case in this section because the issues raised are, at bottom, analogous to issues of trade mark law; not least because bottle shapes can function as three-dimensional trade marks (the 'Coca-Cola' bottle being the classic example). The type of confusion involved in *Prantl* was, moreover, similar to the confusion between conflicting trade marks. That point seems not to have been appreciated by the Court of Justice in *Prantl*, where it did not display the cautious attitude ('leave it to the national court') which has characterised its judgments on trade mark conflicts *stricto sensu*.

As is so often the case, the Court reached a reasonable result, but on the basis of suspect reasoning. The Court adopted a two-step analysis: it examined first whether the German legislation could be saved under the 'mandatory requirements' doctrine on grounds of consumer protection and fair

[254] Case 16/83 [1984] ECR 1299.

trading (Art. 28 and 'Cassis de Dijon'); then it went on to consider whether the measure could be upheld under Article 30 on grounds of public policy or protection of industrial and commercial property.

The Court's 'mandatory requirements' analysis was flawed. It first emphasised the protective and discriminatory effect of the German legislation, which favoured certain domestic producers as against producers in other Member States.[255] The Court then made the surprising statement that, since the legislation had protective effects, it 'therefore' came within the scope of the prohibition laid down by Article 28.[256] The suggestion that a *protective* effect, as opposed to a merely *restrictive* effect, must be proved in order to bring a measure within the scope of Article 28 is surely wrong. Having established the discriminatory and protective nature of the German legislation, the Court should have realised that the relevance of that was not to bring Article 28 into play but to rule out any possibility of regarding the legislation as justified under the 'mandatory requirements' doctrine. The legislation did not apply without distinction to domestic and imported goods, and so did not meet the essential precondition for benefiting from the 'Cassis de Dijon' line of cases. This analysis suggests that legislation which grants producers in a specific locality an exclusive right to use a particular type of container as a means of distinguishing their goods from goods produced in other localities can only find salvation under Article 30. That seems logical enough: such an exclusive right must—if it is worthy of protection in the first place—surely amount to 'industrial and commercial property'. If such an exclusive right is justified, that is because the container functions as an indirect geographical designation of origin or a collective trade mark[257] which helps to distinguish goods produced in the locality in question, prevents outsiders from parasitically trading on the reputation built up by producers in that locality and protects consumers from deception as to the origin of goods. If the exclusive right cannot be justified under Article 30, it cannot be justified at all.

The Court, however, failed to realise that the legislation in question did not apply without distinction to domestic and imported goods[258] and

---

[255] At para. 22 of the judgment.   [256] At para. 23 of the judgment.

[257] There is no reason of principle why a bottle shape should not be registered as a three-dimensional Community collective mark under Arts 64–66 of the Community Trade Mark Regulation, provided that it possesses distinctive character. Article 15 of the Trade Mark Directive makes it clear that Member States have an option to register collective marks. In the United Kingdom s. 49 of the Trade Marks Act 1994 provides for the registration of collective marks.

[258] Thus the Court made exactly the opposite mistake to the one which it was to make a few months later in *Kohl v Ringelhan & Rennett*. In the latter case it held, on the basis of conjecture more than hard evidence, that a measure was being applied in a discriminatory manner. In *Prantl* it held that a measure which openly discriminated between certain domestic goods and imported goods applied without distinction to the two categories of goods. Rather generously, Oliver describes the Court's finding that the legislation at issue in *Prantl* applied without distinction as 'not uncontroversial'. He points out that the case illustrates the difficulty of distinguishing

proceeded to enquire whether it was necessary in order to satisfy mandatory requirements relating in particular to consumer protection and fair trading. The Court began by observing, rather piously, that the justification for adopting legislation to prevent consumers from confusing wines of different quality and origin could not be denied.[259] It went on to state that in determining whether national legislation may, in order to protect an indirect designation of geographical origin in the interests of consumers, prohibit the marketing of wines imported in a certain type of bottle, consumer protection and fair trading must be guaranteed with regard on all sides for the fair and traditional practices observed in the various Member States.[260] The Court then noted that 'bottles which are identical in shape to the Bocksbeutel bottle or differ from it only in ways imperceptible to the consumer are traditionally used to market wines originating in certain regions of Italy'.[261] The Court concluded that 'An exclusive right to use a certain type of bottle granted by the legislation of a Member State may not therefore be used as a bar to imports of wines originating in another Member State put up in bottles of the same or similar shape in accordance with a fair and traditional practice observed in that Member State.'[262] As regards the German government's argument that consumers might be misled if wines from different regions were marketed in the same type of bottle, the Court noted that the provisions of Community law on the labelling of wines were particularly comprehensive and enabled the feared confusion to be avoided.[263]

Finally, the Court considered the possible appraisal of the German legislation in the light of Article 30 of the Treaty. In that regard, it dismissed out of hand the German government's extraordinary argument that the legislation in question was justified under Article 30 on grounds of public policy because it carried penal sanctions.[264] More serious discussion was merited by the German government's arguments that:

(1) the Bocksbeutel bottle functioned as an 'indirect indication of geographic origin' and therefore constituted an industrial property right protected under Article 30; and

(2) an association of Franconian wine producers had registered a picture of the Bocksbeutel bottle bearing an illustrated label as a collective trade mark.

---

between 'distinctly' and 'indistinctly applicable' measures: P. Oliver, 'A Review of the Case Law of the Court of Justice on Articles 30 to 36 EEC in 1984' (1985) 22 CML Rev 301, 315.

[259] At para. 26 of the judgment.   [260] At para. 27 of the judgment.
[261] At para. 28 of the judgment.   [262] Ibid.
[263] At para. 29 of the judgment.
[264] At paras 32 and 33 of the judgment. On that point the court was surely right. If national legislation restricting imports could be justified on grounds of public policy under Art. 30 simply because it carried penal sanctions, Art. 28 would be a dead letter.

Sadly, the Court was not inclined to expend much intellectual energy on analysing those interesting issues. On the first point the Court considered that:

> . . . it need merely be observed, without its being necessary to resolve the questions of law raised by that argument, that producers who traditionally use a bottle of a specific shape may not in any event successfully rely upon an industrial or commercial property right in order to prevent imports of wines originating in another Member State which have been bottled in identical or similar bottles in accordance with a fair and traditional practice in that State.[265]

On the second point, the Court considered that:

> The fact that an association of producers has registered a mark depicting a specific shape of bottle bearing an illustrated label and the protection which such registration provides are . . . irrelevant as regards the question whether national legislation allowing only wine producers in certain regions to use a bottle of the same shape is justified under Article [30] of the EC Treaty.[266]

Those are extraordinary statements. How could the Court say that it was not necessary to resolve the questions of law raised by the German government's argument? If the Franconian producers' exclusive right to use a particular bottle shape constituted an industrial property right (which the Court did not expressly deny), then surely it behoved the Court to give a reason for its decision that the right could not be enforced against imported wine put up in similar bottles 'in accordance with a fair and traditional practice'. And why was the registration of the bottle shape as a collective trade mark irrelevant? If the association of Franconian producers was entitled to invoke trade mark rights against imported wine in infringing bottles (which, again, the Court did not expressly deny), then Mr Prantl could hardly claim that he was selling legitimate goods with an unimpeachable right to be on the market in Germany. If the trade mark rights in the Bocksbeutel bottle prevailed over the free movement of goods, it would be rather pointless to say that the specific provisions of the German wine legislation on the Bocksbeutel bottle did not also prevail over the free movement of goods. How then could the registration of the collective trade mark be described as irrelevant?

The source of the Court's difficulties in *Prantl* lay in its failure to realize at the outset that it was dealing with a form of intellectual property which, as such, should have been appraised in the light of Article 30. The Court's decision to examine the exclusive right mainly from the point of view of fair trading and consumer protection was in any case technically incorrect since, as pointed out above, the basic precondition for applying 'Cassis de Dijon' was not met.

---

[265] At para. 35 of the judgment.   [266] At para. 37 of the judgment.

If the Court had got to grips with the intellectual property issues raised by the case, it would presumably have applied criteria such as the 'specific subject-matter' and 'essential function' of the exclusive right. It would at the very least have had to reflect upon the purpose and *raison d'être* of the exclusive right. Without such reflection it would, after all, have been difficult to determine whether the exclusive right and the resulting import restriction were justified.

The primary purpose of such an exclusive right is presumably to protect producers in a particular locality against competitors who might take advantage of the reputation of the locality's products by using a confusingly similar presentation. It could also be argued that the exclusive right is designed, coincidentally, to protect consumers, who might be misled as to the origin of products if a particular presentation which they have come to associate with the products of a specific locality could be used by producers from other localities. Those two aspects of the exclusive right correspond to the specific subject-matter and essential function of a trade mark, which confirms the analogy between the Franconian wine-growers' exclusive right to the Bocksbeutel bottle and a trade mark (especially a collective trade mark).

What the Court did in *Prantl* was to introduce a doctrine of honest concurrent user as a regards the particular type of exclusive right that was in issue. The Court decided that the Franconian producers' exclusive right to the Bocksbeutel bottle could not be invoked against goods produced in another Member State 'in accordance with a fair and traditional practice'.[267] That was so even if the imported wine was put up in bottles of identical shape or bottles that differed 'in ways imperceptible to the consumer'.[268]

It is interesting to speculate on the scope of that doctrine of honest concurrent user. What exclusive rights does it apply to? Obviously, it does not apply to trade marks (except, apparently, collective trade marks). The Court rejected that possibility in *Terrapin v Terranova*.[269] If the doctrine applies to '*indirect* indications of geographical origin' such as the Bocksbeutel bottle, the question must be asked whether it applies to all indications of geographical origin and to appellations of origin. Suppose, for the sake of argument, that the island of Majorca had a reputation for curing ham and that 'Palma ham' was a protected designation of origin in Spain: could 'Palma ham' be sold in Italy alongside 'Parma ham' on the basis of Article 28 of the Treaty and would the Court of Justice feel entitled to tell an Italian court that there was no risk of confusion? The example may seem far-

---

[267] At paras 28 and 35 of the judgment.   [268] At para. 28 of the judgment.

[269] Two authors have highlighted the contrast between the Court's approach in *Prantl* and in *Terrapin v Terranova*: see Oliver, op. cit. (n. 258), at 317; and J. Turner. 'The Prosecution of Karl Prantl: Bottles on the Incoming Tide' |1985| 4 EIPR 113, 116.

fetched but it does highlight the major flaw in the *Prantl* judgment: just as the Court should limit its role in trade mark conflicts to the definition of general criteria, leaving the final decision to the national court, so too in disputes about confusingly similar, origin-indicating bottle shapes it should exercise a measure of self-restraint and avoid trespassing upon the prerogatives of the national court. In *Prantl* the Court followed its gut reactions and decided, after examining bottles from Franconia and Bolzano,[270] that the risk of confusion was non-existent in view of differences in labelling. On that point it may well have been right, but the fact remains that as a matter of principle the Court should simply have insisted that the imported product should not be excluded unless, having regard to the overall appearance of the bottles, including their labelling, there was a genuine risk of confusion. The final decision should have been left to the national court.

5.3.4 *Pall v Dahlhausen*

Pall v Dahlhausen[271] provides another fine example of how astonishingly broad the concept of unfair competition can be under German law. As in *Kohl v Ringelhan & Rennett*, the relevant provision of German law was paragraph 3 of the Law on Unfair Competition. This time the 'misleading statement regarding the origin of goods' was perceived to lie in the presence of the symbol '®'—standing for 'registered'—alongside the trade mark 'Miropore' on blood filters imported from Italy by Dahlhausen. The trade mark was registered in Italy but not in Germany. Pall (presumably a competitor of Dahlhausen) sought an injunction restraining Dahlhausen from selling the goods in Germany with the symbol '®' after the trade mark on the ground that the use of the symbol constituted a misleading statement, inasmuch as it gave the impression that the trade mark was registered in Germany. The German court took the view that under its own national law the injunction must be granted but questioned whether that was compatible with Articles 28 and 30 of the Treaty. It referred the matter to the Court of Justice.

The Court ruled out the applicability of Article 30 on the ground that the use of the symbol '®' was not regulated by the German trade mark legislation but by the provisions on unfair competition.[272] The ban on using the symbol in relation to a trade mark not registered in Germany applied without distinction to domestic and imported goods.[273] The question,

---

[270] Advocate General Slynn mentions in his opinion in the *Prantl* case (at 1337) that specimens of the bottles were shown to the Court.

[271] Case C-238/89 [1990] ECR I-4827.   [272] At para. 10 of the judgment.

[273] At para. 14 of the judgment. See also point 3 of the opinion of Advocate General Tesauro, at I-4837 *et seq.* The Advocate General carefully explains the criterion of 'applicability without distinction'.

therefore, was whether the ban was necessary in order to satisfy 'mandatory requirements' relating to fair trading and consumer protection.

Most observers would answer that question with an emphatic negative. Who, after all, was being misled and in what material respect? Pall's claim seems to assume that consumers attach great importance to the symbol '®', that their purchasing decisions are influenced by the knowledge that a trade mark is registered, and that they are more likely to buy a product if the trade mark affixed to it is registered in their own country as opposed to some other country. None of those assumptions accords with everyday experience. That enabled the Court to dismiss the argument of consumer protection, observing simply that the symbol was not generally understood as indicating registration in the country of marketing and that consumers were in any case more interested in the qualities of the product than the place of registration of the trade mark.

As regards unfair competition, the Court had to deal with a curious argument put forward by Pall and the United Kingdom (which, for reasons that are not readily discernible, saw fit to submit observations to the Court supporting the position taken by Pall). According to that argument, if registration in one Member State justified using the symbol '®' in other Member States, manufacturers in those Member States where registration was easiest to obtain would be unfairly favoured; moreover, 'forum shopping' would be encouraged, inasmuch as traders would prefer to register in countries where registration was easiest and would avoid registration in Member States with rigorous examination and opposition procedures. Perhaps the proponents of the argument believed that if a trade mark was registered in one Member State and products bearing the trade mark and the symbol '®' could circulate in the other Member States, the trade mark would automatically become protected in the rest of the Community. That is not of course the case. All that the symbol does is to serve notice on competitors who might wish to use an identical or similar sign that the trade mark has been registered somewhere. As the Court pointed out, those competitors can determine whether a trade mark is registered in a particular Member State by checking the register.[274] They are not likely to be deterred from using a potentially infringing sign because they have seen a product on the market with the symbol '®' next to the trade mark. There was thus no way in which Pall or other German traders could claim to be victims of unfair competition through having to compete with imported products bearing the symbol '®' against a trade mark that was not in fact registered in Germany.

---

[274] At para. 21 of the judgment. See also the opinion of Advocate General Tesauro, at I-4842.

5.4 *Misleading trade marks*

5.4.1 *A difficult concept*

Traders frequently choose trade marks which describe certain properties or
characteristics of the goods to which they are applied. If the trade mark
consists exclusively of descriptive elements, it cannot in principle function
as a trade mark, since it lacks the ability to distinguish one undertaking's
goods from those of another, and so cannot be registered as a trade mark.[275]
Sometimes the chosen trade mark denotes properties or characteristics
which the goods do not possess. In that case the trade mark is not descriptive but it may be considered misleading, in which case it will likewise be
barred from registration.[276] A further type of a misleading trade mark is one
that deceives consumers as to the geographical origin of goods.

Misleading trade marks may be regarded as a form of misleading advertising. The whole subject is immensely controversial because perceptions as
to what may be considered deceptive vary widely. A number of questions
arise. By reference to what type of consumer should deceptiveness be
appraised—the average consumer of the goods in question, the exceptionally inattentive consumer, or the highly sceptical one? And what are the
matters in respect of which our relevant consumer, once identified, is likely
to be misled? If, for example, a manufacturer of toilet paper adopts the trade
mark 'Cotonelle', consumers might perhaps associate the name with the
softness of cotton and some might even think that the product contains
cotton. But cotton is not a suitable material for making toilet paper, since
even the most efficient flushing system could not cope with large amounts
of cotton. If a tiny minority of consumers buy 'Cotonelle' in the mistaken
belief that it contains cotton and in the even more mistaken belief that the
presence of cotton is desirable in such a product, are they misled in a way
that can be considered relevant? If consumers buy 'Cotonelle' on the assumption that, with such a name, it must be unusually soft and it turns out
to be no softer than any other toilet paper, are they the victims of a
misleading trade mark or are manufacturers entitled to engage in a little
harmless exaggeration about the quality of their products?

There is no uniform approach to such issues, as the case of *Graffione
v Fransa* illustrates. The trade mark 'Cotonelle' was impugned in France,

---

[275] See Art. 3(1)(c) of the Trade Mark Directive and Art. 7(1)(c) of the Community Trade Mark
Regulation. Such a trade mark can acquire distinctiveness through use: Art. 3(3) of the Directive
and Art. 7(3) of the Regulation.

[276] See Art. 3(1)(g) of the Trade Mark Directive and Art. 7(1)(g) of the Community Trade Mark
Regulation. Both provisions prohibit the registration of 'trade marks which are of such a nature
as to deceive the public, for instance as to the nature, quality or geographical origin of the goods
or service'.

Italy, and Spain: only the Italian judges found it misleading.[277] It is obvious that divergent approaches to the question of misleading trade marks have a capacity to create barriers to intra-Community trade. If a trade mark is considered non-deceptive in some Member States but misleading in others, products bearing the mark which are lawfully on the market in one Member State may become the subject of injunctions prohibiting their resale as soon as they cross an internal frontier of the Community.

In theory, the harmonization of trade mark law and the creation of the Community trade mark offer some prospect of convergence. But one should not be too optimistic. Although the national laws have been harmonized in accordance with Article 3(1)(g) of the Trade Mark Directive, the appraisal of deceptiveness is essentially subjective and judges will continue to be conditioned by their background in national law. Only a limited amount of uniformity can be achieved by preliminary rulings from the Court of Justice on the interpretation of Article 3(1)(g).[278] It is in any event clear that, on account of linguistic differences in Europe, a trade mark may be misleading in one country but harmless in others. 'Cotonelle', for example, could hardly mislead someone who understood only German or Spanish.[279]

Nor will the Community trade mark help much in this respect. Under Article 7(1)(g) and (2) of the Community Trade Mark Regulation, a trade mark cannot be registered if it is misleading only in part of the Community. Moreover, infringement proceedings are conducted before national courts, which have the power to invalidate a Community trade mark if its validity is challenged by way of a counterclaim.[280] Once again there is scope for divergence in view of differences in the mindset of national judges.

5.4.2 *'Clinique' for cosmetics: the Court of Justice decides*

A number of cases on misleading trade marks have come before the Court of Justice. The first of them (*Verband Sozialer Wettbewerb v Clinique Laboratoires and Estée Lauder*)[281] concerned the well-known trade mark 'Clinique', which

---

[277] Case C-313/94 [1996] ECR I-6039. It is perhaps surprising that the Italian courts took such a strict view in the 'Cotonelle' case. Generally, they have a reputation for tolerance as regards consumer deception and apply the maxim *omnis mercator mendax* (every merchant is a liar). On that basis it is assumed that consumers will disbelieve the claims of manufacturers and will not therefore be deceived.

[278] The Court of Justice may also have occasion to rule on the interpretation of the corresponding provision (Art. 7(1)(g)) of the Community Trade Mark Regulation in appeals against judgments of the Court of First Instance concerning decisions of the Boards of Appeal of the Office for Harmonization in the Internal Market.

[279] See the opinion of Advocate General Jacobs in *Graffione*, at para. 10. 'Cotton' is *Baumwolle* and *algodón* in German and Spanish respectively. Presumably the basis for objecting to the trade mark in Spain was that a significant proportion of Spanish consumers understand French or English or are at least familiar with the word 'cotton' from having seen it on clothes labels.

[280] Art. 96 of the Community Trade Mark Regulation.

[281] Case C-315/92 [1994] ECR I-317.

has been used by Estée Lauder since the 1970s on a wide range of cosmetic products in most European countries. Initially, Estée Lauder marketed those products in Germany under the trade mark 'Linique'. It was aware that 'Clinique' might be objected to in Germany, under paragraph 3 of the Law on Unfair Competition, on the ground that it created the misleading impression that the products possessed therapeutic qualities. With a view to reducing packaging and advertising costs arising from the use of different trade marks, Estée Lauder later started to market the products in Germany under the trade mark 'Clinique'. The anticipated difficulties did not take long to materialise. An association for the defence of 'social competition' brought an action seeking to stop the use of the allegedly misleading trade mark. The action was based on paragraph 3 of the Law on Unfair Competition[282] and on a specific legislative provision which prohibited the marketing of cosmetic products under misleading names. Both the German provisions had their equivalents in Community law. The general clause in paragraph 3 of the Law on Unfair Competition corresponded, roughly, to the provisions of Article 4 of Council Directive 84/450/EEC concerning misleading advertising.[283] The specific provision on cosmetic products corresponded to Article 6(2) of Council Directive 76/768/EEC on the approximation of the laws of the Member States relating to cosmetic products,[284] which required Member States to 'take all measures necessary to ensure that in the labelling, presentation for sale and advertising of cosmetic products, the wording, use of names, trade marks, images or other signs, figurative or otherwise, suggesting a characteristic which the products in question do not possess, shall be prohibited'.

All of those legislative provisions—both national and Community—were drafted in extremely general terms. Doubtless, all of them were capable of being construed widely as prohibiting the use of the 'Clinique' trade mark on goods which (it was never contested) did not possess therapeutic properties; just as they were all capable of the opposite construction. It was in any event clear that the Community legislation must be interpreted in the light of the Treaty; so the real issue was whether it was consistent with Articles 28 and 30 of the Treaty to prohibit the importation and marketing of products lawfully manufactured or marketed in another Member State on the ground that the trade mark was misleading. That, essentially, was the question referred to the Court of Justice by the German court.

Articles 28 and 30 of the Treaty are, of course, also general clauses, even vaguer and wider than the legislation discussed above. There were basically two approaches that could have been followed. One approach would have been to lay down general criteria to be applied by the national court in deciding whether the prohibition of the 'Clinique' trade mark was justified on one of the grounds recognised in Community law, leaving the final

---

[282] Cited in n. 249.   [283] OJ 1984 L 250, p. 17.   [284] OJ 1976 L 262, p. 169.

decision to the national court. The alternative approach was to indicate clearly that the prohibition was or was not justified.

Advocate General Gulmann took the first approach—rightly, it is submitted. He contended that the Court would be trespassing on the jurisdiction of the national court if it ruled, as proposed by the Commission, that the prohibition of the 'Clinique' trade mark was contrary to the Treaty.[285] He pointed out, moreover, that it was for the Member States to decide on the degree of protection which they deemed to be correct with a view to safeguarding the overriding interests recognised in Article 30 and in the case law of the Court.[286]

The Court took the alternative approach. It held that Articles 28 and 30 of the Treaty and Article 6 of Directive 76/768 must be interpreted as precluding a national measure which prohibited the importation and marketing of a cosmetic product on the ground that it bore the name 'Clinique'. At first sight it is surprising that the Court should have felt entitled to bind the hands of the national court with such a specific ruling. The Court found justification for that course of action in certain information set out in the order for reference, i.e. 'Clinique' products were sold exclusively in perfumeries and in the cosmetics departments of large stores, and never in pharmacies; they were presented as cosmetic products and not as medicinal products; it was not suggested that, apart from the trade mark used on the products, the presentation did not comply with the rules applicable to cosmetic products; and the use of the trade mark 'Clinique' in other countries did not apparently mislead consumers.[287]

The factors alluded to by the Court hardly seem to provide sufficient justification for a ruling which clearly overstepped the boundaries of the jurisdiction ordinarily exercised by the Court under Article 234 of the Treaty.[288]

5.4.3 *'Cotonelle' for toilet paper: the Court of Justice steps back*

In the light of the above comments one can only welcome the more cautious attitude displayed by the Court in *Graffione v Fransa*. The 'Cotonelle' trade mark, owned by the Scott Group of companies, was attacked by a competitor on grounds of deceptiveness and was declared void by the

---

[285] See para. 25 of the Advocate General's opinion, at I-326.   [286] Ibid.

[287] At para. 21 of the judgment. As D. Simon points out (Europe 1994 Act. No. 141, pp. 7–8), the fact that consumers in other countries did not find the trade marks 'Quattro' and 'Quadra' confusingly similar was accorded no relevance by the Court in *Deutsche Renault v AUDI*. It is difficult to see why the Court took an entirely different approach a few months later in *Clinique*.

[288] For criticism of the Court's approach, see C. Worth and K. Warburton, 'EJC v National Courts: The Division of Powers after Clinique' |1994| 6 EIPR 247. The authors point out that national courts might become reluctant to refer questions to the Court of Justice if they fear that the latter will bind their hands with a ruling on the facts.

Milan Court of Appeal, which ordered Scott to refrain from using it. Scott therefore ceased using the trade mark in Italy. A wholesaler in Liguria, by the name of Graffione, informed its customers that it was no longer able to supply 'Cotonelle'. When Graffione learned that a supermarket in the province of Genoa, owned by a firm called Fransa, was still selling 'Cotonelle', it applied for an injunction to prevent Fransa from selling that product on the ground that its action amounted to unfair competition. Fransa was obtaining its supplies of 'Cotonelle' from France, where the trade mark had not been cancelled. It therefore invoked Article 28 of the Treaty. The Italian court referred questions to the Court of Justice on the interpretation of the Treaty provisions on the free movement of goods and on Article 12(2)(b) of the Trade Mark Directive.

The Court of Justice understood the questions as asking:

(1) whether Articles 28 and 30 of the Treaty preclude a prohibition, under national rules on unfair competition, on the marketing of products coming from another Member State in which they are lawfully marketed, on the ground that they bear a trade mark which the proprietor has been prohibited from using in the Member State of importation because it has been held liable to mislead consumers; and

(2) whether Article 12(2)(b) of the Directive precludes such a prohibition.

The matter was complicated because it was not clear whether the judgment of the Milan Court of Appeal prohibiting the proprietor of the trade mark from using it in Italy also prevented third parties from marketing 'Cotonelle' or whether it was binding only on the proprietor of the trade mark, at least until the judgment became final. If it was not binding on third parties, there was nothing to stop both Fransa and Graffione from selling 'Cotonelle' purchased in France. The Court simply pointed out that Graffione could not complain of unfair competition in that eventuality.

If the judgment of the Milan Court of Appeal was binding on third parties, it was necessary to consider whether a ban on the sale of 'Cotonelle' imported from another Member State could be justified in order to protect consumers who might be misled into believing that the goods contained cotton. On that point the Court carried out a 'Cassis de Dijon' analysis.[289] It observed that a ban on the use of a trade mark, on the ground that it was

---

[289] A. Rigaux ('Marques, concurrence déloyale, protection du consommateur et article 36 CE' (1997) Act. No. 10, Europe 11–13) points out, however, that the Court's approach in *Graffione* was novel inasmuch as it did not distinguish rigorously between a 'Cassis de Dijon' analysis and an Art. 36 analysis. She speculates that the judgment may constitute a first step on the road to integrating the 'mandatory requirements' recognized under the 'Cassis de Dijon' case law into the letter of Art. 30. If that were true, it might not be a bad thing; but a likelier explanation is that the Court sometimes has difficulty in coping with the sophisticated nature of its own case law on Arts 28 and 30.

misleading, was not precluded simply because the trade mark was not considered misleading in other Member States; because of linguistic, cultural, and social differences between the Member States a trade mark might be held to be misleading in one Member State but not in another.[290] The Court then stressed the importance of the principle of proportionality, which meant that an obstacle to free movement could only be justified if it was 'really necessary' for the purpose of protecting consumers and if that aim could not be achieved by measures less restrictive of intra-Community trade.[291] Citing *Clinique*, the Court observed that the risk of misleading consumers could not override the free movement of goods unless the risk was sufficiently serious.[292] The Court ruled that it was for the national court to assess whether that test was satisfied. In carrying out that assessment the national court 'must have regard to all the relevant factors, including the circumstances in which the products are sold, the information set out on the packaging of the products and the clarity with which it is displayed, the presentation and content of advertising material and the risk of error in relation to the group of consumers concerned'.[293]

That approach contrasts markedly with the Court's approach in *Clinique*, in which the Court carried out the assessment itself and came to a firm conclusion that the importation and sale in Germany of products marketed in another Member State under the trade mark 'Clinique' could not be opposed on the ground that the trade mark might mislead consumers into believing that the products possessed medicinal properties. The Court avoided openly contradicting what it had said in *Clinique* by stating in *Graffione* that the documents before the Court did not enable it to assess whether there was a sufficiently serious risk of consumers being misled.[294]

5.4.4 The 'reasonably well-informed, observant and circumspect average consumer'

In *Estée Lauder Cosmetics v Lancaster Group*[295] the Court again exercised self-restraint and avoided telling the national court how to decide the case.[296] It

---

[290] At para. 22 of the judgment. Here there is a neat example of the interaction between judges and advocates general. When stressing the relevance of linguistic, cultural, and social differences, the court cited approvingly the opinion of Advocate General Jacobs, who had in turn cited approvingly the opinion of Advocate General Gulmann in *Clinique*. Mr Gulmann had by now become a judge at the Court of Justice and was in fact the rapporteur in *Graffione*. In *Clinique*, of course, the Court had paid little heed to Mr Gulmann's comments about linguistic, cultural, and social differences. The Gulmann/Jacobs approach is surely correct as regards linguistic differences; it is, however, difficult to see how cultural or social differences should affect the appraisal of an allegedly misleading trade mark, unless one accepts that some nations are more prone to deception than others.

[291] At para. 23 of the judgment.   [292] At para. 24 of the judgment.

[293] At para. 26 of the judgment.   [294] At para. 25 of the judgment.

[295] Case C-200/98 [2000] ECR I-117.

[296] Advocate General Fennelly stressed that the ultimate decision should, as a rule, be left to the national court (see para. 31 of the opinion).

did, however, give a strong hint that the trade mark at issue should not normally be regarded as misleading.[297] The trade mark, which was used for a cosmetic cream, contained the word 'lifting' and was alleged to be capable of deceiving consumers into believing that the cream would produce lasting effects comparable to surgical lifting. As in *Clinique*, the national court was a German *Landgericht*.

The Court of Justice ruled that Article 6(3) of Directive 76/768[298] does not preclude the application of national legislation which prohibits the importation and marketing of a cosmetic product where the 'average consumer, reasonably well-informed and reasonably observant and circumspect', is misled by the name of the product into believing that the product possesses characteristics that it does not have.

The concept of the 'reasonably well-informed, observant, and circumspect consumer' is a welcome addition to the Court's vocabulary. It had already been used in *Gut Springenheide and Tusky v Oberkreisdirektor Steinfurt*.[299] This case concerned the interpretation of a provision in a Council regulation which prohibited the use of misleading statements in the marketing of eggs. There, the Court had left it for the national court (also German) to decide whether the expression 'six-grain—ten fresh eggs' was likely to mislead consumers inasmuch as it implied that the feed given to the hens was made up exclusively of the six cereals indicated, whereas only 60% of the feed was thus composed. Surprisingly, the contentious expression (or, rather, its German equivalent) was considered to be a trade mark by the German court.[300] No less surprising was that court's apparent willingness to condemn the expression as misleading. On the assumption that the eggs really were fresh and that the hens that laid them were fed on a diet composed largely of the six named cereals, it is hard to see where the deception could lie.

The Court of Justice's insistence that the issue must be resolved by reference to the 'reasonably well-informed, observant and circumspect consumer', as opposed to the exceptionally ignorant, dim-witted, and gullible consumer, seems to be designed to encourage the national courts, in particular in Germany, to take a more robust attitude towards claims that consumers are misled by trade marks and descriptive messages on products. If such a test is applied properly, it is difficult to see how any of the trade marks or expressions at issue in *Clinique*, *Graffione*, *Estée Lauder Cosmetics*, or *Gut Springenheide* could be judged misleading.

---

[297] At para. 30 of the judgment.

[298] Article 6 of the Directive was amended by Council Directive 88/667/EEC of 21 December 1988 (OJ 1988 L 382, p. 46). Article 6(3) of the amended version corresponds to Article 6(2) of the original version.

[299] Case C-210/96 [1998] ECR I-4657, at para. 31.

[300] See para. 12 of the judgment. The expression appears to be purely descriptive. There were possibly some additional figurative elements that transformed it into a distinctive sign for trade mark purposes.

The Court's recent case law shows that the concept of the 'average consumer of the category of goods or services in question, who is reasonably well informed and reasonably observant and circumspect', is now well established as the yardstick for use in all areas of trade mark law in which assumptions are made about the expectations of consumers. In particular, the distinctiveness of a trade mark[301] and the likelihood of confusion between trade marks[302] are to be assessed by reference to such a consumer.

---

[301] Joined Cases C-53/01 to C-55/01 *Linde, Winward and Rado,* judgment of 8 April 2003, at para. 41, and *Libertel v Benelux Merkenbureau,* cited in n. 29, at para. 46.

[302] *Lloyd Schuhfabrik Meyer v Klijsen Handel,* cited in n. 114, at para. 26.

9

Patents

1. THE JUSTIFICATION FOR PATENT PROTECTION

1.1 *General*

The rationale of the patent system has been debated for centuries. In a famous report presented to the United States Senate in 1958, Fritz Machlup[1] identified four basic theories justifying the grant of an exclusive right to inventors:

(1) the natural law theory;
(2) the reward theory;
(3) the incentive theory; and
(4) the contract or disclosure theory.

The natural law theory holds that inventors, like authors, are morally entitled to ownership of their intellectual property. The theory is based on 'the assumption that individuals have a natural property right in their ideas, which must be respected by others'.[2]

According to the reward theory, society has an obligation, on grounds of equity, to reward the inventor for his contribution to scientific progress. The simplest way to ensure that he receives a reward commensurate with the value of his contribution is to grant him an exclusive right to exploit his invention.

The incentive theory, which according to Beier is 'the most widely held patent thesis in the western world',[3] is founded on 'the assumption that people, including commercial enterprises, are more likely to invest resources in scientific research if they are guaranteed an exclusive right to exploit their inventions. On this view, the justification for patents is that they stimulate scientific and technical progress by encouraging inventors to invent.

---

[1] F. Machlup, *An Economic Review of the Patent System*, Study No. 15 of the Subcommittee on Patents, Trademarks, and Copyright of the Committee on the Judiciary—United States Senate, 85th Congress, 2nd Session, Washington, 1958. Much quoted but not so easy to track down, Machlup's paper is now available in *The International Intellectual Property System: Commentary and Materials*, Part One, by F. Abbot, T. Cottier and F. Gurry, Kluwer Law International, 1999, at pp. 224–46. For a good summary of Machlup's four theories, see F.-K. Beier, 'Traditional and Socialist Concepts of Protecting Inventions' (1970) 1 IIC 328.
[2] Beier, op. cit. (n. 1), at 330.   [3] Beier, op. cit. (n. 1), at 333.

According to the contract or disclosure theory, the main purpose of the patent system is not so much to stimulate invention but to encourage the inventor to disclose new technical ideas to the rest of the world. The principle that protection is granted to the first to file, rather than to the first to invent, accords with this theory.

There is a degree of overlap between these four theories. In particular, the natural law theory and the reward theory appear to be two ways of saying the same thing, i.e. that in a just and equitable society inventors should enjoy their fair share of the financial benefit to be derived from their inventions. The reward theory and the incentive theory are also closely related. They contemplate society's approach to the inventor *ex post* and *ex ante* respectively. To argue about whether the purpose of the patent system is to reward inventors for inventing or to encourage inventors to invent is rather like arguing about the rationale of the penal system: do we punish crime because society has a moral obligation to ensure that criminals receive their just deserts or because the prospect of punishment deters potential criminals from breaking the law?

To sum up, it is possible to identify one moral reason and two pragmatic reasons for granting patents to inventors. The moral reason is that inventors, rather than free-riders, should enjoy the fruits of their intellectual achievements. The pragmatic reasons are that more will be invented and more inventions will be disclosed if those who invent and then disclose their inventions are rewarded with an exclusive right to exploit them.

1.2 *The Court of Justice's understanding of the rationale of patents*

In the first patent case to come before the Court of Justice (*Parke, Davis v Centrafarm*)[4] the judgment itself was silent about the rationale of the patent system. The case was decided two years before the concept of specific subject-matter made its debut in *Deutsche Grammophon v Metro.*[5] The Advocate General (Mr Roemer) did, however, make some interesting remarks about the purpose of patents. He observed that if Parke, Davis was unable to enforce its patent rights against infringing products manufactured in a Member State where the invention was not patentable 'little would remain of the legal monopoly to exploit an invention, which is intended to guarantee the chance of a reasonable return for the inventor'. He went on as follows:

The consequences which would follow from this for the economy and for legal practice concerning patents would be considerable. A patent law emptied of its substance and devalued to this point could hold up technical progress, since in

---

[4] Case 24/67 [1968] ECR 55.   [5] Case 78/70 [1971] ECR 487.

many cases undertakings would no longer want to bear the increasing costs of research and development, for they would not have any chance of obtaining a reasonable return with the help of an effective legal monopoly for exploiting inventions, granted temporarily. The most one could expect is that inventions would be kept secret (in the hope of thus having a monopoly to exploit them), which would deprive other undertakings not only of the possibility of continuing research on the basis of discoveries already made, but also of the legal possibility of taking part in the exploitation of inventions by means of licences.[6]

The Advocate General was thus subscribing implicitly to the incentive and disclosure theories. All things considered, his approach was commendable, and it is a pity that it was not echoed in the judgment of the Court. In retrospect, the Court's silence appears to have been a missed opportunity, which has stunted the development of the case law to this day.

Certainly, when the Court attempted to address the policy issues underlying the patent system, six years later in *Centrafarm v Sterling Drug*,[7] it came up with a more limited definition of the specific subject-matter of a patent. The Court held that:

'In relation to patents, the specific subject-matter of the industrial property is the guarantee that the patentee, to reward the creative effort of the inventor, has the exclusive right to use an invention with a view to manufacturing industrial products and putting them into circulation for the first time, either directly or by the grant of licences to third parties, as well as the right to oppose infringements.'[8]

Joliet, writing in 1975 (and therefore several years before he was appointed to the bench of the Court of Justice), considered that the Court seemed to be endorsing Machlup's reward theory, apparently to the exclusion of all others.[9] It is doubtful whether that conclusion is correct. Joliet may have been reading too much significance into the Court's use of the word 'reward'. As has been pointed out above, the concepts of reward and incentive are really two sides of the same coin. When the Court says that the patent seeks 'to reward the creative effort of the inventor', there is no reason to suppose that the Court is thinking purely in terms of society's moral obligation to guarantee the inventor a just return; the Court may well have been assuming that the prospect of a reward acts as an incentive to invent. Thus the Court was probably endorsing Machlup's incentive theory as much as his reward theory. What is, however, lacking in the Court's definition of the specific subject-matter of a patent is any reference to the disclosure theory, which is perhaps surprising in view of Advocate General

---

[6] The report, at 78.   [7] Case 15/74 [1974] ECR 1147.
[8] At para. 9 of the judgment.
[9] R. Joliet, 'Patented Articles and Free Movement of Goods within the EEC' (1975) *Current Legal Problems* 15, 30).

Roemer's comments in *Parke, Davis*. Moreover, in the light of the general acceptance of the first-to-file principle in Europe,[10] a definition of the purpose of the patent system which omits any mention of the disclosure theory is incomplete.[11]

It has been argued above (see Chapter 6) that the expression 'specific subject-matter' (*objet spécifique* in French) has a double meaning: as well as referring to the purpose of the patent system (i.e. rewarding inventors and thus stimulating technical progress), the expression describes the core of essential rights granted to the patentee (i.e. the right to manufacture patented products and to place them on the market *for the first time*, either directly or by the grant of licences to third parties, as well as the right to oppose infringements). It was also pointed out above that the Court failed to make it clear whether it was defining the core of essential rights on the basis of the national law in issue (Dutch law) or on the basis of a comparative survey of the national laws of the Member States in general.[12]

From a practical point of view, what really matters is that the Court's definition of the specific subject-matter of a patent enabled it to establish the principle of Community-wide exhaustion, which is doubtless all that it was intended to achieve.

2. PATENTS AS AN OBSTACLE TO THE FREE MOVEMENT OF GOODS

The propensity of patents to act as a barrier to the free movement of goods in the common market is so obvious that it hardly requires explanation. Indeed, such barriers probably constituted the *locus classicus* that led the authors of the Treaty to include a reference to the protection of industrial and commercial property in Article 30. One thinks in the first place of the situation that exists when an inventor has been granted a patent in one or more Member States but has not sought patent protection in some Member States, or has been unable to obtain it (perhaps because of a difference in the substantive law governing the grant of patents). Problems could also arise, as long as differences existed in national laws concerning the term of

---

[10] Under Art. 60(1) of the EPC the right to a European patent belongs in principle to the inventor or his successor in title. If two or more persons make an invention independently of each other, the right to a European patent belongs to the first of them to file, by virtue of Art. 60(2) of the EPC.

[11] Bently and Sherman observe that a first-to-file system may be incompatible with an intellectual property regime predicated on natural rights and that such a system is justified on the basis of the disclosure theory: L. Bently and B. Sherman, *Intellectual Property Law*, Oxford University Press, 2001, p. 346.

[12] Joliet observed (op. cit., n. 9, at 29) that the Court's definition of the essential rights of the patentee summarized the position under Dutch law but did not account for the position under Belgian law.

protection, where a patent expired in one Member State but continued to be valid in another. In such situations products might be lawfully manufactured and placed on the market in one Member State where patent protection did not exist or had ceased to exist, whereas the same products might, by the very act of crossing a frontier, infringe a valid patent in another Member State.

Problems of a different nature arise in the case of parallel patents (i.e. patents obtained by the same person in different Member States in respect of the same invention). If the holder of parallel patents could rely on each national patent to block parallel imports of his own products, patents would be a formidable weapon for partitioning the common market. Then again, the various national patents may be assigned to different persons, perhaps persons between whom no economic or legal link exists beyond the contract of assignment. Can the several proprietors (i.e. the assignees and the assignor, in so far as the latter has retained ownership in some Member States) rely on their national patents to exclude patented products manufactured by the other owners in their respective territories? Licensing raises similar problems.

We have already seen in previous chapters how the Court has resolved some of these issues. Thus it is clear from *Thetford v Fiamma*[13] that, where an invention is patentable in Member State A but not in Member State B, the patent-holder in Member State A may prevent the importation of infringing products manufactured in Member State B. It will be recalled that in that case Thetford owned patents in respect of a portable toilet which it had been able to patent in the United Kingdom by virtue of an old rule of United Kingdom law whereby an invention was deemed not to have been anticipated simply because it had been published in a patent specification filed more than 50 years earlier. The Court rejected Fiamma's argument that such a concept of 'relative novelty' was repugnant to the principles of patent law and that Article 30 of the Treaty only protected patents granted in respect of inventions that were 'absolutely novel'. It followed that Fiamma's infringing articles, manufactured in Italy where the product was not patentable, could be excluded from the United Kingdom market. The Court also rejected the argument that the only relief justified under Article 30 in such a case should be an order for the payment of a reasonable royalty, as opposed to an injunction prohibiting the importation of the infringing article. The Court observed that the right to an injunction was part of the 'substance' of patent law. The expression 'substance', in this context, appears to be a synonym of 'specific subject-matter'.

The *Thetford* case confirmed a principle established 20 years earlier in *Parke, Davis v Centrafarm*,[14] i.e. that, in the absence of harmonization,

[13] Case 35/87 [1988] ECR 3585. [14] Cited in n. 4.

obstacles to free movement caused by discrepancies in national patent laws must be tolerated by virtue of Article 30, provided that they do not entail arbitrary discrimination or a disguised restriction on trade between Member States. In *Parke, Davis* the proprietor of a patent for a pharmaceutical product in the Netherlands was able to enforce its rights against infringing products manufactured without its authorization in Italy where pharmaceutical products were not, at the time, patentable.

In view of the differences that formerly existed in national patent laws it is perhaps surprising that there have not been more such cases. For example, differences in the term of protection of patents might have led to litigation in the Court of Justice. It was clear, in any event, from *EMI Electrola v Patricia Im-und Export*[15] that a patent still in force in Member State A could be invoked against infringing articles manufactured in Member State B, where the patent had already expired either because the term of protection was shorter or because it commenced at an earlier date. That case concerned a right akin to copyright but the same principle must apply to patents.

Fortunately, obstacles to trade due to discrepancies in national patent laws are less and less likely to arise because a high degree of harmonization has now been achieved in the field of patent law. The most remarkable feature of that harmonization is that it has come about largely on a voluntary basis and with limited input from Community law. The main instruments of harmonization have been the 1973 Munich Convention on the Grant of European Patents (the European Patent Convention or EPC) and the 1975 Luxembourg Convention on the European Patent for the Common Market (the Community Patent Convention or CPC),[16] as amended by the Agreement relating to Community Patents of 1989.[17] In a Declaration on the Adjustment of National Patent Law annexed to the 1989 Agreement, the Member States undertook to adjust their law relating to national patents, in so far as they had not already done so, 'so as to bring it into conformity, as far as practicable, with corresponding provisions of the EPC, the Agreement relating to Community Patents and the Patent

---

[15] Case 341/87 [1989] ECR 79.

[16] For further information, see K. Haertel, 'The Harmonizing Effect of European Patent Law on National Patent Laws' (1983) 14 IIC 719; G. Gall, 'Legislative and Judicial Powers in Europe—How Far is Harmonization of Patent Law and Practice Possible and Desirable?' [1988] 5 EIPR 138; K. Bruchhausen, 'Interpretation and Application of European Patent Law and Harmonized National Patent Law' (1983) 14 IIC 732; B. Schwab, 'L'unification et l'harmonisation du droit de brevet' in *La protection de la propriété intellectuelle: aspects juridiques européens et internationaux*, Institut Universitaire International Luxembourg, 1989, p. 169. The CPC never came into force. The Community's legislative organs now intend to create a Community patent by means of a regulation: see the Commission's Proposal for a Council Regulation on the Community Patent (OJ 2000 C 337 E, p. 278).

[17] OJ 1989 L 401, p. 1.

Cooperation Treaty'. A further harmonizing measure is Directive 98/44/EC of the European Parliament and Council of 6 July 1998 on the legal protection of biotechnological inventions.[18]

As a result of those instruments, harmonization has extended to the requirements for patentability, the term of protection, and the scope of protection. The concept of absolute novelty has been adopted and pharmaceutical products are no longer excluded from patentability. Hence the specific problems that arose in *Thetford* and *Parke, Davis* should in principle be a thing of the past.

The other type of trade barrier referred to above (those caused by parallel patents and assignments limited to the territory of individual Member States) will not be removed or alleviated by the harmonization of substantive patent law. Such problems will be with us for as long as national patents—whether granted by national patent offices or by the European Patent Office in accordance with the European Patent Convention—continue to exist.[19]

Yet another type of problem arises from the chauvinistic and protectionist nature of certain provisions of national law in relation to matters such as compulsory licences and licences of right.

3. COMPULSORY LICENCES AND LICENCES OF RIGHT

We have already seen how in *Pharmon v Hoechst*[20] the proprietor (Hoechst) of a patent in the Netherlands was able to prevent the importation of goods manufactured by the holder of a compulsory licence in the United Kingdom, where Hoechst held a parallel patent. That case, like *Thetford v Fiamma*, could be viewed as a classic example of a trade barrier caused by disparities in national patent laws. The British legislation allowed the granting of compulsory licences in circumstances in which the Dutch legislation did not. Presumably, if the laws on compulsory licences had been harmonized, so that the conditions governing the grant of compulsory licences and the rules determining the amount of royalties were the same in all Member States, there would be no case for allowing a patent-holder to oppose imports of products manufactured in another Member State under a compulsory licence. The products could be manufactured in any Member State and the level of royalties would be the same, so there would be no justification for restricting imports. The Court would doubtless hold that the specific subject-matter (or substance) of each national patent had been altered

[18] OJ 1998 L 213, p. 13.
[19] Under Art. 14(1) of the proposed Regulation for a Community Patent, a Community patent may be assigned 'in its entirety, and for the whole of the Community'.
[20] Case 19/84 [1985] ECR 2281.

whenever compulsory licences could be issued under it. The patent-holder was no longer entitled to an exclusive right, but merely to a royalty. That would certainly be consonant with what the Court held in *Allen and Hanbury's v Generics*.[21]

Allen and Hanbury's was the first of series of cases on compulsory licensing which highlighted the exquisitely refined nature of the latent protectionism inherent in the patent laws of certain Member States. The United Kingdom Patents Act 1977 increased the term of protection of patents from sixteen to twenty years. Under transitional provisions, existing patents which still had five years or more to run on 1 June 1978 were extended by four years. However, from the beginning of that four-year period such patents were to be endorsed 'licences of right'. By virtue of section 46(3)(a) of the Patents Act 1977 the effect of that endorsement was that 'any person shall . . . be entitled as of right to a licence . . . on such terms as may be settled by agreement or, in default of agreement, by the Comptroller [General of Patents] on the application of the proprietor of the patent or the person requiring the licence'.

Moreover, section 46(3)(c) of the Act provides that:

. . . if in proceedings for infringement of the patent (otherwise than by the importation of any article) the defendant or defender undertakes to take a licence on such terms, no injunction or interdict shall be granted against him and the amount . . . recoverable against him by way of damages shall not exceed double the amount which would have been payable by him as licensee if such a licence on those terms had been granted before the earliest infringement.

It will be seen that the designation 'licence of right' was a misnomer. The licence in question was in substance a type of compulsory licence, since it could be obtained without the consent of the patent-holder.[22]

Allen and Hanbury's owned a United Kingdom patent for a pharmaceutical product called SALBUTAMOL. The patent had been endorsed 'licences of right' as a result of the provisions described above. Generics wished to import SALBUTAMOL from Italy, where it had been manufactured by a firm which had no financial or contractual links with Allen and Hanbury's.[23] Generics requested a licence to import SALBUTAMOL, first from Allen and Hanbury's and then from the Comptroller General of Patents. Without waiting for the decision of the Comptroller General, Generics informed Allen and Hanbury's of its intention to go ahead with the importation.

Allen and Hanbury's brought patent infringement proceedings against Generics. The case reached the House of Lords, which referred a series of questions to the Court of Justice. The essential question was whether it was

[21] Case 434/85 [1988] ECR 1245 at para. 12.
[22] G. Bonet (1988) *Revue Trimestrielle de Droit Européen* 633, 634.
[23] See para. 2 of the judgment.

compatible with Articles 28 and 30 of the Treaty to grant an injunction prohibiting imports of infringing products from a Member State when the importer had undertaken to take a licence on the terms prescribed by law while no such injunction could be granted against an infringer who manufactured the product in the national territory.

Not surprisingly, the Court had no difficulty in condemning a practice that discriminated so blatantly between products imported from a Member State and products manufactured domestically. The obvious solution would have been to base the judgment on the second sentence of Article 30[24] and the Court did indeed observe that an injunction granted in such circumstances against an importer-infringer would constitute 'arbitrary discrimination'.[25] The principal line of reasoning followed by the Court was, however, rather more ingenious. After reciting its standard definition of the specific subject-matter of a patent, the Court noted that the *substance* of the exclusive rights granted to the patent proprietor was appreciably altered when the patent was endorsed 'licences of right'. In such a case the proprietor merely had the right to a fair return, not the right to prevent a third party from manufacturing the patented product domestically. There was no justification for granting him a more extensive right *vis-à-vis* an importer.[26]

The Court gave short shrift to a number of obviously specious arguments pleaded by Allen and Hanbury's and by the United Kingdom. Thus, it was argued that an importer might not have substantial assets in the State of importation, with the result that the patent proprietor would not be guaranteed payment of his royalties, and that it might be difficult to check the quantity of goods imported. Those arguments might, as the Court pointed out, apply equally to infringers who manufactured domestically; and there was nothing to justify treating them more favourably than importers.[27] A further argument, to the effect that an import ban was justified in order to enable the patent proprietor to check the quality of imported products in the interests of public health, might have been dealt with in similar terms. Instead the Court chose to dismiss the argument on the ground that public health should not be invoked as a means of justifying trade restrictions which are really designed to protect intellectual property.[28] A similar approach had been taken in *Centrafarm v Sterling Drug*,[29] where the point was reasoned more fully. It is in any event clear that health inspections are primarily the responsibility of public authorities and should not be

---

[24] M.-C. Boutard-Labarde (1988) 49, *La Semaine Juridique, édition générale*, II—jurisprudence, No. 21135, 50. The Advocate General also considered that the solution was to be found in the second sentence of Art. 30.

[25] At para. 22 of the judgment. [26] At paras 12–14 of the judgment.
[27] At paras 17 and 19 of the judgment. [28] At para. 21 of the judgment.
[29] Cited in n. 7, at paras 26–30 of the judgment.

delegated to intellectual property owners, who would be subject to an awkward conflict of interest if they had to act as guardians of the public interest while enforcing their private rights and privileges.

The Court also refused to attribute any significance to the fact that the articles in question were pharmaceutical products imported from a Member State where such products were not patentable. It had been argued that manufacturers in such a Member State were free-riders who did not have to bear the cost of research and could therefore manufacture in conditions that distorted competition. The argument was devoid of substance because exactly the same could be said of the domestic infringer who took a licence of right. The very purpose of the royalty payable under the licence of right was to ensure a fair return to the proprietor of the patent as recompense for his research costs. There were no grounds for drawing a distinction according to whether the infringing articles were manufactured domestically or in a Member State where the product in question was not patentable:[30] it could not be pretended that a royalty was sufficient recompense in the one case but that an injunction was essential in the other.

Finally, the Court rejected the surprising argument that, even though an import ban could not be justified on grounds of the protection of industrial and commercial property under Article 30, it could still be justified on grounds of imperative (or 'mandatory') requirements relating to consumer protection and fair trading. The Court simply pointed out that its mandatory requirements doctrine could only save measures which applied without distinction to domestic and imported goods—a condition that was not fulfilled in the instant case.[31] Though one may have reservations about that type of formalistic reasoning, it is clear that if a measure specifically designed to protect industrial and commercial property cannot satisfy the tests elaborated by the Court for appraising the validity of such measures under Article 30, then that should be the end of the matter. The concepts of consumer protection and fair trading should not be misused for the purpose of expanding the rights of intellectual property owners.

The *Allen and Hanbury's* case brought into the public gaze something that had long been known to anyone who looked critically at the patent laws of numerous Member States, i.e. that the rules on compulsory licensing were riddled with protectionism. A central concern of those rules was to encourage the exploitation of patents by means of domestic manufacturing as opposed to supplying the market by imports.[32] Thus, in nine of the twelve

---

[30] At para. 31 of the judgment.   [31] At paras 34 and 35 of the judgment.

[32] For historical and comparative information on this subject, see P. Demaret 'Industrial Property Rights, Compulsory Licences and the Free Movement of Goods under Community Law' (1987) 18 IIC 161, 165 (footnote 8) and 178ff. It appears that the British provisions date back to 1919 and were motivated by a belief that the patent system had been exploited by the Germans and had contributed to the munitions crisis during the First World War: J. Turner, '*Allen and Hanbury's v Generics*: Acte Claire (sic)—and Wrong' [1988] 6 EIPR 186. For a discussion of

Member States in the mid-1980s (Denmark, France, Germany, Greece, Ireland, Italy, Portugal, Spain, and the United Kingdom) a compulsory licence could be granted if the patentee was supplying the domestic market with imports (even imports from another Member State) but not if the patentee was supplying the domestic market with goods manufactured within the Member State in question.[33]

Joliet had pointed out as early as 1975 that a duty to work the patent within national territory was 'a clear violation of Article [28]'.[34] Demaret, in an article published in 1987, demonstrated convincingly that a domestic manufacturing requirement was beyond salvation, under Article 30 of the Treaty, unless perhaps it could qualify for exemption on grounds of 'public security' when imposed for defence reasons.[35]

The Commission finally commenced infringement proceedings under Article 226 of the Treaty against two Member States—Italy and the United Kingdom, in 1987 and 1989 respectively. Those proceedings led to the judgments in *Commission v Italy*[36] and *Commission v United Kingdom*[37] in 1992.

Inevitably, the Court declared that Italy and the United Kingdom had failed to fulfil their obligations under Article 28 of the Treaty by maintaining in force legislation under which a compulsory licence could be granted for failure to exploit a patent sufficiently by domestic manufacture where demand for the patented product on the domestic market was satisfied by imports from other Member States. The principle underlying the judgments is that patent-holders must, like any other undertaking, be free to determine where in the Community they wish to manufacture their products. They cannot be penalised if they choose to manufacture in a Member State other than the one in which they hold a patent. Such a practice would undermine the logic of the common market, which requires that the allocation of production resources is determined by the free play of market forces rather than by government intervention. Moreover, as Advocate General Van Gerven pointed out,[38] Article 30 of the Treaty certainly could not be invoked to justify the contested legislation because the objectionable feature thereof was not designed to enhance the 'protection of industrial and commercial property'; on the contrary, the rules on compulsory licences, which in any event entailed arbitrary discrimination within the meaning of

---

the compatibility of a 'local working' requirement with Art. 27(1) of TRIPS, see M. Halewood, 'Regulating Patent Holders: Local Working Requirements and Compulsory Licences at International Law' (1997) 35 *Osgoode Hall Law Journal* 245.

[33] See the Report for the Hearing in Case C-30/90 *Commission v United Kingdom* [1992] ECR I-829, at I-850 *et seq.*

[34] Joliet, op. cit. (n. 9), at 35.

[35] Op. cit. (n. 32), at 182.

[36] Case C-235/89 [1992] ECR I-818.

[37] Cited in n. 33.

[38] [1992] ECR I-777 at I-813.

the second sentence of Article 30, deprived the patent-holder of a major part of the protection afforded him by the patent.

The Court was rightly unimpressed by arguments which the defendant governments attempted to found on two international conventions. According to the first argument, the contested provisions were in accordance with Article 5 of the Paris Convention for the Protection of Industrial Property. But Article 5 merely authorized members of the Paris Union to provide for the grant of compulsory licences to prevent abuses such as failure to work the patent. There was no obligation on members of the Union to provide for compulsory licences when the patent was exploited by means of manufacture abroad.[39]

The second argument, based on certain provisions of the Community Patent Convention (CPC), was marginally more attractive but flawed nonetheless. Under Article 82 of the CPC in its original form and Article 77 of the CPC as amended at Luxembourg in 1989,[40] a compulsory licence could not be granted in respect of a national patent if the product covered by the patent was put on the market in sufficient quantity to satisfy the needs of a Contracting State, regardless of whether the products in question were manufactured in that or another Contracting State. Article 89 of the CPC in its original form and Article 83 of the amended version allowed Contracting States to reserve the right to delay the application of those provisions for as much as ten years from the entry into force of the CPC. Italy and the United Kingdom, contended that, if the Commission's reasoning were upheld, the result would be that the last-mentioned provisions of the CPC would have to be regarded as contrary to the EC Treaty. The obvious defect in that argument, which the Court did not fail to spot,[41] was that the possibility of an incompatibility between certain provisions of the CPC and Community law was expressly contemplated in Article 93 of the original CPC and in Article 2(1) of the Agreement relating to Community Patents signed in Luxembourg on 15 December 1989.[42] Those provisions expressly state that no provision of the CPC may be invoked against the application of the Treaty. That was sufficient to make the defendant governments' argument untenable.

The peculiar United Kingdom provisions on licences of right came before the Court once more in *Generics and Harris v Smith Kline and French*.[43] Smith Kline and French (SKF) held patents endorsed 'licences of right' for a

[39] See the opinion of Advocate General Van Gerven at I-815.

[40] OJ 1989 L 401, p. 1.

[41] At para. 29 of the judgment in *Commission v Italy* and para. 32 of the judgment in *Commission v United Kingdom*.

[42] That Agreement provided for the original CPC to be replaced by an amended version, which was contained in an annex to the Agreement.

[43] Case C-191/90 [1992] ECR I-5335.

product of which the generic name was 'cimetidine'. Generics and Harris applied for licences of right. The parties could not agree on the licence terms, so the matter was referred to the Comptroller General of Patents and subsequently to the Patents Court. The Patents Court included in the licences a term prohibiting Generics and Harris from importing cimetidine in the form of finished products, from non-member countries and from Spain and Portugal. However, the Patents Court refused to include such a clause as regards the importation of cimetidine in raw-material form. The reason for that distinction was that SKF was manufacturing cimetidine in the form of raw material in Ireland and was making up the finished product in the United Kingdom.

Thus the Patents Court was applying a rule of national law that was clearly inconsistent with the logic of the judgments in *Commission v Italy* and *Commission v United Kingdom*. The patent-holder should not possess a stronger right, as against products imported by a licensee, if he manufactures the patented product in the country where he owns the patent, than he would have if he had the patented product manufactured in another Member State. The effect of the United Kingdom legislation, as interpreted and applied by the Patents Court, was that SKF had an incentive to manufacture the patented product in the United Kingdom rather than in Ireland or some other Member State. The legislation was therefore discriminatory and was capable of hindering intra-Community trade. As such, it was caught by Article 28 and was not capable of justification under Article 30, since the difference in treatment was motivated not by the need to protect industrial and commercial property but by the desire to favour production within the Member State concerned.

That indeed is what the Court of Justice held in response to questions referred to it by the Court of Appeal.[44] That did not, however, mean that the United Kingdom authorities had a positive obligation to allow the licensee to import the patented product from non-member countries. The discrimination inherent in the decision of the Patents Court could be eliminated simply by refusing to allow Generics and Harris to import the patented product from non-member countries in any circumstances; provided that the denial of a licence did not depend on whether the patent-holder was exploiting the patent by manufacturing in the United Kingdom or in another Member State, a ban on imports from a non-member country would not infringe the Treaty. That doubtless explains why Generics and Harris sought to defend the discriminatory practice followed by the Patents Court; it represented their only chance of obtaining a licence to import the patented product from non-member countries.

---

[44] At paras 20 and 24 of the judgment.

As regards the imports from Spain and Portugal, the position was more complicated as a result of Articles 47 and 209 of the Act of Accession of Spain and Portugal. Those provisions have already been encountered in the Chapter 7 on exhaustion of rights. It will be recalled that chemical and pharmaceutical products could not be patented in Spain and Portugal at the time of those countries' accession to the European Community. In protocols to the Act of Accession, Spain and Portugal undertook to amend their laws so as to grant patent protection for chemical and pharmaceutical products. In the meantime it was thought desirable to exclude the principle of exhaustion in relation to products manufactured in those countries without the benefit of patent protection. To that end, Articles 47 and 209 of the Act of Accession provided that the holder of a patent for a chemical or pharmaceutical product filed in a Member State at a time when a product patent could not be obtained in Spain or Portugal for that product, could rely on that patent in order to prevent the import and marketing of the patented product in the Member States where it enjoyed patent protection 'even if that product was put on the market in Spain [Portugal] for the first time by him or with his consent'. That right could only be invoked for a period of three years after such products became patentable in Spain (or Portugal).[45]

It is doubtful whether Articles 47 and 209 of the Act of Accession had any bearing at all on the dispute between SKF and Generics and Harris. The sole purpose of those provisions was to exclude, for a limited period, the operation of the rule in *Merck v Stephar*, i.e. the rule under which a patent-holder could not rely on his patent in order to prevent imports of goods marketed with his consent in another Member State even though the product in question could not be patented in that Member State. Articles 47 and 209 were certainly not intended to limit the application of the rules established in *Allen and Hanbury's* and in the cases brought by the Commission against Italy and the United Kingdom. Apart from the minor fact that all those judgments were delivered several years after the accession of Spain and Portugal, there is nothing in the logic of Articles 47 and 209 to suggest that they should affect the normal application of the Treaty provisions on the free movement of goods in relation to compulsory licences.

Logically, therefore, the Court should have ruled that:

(1) a licence to import the patented product from Spain or Portugal cannot be made dependent on whether the patent-holder manufactures the patented product in the United Kingdom or in another Member State;

(2) where a patent is endorsed 'licences of right', with the result that anyone is entitled to a licence to manufacture the patented product in the Member State in which the patent exists, a person who wishes to

[45] Arts 42(2) and 209(2) of the Act of Accession of Spain and Portugal.

import the patented product from Spain or Portugal must be granted a licence on the same terms.

The first of those points is self-evident. It follows from the logic of *Commission v United Kingdom*. In *Generics and Harris v Smith Kline and French* the Court established such a rule in relation to imports from non-member countries but failed, surprisingly, to realize that the same rule must apply *a fortiori* to imports from Spain and Portugal. The basis for the rule is that the licensing authority may not adopt a practice which distorts trade as between the Member State in which the patent is held and other Member States in which the patent-holder may wish to manufacture the patented product. The country from which the licensee wishes to import the patented product is not of the slightest relevance; it could be an 'old' Member State, a 'new' Member State, or even—as the Court held in *Generics and Harris v Smith Kline and French*—a non-member country. Articles 47 and 209 of the Act of Accession have no bearing on the problem, for they were certainly not intended to legitimise a practice that encouraged patent-holders to manufacture products in the United Kingdom rather than Ireland.

The second point, though not quite so obvious, is equally incontestable. The basic proposition is, of course, derived from the rule in *Allen and Hanbury's*. In that judgment the Court held that, in a situation in which any third party is entitled to a licence to manufacture the patented product in the national territory, subject to payment of a royalty, a prohibition on imports from another Member State is justified under Article 30 of the Treaty only in so far as such a prohibition is necessary in order to ensure that the patent-holder enjoys, *vis-à-vis* importers, the same rights as he enjoys against those who manufacture the patented product in the national territory.[46] In other words, if a licensee who manufactures domestically need only pay a royalty, that is all that can be asked of someone who applies for a licence to import the patented product from another Member State.

There was no reason to interpret Articles 47 and 209 of the Act of Accession of Spain and Portugal as excluding the application of the rule in *Allen and Hanbury's* to imports from Spain or Portugal. To understand that, we need only to look at the mischief which Articles 47 and 209 were intended to correct, i.e. the injustice suffered to by the proprietor of a patent in one Member State when he is unable to block parallel imports of goods that he has placed on the market in another Member State in which he was denied patent protection. As was pointed out in Chapter 7 on the exhaustion of rights, the value of the patent in the first Member State is eroded if the patent-holder has to face competition from his own goods which he has

---

[46] *Allen and Hanbury's*, at para. 14 of the judgment

marketed in the second Member State without the benefit of patent protection. No such injustice would have been suffered by SKF if Generics and Harris had been granted a licence to import the patented product from Spain and Portugal. In respect of those goods SKF would have enjoyed exactly the same compensation—a royalty fixed by agreement or, in the absence of agreement, by the competent authorities—as it received from a licensee of right who manufactured the patented product in the United Kingdom. The unavailability of patent protection in Spain and Portugal made not a scrap of difference. Articles 47 and 209, which were designed solely to alleviate an injustice caused by disparities between the laws of the old and the new Member States with regard to patentable subject-matter, were therefore irrelevant.

Such a position was indeed defended by the governments of Spain, the United Kingdom and the Commission as well as by Generics and Harris. Surprisingly, the Court was not persuaded by those arguments. The Court, following Advocate General Van Gerven, ruled that:

Articles 47 and 209 of the Act concerning the conditions of the accession of the Kingdom of Spain and the Portuguese Republic and the adjustments to the Treaties must be interpreted to the effect that the authorities of the Member States competent to settle, in the absence of agreement, the conditions of licences of right may, on the basis of those provisions and in derogation from the principles laid down by Articles [28] and [30] of the Treaty, prohibit the licensee from importing from Spain and Portugal a patented pharmaceutical product if national law confers upon the proprietor of the patent the right to prevent imports and if the proprietor exercises the right conferred upon him by Articles 47 and 209.

Since the two conditions tagged on to the end of that ruling were obviously fulfilled (otherwise the issue would never have led to litigation, still less to a request for a preliminary ruling), that amounted to saying that SKF was entitled to prevent Generics and Harris from obtaining a licence of right to import the patented product from Spain or Portugal. The Court did not even indicate that the availability of a licence of right could not be made dependent on the Member State in which SKF manufactured the patented product. Sadly, the Court and the Advocate General seem to have experienced difficulty in understanding the true nature of the problem—an impression that is confirmed by the extreme opacity of the remarks in paragraphs 38 to 42 of the judgment.[47]

[47] This very opacity seems to have deterred commentators from criticizing the Court's reasoning. W. Alexander simply describes the Court's ruling on Arts 47 and 209 of the Act of Accession without offering any analysis or critical comment: (1994) CML Rev. 173, 187. G. Bonet considers the Court's position 'très logique' without, however, explaining why or attempting to identify the issues raised by Arts 47 and 209: (1993) *Revue Trimestrielle de Droit Européen* 538, 543.

4. A FAIR DEAL FOR PHARMACEUTICAL PATENTS?

Life is not always easy for the makers of pharmaceutical products. As we saw in Chapters 7 and 8 on exhaustion of rights and on trade marks, their products are often subject to price controls. These cause price discrepancies which stimulate parallel imports. The pharmaceutical companies cannot invoke their patents to block parallel imports of their products even though those products were first marketed in a country where no patent protection existed. And in many situations they cannot invoke their trade marks to prevent the parallel importers from repackaging their products.

Although it is fashionable in certain quarters to stigmatize pharmaceutical companies as corporate giants exploiting the downtrodden, it should not be forgotten that without their research the battle to cure disease and sickness and to reduce physical suffering could not be won. Medical science advances largely because corporate funds are made available to finance research into new drugs and treatments. Investment in research is unlikely to take place on a significant scale unless there is a prospect of profit. Seen in that light, a twenty-year monopoly on new pharmaceutical products does not seem excessively generous as a reward for past efforts and an incentive to further investment.

Unfortunately, the proprietors of pharmaceutical patents rarely enjoy anything approaching a twenty-year monopoly. Before a medicinal product may be placed on the market, a marketing authorization must be obtained either from the competent national authorities in accordance with Directive 2001/83/EC of the European Parliament and Council on the Community code relating to medicinal products for human use[48] or from the Community authorities in accordance with Council Regulation (EEC) No. 2309/93 laying down Community procedures for the authorization and supervision of medicinal products for human and veterinary use and establishing a European Agency for the Evaluation of Medicinal Products.[49] The delay involved in obtaining a marketing authorization 'substantially shortens the useful period of the patentee's exclusive right to market his patented product since the period of patent protection, which runs from the date of filing the application for the patent, continues running throughout the authorization procedure'.[50]

To compensate patent proprietors for the reduction in the useful life of their patents due to the delay in obtaining marketing authorization, the Council introduced the Supplementary Protection Certificate (SPC) in

---

[48] OJ 2001 L 311, p. 67.   [49] OJ 1993 L 214, p. 1.
[50] See para. 2 of the opinion of Advocate General Jacobs in Case C-316/95 *Generics v Smith, Kline and French* |1997| ECR I-3929.

1992.[51] The effect of an SPC is to prolong the exclusive rights of the proprietor of a patent for a medicinal product by a maximum of five years. Since the average period for approval of medicines was twelve years in 1990,[52] it is doubtful whether the scheme is sufficiently generous to patentees.

To some extent the delay in obtaining a marketing authorization is offset at the end of the life of the patent, inasmuch as competitors who wish to manufacture the patented product after it has ceased to be protected must themselves obtain a marketing authorization. Sometimes competitors of the patentee seek to advance the date on which they can effectively enter the market by submitting their request for a marketing authorization before the patent has expired. That will normally necessitate the provision of a sample of the medicinal product to the competent authority. The question arises whether the provision of such a sample, while the patent is still running, amounts to a patent infringement.

In *Generics v Smith Kline and French*[53] the Dutch courts took the view that Generics had indeed infringed two of SKF's patents (one of which related to cimetidine) by providing samples of the patented products to the competent Dutch authority when they applied for a marketing authorization some time before the patents expired. In order to make good the damage to SKF, a Dutch court made an order prohibiting Generics from offering or supplying cimetidine for consumption on the market in the Netherlands until a period of fourteen months had elapsed after the expiry of the patent for cimetidine. That period was selected on the basis that it usually took at least fourteen months to obtain a marketing authorization. Thus, fourteen months after the expiry of the patent was the earliest point at which Generics would have been able to market cimetidine if it had applied for a marketing authorization immediately after the expiry of SKF's patent.

Generics argued that the fourteen-month moratorium imposed on its marketing of cimetidine was a barrier to intra-Community trade incompatible with Articles 28 and 30 of the Treaty. Presumably the basis of that view was that the cimetidine that it was thereby prevented from marketing in the Netherlands might have been imported from another Member State. The *Hoge Raad* sought guidance from the Court of Justice on the interpretation of Articles 28 and 30.

---

[51] Council Reg. (EEC) No. 1768/92 of 18 June 1992, concerning the creation of a supplementary protection certificate for medicinal products (OJ 1992 L 182, p. 1). A similar scheme applies to plant protection products by virtue of Council Reg. (EC) No. 1610/96 of the European Parliament and the Council of 23 July 1996 (OJ 1996 L 198, p. 30). An action for the annulment of Reg. No. 1768/92, commenced by Spain on grounds of lack of competence, was dismissed by the Court of Justice: Case C-350/92 *Spain v Council* [1995] ECR I-1985.

[52] Bently and Sherman, op. cit. (n. 11), at p. 551.   [53] Cited in n. 50.

The Court had no difficulty in holding that the Dutch practice amounted to a measure equivalent in effect to an import restriction under Article 28 of the Treaty in so far as the submission of a sample in support of a marketing authorization was treated as a patent infringement. That had to be the case, since the rule could have the effect of preventing the marketing of imported goods immediately after the expiry of the patent.

The Court also had no difficulty in finding that the practice of the Dutch courts was justified under Article 30 of the Treaty. The Court's reasoning was to some extent formalistic. It went through the ritual of invoking the concept of 'specific subject-matter' and observed that 'the right of the proprietor of a patent in respect of a manufacturing process for a medicinal product to oppose the use by another person of samples of medicinal products manufactured in accordance with that process for the purpose of obtaining a marketing authorization falls within the specific subject-matter of the patent right in so far as such samples have been used without the direct or indirect consent of the patentee'. What the Court presumably meant is that it was perfectly consonant with the patent laws of Europe for the patentee to be able to prevent third parties from using the patented product or process in support of an application for a marketing authorization. The Court referred in this regard to Article 25 of the Community Patent Convention and to Article 28 of the TRIPS Agreement.

The point was dealt with more fully by Advocate General Jacobs. He noted that the Court had generally been willing to take account of the CPC even though it had not entered into force.[54] He then cited Article 25 of the CPC, which provides that the proprietor of a Community patent has the right, *inter alia*, to prevent all third parties not having his consent from 'making, offering, putting on the market or using a product which is the subject-matter of the patent, or importing or stocking the product for these purposes'. As the Advocate General observed, the exceptions to that right are very limited. The only ones which might be regarded as relevant, according to the Advocate General, were 'acts done privately and for non-commercial purposes' and 'acts done for experimental purposes relating to the subject-matter of the patented invention', under Article 27(a) and (b). The act of submitting a sample of the patented product to a public authority in support of an application for a marketing authorization could not be performed without first making the product or importing it. Moreover, the act would in any case amount to 'using' the product. Hence the view that Generics had infringed SKF's patent would be difficult to challenge.

The Court also found that the Dutch practice was not disproportionate in so far as it prevented Generics from marketing the patented product for a

---

[54] At para. 38 of the Advocate General's opinion, where he cites para. 32 of the judgment in C-30/90 *Commission v United Kingdom*.

period of fourteen months. All that the moratorium aimed to do was to place the proprietor of the patent in the position in which it would have been if its rights had been respected.[55] Although the period of fourteen months exceeded the maximum period permitted by the relevant Community legislation for the procedure leading to the grant of a marketing authorization, it was nonetheless justified because it corresponded to the actual average duration of the procedure in the Member State concerned.[56]

---

[55] At para. 28 of the judgment.   [56] At para. 31 of the judgment.

10

Copyright

1. COPYRIGHT; *DROIT D'AUTEUR*; NEIGHBOURING RIGHTS

'Copyright' is the term used in English law to describe a whole series of exclusive rights granted to:

- authors, composers, artists, architects, etc. ('the creators');
- musicians, singers, dancers, etc. ('the performers'); and
- publishers, record producers, film-makers, etc. ('the entrepreneurs').

Dictionaries tell us that 'copyright' translates into French as *droit d'auteur*. The translation is inaccurate—at least in part—because the term *droit d'auteur*, as the name implies, refers only to the rights of the first category: the creators of *la propriété littéraire et artistique*. The rights accorded to performers and entrepreneurs are called *droits voisins* in French, which is often rendered literally as 'neighbouring rights' in English, though a more idiomatic translation would be 'related rights'.[1]

Comparativists are wont to emphasize the differences of substance between the laws of the United Kingdom (and other common law countries) in this field and those of continental Europe. It is often said that the common law is primarily concerned with the protection of economic rights, whereas countries that follow the civil law tradition concentrate on the moral rights of the author and analogous creators. While there is doubtless a great deal of oversimplification in these views, and maybe even a measure of racial stereotyping, there is also more than a grain of truth. Certainly English law has historically been reluctant to recognize such 'moral rights' as the author's rights to be identified as the author of his work and to oppose unauthorized adaptations of the work.[2] French law, on the other hand,

---

[1] Some authors see significance in the use of the expression 'related rights' (as opposed to 'neighbouring rights') in the TRIPS Agreement, the argument appearing to be that this is evidence of an Anglo-American tendency to place performers' and entrepreneurs' rights on the same footing as authors' rights: see, e.g., A. Bercovitz, in *Intellectual Property and International Trade: The TRIPS Agreement* (eds. C. M. Correa and Abdulquairi A. Yusuf), Kluwer Law International, 1998, p. 145 at p. 156, and P. A. Maier in *L'Europe et les enjeux du GATT dans le domaine de l'audiovisuel* (under the direction of Carine Doutrelepont), p. 141 at p. 143. In fact, the expression 'related rights' has been consistently used, as the equivalent of *droits voisins* in the English version of Community legislation since at least 1992.

[2] The right to be identified as the author of a work or director of a film is now laid down in ss. 77–79 of the Copyright, Designs and Patents Act 1998. Ss. 80–84 of the Act allow the author of a work or the director of a film to object to derogatory treatment of the work or film. Even before the passing of that Act, there were means of protecting such rights in English law: see D. I. Bainbridge, *Intellectual Property*, 4th edn, Financial Times/Pitman publishing 1999, at p. 99.

appears to have been less enthusiastic than English law in protecting the purely economic rights of the entrepreneurs who make literary and artistic works available to the public. That is illustrated by the *Deutsche Grammophon*[3] case, where the alleged justification for not applying the exhaustion principle to gramophone records first marketed in France was that the record manufacturer enjoyed no exclusive right to exploit the product in that country.

Perhaps the case that most strikingly highlights the difference of approach between the common law and the civil law tradition is *Magill*.[4] Continental lawyers have difficulty in understanding how something as mundane and devoid of literary or artistic inspiration as a schedule of television programmes can be protected by copyright. That lack of understanding perhaps explains the incoherence of the judgments delivered by the Court of Justice and the Court of First Instance. After paying lip service to the principle that national law governs the creation of intellectual property rights in the absence of harmonization, the judges went on to uphold a Commission decision that effectively deprived the television companies of their exclusive right to publish their programme schedules in full.

This is not the place to engage in a detailed comparative study. The one thing that must be emphasized in this context is that there were—before the spate of harmonizing directives issued in the 1990s—major differences between the laws of the Member States in the field of copyright. These differences concerned, *inter alia*, the type of work protected, the standard of originality, the scope of the exclusive right, the persons for whose benefit the exclusive right inured, the term of protection, and the remedies available against infringers. Many differences remain. It goes without saying that disparities in the laws of the Member States pose problems in connection with the free movement of goods. We have already seen several examples. In *Deutsche Grammophon* it was argued that the value of the phonogram producer's exclusive right in Germany would be undermined if goods which he had placed on the market in France without the benefit of an equivalent exclusive right could be resold in Germany. The Court was not persuaded and gave priority to the free movement of goods. It did likewise in *Musik-Vetrieb Membran v GEMA*,[5] even though the British statutory provisions on royalties forced the copyright owner to accept a lower royalty in the United Kingdom than the one that he could negotiate in Germany; in that case the value of the copyright owner's right in the Member State of importation was clearly undermined on account of the less generous protection in the Member State where the first sale had taken place.

---

[3] Case 78/70 *Deutsche Grammophon v Metro* [1971] ECR 487.
[4] Joined Cases C-241/91 P and C-242/91 P *RTE and ITV v Commission* [1995] ECR 743.
[5] Case 55/80 [1981] ECR 147.

In two other cases where the root of the problem lay in disparities between national law, the scales were tipped in favour of the copyright owner. In *EMI Electrola v Patricia Im-und Export*[6] the claimant's copyright in recordings by Cliff Richard had expired in Denmark but not in Germany; it was able to prevent the importation into Germany of records marketed *without its authorization* in Denmark. In *Warner Brothers and Metronome v Christiansen*[7] the owner of the copyright in a James Bond film was able to enforce its right under Danish law to prohibit rentals of a video-cassette of the film, notwithstanding that the video-cassette had been sold with the copyright owner's consent in the United Kingdom, where the law did not then recognize an exclusive right to control rentals of the protected work.

Those four examples are sufficient to illustrate the extent to which disparities in national law can interfere with the free movement of goods. Such is the scale of the harmonization undertaken in recent years that those particular problems, and many others, appear to have been eliminated at source. While these matters may therefore be of largely historical interest, there are still some lessons to be drawn from the case law. In the first three of the four cases cited, the Court found a convenient solution in its consent-based conception of the exhaustion principle. In *Deutsche Grammophon* and *GEMA* the right-holder had consented to the first sale in the Member State of exportation and could not therefore prevent resale in another Member State in spite of the alleged hardship. In *EMI Electrola* the records had been marketed in Denmark without the consent of the copyright owner, who could therefore block their importation into Germany. In those cases, as in *Merck v Stephar*,[8] *Pharmon v Hoechst*[9] and *Merck v Primecrown*,[10] the Court was consistent, even though some would maintain that its fondness for the apparent simplicity and legal certainty of a consent-based test has led to injustice and to an undermining of intellectual property rights.

2. THE TERRITORIALITY OF COPYRIGHT

Copyright protection is not dependent on registration. As a result of the wide acceptance of the leading conventions, in particular the Berne Convention, literary and artistic works enjoy a similar level of protection in large parts of the world from the moment of creation. It is tempting to assume, therefore, that copyright is somehow more 'universal' and less territorial in nature than other forms of intellectual property, such as patents and trade marks, which are generally dependent on registration

[6] Case 341/87 [1989] ECR 79.
[7] Case 158/86 [1988] ECR 2605.
[8] Case 187/80 [1981] ECR 2063.
[9] Case 19/84 [1985] ECR 2281.
[10] Case C-267/95 [1996] I-6285.

with administrative authorities whose jurisdiction is by definition territorially limited.[11]

While there may be some truth in that, it must always be remembered that copyright protection depends ultimately on national law. The harmonisation achieved by international conventions is only partial. Even in apparently harmonized areas, differences may arise through divergent judicial interpretation. Assignments of copyright may, moreover, be limited to specific territories. Enforcement of copyright is in any event necessarily dependent on national courts whose jurisdiction is territorial by definition. In short, there are plenty of situations in which a work or a performance may give rise to an exclusive right in one country but not in another, just as there are situations in which the ownership of the right varies from country to country. Thus copyright, like registration-based intellectual property rights, is capable of interfering with the free movement of goods by virtue of its territoriality. It is also capable, as we shall see, of interfering with the free movement of services.

3. THE SPECIFIC SUBJECT-MATTER AND ESSENTIAL FUNCTION OF COPYRIGHT

Attempts to justify granting exclusive rights to authors, performers and entrepreneurs focus on two central themes. First, there is the moral imperative of rewarding those who enrich the cultural heritage of mankind. Secondly, there is the economic argument that without the incentive of financial gain certain types of work would not be created at all or would not be made available to the general public. The moral argument tends to apply above all to authors, whereas the economic argument is the most satisfactory explanation for the protection now accorded to certain entrepreneurs and performers. The dichotomy between moral and economic justifications probably explains the huge disparity in the terms of protection granted to authors, on the one hand, and to entrepreneurs and performers, on the other.[12] A term of seventy years after the death of the author cannot possibly be justified as an incentive to literary production; no author writes with a view to enriching his great grandchildren. The only explanation for

---

[11] There is, of course, some protection for unregistered trade marks by means of an action for passing-off in English law and an action for unfair competition in some continental jurisdictions. However, most litigation nowadays concerns registered trade marks.

[12] See W. R. Cornish, *Intellectual Property: Patents, Copyright, Trade Marks and Allied Rights*, 4th edn, Sweet and Maxwell, London, 1999, p. 365. Rather more difficult to explain and justify is the disparity between the terms of protection for copyright and patents: see E. C. Walterscheid, 'The Remarkable—and Irrational—Disparity between the Patent Term and the Copyright Term' (2001) JPTOS 233.

such a term of protection is that society values authors so highly that it esteems them worthy of a reward that can be passed on for several generations. Broadcasting organisations, producers of films, phonograms and the like are viewed purely as economic agents; they are given an exclusive right of much shorter duration as an incentive to make the investment needed to communicate authors' works to the public. The term of protection need not be so long because businesses, even when planning a long-term strategy, do not generally think more than twenty-five years ahead.

The Court of Justice has, predictably, not spent much time agonizing about the underlying justification for copyright. One might have expected the Court to work a reference to the purpose of copyright into its definition of the *objet spécifique* ('specific subject-matter') of copyright, just as it has done in the case of patents and trade marks. In the early years the Court was decidedly reluctant to say anything at all about the purpose of copyright protection. The most glaring example of that is the *Deutsche Grammophon* judgment, which held that derogations from the free movement of goods were only permissible if they were justified for the purpose of safeguarding the specific subject-matter of an intellectual property right, but then failed to make any attempt to define the specific subject-matter of copyright.[13] As a result, the judgment makes no sense. One possible explanation is that the first draft may have contained a definition but this was removed because the judges could not agree on its terms.

One of the oddities of the Court's case law on intellectual property and the free movement of goods in the 1970s and 1980s is that the Court felt able to resolve patent and trade mark issues by recourse to arcane, self-serving definitions of the specific subject-matter of those intellectual property rights but shied away from any attempt to do the same with copyright. This blatant discrepancy confirms that the Court's constant invocations of the specific subject-matter test in relation to patents and trade marks are nothing but cant.

In fact, after *Deutsche Grammophon* in 1971 one has to wait until the *Phil Collins* judgment in 1993 for another reference to the specific subject-matter of copyright in a judgment of the Court.[14] By then there had been

---

[13] At para. 11 of the judgment.

[14] In the years between *Deutsche Grammophon* and *Phil Collins* various advocates general had made half-hearted attempts to use the specific subject-matter criterion in relation to copyright. See, e.g., the opinions of Advocate General Warner in Case 62/79 *Coditel v Ciné Vog Films* ('Coditel I') [1980] ECR 881 at 879, and in *Musik-Vertrieb Membran v GEMA* at 177; Advocate General Reischl in Case 262/81 *Coditel v Ciné Vog Films* ('Coditel II') [1982] ECR 3381 at 3406, 3409 and 3413; Advocate General Lenz in Case 402/85 *Basset v SACEM* [1987] ECR 1747 at 1759; and Advocate General Darmon in Case 341/87 *EMI Electrola v Patricia Im- und Export* [1989] ECR 79 at 88. The Court of First Instance also paid homage to the specific subject-matter of copyright in the *Magill* cases (see, e.g., para. 70 of the judgment in Case T-69/89 *RTE v Commission* [1991] ECR II-485).

sufficient harmonization of copyright law for the Court to attempt a definition of the specific subject-matter of copyright that encompassed both moral and economic rights. The Court stated as follows:

> The specific subject-matter of [copyright and related rights], as governed by national legislation, is to ensure the protection of the moral and economic rights of their holders. The protection of moral rights enables authors and performers, in particular, to object to any distortion, mutilation or other modification of a work which would be prejudicial to their honour or reputation. Copyright and related rights are also economic in nature, in that they confer the right to exploit commercially the marketing of the protected work, particularly in the form of licences granted in return for payment of royalties.[15]

In the meantime the Court had made a fleeting reference to the 'essential function' of copyright. This occurred in *Coditel I*,[16] where the Court said that 'the right of a copyright owner and his assigns to require fees for any showing of a film is part of the essential function of copyright in this type of literary or artistic work'.[17] That is a curious statement. One might just as well say that the essential function of breathing is to suck air into the lungs. Although the Court spoke in that passage of the essential function of copyright, it was in reality simply describing the basic rights conferred on the copyright owner. That is of course what the Court normally refers to as the 'specific subject-matter' of an intellectual property right.

Many years after *Coditel I* the concept of 'essential function' made a dramatic reappearance in the *Magill* cases, which concerned the application of the EC competition rules. There the Court of First Instance made a remarkably bold statement—in fact the first statement in which the Community judicature had said anything about the real purpose of copyright and its underlying justification. The Court said that the 'essential function [of copyright] . . . is to protect the moral rights in the work and ensure a reward for the creative effort [of the author]'.[18] The Court of Justice cited that passage approvingly, when it confirmed the judgment of the Court of First Instance.[19]

The term 'essential function' had played a role in the Court's case law on trade marks since the 1970s. There the Court made a distinction between the specific subject-matter of the trade mark right and the essential function of the trade mark. The former was defined as the exclusive right of the proprietor to market products under the trade mark and thus protect his

---

[15] Joined Cases C-92/92 and C-326/92 *Phil Collins and others* [1993] ECR I-5145. It is interesting to note that moral rights enjoy pride of place in this definition, perhaps because the judge rapporteur was French. The facts of the case suggest that the English claimant was more concerned about his economic rights.

[16] Cited in n. 14.   [17] At para. 14 of the judgment.

[18] *RTE v Commission* (cited in n. 14), at para. 71.

[19] Joined Cases C-241/91 P and C-242/91 P *RTE and ITP v Commission* [1995] ECR I-743 at para. 28.

commercial reputation against counterfeiters. The latter was defined as the guarantee, to consumers, that all products bearing the trade mark had the same commercial origin.

In his opinion in *Magill*, Advocate General Gulmann appeared to believe that this distinction between specific subject-matter and essential function applied not just to trade marks but also to copyright and, presumably, to intellectual property rights in general. The Advocate General seemed to suggest that it is first necessary to identify the rights that constitute the specific subject-matter of an intellectual property right (i.e. the core rights that are in principle immune to the effects of EC law), and that the essential function of the intellectual property right may then be used as an auxiliary concept which enables the Court to determine whether the exercise of a right that belongs to the specific subject-matter is none the less incompatible with the Treaty rules.

The Advocate General's analysis is surely over-sophisticated. A first objection is that the distinction between specific subject-matter and essential function, which the Court had made in the field of trade marks, was artificial, since the two concepts represented opposite sides of the same coin. Secondly, the concept of the essential function of copyright had never played a major role in the Court's case law, having had nothing more than a walk-on part in *Coditel I*, where the expression was moreover used in an obscure and misleading fashion. Gulmann's analysis assumes a coherence in the case law that simply does not exist.

It is significant that the Court's one and only reference to copyright as a means of rewarding creative effort was made in the context of a case in which it was difficult to discern any creative effort, on the part of the copyright owners, that was worthy of reward. The copyright owners were television companies which invoked copyright in weekly listings of their programmes so as to prevent an independent publisher from producing a weekly television magazine that would compete with their own magazines. In granting the injunction sought by the television companies Mr Justice Lardner, of the Irish High Court, stated:[20] 'I am satisfied that each weekly schedule is the result of a great deal of preliminary consideration and work and the exercise of skill and judgment.'

The Irish judge thus applied the traditional common law test for determining whether an original work protectable by copyright existed, i.e. whether 'skill, labour and judgment' had been expended in the creation of the work. In continental Europe it is clear that a higher standard of creativity is required. In French law, for example, a work is original, and eligible for protection by way of *droit d'auteur*, if it bears the imprint of the

[20] The judge's comments were quoted in para. 10 of the judgment of the Court of First Instance in *RTE v Commission* (cited in n. 14), at 495.

personality of its author.[21] German law requires a work to be a 'personal intellectual creation'.[22] A list of television programmes clearly does not meet these requirements.

No one should be surprised therefore if the Community Courts were sceptical about the desirability of according a high level of protection to this particular manifestation of 'intellectual' property. The difficulty facing the Courts was that they were bound by the abundant case law stating that:

(1) in the absence of harmonization, national law alone governs the grant of intellectual property rights; and

(2) Community law cannot call in question the existence, substance, specific subject-matter, etc. of intellectual property rights recognized by national law.

As we have seen, the Courts did indeed destroy the substance of the television companies' 'intellectual' property right in the *Magill* judgments by forcing them to surrender their exclusive right of reproduction. The Courts tried of course to disguise that fact by alluding to various special circumstances which allegedly showed that the television companies were exercising their rights abusively (consumer demand for a comprehensive weekly television guide, absence of any alternative, possible emergence of a new product, ancillary nature of magazine publishing in relation to the television companies' principal activity).

Easy though it is to understand and share the judges' sympathy for the 'little man' battling against the 'big corporations', their inability to produce judgments that even approach intellectual coherence is deeply unsatisfactory. The judges simply do not explain what basis there is for allowing Community law to destroy something which Community law cannot—so we have been told a few paragraphs earlier—call into question. Is it not significant, therefore, that this is the one case in which the Court of Justice pointed out that one of the essential functions of copyright is to reward creativity? By mentioning that aspect of copyright law the Court seems to have betrayed its subconscious feeling that the protected 'work' (a schedule of television programmes) was not worthy of protection because there was no creative effort to reward. Indeed, Advocate General Gulmann openly stated that in his view the Court of First Instance had been swayed by the unmeritorious nature of the protected work.[23]

---

[21] A. Françon. *Le droit d'auteur: aspects internationaux et comparatifs*. Les Editions Yvon Blais Inc., Québec, 1992, p. 145.

[22] Bainbridge, op. cit. (n. 2), at p. 43.

[23] [1995] ECR I-743 at I-782, where the Advocate General stated: 'I am . . . inclined to endorse the . . . view that the actual grounds for applying Article [82] in the present circumstances must . . . be that the programme listings were not regarded as meriting protection.'

4. REPRODUCTION RIGHT AND PERFORMANCE RIGHT: THE LIMITATIONS OF THE EXHAUSTION PRINCIPLE

In *Warner Brothers* the Court found—rightly, it is submitted—that consent to the first marketing within the Community was not the key to the problem. The reason lay in a fundamental feature of copyright which distinguishes it from other types of intellectual property and causes it to throw up problems that cannot be solved by the straightforward application of the exhaustion principle. The copyright owner enjoys two basic rights: the reproduction right and the performance right. The former constitutes copyright in its most literal sense; it refers to the exclusive right to make copies of the protected work in material form. This is the right that is infringed by, for example, the video or audio pirate who makes and distributes copies of films or musical recordings. The performance right refers to the exclusive right to perform the protected work in public (e.g. to put on a play in a theatre, to perform a song or symphony in a concert hall, to play gramophone records in a discotheque, and so forth). These two distinct categories of exclusive right appear to be recognized by most legal systems. Even the terminology differs but little. French law, for example, speaks of *droit de reproduction* and *droit de représentation*. As far as the free movement of goods is concerned, the reproduction right does not pose problems that differ very much from those that arise in relation to patents, trade marks, design rights, and other types of intellectual property right. The infringing acts bring into existence physical goods which then become the subject of commerce, including of course commerce between Member States. The ordinary rules of exhaustion will determine whether goods protected by copyright which are on the market in one Member State may be resold in the rest of the common market.

Admittedly it was once suggested, in the early days of EC law, that copyright (or, to be more accurate, *droit d'auteur*) lay entirely outside the scope of the Treaty because authors' rights were essentially of a moral, non-economic nature. There was little in the wording of the Treaty to support this view. In fact, Annex III to the Treaty expressly mentioned copyright royalties among the payments on which Member States were not allowed to introduce new restrictions in accordance with Article 106 of the original Treaty. It is true that Article 30 speaks of 'industrial and commercial property' (*propriété industrielle et commerciale* in French), which in the terminology of continental Europe would not normally include copyright and related rights. However, the only consequence of such an interpretation would be to deny copyright owners the benefit of Article 30. Trade barriers caused by copyright would be caught by Article 28 but would not

be capable of justification under Article 30.[24] Not surprisingly, the Court
has avoided such a bizarre result. It did so, at first hesitatingly, in *Deutsche
Grammophon* in 1971, where it used the formula 'on the assumption that
those provisions [i.e. the provisions of Article 30] apply to a right related to
copyright'.[25] Any doubt was removed eleven years later in *Musik-Vertrieb
Membran v GEMA*, where the Court said that the expression 'industrial and
commercial property' in Article 30 'includes the protection conferred by
copyright, especially when exploited commercially in the form of licences
capable of affecting distribution in the various Member States of goods
incorporating the protected literary or artistic work'.[26]

There is thus no doubt that Article 30 applies to copyright and that the
copyright owner may invoke his exclusive reproduction right to prevent the
importation and sale of copies made without his authorization, even though
the copies are lawfully on the market in another Member State, e.g. because
the term of protection has expired in the other Member State. No doubt
either that, if the author consented to the marketing in the other Member
State, he loses the benefit of Article 30 under the exhaustion principle, even
though—as in *Musik-Vertrieb Membran v GEMA*—the consent was given in
an adverse legal environment that denied him a part of his 'just reward'.

But what of the performance right? This does not lend itself to conventional exhaustion analysis. No one would suggest that, if an author allows
his play to be performed in London, he must be deemed to have consented to
its performance throughout Europe—with the result that a theatre in Paris
or Dublin can put the play on without bothering to obtain the author's
separate consent. No one would suggest that, if a concert is illegally
recorded in Copenhagen, the composer and musicians should be unable
to prevent the distribution of the bootleg recordings in the rest of Europe
because they consented to, or took part in, the original performance.

The very essence of the performance right is that it does not exhaust itself
in a single performance. The author may allow his work to be performed as
often, or as rarely, as he likes, in whatever places he chooses. The performing artist may allow his performance to be broadcast on television or radio.
He may allow it to be fixed in a recording, in which case he may allow the
recording to be broadcast on the airwaves or shown in cinemas or played in
a discotheque. If, of course, he allows copies of the fixation (vinyl records,
CDs, video-cassettes, DVDs, etc.) to be sold somewhere in the EEA, then he
cannot prevent the resale of those copies anywhere within the EEA. But that
does not mean that he cannot object or demand royalties if the recording is
played in a public place.

---

[24] See R. Joliet and P. Delsaux. 'Le droit d'auteur dans la jurisprudence de la Cour de justice des
Communautés européennes' (1985) 4 *Cahiers de Droit Européen* 381 at 391.
[25] At para. 11 of the judgment.   [26] At para. 9 of the judgment.

5. *CODITEL I:* PERFORMANCE RIGHT, BROADCASTING, AND THE FREEDOM TO PROVIDE CROSS-FRONTIER SERVICES

The Court of Justice recognized the special nature of the performance right in *Coditel I*,[27] where it stated:

A cinematographic film belongs to the category of literary and artistic works made available to the public by performances which may be infinitely repeated. In this respect the problems involved in the observance of copyright in relation to the requirements of the Treaty are not the same as those which arise in connexion with literary and artistic works the placing of which at the disposal of the public is inseparable from the circulation of the material form of the works, as in the case of books or records.

In these circumstances the owner of the copyright in a film and his assigns have a legitimate interest in calculating the fees due in respect of the authorization to exhibit the film on the basis of the actual or probable number of performances and in authorizing a television broadcast of the film only after it has been exhibited in cinemas for a certain period of time.[28]

The *Coditel* litigation was all about the copyright in a film called *Le Boucher*. The copyright was owned by a French company called 'Les Films La Boétie' ('La Boétie' for short), which granted the exclusive distribution rights in the film for Belgium to Ciné Vog Films ('Ciné Vog' for short) for a period of seven years. The agreement covered both cinema showings and television broadcasts. It provided, however, that the film was not to be shown on television in Belgium until forty months after its first showing in a Belgian cinema. La Boétie granted the right to distribute the film in Germany to another company (Filmedis).[29] This company was, it seems, allowed to exploit the television rights in the film in Germany immediately. The film was shown on German television eighteen months before it could be shown on Belgian television under the contract between La Boétie and Ciné Vog. Coditel provided cable television services in Belgium. One of the stations that it relayed to its subscribers was the German station that had shown *Le Boucher*. As a result, viewers in Belgium were able to see the film on television at a time when it was not supposed to be shown on television in Belgium according to the contract between La Boétie and Ciné Vog. Ciné Vog had not authorized this showing of the film on Belgian television screens and did not receive any remuneration in respect of it. Ciné Vog brought proceedings in the Belgian courts against La Boétie for breach of contract and against Coditel for copyright infringement.

The Brussels *Cour d'Appel* took the view that, under Belgian copyright law, Coditel was not entitled to relay the broadcast of *Le Boucher* in Belgium

---

[27] Cited in n. 14.   [28] At paras 12 and 13 of the judgment.
[29] See the opinion of Advocate General Warner, at 866.

without the consent of Ciné Vog. The *Cour d'Appel* based that view on Article 11 *bis* (1) of the Berne Convention on the Protection of Literary and Artistic Works,[30] which provides that:

Authors of literary and artistic works shall enjoy the exclusive right of authorizing:
(i) the broadcasting of their works or the communication thereof to the public by any means of wireless diffusion of signs, sounds or images;
(ii) any communication to the public by wire or by rebroadcasting of the broadcast of the work, when this communication is made by an organization other than the original one;[31]

. . .

The *Cour d'Appel* considered that the cable company (Coditel) was an organization other than the original German television station which had broadcast the film in Germany; the holder of the copyright was therefore able to prevent the cable retransmission of the film by virtue of Article 11 *bis* (1) (ii). That interpretation of Article 11 *bis* appears to be correct.[32]

The *Cour d'Appel* referred questions to the Court of Justice, designed essentially to ascertain whether Ciné Vog was entitled to prevent Coditel from retransmitting the film in the light of Article 49 of the Treaty, which prohibits restrictions on the free movement of services between Member States.

Article 30 of the Treaty was not directly relevant. The case had nothing to do with the free movement of goods since television broadcasts are not goods. This again highlights the special nature of the performance right in Community law. Performances are not goods, though a fixation of a performance may of course give rise to goods (e.g. CDs, cassettes, video-cassettes, DVDs). A performance will often involve the provision of a service. La Boétie was engaged in the provision of services when it sold the distribution rights in the film *Le Boucher* to different companies in Belgium and Germany. The acquirer of the German rights was engaged in the provision of services when it allowed a German television company to broadcast the film. Coditel was likewise engaged when it relayed the broadcast to its subscribers in Belgium.[33]

---

[30] Art. 11 *bis* was added to the Berne Convention by the Rome revision of the Convention in 1928 and was amended by the Brussels revision in 1948.
[31] The English version of the judgment in *Coditel I* contains a non-authentic translation of Art. 11 *bis* of the Berne Convention.
[32] See C. Doutrelepont, 'Les arrêts Coditel face au droit interne et au droit européen' (1984) *Journal des Tribunaux*, No. 5299, 397–409; P. Goldstein, *International Copyright: Principles, Law and Practice*, Oxford University Press, 2001, at p. 266; and R. Plaisant, (1980) 43 *Recueil Dalloz-Sirey, jurisprudence* 600 at 602.
[33] See the analysis of Advocate General Warner, at 874–876. The Court did not have to decide whether there was a restriction on the cross-border provision of services, since it went on to hold that, even if there was a restriction, it was justified.

Clearly, then, this was a case about the cross-border provision of services.[34] Article 49 was therefore the relevant provision. The problem was that the Treaty provisions on the free movement of services do not contain any real equivalent of Article 30. Article 55 makes Articles 45 to 48—which belong to the chapter on the right of establishment—applicable to services.

Paragraph (1) of Article 46 is the 'derogating' provision which corresponds roughly to Article 30. Its wording is, however, hopelessly inadequate to deal with problems of the type that arose in *Coditel*. Article 46(1) simply saves 'provisions laid down by law, regulation or administrative action providing for special treatment for foreign nationals on grounds of public policy, public security or public health'. There is no mention of intellectual—or, to use the language of Article 30, 'industrial and commercial'—property.

The authors of the Treaty doubtless had in mind, when drafting the provisions on the free movement of services, the *locus classicus* of the service-provider (plumber, doctor, television repair man, or whatever) who occasionally crosses a frontier to provide a service to a client established in another Member State. Such persons were unlikely to be impeded in their activities by intellectual property rights. Hence the absence of any reference to such rights in the chapter on services. Advocate General Warner expressed the view, in his opinion in *Coditel I*, that the lacuna was due to an oversight on the part of the authors rather than a deliberate intention.[35] He invited the Court to apply Article 30 by analogy. That in effect is what the Court did, but without saying so expressly. The Court stated as follows:

Whilst Article [49] of the Treaty prohibits restrictions upon freedom to provide services, it does not thereby encompass limits upon the exercise of certain economic activities which have their origin in the application of national legislation for the protection of intellectual property, save where such application constitutes a means of arbitrary discrimination or a disguised restriction on trade between Member States. Such would be the case if that application enabled parties to an assignment of copyright to create artificial barriers to trade between Member States.[36]

The language used by the Court in this passage is borrowed directly from Article 30. It is obviously desirable that the law governing restrictions on the freedom to provide services should, so far as possible, parallel the law governing the free movement of goods. The Court should therefore be applauded for ensuring such a result in spite of the defective wording of

---

[34] Surprisingly, one author considers that a cross-border movement of goods is involved and that Art. 28 is the relevant Treaty provision: see N. March Hunnings (1980) CML Rev. 564. That view is, to say the least, eccentric.

[35] At 878.   [36] At para. 15 of the judgment.

the Treaty provisions on services. It is surprising, in fact, that the Court did not expressly mention Article 30 and say that it was applying the provision by analogy. Perhaps the explanation is that the Court had always refused to apply the terms of Article 30 extensively in relation to the free movement of goods, on the ground that they derogate from a fundamental principle of Community law.[37]

More controversial is the Court's view on what may constitute 'artificial barriers to trade between Member States' due to an assignment of copyright. In the following paragraph of its judgment in *Coditel I* the Court went on to state:

> . . . whilst copyright entails the right to demand fees for any showing or performance, the rules of the Treaty cannot in principle constitute an obstacle to the geographical limits which the parties to a contract of assignment have agreed upon in order to protect the author and his assigns in this regard. The mere fact that those geographical limits may coincide with national frontiers does not point to a different solution in a situation where television is organised in the Member States largely on the basis of legal broadcasting monopolies, which indicates that a limitation other than the geographical field of application of an assignment is often impracticable.[38]

The Court's willingness to tolerate trade barriers due to the assignment[39] of copyright is a little surprising, to say the least. The Court seems to have accepted that the owner of the copyright in a film may assign the exploitation rights to different persons in different Member States and that each assignee may then enforce his rights when a broadcast in one Member State is relayed to televiewers in another Member State. It is extremely unlikely that the Court would show the same degree of tolerance towards copyright owners who attempted to partition the market in physical goods (books, CDs, video-cassettes, etc.) along the lines of national frontiers.

At the heart of the Court's reasoning in the *Coditel* cases is the recognition that the problems entailed by the performance right are fundamentally different from those caused by the reproduction right. The latter are exhausted by each sale of the protected work when it is fixed in a physical product. The former are not exhausted because 'copyright entails the right to demand fees for any showing or performance'.

As was noted above, it appears that under Article 11 *bis* (1)(ii) of the Berne Convention the copyright owner who allows his work to be broadcast

---

[37] See, e.g., Case 46/76 *Bauhuis v Netherlands* [1977] ECR 52 and Case 113/80 *Commission v Ireland* ('Irish souvenirs') [1981] ECR 1625.

[38] At para. 16 of the judgment.

[39] Strictly speaking the copyright had not been *assigned*: Ciné Vog had been granted an exclusive licence and the right to bring infringement proceedings. The distinction is not, however, relevant from the point of view of the provisions on the freedom to provide services: R. Joliet and P. Delsaux, op. cit. (n. 24), at 397.

enjoys the right to authorise (or to refuse to authorise) the simultaneous cable retransmission of the work where the retransmission is to be carried out by 'an organization other than the original one'. This would mean, for example, that where the copyright owner allows a film to be broadcast by a German broadcasting organization, he cannot object or demand extra royalties if that broadcasting organization boosts reception in remote, mountainous areas by means of cable transmission. But he may object if a different organization (such as Coditel) retransmits the programme by cable, without blacking out the protected work, either in Germany or elsewhere.

As will be argued later in this chapter, the Berne Convention is not an instrument that can simply be ignored in Community law. An attempt should be made to construe the provisions of Community law in a manner that is compatible with the Convention. Surprisingly, Ciné Vog did not place much emphasis on the Berne Convention in its arguments before the Court of Justice. The Court did not therefore address the point. On the view taken by the Court there was in any case no question of a clash between the Berne Convention and Community law, because the rules on the freedom to provide services did not prevent the assignee/licensee of the Belgian copyright from blocking the cable retransmission of the film in Belgium.

To the extent that the Court's judgment was based on the special nature of the television market, it is arguable that the situation alluded to by the Court has now changed so radically that an important part of the rationale for the *Coditel* case law has ceased to exist. It is no longer true that 'television is organised in the Member States largely on the basis of legal broadcasting monopolies'. One can only speculate as to whether the Court might take a different approach to market-partitioning assignments of film rights now that national broadcasting monopolies are largely a thing of the past and satellite footprints straddle frontiers with consummate ease.

6. COUNCIL DIRECTIVE 93/83/EEC

The legislative framework has evolved since the *Coditel* litigation. Cable retransmission is dealt with in Council Directive 93/83/EEC of 27 September 1993 on the coordination of certain rules concerning copyright and rights related to copyright applicable to satellite broadcasting and cable retransmission.[40] Article 8(1) of the Directive provides that 'Member States shall ensure that when programmes from other Member States are retransmitted by cable in their territory the applicable copyright and related rights are observed and that such retransmission takes place on the basis of

[40] OJ 1993 L 248, p. 15.

individual or collective contractual agreements between copyright owners, holders of related rights, and cable operators'.

Article 9 provides as follows:

1. Member States shall ensure that the right of copyright owners and holders or related rights to grant or refuse authorization to a cable operator for a cable retransmission may be exercised only through a collecting society.
2. Where a right-holder has not transferred the management of his rights to a collecting society, the collecting society which manages rights of the same category shall be deemed to be mandated to manage his rights. Where more than one collecting society manages rights of that category, the right-holder shall be free to choose which of those collecting societies is deemed to be mandated to manage his rights. A right-holder referred to in this paragraph shall have the same rights and obligations resulting from the agreement between the cable operator and the collecting society which is deemed to be mandated to manage his rights as the rightholders who have mandated that collecting society and he shall be able to claim those rights within a period, to be fixed by the Member State concerned, which shall not be shorter than three years from the date of the cable retransmission which includes his work or other protected subject-matter.
3. A Member State may provide that, when a right-holder authorizes the initial transmission within its territory of a work or other protected subject-matter, he shall be deemed to have agreed not to exercise his cable retransmission rights on an individual basis but to exercise them in accordance with the provisions of this Directive.

If the facts of the *Coditel* litigation were to occur now, Ciné Vog's authorization for the cable retransmission of the film in Belgium would be required by virtue of Article 8(1). Ciné Vog would have to exercise its rights through a collecting society under Article 9(1). If Ciné Vog did not expressly authorize a collecting society to manage its rights, a collecting society which managed rights of the same category would be competent to act under Article 9(2).

The Directive takes a realistic approach. It recognizes that the right-holder is entitled to remuneration if the protected work is retransmitted by cable. It also recognizes that, from a practical point of view, the best solution is to entrust copyright management to a collecting society which can negotiate collectively on behalf of the numerous right-holders who are likely to be involved whenever television programmes are retransmitted by cable.

7. PERFORMANCE RIGHT AND THE FREE MOVEMENT OF GOODS

The performance right raises problems concerning not only the free movement of services but also the free movement of goods. That is illustrated by a pair of cases decided in the late 1980s—*Basset v SACEM* and *Warner Brothers and Metronome v Christiansen*. The two cases are not often bracketed together. And yet they raise surprisingly similar issues. *Warner Brothers* has already been considered above in Chapter 4. It will be recalled that the case concerned the exclusive right, under Danish law, of the owner of the copyright in a film to control the renting of the film. No such right existed in the United Kingdom at the time and the question was whether the copyright owner could prevent the renting in Denmark of a copy of the film which had been marketed in the United Kingdom with the copyright owner's consent.

Although the facts of *Basset v SACEM*[41] were rather different, the legal issue was remarkably similar. Mr Basset operated a discotheque in France. SACEM—the Society of Authors, Composers and Music Publishers—collected royalties on behalf of copyright owners in France. Under French law, when a musical work has been recorded and the recording is played in a public place (e.g. a discotheque), the author is allowed to claim, in addition to a royalty for the performance of the work, a royalty known as a 'supplementary mechanical reproduction fee' (*droit complémentaire de reproduction mécanique*). What this appears to mean in practice is that if songs are performed by a band in a dance hall SACEM claims a royalty of 6.6 per cent of the gross takings. If recordings are played in a discotheque, SACEM claims a royalty of 8.25 per cent of the gross takings, the extra 1.65 per cent being ascribed to the supplementary mechanical reproduction fee. The question in *Basset v SACEM* was whether the supplementary mechanical reproduction fee could be charged in respect of records which had been marketed with the copyright owner's consent in a Member State in which no corresponding right existed.

In both cases the law of one Member State allowed the copyright owner to prevent, or to authorize subject to payment of a royalty, a particular use of products incorporating the protected work. In both cases the issue was whether the copyright owner could enforce that right when the products in question had been marketed with the copyright owner's consent in another Member State in which a corresponding right to restrict the use of the products in a particular way did not exist. In both cases the Court answered that question in the affirmative.

The Court's reasoning in the two judgments was somewhat different, and was altogether more elaborate in *Warner Brothers*. In that case the Court did at least come to a clear finding that there was a measure equivalent in effect to a quantitative restriction on imports. It reached that finding on the basis of an observation that the commercial exploitation of video-cassettes increasingly takes the form of hiring-out to individuals who

---

[41] Cited in n. 14.

possess video-cassette recorders (VCRs). Therefore the right to prohibit hiring-out was liable to affect the domestic trade in video-cassettes and hence, indirectly, intra-Community trade. In *Basset v SACEM* the Court made no clear finding as to the existence of a measure equivalent in effect to a quantitative restriction on imports, but merely observed that, even if the charging of the supplementary mechanical reproduction fee were to be capable of restricting imports within the meaning of Article 28, it was justified under Article 30.

The Court's hesitation is understandable. The measures at issue in *Basset v SACEM*, or in *Warner Brothers*, did not restrict imports in any meaningful sense. The contested French and Danish laws did not prevent or restrict the importation or sale of records or video-cassettes from other Member States. Admittedly, if the operator of a discotheque or a video rental store could circumvent the national laws which restricted their freedom, respectively, to play records in public and to rent out video-cassettes, by buying the articles in question in another Member State, then a small increase in imports would doubtless ensue. But that would be an artificial trade pattern, dictated not by any competitive advantage existing in the exporting State but by the happy circumstance that the imported product would—on the view canvassed by the discotheque owner and the video-cassette renter in the two cases—continue to be subject, after importation, to the intellectual property laws of the exporting State, which happened to provide for a lower standard of protection. It should in any case be apparent that not every restriction on the use of an imported product amounts to a quantitative restriction on imports.

Perhaps if these cases came before the Court now, it would further develop the *modalités de vente* doctrine that saw the light of day in *Keck and Mithouard*. Restrictions on mere *modalités d'exploitation* would lie outside the reach of Article 28, unless they were discriminatory in fact or in law. The issue of justification would then become otiose. These cases were, however, decided several years before *Keck*, so the Court dutifully concluded that there was a restriction on imports in *Warner Brothers* and that such a restriction could not be ruled out in *Basset v SACEM*.

On the issue of justification, the absence of discrimination was in any event a major consideration. In both cases the Court stressed that the measure in issue applied to domestic goods in the same way as to goods manufactured in another Member State.[42] In *Basset v SACEM* the Court found justification for the supplementary mechanical reproduction fee by analysing it, correctly, as 'part of the payment for an author's rights over the public performance of a recorded musical work'.[43] Since this 'must be

---

[42] See para. 14 of *Basset v SACEM* and para. 12 of *Warner Brothers*.
[43] At para. 15 of the judgment.

regarded as a normal exploitation of copyright', it was justified under Article 30.[44] The Court's analysis in *Warner Brothers* was more sophisticated.[45] It emphasized the emergence of a specific market for video rentals, noted that an exclusive rental right was the only way to guarantee for film-makers a fair share of the income from that market and observed finally that the exclusive right would be rendered worthless if it did not apply to video-cassettes marketed with the copyright owner's consent in a Member State that did not recognize such a right.

Implicit in the Court's judgment is the idea that the video rental right is similar in nature to the performance right and should not therefore be exhausted when the copyright owner sells a copy of the protected work. The logic of that becomes apparent if the substance of the rental business is considered. If a film is rented out to a hundred persons in succession and each of those persons views the film at home, accompanied perhaps by family and friends, the result is substantially the same as when the film is shown in a cinema.

8. VIDEO RENTAL AND LENDING RIGHTS AFTER HARMONIZATION

In *Warner Brothers* the Court was doubtless aware of the policy arguments in favour of the copyright owners. Morally and economically their case was strong. The essential point to bear in mind is that even the most devoted film buff rarely watches a film more than once or twice. Such persons have no interest in buying a copy of a film if they can rent one for long enough to view the contents at a fraction of the price. Renting is potentially the most lucrative part of the market. It would be wrong to deny the film-maker a share of the proceeds of renting. Ultimately it is in the interest of everyone concerned—film-makers, firms that sell or rent out video-cassettes, and customers of the latter—that the copyright owner has the means to extract some remuneration from the renting of his work. Fortunately, such a result has now been ensured, at Community level, by Council Directive 92/100/EEC of 19 November 1992 on rental and lending right and on certain rights related to copyright in the field of intellectual property.[46] Article 2(1), fourth indent, of the Directive, in conjunction with Article 1(1) thereof, confers on the producer[47] of the first fixation of a film the exclusive right to

---

[44] At para. 16 of the judgment.   [45] See section 8 of Chap. 4.

[46] OJ 1992 L 346, p. 61.

[47] A parallel right to control the renting and lending of films is conferred on the 'principal director', *qua* author, by Art. 2(2). The actors also enjoy parallel rights as performers under Art. 2(1). The existence of parallel exclusive rights is a normal phenomenon in the field of copyright and is dealt with by means of contractual assignments. It is assumed that the other right-holders will assign their rental and lending rights to the producer: see J. Reinbothe and S. von Lewinski,

authorize or prohibit the rental and lending of the original and copies of the film.[48] 'Rental' means making available for use, for a limited period of time and for direct or indirect economic or commercial advantage. 'Lending' means making available for use, for a limited period of time and not for direct or indirect economic or commercial advantage, when it is done through establishments which are accessible to the public.

It might have been thought that the introduction of a harmonized right to control video renting and lending throughout the European Community would have meant that obstacles to the free movement of goods would no longer arise in this field. Certainly one would have expected that the type of dispute that was litigated in *Warner Brothers* would be a thing of the past. The case of *FDV v Laserdisken*[49] shows that such optimism is unfounded. The basic question referred to the Court in that case, once again by a Danish court, was whether 'it is contrary to the [Treaty rules on the free movement of goods and competition law] or to the Directive for the holder of an exclusive rental right to prohibit copies of a film from being offered for rental in a Member State even where offering those copies for rental has been authorized within another Member State'.[50]

Laserdisken rented video disks in Denmark. The video disks had been imported from the United Kingdom. The copyright owners had, allegedly, authorized the renting of the disks in the United Kingdom but not in Denmark. FDV (the Association of Danish Video Distributors), acting on behalf of the copyright owners, applied for an injunction prohibiting Laserdisken from renting out films in breach of the copyright owners' exclusive rental right under Danish law.

The Court ruled that: 'It is not contrary to Articles [28 and 30] of the EC Treaty or to Council Directive 92/100/EEC . . . for the holder of an exclusive rental right to prohibit copies of a film from being offered for rental in a Member State even where the offering of those copies for rental has been authorised in the territory of another Member State.'

The basis for the Court's reasoning was that the rental right is not exhausted when the product is sold or when it is first offered for rental.[51] The Court thought that the adoption of the Directive made no difference. It noted that the Directive distinguished between the exclusive distribution right provided for in Article 9 and the exclusive rental right provided for in Article 1. Whereas the former is exhausted by the first sale in the

---

The E.C. Directive on Rental and Lending Rights and on Piracy, Sweet and Maxwell, 1993, p. 49. Express provisions are contained in Art. 2(4), (5) and (6).

[48] In Case C-200/96 *Metronome Music v Music Point Hokamp* [1998] ECR I-1953 the Court rejected the argument that Art. 1(1) of Directive 92/100 was invalid on the ground that it was contrary to fundamental rights, in particular the freedom to pursue a trade or profession.

[49] Case C-61/97 [1998] ECR I-5171. The case is also known as *Egmont Film*.

[50] At para. 8 of the judgment.   [51] At para. 18 of the judgment.

Community (Art. 9(2)), the latter is not (Art. 1(4)). According to the Court, that is justified by the very nature of rental right, 'which would be rendered worthless if it were held to be exhausted as soon as the object was first offered for rental'.[52] It is true that Article 1(4) of the Directive states that the rental right 'shall not be exhausted by any sale or other act of distribution of originals and copies of copyright works and other subject-matter'.

The issue is not, however, as simple and straightforward as the Court appeared to think. The authors of the Directive probably did not appreciate the complexity of the matter either. Certainly the wording of Article 1(4) is unhelpful. The problem is that the Directive uses technical jargon (the concept of 'exhaustion') which does not have any precise, well understood meaning in relation to rental right.

Obviously the copyright owner does not lose his right to prohibit renting simply because he places copies of a film on the market with a view to their being resold to members of public. The whole point of a specific rental right is to prevent such a consequence. It is equally obvious that if the copyright owner allows a number of copies of a film to be rented out a number of times, he is not required to authorize the further renting of those copies or the renting of other copies of the same film. The situation is different if the copyright owner sells copies of the film on the understanding that the person who buys them may rent them out an unlimited number of times. In that case the copyright owner will presumably include in the selling price an amount that he considers an appropriate remuneration for authorizing the rental of the film. It is not clear whether the copyright owners involved in *FDV v Laserdisken* had in fact authorized the rental of the video disks which had been sold with their authorization in the United Kingdom. Laserdisken contended that they had, but this was denied by the copyright owners.[53] The Court worked on the assumption that the copyright owners had implicitly authorized the rental of films in the United Kingdom.[54]

It could certainly be argued that if the copyright owners had authorized the rental, in the United Kingdom, of the copies sold in the United Kingdom, they should not be allowed to block the rental of those copies in another Member State. If the copyright owner obtains a remuneration, through the selling price, for an unlimited number of rentals, one may well ask why he should be allowed to specify in which part of the common market rental should take place.

According to its preamble, the purpose of the Directive was to remove disparities in national law because 'such differences are sources of barriers to trade and distortions of competition which impede the achievement and

---

[52] At para. 21 of the judgment.
[53] See para. 2 of the opinion of Advocate General La Pergola.
[54] See para. 5 of the judgment.

proper functioning of the internal market'.[55] By eliminating those discrepancies, the Directive sought to contribute to 'the objective of introducing an area without internal frontiers as set out in Article [14] of the Treaty so as to institute, pursuant to Article [3(g)] of the Treaty, a system ensuring that competition in the common market is not distorted'.[56]

The position taken by the Court in *FDV v Laserdisken* seems to imply that the copyright owner is free to divide up the rental market along the lines of national frontiers. He may sell copies of a film and insert in the contract a clause authorizing its rental in the United Kingdom but prohibiting its rental in the rest of the common market. It is doubtful whether Article 1(4) of the Directive was intended to permit that sort of result, especially if account is taken of the terms of the preamble to the Directive. It is also doubtful whether such a result is compatible with the Treaty provisions on the free movement of goods or competition law.[57]

9. INTERNATIONAL AGREEMENTS CONCERNING COPYRIGHT AND RELATED RIGHTS

The desire to unify and harmonize copyright law at the international level goes back a long way. A number of important international conventions have been concluded and have gained many adherents. Their influence on the laws of the Member States and their relationship to EC law cannot be neglected. For that reason their main provisions are examined here.

9.1 *The Berne Convention*

The most venerable of these instruments is the 1886 Berne Convention for the Protection of Literary and Artistic Works, which has been revised on a number of occasions—at Berlin (1908), Rome (1928), Brussels (1948), Stockholm (1967), and Paris (1971). Adherents to the Berne Convention, which is administered by the World Intellectual Property Organization (WIPO) in Geneva, include all countries in western Europe and, since 1989, the United States. The protection granted by the Berne Convention extends to (a) all authors who are nationals of, or habitually resident in, a Contracting State and (b) other authors, as regards works first published in

---

[55] See the first recital in the preamble to the Directive.

[56] See the third recital in the preamble to the Directive.

[57] As regards competition law, the national court in *FDV v Laserdisken* did indeed refer to Arts 81 and 82 of the Treaty. However, the Court of Justice refused to deal with the competition issues because the national court had not explained why it thought the competition rules relevant: see para. 17 of the opinion of Advocate General La Pergola.

a Contracting State or published simultaneously in a Contracting State and in some other country (Article 3). According to Article 2(1), the Convention protects 'literary and artistic works', a term which includes:

. . . every production in the literary, scientific and artistic domain, whatever may be the mode or form of its expression, such as books, pamphlets and other writings; lectures, addresses, sermons and other works of the same nature; dramatic or dramatico-musical works; choreographic works and entertainments in dumb show; musical compositions with or without words; cinematographic works to which are assimilated works expressed by a process analogous to cinematography; works of drawing, painting, architecture, sculpture, engraving and lithography; photographic works to which are assimilated works expressed by a process analogous to photography; works of applied art; illustrations, maps, plans, sketches and three-dimensional works relative to geography, topography, architecture or science.

In order to understand how the Convention works it is necessary to explain the key concept 'country of origin'. Essentially the country of origin of a work is:

(1) for works first published in a contracting State, that country;
(2) for unpublished works and for works first published in a non-Contracting State, the Contracting State of which the author is a national (Art. 5(4)).

Protection in the country of origin is governed by the law of that country. However, if the author is neither a national nor a habitual resident of that country, he enjoys the same protection in the country of origin as authors who have the nationality of that country (Art. 5(3)). In each Contracting State other than the country of origin, the author enjoys in respect of protected works the same rights as authors who have the nationality of the respective country, together with certain specific rights granted by the Convention (Art. 5(1)). Thus the Convention operates the twin principles of 'national treatment' and a 'minimum standard'.

One of the fundamental principles of the Berne Convention is that the enjoyment and exercise of the rights governed by it may not be made subject to any formalities such as registration, deposit of a copy of the protected work or payment of a fee (Art. 5(2)). The idea is that copyright comes into being by the very act of creation of the protected work. In this respect copyright differs fundamentally from patent and trade mark law.

As regards the minimum standard referred to above, the Convention provides for both moral rights and economic rights. The basic moral rights are the right to be identified as the author of the work and to object to any modification of the work which would be detrimental to the author's honour or reputation (Art. 6 *bis*). Moral rights were introduced by the 1928 Rome revision.[58]

The basic economic rights conferred on authors by the Convention are:

- the exclusive right to reproduce the protected work in whatsoever form, including audio and video recording (Art. 9(1));
- the exclusive right to have the work translated (Art. 8);
- the exclusive right to have the work adapted (Art. 12); and
- the exclusive right to have the work performed (Art. 11).

Compulsory licensing may, however, be authorized, subject to the payment of an equitable remuneration (Art. 9(2).

The Convention provides for a minimum term of protection consisting of the life of the author plus fifty years (Art. 7). Contracting States which granted a shorter term of protection before the entry into force of the 1971 Paris revision were allowed to retain that shorter term (Art. 7(7)). In principle the term of protection is governed by the law of the country in which protection is claimed (subject to compliance with the minimum of fifty years *post mortem auctoris*). However, in the absence of any provision to the contrary in the law of that country, the term of protection is not to exceed the term fixed in the country of origin (Art. 7(8)).

For certain categories of work the Convention lays down special rules. In particular, for cinematographic works Contracting States may provide that the term of protection expires fifty years after the work was made available to the public with the author's consent or, if that condition is not fulfilled, fifty years after the creation of the work.

Finally, the Convention contains a number of special rules in favour of developing countries.

9.2 *The Universal Copyright Convention (UCC)*

This Convention was signed in Geneva in 1952 and revised in Paris in 1971. It was promoted by the United Nations Educational, Scientific and Cultural Organization (UNESCO). The UCC is generally less onerous than the Berne Convention. Indeed, its *raison d'être* was to provide a framework of international co-operation in the field of copyright for countries which, for one reason or another, were unwilling to grant the high standard of protection required by the Berne Convention. Until 1989 those countries included the United States.

The Berne Convention and the UCC are not mutually exclusive: many countries belong to both. Article XVII of the UCC lays down the principle

---

[58] Bainbridge observes that it took the United Kingdom 60 years to comply with its obligation to protect moral rights: op. cit (n. 2), at p. 264, note 65.

that the UCC in no way affects the provisions of the Berne Convention. A declaration annexed to the UCC states that the UCC is not applicable, as between members of the Berne Union, to works whose country of origin is a member of the Berne Union. Moreover, works which have as their country of origin a country which left the Berne Union after 1 January 1951 are not protected by the UCC in countries which belong to the Berne Union. That is intended as a disincentive for countries minded to leave the Berne Convention in favour of the less onerous UCC: the effect of abandoning Berne would be to prevent many of their citizens from enjoying the protection of either Convention.

As to substance, it has been said that the UCC 'lacks the detail of the Berne . . . Convention and takes a more "broad brush" approach'.[59] In spite of drafting differences, the basic principles are rather similar. The UCC, like the Berne Convention, provides both for 'national treatment' and for a minimum standard of protection. The main differences concern the issue of formalities and the term of protection.

Any Contracting State which makes the protection of copyright conditional on compliance with formal requirements such as deposit, registration, payment of fees, manufacture, or publication on national territory must deem those requirements to be satisfied if, upon first publication of the work, all copies bear the symbol © accompanied by the name of the author and the year of first publication (Art. III(1)). Contracting States may, however, continue to require compliance with formal requirements for works first published on their territory and for all works by their own nationals, regardless of the place of first publication (Art. III (2)).

The term of protection, under the UCC, must not be less than the life of the author plus twenty-five years (Art. IV (2)). Any Contracting State which, before the entry into force of the UCC, granted protection for a period calculated from the first publication of the work is allowed to maintain that practice, but the term of protection must not be less than twenty-five years calculated from the first publication.

9.3 *The International Convention for the Protection of Performers, Producers of Phonograms and Broadcasting Organizations (the 1961 Rome Convention)*

9.3.1 *Performers*

As the title implies, the Rome Convention protects three distinct categories, of which the first are, by definition, natural persons. 'Performers' are actors, singers, musicians, dancers, and other persons who perform literary or artistic works (Art. 3(a)). One author observes that this definition appears

---

[59] Bainbridge, op. cit. (n. 2), at p. 264.

to include practically everyone, except circus performers—though it is not entirely clear why a clown's performance should be considered less artistic than a dancer's—and sportsmen.[60]

The Rome Convention provides for 'national treatment', in the sense that a Contracting State must, in respect of protected works, grant the nationals of other Contracting States the same treatment that it grants its own nationals. The particularity of the Convention is that the connecting factor for determining what is a protected work is the country where the performance took place rather than the nationality of the performer: the performer is entitled to national treatment in respect of performances which took place on the territory of a Contracting State (Art. 4).[61]

Under Article 7, performers must be able to object to certain acts done without their consent: notably, the fixation or live broadcasting of their performance and the reproduction of a fixation that was made without their consent.

9.3.2 *Producers of phonograms*

A phonogram is defined as any exclusively aural fixation of a performance or of other sounds (Art. 3(b)). Thus the Convention is concerned with audio—as opposed to video—recordings. In popular parlance the word 'phonogram' covers things such as vinyl records, audio cassettes, CDs and mini-discs, but not video-cassettes or DVDs. The producer of a phonogram is the natural or legal person who first fixes the sounds of a performance or other sounds.

Contracting States must grant 'national treatment' in respect of a phonogram if (a) the producer of the phonogram is a national of another Contracting State, or (b) the first fixation took place in another Contracting State, or (c) the phonogram was first published in another Contracting State (Art. 5).[62] Where any of those three conditions is fulfilled, the producer is entitled to the treatment that the Contracting State grants to phonogram producers who are nationals of that State in respect of phonograms of which the first fixation or first publication took place in that State (Art. 2(1)(b)).

As regards the minimum standard of protection, phonogram producers must be granted an exclusive right to authorize or prohibit the direct or indirect reproduction of their phonograms (Art. 10).

---

[60] C. Colombet, *Grands principes du droit d'auteur et des droits voisins dans le monde: approche de droit comparé*, Paris, 1990, p. 162.

[61] The performer is also protected if the performance was recorded in a protected phonogram or broadcast in a protected broadcast.

[62] Where the phonogram is first published in a non-Contracting State but is then published in a Contracting State within the next 30 days, it is deemed to have been first published in the latter country.

9.3.3 *Broadcasting organizations*

'Broadcasting' is defined as the transmission by wireless means for public reception of sounds or of images and sounds (Art. 3(f)). Thus cable broadcasting is excluded. To benefit from 'national treatment' in a Contracting State, the broadcasting organization must either have its headquarters in another Contracting State or the broadcast must have been transmitted from a transmitter situated in another Contracting State (Art. 6(1)). A Contracting State may, however, decide to grant national treatment only if both those conditions are satisfied (Art. 6(2)). As regards the scope of this national treatment, the beneficiaries must enjoy the rights that the Contracting State grants to broadcasting organizations which have their headquarters on its territory in respect of broadcasts transmitted by transmitters situated on its territory (Art. 2).

As regards the minimum standard of protection, broadcasting organizations must be granted an exclusive right to authorize or prohibit the retransmission of their broadcasts, the fixation of their broadcasts and the reproduction of fixations of their broadcasts made without their consent (Art. 13).

9.3.4 *Term of protection*

The minimum term of protection under the Rome Convention is twenty years. The term runs from the end of the year in which the performance was recorded (as regards the rights of performers and phonogram producers) and from the end of the year in which the broadcast took place (as regards the rights of broadcasting organizations) (Art. 14).

9.3.5 *Formalities*

Where the law of a Contracting State subjects the protection of performers or phonogram producers to compliance with formal requirements, these are deemed to be satisfied if each published copy of the phonogram, or the case containing it, bears the symbol 'Ⓟ' accompanied by the year of first publication and the name of the producer or the right owner (Art. 11).

9.4 *The 1971 Phonograms Convention*

The object of this Convention is to protect phonogram producers against certain forms of piracy.

Each Contracting State is required to protect phonogram producers who are nationals of other Contracting States against the production of copies of phonograms without the consent of the producer and against the importation of such copies, when the production or importation is done with a view to distribution to the public, and against the distribution of such copies to the public (Art. 2). The Convention applies only to sound recordings, thus excluding audio-visual material.

The Convention does not require 'national treatment'. It does not therefore prevent Contracting States from granting more favourable treatment to their own nationals.[63]

9.5 *The 1974 Satellite Convention*

The purpose of this Convention is to protect organizations which broadcast, by satellite, television or radio programmes which are not intended to be received directly by the public from the satellite. In other words, it is concerned only with indirect satellite broadcasts, i.e. broadcasts which, after passing through a satellite, are picked up by a terrestrial receiver which then relays them to the public. Each Contracting State is required to take the necessary measures to prevent the distribution on or from its territory of signals carrying programmes by any distributor for whom the signals, transmitted via satellite, are not intended (Art. 2).

9.6 *The Agreement on Trade-related Aspects of Intellectual Property Rights, including trade in Counterfeit Goods (TRIPS)*

Articles 9 to 14 of the TRIPS agreement contain important provisions on copyright and related rights. Article 9 requires members of the World Trade Organization (WTO) to comply with Articles 1 to 21 of the Berne Convention, with the exception of Article 6 *bis*. As a result of this exception, which was due to opposition from the United States,[64] TRIPS does not impose any obligation to recognize moral rights. The incorporation into TRIPS of the essential obligations under the Berne Convention is significant inasmuch as TRIPS is subject to the WTO's arrangements for the settlement of disputes.[65] Moreover, the TRIPS provisions on copyright and related rights do not derogate from WTO members' obligations under the Berne and Rome Conventions (Art. 2).

Article 10(1) requires computer programs to be protected as literary works under the Berne Convention. Compilations of data or other material, whether in machine-readable or other form, which by reason of the selec-

---

[63] Colombet, op. cit. (n. 60), at p. 171. [64] Maier, op. cit. (n. 1), at p. 144.

[65] This may explain why the United States was reluctant to include moral rights in the TRIPS Agreement even though it had already acceded to the Berne Convention. Obligations under the Berne Convention are more difficult to enforce. In theory the International Court of Justice has jurisdiction over disputes between members of the Berne Union but this jurisdiction has never been invoked: P. E. Geller, 'Can the GATT Incorporate Berne Whole?' [1990] 11 EIPR 423 at 425.

tion or arrangement of their contents constitute intellectual creations, are to be protected as such (Art. 10(2)).

Article 11 requires WTO members to grant authors and their successors in title the right to authorize or to prohibit commercial rental 'in respect of at least computer programs and cinematographic works'. However, in respect of cinematographic rights members are exempted from that obligation 'unless such rental has led to widespread copying of such works which is materially impairing the exclusive right of reproduction conferred in [the member in question] on authors and their successors in title'. The vagueness of this wording makes it very difficult to establish in what circumstances a member is actually required to establish a rental right in respect of cinematographic works.[66] Under Article 14(4) producers of phonograms and 'any other right holders in phonograms as determined in domestic law' are also to enjoy a rental right, though this may be replaced by a right to equitable remuneration in equally vaguely defined circumstances.

Article 14 deals with the rights of performers, producers of phonograms and broadcasting organizations. Instead of incorporating by reference the main provisions of the Rome Convention (a technique which might not have been appropriate, since the United States does not belong to the Rome Convention), Article 14 lays down obligations which are generally similar to those of the Rome Convention. In some respects TRIPS is more generous (e.g. in relation to the term of protection for performers and producers of phonograms, which is set at fifty years computed from the end of the calendar year in which the fixation was made or the performance took place).[67]

In other respects TRIPS provides a lower standard of protection than the Rome Convention. For example, Article 14(3) reproduces, with less precise wording, rights granted to broadcasting organizations under Article 13 of the Rome Convention.[68] However, the next sentence of Article 14(3) allows the exclusion of those rights for broadcasting organizations, provided that 'owners of copyright in the subject-matter of broadcasts [have] the possibility, under the Berne Convention, of preventing the acts that they could otherwise prohibit'.

9.7 *The status and significance of the main international agreements in EC law*

Of the above agreements, the Berne and Rome Conventions and TRIPS are particularly significant in EC law. The Council Resolution of 14 May 1992

---

[66] Bercovitz, op. cit. (n. 1), at p. 153.

[67] For broadcasting organizations, however, the term of protection remains at 20 years from the end of the calendar year in which the broadcast took place, as in the Rome Convention (Art. 14(5)).

[68] C. M. Correa, 'The TRIPS Agreement: Copyright and Related Rights' (1994) IIC 543 at 551.

on increased protection for copyright and neighbouring rights noted that the Member States, in so far as they had not already done so, undertook, subject to their constitutional provisions, to become by 1 January 1995 parties to the Paris Act of the Berne Convention, and to introduce national legislation to ensure effective compliance therewith. Protocol No. 28 to the EEA Agreement requires Contracting States to become party, by the same date, to the 'major international conventions' dealing with intellectual property.

Although the European Community, as such, is not a party to the Berne and Rome Conventions, the participation of all the Member States means that they cannot be ignored by the Community's legislative and judicial organs. In fact, the preambles to the harmonization directives adopted by the Council in the field of copyright and related rights almost invariably refer to those Conventions and articulate the Community legislature's intention to avoid enacting any provision which conflicts with them.[69] The express reference to such an intention in the legislation probably means that, if there were any incompatibility between a provision of the legislation and the international convention in question, the Court of Justice could be invited to declare the provision invalid, even though the convention does not have direct effect in Community law.[70]

The TRIPS agreement has an even higher status in Community law since the European Community, in addition to the Member States, is a party to the WTO Agreement and its annexes (including TRIPS).

It is true that the WTO Agreement and its annexes do not have direct effect in Community law.[71] Thus neither an individual[72] nor a Member

---

[69] See, e.g., the tenth recital in the preamble to Council Directive 92/100/EEC of 19 November 1992 on rental and lending right and on certain rights related to copyright in the field of intellectual property (OJ 1992 L 346, p. 61) and recitals 1, 4, 5, 12, 15, 17 and 22 of Council Directive 93/98/EEC of 29 October 1993 harmonizing the term of protection of copyright and certain related rights (OJ 1993 L 290, p. 9).

[70] See Case C-69/89 *Nakajima v Council* [1991] ECR I-2069; that case concerned a regulation which expressly stated its intention to comply with the GATT anti-dumping code. See also Case C-149/96 *Portugal v Council* [1999] ECR I-8395 at para. 49.

[71] See the last recital in Council Decision 94/800 of 22 December 1994 concluding the WTO Agreement on behalf of the Community (OJ 1994 L 336, p. 1). See also the judgment of Jacob, J., in *R v Comptroller General of Patents, ex p Lenzing* [1996] RPC 245. As to the arguments for and against direct effect, see P. Eeckhout, 'The Domestic Legal Status of the WTO Agreement: Interconnecting Legal Systems' (1997) CML Rev. 11; P. Manin, 'A propos de l'accord instituant l'Organisation mondiale du commerce et l'accord sur les marchés publics: la question de l'invocabilité des accords internationaux conclus par la Communauté européenne' (1997) *Revue Trimestrielle de Droit Européen* 399; and J. Drexl, 'Nach "GATT und WIPO": Das TRIPS-Abkommen und seine Anwendung in der Europäischen Gemeinschaft' (1994) GRUR Int. 778. See also W. Coole, 'Judicial Review of the EPO and the Direct Effect of TRIPS in the European Community' [1997] EIPR 367.

[72] Joined Cases C-300/98 and C-392/98 *Parfums Christian Dior v Tuk Consultancy* [2000] ECR I-11307, at para. 46, and Case 89/99 *Schieving-Nijstad v Groeneveld* [2001] ECR I-5851 at para. 53.

State[73] can challenge the validity of a Community provision on the ground that it is contrary to TRIPS.[74] Community legislation must, however, be construed, so far as possible, in a manner that is consistent with the Community's obligations under international agreements.[75] In *Metronome Music v Music Point Hokamp* the Court, when invited to consider the validity of the Community provisions introducing an exclusive rental right, observed that they were in accordance with Articles 11 and 13 of the TRIPS Agreement.[76]

The European Community's participation in the TRIPS Agreement has the effect of requiring the Community to comply with certain provisions of other international instruments. In particular, Article 9 of the TRIPS Agreement requires compliance with Articles 1 to 21, except Article 6 *bis*, of the Berne Convention (1971) and the Appendix thereto. The Court has held that it has jurisdiction to interpret TRIPS for the purpose of defining the obligations that the Community assumed by becoming a party to TRIPS.[77] Presumably this means that the Court has jurisdiction to interpret the provisions of the Berne Convention that have become binding on the Community via TRIPS.

In view of the undeniable status that the Berne Convention has in Community law, it is regrettable that the Court of Justice and the Court of First Instance were so dismissive of arguments based on the Convention in the *Magill* case. RTE contended that its copyright in listings of television programmes enjoyed protection under Article 9 of the Convention. As we have seen, Article 9(1) grants authors of literary and artistic works the

---

[73] Case C-280/93 *Germany v Council* [1994] ECR I-4973, at para. 109, and *Portugal v Council* (cited in n. 70) at para. 47.

[74] The reasons given by the Court for excluding the direct effect of the WTO Agreement and its Annexes are purely political. The Court thought that there would be a lack of reciprocity if the Agreement had direct effect in the Community and the courts in other countries held that it did not (at para. 45 of *Portugal v Council*, cited in n. 70). If the Community judicature were responsible for ensuring that Community law complies with the WTO Agreement, that would deprive the Community's legislative or executive organs of the scope for manoeuvre enjoyed by their counterparts in the Community's trading partners (at para. 46 of *Portugal v Council*, the English version of which contains a serious translation error).

[75] See Eeckhout (cited in n. 71), at 41, and Manin (cited in n. 71), at 412. See also Case C-61/94 *Commission v Germany* [1996] ECR I-3989 at para. 52, and Case C-70/94 *Werner v Germany* [1995] ECR I-3189 at para. 23, and Case C-83/94 *Leifer* [1995] ECR I-3231 at para. 24. A similar principle exists in the law of the United Kingdom: *The Zamora* [1916] AC 77.

[76] Cited in n. 48, at para. 25. The Court has also held that in a field to which TRIPS applies and in respect of which the Community has already legislated, the judicial authorities of the Member States are required by virtue of Community law, when called upon to apply national rules with a view to ordering provisional measures for the protection of rights falling within such a field, to do so as far as possible in the light of the wording and purpose of Art. 50 of TRIPS: Case C-53/96 *Hermès v FHT* [1998] ECR I-3603 at para. 28; *Parfums Christian Dior v Tuk Consultancy* (cited in n. 72) at para. 47; and *Schieving-Nijstad v Groeneveld* (cited in n. 72) at para. 54.

[77] *Hermès* (cited in n. 76), at para. 30, and *Parfums Christian Dior v Tuk Consultancy* (cited in n. 72), at para. 33.

exclusive right to authorize the reproduction of their works. Article 9(2) provides that: 'It shall be a matter for legislation in the countries of the Union to permit the reproduction of such works in certain special cases, provided that such reproduction does not conflict with a normal exploitation of the work and does not unreasonably prejudice the legitimate interests of the author.' According to RTE, the Commission decision requiring it to license the reproduction of its listings by Magill was contrary to Article 9(1) and (2) and therefore unlawful.

There were several ways in which the Courts could have dealt with this point without calling into question the status of the Berne Convention in Community law. In the first place, it is questionable whether listings of television programmes constitute 'literary and artistic works' within the meaning of Articles 1, 2(1) and 9(1) of the Convention. It is probable that the vast majority of Berne Convention countries do not protect such works, and their failure to do so is hardly likely to be considered a breach of the Convention. Moreover, according to Article 2(8), the protection of the Convention does not apply to 'news of the day or to miscellaneous facts having the character of mere items of press information'. That expression might be broad enough to cover a listing of television programmes.

Secondly, Article 9(2) expressly envisages the grant of compulsory licences 'in certain special cases'. Admittedly, Article 9(2) refers to 'legislation in the countries of the Union'. Neither Article 82 of the EC Treaty nor a Commission decision implementing it constitute 'legislation' *stricto sensu*.

RTE contended that, to comply with Article 9(2), compulsory licences could be granted only under specific legislation which clearly set out how and when they could be granted. Advocate General Gulmann argued convincingly that such a view was excessively narrow.[78] Article 9(2) was merely intended to reserve to the countries of the Berne Union the power to provide for compulsory licences in certain cases. The term 'legislation' is wide enough to include a general provision allowing an executive body such as the Commission to apply the rules of competition law.

It was not therefore necessary to address the question whether precedence should be given to the Berne Convention or to EC competition law. The Courts could easily have arrived at the view that the Commission decision requiring certain television companies to allow a magazine publisher to reproduce their programme schedules was compatible with the Berne Convention. Sadly, they chose a different solution.

The Court of Justice, upholding the position taken by the Court of First Instance, thought it appropriate to start by observing that the Community

---

[78] See paras 161–167 of Advocate General Gulmann's opinion in Joined Cases C-241/91 P and C-242/91 P *RTE and ITP v Commission ('Magill')*. Mr Gulmann also pointed out that Ireland had not ratified the Paris Act of the Berne Convention, which introduced Art. 9 into the Convention: see para. 151 of the opinion.

is not a party to the Berne Convention.[79] That seems a strange starting-point for the Court's deliberations, given the fact that all the Member States of the European Community were parties to the Berne Convention and that a Council Resolution adopted in 1992 urged all the Member States to become parties to the Paris Act of the Berne Convention. It would be absurd to encourage the Member States to adhere to an international Convention and yet allow the Community to disregard the provisions of the same Convention. Moreover, the Community was, by the time when the Court of Justice gave judgment in *Magill*, bound to comply with most of the provisions of the Berne Convention, including Article 9, as a result of the Community's accession to the WTO Agreement and TRIPS.

In spite of all this the Court decided to treat the Berne Convention as just another international agreement imposing on some Member States a number of obligations, some of which might be incompatible with Community law. The Court applied its established case law on Article 307 of the Treaty, the first paragraph of which provides: 'The rights and obligations arising from agreements concluded before 1 January 1958 or, for acceding States, before the date of their accession, between one or more Member States on the one hand, and one or more third countries on the other, shall not be affected by the provisions of this Treaty.'

According to that case law, the provisions of an agreement concluded before the entry into force of the Treaty or before a Member State's accession cannot be relied on in intra-Community relations, if the rights of non-member countries are not involved.[80] The Court therefore concluded that Article 9 of the Berne Convention could not be relied on to limit the powers of the Community, 'since the Treaty can be amended only in accordance with the procedure laid down in Article 236'.[81]

The Court's reference to amending the Treaty is puzzling, since no one was suggesting that the Treaty should be amended in order to safeguard RTE's intellectual property rights. All that was being suggested was that the Commission, in the exercise of its powers under competition law, should have regard to the leading instrument of international co-operation in the field of copyright. That seemed an eminently reasonable request, especially since the Commission had itself put forward a proposal in 1990 for a Council Decision requiring the Member States to accede to the Paris Act of the Berne Convention and to the Rome Convention.[82]

---

[79] See *Magill* (cited in n. 78) at para. 83.

[80] At para. 84 of the judgment.

[81] At para. 86 of the judgment. Art. 236 of the EEC Treaty was replaced by Art. N of the Treaty on European Union, signed in Maastricht in 1992. Art. N was renumbered as Art. 48 by the Amsterdam Treaty of 1997. Thus the provision governing the amendment of the EC Treaty is now to be found in Art. 48 of the Treaty on European Union.

[82] OJ 1999 C 24, p. 5. The Council opted instead for a resolution noting that the Member States undertook to accede to the Convention by 1 January 1995.

It is regrettable that the Court could not avoid giving a judgment that shows scant respect for the international legal order. To suggest that the Community institutions may ignore obligations accepted by all the Member States in relation to copyright is deplorable.[83] The aims of the EC Treaty—to create a common market based on free trade and undistorted competition—are commendable, but they should not be pursued at the expense of the Berne Convention. That Convention, which created a Union both older[84] and wider[85] than the European Community, pursues an equally commendable aim, i.e., to 'protect, in as effective and uniform manner as possible, the rights of authors in their literary and artistic works'.[86]

The Court's attitude to the Berne Convention is in stark contrast to its treatment of the European Human Rights Convention. In a series of judgments stretching back to *Nold v Commission*,[87] the Court has held that international treaties for the protection of human rights on which the Member States have collaborated or of which they are signatories, can supply guidelines, which should be followed within the framework of Community law. The European Human Rights Convention is the primary example of such a treaty and has consistently been used by the Court to test the validity of acts of the Community institutions.[88] The Berne Convention is just as fundamental in the field of copyright. It is difficult therefore to see why it could not be accorded a similar status.[89]

---

[83] For an excellent critique of the Court's attitude towards the Berne Convention, see H. Calvet and T. Desurmont, 'L'arrêt Magill: une décision d'espèce?' (1996) 167 *Revue internationale du droit d'auteur* 2 at 47–63. See also H. Cohen Jehoram and K. Mortelmans, 'Zur 'Magill'-Entscheidung des Europäischen Gerichtshofs' (1997) GRUR Int., Heft I, 11 at 14.

[84] The Berne Convention dates back to 1886.

[85] The Berne Union now has 150 members (status on 15 April 2003 according to the WIPO website).

[86] See the first sentence in the preamble to the Convention.

[87] Case 4/73 *Nold v Commission* [1974] ECR 491.

[88] See, e.g., Case 63/83 *R v Kirk* [1984] ECR 2689.

[89] Such a suggestion was advanced by RTE (see para. 79 of the judgment) but elicited no comment from the Court. The idea found favour with Advocate General Gulmann (see para. 154 of the opinion and footnote 81).

11

Competition law

1. INTRODUCTION

The EC Treaty is founded on the twin principles of free trade and undistorted competition. The former is guaranteed by the provisions on free movement of goods and services that have been examined in the preceding chapters. The latter is protected by the competition rules of the Treaty laid down in Articles 81 to 89. Just as we have seen that intellectual property rights frequently clash with the principle of the free movement of goods and services, so too there is a tendency for them to enter into conflict with the competition rules of the Treaty.

The principal rules that we are concerned with are Articles 81 and 82. The former prohibits, *inter alia*, agreements between undertakings that restrict competition. The latter prohibits undertakings that have exceptional market power from abusing their dominance. As we shall see, intellectual property rights have a role to play in relation to both of these prohibitions.

2. THE TREATY PROHIBITION ON ANTI-COMPETITIVE COLLUSION BETWEEN UNDERTAKINGS

2.1 *The structure of Article 81*

Article 81 of the Treaty provides as follows:

1. The following shall be prohibited as incompatible with the common market: all agreements between undertakings, decisions by associations of undertakings and concerted practices which may affect trade between Member States and which have as their object or effect the prevention, restriction or distortion of competition within the common market, and in particular those which:
   (a) directly or indirectly fix purchase or selling prices or any other trading conditions;
   (b) limit or control production, markets, technical development, or investment;
   (c) share markets or sources of supply;
   (d) apply dissimilar conditions to equivalent transactions with other trading parties, thereby placing them at a competitive disadvantage;
   (e) make the conclusion of contracts subject to acceptance by the other parties of supplementary obligations which, by their nature or according to commercial usage, have no connection with the subject of such contracts.

2. Any agreements or decisions prohibited pursuant to this Article shall be automatically void.
3. The provisions of paragraph 1 may, however, be declared inapplicable in the case of:

—any agreement or category of agreements between undertakings;

—any decision or category of decisions by associations of undertakings;

—any concerted practice or category of concerted practices;

which contributes to improving the production or distribution of goods or to promoting technical or economic progress, while allowing consumers a fair share of the resulting benefit, and which does not:

(a) impose on the undertakings concerned restrictions which are not indispensable to the attainment of these objectives;

(b) afford such undertakings the possibility of eliminating competition in respect of a substantial part of the products in question.

Article 81 contains three paragraphs. The first sets out the prohibition. Basically, this prohibition covers agreements, decisions and practices which restrict competition.

The second paragraph decrees one of the consequences of infringing the prohibition: a prohibited agreement or decision is automatically void. This means, *inter alia*, that a contractual agreement which infringes Article 81(1) cannot be enforced in court. The Court of Justice has held, however, that the nullity affects only those clauses in the agreement that restrict trade. The whole agreement is void only if the prohibited clauses cannot be severed from the rest of the agreement. Severability is a question governed by national law.[1]

The third paragraph provides that the prohibition may be declared inapplicable to agreements, decisions, and concerted practices that fulfil certain conditions. Basically, this means that the agreement, decision or practice (or category thereof) must be 'pro-competitive'. The use of the passive voice in Article 81(3) ('The provisions . . . may . . . be declared inapplicable') leaves open the question who may grant such an exemption. That issue was left to be decided by implementing legislation, which the Council was empowered to adopt under Article 83.

2.2 The implementation of the prohibition under Regulation No. 17

2.2.1 The role of the Commission

The main implementing measure adopted under Article 83 was, until recently, Council Regulation No. 17 (First Regulation implementing Articles [81] and [82] of the Treaty).[2] As the title reveals, Regulation

---

[1] Case 56/65 *Société La Technique Minière v Maschinenbau Ulm GmbH* [1966] ECR 234.

[2] OJ 1962 No 204, p. 62; OJ (English Special Edition) 1959–1962, p. 87.

No. 17 implemented Article 82 as well as Article 81. Although this regulation has now been repealed, with effect from 1 May 2004, the system established by it is still worth studying because much of the case law developed during the four decades when it was in force continues to be relevant. Article 9(1) of the Regulation conferred on the Commission exclusive power to grant an exemption under Article 81(3), subject to review of its decisions by the Court of Justice.[3] Agreements, decisions, and concerted practices of the kind described in Article 81(1) were to be notified to the Commission if the parties wished to obtain an exemption. Without notification no exemption could be granted.[4]

The exclusivity of the Commission's power to grant exemption was widely perceived as a major weakness in the system for implementing Community competition law because the Commission lacked the resources to scrutinize fully all the agreements that were notified to it. Approximately 200 agreements were notified each year and the Commission appeared unable to adopt more than around 20 decisions a year.[5] Between 1962 and 1999 the Commission issued only 222 decisions expressly exempting an agreement under Article 81(3).[6]

Article 2 of Regulation No. 17 empowered the Commission to grant 'negative clearance'. This meant that the Commission certified that on the basis of the facts in its possession there were no grounds under Article 81(1) or Article 82 of the Treaty for action on its part in respect of an agreement, decision, or practice. The difference between negative clearance and exemption was that the former involved a finding that the agreement, decision, or practice did not appear to infringe Article 81(1), whereas the latter assumed that the agreement, decision, or concerted practice did so infringe but declared the prohibition laid down by that provision inapplicable.[7] At first sight a negative clearance might appear preferable to an exemption, from the point of view of the undertakings concerned. However, a negative clearance had the serious disadvantage that it was thought not to be binding on national courts, which might take a different view.[8]

In fact, those who notified agreements to the Commission with a view to obtaining an exemption or negative clearance were likely to obtain neither; instead they had to content themselves with a 'comfort letter'. This is an informal communication by which the Commission indicated that an

---

[3] Since 1989 this jurisdiction has been exercised at first instance by the Court of First Instance.
[4] Art. 4(1) of Reg. No. 17. The obligation to notify did not apply to certain agreements relating to the exercise of industrial property rights: Art. 4(2)(b).
[5] A. Jones and B. Sufrin, *EC Competition Law: Text, Cases and Materials*, Oxford, 2001, p. 212.
[6] I. Forrester, 'Modernization of EC Competition Law' (2000) 23 *Fordham International Law Journal* 1028 at 1032.
[7] A further difference was that a negative clearance also entailed a finding that the agreement, decision, or practice did not appear to infringe Art. 82 of the Treaty.
[8] Jones and Sufrin, op. cit. n. 5, at p. 201.

agreement was not caught by Article 81(1) or was covered by a block exemption or would qualify for exemption.

Regulation No. 17 also conferred on the Commission investigating powers[9] and the power to impose substantial fines for intentionally or negligently infringing Article 81(1) or 82 of the Treaty.[10] The Commission could require those who infringed the competition rules to bring the infringement to an end. It could open proceedings to establish the existence of an infringement of its own motion or upon application by a Member State or by a natural or legal person who claimed a legitimate interest.[11]

In addition to authorizing the Commission to grant individual exemptions following notification, the Council adopted a number of regulations which empower the Commission to exempt certain 'categories of agreement' (a possibility expressly envisaged by Article 81(3)). These are known as 'block exemptions' or 'group exemptions'. In particular, Council Regulation No. 19 of 2 March 1965 on the application of Article [81(3)] to certain categories of agreements[12] empowers the Commission to exempt, by regulation, categories of distribution and exclusive purchasing agreements and categories of intellectual property licensing agreements. The Commission has accordingly adopted several block exemption regulations, in particular in the field of patent and know-how licensing.[13]

2.2.2 *The role of the national authorities*

Article 84 provides that, until the entry into force of the implementing measures provided for in Article 83, 'the authorities in Member States shall rule on the admissibility of agreements, decisions and concerted practices and on abuse of a dominant position in the common market in accordance with the law of their country and with the provisions of Article 81, in particular paragraph 3, and of Article 82'.

Although clearly intended as a transitional provision, Article 84 remains relevant in those areas to which the implementing legislation adopted under Article 83 does not apply.[14] Under Regulation No. 17 national authorities also retained a general competence to act, in accordance with Article 84, as long as the Commission had not initiated any procedure with a view to issuing a negative clearance, ordering the termination of an infringement or granting an exemption.[15]

---

[9] Art. 14.

[10] Art. 15. The maximum fine was 10 % of the turnover in the preceding year of each of the undertakings participating in the infringement.

[11] Art. 3.   [12] OJ 1965, p. 533; OJ (English Special Edition) 1965, p. 35.

[13] See sections 3.5.3 and 3.5.4 below.   [14] Jones and Sufrin, op. cit. (n. 5), at p. 74.

[15] Art. 9(3) of Reg. No. 17. As to the meaning of the expression 'initiate a procedure', see M. Waelbroeck and A. Frignani, *European Competition Law*, Transnational Publishers, Inc., Ardsley, NY, 1999, para. 506.

2.2.3 *The role of the national courts*

Both Article 81(1) and Article 82 were held to have direct effect and might therefore be relied on in proceedings before national courts.[16] This meant in particular that contracts which infringed Article 81(1) and had not been exempted by the Commission might not be enforceable in court.

Under the system established by Regulation No. 17, Article 81(3) could not have direct effect since that would be incompatible with the Commission's exclusive power to grant exemptions.[17] In practice this led to difficulties. The national court might decide that an agreement was caught by Article 81(1) even though its pro-competitive aspects made it worthy of exemption. Since the national court could not itself grant an exemption, it was obliged to treat the agreement as null and void under Article 81(2), unless the agreement came within the terms of a block exemption. The regulations granting block exemptions are directly applicable in all the Member States by virtue of Article 219 of the Treaty.

A further complication resulted from the Court of Justice's ruling that the ordinary national courts before which the direct effect of the Community competition rules was pleaded did not constitute 'authorities of/in Member States' within the meaning of Article 84 of the Treaty and Article 9(3) of Regulation No. 17.[18] The Court held that the term 'authorities' only included 'the administrative authorities entrusted, in most Member States, with the task of applying domestic legislation on competition subject to the review of legality carried out by the competent courts, or else the courts to which, in other Member States, the task has been especially entrusted'.[19] This meant that only administrative authorities and specialist competition courts ceased to be competent, by virtue of Article 9(3) of Regulation No. 17, to apply Articles 81(1) and 82 once the Commission had initiated proceedings. The ordinary courts, on the other hand, retained their competence to apply Community competition law in those circumstances. There was thus a danger, for example, that a national court which was asked to enforce a contract would declare the contract void under paragraphs (1) and (2) of Article 81, while the Commission went on to exempt it under paragraph (3) with effect from the date of notification.[20]

To obviate the danger of conflicting decisions the Court of Justice pointed out in *Delimitis v Henninger Bräu* that the national court could suspend its

---

[16] Case 127/73 *BRT v SABAM* [1974] ECR 51.
[17] Case C-234/89 *Delimitis v Henninger Bräu* [1991] ECR I-935 at paras 44–46.
[18] *BRT v SABAM*, cited in n. 16.
[19] Joined Cases 209 to 213/84 *Ministère Public v Asjes (Nouvelles Frontières)* [1986] ECR 1425 at para. 55.
[20] This back-dating of an exemption was expressly permitted by Art. 6(1) of Reg. No. 17.

proceedings or adopt provisional measures, and went on to suggest that the national court could also ask the Commission for information about the state of any proceedings initiated by the Commission and seek to 'obtain legal and economic facts which the Commission is able to give it'.[21]

2.3 *The reforms introduced by Regulation No. 1/2003*

2.3.1 *Outline*

The need to reform the above system became so obvious that the Commission published a White Paper[22] in 1999 in which it proposed a radically different approach to the enforcement of the competition rules of the Treaty. The White Paper led to the adoption of Council Regulation (EC) No. 1/2003 on the implementation of Articles 81 and 82 of the Treaty.[23] Regulation No. 1/2003 comes into force on 1 May 2004. It repeals Regulation No. 17 and replaces it with a new system. The main feature of the new system is decentralization. The national courts and national competition authorities may now apply Article 81(3) as well as Article 81(1). The procedure for notifying agreements to the Commission and seeking an individual exemption is abolished. Agreements that satisfy the requirements of Article 81(3) 'are legally valid and enforceable without the intervention of an administrative decision'.[24] This result is achieved by Article 1 of the Regulation, which provides:

1. Agreements, decisions and concerted practices caught by Article 81(1) of the Treaty which do not satisfy the conditions of Article 81(3) of the Treaty shall be prohibited, no prior decision to that effect being required.
2. Agreements, decisions and concerted practices caught by Article 81(1) of the Treaty which satisfy the conditions of Article 81(3) of the Treaty shall not be prohibited, no prior decision to that effect being required.
   . . .

Article 2 of the Regulation imposes the burden of proving an infringement of Article 81(1) on the party or authority alleging the infringement. The burden of proving that the agreement in question is eligible for an exemption rests with the party invoking the benefit of Article 81(3).

---

[21] Cited in n. 17, at paras 52 and 53. The suggestion that the national court should seek legal advice from the Commission has been criticized: see V. Korah, *An Introductory Guide to EC Competition Law and Practice*, 5th edn, Sweet and Maxwell, London, 1994, p. 141.

[22] White Paper on Modernization of the Rules Implementing Articles |81| and |82| of the EC Treaty, Commission Programme No. 99/027, OJ 1999 C 132, p. 1. On the need for reform, see Forrester, op. cit. (n. 6).

[23] OJ 2003 L 1, p. 1.

[24] C. Gauer, D. Dalheimer, L. Kjolbye and E. de Smijter, 'Regulation 1/2003: A Modernized Application of EC Competition Rules' (2003) *Competition Policy Newsletter* 3.

2.3.2 *Powers of the Commission*

The basic powers of the Commission under the new system are defined in Article 7 of the Regulation, which provides:

1. Where the Commission, acting on a complaint or on its own initiative, finds that there is an infringement of Article 81 or of Article 82 of the Treaty, it may by decision require the undertakings and associations of undertakings concerned to bring such infringement to an end. For this purpose, it may impose on them any behavioural or structural remedies which are proportionate to the infringement committed and necessary to bring the infringement effectively to an end. Structural remedies can only be imposed either where there is no equally effective behavioural remedy or where any equally effective behavioural remedy would be more burdensome for the undertaking concerned than the structural remedy. If the Commission has a legitimate interest in doing so, it may also find that an infringement has been committed in the past.
2. Those entitled to lodge a complaint for the purposes of paragraph 1 are natural or legal persons who can show a legitimate interest and Member States.

The Commission may also order interim measures, on the basis of a *prima facie* finding of infringement, in cases of urgency.[25]

The use of unexplained jargon such as 'behavioural or structural remedies' in a legislative text is regrettable. Presumably a behavioural remedy is one which is intended to modify the future behaviour of the undertakings concerned, such as a fine or periodic penalty payment. The Commission is empowered to impose fines for supplying incorrect or misleading information[26] and for infringing Article 81 or Article 82.[27] It may also impose periodic penalty payments, *inter alia*, in order to compel undertakings to put an end to an infringement of Article 81 or Article 82.[28] A structural remedy is presumably one which modifies the structure of the undertaking or undertakings concerned, e.g. an order requiring a company to divest itself of a subsidiary company.

A novel feature of the new legislation is the Commission's power to impose binding commitments on undertakings that are infringing the competition rules. Article 9(1) provides:

Where the Commission intends to adopt a decision requiring that an infringement be brought to an end and the undertakings concerned offer commitments to meet the concerns expressed to them by the Commission in its preliminary assessment, the Commission may by decision make those commitments binding on the undertakings. Such a decision may be adopted for a specific period and shall conclude that there are no longer grounds for action by the Commission.

---

[25] Art. 8.
[26] Up to 1% of total turnover in the previous business year: Art. 23(1).
[27] Up to 10% of total turnover in the previous business year: Art. 23(2)(a).
[28] Art. 24(1)(a).

Such commitments are enforceable by means of fines and periodic penalty payments.[29]

The Commission's investigating powers have been reinforced by the Regulation.[30]

2.3.3 *Powers of the national competition authorities*

Article 5 of the Regulation empowers the competition authorities of the Member States to apply Articles 81 and 82 of the Treaty in individual cases. Acting on their own initiative or on a complaint, they may take decisions:

- requiring that an infringement be brought to an end;
- ordering interim measures;
- accepting commitments; and
- imposing fines, periodic penalty payments, or any other penalty provided for in their national law.

'Commitments' presumably has the same meaning that it has in Article 9. Thus the national authorities have the same power as the Commission to require undertakings that infringe competition law to accept binding commitments.

The Member States are required, by Article 35 of the Regulation, to designate the competition authority or authorities responsible for the application of Articles 81 and 82 in such a way that the provisions of the Regulation are effectively complied with. The necessary measures must be taken before 1 May 2004. The authorities designated may include courts.

2.3.4 *Powers of the national courts*

Article 6 of the Regulation states: 'National courts shall have the power to apply Articles 81 and 82 of the Treaty.' Notwithstanding its brevity, that provision is of enormous significance. Previously, the national courts could apply Article 81(1)—which was held to have direct effect—but they could not apply Article 81(3). The national courts are, as a result of Article 6 of the Regulation, no longer going to find themselves in the unfortunate situation of having to treat as null and void agreements which on balance are beneficial to competition. Instead they may decide that, although the agreement restricts competition within the meaning of Article 81(1), that provision should be declared inapplicable because the agreement satisfies the requirements of Article 81(3).

---

[29] Arts 23(2)(c) and 24(1)(c).   [30] Arts 17–21.

This, of course, raises the awkward question whether Article 81(3) is capable of having direct affect, i.e. capable of being relied on in the courts.[31] Article 6 of the Regulation appears to assume that it is. A Council regulation cannot, however, determine whether a particular provision of Community law is capable of having direct effect. Ultimately that is an issue for the Court of Justice. It would be easy to object that Article 81(3) is not sufficiently clear and precise to allow of judicial application.[32] For example, the question whether an agreement promotes economic progress 'while allowing consumers a fair share of the resulting benefit' is not the sort of issue that judges are used to pronouncing on. Against that it could be said that an analysis under Article 81(3) is no more complex and subjective than an analysis under Article 81(1). Moreover, even if the applicability of Article 81(3) were entrusted at first instance to a purely administrative body, the decisions taken by such a body would still have to be subject to some sort of judicial review; so, whatever system is used, the task of applying Article 81(3) cannot be avoided by the courts.

2.3.5 Co-operation between the Commission and the national courts and authorities

The decision to decentralize the application of Articles 81 and 82 is a bold one. The obvious danger is that it may lead to divergent approaches and to conflicting decisions. To reduce that risk, the Regulation contains a number of provisions on co-operation between the Commission and the national competition authorities and courts.

Article 11(1) proclaims that 'the Commission and the competition authorities of the Member States shall apply the competition rules in close cooperation'. The Commission is to transmit to the competition authorities of the Member States copies of the most important documents it collects with a view to applying various provisions of the Regulation.[33] The national competition authorities must, when acting under Article 81 or Article 82, inform the Commission in writing before, or without delay after, commencing the first formal investigative measure.[34] No later than 30 days before the adoption of a decision requiring that an infringement be brought to an end, accepting commitments or withdrawing the benefit of a block exemption regulation,[35] the national competition authorities must

---

[31] For an interesting discussion of this issue, see Jones and Sufrin, op. cit. (n. 5), at. p. 1035.
[32] That is the essential criterion for determining whether a Treaty provision has direct effect: Case 26/62 *Van Gend en Loos v Nederlandse Administratie der Belastingen* [1963] ECR 1.
[33] Art. 11(2).   [34] Art. 11(3).
[35] The power to withdraw the benefit of a block exemption regulation is conferred on the national competition authorities by Art. 29(2).

inform the Commission.[36] Curiously, this obligation to notify the Commission in advance does not apply if the competition authority of a Member State envisages imposing a fine or a periodic penalty payment.

The competition authorities of the Member States may consult the Commission on any case involving the application of Community law.[37] The initiation of proceedings by the Commission relieves the national competition authorities of their competence to apply Articles 81 and 82 of the Treaty. When the national competition authorities rule on agreements which are already the subject of a Commission decision, they cannot take decisions which would run counter to the Commission's decision.[38]

National courts may ask the Commission to send them information in its possession or its opinion on questions concerning the application of the Community competition rules.[39] The Member States are required to send the Commission a copy of any written judgment of a national court deciding on the application of Article 81 or Article 82.[40]

The Commission is empowered to submit written observations to national courts, where 'the coherent application of Article 81 or Article 82 of the Treaty so requires'.[41] The national courts, like the national competition authorities, are barred from taking decisions which run counter to a decision of the Commission when they rule on an agreement which is already the subject of a Commission decision.[42] They must also avoid giving a decision which would conflict with a decision which the Commission contemplates taking.[43]

2.4 *The substance of the prohibition*

Article 81 is based on the idea that a healthy market economy depends on a never-ending struggle between independent undertakings which compete with each other in an attempt to produce the goods and services that consumers require. Those who best respond to consumers' demands and produce the right goods and services most efficiently will, by offering the most favourable conditions, be able to gain a share of the market, thus ensuring their survival and their ability to go on satisfying consumer needs. These are the 'winners'. Firms that do not adapt themselves sufficiently to the demands of consumers, or do not operate efficiently enough to trade at a profit, will cease to exist. They are the 'losers'. Their disappearance will liberate resources that can be reallocated among other firms that are better adapted to the needs of the market-place. Ultimately there will be greater overall prosperity because there will be a greater supply of the goods and services that people want to buy.

[36] Art. 11(4).   [37] Art. 11(5).   [38] Art. 16(2).
[39] Art. 15(1).   [40] Art. 15(2).   [41] Art. 15(3).
[42] Art. 16(1), first sentence.   [43] Art. 16(1), second sentence.

This market mechanism can only function properly if each competitor strives to be a 'winner', thereby accepting, of course, the risk of ending up as a 'loser'. If the competitors get together and agree not to compete flat-out so that none of them suffers the fate of losers, they will no longer have any incentive to produce what the consumer requires as efficiently as possible. As a result, inefficient firms will stay in business, thus tying up resources that could otherwise be reallocated, and no firm is likely to perform as efficiently as it would if it was spurred on by the threat of losing market share to competitors.

The purpose of Article 81 is to prevent that kind of collusion between competitors. Article 81 identifies three forms of collusion:

(1) agreements between undertakings;
(2) decisions by associations of undertakings; and
(3) concerted practices between undertakings.

In the present context we are concerned largely with the first category. The distinction between an agreement and a concerted practice in blurred. The term 'concerted practice' catches all 'coordination between undertakings which, without having reached the stage where an agreement, properly so called, has been concluded, knowingly substitutes practical cooperation between them for the risk of competition'.[44] The other category of prohibited collusion ('decisions of associations of undertakings') covers, for example, conduct by which the members of a trade association co-ordinate their conduct, 'whether engaged in through resolutions of the association, recommendations, the operation of certification schemes or through the association's constitution itself'.[45]

While French has the convenient term *entente* to cover the three categories of collusion referred to in Article 81, English unfortunately lacks a corresponding term. In the rest of this chapter the word 'agreement' is used loosely to cover all three categories.

For an agreement to be caught by Article 81 two conditions must be fulfilled:

(1) it must have as its object or effect the prevention, restriction, or distortion of competition;
(2) it must affect trade between Member States.

Happily, neither the Commission nor the Court of Justice seem to engage in semantic exercises to distinguish between the terms 'prevention', 'restriction', and 'distortion'. Nothing of substance would be lost if the terms 'prevention' and 'distortion' had been omitted from the text of Article 81.

---

[44] Joined Cases 48, 49 and 51 to 57/69 *ICI v Commission* ('the dyestuffs case') [1972] ECR 619 at paras 64 and 65.
[45] Jones and Sufrin, op. cit. (n. 5), at pp. 118 *et seq.*

Most authors, for the sake of simplicity, speak about agreements that *restrict* competition.

Article 81(1) gives five examples, under letters (a) to (e), of agreements that restrict competition. It is clear from the words 'in particular' that this list is not exhaustive. Although the word 'appreciably' does not appear in the text of Article 81, the Court of Justice has held that for an agreement to come within the prohibition it must 'affect trade between Member States and the free play of competition to an appreciable extent'.[46]

The requirement of an effect on trade between Member States is intended to define 'the boundary between the areas respectively covered by Community law and national law'.[47] It is thus a jurisdictional test. The test has been construed broadly. In *Société La Technique Minière v Maschinenbau Ulm* the Court stated that 'it must be possible to foresee with a sufficient degree of probability on the basis of a set of objective factors of law or of fact that the agreement in question may have an influence, direct or indirect, actual or potential, on the pattern of trade between Member States'.[48] It is the agreement as a whole that must affect trade between Member States. If that is the case, it is not necessary to show that the clause which restricts competition itself affects trade.[49]

In *Consten and Grundig* it was argued that the agreement did not affect trade, within the meaning of Article 81(1), because it actually increased the volume of trade between Member States. The Court rejected the argument. Although the effect on competition must be adverse, the effect on trade between Member States may be neutral. The aim of Article 81 is not to increase the volume of trade between Member States but to ensure that competition in the common market is not distorted.

In addition to this 'pattern of trade' test, the Court has held that trade between Member States is affected if an agreement interferes with the structure of competition in the common market.[50]

3. ANTI-COMPETITIVE AGREEMENTS AND INTELLECTUAL PROPERTY RIGHTS

3.1 *Introduction*

An intellectual property right is an exclusive right recognized by the State. Its existence is not dependent on any agreement between undertakings, so

---

[46] Case 22/71 *Béguelin Import v GL Import-Export* |1971| ECR 949.
[47] Joined Cases 56 and 58/64 *Consten and Grundig v Commission* |1966| ECR 299 at 341.
[48] Case 56/65 |1966| ECR 235 at 249.
[49] Case 193/83 *Windsurfing v Commission* |1986| ECR 611 at paras 96 and 97.
[50] Joined Cases 6 and 7/73 *Commercial Solvents v Commission* |1974| ECR 223 at para. 33.

it is not directly caught by the prohibition of Article 81. An intellectual property right may none the less be the subject of an agreement between undertakings, and such an agreement may prevent, restrict, or distort competition. Indeed, the power and privileges associated with exclusivity make intellectual property rights uniquely suited to that purpose. This explains why the Commission has sometimes tended to view intellectual property rights with a certain hostility and suspicion.

One of the earliest cases before the Court of Justice in which an attempt was made to apply Article 81 to an intellectual property right was *Parke, Davis v Centrafarm*.[51] In that case the plaintiff relied on its Dutch patent to block imports of infringing products from Italy. The infringing products had not been made by the patent-holder, or with its consent, so there was no question of applying the exhaustion doctrine under Articles 28 and 30 of the Treaty. As regards the Treaty prohibition on agreements restricting competition, the Court observed:

A patent taken by itself and independently of any agreement of which it may be the subject, is unrelated to any of [the categories of agreement contemplated in Article 81], but is the expression of a legal status granted by a State to products meeting certain criteria, and thus exhibits none of the elements of contract or concerted practice required by Article [81(1)]. Nevertheless it is possible that the provisions of this article may apply if the use of one or more patents, in concert between undertakings, should lead to the creation of a situation which may come within the concepts of agreements between undertakings, decisions of associations of undertakings or concerted practices within the meaning of Article [81(1)].[52]

A few years later in *Deutsche Grammophon v Metro* the Court used a formula that has since been repeated in a number of judgments:[53] 'The exercise of the exclusive right . . . might fall under the prohibition set out by [Article 81(1)] each time it manifests itself as the subject, the means or the result of an agreement which, by preventing imports from other Member States of products lawfully distributed there, has as its effect the partitioning of the market.'[54]

3.2 *Assignments and licences in general*

So the exercise of an intellectual property right may be caught by Article 81 whenever it manifests itself as *the subject, the means, or the result* of an agreement that restricts competition. The classic examples of agreements relating to intellectual property rights that are capable of restricting

---

[51] Case 24/67 [1968] ECR 55. [52] At 71, *in fine*.
[53] See. e.g.. Case 51/75 *EMI Records v CBS United Kingdom* [1976] ECR 811 at para. 27; and Case 258/78 *Nungesser v Commission* [1982] ECR 2015 at para. 28.
[54] Case 78/70 [1971] ECR 487 at para. 6.

competition are licensing agreements and assignments. An assignment implies the outright transfer of ownership to another person. A licence merely implies that a person other than the owner is allowed to perform acts that would otherwise amount to an infringement of the owner's intellectual property right.

At first sight the distinction between an assignment and a licence might appear clear-cut. There are, however, transactions which have the outward appearance of an assignment but are in substance much closer to a licensing agreement.[55] Suppose, for example, a trade mark owner assigns his mark in a certain territory to another person but stipulates in the contract of assignment what production methods must be used and how the product must be presented and marketed, and provides for the trade mark to be reassigned to the original owner in certain circumstances. Such a transaction would be much closer, in substance, to a licensing agreement than an assignment, especially if the assignee is required to make regular royalty payments to the assignor.

Both the Court and the Commission have demonstrated a willingness to look at substance rather than appearance when determining whether a transaction involves an assignment or a licence.[56] In *Nungesser v Commission*[57] the French institute 'INRA' had assigned its plant breeder's rights to its German distributor, who was allowed to register them in his own name. The Court affirmed that the assignee/distributor's position on the German market was, in economic terms, that of an exclusive licensee.[58]

The Commission has taken a similar approach in its legislation. Article 11(2) of Commission Regulation (EC) No. 2349/84 of 23 July 1984 on the application of Article [81(3)] of the Treaty to certain categories of patent licensing agreements[59] provided that the regulation also applied to 'assignments of a patent or of a right to a patent where the sum payable in consideration of the assignment is dependent upon the turnover attained by the assignee in respect of the patented products, the quantity of such products manufactured or the number of operations carried out employing the patented invention'.

That regulation has now been replaced by Commission Regulation (EC) No. 240/96 of 31 January 1996 on the application of Article [81(3)] of the Treaty to certain categories of technology transfer agreements.[60] Article 6(2) of the new Regulation provides:

---

[55] For examples of this in relation to know-how agreements, see G. Cabanellas and J. Massaguer, *Know-how Agreements and EEC Competition Law*, IIC Studies in Industrial Property and Copyright Law, Vol. 12, Munich, 1991, p. 58.

[56] This seems to accord with the practice of the English courts: see *Jonathan Cape Ltd v Consolidated Press Ltd* [1954] 3 All ER 253 and the interesting discussion of that case in D. I. Bainbridge, *Intellectual Property*, 4th edn, Financial Times/Pitman Publishing 1999, p. 91.

[57] Cited in n. 53.

[58] At para. 47.

[59] OJ 1984 L 219, p. 15.

[60] OJ 1996 L 31, p. 2.

This Regulation shall also apply to:

. . .

(2) assignments of know-how, patents or both where the risk associated with exploitation remains with the assignor, in particular where the sum payable in consideration of the assignment is dependent on the turnover obtained by the assignee in respect of products made using the know-how or patents, the quantity of such products manufactured or the number of operations carried out employing the know-how or patents.

There is no reason to assume that contracts assigning or licensing intellectual property rights are necessarily detrimental to competition. An assignment simply transfers an exclusive right from one person to another: the assignee does not acquire greater power to impede competition than the previous owner. A licence brings another operator into the market, which means that an exclusive right hitherto in the hands of a single undertaking is now exercised by at least two undertakings. At first sight, that ought to strengthen competition or at least not weaken it. It might be tempting therefore to think that, whatever damage may be done to competition by intellectual property rights, the competitive situation is not likely to deteriorate because these rights change ownership or are licensed to other users.

The reality is, of course, more complex. Once again the conflict between intellectual property rights and EC law is due essentially to the territoriality of those rights. Unitary rights, capable of being assigned or licensed for the whole of the common market rather than a part of it, would be much less likely to fall foul of Article 81. A series of parallel national rights, each capable of being assigned or licensed to a different person, could become a magnificent instrument for partitioning the common market. That largely explains why the Commission and the Court have, over the years, shown varying degrees of hostility and suspicion to agreements for the assignment or licensing of intellectual property rights.

3.3 *Trade mark assignments*

The suitability of trade mark assignments for the purpose of dividing up the common market is evident from the well-known case *Consten and Grundig v Commission*.[61] It will be remembered that in that case Grundig allowed its French distributor (Consten) to register a Grundig trade mark (GINT), so that Consten could use its rights as proprietor of the registered trade mark to block parallel imports. Although not technically a trade mark assignment, that transaction produced the same effects as a trade mark assignment. The Court rightly upheld the Commission decision prohibiting Consten from asserting its trade mark rights in order to prevent parallel imports.

---

[61] Cited in n. 47.

Obviously, if manufacturers were allowed to assign their national trade mark rights to their distributors in each Member State and each distributor were allowed to treat parallel imports as trade mark infringements, the various national markets could be sealed off hermetically. It would be hard to imagine a clearer case for applying Article 81(1) to an agreement concerning intellectual property rights.

The vital factor, when appraising the legality of Consten and Grundig's conduct, is that legal and economic links continued to exist between the two undertakings after the execution of the contract by which Consten acquired the rights in the GINT trade mark for France. The relationship (manufacturer and exclusive distributor) could hardly have been closer.

The stance taken by the Court a few years later in *Sirena v Eda*[62] is much more questionable. In that case the American owner of the trade mark 'Prep Good Morning', for shaving cream in Italy and Germany, assigned the Italian registration to Sirena in 1937. Some time later it licensed Eda to use the trade mark in Germany. When Eda began exporting products bearing the trade mark to Italy, Sirena sued for trade mark infringement. The Court of Justice held that the practice of assigning a trade mark to different persons in different Member States was contrary to Article 81(1) since it would recreate 'impenetrable barriers' between the Member States. The implication of the ruling was that Eda was free to use the trade mark in Italy even though it had belonged exclusively to Sirena in that territory for over 30 years (and presumably Sirena was free to use it in Germany). The fact that consumers might have been a little confused and possibly misled appears not to have troubled the Court.

There is nothing in the text of the judgment to suggest that there was a continuing relationship between Sirena and Eda or between Sirena and the American company that had, in the days of Mussolini and Hitler, owned the trade mark in both Italy and Germany. The Court seems to have approached the case on the basis that the trade mark had, since 1937, been under the control of separate undertakings in Italy and Germany and that there were no legal, economic, or financial links between those undertakings.[63]

---

[62] Case 40/70 |1971| ECR 69.

[63] Advocate General Dutheillet de Lamothe indicated in his opinion in *Sirena v Eda* that there were concerted practices between the various European assignees of the trade mark. Advocate General Mayras, in his opinion in Case 192/73 *Van Zuylen v HAG ('HAG I')* |1974| ECR 731 at 750, suggested that the Court must have accepted that interpretation of the facts in *Sirena v Eda*. In *EMI Records v CBS United Kingdom* Advocate General Warner pointed out (at 865) that the Italian court which referred *Sirena v Eda* to the Court of Justice also assumed the existence of concerted practices. None the less, the fact remains that nothing in the text of the Court's judgment in *Sirena v Eda* suggests that the Court made any such assumption or that its ruling was confined to that type of situation.

The Court's willingness to give retroactive effect to Article 81 of the EC Treaty met with almost universal criticism.[64] The Court attempted to justify its position by saying that for Article 81 to apply to agreements concluded before the entry into force of the Treaty it was sufficient that the agreement continued to produce effect after that date. The Court presumably thought that a trade mark assignment executed in 1937 continued to produce effect in 1971 simply because the assignee continued to enjoy exclusive rights in the trade mark even against the assignor. That is true so far as it goes, just as it is true that the purchaser of a house may bar the previous owner from entering the house 30 years later if he wishes, but it hardly seems a valid reason for applying Article 81 to an agreement that was fully consummated in the distant past, long before the Treaty's entry into force. If the principle of legal certainty means anything at all, it must surely imply that property rights acquired under a contract which complied with the law in force at the time of its conclusion should not be nullified simply because the law governing such contracts is later modified.

Fortunately, the Court mitigated the potentially damaging effects of *Sirena v Eda* a few years later in the *EMI v CBS Records*[65] series of cases. These concerned the trade mark 'Columbia', which a United States company registered in the United States, the United Kingdom, and other countries in Europe and elsewhere. The European registrations of the trade mark were assigned to other companies many years before the entry into force of the EC Treaty.[66] By the 1970s they were owned by EMI Records Limited or by a member of the same group of companies (hereafter 'EMI'), while in North and South America the trade mark was owned by CBS, Inc. (hereafter 'CBS'). There had certainly been a history of agreements, including global market-sharing agreements, between the various owners of the 'Columbia' trade mark but these seem to have been terminated in 1974. At around that time CBS started exporting to Europe, from the United States, gramophone records bearing the 'Columbia' trade mark which it then marketed through its various European subsidiaries. Not surprisingly, EMI sued the CBS companies for trade mark infringement. The defendants argued that EMI's reliance on its trade mark rights was contrary to the free movement of goods and to the Treaty rules on competition, including

---

[64] One author refers to *Sirena v Eda* as 'an erroneous aberration . . . which we now pass over in embarrassed silence as a half-baked judicial fish': I. S. Forrester, 'Magill, "A Famous Victory"? Third Party Access to Intellectual Property Rights' in *International Intellectual Property Law and Policy*, Vol. 2 (ed. H. C. Hansen, Fordham University School of Law), Juris Publishing, Sweet and Maxwell, p. 35–10.

[65] Case 51/75 *EMI Records v CBS United Kingdom* [1976] ECR 811, Case 86/75 *EMI Records v CBS Grammofon* [1976] ECR 871 and Case 96/75 *EMI Records v CBS Schallplatten* [1976] ECR 913.

[66] For a full account of the history of the 'Columbia' trade mark see the opinion of Advocate General Warner in *EMI Records v CBS United Kingdom*, at 855 *et seq.*

Article 81. Danish, German, and English courts referred questions of interpretation to the Court of Justice.

CBS's argument concerning the free movement of goods amounted to an attempt to extend the geographical scope of the infamous doctrine of common origin.[67] The attempt was doomed to failure: the goods in question were imported from outside the Community and there was no barrier to trade between Member States. The argument based on Article 81 was much stronger.

The question, essentially, was whether the agreements which led to the trade mark being owned by different companies in Europe and in the Americas:

(1) had as their object or effect to prevent, restrict or distort competition within the common market; and
(2) were capable of affecting trade between Member States.

The Court ruled that such agreements might impair competition within the common market if they led to the isolation of the common market as a whole and reduced the supply of trade-marked products originating in a non-member country.[68] And they might affect trade between Member States if the proprietor of the trade mark in question in the non-member country owned subsidiaries in various Member States which were able to market the products in Europe.[69]

The actual language used by the Court is convoluted and verges on the incomprehensible.[70] What the Court seems to have meant is simply that an agreement which effects a carve-up of the world market, giving Europe to one party and the Americas to another, with the aid of trade mark assignments, may restrict competition within Europe and may affect trade within Member States. That proposition is hardly controversial as regards agreements and assignments executed after the entry into force of the Treaty. The difficult point was whether, and on what conditions, to apply it to events that occurred in the dim and distant past. On that point the Court started by repeating the formula in *Sirena v Eda*: 'For Article [81] to apply to a case, such as the present one, of agreements which are no longer in force it is sufficient that such agreements continue to produce their effects after they have formally ceased to be in force.'[71] But the Court added an important qualification:

---

[67] See Chap. 8, section 2.2.   [68] At para. 28 of the judgment in Case 51/75.
[69] At para. 29 of the judgment.
[70] The summary in the previous paragraph represents an attempt to make sense of what the Court said in paras 28 and 29 of the judgment.
[71] At para. 30 of the judgment.

An agreement is only regarded as continuing to produce its effects if from the behaviour of the persons concerned there may be inferred the existence of elements of concerted practice and of coordination peculiar to the agreement and producing the same result as that envisaged by the agreement. This is not so when the said effects do not exceed those flowing from the mere exercise of the national trade-mark rights.[72]

It is clear from that passage of the judgment that an assignment which took place before the entry into force of the Treaty and led to the split ownership of a trade mark is not in itself objectionable. The resulting legal situation must be accepted. The trade mark belongs to different persons and each has the exclusive right to use it in his territory. If that impedes the free movement of goods and impairs competition, those effects must be tolerated because they result from historical events that the Treaty does not pretend to reverse. Article 81 only bites if the various owners of the trade mark engage in concerted practices.

Quite what would amount to a concerted practice in this context is not easy to say. Moreover, the language used by the Court in paragraph 31 of its judgment in *EMI Records v CBS United Kingdom* is not helpful. The classic definition of a concerted practice is 'coordination between undertakings which, without having reached the stage where an agreement properly so called has been concluded, knowingly substitutes practical cooperation between them for the risks of competition'.[73]

Although there had been ample collaboration between EMI and CBS over the years, the two groups appeared to have been operating at arm's length for some time when the case came before the Court of Justice. They each sold gramophone records under a different trade mark in the territory in which the 'Columbia' trade mark belonged to the other party.[74] That fact alone suggests that they were not using the trade mark as the basis for a cozy market-sharing arrangement. CBS's action in making direct sales in Europe under the 'Columbia' trade mark and EMI's resulting infringement actions confirm that the two undertakings were not 'substituting practical cooperation between them for the risks of competition'.

It is not difficult to imagine an entirely different scenario in which all the indicia point to post-assignment co-operation between the various proprietors of the fragmented trade mark. The following would be an example:

- Each proprietor sticks to the territory in which he owns the mark and makes no attempt to sell the type of product in question in the other party's territory under a different trade mark.

---

[72] At paras 31 and 32 of the judgment.   [73] *ICI v Commission* (cited in n. 44).
[74] See the opinion of Advocate General Warner at 853.

- The various proprietors use a similar get-up for the product and generally seek to create the impression that the products emanate from a common source.
- Each proprietor brings trade mark infringement actions against parallel importers.

In such a scenario one would surely have to conclude that the parties were engaged in a concerted practice. The object of the practice would be to share out the goodwill associated with the mark along geographical lines. Such a practice would be bound to restrict competition and could only escape the prohibition laid down in Article 81(1) on the ground that it did not have an appreciable effect on trade between Member States. That might be the case if turnover in the trade-marked goods represented an insignificant share of the relevant market.[75]

In *Consten and Grundig* and *Sirena v Eda* the Court seems to have assumed that any agreement which ends the unitary ownership of a trade mark within the common market automatically restricts competition.

The *Ideal Standard*[76] case shows that there are situations in which that may not be the case. The judgment has already been fully analysed in Chapter 8 on trade marks.[77] Only one paragraph of the judgment dealt with competition law. The Court stated:

. . . where undertakings independent of each other make trade-mark assignments following a market-sharing agreement, the prohibition of anti-competitive agreements under Article [81] applies and assignments which give effect to that agreement are consequently void. However, . . . that rule and the accompanying sanction cannot be applied mechanically to every assignment. Before a trade-mark assignment can be treated as giving effect to an agreement prohibited under Article [81], it is necessary to analyse the context, the commitments underlying the assignment, the intention of the parties and the consideration for the assignment.[78]

The Court can only be praised for recognizing the need to look at a trade mark assignment in its legal and economic context. The passage cited is not, however, free of difficulty. It focuses totally on the intention of the parties. While the Court was right to stress that a deliberate strategy to divide up the common market by means of trade mark assignments would fall foul of Article 81, it should always be remembered that that provision applies to agreements which have as their object *or effect* the prevention, restriction, or distortion of competition. Thus the parties' intention is irrelevant if the

---

[75] See Case 5/69 *Völk v Vervaecke* [1969] ECR 295 and the discussion in Jones and Sufrin, op. cit. (n. 5), at p. 127.
[76] Case C-9/93 *IHT Internationale Heiztechnik v Ideal Standard* [1994] ECR I-2789.
[77] See Chap. 8, section 2.2.5.
[78] At para. 59 of the judgment.

effect of the assignment is anti-competitive.[79] Quite what the Court's think-ing was on this point is unclear. In practice, however, the difference between effect and intention may not be important. If, for example, X registers the trade mark GADZOOKS for winged gudgeons in the whole of the common market and assigns the German, Danish, Swedish, and Finnish registrations to Y but retains the other registrations, the effect is likely to be anti-competitive; but so too is the intention. There will be little need to analyse the parties' 'underlying commitments' in order to conclude that they intended to achieve a pan-European carve-up of the market in winged gudgeons. In many situations it will be relatively easy to infer a market-sharing intention from an agreement to split up the ownership of a trade mark. One author asks the rhetorical question: 'what trade mark holder of sound mind would today split his mark unless his purpose was to divide up the market?'[80]

As to the consequences of a breach of Article 81 in this area, it is arguable that the Court went too far by stating that the assignment would be void. The nullity of the anti-competitive agreement itself is decreed by Article 81(2). In the case of a trade mark assignment, the assignee will normally be entered on the trade mark register as the new proprietor of the mark. If the assignment agreement is void, does that mean that the assignee is legally obliged to re-assign the mark to its original owner? And who is entitled to be regarded as the proprietor of the mark until the register has been amended? The judgment is silent on those questions. One commen-tator has argued that to treat the assignment as void infringes the principle of proportionality, since it would be 'sufficient merely to prohibit the use of the trade mark'.[81]

3.4 Copyright assignments and licences

Authors are rarely in a position to exploit their works themselves. Like inventors, they are forced to seek their reward through the agency of others, to whom they assign their intellectual property rights or grant

---

[79] For criticism of the *Ideal Standard* judgment on this point, see P. Auteri, 'La cessione del marchio per Stati fra divieto delle intese e controllo delle concentrazioni: considerazioni in margine al caso "Ideal Standard" ' (1996) I *Rivista di Diritto Industriale* 5 at 28 *et seq.*, and W. Alexander (1995) CML Rev. 327, 345.

[80] P. Oliver, 'Of Split Trade Marks and Common Markets' (1991) MLR 587, 592. In that article Oliver defended *HAG II* but argued that the exhaustion-of-rights principle should prevail where a trade mark was split up as a result of a contractual assignment effected after the entry into force of the Treaty. Not surprisingly he has strongly criticized the *Ideal Standard* judgment: see P. Oliver, *Free Movement of Goods in the European Community*, 3rd edn, Sweet and Maxwell, 1996, pp. 281–284.

[81] Alexander, op. cit. (n. 79), at 346. He presumably means that it would be sufficient to prohibit each proprietor from using the mark to exclude from his territory the products of the other.

licences. Licences and assignments are the norm in this field, rather than an exception. Moreover, in the case of cinematographic works and recorded music the existence of various overlapping rights and the complexity of collecting royalties for each performance of a protected work mean that licences or assignments are essential if rights are to be enforced efficiently.

The above considerations suggest that the authorities responsible for applying competition law should be willing to exercise leniency, where appropriate, in relation to copyright licences and assignments. That is not to say, of course, that such operations cannot fall foul of Article 81. As with other intellectual property rights, assignments of copyright provide an excellent tool for dividing up markets. Different scenarios can be envisaged:

A. An author writes a book. He retains the copyright in his own country but assigns the copyright, for a lump sum, to a different publisher in each of the Member States.
B. Company X owns the copyright in the works of a number of popular songwriters. It assigns the copyright for North and South America to Company Y, keeps the European rights itself and assigns the copyright for the rest of the world to Company Z. Consideration again is in the form of a lump sum.
C. A film maker owns the right to exploit a film—on television, in the cinema, and by the sale and rental of video-cassettes and DVDs— throughout Europe. He assigns the right to different companies in each Member State.
D. A designer of furniture licenses someone to manufacture items of furniture which are protected by copyright. The designer agrees not to grant further licences for the allotted territory and undertakes not to sell furniture in that territory. The licensee is prohibited from selling directly outside the allotted territory.

Many other examples could be given. In the first three scenarios described above, the outright assignment of the right has been postulated. The same results could be achieved by means of an exclusive licence. If the consideration was for a lump sum and the licence was valid for a relatively long period, it would be difficult to see any reason for treating it differently from an assignment for the purpose of competition law. Conversely, an assignment might be more in the nature of a licence if the consideration took the form of a royalty and if there was a continuing business relationship between the two parties.

All of the examples may concern trade in physical goods (books, records, video-cassettes, DVDs, and furniture). In the second and third examples less tangible forms of commerce are likely to be at least as relevant, i.e. performance of the protected work in concert-halls, discotheques, or cinemas, and broadcasting of the work, either by wireless means (terrestrial or satellite) or by cable.

Surprisingly there has been little case law involving the situations described in the first and second examples. In Scenario A, the obvious question that arises is whether the exhaustion principle applies. If it does, the copyright owner in each Member State will have to tolerate parallel imports of books marketed by the copyright owners in the other Member States. Probably the exhaustion principle does apply in this type of case. The special reasons that led the Court to exclude exhaustion in the *Ideal Standard* case— the inability of each owner of the trade mark to control the quality of goods marketed by the other owner—do not apply to copyright. There is no compelling reason therefore to exclude the exhaustion principle.

The same solution would apply in Scenario C as regards video-cassettes and DVDs marketed in a Member State by one of the assignees. Exhaustion would certainly apply in Scenario D. Irrespective of whether the licence complies with competition law, it is clear that neither the licensor nor the licensee may oppose parallel imports of furniture that has been manufactured and marketed by the other. They will also be unable to oppose direct sales, on the basis of breach of contract, if the licence is held to infringe Article 81(1) and is not exempted under Article 81(3).

In Scenario B the exhaustion principle does not come into play because the integrity of the common market is not in issue: the European copyrights have been kept under common ownership. The principle of the free movement of goods does not prevent Company X from relying on the copyright to exclude goods incorporating the protected works that have been marketed outside the EEA by Companies Y and Z.

As regards the application of competition law, it is unlikely that assignment of the works of a single author, as in Scenario A, would have an appreciable effect on competition or on trade between Member States. Article 81 would not therefore come into play. The assessment might of course be different if a major publisher who owned the rights in the works of many popular authors used assignments to partition the common market. The definition of the relevant product market would be crucial.[82] Not all books are in competition with each other. The reader who wants a cookery book is hardly likely to buy a detective novel instead.

The *EMI v CBS* cases suggest that Article 81 might have something to say about Scenario B, at least if the protected works were sufficiently significant for the effect on trade between Member States and competition to be appreciable.[83] Although in that case the Court was addressing trade mark issues, the same principles would seem to apply to copyright.

[82] This is dealt with below in section 4.2.2.
[83] See nn. 68–70 and the accompanying text.

Even if Article 81 were found to apply, it is not easy to say what consequences that would have. The anti-competitive agreements are the contracts assigning the rights outside Europe to Companies Y and Z. According to the *Ideal Standard* judgment, the applicability of Article 81 renders the assignments void (though that may not apply to extra-Community intellectual property rights). Presumably, if the assignments were void, that would mean that the assigned copyrights would revert to Company X, which would have to repay the consideration received from Companies Y and Z. One may wonder what would happen to any royalties or other profits which had accrued to Companies Y and Z in the meantime. To avoid such complications it might be preferable just to say that Company X cannot exclude from the common market products marketed outside Europe with the consent of Companies Y and Z. In other words exhaustion would apply as a sanction for infringing the competition rules of the Treaty, even though it did not apply as a result of the free movement of goods.

Scenario C is loosely based on the facts of the *Coditel* cases decided by the Court of Justice in the early 1980s. It will be recalled that in *Coditel I*[84] the Court held that the Treaty rules on the free movement of services are not breached when the person who owns the copyright in a film in one Member State blocks the simultaneous cable transmission in that State of a television channel which has broadcast the film in another Member State where the copyright has been assigned to a different person.

The referring court in *Coditel I* was the Brussels Court of Appeal. That court had rejected an attempt by the cable transmitter (Coditel) to invoke EC competition law and only referred to the Court of Justice questions on the freedom to provide services. The refusal to entertain Coditel's argument based on Article 81 of the Treaty was challenged in the Belgian Court of Cassation, which sought guidance from the Court of Justice, thus giving rise to the case known as *Coditel II*.[85] The question referred to the Court of Justice read as follows:

Where a company which is the proprietor of the rights of exploitation of a cinematographic film grants by contract to a company in another Member State an exclusive right to show that film in the State, for a specified period, is that contract liable, by reason of the rights and obligations contained in it and of the economic and legal circumstances surrounding it, to constitute an agreement, decision or concerted practice which is prohibited between undertakings pursuant to Article [81(1) and (2)] of the Treaty or are those provisions inapplicable either because the right to show the film is part of the specific subject-matter of copyright and accordingly Article [30] of the Treaty would be an obstacle to the application of Article [81], or because the right relied on by the assignee of the right to show the film derives from

[84] Case 62/79 *Coditel v Ciné Vog Films* ('*Coditel I*') [1980] ECR 881. See Chap. 10, section 5.
[85] Case 262/81 *Coditel v Ciné Vog Films* ('*Coditel II*') [1982] ECR 3381.

a legal status which confers on the assignee protection *erga omnes* and which does not fall within the class of agreements and concerted practices referred to by the said Article [81].

The Belgian court's reference to the 'specific subject-matter of copyright' is interesting. The concept of specific subject-matter has, as we have seen, never played a prominent role in the Court of Justice's case law on copyright. Moreover, it had not at the time been used by the Court of Justice in relation to competition law.[86]

In spite of the Belgian court's prompting, the Court of Justice did not make use of the concept of specific subject-matter in *Coditel II*. In fact the Court engaged in remarkably little theorizing about the relationship between competition law and intellectual property rights. It began with the trite observation that it is conceivable that certain aspects of the manner in which the right is exercised may prove to be incompatible with Article 81 'where they serve to give effect to an agreement, decision or concerted practice which may have as its object or effect the prevention, restriction or distortion of competition within the common market'.[87] The Court then asserted that 'the mere fact that the owner of the copyright in a film has granted to a sole licensee the exclusive right to exhibit that film in the territory of a Member State and, consequently, to prohibit, during a specific period, its showing by others, is not sufficient to justify the finding that such a contract must be regarded as the purpose, the means or the result of an agreement, decision or concerted practice prohibited by the Treaty.'[88]

All that that means is that there is no *per se* prohibition, under Article 81, against granting an exclusive licence to exhibit a film in a Member State during a specific period. That hardly seems a controversial proposition. To justify it the Court observed, nonetheless, that: 'The characteristics of the cinematographic industry and of its markets in the Community, especially those relating to dubbing and subtitling for the benefit of different language groups, to the possibilities of television broadcasts, and to the system of financing cinematographic production in Europe serve to show that an exclusive exhibition licence is not, in itself, such as to prevent, restrict or distort competition.'[89]

The relevance of some of the factors referred to by the Court is questionable. It is, for example, common knowledge that film making is an expensive business and that some film makers have difficulty raising finance. It is not easy to see why that should justify granting special treatment to film makers in general as regards the application of competition law. There

---

[86] The specific subject-matter test seems to have made its debut in competition law in Case 193/83 *Windsurfing International v Commission* [1986] ECR 611 at paras 45, 72, 80, 85 and 92.
[87] At para. 14 of the judgment.   [88] At para. 15 of the judgment.
[89] At para. 16 of the judgment.

are many other economic sectors which involve heavy investment of capital and major risk taking.

The need for dubbing or subtitling seems, at first sight, to offer a stronger justification for permitting exclusive licences that are limited to a specific part of the territory of the common market. One wonders nonetheless why such licences have to coincide with national frontiers instead of following Europe's natural linguistic cartography.[90] Belgium illustrates the point perfectly. If the European copyright in a film has to be split up on account of language, would it not be more natural to grant separate licences covering (a) the Netherlands and Flanders and (b) France and Wallonia? The logic of producing a special Belgian version with subtitles in French and Dutch is not self-evident.[91]

The reference to 'the prohibition of television broadcasts' echoes a remark made in *Coditel I* to the effect that a copyright assignment may, for practical reasons, have to coincide with national frontiers 'in a situation where television is organized in the Member States largely on the basis of legal broadcasting monopolies'.[92] It seems a trifle perverse to allow that unfortunate situation to serve as justification for a practice which prevented cable transmitters such as Coditel from doing the one thing which, before the advent of satellite broadcasting, offered some hope of breaking down national broadcasting monopolies.[93]

Fortunately, the Court recognized in *Coditel II* that, while an exclusive licence limited to the territory of a Member State is not *per se* contrary to Article 81(1), the exercise of the copyright in a film might infringe that provision 'where there are economic or legal circumstances the effect of which is to restrict film distribution to an appreciable degree or to distort competition on the cinematographic market, regard being had to the specific characteristics of that market'.[94] Obviously the assessment of the economic and legal context of a copyright assignment or licence is a matter for the national court. The Court of Justice offered the following guidance:

... it is for national courts, where appropriate, to make such inquiries and in particular to establish whether or not the exercise of the exclusive right to exhibit a cinematographic film creates barriers which are artificial and unjustifiable in terms of the needs of the cinematographic industry, or the possibility of charging fees which exceed a fair return on investment, or an exclusivity the duration of which is disproportionate to those requirements, and whether or not, from a general point of

[90] See, in this sense, F. Sturm, 'Belgisches Kabelfernsehen vor dem Forum des Europäischen Gerichtshofs' (1980) 11 *Archiv für Presserecht 1980* 190 at 193.

[91] It could be argued that bilingual subtitles are necessary to cater for Walloons who travel to Flanders and Flems who travel to Wallonia. The irony of the argument will not be lost on anyone who has driven around Flanders looking for roadsigns to Mons or Liège.

[92] At para. 16.   [93] Similar criticism is expressed by Sturm, op. cit. (n. 90), at 193.

[94] At para. 17 of the judgment.

view, such exercise within a given geographic area is such as to prevent, restrict or distort competition within the common market.'[95]

The main defect in the Court's reasoning is that it focuses entirely on the needs of the cinematographic industry. The needs of the television broadcasters, the cable companies and above all the televiewing public are neglected. Consumers are, of course, the ultimate losers. If a Belgian cable company is unable to retransmit the programmes of a German station without fear of being sued for breach of copyright by the person who is exclusively entitled to exploit in Belgium a film that the German station has broadcast with the consent of the copyright owner, the result is that consumers will be deprived of choice. What happened in practice is that after the *Coditel* litigation cable companies began to scramble the images of films included in foreign television schedules, where they were unable to secure the copyright owner's consent to cable retransmission.

One must not, of course, neglect the legitimate rights of copyright owners or forget that without adequate copyright protection the film makers would be unable to secure a fair return on their investment and there would soon be no films for the consumer to enjoy, either on television or in the cinema. But one must also remember that if the copyright in a film is split up by means of a series of assignments or exclusive licences, the responsibility for that lies entirely with the copyright owner.

The film makers argue in their defence that each national market has its own characteristics and that the moment when they release a film for showing in the cinema may need to vary from one country to another (which has repercussions as regards the moment when the film can be shown on television, since a television showing would reduce the film's capacity to attract a live cinema audience).[96] It is questionable whether the cinematographic industry has proved its case. It is difficult to see why, for example, a film has to be released in Germany earlier than in Belgium or why it should be shown on German television earlier than on Belgian television.

In *Coditel I* the Court recognized that the performance right is different in nature from the reproduction right and is not exhausted upon its first exercise in the common market. That is of course true but it does not mean that film makers should be free to divide up the common market into a series of watertight national markets and exploit each one separately, to the detriment of consumers and cross-border providers of services. There is much to be said for the Commission's suggestion in *Coditel I* that the cable company should be allowed to retransmit the film in question but that the

---

[95] At para. 19 of the judgment.

[96] In fact, Coditel's retransmission of *Le Boucher* probably had very little effect on cinema audiences for the film in Belgium since the film was presumably dubbed into German.

owner of the Belgian copyright should be entitled to claim an equitable remuneration.[97]

In both of the *Coditel* judgments the Court seems to have approached the case on the basis that the copyright in the film *Le Boucher* belonged, in Germany and Belgium, to companies between which there were no legal or economic relations. The exact relationship between the original owner of the copyright (La Boétie) and the assignees or licensees of the German and Belgian rights (Filmedis and Ciné Vog, respectively) is unclear. Nor should it matter, as regards the application of the provisions on the free movement of services. On the view canvassed above, the copyright owner should not be able to block the simultaneous cable retransmission in Belgium of a film broadcast with his consent in Germany. There is no reason to take a different view where the copyright owner has assigned the copyright to different persons in Germany and Belgium. It is true that, in the field of trade marks, special considerations preclude the application of the exhaustion principle to goods produced by the respective owners of trade marks which belong to different persons as a result of an assignment.[98] Those special considerations (i.e. the need to protect consumers against confusion as to the origin of goods) do not apply to copyright.

It is tempting to speculate what the Court would have done in *Coditel I* if the German and Belgian copyrights had still belonged to the original owner. Perhaps the Court would not have had so much sympathy for a copyright owner who allowed a film to be broadcast on German television but himself objected to the simultaneous cable retransmission of the film in neighbouring Belgium. Perhaps the justification for applying some sort of exhaustion principle would have been more evident.

3.5 *Patent and know-how licensing*

3.5.1 *The Commission's early attitude to patent licensing*

In the early years, the Commission took a benevolent attitude towards patent licensing agreements. That attitude manifested itself in a Notice issued by the Commission in 1962 (known as 'the Christmas Message' because it was issued on 24 December).[99] The Commission stated that, on the basis of the facts known to it, various clauses in patent licensing agreements did not appear to be caught by Article 81(1). That applied, in particular, to obligations imposed on the licensee which were intended to:

---

[97] *Coditel I* at 898. One author criticizes the Commission for proposing, in effect, a statutory licence which would seriously reduce the level of protection for authors: R. Plaisant (1980) 43 *Recueil Dalloz Sirey*, jurisprudence, 600 at 602. It could be argued that a statutory licence would be justified because it is the most practical way of enabling consumers to benefit from a cable relay service.

[98] See *Ideal Standard*, cited in n. 76.   [99] OJ 2922/62.

(1) limit the exploitation of the invention to only some of the forms provided for by patent law (manufacture, use, sale);
(2) limit use of the patented process to certain technical applications;
(3) limit the quantity of production or the number of acts of exploitation of the patent;
(4) limit exploitation to a part of the territory covered by the patent.

The last point was particularly significant because it meant that the licensor could give an exclusive licence to a licensee for a specific territory, i.e. 'a licence which restricted the licensor not only from appointing any other licensee in that territory but also from making, using or selling itself in that territory'.[100]

The same benevolent approach is found in Article 4(2)(2)(b) of Regulation No. 17, which classed as 'non-notifiable' agreements to which no more than two undertakings were party and which imposed 'restrictions on the exercise of the rights of the assignee or user of industrial property rights—in particular patents, utility models, designs or trade marks—or of a person entitled under a contract to the assignment, or grant, of the right to use a method of manufacture or knowledge relating to the use and to the application of industrial processes'. The importance of that provision should not, however, be overestimated. It merely meant that such agreements did not have to be notified. It did not exempt them from the prohibition laid down in Article 81(1). The practical significance of this was that the Commission might, if it decided that an agreement merited exemption under Article 81(3), grant exemption as from the date when the agreement was concluded.[101] Otherwise, under Article 6(1) of Regulation No. 17, exemption could only take effect from the date of notification.

In the early 1970s the Commission became much more sceptical about the licensing of intellectual property rights and began to treat certain clauses in licence agreements as being automatically caught by Article 81(1), and therefore null and void unless exempted under Article 81(3). The *Davidson Rubber*[102] case provides a typical example of the Commission's attitude. In that case an American company which owned two patents relating to the manufacture of padded objects, such as arm rests and car seats, granted patent and know-how licences to a series of companies in various Member States. Each licence was exclusive for the territory in question. The agreements were notified to the Commission, which adopted

---

[100] S. D. Anderman, *EC Competition Law and Intellectual Property Rights*, Clarendon Press, Oxford, 1998, p. 53.
[101] Jones and Sufrin, *op. cit.* (n. 5), at p. 210.
[102] OJ 1972 L 143, p. 31. For other examples of the Commission's policy, see *Burroughs-Delplanque* (OJ 1972 L 13, p. 50); *AOIP/Beyrard* (OJ 1976 L 6, p. 8); and *Velcro/Aplix* (OJ 1985 L 233, p. 22).

a decision exempting them under Article 81(3). It might have been more reasonable to hold that no exemption was needed since the agreements did not restrict competition within the meaning of Article 81(1). The Commission, however, considered that the agreements restricted competition and affected trade between Member States because Davidson Rubber had, by granting a series of exclusive licences, deprived itself of the power to license other undertakings to exploit the patents and know-how in the territory concerned; these other potential licensees would have been able to export products to other Member States, so the restriction of competition must be deemed capable of affecting trade between Member States in a way that was capable of damaging the attainment of the aims of a single market.[103]

The Commission's reasoning in *Davidson Rubber*, as in other decisions of that period, is wholly deficient. Its approach is dogmatic and formalistic. Notable is the absence of any form of economic analysis. The Commission seems to forget that a patent, by its very nature, confers an exclusive right. Before concluding licensing agreements, Davidson Rubber was alone entitled to exploit the patents in the territories concerned. It alone was able to exploit the secret know-how, assuming of course that it was secret. It makes little sense therefore to talk of competition and trade between Member States being impaired by exclusive licences because other potential licensees were prevented from using the licensed technology and exporting products made with that technology to other Member States.

But the most serious defect in the Commission's approach is that it neglected to take into account the fact that many licensees—operating in the real world where competition is a matter of economic survival rather than a subject for bureaucratic theorizing—will not entertain any licence but an exclusive one.[104] To exploit the licensed technology the licensee has to invest. Production facilities have to be tooled up. The potential licensee might not be willing to accept the commercial risk, unless he has the exclusive right to exploit the licensed technology in the territory concerned.[105]

A further objection to the Commission's approach is that it comes close to threatening the existence of the intellectual property right. Many patentees will not be in a position to exploit the patent themselves; their only hope is to find licensees who will assume the commercial risk and offer a royalty to the patentee. If they are prevented from exploiting the patent in that way because the only licence agreements of interest to potential licensees are deemed unlawful, then what is left of the substance of the patent and where is the patentee's 'just reward'?

---

[103] At section II.8 of the Commission's decision.
[104] Jones and Sufrin, op. cit. (n. 5), at p. 582.
[105] V. Korah, op. cit. (n. 21), at p. 212.

To make matters worse, the Commission's hostility was not confined to territorial restraints. A whole range of non-territorial restraints also incurred the Commission's displeasure in the 1970s. In *AOIP/Beyrard* the Commission refused to exempt a no-challenge clause, a non-competition clause and a clause containing an obligation to pay royalties after the expiry of the most recent patent in force when the agreement was concluded.[106] In *Vaessen/Moris* the Commission held that a tie-in of certain products to a patented process was contrary to Article 81(1) because it was not essential to the proper exploitation of the patent.[107]

3.5.2 *The* Nungesser *case*

The Commission's hostile attitude towards patent licensing agreements came under steady fire throughout the 1970s. The criticism doubtless helped to produce a more nuanced approach in the regulation on group exemption for patent licensing agreements which the Commission finally managed to adopt in 1984[108] after 'a long and tortuous history of negotiation between the Commission and the Member States, both fiercely lobbied by the business community'.[109] An even greater influence, perhaps, was exerted by the Court of Justice through its judgment in *Nungesser v Commission*, delivered in 1982.

The *Nungesser* case was concerned, not with patents but with a more esoteric species of intellectual property: namely, plant breeders' rights. A French organization called INRA developed certain new varieties of hybrid maize seed. It entered into two contracts, in 1960 and 1965, with Mr Kurt Eisele, who was the principal shareholder of a company called L. C. Nungesser KG. By virtue of those contracts INRA granted Mr Eisele the exclusive right to propagate and sell the new varieties of maize seed in Germany. INRA also allowed Mr Eisele to register those varieties in his own name with the German Plant Varieties Office (the *Bundessortenamt*). Registration conferred an exclusive right on the registered proprietor to produce for commercial purposes the reproductive material of the new variety and to offer it for sale.

Mr Eisele, as registered owner of the plant breeders' rights over the maize varieties developed by INRA, sued a parallel importer for infringing his intellectual property rights and published a notice in a German magazine stating that parallel imports of the protected seeds constituted an infringement of those rights. A parallel importer complained to the Commission.

---

[106] *AOIP/Beyrard* (cited in n. 102).   [107] See Anderman, op. cit. (n. 100), at p. 61.
[108] Commission Reg. (EC) No. 2349/84, OJ 1984 L 219, p. 15.
[109] Anderman, op. cit. (n. 100), at p. 76.

The Commission adopted a decision declaring that various clauses of the contracts were contrary to Article 81(1). Moreover, it refused to grant an exemption under Article 81(3). Essentially the Commission condemned the contracts in so far as:

(1) INRA undertook not to produce the protected seeds in Germany;
(2) INRA undertook not to license other persons to produce or sell seeds in Germany; and
(3) both parties undertook to take steps to prevent parallel imports of the seeds into Germany.

Mr Eisele and the Nungesser company challenged the Commission decision before the Court of Justice, and were partially successful.

The Court took a more balanced view than the Commission. It held that the contracts infringed Article 81(1) only in so far as the parties undertook to attempt to prevent parallel imports. The Court did not feel it necessary to give extensive reasons for considering such attempts illegal *per se*. Citing only *Consten and Grundig* by name, the Court referred to its consistent case law according to which 'absolute territorial protection granted to a licensee in order to enable parallel imports to be controlled and prevented results in the artificial maintenance of separate national markets contrary to the Treaty'.[110] The Court rightly rejected a curious argument advanced by the United Kingdom, which had intervened in the case. According to that argument, the contracts could not be contrary to Article 81(1) since any attempt to block parallel imports would be frustrated on account of the principle of the exhaustion of rights, which was firmly established in the case law of the Court of Justice.[111] Apart from the minor detail that no such principle had been established at the time when the contracts were concluded, there was an obvious flaw in the United Kingdom's argument: attempts to block parallel imports might well be successful, in spite of the exhaustion principle, because the undertakings involved in the parallel trade might be intimidated by the threat of court action. The facts of the *Nungesser* case illustrate that point: the parallel importer sued by Mr Eisele acceded to an in-court settlement whereby he undertook to desist from importing the seed variety in question without Mr Eisele's authorization. Presumably the parallel importer was ignorant of the exhaustion principle when he settled the action, just as Mr Eisele was ignorant of Article 81 when he commenced the action.

As for the possibility of exempting a contractual agreement to obstruct parallel imports, the Court ruled that out by referring to the proportionality test laid down in Article 81(3). Article 81(3), it will be recalled, allows for the prohibition contained in Article 81(1) to be declared inapplicable to an

---

[110] At para. 61 of the judgment.   [111] At para. 62 of the judgment.

agreement which contributes to improving the production or distribution of goods or promoting technical progress, and which does not impose on the undertakings concerned restrictions which are not indispensable to the attainment of those objectives. The Court observed as follows:

As it is a question of seeds intended to be used by a large number of farmers for the production of maize, which is an important product for human and animal foodstuff, absolute territorial protection manifestly goes beyond what is indispensable for the improvement of production or distribution or the promotion of technical progress, as is demonstrated in particular in the present case by the prohibition, agreed to by both parties to the agreement, of any parallel imports on INRA maize seeds into Germany even if those seeds were bred by INRA itself and marketed in France.[112]

Economic analysis is singularly lacking here. The argument is, moreover, circular: to prove that a ban on parallel imports exceeds what is indispensable for the improvement of production or distribution or the promotion of technical progress, the Court points out that the litigious contracts banned parallel imports. It might have made more sense to say that in order to preserve the coherence of the law the Commission should not exempt, under Article 81(3), contractual provisions which are diametrically opposed to the fundamental aims of Article 28 of the Treaty. In any event, an agreement to obstruct parallel imports is, as the United Kingdom pointed out, unenforceable as a result of the Court's case law on Article 28. A contractual provision which is legally unenforceable can hardly be indispensable for the attainment of any objective.

But the main interest in the *Nungesser* case lies in the arguments used by the Court to justify the finding that Article 81(1) was not infringed by a licence under which INRA undertook (a) not to produce seeds of the protected varieties in Germany and (b) not to license other persons to produce or sell the seeds in Germany.

The Court characterized such a licence as an 'open' exclusive licence, as opposed to a 'licence with absolute territorial protection', i.e. a licence by which 'the parties to the contract propose, as regards the products and the territory in question, to eliminate all competition from third parties, such as parallel importers or licensees for other territories'.[113]

The Court held that an open exclusive licence was not in itself incompatible with Article 81(1). The reason for that finding was as follows:

. . . in the case of a licence of breeders' rights over hybrid maize seeds newly developed in one Member State, an undertaking established in another Member State which was not certain that it would not encounter competition from other licensees for the territory granted to it, or from the owner of the right himself, might

---

[112] At para. 77 of the judgment. [113] At para. 53 of the judgment.

be deterred from accepting the risk of cultivating and marketing that product; such a result would be damaging to the dissemination of a new technology and would prejudice competition in the Community between the new product and similar existing products.[114]

The logic of that reasoning is not, of course, confined to plant breeders' rights. It applies with equal force to patents and know-how. Therein lies the importance of the *Nungesser* judgment, which arrived just as the draft regulation on the group exemption of patent licensing agreements was being debated. In fact, the Commission deliberately waited for the outcome of the *Nungesser* case before adopting Regulation No. 2349/84.

There was a sequel to *Nungesser* a few years later, namely *Erauw-Jacquéry v La Hesbignonne*,[115] which also concerned plant-breeders' rights. In that case the Court held that Article 81(1) was not infringed by a clause under which the licensee was prohibited from selling or exporting 'basic seed', i.e. seed which is propagated so that the next generation can be sold to growers. It is sometimes suggested that in *Erauw-Jacquéry* the Court tolerated a licence with 'absolute territorial protection'.[116] That is not, however, correct. The Court did not say that a licence involving 'absolute territorial protection' in the sense in which that term had been used in *Nungesser* was acceptable. The Court was dealing with a licence under which basic seed could not be sold at all[117] but was to be used to produce second-generation seed for sale to growers. The Court did not suggest that a restriction on parallel imports of second-generation seed would lie outside the scope of Article 81(1).[118]

3.5.3 *The old block exemptions on patent licensing and know-how licensing*

Commission Regulation (EC) No. 2349/84 of 23 July 1984 on the application of Article [81(3)] of the Treaty to certain categories of patent licensing agreement ('the Patent Licensing Regulation')[119] was the first block exemption in the field of intellectual property rights. It established a pattern—with a white list, a black list, and an opposition procedure—which has been adhered to ever since. It was followed five years later by Commission Regulation (EC) No. 556/89 of 30 November 1988 on the application of Article [81(3)] of the Treaty to certain categories of know-how licensing agreements ('the Know-how Licensing Regulation').[120]

---

[114] At para. 57 of the judgment.   [115] Case 27/87 [1988] ECR 1919.

[116] Jones and Sufrin, op. cit. (n. 5), at p. 587.

[117] The licensee was required not to use the basic seed supplied by the breeder for any purpose other than propagation: see the opinion of Advocate General Mischo at para. 10 (at 1928).

[118] The Advocate General assumed that the licence in issue banned parallel imports and took it for granted that such a clause was beyond redemption: see para. 29 of the opinion (at 1931).

[119] OJ 1984 L 219, p. 15.   [120] OJ 1989 L 61, p. 1.

The wisdom of having separate regulations for patent licensing and know-how licensing was never apparent. One of the problems this engendered was that it was not always easy to ascertain which regulation applied to a specific transaction. The Patent Licensing Regulation applied to pure patent licensing agreements and also to 'mixed' agreements licensing patents and non-patented know-how.[121] The regulation only applied to mixed agreements:

(1) if the know-how permitted a better exploitation of the patents;
(2) if the licensed patents were necessary in order to achieve the objects of the licensed technology; and
(3) for as long as the patents were in force.[122]

The Know-how Licensing Regulation applied to pure know-how licensing agreements and to mixed agreements not already exempted by the Patent Licensing Regulation.[123]

The Patent Licensing and Know-how Licensing Regulations were both replaced by Council Regulation (EC) No. 240/96 of 31 January 1996 on the application of Article [81(3)] of the Treaty to certain categories of technology transfer agreements ('the Technology Transfer Regulation').[124] Agreements in force on 31 March 1996 which fulfilled the exemption requirements laid down in the old regulations continue to be exempt.[125] The Technology Transfer Regulation applies to agreements concluded after 1 April 1996.[126]

3.5.4 *The Technology Transfer Regulation*

3.5.4.1 *Scope of the Regulation*

The Technology Transfer Regulation applies to pure patent licensing agreements, to pure know-how licensing agreements and to mixed patent and know-how licensing agreements, including those agreements containing ancillary provisions relating to intellectual property rights other than patents.[127]

As in the case of the two regulations that it replaces, the Technology Transfer Regulation applies only to agreements to which two undertakings are party.[128] Thus a licensor who is contemplating granting a series of exclusive licences to undertakings in a number of Member States should

---

[121] Art. 1(1) of Reg. No. 2349/84.
[122] The ninth recital in the preamble to Reg. No. 2349/84.
[123] Art. 1(1) of Reg. No. 556/89.   [124] OJ 1996 L 31, p. 2.
[125] Art. 11(3) of Reg. No. 240/96.   [126] Art. 13(1) of Reg. No. 240/96.
[127] Art. 1(1).   [128] Ibid.

take care to conclude a separate agreement with each licensee. The regulation is capable of applying to such a network of bilateral agreements.[129]

To be covered by the Regulation the know-how must be 'secret, substantial and identified in any appropriate form'.[130] 'Secret' means that 'the know-how package as a body or in the precise configuration and assembly of its components is not generally known or easily accessible, so that part of its value consists in the lead which the licensee gains when it is communicated to him'.[131] 'Substantial' means that the know-how includes information which 'can reasonably be expected at the date of conclusion of the agreement to be capable of improving the competitive position of the licensee, for example by helping him to enter a new market or giving him an advantage in competition with other manufacturers or providers of services who do not have access to the licensed secret know-how or other comparable secret know-how'.[132] 'Identified' means that the know-how is 'described or recorded in such a manner as to make it possible to verify that it satisfies the criteria of secrecy and substantiality'.[133]

The Regulation is concerned only with the *industrial* licensing of technology, as opposed to commercial licensing. It applies only where the licensee himself manufactures the licensed products or has them manufactured for his account.[134] It does not apply to 'agreements solely for the purpose of sale' or to 'agreements relating to marketing know-how communicated in the context of franchising arrangements'.[135] Such agreements are likely to be covered by Commission Regulation (EC) No. 2790/99 of 22 December 1999 on the application of Article 81(3) of the Treaty to categories of vertical agreements and concerted practices.[136]

The Regulation also applies to patent and know-how licensing agreements which contain 'ancillary provisions relating to intellectual property rights other than patents'.[137] The preamble expressly mentions, as examples of other intellectual property rights, 'trade marks, design rights and copyright, especially software protection . . . when such additional licensing contributes to the achievement of the objects of the licensed technology and contains only ancillary provisions'.[138] The requirement that the provisions relating to other intellectual property rights should be ancillary has been interpreted strictly by the Commission.[139]

3.5.4.2 *Structure of the Regulation*

The Regulation follows the classic structure of 'white list', 'black list', and opposition procedure.

---

[129] P. A. Stone, 'The EEC Block Exemption for Patent Licences' [1985] 6 EIPR 173, 175.
[130] Art. 10(1).   [131] Art. 10(2).   [132] Art. 10(3).   [133] Art. 10(4).
[134] Para. 8 of the preamble.   [135] Ibid.   [136] OJ 1999 L 336, p. 21.
[137] Art. 1(1).   [138] The sixth recital in the preamble.
[139] See below in section 3.6.2.

Article 1(1) exempts from the prohibition laid down in Article 81(1) of the Treaty licensing agreements which impose certain obligations, in particular territorial restraints, on the licensor or licensee. The central concern of that provision (and of the whole Regulation) is to determine the degree of exclusivity that can be granted to licensees in their allocated territory. The maximum period of time from which the various obligations may be imposed is laid down in Article 1(2) to (4).

Article 2 specifies a number of obligations on the licensee or licensor which are generally not restrictive of competition but which are exempted in any case. Article 2, which deals essentially with non-territorial restraints, is generally referred to as the 'white list', although it might be more logical to regard Articles 1 and 2 together as constituting the white list, since both of them define the clauses that are positively permitted in a licensing agreement. Tritton refers to the exempted clauses in Article 1 of the Regulation as the white list and uses the expression 'super white list' to describe the clauses which, according to Article 2 of the Regulation, lie outside the scope of the prohibition decreed by Article 81(1) of the Treaty.[140]

Article 3 lists seven provisions whose presence in a licensing agreement will deprive the agreement of the benefit of the block exemption. This is known as the 'black list'. The inclusion of a black-listed clause does not necessarily mean that an agreement is not eligible for exemption under Article 81(3) of the Treaty. Under the old system (i.e. before the adoption of Regulation No. 1/2003) a licensing agreement which contained a black-listed clause could still be notified and obtain an individual exemption. Following the 'modernisation' of competition law by Regulation No. 1/2003 the parties to a licensing agreement that contains a black-listed clause will be able to argue, in proceedings before the Commission or the national competition authorities, including the courts, that the agreement qualifies for exemption under Article 81(3) in spite of the presence of the black-listed clause. From a practical point of view, however, the parties to the agreement might be better advised to remove the black-listed clause and claim the benefit of the block exemption.

Article 4 provides for what is known as the 'opposition procedure'. Under this procedure an agreement which contains obligations 'restrictive of competition' which are not exempted by Articles 1 or 2 and are not black-listed by Article 3 may be notified to the Commission in accordance with the provisions of Articles 1, 2, and 3 of Commission Regulation (EC) No. 3385/94.[141] The agreement is exempted if the Commission does not oppose the granting of exemption within a period of four months from notification. The Commission must oppose exemption if it is asked to do so

---

[140] G. Tritton. *Intellectual Property in Europe*. Sweet and Maxwell. London. 1996. p. 495.
[141] OJ 1994 L 377. p. 28.

by a Member State on the basis of considerations relating to the competition rules of the Treaty.[142] The Commission may withdraw the opposition at any time. However, if the opposition was raised at the request of a Member State and the request is maintained, the opposition may only be withdrawn after consultation of the Advisory Committee on Restrictive Practices and Dominant Positions.[143]

It is clear that the opposition procedure will have to be discontinued as a result of the reforms introduced by Regulation No. 1/2003. The procedure is dependent on notification. Since the whole concept of notification has been swept away, the opposition procedure is no longer appropriate. The Commission has recognized that the procedure will have to be abolished.[144]

3.5.4.3 *Withdrawal of the exemption*

Article 29(1) of Regulation No. 1/2003 allows the Commission to withdraw the benefit of a block exemption regulation (including the Technology Transfer Regulation) 'when it finds that in any particular case an agreement, decision or concerted practice to which the exemption Regulation applies has certain effects which are incompatible with Article 81(3) of the Treaty'.

Where an agreement, decision or concerted practice has effects which are incompatible with Article 81(3) of the Treaty 'in the territory of a Member State, or in a part thereof, which has all the characteristics of a distinct geographic market', the competition authority of that Member State may withdraw the benefit of a block exemption regulation in respect of that territory.[145]

The above provisions replace Article 7 of the Technology Transfer Regulation (and the corresponding provisions of other block exemption regulations), which allowed the Commission to withdraw the benefit of a block exemption regulation in the case of an agreement that had effects incompatible with Article 81(3) of the Treaty.

3.5.4.4 *Territorial exclusivity under the Regulation*

The *Nungesser* judgment recognized that a certain degree of territorial protection could be compatible with Article 81(1). The licensor could undertake not to exploit the licensed technology himself in the licensee's territory and not to license other undertakings for that territory, provided

---

[142] Art. 4(5).   [143] Art. 4(6).

[144] Commission Evaluation Report on the Transfer of Technology Block Exemption Regulation No 240/96, section 1, para. 7.

[145] Art. 29(2) of Reg. No. 1/2003. On the concept of the 'geographic market', see section 4.2.2 below.

that parallel imports were not impeded. That basic concept of 'open' exclusive licences was elaborated upon in the Patent Licensing Regulation, the provisions of which served as a model for the Know-how Licensing Regulation. The provisions of the Technology Transfer Regulation are identical in substance.

The basic rules are to be found in Article 1(1), points 1 to 6. These are not the easiest of provisions to read because some of the terminology used is confusing. Points 1 to 3 deal with the relationship between the licensor and the licensees. Points 4 to 6 deal with the relationship between licensees:

- Points 1 to 3 of Article 1(1) exempt clauses whereby the licensor undertakes not to license other undertakings to exploit the licensed technology in the licensed territory or to exploit the licensed technology in the licensed territory himself and clauses whereby the licensee undertakes not to exploit the licensed technology in territories reserved for the licensor. The term 'exploit' has a wide meaning: it refers to any use of the licensed technology, in particular in the manufacture, active marketing, passive marketing, or leasing of the licensed product.[146]
- Point 4 of Article 1(1) exempts clauses whereby the licensee undertakes not to manufacture or use the licensed product, or use the licensed process, in territories which are licensed to other licensees.
- Point 5 of Article 1(1) exempts clauses whereby the licensee undertakes not to pursue an active policy of marketing the licensed product in territories which are licensed to other undertakings, and in particular not to engage in advertising specifically aimed at those territories or to establish a branch or maintain a distribution depot there.
- Point 6 of Article 1(1) exempts a clause whereby the licensee undertakes 'not to put the licensed product on the market in the territories licensed to other licensees . . . in response to unsolicited orders'. This is what is known as a ban on 'passive sales'.

The duration of the permitted exclusivity depends on whether the agreement is a pure patent licensing agreement, a pure know-how licensing agreement or a mixed patent and know-how licensing agreement.

In the case of a pure patent licensing agreement, exclusivity is permitted for as long as the licensed product is protected by parallel patents in the relevant territories. However, a clause obliging the licensee not to effect 'passive' sales in territories licensed to other undertakings is permitted for a maximum of five years from the date when the product is first put on the market within the common market by one of the licensees.[147] The five-year

---

[146] See Art. 10, point 10.

[147] Art. 1(2). According to one author, the different treatment of active and passive sales bans is not justified from an economic point of view: Y. Jeanrenaud, 'Exclusive Licences of Patent

limit also applies to a ban on passive sales in a pure know-how licensing agreement and in mixed agreements.[148]

For pure know-how licensing agreements, the maximum duration of the permitted exclusivity (except for a passive sales ban) is ten years from the date when the licensed product is first put on the market within the common market by one of the licensees.[149]

In the case of mixed agreements, exclusivity is permitted in the Member States in which the licensed technology is protected by necessary patents for as long as the licensed product is protected in those Member States by such patents if the duration of such protection exceeds the ten-year period applicable to pure know-how licensing agreements.[150] As noted above, passive sales bans, as between licensees, are excluded from the benefit of this provision: they are always subject to a five-year period.

By virtue of the rules on the maximum duration of the exclusivity, in conjunction with the definition of 'exploit' given by Article 10, point 10, it is clear that a greater degree of territorial protection is permitted in relations between licensor and licensee than in relations between licensees.[151] The licensor and licensee may, for example, agree to ban each other from making even passive sales into each other's territory for as long as the licensed product is protected by parallel patents in those territories (in the case of a pure patent licensing agreement). Licensees cannot in any circumstances be banned from making passive sales into each other's territory for longer than five years.

It is important to stress that if the maximum periods laid down in Article 1(2) to (4) are exceeded, the agreement loses the benefit of the block exemption completely. Article 3, point 7, black-lists clauses providing for longer periods. Nor could the agreement obtain exemption under the opposition procedure provided for in Article 4; that procedure does not apply to agreements which contain any of the black-listed clauses.[152] Hence, under the old system, if a longer period of exclusivity was required, the only possibility was to notify the agreement and seek individual exemption. After Regulation No. 1/2003 becomes applicable on 1 May 2004, the parties to a licensing agreement that provides for a longer period of exclusivity may argue, in proceedings before the Commission or the national authorities, that the agreement qualifies for exemption under Article

---

Rights and Territorial Restraints in the EEC: Certainty vs Flexibility' (1986) 26 *Swiss Review of International Competition Law* 21 at 43.

[148] Art. 1(3), second subpara., and Art. 1(4), second subpara.
[149] Art. 1(3), first subpara.   [150] Art. 1(4), first subpara.
[151] Korah speaks of 'absolute territorial protection as between licensor and licensee': see V. Korah, *Technology Transfer Agreements and the EC Competition Rules*, Clarendon Press, Oxford, 1996, p. 140.
[152] Art. 4(1).

81(3) of the Treaty. They may, however, find it more prudent to keep the period of exclusivity within the limits provided for in the Technology Transfer Regulation and thus obtain the benefit of the block exemption.

The Commission has shown a willingness to exempt agreements which provide for a longer period of exclusivity in appropriate circumstances. In *Pasteur Mérieux-Merck*[153] the Commission exempted a know-how licensing agreement under which territorial exclusivity was capable of lasting longer than the ten years permitted by Article 1(2) of the Know-how Licensing Regulation. The justification given for the exemption was that the licensee had an incentive, as a result of the agreement, to develop new multivalent vaccines. That would lead to a second source of such vaccines and would therefore be beneficial to the consumer.

3.5.4.5 *Non-territorial restraints under the Regulation*

Quantitative restrictions   An obligation on the licensee to pay a minimum royalty or to produce a minimum quantity of the licensed product or to carry out a minimum number of operations exploiting the licensed technology is white-listed by Article 2(1), point 9. The justification for such an obligation is particularly strong in the case of an exclusive licensee, since the technology might otherwise not be exploited at all in the territory concerned.[154] An obligation to produce a minimum quantity can, however, become so onerous that it effectively prevents the licensee from using competing technology. When that happens the Commission may withdraw the exemption, but only if the licensor and licensee were competing manufacturers at the date of the grant of the licence.[155]

A clause imposing a maximum quantity of the licensed products that one party may manufacture or sell or limiting the number of operations exploiting the licensed technology is black-listed by Article 3, point 5. There are, however, two exceptions. First, the licensee may be obliged to 'limit his production of the licensed product to the quantities he requires in manufacturing his own products and to sell the licensed product only as an integral part of or a replacement part for his own products or otherwise in connection with the sale of his own products, provided that such quantities are freely determined by the licensee'.[156]

The second exception concerns what is known as 'second sourcing'. The rationale of this is to enable component manufacturers who hold patents or secret know-how to guarantee their customers a second source of supply.[157] Article 2(1), point 13, therefore white-lists:

---

[153] OJ 1994 L 309, p. 1, at paras 104–10.
[155] Art. 7(4).   [156] Art. 1(1), point 8.
[154] Korah, op. cit. (n. 151), at p. 194 *et seq.*
[157] Korah, op. cit. (n. 151), at p. 203 *et seq.*

'. . . an obligation on the licensee to supply only a limited quantity of the licensed product to a particular customer, where the licence was granted so that the customer might have a second source of supply inside the licensed territory; this provision shall also apply where the customer is the licensee, and the licence which was granted in order to provide a second source of supply provides that the customer is himself to manufacture the licensed products or to have them manufactured by a subcontractor.'

Price restrictions   Price-fixing agreements are treated as anathema in competition law. Article 81(1)(a) of the Treaty prohibits agreements which 'directly or indirectly fix purchase or selling prices'. It is not surprising therefore that Article 3(1) of the Regulation black-lists clauses whereby 'one party is restricted in the determination of prices, components of prices or discounts for the licensed products'. This wording clearly applies to maximum prices as well as minimum prices.[158]

Price recommendations are not black-listed. In *Pronuptia* the Court held that mere recommendations of resale prices which were not binding on franchisees did not infringe Article 81(1).[159]

Field-of-use restrictions   Technology can often be used in several different fields (e.g. astronomical telescopes and binoculars for bird-watching). The term 'field-of-use restriction' refers to a licence provision whereby the licensee is allowed to use the licensed technology only in a particular technical field. Such a restriction is white-listed by Article 2(1), point 8, which permits 'an obligation on the licensee to restrict his exploitation of the licensed technology to one or more technical fields of application covered by the licensed technology or to one or more product markets'.

Field-of-use restrictions can sometimes be difficult to distinguish from customer allocation clauses.[160] These are black-listed by Article 3, point 4, where the licensor and licensee 'were already competing manufacturers before the grant of the licence and one of them is restricted, within the same technical field of use or within the same product market, as to the customers he may serve, in particular by being prohibited from supplying certain classes of user, employing certain forms of distribution or, with the aim of sharing customers, using certain types of packaging for the products, save as provided in Article 1(1), point 7, and Article 2(1), point 13'.

The reference to Articles 1(1), point 7, and 2(1), point 13, means that the ban on customer allocation ceases to apply if the packaging restriction is due to an obligation to use the licensor's trade mark or get-up or if the exemption for second sourcing applies.

---

[158] Korah thinks that maximum prices are 'probably black-listed': op. cit. (n. 151), at p. 207.
[159] Case 161/84 *Pronuptia de Paris v Schillgalis* [1986] ECR 353 at para. 25. Korah questions whether that precedent can be extended beyond franchising: op. cit. (n. 151), at p. 208.
[160] Korah, op. cit. (n. 151), at p. 193; Jones and Sufrin, op. cit. (n. 5), at p. 602.

Minimum quality specifications and tie-ins   Article 2(1), point 5, white-lists clauses which impose:

> . . . an obligation on the licensee to observe minimum quality specifications, includ-ing technical specifications, for the licensed product or to procure goods or services from the licensor or from an undertaking designated by the licensor, in so far as these quality specifications, products or services are necessary for:
> (a) a technically proper exploitation of the licensed technology; or
> (b) ensuring that the product of the licensee conforms to the minimum quality specifications that are applicable to the licensor and other licensees;
> and to allow the licensor to carry out related checks.

A licence clause whereby the licensee is obliged to purchase certain goods or services from the licensor (or from the licensor's nominee) is known as a 'tie-in'. Community competition law is traditionally hostile to tie-ins. Tie-ins are expressly condemned, in more general terms, by Articles 81(1)(e) and 82(d) of the Treaty.

The Commission has, predictably, treated tie-ins with suspicion. The classical example of the Commission's hostility is *Vaessen/Moris*.[161] Mr Moris owned a patent on a device for making sausages. He licensed the patent to various sausage manufacturers, free of charge, on condition that they bought all the sausage casings used with the device from his company. He ensured that the number of the patent was printed on the sausage casings. On the face of things, that seems a perfectly reasonable arrange-ment from everyone's point of view. The tie-in was a simple means for Mr Moris to obtain a reward for the use of his patent. It was the easiest way for him to check how much use was made of the patented device. When, however, a rival manufacturer of sausage casings (Vaesen) complained to the Commission that it could not break into the market because the sausage makers were tied to Mr Moris's company, the Commission held that the tie-in infringed Article 81(1), inasmuch as it deprived the licensees of their 'business freedom to obtain supplies from other undertakings, perhaps on more favourable terms'.[162]

The Commission's reasoning is specious. Vaesen's casings might well have been cheaper than Mr Moris's, since Vaesen did not have to bear the cost of developing the sausage-making device.[163] Moreover, the sausage makers were not deprived of freedom of choice. They could buy casings from other suppliers when the patented device was not used. They had a choice between using Mr Moris's device and casings or using cheaper casings without the benefit of Mr Moris's more efficient manufacturing process.[164]

---

[161] OJ 1979 L 19, p. 32. For a similar attitude, see *Velcro/Aplix*, cited in n. 102.
[162] At para. 15.
[163] L. Zanon, 'Ties in Patent Licensing Agreements' (1980) 5 EL Rev. 391, 392.
[164] Ibid.

Fortunately the Commission adopted a more reasonable attitude in *Campari*.[165] In that case the licensee was required to obtain secret ingredients from the licensor. The justification accepted by the Commission was that the secret ingredients were needed in order to maintain the consistency of the franchised beverage.

At first sight, the link between tie-ins and minimum quality specifications is not obvious. They are, however, connected because, as the *Campari* case shows, the tied product may be necessary in order to guarantee the quality of the end product manufactured with the licensed technology. That is particularly important in the case of franchises and other arrangements that involve the use of the licensor's trade mark.

The link between tie-ins and minimum quality specifications is recognized by Article 2(1), point 5, the wording of which is clumsy, to say the least. It offers two possible justifications for tie-ins or minimum quality specifications. They must either be necessary for a technically proper exploitation of the licensed technology or be necessary in order to ensure that the licensee's product conforms to minimum quality specifications that are applicable to the licensor and other licensees. It could be argued that there are situations in which the licensor could legitimately impose different quality specifications on its licensees.[166] It sometimes happens that requirements differ from one territory to another. The Commission is maybe reluctant to acknowledge the existence of that fact since it appears to be at odds with the concept of a common market.

In one respect the Technology Transfer Regulation represented real progress in comparison with the Patent Licensing Regulation and the Know-how Licensing Regulation. Article 3, point 3, of the latter, blacklisted quality specifications and tie-ins that were not necessary for a technically satisfactory exploitation of the licensed technology or for ensuring that the licensee's products conformed to quality standards respected by the licensor and other licensees. Article 3, point 9, of the former dealt similarly with tie-ins. Article 4(2)(a) of the Technology Transfer Regulation, by contrast, provides that the opposition procedure applies to clauses whereby 'the licensee is obliged at the time the agreement is entered into to accept quality specifications or further licences or to procure goods or services which are not necessary for a technically satisfactory exploitation of the licensed technology or for ensuring that the production of the licensee conforms to the quality standards that are respected by the licensor and other licensees'.

This meant—at least before the advent of Regulation No. 1/2003—that the Commission could evaluate, on a case-by-case basis, whether a tie-in or

---

[165] OJ 1978 L 70, p. 69. See also *Rich Products/Jus-Rol* (OJ 1988 L 69, p. 21).
[166] Korah, op. cit. (n. 151), at p. 179 *et seq.*

minimum quality specification, which did not comply with the terms of Article 2(1), point 5, was none the less worthy of exemption. According to Anderman, the main concern of the Commission would be to distinguish between licensors with considerable market power and those without such power in the market for the licensed technology.[167] The former were likely to find their agreements being opposed, especially if they were in a dominant position. According to Korah, some Commission officials now recognize that tie-ins may be a good way of monitoring royalties.[168] As was pointed out above,[169] the opposition procedure will have to be discontinued following modernisation.

A tie-in and quality control clause was in issue in *Windsurfing International v Commission*.[170] The patent at issue in that case covered a rig for mounting on a sailboard. One clause of the licence agreement obliged the licensee to mount the patented rig only on certain types of board specified in the agreement and to seek the licensor's prior approval before marketing any new type of board with the patented rig. The licensor argued that the clause was intended to guarantee the quality of the manufactured product. The Court found the clause contrary to Article 81(1). It held that quality controls were only justified in so far as they related to a product covered by the patent; a patent that covered a rig for a sailboard could not justify controls relating to the quality of the board.[171] More generally, the Court observed that quality controls were only acceptable if they were based on objectively verifiable criteria laid down in advance; if it were otherwise, the discretionary nature of the quality controls would enable the licensor to impose his own selection of models.[172] What the Court meant is that quality control would just become an excuse for a tie-in for which there was no objective justification. The Court also held that an obligation on the licensee to sell the patented rigs only in conjunction with a board approved by the licensor was contrary to Article 81(1) on account of its arbitrary nature.[173]

Improvements on the licensed technology It is in the nature of technology that it goes on being developed. Both licensor and licensees may discover improvements on the licensed technology. All are likely to have an interest in acquiring access—possibly exclusive—to such improvements. The licence may contain clauses concerning their fate.

The basic principle laid down in the Technology Transfer Regulation (as in its predecessors) is that the licensee may be obliged to grant the licensor a licence on improvements made by the licensee[174] but that he cannot be

---

[167] Op. cit. (n. 100), at p. 106.
[169] See section 3.5.4.2 above.
[171] At para. 45 of the judgment.
[173] At para. 57 of the judgment.

[168] Op. cit. (n. 151), at p. 177.
[170] Cited in n. 86.
[172] At para. 46 of the judgment.
[174] Art. 2(1)(4).

obliged to assign improvements to the licensor.[175] Article 2(1), point 4, white-lists:

. . .

an obligation on the licensee to grant to the licensor a licence in respect of his own improvements to or his new applications of the licensed technology, provided:
—that, in the case of severable improvements, such a licence is not exclusive, so that the licensee is free to use his own improvements or to license them to third parties, in so far as that does not involve disclosure of the know-how communicated by the licensor that is still secret,
—and that the licensor undertakes to grant an exclusive or non-exclusive licence of his own improvements to the licensee.

Article 3, point 6, black-lists a clause whereby 'the licensee is obliged to assign in whole or in part to the licensor rights to improvements to or new applications of the licensed technology'.

There is an important distinction in Article 2(1), point 4, between severable and non-severable improvements. An improvement is severable if it is capable of being exploited independently of the technology transferred by the original licence. It is non-severable if it is only capable of being used in conjunction with that technology.[176] The distinction is important for at least two reasons.

First, a severable improvement has a life of its own and should rightly be regarded as the intellectual property of the person who made the improvement. The licensee who makes a severable improvement may, quite reasonably, be required to license it to the licensor but he should not have to let the licensor go on using it after the expiry of the original licence. In *Delta Chemie/DDD*[177] the Commission required the parties to amend a know-how licence so that the licensor could not continue to exploit the licensee's improvements after the expiry of the original licence.

Secondly, in the case of a know-how licence it should be possible to communicate a severable improvement to third parties without disclosing the secret know-how; by the same token, in the case of a patent licence it should be possible for third parties to exploit a severable improvement without infringing the licensed patent. The same cannot be said of non-severable improvements. For that reason Article 2(1), point 4, recognizes that the licensee may be required to grant the licensor an exclusive licence of his own non-severable improvement. If the licensee were allowed to license the improvement to third parties, the latter would not be able to exploit the improvement without using the technology covered by the original licence. It is reasonable, therefore, to permit the original licensor to retain control over non-severable improvements. Without such control his own intellectual property rights would be endangered.

---

[175] Art. 3(6).   [176] Anderman, op. cit. (n. 100), at p. 110.
[177] OJ 1988 L 309, p. 34.

That argument does not apply, however, to severable improvements. Since these can be regarded as the independently created intellectual property of the licensee, he should be free to license them to third parties, provided of course that this is done without communicating the original licensor's secret know-how.

The further condition imposed by the second indent of Article 2(1), point 4—i.e. that the licensor must undertake to license his own improvements to the licensee—reflects the Commission's concern to ensure balance and reciprocity in technology licensing agreements. That concern was evident in *Boussois/Interpane*,[178] where the Commission exempted a reciprocal obligation, in a mixed patent and know-how licence, to grant non-exclusive licences for improvements made by either party.

A further question that arises is whether clauses relating to improvements can be used to extend the duration of the territorial protection permitted by the Regulation. The answer is basically negative, though the preamble seems to admit of one exception (see below).

Article 3, point 7, black-lists a provision whereby 'the licensor is required, albeit in separate agreements or through automatic prolongation of the initial duration of the agreement by the inclusion of any new improvements, for a period exceeding that referred to in Article 1(2) and (3) not to license other undertakings to exploit the licensed technology in the licensed territory, or a party is required for a period exceeding that referred to in Article 1(2) and (3) or Article 1(4) not to exploit the licensed technology in the territory of the other party or of other licensees'.

Moreover, Article 10, point 7, defines the term 'licensed technology' as including improvements, so the maximum exemption periods laid down in Article 1(2), (3), and (4) are applicable to any improvements as well as to the technology covered by the original licence.

The exception is to be found in paragraph 14 of the preamble, which states:

Exemption under Article [81(3)] of longer periods of territorial protection for know-how agreements, in particular in order to protect expensive and risky investment or where the parties were not competitors at the date of the grant of the licence, can be granted only by individual decision. On the other hand, parties are free to extend the term of their agreements in order to exploit any subsequent improvement and to provide for the payment of additional royalties. However, in such cases, further periods of territorial protection may be allowed only starting from the date of licensing of the secret improvements in the Community, and by individual decision. Where the research for improvements results in innovations which are distinct from the licensed technology the parties may conclude a new agreement benefiting from an exemption under this Regulation.

---

[178] OJ 1987 L 50, p. 30.

The practice of putting substantive provisions into the preamble, rather than the body of the Regulation, is unorthodox and does not contribute to legal certainty. Nor does the vagueness of the term 'innovations which are distinct from the licensed technology'. No-one seems to know what this term means.[179] It would be tempting to suggest that it equates with the term 'severable improvements' in Article 2(1), point 4. However, the use of a different term might imply a difference of meaning, at least under English canons of interpretation.

Non-competition clauses   Article 3, point 2, black-lists a provision whereby 'one party is restricted from competing within the common market with the other party, with undertakings connected with the other party or with other undertakings in respect of research and development, production, use or distribution of competing products without prejudice to the provisions of Article 2(1), points 17 and 18'. This means, for example, that the dominant party to a licensing agreement (who may not necessarily be the licensor) cannot restrain the other party from carrying out further research with a view to developing competing products; nor can he be restrained from using or distributing products that will compete with the licensed products.

Article 3, point 2, is expressly subject to points 17 and 18 of Article 2(1). Article 2(1), point 18, allows the licensor to reserve the right to terminate the exclusivity granted to the licensee and to stop licensing improvements to him when the licensee enters into competition within the common market with the licensor, with undertakings connected with the licensor or with other undertakings in respect of research and development, production, use or distribution of competing products. The licensor may also reserve the right to require the licensee to prove that the licensed know-how is not being used for the production of products and the provision of services other than those licensed. These provisions constitute a serious deterrent to licensees who might wish to engage in competing activities.[180] A licensee who has an exclusive territory is hardly likely to sacrifice his exclusivity or renounce the right to improvements, unless of course he finds the competing technology more attractive than the technology originally licensed to him.

Article 2(1), point 17, white-lists a clause which imposes 'an obligation on the licensee to use his best endeavours to manufacture and market the licensed product'.

---

[179] The lack of clarity is criticized by Korah, op. cit. (n. 151), at p. 150, and Anderman, op. cit. (n. 100), at p. 118.

[180] Tritton, op. cit. (n. 140), at p. 532. Anderman, op. cit. (n. 100), at p. 128. See also the article (cited by Anderman) by T. Frazer, 'Vorsprung durch Technik: The Commission's Policy on Know-How Agreements' (1989) 1 *Oxford Yearbook of European Law* 18.

At first sight, the relationship between a non-competition clause and a 'best endeavours' clause is not self-evident, at least to the uninitiated. The explanation is that, if the licensee started to compete with the licensor by developing alternative technology or distributing competing products, he would not be using his best endeavours to manufacture and market the licensed product.[181] A further point to bear in mind is that Article 2(1), point 9, white-lists an obligation on the licensee to produce a minimum quantity of the licensed product. That too can make it difficult in practice for the licensee to produce competing products; his production capacity may have to be devoted entirely to manufacturing the licensed product in order to comply with the minimum quantity clause.

According to one view, there is no cause for concern if the licensee is effectively prevented from developing or producing competing products, provided that the relationship between the parties is truly vertical.[182] The owner of valuable technology would have little incentive to grant an exclusive licence if the licensee were free to abstain from exploiting the technology (which no one else could exploit in the relevant territory on account of the exclusivity), while instead developing and promoting rival technology. Furthermore, if the parties were not competitors, either actual or potential, before the grant of the licence, there is no compelling reason why they should be expected to become competitors thereafter.

The Commission appears to have recognized that clauses equivalent in effect to an obligation not to compete are only objectionable when the licence is concluded between undertakings which are in a horizontal relationship. Article 7, point 4, of the Regulation allows the Commission to withdraw the exemption where the parties were competing manufacturers at the date of the grant of the licence and the Commission finds that obligations on the licensee to produce a minimum quantity or to use his 'best endeavours' have the effect of preventing the licensee from using competing technologies. Since such obligations are considered by some authorities to be automatically equivalent to a ban on using alternative technologies, the best advice one can give to licence partners who are in a horizontal relationship is to omit a best endeavours clause from their licence and to set any minimum quantity at a relatively low level.

Most-favoured licensee clauses   Article 2(1), point 10, white-lists 'an obligation on the licensor to grant the licensee any more favourable terms that the licensor may grant to another undertaking after the agreement is entered into'.

---

[181] Korah, op. cit. (n. 151), at p. 196. According to Korah, a 'best endeavours' clause and a non-competition clause have identical effects. That might be overstating the case somewhat in view of the vagueness of the term 'best endeavours'.

[182] Anderman, op. cit. (n. 100), at p. 129.

There is some disagreement as to whether most-favoured customer clauses are, in general, capable of being detrimental to competition. On one view they dampen competition because a firm is less likely to give a discount to one customer if it has to offer the same terms to others.[183] In the field of intellectual property licensing within the common market it could, however, be argued that a licensee might be reluctant to invest in exploiting new technology if there was a possibility that a licensee in another territory might be offered more favourable terms (e.g. lower royalties). Here it must be remembered that the goods marketed by the other licensee could, as a result of parallel imports, be offered for sale anywhere in the Community, so the territorial exclusivity enjoyed by the licensee who has to pay higher royalties would not shield him against competition from the licensee who pays lower royalties.

In *Kabelmetal/Luchaire*[184] the Commission held that Article 81(1) was not infringed by an undertaking in a patent and know-how licensing agreement not to grant more favourable terms to another licensee anywhere in the world. The Commission suggested that there might, however, be specific situations in which the only way to find further licensees would be to grant them more favourable terms, in which case a most-favoured licensee clause could be an appreciable restriction on trade. The defect in that reasoning is that the Commission analyses the legality of the clause *ex post* (i.e. at the time when the licensor is seeking further licensees). The clause should be appraised *ex ante*, at the time when the original licensing agreement is concluded. It is all very well to worry about whether subsequent licensees could be wooed with more favourable terms; the question that has to be asked is whether the first licensee would risk the necessary investment without a guarantee that subsequent licensees would not obtain better terms.

No-challenge clauses   Licensors of intellectual property rights have an understandable enthusiasm for including in the licence agreement a clause prohibiting the licensee from challenging the validity of the licensed patent or questioning the secret and substantial nature of the licensed know-how.[185] A licensee might, of course, wish to attack the validity of the licensed intellectual property rights in order to escape from his obligation to pay royalties, while at the same time continuing to exploit the licensed technology.

No-challenge clauses have long been the subject of controversy. One argument in favour of them is that it would be inequitable to allow the licensee to use the intimate knowledge acquired through exploiting the technology to attack the validity of the licensed rights. American law

---

[183] Korah, op. cit. (n. 151), at p. 199.   [184] OJ 1975 L 222, p. 34.
[185] Such clauses used to be so common that models appeared in books of precedents: J. Ferry, 'Patent Agreements: No-challenge Clauses' [1989] 4 EIPR 138.

had a doctrine of 'licensee estoppel', whereby the licensee—even without an express provision in the licence—was estopped from challenging the validity of the patent. That doctrine was abandoned by the Supreme Court, in 1969, in *Lear v Adkins*.[186] A further argument in favour of no-challenge clauses is that the owner of intellectual property rights might be reluctant to grant a licence at all if the validity of his rights could be challenged by the licensee.[187] The argument against no-challenge clauses is that there is a public interest in not allowing commercial freedom to be impeded by invalid intellectual property rights.

In the past, the Commission has displayed predictable hostility to no-challenge clauses. In *Davidson Rubber*[188] the Commission refused to exempt a series of licensing agreements until the parties had removed an undertaking, on the part of the licensee, not to challenge the licensor's patents.

AOIP/Beyrard[189] is a particularly interesting example of the Commission's attitude. Mr Beyrard was a self-employed inventor who owned a number of patents which he licensed to AOIP. The licensee was a relatively large company with a staff of 3,500 and a turnover in 1972 of approximately FF189 million. The Commission found that several clauses of the licence agreements were contrary to Article 81(1) and were not exemptible. In particular, the Commission objected to the no-challenge clause in the following terms:

Clause 5(2) of the licensing agreement prohibits the licensee from challenging the validity of the patents directly or indirectly. Such a no-challenge clause is not a matter pertaining to the existence of the patent. Rather, it constitutes a contractual restriction of competition in that it deprives the licensee of the possibility, which is available to everyone else, of removing an obstacle to his freedom of action in the commercial field by means of an action for revocation of the patents. This is no less the case where the relevant authority examines an application for novelty and degree of inventiveness before granting a patent, since such an examination does not affect the right of firms who might profit from the non-existence of the patent to oppose it or to bring actions for its revocation. Even if it is the licensee who is best placed to attack the patent on the basis of the information given to him by the licensor, the public interest in the revocation of patents which ought not to have been granted requires that the licensee should not be deprived of this possibility.[190]

It seems a trifle far-fetched to imagine that competition might be damaged by a clause in a licensing agreement between a private inventor and a large manufacturing company whereby the latter promises not to challenge the validity of the former's patents. Presumably the company had sufficient

---

[186] 395 US 693 (1969), 162 USPQ 1. That does not, however, mean that no-challenge clauses are prohibited *per se* under American antitrust law: B. I. Cawthra, *Patent Licensing in Europe*, 2nd edn, Butterworths, London, 1986, p. 175.

[187] Korah, op. cit. (n. 151), at p. 183.

[188] OJ 1972 L 143, p. 31.

[189] OJ 1976 L 6, p. 8.

[190] At 12.

resources and expertise to assess whether the patents were valid *prima facie* and worth paying for before entering into the agreement. The company was unlikely to strike a bad bargain, and if it did, why should competition law intervene to protect it? From the inventor's point of view a no-challenge clause is an essential safeguard in such a context. He is almost certainly the weaker party. He has no manufacturing facilities himself and a licence is the only practical means of exploiting the invention. He has no in-house lawyers to fight a patent invalidation action and may lack the financial resources to litigate against a big corporation.

The Commission's reasoning in *AOIP/Beyrard* is unconvincing. When the Commission said that the no-challenge clause was 'not a matter pertaining to the existence of the patent', it was presumably attempting to build an argument on the distinction made by the Court of Justice between the existence of an intellectual property right and its exercise. That distinction is notoriously unhelpful but if it was to be used at all in this case it was surely an argument for upholding the no-challenge clause. Without such a clause the existence of the patents might well have been jeopardized, and perhaps unfairly if the owner of the patents were to capitulate in invalidation proceedings for want of funds.

The Commission was admittedly right to recognize that an invalid patent is capable of creating an unjustifiable restriction on commercial freedom. Historically there are plenty of examples of bogus patents being used by unscrupulous inventors to extract royalties from *bona fide* manufacturers.[191] That is particularly likely to happen in a registration-only system and is a powerful argument for having a thorough pre-grant examination.[192] However, in *AOIP/Beyrard* the Commission expressly stated that the existence of a pre-grant examination for novelty and degree of inventiveness made no difference.

The Commission's hostility to no-challenge clauses was enthusiastically endorsed by the Court of Justice in *Windsurfing International v Commission*.[193] The Court held that 'such a clause clearly does not fall within the specific subject-matter of the patent, which cannot be interpreted as also affording protection against actions brought in order to challenge the patent's validity, in view of the fact that it is in the public interest to eliminate any obstacle to economic activity which may arise where a patent was granted in error'.[194]

---

[191] For an entertaining account of an early American example, see E. C. Walterscheid, 'The Winged Gudgeon—An Early Patent Controversy' (1997) JPTOS 533.

[192] One author, writing in 1986, suggested that no-challenge clauses would decline in importance because the examination standard prescribed by the European Patent Convention would lead to stronger national patents and an increased presumption of validity: see Cawthra, op. cit. (n. 186), at p. 176.

[193] Cited in n. 86.   [194] At para. 92 of the judgment.

The Court expressly rejected the licensor's argument that the public interest in a free system of competition was better served by a no-challenge clause, which made it easier for the patentee to grant a licence, especially since there was a thorough and extensive patent examination under the relevant national law.

The court's reasoning in *Windsurfing* is exceptionally formalistic. The statement that a no-challenge clause does not fall within the specific subject-matter of the patent is meaningless. Presumably the term 'specific subject-matter' refers to the essential rights of the patentee, determined in the light of the purpose of the patent, which is to reward the creative effort of the inventor. The Court considered that those essential rights cannot include the right to preclude a challenge to validity by the licensee because of the public interest in eliminating obstacles to economic activity due to patents granted in error. Important though that interest might be, the Court should none the less have explained why it should necessarily prevail over the public interest in encouraging the diffusion of technology by means of licensing, bearing in mind that the patentee might be reluctant to grant licences without the protection of a no-challenge clause.

The Court adopted a more flexible approach in *Bayer v Süllhöfer*.[195] In that case a no-challenge clause was included in a licence agreement which settled litigation between the parties concerning the validity of a patent. The parties later fell out and litigation recommenced in the German courts. The question of the validity of the no-challenge clause arose and was referred to the Court of Justice. The Commission, which submitted observations to the Court, argued that a no-challenge clause was normally contrary to Article 81(1) but might be legitimate when it formed part of a settlement of litigation and there were genuine doubts about the validity of the patent. The alleged justification for this point of view was that there is a public interest in encouraging the settlement of litigation.

The Court rightly rejected the Commission's contention. A settlement agreement, even if judicially approved, is a contract and cannot be exempt from the mandatory provisions of law that govern the validity of contracts in general.[196] The Court did, however, avoid condemning no-challenge clauses outright and thus implicitly overruled *Windsurfing International* on this point. The Court ruled that a no-challenge clause must be appraised 'in its legal and economic context'.[197] That is surely the correct approach. Unfortunately, the Court went on to identify two aspects, specific to the case

---

[195] Case 65/86 [1988] ECR 5249.

[196] It appears that the Commission has even ordered parties who settled litigation on terms incompatible with competition law to return to court and have the court order amended: see J. Ferry, op. cit. (n. 185), at 139 (footnote 7).

[197] At para. 16 of the judgment.

in point, which were arguably[198] no more relevant than the fact that the agreement came about in the context of settling litigation. The aspects referred to were the royalty-free nature of the licence and the obsolescence of the patent.

The Patent Licensing Regulation black-listed no-challenge clauses, but without prejudice to the licensor's right to terminate the licensing agreement in the event of such a challenge.[199] Curiously a clause reserving the licensor's right to terminate the agreement in the event of a challenge was not expressly white-listed, raising doubts about whether an agreement containing such a clause had to be cleared through the opposition procedure.[200]

The Technology Transfer Regulation evidences a considerable softening in the Commission's attitude towards no-challenge clauses. These are no longer black-listed; instead they are subject to the opposition procedure. Under Article 4(2)(b), the opposition procedure[201] applies in particular where 'the licensee is prohibited from contesting the secrecy or the substantiality of the licensed know-how or from challenging the validity of patents licensed within the common market belonging to the licensor or undertakings connected with him'. Moreover, the ambiguity about a clause reserving the licensor's right to terminate a licensing agreement if the licensee challenges the validity of the licensor's intellectual property rights has been removed. Article 2(1), point 15, of the Regulation expressly white-lists a clause containing 'a reservation by the licensor of the right to terminate the agreement if the licensee contests the secret or substantial nature of the licensed know-how or challenges the validity of licensed patents within the common market belonging to the licensor or undertakings connected with him'. Article 2(1), point 16, white-lists a clause containing 'a reservation by the licensor of the right to terminate the licence agreement of a patent[202] if the licensee raises the claim that such a patent is not necessary'. The necessity of the patent is relevant for the purpose of determining the maximum permitted duration of territorial restraints in a mixed patent and know-how licence.[203]

These provisions appear to strike the right balance. There is no longer a *per se* prohibition on no-challenge clauses. Instead such a clause can be struck down when it is clear from the economic and legal context that it is detrimental to competition. Moreover, the fact that the licensor may reserve

---

[198] Korah, op. cit. (n. 151), at p. 195; Ferry, op. cit. (n. 185), at 139.

[199] Art. 3, point 1, of Reg. No. 2349/84.

[200] Korah, op. cit. (n. 151), at p. 182.

[201] As to the continued applicability of the opposition procedure, see section 3.5.4.2 above.

[202] This appears to have been translated literally from the French. For 'licence agreement of a patent' read 'patent licensing agreement'.

[203] Art. 1(4).

the right to terminate the agreement in the event of a challenge should offer the licensor a large measure of protection. Such a prospect will deter the licensee from mounting a challenge except in the clearest of cases.

An obligation to use the licensor's trade mark and get-up   Article 1(1), point 7, exempts 'an obligation on the licensee to use only the licensor's trade mark or the get-up determined by the licensor to distinguish the licensed product during the term of the agreement, provided that the licensee is not prevented from identifying himself as the manufacturer of the licensed products'. Similarly, Article 2(1), point 11, permits 'an obligation on the licensee to mark the licensed product with an indication of the licensor's name or of the licensed patent'.

The wording of Article 1(1), point 7, is self-contradictory in one respect. The word 'only' implies that the licensee may be prevented from using any trade mark other than that of the licensor. Yet the proviso at the end of the clause confers on the licensee a positive right to identify himself as the manufacturer of the licensed products—something which he may not be able to do without using a trade mark of his own.

In *Windsurfing* the Court condemned a clause requiring the licensee to affix to sailboards a notice stating 'licensed by Windsurfing International'. The Court considered that the licensee could be required to place such a notice only on the component covered by the patent (i.e. the rig). Otherwise the notice would encourage uncertainty as to whether the board too was covered by the patent and diminish the consumer's confidence in the licensees so as to gain a competitive advantage for the licensor.[204]

3.6 *Trade mark licensing*

3.6.1 *Community legislation which positively authorizes trade mark licensing*

Both of the major pieces of Community legislation on trade mark law expressly authorize licensing. Article 8(1) of Council Directive 89/104/ EEC of 21 December 1988 to approximate the laws of the Member States relating to trade marks[205] provides: 'A trade mark may be licensed for some or all of the goods or services for which it is registered and for the whole or part of the Member State concerned. A licence may be exclusive or non-exclusive.' Article 22(1) of Council Regulation (EC) No. 40/94 of 20 December 1993 on the Community trade mark[206] contains a similar provision regarding Community trade marks.

---

[204] At para. 73 of the judgment.   [205] OJ 1989 L 40, p. 1.
[206] OJ 1994 L 11, p. 1.

Both aforementioned articles contain a second paragraph which allows the trade mark proprietor to invoke the rights conferred by the trade mark against a licensee who 'contravenes any provision in his licensing contract with regard to its duration, the form covered by the registration in which the trade mark may be used, the scope of the goods or services for which the licence is granted, the territory in which the trade mark may be affixed, or the quality of the goods manufactured or of the services provided by the licensee'. That means that in addition to an action for breach of contract the licensor may bring trade mark infringement proceedings against the licensee in the circumstances specified.

The Directive and Regulation cannot of course derogate from the EC Treaty. The fact that a licensing agreement complies with the above legislative provisions does not mean that it necessarily escapes sanction under Article 81 of the Treaty.[207] The compatibility of the agreement with EC competition law must still be appraised in the usual way.

It may be noted that care has been taken to ensure that the legislation is compatible with the Treaty provisions on the free movement of goods. The territorial restrictions which may be imposed on the licensee relate to 'the territory in which the trade mark *may be affixed*' (emphasis added). Thus if P, the proprietor of a Community trade mark, grants a licence to L to use the trade mark in Spain and L makes the trade-marked products in France, P may sue for trade mark infringement under Article 22(2) of the Regulation. Anyone who purchases the goods from L and resells them will, presumably, also infringe the trade mark. But if L makes the products in Spain and exports them to France for resale, L is not infringing P's trade mark. P will, at most, have a contractual claim against L. In the second hypothesis the products made by L will be able to circulate freely in the rest of the Community by virtue of the exhaustion principle laid down in Article 13(1) of the Regulation.[208] It is arguable that Article 28 of the Treaty would have been infringed if the legislation had been drafted in such a way as to allow P to use trade mark infringement proceedings to prevent L's goods from being further marketed in the common market in that situation.

3.6.2 *The possible application of the Technology Transfer Regulation to trade mark licences*

For reasons that no one seems able to explain, the Commission has never adopted a block exemption regulation for trade mark licensing agreements.

---

[207] It is sometimes suggested that a licensing agreement which complies with the relevant provisions of the Directive and Regulation is presumed not to fall foul of Art. 81: see N. J. Wilkof, *Trade Mark Licensing*, Sweet and Maxwell, London, 1995, p. 260.

[208] T. de las Heras Lorenzo, *El agotamiento del derecho de marca*, Editorial Montecorvo S. A., Madrid, 1994, p. 310.

In spite of that regrettable lacuna, certain provisions relating to the licensing of trade marks may nonetheless be covered by other block exemption regulations, i.e. the Technology Transfer Regulation and Commission Regulation (EC) No. 2790/1999 of 22 December 1999 on the application of Article 81(3) of the Treaty to categories of vertical agreements and concerted practices[209] ('the Vertical Agreements Regulation').

Recital 6 of the Technology Transfer Regulation states that it is appropriate to extend the scope of the Regulation to patent and know-how licensing agreements which license 'intellectual property rights other than patents (in particular, trade marks, design rights and copyright, especially software protection), when such additional licensing contributes to the achievement of the objects of the licensed technology and contains only ancillary provisions'. That extension is effected by Article 1(1) of the Regulation. The term 'ancillary provisions' is defined by Article 10(15) as 'provisions relating to the exploitation of intellectual property rights other than patents, which contain no obligations restrictive of competition other than those also attached to the licensed know-how or patents and exempted under this Regulation'.[210]

Similar provisions were contained in the Patent Licensing Regulation and the Know-how Licensing Regulation. The concept of 'ancillary provisions' in Article 1(1) of the latter Regulation was interpreted restrictively by the Commission in the *Moosehead* decision.[211] There the Commission held that the block exemption granted by the Know-how Licensing Regulation did not apply to an agreement whereby the Canadian brewery Moosehead licensed the British brewery Whitbread to use its know-how to brew beer in the United Kingdom and to sell it under the trade mark 'Moosehead'. The Commission based that interpretation on the use of the word 'ancillary' in Article 1(1) of the Regulation. It stated that 'the principal interest of the parties lies in the exploitation of the trade mark rather than of the know-how. The parties view the Canadian origin of the mark as crucial to the success of the marketing campaign, which promotes the product as a Canadian beer'.[212]

It is regrettable that the Commission interprets so narrowly the concept of ancillary provisions in relation to trade marks. A broader view would go some way to compensate for the Commission's failure to adopt a block exemption regulation dealing specifically with trade mark licences. Moreover, the finding that Moosehead and Whitbread were primarily interested in exploiting the trade mark rather than the know-how seems somewhat

---

[209] OJ 1999 L 336, p. 21.

[210] The definition is criticized by Korah, op. cit. (n. 151), at p. 118.

[211] Commission Decision 90/186/EEC of 23 March 1990 (OJ 1990 L 100, p. 32).

[212] At point 1 of para. 16 of the decision.

arbitrary. The trade mark 'Moosehead' was virtually unknown in the United Kingdom at the time, so the goodwill attached to it was minimal. It could have been argued that Whitbread was primarily interested in gaining access to know-how (in the form of brewing formulas and special yeast) that would give the beer a distinctive Canadian taste.

3.6.3 *The possible application of the Vertical Agreements Regulation*

The Vertical Agreements Regulation replaced three group exemption regulations which dealt separately with agreements on exclusive distribution,[213] exclusive purchasing,[214] and franchising.[215] Article 2(1) of the Regulation declares Article 81(1) of the Treaty to be inapplicable to 'agreements or concerted practices entered into between two or more undertakings each of which operates, for the purposes of the agreement, at a different level of the production or distribution chain, and relating to the conditions under which the parties may purchase, sell or resell certain goods or services'. Article 2(3) provides:

The exemption provided for in paragraph 1 shall apply to vertical agreements containing provisions which relate to the assignment to the buyer or use by the buyer of intellectual property rights, provided that those provisions do not constitute the primary object of such agreements and are directly related to the use, sale or resale of goods or services by the buyer or its customers. The exemption applies on condition that, in relation to the contract goods or services, those provisions do not contain restrictions of competition having the same object or effect as vertical restraints which are not exempted under this Regulation.

The exemption applies only if the market share held by the supplier does not exceed 30 per cent of the relevant market on which it sells the contract goods or services.[216] In the case of vertical agreements concerning 'exclusive supply obligations', the exemption applies only if the market share held by the buyer does not exceed 30 per cent of the relevant market on which it purchases the contract goods or services.[217] The term 'exclusive supply obligation' means 'any direct or indirect obligation causing the supplier to sell the goods or services specified in the agreement only to one buyer inside the Community for the purposes of a specific use or for resale'.[218]

The Commission published 'Guidelines on Vertical Restraints'[219] soon after the adoption of the Regulation. These outline the Commission's policy

---

[213] Commission Regulation (EEC) No. 1983/83 of 22 June 1983 on the application of Article |81(3)| of the Treaty to categories of exclusive distribution agreements (OJ 1983 L 173, p. 1).
[214] Commission Regulation (EEC) No. 1984/83 of 22 June 1983 on the application of Article |81(3)| of the Treaty to categories of exclusive purchasing agreements (OJ 1983 L 173, p. 5).
[215] Commission Regulation (EEC) No. 4087/88 of 30 November 1988 on the application of Article |81(3)| of the Treaty to categories of franchise agreements (OJ 1988 L 359, p. 46).
[216] Art. 3(1).   [217] Art. 3(2).   [218] Art. 1(c).   [219] OJ 2000 C 291, p. 1.

on vertical agreements in general. Paragraphs 30 to 44 deal with intellectual property rights. The Guidelines indicate that commercial franchise agreements will normally meet the conditions set out in Article 2(3) for the applicability of the Regulation, in particular 'where the franchisor sells to the franchisee goods for resale and in addition licenses the franchisee to use his trade mark and know-how to market the goods'.[220] The Guidelines go on to state: 'Also covered is the case where the supplier of a concentrated extract licenses the buyer to dilute and bottle the extract before selling it as a drink.'[221] The Regulation does not, however, cover 'the pure licence of a trade mark or sign for the purposes of merchandising'.[222]

Article 4 of the Regulation contains the equivalent of the 'black list' in the old-style block exemption regulations. The presence of any of the clauses specified in Article 4 deprives the whole agreement of the benefit of the block exemption. In particular Article 4 prohibits restrictions on the buyer's freedom to fix his own sale price. The supplier may, however, impose a maximum sale price or recommend a sale price. Article 4 also prohibits territorial restrictions and restrictions as to the customers to whom the buyer may sell the contract goods or services. The buyer may, however, be banned from making active sales into the exclusive territory or to an exclusive customer group reserved to the supplier or to another buyer, provided that sales by the buyer's customers are not restricted. A buyer operating at the wholesale level may also be banned from making sales to end-users. The members of a selective distribution system may be banned from selling to unauthorized distributors. Members of a selective distribution system operating at the retail level may not be banned from making active or passive sales to end-users, but such members may be banned from operating out of an unauthorized place or establishment. Distributors within a selective distribution system may not be banned from supplying each other.

3.6.4 *The possibility of an individual exemption under Regulation No. 17*

Under the old system, if a trade mark licence could not be brought within the scope of a block exemption regulation, and the parties required the legal certainty of knowing that their arrangements did not fall foul of EC competition law, the only course open to them was to notify the agreement to the Commission and seek an individual exemption (or possibly negative clearance) under Regulation No. 17. That procedure had two major disadvantages: it was time-consuming and it was likely to lead to nothing better than a comfort letter.

---

[220] At para. 35 of the Guidelines.   [221] Ibid.   [222] At para. 32 of the Guidelines.

The Commission's general approach was to be extremely severe—excessively so, it is submitted—when deciding whether a particular clause restricted competition and was therefore caught by Article 81(1), but correspondingly generous when deciding whether the clause satisfied the conditions for exemption under Article 81(3). Thus, in the *Campari* decision,[223] the Commission found that agreements whereby Campari-Milano appointed exclusive licensees of its trade marks in various Member States restricted competition because they prevented Campari-Milano from licensing other undertakings to use its trade mark in the territories concerned. But the notion that the proprietor of a well-known trade mark should license a multiplicity of firms to use the mark in the same territory in order to maintain effective competition is absurd. The *Campari* decision had the excuse that it pre-dated *Nungesser* but the *Moosehead* decision did not. Yet it contained the same dubious argument: 'the exclusive character of the licence has, as a consequence, the exclusion of third parties, namely the five other large brewers in the [United Kingdom], from the use, as licensees, of the Moosehead trade mark, in spite of their potential interest and their ability to do so'. The notion that all the leading British brewers should be allowed to brew beer under the trade mark 'Moosehead' is contrary to economic reality.

Presumably the Commission thought that the logic of *Nungesser* (i.e. that an exclusive licence of plant breeder's rights promotes the dissemination of technology) did not apply to trade marks. It is submitted, however, that the *Nungesser* logic is transposable to trade marks and other forms of intellectual property rights.[224] Without exclusivity, the licensee would be unwilling to invest in plant and advertising in order to develop the reputation of a new mark. The result would be detrimental to investment, to employment, and to competition.

Fortunately, in both *Campari* and *Moosehead*, the Commission recognized the economic advantages of exclusive licences and granted exemptions. But that is beside the point. It should not have been necessary for undertakings which wished to enter into perfectly ordinary business transactions, such as trade mark licences, to subject themselves to the time-consuming procedure of notification and exemption.

As to the permissible degree of exclusivity in trade mark licensing, the Commission's practice has been broadly similar to that outlined above in relation to patent licences, know-how licences, and mixed patent and know-how licences. Thus, in the *Campari* case, Campari-Milano undertook

---

[223] Decision 78/253/EEC of 23 December 1977 (OJ 1978 L 70, p. 69). See also Decision 84/381/EEC of 12 July 1984 (*Carlsberg*) (OJ 1984 L 207, p. 26).

[224] See R. Joliet, 'Trade Mark Licensing Agreements under the EEC Law of Competition', (Winter 1983–84), Vol. 5, No. 4 *Northwestern Journal of International Law and Business* 755 at 799.

not to manufacture Campari Bitter in the licensed territories itself and not to license other undertakings for those territories, and Campari-Milano and the licensees undertook not to pursue an active sales policy in each other's territories, while at the same time agreeing to do everything possible to meet unsolicited orders from those territories. The Commission had no difficulty in exempting the agreements. Arguably a five-year ban on passive sales to other licensees' territories ought to be permitted by analogy with the Technology Transfer Regulation.

As for the likely duration of an exemption obtained under Article 81(3), it is to be noted that Article 8(1) of Regulation No. 17 required the Commission to specify the period for which an exemption was granted. The exemption could be renewed on application if the requirements of Article 81(3) continued to be satisfied.[225] In the *Campari* decision the Commission held that nine years was a reasonable period for the exemption. In *Moosehead* the exemption was granted for ten years. In *Carlsberg* a period of eight years was considered sufficient on the dubious ground that it was long enough for the licensor to build up its own distribution network so that it was no longer dependent on the licensee for the marketing of its output in the licensed territory.

3.6.5 *The appraisal of trade mark licences after the entry into force of Regulation No. 1/2003*

Following the entry into force of Regulation No. 1/2003 the possibility of notifying an agreement to the Commission and seeking an individual exemption no longer exists. Instead the parties to trade mark licensing agreements (like the parties to any other type of agreement) will have to attempt to draft their contracts in such a way that they either lie outside the reach of Article 81(1) or satisfy the conditions of Article 81(3). The parties will then be in a position to argue, in proceedings before the Commission or the national authorities, including the courts, that their contracts are legally valid and enforceable.

To some extent the parties to trade mark licensing agreements will be able to seek inspiration from the Technology Transfer Regulation and from the Commission decisions cited in the previous section. They should not, however, be afraid of arguing that a more liberal, less formalistic approach should be taken to trade mark licensing. On balance, the new system may suit those in business better than the old notification system. Decentralization may be one way of loosening the straitjacket previously imposed on industry by the Commission without necessarily leading to greater

---

[225] Art. 8(2) of Reg. No. 17.

uncertainty. The following comments by serving officials of the Commission's Directorate General for Competition are of interest:

'The abolition of notifications does not entail a loss in legal certainty for companies. This perception is mistaken. By extending validity and enforceability to all agreements that fulfil the conditions of Article 81(3), the new regulation ensures legal certainty for a large number of agreements that remained in a legal limbo under the old system inasmuch as only a minuscule number of agreements were covered by a formal exemption decision of the Commission.'[226]

3.7 Trade mark delimitation agreements

Trade mark infringement actions and opposition proceedings are often settled amicably. Approximately 80 per cent of oppositions against applications to register Community trade marks are, for example, settled by the parties without a decision by the Office for Harmonization in the Internal Market (OHIM). The relevant legislation actively encourages such an outcome by providing for a 'cooling-off period' of two months.[227] If the opposition is settled in that period the opposition fee is refunded and no order for costs is made.

The normal basis of settlement is that the parties agree that their respective marks can coexist by delimiting the goods or services in respect of which each mark is to be used and registered. The parties may agree to use additional distinguishing material in their product get-up as a means of avoiding confusion.[228] Sometimes there will be an undertaking not to challenge the validity of the other party's trade mark.

It is clear from *Bayer v Süllhöfer* that an agreement is not taken outside the scope of Article 81 of the Treaty simply because it is concluded for the purpose of terminating patent infringement proceedings. The same must apply to agreements terminating trade mark infringement proceedings and oppositions at the pre-registration stage. Policy considerations dictate, nonetheless, that such agreements—in particular trade mark delimitation agreements—should be treated as binding and should at least enjoy a presumption of validity. The Community Trade Mark Regulation, which does not provide for any *ex officio* review of relative obstacles to registration, is founded on the assumption that primary responsibility for preventing consumer confusion due to similar trade marks lies with the individuals concerned. The Community's antitrust authorities should not lightly assume that agreements which are ostensibly designed to avoid confusion

---

[226] Gauer, Dalheimer, Kjolbye and de Smijter, op. cit. (n. 24), at 4.

[227] Rule 19 of Commission Reg. (EC) No. 2868/95 of 13 December 1995 implementing Council Reg. (EC) No. 40/94 on the Community trade mark, OJ 1995 L 303, p. 1.

[228] See, e.g., the agreement between Henkel and Unilever concerning the trade mark 'Persil' for washing powder: (1978) 9 IIC 287.

between trade marks are really a device for sharing out markets. Only if there is plainly no likelihood of confusion could such an intention be inferred.

Predictably the Commission has tended to view trade mark delimitation agreements with suspicion, especially when they have been based on a geographical division rather than product delimitation. A number of cases have come to the Commission's attention.

The first case was *Sirdar/Phildar*. A British company (Sirdar Wools Ltd) used the trade mark 'Sirdar' for knitting yarn. A French company (Les Fils de Louis Mulliez S.A.) used the trade mark 'Phildar' for the same product. After the British company opposed the French company's attempt to register 'Phildar' in the United Kingdom on the ground that the marks were confusingly similar, the parties concluded an agreement in 1964 whereby Sirdar Wools undertook not to use the trade mark 'Sirdar' in France and Les Fils de Louis Mulliez undertook not to use the trade mark 'Phildar' in the United Kingdom. In 1973 Sirdar Wool registered its trade mark in France unopposed by Les Fils de Louis Mulliez, which then started to use its trade mark Phildar in the United Kingdom and applied to register it there. Sirdar Wools, which seems to have been determined to have its cake and eat it, brought a trade mark infringement action against the French company and notified the delimitation agreement to the Commission.

The Commission adopted a decision[229] in which it held that the agreement infringed Article 81(1) and was not eligible for an exemption under Article 81(3). The Commission was not impressed by the argument that competition was not restricted because the parties were free to market their products under different trade marks. It gave two reasons for that finding:

(1) the parties would lose the goodwill attached to their existing trade marks; and
(2) parallel imports would be practically impossible if the trade mark on each pack of yarn had to be changed.

As Smulders and Glazener point out,[230] those arguments are unconvincing. Loss of goodwill would be minimal since neither party's trade mark was known in the other's territory. As for parallel imports, they—like direct sales by the trade mark owners—could not have taken place if there was a likelihood of confusion between the trade marks.[231]

The *Sirdar/Phildar* case reveals the essential difficulty in applying Article 81 to trade mark delimitation agreements: it is impossible to judge whether there is an unwarranted restriction of competition without first determining

---

[229] OJ 1975 L 125, p. 27.

[230] B. P. M. Smulders and P. Glazener. 'Trademark Delimitation Agreements and the EEC Rules on Free Movement of Goods and Competition' (1991) 4 LJIL 3, 6.

[231] That point was established one year later in Case 119/75 *Terrapin v Terranova* [1976] ECR 1039; see Chap. 8, section 2.2.3.

whether there is a genuine likelihood of confusion between the trade marks. If consumers are likely to confuse the marks, it is in everyone's interest that the marks should not be used in the same territory. The competition authorities should not attempt to prevent the parties from mutually agreeing on a solution that each of them could obtain judicially. On the other hand, if the trade marks are clearly not likely to be confused, a trade mark delimitation agreement might look suspiciously like a device for agreeing not to compete in each other's territory. Unfortunately, the Commission, which has no experience of handling trade mark oppositions or infringement actions, is hardly qualified to judge whether the likelihood of confusion is genuine. In *Sirdar/Phildar*, however, there was one additional factor that excited suspicion that the agreement was about market sharing as much as the avoidance of consumer confusion. The trade marks 'Phildar' and 'Sirdar' coexisted peacefully in several other Member States and third countries. That was, in fact, expressly provided for in the agreement between the parties. When two parties agree that each will refrain from using its principal trade mark in the home territory of the other but agree at the same time that the two trade marks can coexist in other territories, that does look remarkably like a market-sharing arrangement.[232] That impression would be reinforced if the parties made no serious attempt to compete in each other's territories under different trade marks.

In *Penneys* the Commission granted negative clearance for a trade mark delimitation agreement between J. C. Penney Company (a US corporation) and Associated British Foods Ltd and its related companies. The parties had been in dispute about the trade mark 'Penneys' in various countries. They settled their dispute by an agreement which they notified to the Commission. The gist of the agreement was that J. C. Penney would own the mark in countries other than Ireland, where it would belong to Associated British Foods. The agreement contained a no-challenge clause of unlimited duration whereby Associated British Foods undertook not to contest J. C. Penney's registrations of the trade mark 'Penney' or to use the trade mark even if J. C. Penney ceased to use the mark or allowed its registrations to lapse. The duration of that clause was reduced to five years at the request of the Commission.

On the whole, the Commission's attitude in *Penney* was enlightened. At least it did not attempt to interfere with an obviously reasonable solution adopted by the parties to a genuine dispute over a trade mark that each party was entitled to use in different countries of the world. The Commission none the less revealed its underlying suspicion of trade mark delimitation agreements by stating that the parties to trade mark disputes should 'in general . . . seek the least restrictive solution possible, such as incorpor-

---

[232] Smulders and Glazener, op. cit. (n. 230), at 7.

ating distinguishing marks, shapes or colours to differentiate the products of the two enterprises which bear identical or confusingly similar marks'. The Commission seems to have believed, in the 1970s, that manufacturers of goods should aim to use the same trade mark throughout the Community (presumably so that parallel imports could take place); on this view, if a trade mark conflict arose in a particular Member State the undertakings concerned should tinker with their marks or product get-up, perhaps by means of 'stickering', rather than adopt a different trade mark. It is difficult to see any legal basis for such an obligation. Moreover, as Beier demonstrated in an article published in 1978, it is doubtful whether additional distinguishing matter can protect consumers from confusion.[233]

Persil[234] is one of the rare cases in which the owners of conflicting trade marks have agreed to solve the problem by means of additional distinguishing matter. It surely demonstrates that Beier's scepticism on that subject was justified. The trade mark 'Persil' was owned by Unilever in the United Kingdom and France and by Henkel in Germany, Benelux, Italy, and Denmark. Both firms attempted, in countries where they owned the trade mark, to prevent imports of Persil washing powder made by the other. In correspondence they exchanged promises to do everything possible to prevent their products from entering each other's markets under the trade mark 'Persil'. The Commission concluded that geographical market sharing was taking place and initiated proceedings under Article 81(1).

The proceedings were concluded—to the Commission's immense satisfaction—when Henkel and Unilever agreed to differentiate their trade marks. Henkel would use red letters for the trade mark 'Persil' accompanied by the name 'Henkel' in small letters in a red oval, while Unilever would use a green 'Persil' trade mark.

The Commission, which clearly considered this a shining example of how to settle a trade mark conflict without compromising the integrity of the common market, thereupon terminated the proceedings. It is a pity that no consumer surveys appear to have been done to establish what percentage of consumers believed that red and green 'Persil' emanated from unrelated companies. It is likely to have been extremely low.[235]

The only case on trade mark delimitation agreements that has reached the Court of Justice is *BAT v Commission*,[236] which concerned a trade mark dispute between one of the world's biggest tobacco companies (BAT) and a small Dutch tobacco firm run by Mr Antonius Segers. The latter sought

---

[233] F.-K. Beier, 'Trademark Conflicts in the Common Market: Can They Be Solved by Means of Distinguishing Additions?' (1978) 9 IIC 221.

[234] (1978) 9 IIC 287.

[235] See the comments of Advocate General Jacobs in Case C-10/89 *CNL Sucal v HAG GF* ('HAG II') [1990] ECR I-3711, at para. 43 of the opinion.

[236] Case 35/83 [1985] ECR 36.

protection in Germany for the trade mark 'Toltecs Special' for 'raw tobacco and tobacco products, including fine tobacco products' in Class 34. He encountered an opposition from BAT based on its registration of the trade mark 'Dorcet' for 'raw tobacco, tobacco products and cigarette paper'. The opposition was settled by means of an agreement whereby Mr Segers undertook to register and use his trade mark only in respect of 'curly cut tobacco (shag)' and not to advertise his products as being suitable for rolling cigarettes. He also undertook not to claim any right against BAT arising from registration of the trade mark 'Toltecs Special' even if BAT did not use the trade mark 'Dorcet' for more than five years. In return BAT undertook to withdraw its opposition to the registration of the trade mark 'Toltecs Special'.

Mr Segers subsequently encountered all manner of difficulties when he attempted to market tobacco in Germany under the trade mark 'Toltecs Special'.[237] BAT appears to have believed that the agreement entitled it to determine who should be allowed to distribute tobacco products in Germany under that trade mark.

As a result of those difficulties, Mr Segers complained to the Commission, which adopted a decision holding that the agreement infringed Article 81(1) in so far as:

(1) it prevented Mr Segers from selling fine tobacco in Germany under the 'Toltecs Special' trade mark;
(2) it prevented Mr Segers from challenging BAT's 'Dorcet' trade mark even if it was not used for more than five years.

The Commission fined BAT 50,000 ECUs in respect of the second infringement. The Commission did not fine Mr Segers because he was the owner of a small firm and was inadequately informed about German and Community law. Clearly the Commission regarded Mr Segers—not without good reason—as the victim of bullying by a large corporation not afraid to take advantage of its unequal bargaining power. Although the Court of Justice quashed the fine (for reasons that are not easy to understand[238]), it upheld the Commission's decision on the substance.

One of the most positive aspects of the judgment is that the Court expressly recognized that trade mark delimitation agreements are 'lawful and useful if they serve to delimit, in the mutual interest of the parties, the spheres within which their respective trade marks may be used, and are intended to avoid confusion or conflict between them'.[239]

The *Dorcet/Toltecs Special* case confirms, once again, that the essential difficulty facing the Commission and the Court, when attempting to rule on

---

[237] For a full summary of these difficulties, see the opinion of Advocate General Slynn in *BAT v Commission*, at 365–6.

[238] At para. 46 of the judgment.　　　　　　[239] At para. 33 of the judgment.

the application of Article 81 to trade mark delimitation agreements, is that it is generally impossible to do so without pronouncing on the likelihood of confusion between the trade marks in question. The Commission was quite happy to rule that there was no 'serious risk of confusion' in this case—a view that few would disagree with. The Court, however, managed to avoid expressing a view on that issue by pointing out that BAT's registration of the trade mark 'Dorcet' could have been revoked on grounds of non-use at the time when the agreement with Mr Segers was concluded.[240] Its opposition to the registration of 'Toltecs Special' was therefore 'an abuse of the rights conferred upon it by its trade mark ownership'[241] and the agreement was based on 'a contrived conflict involving trade mark law'.[242] The case demonstrates that, while trade mark delimitation agreements are generally harmless and often in the public interest, they can occasionally be used for anti-competitive practices. That is likely to happen in particular when the parties have grossly unequal bargaining power.[243]

3.8 *Software licensing*

Software licensing raises special problems on account of the nature of software. Software is protected mainly through copyright by virtue of Council Directive 91/250/EEC of 14 May 1991 on the legal protection of computer programs.[244] Article 1(1) of the Directive states: 'Member States shall protect computer programs, by copyright, as literary works within the meaning of the Berne Convention for the Protection of Literary and Artistic Works.'

Since software is merely 'a set of instructions, the purpose of which is to cause . . . a computer to perform its functions',[245] its characterisation as 'literary works' is questionable. It is certainly a very special type of literary work.[246] It is a 'utilitarian tool which must perform certain tasks in a certain environment'.[247] As such, a computer program must be capable of interacting with other programs and with hardware: it must be *interoperable*. Software is also extraordinarily easy to copy, once it is recorded in electronic form, and the copy is usually equal in quality to the original.[248]

---

[240] At para. 35 of the judgment.   [241] Ibid.   [242] At para. 37 of the judgment.
[243] The *Chiquita/Fyffes* agreement seems to be another example of a market-sharing trade mark agreement designed to protect the more powerful party: see Waelbroeck and Frignani, op. cit. (n. 15), at p. 781.
[244] OJ 1991 L 122, p. 42.
[245] See Part I, section 1.1, of the Explanatory Memorandum to the Commission proposal for a Council Directive on the Legal Protection of Computer Programs (COM(88)816 final—SYN 183).
[246] For a detailed account of the special nature of software, see I. S. Forrester, 'Software Licensing in the Light of Current EC Competition Law Considerations' [1992] ECLR 5.
[247] Ibid., at 6.
[248] Jennifer Darbyshire, 'Computer Programs and Competition Policy: A Block Exemption for Software Licensing' [1994] 9 EIPR 374, 376.

Indeed, the normal use of software involves an act of copying, since loading it on to a computer reproduces the object code of the program.[249]

On the face of it, Directive 91/250 grants very extensive rights to the author (or other right-holder) of a computer program. These include the exclusive right to authorize (or not to authorize) 'the permanent or temporary reproduction of a computer program by any means and in any form, in part or in whole', even when the 'loading, displaying, running, transmission or storage of the computer program necessitate such reproduction'.[250] The right-holder may also control the 'translation, adaptation, arrangement and any other alteration of a computer program and the reproduction of the results thereof'.[251] Subject to the usual exhaustion rule, the right-holder has the exclusive right to authorize 'any form of distribution to the public, including the rental, of the original computer program or of copies thereof'.[252]

These exclusive rights are defined so broadly that the purchaser of software requires a licence from the right-holder in order to use it for its intended purpose. Dolmans states: 'End-users need a licence to the extent that use of the software requires a permanent or temporary reproduction of code in the working memory of the computer—which is normally the case when one loads and runs software.'[253] In fact, the end-user will normally acquire an automatic licence by virtue of Article 5(1) of the Directive, which provides: 'In the absence of specific contractual provisions, the acts referred to in Article 4(a) and (b) shall not require authorization by the right-holder where they are necessary for the use of the computer program by the lawful acquirer in accordance with its intended purpose, including for error correction.'

The first seven words of Article 5(1) make it clear that this automatic licence can be excluded by contract. Bizarrely, that is contradicted by the wording of the seventeenth and eighteenth recitals in the preamble to the Directive, which state that the acts of loading and running a computer program and correcting errors cannot be prohibited by contract. Various attempts have been made to explain the contradiction.[254] A rational businessman would not, of course, sell a computer program and prohibit the purchaser from using it. He might, however, prohibit maintenance, and the opening words of Article 5(1) seem to make that possible. Forrester suggests that a clause prohibiting maintenance necessary for use amounts to a tie-in, since the licensee is compelled to acquire both program and maintenance

---

[249] Ibid., at 376.   [250] Art. 4(a).   [251] Art. 4(b).   [252] Art. 4(c).

[253] Meurits Dolmans, 'Software Licensing in Europe—Do We Need a Block Exemption?' in *International Intellectual Property Law & Policy*, Vol. 1, (ed. by H. C. Hansen), Juris Publishing, Inc., Sweet and Maxwell, 1996, p. 412.

[254] See Forrester, op. cit. (n. 246), at 14, and B. Czarnota and R. Hart, *Legal Protection of Computer Programs in Europe—A Guide to the EC Directive*, Butterworths, 1991, pp. 65 *et seq.*

from the licensor, and might therefore be condemned under Article 81(1).[255]

One of the central concerns of the Software Directive is to ensure interoperability. Thus Article 6(1) provides:

The authorization of the right-holder shall not be required where reproduction of the code and translation of its form within the meaning of Article 4(a) and (b) are indispensable to obtain the information necessary to achieve the interoperability of an independently created computer program with other programs, provided that the following conditions are met:
(a) these acts are performed by the licensee or by another person having a right to use a copy of a program, or on their behalf by a person authorized to do so;
(b) the information necessary to achieve interoperability has not previously been readily available to the persons referred to in subparagraph (a); and
(c) these acts are confined to the parts of the original program which are necessary to achieve interoperability.

This wording allows the licensee to develop a competing product. Such a program may connect to the licensed program or with 'other programs'.[256]

4. THE TREATY PROHIBITION ON ABUSE OF MARKET POWER

4.1 *The essentials of Article 82*

Article 82 of the Treaty provides as follows:

Any abuse by one or more undertakings of a dominant position within the common market or in a substantial part of it shall be prohibited as incompatible with the common market insofar as it may affect trade between Member States:
   Such abuse may, in particular, consist in:
(a) directly or indirectly imposing unfair purchase or selling prices or other unfair trading conditions;
(b) limiting production, markets or technical development to the prejudice of consumers;
(c) applying dissimilar conditions to equivalent transactions with other trading parties, thereby placing them at a competitive disadvantage;
(d) making the conclusion of contracts subject to acceptance by the other parties of supplementary obligations which, by their nature or according to commercial usage, have no connection with the subject of such contracts.

Article 82 postulates three essential elements:

(1) an undertaking or group of undertakings must hold a dominant position within the common market or in a substantial part of it;

---

[255] Op. cit. (n. 246), at 14. [256] Forrester, op. cit. (n. 246), at pp. 12, 13.

(2) the dominant position must be abused; and

(3) the abuse must affect trade between Member States.

The first two elements will be examined in the rest of this chapter. As regards the third element, reference may be made to the case law on Article 81 since the requirement of an appreciable effect on trade between Member States has been interpreted in the same way in Articles 81 and 82.[257] According to Jones and Sufrin, there is a tendency to apply the 'structure of competition' test rather than the 'pattern of trade' test in relation to Article 82.[258]

4.2 *Establishing the existence of a dominant position*

4.2.1 *The vagueness of the term*

The term 'dominant position' is notoriously imprecise. The basic concern of Article 82 is to prevent firms which have 'market power' from acting in a manner that is detrimental to competition. This is based on the assumption that a market economy only works if consumers and traders can choose between alternative sources of supply. Competition between the various suppliers will drive prices down and improve the quality of their products and services. A supplier who is insulated from competitive forces will have little incentive to operate at maximum efficiency and will not be compelled to offer attractive conditions of business to his customers.

It follows that the classic test for identifying a dominant position is whether an undertaking holds such power on the market that it is not restrained by competition, or the fear of competition. In *United Brands v Commission* the Court ruled that: 'The dominant position referred to in this article relates to a position of economic strength enjoyed by an undertaking which enables it to prevent effective competition being maintained on the relevant market by giving it the power to behave to an appreciable extent independently of its competitors, customers and ultimately of its consumers.'[259]

The obvious starting point for assessing market power is market share. In *Hoffmann-La Roche v Commission* the Court of Justice observed that market shares of 75 to 87 per cent were 'so large that they are in themselves evidence of a dominant position'.[260] Nonetheless, although it is sometimes casually assumed that a monopoly is the classic example of a dominant position, there is rather more to the assessment than measuring market share in percentage terms. Korah points out that an undertaking can have

---

[257] Jones and Sufrin, op. cit. (n. 5), at p. 255.   [258] Ibid.

[259] Case 27/76 [1978] ECR 207, at para. 65.

[260] Case 85/76 [1979] ECR 461, at paras 53–56 of the judgment.

100 per cent of the market and yet still not enjoy market power if entry barriers are low: 'Even a sole supplier may be constrained by fear of entry and charge only competitive prices where barriers to entry are not high; in which case, the market is already operating competitively.'[261]

4.2.2 *The importance of defining the relevant market*

The concept of the 'relevant market' is always important in competition law because it is impossible to determine whether effective competition exists without first identifying the market on which competition is to be assessed. The concept is particularly crucial for the purpose of establishing whether a dominant position exists. The question 'Does X have a dominant position?' means nothing by itself. It becomes meaningful if, for example, we ask 'Did X have a dominant position on the market for ladies' fashion shoes in the Benelux countries in the second half of 2002?'. There may thus be three elements that together define the relevant market: the products, the territory, and the period.

The classic test for defining the relevant product market is the substitutability test, which can also help to determine the relevant geographical market. Men's shoes are, for example, no substitute for ladies' shoes. A maker of ladies' shoes will not shrink from a price rise for fear that his customers will desert him and start to buy men's shoes instead. Ladies' walking shoes are likewise no substitute for ladies' fashion shoes. Shoes are, however, cheap to transport and retailers will readily look for alternative sources of supply from other countries. The Benelux countries are unlikely therefore to constitute a separate geographical market; a firm that enjoyed a large market share in Benelux could not disregard competition from other countries. The relevant market would have to be defined more widely; it might in fact be the market for ladies' fashion shoes in the European Union as a whole.

The substitutability test has been approved by the Court of Justice in numerous judgments. In *Hoffmann-La Roche v Commission* the Court stated: 'The concept of the relevant market in fact implies that there can be effective competition between the products which form part of it and this presupposes that there is a sufficient degree of interchangeability between all the products forming part of the same market in so far as a specific use of such products is concerned.'[262]

In *United Brands v Commission* the Court stated: 'For the banana to be regarded as forming a market which is sufficiently differentiated from other

---

[261] V. Korah, 'The Concept of a Dominant Position within the Meaning of Article 86' [1980] 17 CML Rev. 395, 396. See also Jones and Sufrin, op. cit. (n. 5), at p. 297.

[262] At para. 28 of the judgment.

fruit markets it must be possible for it to be singled out by such special features distinguishing it from other fruits that it is only to a limited extent interchangeable with them and is only exposed to their competition in a way that is hardly perceptible.'[263]

In the same judgment the Court applied the 'homogeneous conditions' test for defining the relevant geographical market:

The opportunities for competition under Article [82] of the Treaty must be considered having regard to the particular features of the product in question and with reference to a clearly defined geographic area in which it is marketed and where the conditions of competition are sufficiently homogeneous for the effect of the economic power of the undertaking concerned to be able to be evaluated.

. . .

The conditions for the application of Article [82] to an undertaking in a dominant position presuppose the clear delimitation of the substantial part of the Common Market in which it may be able to engage in abuses which hinder effective competition and this is an area where the objective conditions of competition applying to the product in question must be the same for all traders.[264]

The 'homogeneous conditions' test may sound esoteric but it is by no means without logic. Suppose, for example, that the market in ladies' fashion shoes in Europe in general is characterized by very high demand and strong competition between numerous manufacturers and retailers but demand in Benelux is sluggish and 80 per cent of the market is controlled by three manufacturers and a handful of retailers, with no sign that other firms are able to penetrate. There would be a strong case for saying that Benelux is the relevant geographical market. In that scenario, the Benelux market would be so peculiar and apparently immune to external influences, that the obviously correct approach would be to ask whether an undertaking or group of undertakings has a dominant position on the Benelux market in ladies' fashion shoes. To define the relevant geographical market more widely would be illogical.

The temporal dimension of the relevant market is frequently ignored.[265] In one sense, of course, the time factor is always present because a dominant position has to be assessed in relation to a particular period. According to Waelbroeck and Frignani, this is not what is meant when competition lawyers speak about the temporal aspect of the relevant market.[266] They maintain that this concept should only be used to refer to markets that differ substantially according to the time of day (e.g. electricity or public transport, where peak periods or rush hours are followed by periods of relative quiet) or the season of the year (e.g. fruit or the hotel business).

---

[263] At para. 22 of the judgment.   [264] At paras 11 and 44 of the judgment.
[265] Jones and Sufrin, op. cit. (n. 5), at p. 290.
[266] Waelbroeck and Frignani, op. cit. (n. 15) at p. 256.

The traditional approach outlined above may have to give way to the supposedly more scientific methods now espoused by the Commission, such as the SSNIP test. This is set out in a Commission Notice published in 1997.[267] SSNIP stands for 'Small but Significant Non-transitory Increase in Price'. The test invites us to assume that a small but significant increase in the price of product A occurs. We must then ask whether such an increase would cause customers to switch to product B on such a scale that the price rise would be unprofitable. If the answer is in the affirmative, products A and B form part of the same market.

The SSNIP test has its advocates and has been adopted in various parts of the globe.[268] Whether it really is more scientific and objective than traditional criteria such as product characteristics, intended use, and functional interchangeability—which, according to the above-mentioned Commission Notice, are no longer likely to play an important role in the definition of the relevant market—may be doubted. No matter how much economic analysis is practised, the relevant market will remain an elusive concept—resistant to arithmetical calculations and genuinely scientific methodology. Ultimately the assessment will be of a partly subjective nature. This is unfortunate because so much turns on the definition of the relevant market; the more narrowly it is defined, the easier it will be to establish market dominance.

4.2.3 *Entry barriers*

There is much debate about what constitutes an entry barrier. There are basically two schools of thought.[269] One holds that any cost which is higher for a new entrant than an existing operator is an entry barrier. The other takes a much narrower view and holds that many perceived entry barriers are simply the natural result of the efficiency attained by the existing operators.[270] On this view, an undertaking which has a large market share reached that position by being efficient. If the presence of such an undertaking on the market means that it is difficult for a newcomer to enter the market, that should be accepted as part of the reward for being efficient.

The narrow view of entry barriers tends to regard only legal impediments as objectionable entry barriers. The classic example of such a legal

---

[267] Commission Notice on the definition of the relevant market for the purposes of Community competition law, OJ 1997 C 372, p. 5.

[268] Jones and Sufrin, op. cit. (n. 5), at pp. 44 *et seq.*

[269] B. J. Rodger and A. MacCulloch, *Competition Law and Policy in the European Community and United Kingdom*, 2nd edn Cavendish Publishing Company, London, 2001, p. 86.

[270] See, e.g., R. Bork, *The Antitrust Paradox: A Policy at War with Itself*, Maxwell MacMillan, Oxford, 1993.

impediment is, of course, provided by intellectual property rights, in particular patents,[271] design rights, and trade marks. Chicago school economists would, however, regard even these barriers as nothing more than the legitimate reward for innovation and investment. They would presumably be less enthusiastic about entry barriers caused by statutory monopolies (such as the monopoly in funeral services at issue in *Bodson v Pompes Funèbres*).[272] Government restrictions in relation to radio frequencies[273] and take-off and landing slots at airports[274] are examples of entry barriers imposed in order to further some perceived public interest.

Not surprisingly, the Commission and Court of Justice have not adhered to the Chicago school[275] and have tended to adopt a broad view of entry barriers as indicia of market dominance. In *United Brands* the Court made the following observations:

The particular barriers to competitors entering the market are the exceptionally large capital investments required for the creation and running of banana plantations, the need to increase sources of supply in order to avoid the effects of fruit diseases and bad weather (hurricanes, floods), the introduction of an essential system of logistics which the distribution of a very perishable product makes necessary, economies of scale from which newcomers to the market cannot derive any immediate benefit and the actual cost of entry made up *inter alia* of all the general expenses incurred in penetrating the market such as the setting up of an adequate commercial network, the mounting of very large-scale advertising campaigns, all those financial risks, the costs of which are irrecoverable if the attempt fails.[276]

In *Nederlandsche Banden-Industrie Michelin v Commission*[277] the Court found that Michelin's 'lead . . . over its competitors in matters of investment research and the special extent of its range of products' constituted entry barriers that immunized it against competition.[278] In response to the argument that such a finding penalized Michelin for the quality of its products and services, the Court observed that: 'A finding that an undertaking has a dominant position is not in itself a recrimination but simply means that, irrespective of the reasons for which it has a dominant position, the undertaking concerned has a special responsibility not to allow its conduct to impair genuine undistorted competition on the common market.'[279]

---

[271] See, e.g., Case T-30/89 *Hilti v Commission* [1991] ECR II-1439 at para. 71, where the Court of First Instance observed 'Hilti's market power and dominance stem principally from its large share of sales of nail guns coupled with patent protection for its cartridge strips.'

[272] Case 30/87 [1988] ECR 2479.

[273] See, e.g., Commission Decision 89/113/EEC (*Decca Navigator System*), OJ 1989 L 43, p. 27, at para. 8.

[274] *British Midland-Aer Lingus*, OJ 1992 L 96, p. 34.

[275] Jones and Sufrin, op. cit. (n. 5), at p. 298.

[276] At para. 122 of the judgment.

[277] Case 322/81 [1983] ECR 3461.

[278] At para. 55 of the judgment.

[279] At para. 57 of the judgment.

4.2.4 *The role of intellectual property rights in establishing dominance*

The point made by the Court in the passage just quoted is that Article 82 prohibits the abuse—not the existence—of a dominant position. There is no stigma attached to the phenomenon of market dominance and the Court should not be reluctant to recognize dominance and its causes, regardless of whether they are perceived as good or bad.

Seen in this light, the question whether an intellectual property right can by itself confer dominance on its owner should not be controversial. Plainly it can and there is no point in denying such an obvious truth. The simplest of examples serves to prove this proposition. Suppose someone patents, throughout Europe, a pharmaceutical that is capable of curing AIDS. If no other pharmaceutical capable of curing AIDS exists, the proprietor of the patent will inevitably hold a dominant position. The relevant product market can only be defined as the market in pharmaceuticals for success-fully treating AIDS, since no other product could be substituted for the patented pharmaceutical. The patentee would enjoy a legal monopoly on the relevant market throughout Europe and the entry barrier would be insuperable during the life of the patent (unless, of course, someone else developed a non-infringing drug also capable of curing AIDS).

Various authors have recognized this point. Govaere, for example, states:

There are . . . cases in which the enforcement of intellectual property rights funda-mentally affects the definition of the relevant market. This will be so if an exclusive right is granted in relation to a product for which no non-infringing substitutes exist. In other words, the conferring of an intellectual property right in those cases comes down to the grant of a legal monopoly in the relevant market because all competitors can be lawfully excluded. This is a situation which is most likely to occur with regard to patents as the objective of the latter is to confer an exclusive right on a new product or process.[280]

Friden writes: 'The crucial point . . . is the definition of the relevant market. If it can be defined with reference to the supply of products or the provision of services, subject to the right in question, then the right can in practice be said to make the holder dominant . . . such absence of substi-tutes logically implies dominance.'[281]

In spite of the obviousness of the above conclusion, the Court has been strangely reluctant to admit that an intellectual property right can by itself create a dominant position. In *Deutsche Grammophon* the Court stated that: 'A manufacturer of sound recordings who holds a right related to copyright does not occupy a dominant position within the meaning of Article [82] of

---

[280] I. Govaere, *The Use and Abuse of Intellectual Property Rights in EC Law*, Sweet and Maxwell, London, 1996, p. 247.

[281] G. Friden, 'Recent Developments in EEC Intellectual Property Law: The Distinction between Existence and Exercise Revisited' (1989) CML Rev. 193, 209.

the Treaty merely by exercising his exclusive right to distribute the protected articles.'[282] In the same vein the Court stated in *EMI Records v CBS United Kingdom*:

Although the trade-mark right confers upon its proprietor a special position within the protected territory this, however, does not imply the existence of a dominant position within the meaning of the abovementioned article, in particular where, as in the present case, several undertakings whose economic strength is comparable to that of the proprietor of the mark operate in the market for the products in question and are in a position to compete with the said proprietor.[283]

The intellectual property rights at issue in *Deutsche Grammophon* and in the *EMI v CBS* cases were clearly not likely to give rise, by themselves, to a dominant position. Deutsche Grammophon was an important manufacturer of recorded music but there was no suggestion that its portfolio of copyrights was so substantial as to empower it to act as though its competitors did not exist. In the *EMI v CBS* cases the 'Columbia' trade mark for gramophone records was in issue; it was one of numerous record labels present on a market that was characterized by keen competition at the time. In both of those cases the relevant product market was presumably the market in recorded music. The relevant market might, of course, be defined more narrowly as the market in recorded classical music or recorded rock music or jazz (on the ground that the mutual substitutability of the different *genres* is limited by the non-eclectic nature of most consumers' tastes); but it would still be a relatively broad market and dominance would not be so easy to establish.

In *Volvo v Veng*[284] there was a much stronger argument for saying that the intellectual property right at issue automatically conferred a dominant position on its proprietor. Veng was an independent supplier of body panels as spare parts for cars. Volvo, the Swedish car manufacturer, was the proprietor of a registered design in the United Kingdom in respect of body panels for Volvo cars. Veng imported infringing panels (i.e. panels made without Volvo's authorization) from other Member States and sold them in the United Kingdom. Volvo sued Veng for infringement of its registered design. The Patents Court referred three questions to the Court of Justice on the interpretation of Article 82. Essentially, it asked:

(1) whether a car manufacturer who held registered design rights over body panels, and could thus prevent anyone else from making or selling matching parts for the models in question, held a dominant position in the market for such parts;

[282] Case 78/70 *Deutsche Grammophon v Commission* [1971] ECR 487, at para. 16 of the judgment.
[283] Case 51/75 [1976] ECR 811 at para. 36 of the judgment.
[284] Case 238/87 [1988] ECR 6211.

(2) whether such a dominant position was *prima facie* abused if the manufacturer refused to license others to supply such body panels in return for a reasonable royalty; and

(3) whether such an abuse was likely to affect trade between Member States by reason of the fact that the intending licensee was prevented from importing body panels from another Member State.

In a carefully reasoned opinion, Advocate General Mischo argued that question (1) required an affirmative answer. He pointed out that the owner of a particular model who needed to repair the bodywork of his car was obliged to purchase a body panel identical in shape and appearance to the original panel. No substitutable goods existed which did not infringe the design rights of the manufacturer. The relevant market was therefore the market in parts for the model in question and the proprietor of the registered design had a statutory monopoly that was coextensive with the relevant market. With a market share of 100 per cent and an insurmountable entry barrier for potential competitors, that person clearly held a dominant position as a direct consequence of the registered design.[285]

Strangely the Court of Justice chose to deal first with the Patent Court's second question, which it answered in the negative. It went on to identify certain forms of conduct which might, if practised by the proprietor of a registered design for car body panels, amount to abuse of a dominant position. It then noted that the national court had not mentioned any instance of such conduct and held that in view of that circumstance, and having regard to the answer given to the Patent Court's second question, there was no need to answer that court's first question (or the third one either).

The Court's performance in *Volvo v Veng* was extraordinary. The question whether a dominant position exists is surely preliminary to the question whether a dominant position is abused. Presumably the Court thought that the question whether ownership of an intellectual property right could by itself give rise to a dominant position was so horrendously controversial and difficult that it was preferable to say that, even if a dominant position existed, it was not abused simply because the owner of an exclusive right exercised it. If anything though, the latter question was surely the more controversial of the two. Moreover, if the Court was anxious to avoid making unnecessary pronouncements in this field, why did it choose to identify certain forms of conduct not mentioned by the national court and condemn them as abusive of a (purely hypothetical) dominant position?

---

[285] See paras 8 and 14 of the opinion. See also paras 48 and 54 of Advocate General Mischo's opinion in Case 53/87 *CICRA v Renault* [1988] ECR 6039. Surprisingly the Advocate General did not mention Case 22/78 *Hugin v Commission* [1979] ECR 1869 in which the Court had defined the relevant market narrowly as the market in spare parts for cash registers made by Hugin.

The *Magill*[286] case is a further example of the Court of Justice's surprising reluctance to recognize that ownership of an intellectual property right can by itself create a dominant position. The facts are set out in Chapter 5.[287] It will be recalled that Magill published an independent weekly television guide which listed programmes transmitted by the British and Irish television companies. The latter claimed copyright in their listings of television programmes and invoked their copyright in order to prevent the publication of an independent weekly television guide, which they saw as an unwanted competitor for the separate weekly guides that they each published. Magill's complaint was upheld by the Commission, which took the view that the television companies held a dominant position in the market for advance weekly listings of their own programmes and that their refusal to license Magill to publish those listings in its independent guide constituted an abuse of that dominant position.

As usual, much depended on the definition of the relevant market. The television companies allowed newspapers to publish full details of the day's programmes (plus details of the programmes for the following day if it was a public holiday) together with highlights of the week's programmes. They argued that the relevant product market comprised 'all advance programme information supplied to the public on a weekly or daily basis, since there exist[ed] a high degree of substitutability between the various forms of programme information'.[288] RTE (the Irish television company) pointed out that, according to a market survey, only 19 per cent of television viewers used RTE's weekly guide and most viewers relied mainly on the daily press for information about programmes. If daily newspapers with information about television programmes were included in the definition of the relevant market, it would of course be more difficult to show that the television companies held a dominant position.

The Commission and the Court of First Instance found that the relevant product market comprised each television company's weekly programme listings and the television guide in which they were published. The Court of First Instance held that the markets for weekly listings and for the television magazines in which they were published constituted 'sub-markets within the market for television programme information in general'.[289] There was a specific demand for a weekly guide; information covering a 24-hour or 48-hour period was only to a limited extent substitutable.[290]

The Court of First Instance, like the Commission, had no difficulty in holding that each television company held a dominant position in the

---

[286] Joined Cases C-241/91 P and C-242/91 P *RTE and ITP v Commission* [1995] ECR I-808.
[287] See Chap. 5, section 6.
[288] See para. 30 of the judgment of the Court of First Instance in Case T-69/89 *RTE v Commission* [1991] ECR II-485.
[289] At para. 62 of the judgment in Case T-69/89.   [290] Ibid.

market so defined. Whereas the Commission had referred to the broadcast-ers' *factual and legal* monopoly on the production and publication of their weekly listings, the Court of First Instance had no hesitation in recognizing that the real basis for the television companies' dominant position was the *legal* monopoly created by their ownership of copyright in their programme listings. The following quotation is significant:

With regard to the applicant's position on the relevant market, the Court, notes that RTE enjoyed, as a consequence of its copyright in its programme listings, the exclusive right to reproduce and market those listings. It was thus able, at the material time, to secure a monopoly over the publication of its weekly listings in the *RTE Guide*, a magazine specializing in its own programmes. Consequently, the applicant clearly held at that time a dominant position both on the market repre-sented by its weekly listings and on the market for the magazines in which they were published in Ireland and Northern Ireland.[291]

The Court of First Instance was surely right to recognize that the decisive element in the creation of the broadcasters' dominant position was the legal monopoly flowing from their copyright. That is what enabled them to keep a competing product off the market. The factual monopoly—due to the broadcasters' unique knowledge of their own programme schedules—was hardly sufficient to achieve that purpose because the broadcasters made the information available to newspaper publishers so that they could publish details on a daily basis. That was something that the broadcasters evidently found to be in their own interest since it stimulated interest in their programmes. The advantage of copyright protection, from the broadcasters' point of view, was that it allowed them to disclose information about their programme listings for publication on their terms without any fear that the information would be reproduced in a weekly programme guide. The legal monopoly was crucial to their purpose.

When RTE appealed to the Court of Justice, the latter predictably—but without much fanfare—stuck to its traditional case law, observing: 'So far as dominant position is concerned, it is to be remembered at the outset that mere ownership of an intellectual property right cannot confer such a position.'[292] The Court then went on to state that the broadcasters' domin-ant position was due to their '*de facto* monopoly over the information used to compile listings for the television programmes'.[293]

Advocate General Gulmann likewise was happy to recite the old case law uncritically. Moreover, he censured the Court of First Instance on the ground that it appeared 'to have attached decisive weight to the undertak-ings' copyright, an approach which . . . is not in accordance with the case

---

[291] At para. 63 of the judgment in Case T-69/89.
[292] At para. 46 of the judgment in Joined Cases C-241/91 P and C-242/91 P.
[293] At para. 47 of the judgment.

law of the Court of Justice'.[294] He nonetheless agreed with the Court of First Instance's finding that the broadcasters held a dominant position but preferred to base that finding on their factual monopoly.

The Court of Justice's stubborn refusal to recognize that an intellectual property right can by itself confer a dominant position on its proprietor is difficult to understand. The cases of *Volvo v Veng* and *Magill* appear to show that whenever the products covered by the exclusive right are coextensive with the relevant market, a dominant position will ensue.[295] The Court has at least recognized that intellectual property rights can help an undertaking to acquire a dominant position. In *Parke, Davis v Centrafarm*—which was one of the earliest judgments of the Court on intellectual property rights— the Court acknowledged the ability of a patent to contribute to market dominance 'since the existence of patent rights is at present a matter solely of national law, the use made of them can only come within the ambit of Community law *where such use contributes to a dominant position*, the abuse of which may affect trade between Member States' (emphasis added).[296]

The Commission too has long been aware of the ability of intellectual property rights to contribute to market power. One of the classic statements on the concept of dominance, in the Commission's *United Brands* decision, mentioned know-how and registered trade marks as elements that were capable—along with market share, access to raw materials, and capital—of placing an undertaking in a dominant position.[297]

4.3 *Can the exercise of an intellectual property right constitute an abuse of a dominant position?*

4.3.1 *The basic problem*

The idea that an undertaking may commit an unlawful abuse of its domin- ant position by exercising its intellectual property rights is problematical. The very essence of an intellectual property right is that the State grants a limited monopoly to someone for a specific purpose, e.g. to reward

---

[294] At para. 184 of the Advocate General's opinion.

[295] A similar position is taken by Friden, op. cit. (n. 281), at 203. See also Anderman, op. cit. (n. 100), at p. 173. Tritton defends the Court's position in *Magill* by arguing that copyright is only a qualified monopoly, as opposed to an absolute one, inasmuch as it merely prevents third parties from copying the protected material: op. cit. (n. 140), at p. 628. The idea that Magill could have compiled a useful television guide without infringing the broadcasters' copyright, were it not for the latters' *de facto* monopoly over the necessary information, seems far-fetched.

[296] Cited in n. 51.

[297] OJ 1975 L 95, p. 1; [1976] CMLR 28. The Commission also recognized the role of intellectual property rights in helping to achieve a dominant position in the *Hilti* case, where the Commission said: 'Hilti's market power and dominance stem principally from its large share of the sales of nail guns coupled with the patent protection for its cartridge strips.' Commission Decision 88/138/EEC, OJ 1989 L 65, p. 19 at para. 71.

inventiveness, creativity, investment in research, or to help firms to protect their goodwill. The laws governing the grant of intellectual property rights generally involve a balancing exercise. Patent laws, for example, balance the need to reward and stimulate innovation against the need to grant public access to knowledge and to encourage competition in the production of goods. Similar considerations apply to design rights and to copyright. In all these cases the law, as an act of policy, places the intellectual property owner in a privileged position, partially exempting him from competition. It does so with the deliberate intention of allowing him to exploit his statutory monopoly and thereby obtain his just reward.

The objectives of trade mark law are rather different. But here too, one of the underlying aims of the intellectual property right is to allow its proprietor to obtain a fair return on his investment. Branding—to use the economist's term—is the means by which one undertaking can make its goods recognizably different from its competitors' goods and charge a higher price, if the consumer thinks, or can be persuaded, that they are worth it. The public interest is not, of course, neglected by trade mark law, for consumers have every interest in distinguishing between the different products on the market-place. They also have an interest in a system that rewards those who produce the goods and services that correspond to their aspirations.

It is legitimate, then, to ask whether competition law should be allowed to censure the exploitation of intellectual property rights when intellectual property law has itself attempted to strike a balance between public and private interests.[298] Anderman answers the question—correctly, it is submitted—in the following terms:

> . . . it seems to be overly optimistic to expect that IPR [intellectual property rights] legislation by itself can regulate the exercise of IPRs so comprehensively that it meets the objectives of public policy generally and competition policy in particular in relation to markets. The offer of an exclusive right to an undertaking or individual for a fixed period of time by IPR legislation is granted irrespective of the market power of the owner or the quality of the innovation, assuming that minimum standards of qualification are met.[299]

The point is that intellectual property rights are a fairly crude method of rewarding innovation and excellence in the market-place. They are granted on the basis of general criteria, no account being taken of the particular circumstances of each case. Intellectual property legislation cannot address all the concerns that fall within the province of competition law. Above all, intellectual property legislation cannot examine whether

---

[298] Jones and Sufrin, op. cit. (n. 5), at p. 625.

[299] Anderman, op. cit. (n. 100), at p. 249. Govaere, op. cit. (n. 280), at p. 305, answers the question in the opposite sense.

effective competition in a particular market is being damaged as a result of the manner in which a dominant undertaking is exercising its intellectual property rights.

It follows that there is a legitimate role for Article 82 in relation to the exercise of intellectual property rights by dominant undertakings. The problem is to determine precisely what that role should be. Not surprisingly, the Court of Justice has generally taken a cautious approach. It has been reluctant to accept that mere exercise of an intellectual property right can constitute abuse of a dominant position, except in very specific circumstances. In *Parke, Davis* the Court made the following rather obvious statement: 'Although the sale price of the protected product may be regarded as a factor to be taken into account in determining the possible existence of an abuse, a higher price for the patented product as compared with the unpatented product does not necessarily constitute an abuse.'[300]

In *Deutsche Grammophon* the Court said that a difference between the controlled price which a record manufacturer attempted to impose on its distributors and the price of the product reimported from another Member State did not necessarily suffice to disclose an abuse of a dominant position, even if such a position existed.[301] In *EMI Records v CBS United Kingdom* the Court stated that 'in so far as the exercise of a trade-mark right is intended to prevent the importation into the protected territory of products bearing an identical mark, it does not constitute an abuse of a dominant position within the meaning of Article [82] of the Treaty'.[302]

In none of the three cases just mentioned was there much of an argument for saying that the intellectual property owner had abused a dominant position as a result of the manner in which the intellectual property was being exercised. In later cases—notably *Volvo v Veng and Magill*—the Court has been more willing to recognize situations in which the exercise of an intellectual property right can amount to the abuse of a dominant position. Also of interest is the judgment of the Court of First Instance in *Tetra Pak Rausing v Commission.*[303]

In the light of this case law a number of situations may be examined.

4.3.2 *Unfair prices*

Article 82(a) of the Treaty refers expressly to the imposition of unfair purchase or selling prices as an example of abusive conduct. It is obviously necessary to exercise caution before holding that an intellectual property owner has abused a dominant position by charging excessive prices for the protected products. One of the assumptions at the heart of patent law is that

---

[300] [1968] ECR 55, 72.
[302] At para. 37 of the judgment.
[301] At para. 19 of the judgment.
[303] Case T-51/89 [1990] ECR II-309.

the patentee, being in a monopoly position, will be able to sell the patented product at a relatively high price and thus obtain his just reward. It is therefore perfectly normal if the patented product sells at a higher price than similar unpatented products, as was indeed recognized by the Court of Justice in the passage from *Parke, Davis* quoted above. It must also be remembered that for every invention that is successful in the market-place there are many others that fail. That is especially true in the field of pharmaceuticals. No drug company deliberately throws away money on useless research. The problem is that when research projects are started there is no way of knowing whether a profitable drug will emerge or not. The successful products have to pay for the failures; they also have to finance further research, the outcome of which is equally uncertain.

In *Volvo v Veng* Advocate General Mischo inferred from the *Parke, Davis* judgment that 'the "inventor" is entitled to recover not only his production costs in the strict sense and a reasonable profit margin but also his research and development expenditure'.[304] *Volvo v Veng* was concerned, not with patents, but with registered designs in respect of body panels for a car. Research and development costs in the car industry are perhaps not comparable to those of the pharmaceutical industry. Moreover, the problems involved in designing new vehicle models are not of the same order as those faced by biochemists and pharmacologists who strive to combat constantly evolving microbes. The challenges are aesthetic as much as technical. But here too the outlay can be enormous and success is not guaranteed.

A special issue that arose in *Volvo v Veng* was whether a car maker with an exclusive right to make body panels for its own models, by virtue of design rights, could legitimately go on earning the extra profits of a monopolist when it had already—so it is presumed—recovered its research and development costs, or at least a part of them, through the sale of new cars. Advocate General Mischo thought that in principle there was no reason 'why a manufacturer should be prohibited from charging the amortisation to income both from new vehicles and from spare parts, provided that the apportionment is equitable'.[305] He referred nonetheless to an enquiry by the United Kingdom Monopolies and Mergers Commission[306] which had found that the prices of bodywork components were sometimes fixed at an excessively high level.[307]

The Court held in *Volvo v Veng* and in the parallel case decided on the same day—*CICRA v Renault*—that 'the fixing of prices for spare parts at an unfair level' might amount to abusive conduct on the part of a dominant

---

[304] At para. 32 of the opinion.   [305] At para. 33 of the opinion.

[306] The Monopolies and Mergers Commission has now been replaced by the Competition Commission under the Competition Act 1998: see Rodger and MacCulloch, op. cit. (n. 269), at p. 67.

[307] At para. 33 of the opinion.

undertaking.[308] In *CICRA v Renault* the Court added the following, rather significant comment:

> With reference more particularly to the difference in prices between components sold by the manufacturer and those sold by the independent producers, it should be noted that . . . a higher price for the former than for the latter does not necessarily constitute an abuse, since the proprietor of protective rights in respect of an ornamental design may lawfully call for a return on the amounts which he has invested in order to perfect the protected design.'[309]

It might be objected that the Court fails to take into account the need for a sufficiently substantial return from successful designs in order to compensate for less successful ones.[310]

In any event, it is clear that spare parts for cars constitute a special case. Dishwashers and lawnmowers break down and occasionally need spare parts for repairs. But they do not move around on roads regularly colliding with each other and necessitating new 'must fit' and 'must match' body panels. Only cars do that. As Advocate General Mischo demonstrated in *Volvo v Veng*, each car maker has a dominant position on the market in spare parts for its own models. The consumer who invests a substantial part of his assets in a car and needs spare parts for it has no freedom of choice. He is a captive consumer with a unique potential to become a victim of abusive practices. Defenders of *laissez-faire* economics would argue that car buyers take into account the cost of spare parts when deciding which car to buy and that car makers are free to look for a return on investment and a reasonable profit either through sales of new cars or sales of spare parts or a combination of both. The argument is fallacious because consumers probably do not have sufficient data about the cost of spare parts and do not factor that into their calculations. The competition authorities should therefore be willing to protect them if car makers take advantage of their situation as 'captives' and impose unfair prices for spare parts.

The task of determining when a price is 'unfair' is not of course easy. But it is absurd to argue that the task is impossible or that the concept of unfair prices for products protected by intellectual property rights is unworkable.[311] All notions pertaining to the abuse of a dominant position are subjective and difficult to quantify. That is not a reason for giving up and ceasing to apply the law. These are matters that can be determined by the administrative authorities in the usual way, with input from economic experts, cost accountants and so forth, and subject always to judicial review.

---

[308] See para. 9 of *Volvo v Veng* and para. 16 of *CICRA v Renault*.
[309] At para. 17 of the judgment.   [310] Govaere, op. cit. (n. 280), at p. 219.
[311] Such an argument is, however, defended by Govaere, op. cit. (n. 280), at p. 260.

4.3.3 *Refusal to license*

4.3.3.1 *The general rule: a dominant undertaking is not obliged to license*

The general rule in intellectual property laws is that the right-holder is not obliged to license the use of the right by others. The very essence of an intellectual property right is exclusivity. From that position of strength the right-holder is free to negotiate the best bargain he can with those who wish to use his intellectual property. That is how intellectual property functions. That is how, for example, inventors, designers, and authors obtain their 'just reward'. There are, of course, circumstances in which the State intervenes and, instead of an absolute monopoly, grants only a right to a reasonable royalty. Such interventions are rare and normally occur because some overriding public interest is deemed to be at stake. Bently and Sherman, writing on the subject of copyright, explain why compulsory licences are generally an unsatisfactory way of rewarding or compensating intellectual property owners:

. . . in contrast to exclusive property rights, the existence and terms of compulsory licences require some administrative procedure, which is costly and time-consuming when compared to free-market negotiations. Critics of the compulsory licence also complain that the value of a licence can only ever be accurately determined by negotiations in the market-place. It is also argued that compulsory licences unfairly deprive the copyright holder of the most significant element of their rights, namely the right to bargain.[312]

Not surprisingly, the Court of Justice has generally taken the line that Community law does not require the right-holder to grant licences to others who wish to use his intellectual property. To hold otherwise would be contrary to the fundamental principles that the Treaty safeguards the existence of the right and does not call in question the substance or 'specific subject-matter' of the right. In *Volvo v Veng* the Court stated in the clearest possible terms that Article 82 is not a vehicle for imposing compulsory licences on dominant undertakings:

. . . the right of the proprietor of a protected design to prevent third parties from manufacturing and selling or importing, without [his] consent, products incorporating the design constitutes the very subject-matter of his exclusive right. It follows that an obligation imposed upon the proprietor of a protected design to grant to third parties, even in return for a reasonable royalty, a licence for the supply of products incorporating the design would lead to the proprietor thereof being deprived of the substance of his exclusive right, and that a refusal to grant such a licence cannot in itself constitute an abuse of a dominant position.[313]

---

[312] L. Bently and B. Sherman, *Intellectual Property Law*, Oxford University Press, 2001, p. 262.
[313] At para. 8 of the judgment.

4.3.3.2 Magill: *an exceptional case*

If *Volvo v Veng* established the principle that a mere refusal to license a third party is not an abuse of a dominant position, the *Magill* case soon demonstrated that the principle is by no means absolute.

Magill has been dealt with extensively in earlier chapters, to which reference is made for the avoidance of needless repetition.[314] In *Magill* the broadcasting companies relied heavily on the passage from *Volvo v Veng* quoted above. The Court of First Instance attempted to square its ruling in *Magill* with *Volvo v Veng* by pointing out that the broadcasters' refusal to license copyright in their programme listings to Magill excluded competition on the derivative market for weekly television guides. The Court likened that to a car maker's refusal to supply spare parts to an independent repairer. The analogy is false.[315] A refusal to supply the protected product is not the same as a refusal to license a third party to make the protected product.[316] If a refusal to supply is unlawful, the remedy is an order requiring the right-holder to supply the protected product on demand at a reasonable price. If a refusal to license is unlawful, the remedy is a compulsory licence allowing a third party to make the product in return for a reasonable royalty. In both cases the substance of the exclusive right is affected, but it is affected in different ways.

In *Magill* the Court of First Instance and Court of Justice identified the following elements as indicia of abuse:[317]

(1) There was no substitute for a weekly television guide offering information about programmes on all stations.
(2) There was proven demand for such a guide on the part of consumers.
(3) The broadcasters gave consumers no choice but to buy the weekly guides for each station.
(4) The broadcasters' refusal to allow the publication of a composite weekly television guide prevented the appearance of a new product for which there was a demand.
(5) 'There was no justification for such refusal either in the activity of television broadcasting or in that of publishing television magazines.'
(6) The broadcasters, by refusing to license *Magill*, reserved to themselves the secondary market in weekly television guides, contrary to the judgment of the Court of Justice in *Commercial Solvents v Commission*.[318]

---

[314] See Chaps 5 and 10.

[315] See para. 110 of the opinion of Advocate General Gulmann in Joined Cases C-241/91 P and C-242/91 P (*Magill*); see also Tritton, op. cit. (n. 140), at p. 645, and J. Flynn, 'Intellectual Property and Anti-trust: EC Attitudes' [1992] 2 EIPR 33, 53 *et seq.*

[316] R. Subiotto, 'The Right to Deal with Whom One Pleases under EEC Competition Law: A Small Contribution to a Necessary Debate' [1992] 6 ECLR 234, 241; see also P. Crowther, 'Compulsory Licensing of Intellectual Property Rights' (1995) EL Rev. 521, 526.

[317] At paras. 52–56 of the judgment in Joined Cases C-241/91 P and C-242/91 P.

[318] Joined Cases 6/73 and 7/73 [1974] ECR 223 at para. 25.

On that basis the Court of Justice held that the broadcasters had abused their dominant position, by refusing to license *Magill* to reproduce their copyright information, while at the same time reaffirming that 'refusal to grant a licence, even if it is the act of an undertaking holding a dominant position, cannot in itself constitute abuse of a dominant position'.[319]

The Court's attempt to square *Magill* with *Volvo v Veng* is unconvincing. There is a contradiction between the two judgments and it is pointless to deny it. In fact, there is a contradiction between *Magill* and all the case law holding that Community law does not call in question the substance of intellectual property rights granted by national law.

That is not to say that *Magill* was wrongly decided. On the contrary, there is a lot to be said for the Court's consumer-oriented approach. Few will have any sympathy for the television companies. Their attempt to exclude all competition on a derivative market and to deprive the consumer of a product that consumers clearly found useful was deplorable. A practice which meant that Irish television viewers were obliged to buy three separate magazines in order to find out what would be on their screens each week is hard to justify. If intellectual property laws sanction such a result there is clearly something wrong with them. This explains why the law was amended in the United Kingdom following a report by the Monopolies and Mergers Commission.[320] The Broadcasting Act 1990 requires broadcasters to make information about television programmes available to publishers and allows publishers to reproduce the information, either on the basis of a negotiated licence or, if agreement cannot be reached, on terms settled by the Copyright Tribunal.[321]

The problem with *Magill* is not that it was wrongly decided but that the reasoning was incoherent and contradictory. The Commission and both Courts paid lip service to the inviolability of intellectual property rights created by national law. In reality, however, they clearly thought that copyright protection for a list of television programmes was a dubious form of intellectual property. That is what the Courts meant when they said that there was no justification for the broadcasters' refusal to license

---

[319] At para. 49 of the judgment.

[320] *The British Broadcasting Commission and Independent Television Publications: A Report on the Policies and Practices of the BBC and ITP of Limiting the Publication of Advance Programme Information* (1985) (Cmnd. 9614).

[321] Broadcasting Act 1990, ss. 175 and 176. For an example of the application of these provisions, see *News Group Newspapers v ITP* [1993] RPC 173. Bently and Sherman (op. cit. (n. 312), at p. 263) suggest that as a result of the Database Regulations adopted pursuant to Directive 96/9/EC on the legal protection of databases (OJ 1996 L 77, p. 20) the compulsory licence is no longer available since programme listings are protected by the new *sui generis* right and no provision for compulsory licences is made by the Database Regulations (or, one might add, by the Directive). It is true that programme listings seem to fall within the broad definition of 'database' in Art. 1(2) of the Directive. It is clear none the less that neither the Directive nor the Regulations intended to abolish a compulsory licensing scheme that was mandated by *Magill* and expressly adopted by Parliament a few years earlier.

their rights to Magill 'either in the activity of television broadcasting or in that of publishing television magazines'.[322] The same idea was expressed by the Court of First Instance, when it indicated that the broadcasters' copyright was not being 'exercised in a manner which corresponds to its essential function, within the meaning of Article [30] of the Treaty, which is to protect the moral rights in the work and ensure a reward for the creative effort, while respecting the aims of Article [82]'.[323] The reference to 'moral rights' and 'creative effort' seems to be a subtle way of suggesting that the laws of Ireland and the United Kingdom were out of kilter with the rest of Europe in this area.[324] It is difficult to avoid the conclusion that the one truly 'exceptional circumstance', in the Court's eyes, was the existence of copyright in a list of television programmes.[325]

4.3.3.3 *The implications of* Magill: *an essential facilities doctrine?*

Following *Magill* there was considerable debate about the scope of the ruling. Some expressed fears that intellectual property was no longer safe from the Commission's marauding reach; that authors would be compelled to authorize anthologies of their works, that patent-holders would not be able to prevent the subject-matter of their patent from being incorporated into a more complex product; in short, that a judge-made system of compulsory licences would be imposed in defiance of national law.[326]

In fact, there was never much danger of such fears being realized. There are two reasons for that. First, Article 82 only applies to dominant undertakings; so not every poet, inventor, and designer is likely to be coshed by the Commission at the behest of a Magill. Secondly, while it is true that the Community Courts showed scant regard in *Magill* for a right that Irish law characterized as intellectual property, that does not mean that intellectual property rights in general are likely to be treated in the same way. Between

---

[322] At para. 55 of the judgment of the Court of Justice, where reference is made to the relevant paragraphs of the judgments of the Court of First Instance. According to Flynn, op. cit. (n. 315), 'the subtext of the case is one of hostility to the underlying intellectual property rights (the proposition that Irish law was wrong in giving copyright protection to a compilation of factual matter that as a practical question could be expressed in only one way).'

[323] At para. 71 of the judgment in Case T-69/89 *RTE v Commission* [1991] ECR II-485 and para. 56 of the judgment in Case T-76/89 *ITP v Commission* [1991] ECR II-575.

[324] Laddie, J., has suggested that, like the animals in *Animal Farm*, some intellectual property rights are more equal than others and that the *Magill* ruling would not be applied to patents: *Philips Electronics NV v Ingham Ltd and The Video Duplicating Co Ltd*, quoted by F. Wooldridge in 'The Essential Facilities Doctrine and *Magill II*: The Decision of the ECJ in *Oscar Bronner*' (1999) IPQ 256, 258.

[325] H. Calvet and T. Desurmont, 'L'arrêt Magill: Une décision d'espèce?' (1996) 167 *Revue Internationale du Droit d'Auteur* 2 at 45. A similar idea is expressed by H. Cohen Jehoram and K. Mortelmans, 'Zur Magill-Entscheidung des Europäischen Gerichtshofs' (1997) 1 GRUR Int. 11 at 15.

[326] G. Bonet, RTD eur. 29(3) juill.-sept. 1993, 525 at 529.

them, the Courts confirmed all the old case law safeguarding intellectual property rights:

- in the absence of harmonization, national law governs the creation of intellectual property rights;[327]
- the 'actual substance' and specific subject-matter of such rights are protected in Community law;[328]
- refusal to grant a licence cannot in itself constitute abuse of a dominant position.[329]

Some judicial sleight of hand then produced a result that accorded with the judges' sense of justice and reasonableness. The above principles were stood on their heads somewhat but that does not mean that the Court is likely to take similar liberties with more deserving intellectual property rights. Copyright in literary, artistic, and musical works (*créations de l'esprit* in French terminology) as opposed to more utilitarian forms of copyright will not be threatened. Nor will patents and design rights. Trade marks are in any event exempt from the whole *Magill* rationale because compulsory licensing is out of the question.[330]

The better view therefore is that of the numerous commentators who have argued that the *Magill* doctrine will be applied restrictively[331]—only in fact when 'exceptional circumstances' exist. In particular, it is likely to be applied in the field of information technology and telecommunications.[332] It is also liable to be invoked in any area where a dominant undertaking is able to use intellectual property rights to prevent access to ancillary[333] markets. *Magill* belongs to a series of cases in which the Commission has developed an 'essential facilities' doctrine. This concept has been defined in the following terms: 'An essential facility means one to which undertakings require access in order to produce goods or provide services for their customers, but which they could not reproduce themselves without prohibitive expense or inordinate delay.'[334]

---

[327] Para. 66 of the *RTE* judgment at first instance and para. 49 of the judgment on appeal.

[328] Para. 69 of the *RTE* judgment at first instance.

[329] Para. 49 of the judgment on appeal.

[330] Art. 21 of TRIPS expressly prohibits the compulsory licensing of trade marks.

[331] See, e.g., T. C. Vinje, 'The Final Word on Magill: The Judgment of the ECJ' [1995] 6 EIPR 297, 302; Subiotto, op. cit. (n. 316); Jones and Sufrin, op. cit. (n. 5), at p. 407; W. R. Cornish, *Intellectual Property: Patents, Copyright, Trade Marks and Allied Rights*, 4th edn, Sweet and Maxwell, London, 1999, p. 766.

[332] S. M. Taylor, 'Copyright versus Right to Compete: The Judgment of the ECJ in Magill' [1995] 3 CTLR 99, 100; Subiotto, op. cit. (n. 316), at 239; and Vinje, op. cit. (n. 331), at 302.

[333] Also known as 'downstream' or 'derivative' markets.

[334] Wooldridge, op. cit. (n. 324), at 256. One author (R. Greaves, 'The Herchel Smith Lecture 1998: Article 86 of the EC Treaty and Intellectual Property Rights' [1998] EIPR 379, 383) rejects the concept of essential facilities on the ground that it is of American origin. It would surely be better to judge it on its merits.

The essential facilities doctrine is sometimes said to have originated in the _Commercial Solvents_ case.[335] In that case a manufacturer (Commercial Solvents) of a raw material needed for the manufacture of ethambutol, a drug for treating tuberculosis, stopped supplying one of its long-standing customers (Zoja), the reason being that Commercial Solvents had decided to start manufacturing ethambutol itself. The Court of Justice upheld the Commission's decision, holding that Commercial Solvents had abused its dominant position on the market for the raw material by refusing to supply the raw material to its former customer with a view to eliminating that undertaking's competition on the market for the derivative product.

It will be recalled that in _Magill_ the Court of First Instance and Court of Justice attached some importance to _Commercial Solvents_ as a precedent. Of course they glossed over an obvious difference between the cases. Commercial Solvent's dominance was not caused or strengthened by an intellectual property right and the company was not exercising such a right when it cut off supplies to Zoja. The fact that the Courts made an analogy between the two cases confirms that they did not attach any value to the broadcasters' intellectual property rights in _Magill_. The analogy only makes sense if the intellectual property aspect of _Magill_ is disregarded.

The essential facilities doctrine was developed by the Commission in a series of decisions in the 1990s concerning access to port and airport facilities.[336] In _Sealink/B&I Holyhead_ the Commission said:

'A dominant undertaking which both owns or controls and itself uses an essential facility i.e. a facility or infrastructure without access to which competitors cannot provide services to their customers, and which refuses its competitors access to that facility or grants access to competitors only on terms less favourable than those which it gives its own services, thereby placing the competitors at a competitive disadvantage, infringes Article [82], if the other conditions of that Article are met.'[337]

4.3.3.4 Oscar Bronner _and_ Tiercé Ladbroke: _the limitations of the essential facilities doctrine_

The essential facilities doctrine was reined in somewhat by the Court of Justice in _Oscar Bronner v Mediaprint_.[338] Mediaprint had a dominant position on the Austrian newspaper market. It distributed two mass-circulation daily newspapers via a home-delivery scheme that it had set up. Oscar Bronner, the publisher of a newspaper with a much smaller circulation, asked Mediaprint to include its newspaper in the home-delivery scheme but

---

[335] Joined Cases 6 and 7/73 _Commercial Solvents v Commission_ [1974] ECR 223.

[336] _British Midland/Aer Lingus_, OJ 1992 L 96, p. 34; _Sealink/B & I Holyhead_ [1992] 5 CMLR 255 at para. 41 of the decision; _Sea Containers/Stena Sealink_, OJ 1994 L 15, p. 8; _Port of Rødby_, OJ 1994 L 55, p. 52; _Morlaix (Port of Roscoff)_ [1995] 5 CMLR 177.

[337] At para. 41 of the decision.   [338] Case 7/97 [1998] ECR I-7791.

Mediaprint refused. Oscar Bronner commenced proceedings against Mediaprint in the Austrian courts for breach of the Austrian equivalent of Article 82. Guidance from the Court of Justice was sought. The essential question was whether a refusal to admit a competitor to a home-delivery system in such circumstances amounted to an abuse of a dominant position.

The Court of Justice answered that question in the negative. The case is of interest for present purposes because both the Court and the Advocate General commented on *Magill* and on the circumstances in which a dominant undertaking may be required to license intellectual property rights. Advocate General Jacobs emphasized that 'the right to choose one's trading partners and freely to dispose of one's property are generally recognized principles in the laws of the Member States, in some cases with constitutional status'.[339] He rightly pointed to the reasons of competition policy for not, as a rule, forcing a dominant undertaking to share with its competitors facilities that it has developed: if things were otherwise, there would be no incentive for a competitor to develop its own facilities[340] and the incentive for the dominant undertaking to invest in efficient facilities would be reduced if its competitors were, upon request, able to share the benefits.[341]

As regards intellectual property rights, the Advocate General pointed out that the grant of such rights normally involves a balancing exercise, at least when they are granted for a limited period. In *Magill*, however, the limited duration of the broadcasters' copyright was purely notional because the useful life of a programme guide was so short. As a result, the exercise of copyright created a permanent barrier to the entry of a new product on the market.[342] The Advocate General argued that intellectual property rights would generally restrict competition for a limited period only, whereas control over an essential facility might lead to permanent exclusion of competition on an ancillary market.[343] That argument might hold good for patents but with the duration of copyright fixed at 70 years *post mortem auctoris* it looks unconvincing. An entry barrier that might last 100 years or more has an air of permanence about it.

The Court, for its part, interpreted *Magill* restrictively, stating that a refusal to grant access to a home-delivery system would only be an abuse if it was likely to eliminate all competition in the daily newspaper market on the part of the person requesting the service, if the refusal was incapable of being objectively justified, and the service was indispensable to carrying on that person's business inasmuch as there was no actual or potential substitute.[344]

---

[339] At para. 56 of the opinion.
[340] At para. 57 of the opinion. Here it must be assumed that the duplication of facilities would be advantageous to the consumer. Competition law should not seek to duplicate facilities (such as ports or home-delivery systems) purely for the sake of it.
[341] Ibid.   [342] At para. 63 of the opinion.   [343] At para. 64 of the opinion.
[344] At para. 41 of the judgment.

Further evidence that *Magill* will be interpreted restrictively lies in *Tiercé Ladbroke v Commission*.[345] Ladbroke wanted to show live television pictures of French horse races in its betting shops in Belgium. The owner of the copyright (PMI) refused permission. PMI granted the exclusive right to televise French horse races in Germany and Austria to DSV. DSV refused to retransmit to Ladbroke. Ladbroke complained to the Commission, alleging that this amounted to an abuse of a dominant position. The Commission rejected the complaint and that decision was upheld by the Court of First Instance. Some of the Court's reasoning was questionable, in particular that part which dismissed Ladbroke's argument that PMI's policy was discriminatory. The Court held that there was no partitioning of the common market 'since on the basis of its structure, which is determined according to criteria relating to the conditions of competition and, in particular, the pattern of demand on the market in the sound and pictures of races in general, the geographical market is divided into distinct national markets'.[346]

The Court does not explain how the pattern of demand varies. Its finding that the market was not partitioned seems arbitrary. It is interesting to note that the Court could no longer rely on the rationale of *Coditel II* in order to justify separate assignments of broadcasting rights in accordance with national frontiers. In *Coditel II* the decisive point was that television was the subject of national monopolies, which is no longer the case in the digital and satellite age.

As for *Magill*, the Court held that Ladbroke could not invoke that precedent because, far from being barred access to the main betting market in Belgium, Ladbroke had the biggest share of the market, while PMI was not present on the market at all.[347] Moreover, the televised broadcasting of horse races was not indispensable for the exercise of a bookmaker's main activity.[348]

4.3.3.5 *Essential facilities in relation to information technology and telecommunications*

If the essential facilities doctrine is likely to have the greatest impact in the area of information technology and telecommunications, that is because the dominant undertaking's system frequently imposes itself as the 'industry standard'. Anyone who wishes to compete needs to be able to use that system because otherwise his products will not work in conjunction with other products: 'Basically, computer products, such as operating system programs, application programs, CPUs and peripheral devices, interact

---

[345] Case T-504/93 [1997] ECR II-923.
[346] At para. 125 of the judgment.
[347] At para. 130 of the judgment.
[348] At para. 132 of the judgment.

through 'interfaces', which establish the rules for interaction for such components. For various historical reasons, certain companies' interfaces have become established as *de facto* interface standards with which other companies' products must comply.'[349]

The *IBM System 370* case was a classic example of this phenomenon. IBM sold a central processing unit (CPU) called 'IBM System 370'. It also sold software for use with that system. Independent software makers complained about some of IBM's practices. It was alleged that IMB failed to supply other software makers in sufficient time with the technical information needed to permit competing software to be used with System 370. They also complained that IBM refused to supply certain software installation services to users of CPUs not made by IBM. The Commission closed its investigation into IBM's practices when IBM undertook, *inter alia*, to disclose adequate information to competitors in sufficient time to enable them to attach both hardware and software to System 370.[350]

In *Decca Navigator System*[351] the owner of a marine navigation system claimed copyright in certain frequency charts supplied with receivers of radio signals. Other firms started to make receivers that were compatible with the Decca system. Decca sued them for copyright infringement and then, to settle the litigation, granted licences which contained market-sharing provisions. Decca also changed the signals used by its navigation equipment so that receivers made by other firms did not enjoy proper reception. The Commission held that Decca had abused its dominant position on the market for the provision of navigation signals by imposing market-sharing provisions on its licensees and by denying users of competing receivers proper access to its navigation signals.

4.3.3.6 IMS: *must access to the 'industry standard' be granted?*

A recent example of an 'industry standard' protected by intellectual property rights is provided by the *NDC Health/IMS Health* case which, at the time of writing, was still pending before the Court of First Instance. IMS provided a sales monitoring service to the pharmaceutical industry. This service enabled pharmaceutical undertakings to track sales of their products and to ascertain, *inter alia*, how each product performed in each part of the geographical market. IMS, which had achieved a dominant position on that market, used a highly complicated system known as the '1,860 brick structure'. This divided the German market into 1,860 regional segments

---

[349] Vinje, op. cit. (n. 331), at 302.

[350] [1984] 3 CMLR 147; Commission's XIVth Report on Competition Policy, 1984, at pp. 94 *et seq.* See also C. Reed, 'EC Anti-trust Law and the Exploitation of Intellectual Property Rights in Software' (1992) 32 *Jurimetrics Journal* 431.

[351] Decision 89/113/EEC, OJ 1989 L 43, p. 27; [1990] 4 CMLR 627.

which were used to report sales information. The 1,860 brick structure has been characterized by a German court as a database.[352] As such it is protected by copyright pursuant to Directive 96/9/EC. The 1,860 brick structure appears to be regarded as the industry standard in Germany.[353] Any competitor of IMS that attempted to enter the market using a different system would encounter difficulties because the pharmaceutical suppliers are reluctant to work with anything other than the industry standard. NDC entered the market in 1999 with a brick structure of 2,201 segments but that structure was rejected by potential customers, who claimed that the data were not usable unless they could be presented within the format of the industry standard.[354] As a result, NDC requested a licence from IMS. When IMS refused, NDC complained to the Commission, alleging that IMS's refusal amounted to abuse of a dominant position. NDC also claimed that IMS had threatened copyright infringement proceedings against pharmaceutical suppliers who accepted regional sales reports from any third party in a 1,860 brick structure or any derivative one.

The Commission adopted an interim decision under Article 3(1) of Regulation No. 17. The decision required IMS to grant licences without delay to all undertakings currently present on the market for German regional sales data services, on request and on a non-discriminatory basis, for the use of the 1,860 brick structure, in order to permit them to use and sell regional sales data formatted according to that structure.[355] Royalties were to be determined by agreement or, failing that, by independent experts.[356]

IMS challenged the decision in the Court of First Instance. The operation of the decision was suspended by an order of the President of the Court of First Instance.[357] That order was confirmed by the President of the Court of Justice.[358] Quite apart from the substantive issues, the case is of great interest because of the approach taken by the judges in relation to interim measures in the field of competition law and intellectual property. Basically, the judges considered that the balance of interests militated in favour of a suspension. There was a risk that IMS would suffer serious and irreparable

---

[352] See para. 36 of Commission Decision 2001/165/EC of 3 July 2001 (Case COMP D3/38.044—*NDC Health/IMS Health*: interim measures), OJ 2002 L 59, p. 18.

[353] Ibid., at paras 86–92.

[354] Ibid., at para. 20. One of the issues is that industry needs a standard. IMS's 1,860 brick structure became the standard, not necessarily because of its inherent advantages, but because it was available and because the pharmaceutical companies had helped to develop it and had a vested interest in preserving it: M. R. Patterson, 'Inventions, Industry Standards, and Intellectual Property' (2002) *Berkeley Technology Law Journal*, Issue 17:3, footnote 115 and the accompanying text.

[355] Art. 1 of the Decision cited in n. 352.   [356] Art. 2 of the Decision.

[357] Case T-184/01 R [2001] ECR II-3193.

[358] Case C-481/01 P(R) [2002] ECR I-3401.

damage if it was forced to give its competitors access to the 1,860 brick structure while the legality of the Commission's decision was being challenged in court. Since the abusive nature of IMS's conduct was not certain in the light of the case law, its copyright should be preserved without impairment until judgment in the main action.[359]

As to the substantive issues, the IMS case gives the Court of First Instance an excellent opportunity to develop and clarify the existing case law. Essentially, the Court will have to decide whether there are 'exceptional circumstances' to justify derogating from the general rule that intellectual property owners are not required to license other undertakings that wish to compete with them. The exceptional circumstances do not have to be the same as in *Magill*. Thus the fact that no new product is being kept off the market does not necessarily mean that IMS has not abused its dominant position. The exceptional circumstances invoked by the Commission are as follows:

(1) IMS has created, in collaboration with the pharmaceutical industry over a long period of time, a brick structure which has become the *de facto* industry standard for the presentation of regional data services.
(2) IMS is excluding all competition from the market for regional data services by refusing 'without objective justification' to license the structure to competitors.[360]

The Commission's statement that IMS's refusal to license lacks any objective justification is controversial. It assumes that the intellectual property owner who occupies a dominant position is obliged to justify a refusal to license and that the mere desire to retain the exclusivity conferred by the intellectual property right is not in itself a sufficient justification. Such assumptions were, of course, made by the Community Courts in *Magill*. It remains to be seen whether they will take the same attitude in *IMS*, where the intellectual property right in issue appears to be rather more substantial and more deserving of protection.

4.3.4 *Refusal to supply*

The *Commercial Solvents* case established that a refusal to supply is capable of infringing Article 82. Since then the principle has been reaffirmed in a number of cases. One of the abuses for which the United Brands Corporation (UBC) was condemned was its decision to cut off supplies of bananas to its Danish distributor (Olesen) when the latter took part in an advertising campaign for a rival brand. Although intellectual property rights were

---

[359] At para. 144 of the order in Case T-184/01 R.   [360] At para. 180 of the Decision.

not in issue, the Court's reasoning is worth quoting *in extenso* because it illustrates the anti-business culture that has at times pervaded the Court:

Although it is true, as the applicant points out, that the fact that an undertaking is in a dominant position cannot disentitle it from protecting its own commercial interests if they are attacked, and that such an undertaking must be conceded the right to take such reasonable steps as it deems appropriate to protect its said interests, such behaviour cannot be countenanced if its actual purpose is to strengthen this dominant position and abuse it.

Even if the possibility of a counter-attack is acceptable that attack must still be proportionate to the threat taking into account the economic strength of the undertakings confronting each other.

The sanction consisting of a refusal to supply by an undertaking in a dominant position was in excess of what might, if such a situation were to arise, reasonably be contemplated as a sanction for conduct similar to that for which UBC blamed Olesen.

In fact UBC could not be unaware of [the] fact that by acting in this way it would discourage its other ripener/distributors from supporting the advertising of other brand names and that the deterrent effect of the sanction imposed upon one of them would make its position of strength on the relevant market that much more effective.

Such a course of conduct amounts therefore to a serious interference with the independence of small and medium sized firms in their commercial relations with the undertaking in a dominant position and this independence implies the right to give preference to competitors' goods.[361]

Quite why UBC should go on supplying a customer who was advertising a competitor's product is not easy to see. The Court says that UBC's response to Olesen's conduct was disproportionate but it does not indicate what steps would have been proportionate and 'reasonable' as a way of 'protecting its own commercial interests if they are attacked'. The statement in the above extract that 'such behaviour cannot be countenanced if its actual purpose is to strengthen this dominant position and abuse it' is self-serving and circular. What evidence was there that UBC's decision to cut off supplies to Olesen was intended to strengthen UBC's dominant position rather than simply maintain it? Did the Court not display bias, or at least a lack of judicial objectivity, by assuming at the start of its analysis that UBC's purpose was to abuse its dominant position?

Another leading case on refusal to supply is *Hugin v Commission*.[362] Hugin, a Swedish manufacturer of cash registers, had only 12 per cent of the EC market in cash registers. Hugin decided to stop supplying cash registers or spare parts to Lipton, a small English firm which sold, rented, serviced, and repaired cash registers. This was held by the Commission to constitute an abuse of Hugin's dominant position on the market in spare

---

[361] At paras 189–193 of the judgment.   [362] Cited in n. 285.

parts for Hugin cash registers.[363] The spare parts at issue in *Hugin* were the subject of design rights in the United Kingdom. In *Volvo v Veng* and *CICRA v Renault* the Court confirmed that an 'arbitrary refusal to deliver spare parts to independent repairers' is abusive conduct on the part of a dominant undertaking.

In principle, the question whether a refusal to supply is an abuse does not depend on whether the products are protected by intellectual property rights.[364] The only difference is that if one accepts the narrow definition of the relevant market used in *Hugin* and in the *Volvo* and *Renault* cases, the result must be that whenever spare parts are protected by design rights, the manufacturer will automatically be deemed to be in a dominant position; as such he will be required to supply spare parts to independent repairers of his equipment, unless he can show that a refusal to supply is not arbitrary. One way of justifying a refusal might be to show that the repairer does not have the expertise or resources to carry out repairs satisfactorily. A reputable car maker might have grounds for refusing to supply spare parts to a back-street garage. That would hardly be arbitrary.

On a more general level, it might also be argued that the competition authorities should not blindly assume that the consumer invariably benefits from the existence of independent repairers. Hugin wanted to integrate vertically. Its aim was to set up a network of subsidiaries and authorized dealers which alone would be entitled to receive spare parts. They would thus monopolize the 'downstream' market in servicing cash registers. But was competition really threatened by such arrangements since Hugin had only 12 per cent of the market in cash registers? The car market, of course, is thought of as a special case (mainly perhaps because of our peculiarly emotional relationship to the motor car). One striking feature of the car market is that, in spite of constant mergers, it remains ferociously competitive. With a number of manufacturers desperately fighting for market share, it is not surprising that some commentators ask whether any real damage is done to consumers' interests if each maker has an exclusive right to make spare parts for its models and supply them only to its authorized dealers. Commenting on the *Hugin* case, Jones and Sufrin state: 'It seems that the Commission's objective was Lipton's continued presence on the market: the protection of competitors rather than competition.'[365] This is

---

[363] Commission Decision 78/68/EEC (*Hugin/Lipton*), OJ 1978 No L 22, p. 23. The Court of Justice annulled the decision on the ground that trade between Member States was not affected appreciably, without ruling on whether Hugin's conduct was abusive.

[364] Tritton, op. cit. (n. 140), at p. 652.

[365] Jones and Sufrin, op. cit. (n. 5), at p. 385. The same point was made by Advocate General Jacobs in *Oscar Bronner* (at para. 58 of the opinion). His comments were cited approvingly by the President of the Court of First Instance in *IMS Health* (at para. 145 of the order in Case T-184/01 R).

an important point. The preservation of independent repairers is not an end in itself. It is only desirable if, on balance, it is beneficial to consumers.

In the *Volvo* and *Renault* cases the Court also cited as an instance of abusive conduct 'a decision no longer to produce spare parts for a particular model even though many cars of that model remain in circulation'. Such a decision might be characterized as a general refusal to supply. It differs from a selective refusal to supply in two respects. First, it is less likely to be condemned as arbitrary and discriminatory, since it affects all potential purchasers in the same degree. Secondly, the remedy is likely to be a compulsory licence, whereas the remedy for a selective refusal to supply will normally be an order to supply the customer in question.[366]

4.3.5 *Excessive royalties: the role of copyright collection societies*

If a refusal to license can be an abuse, it is obvious that an offer to license in return for a manifestly unrealistic royalty can also be an abuse: if the royalty is set at such a rate that no one is likely to take a licence, it is in effect a refusal to license.

The issue of excessive royalties has arisen above all in relation to copyright collection societies.[367] The nature of these organizations needs briefly to be explained. They owe their existence to the fact that typical copyright owners (e.g. songwriters and performers) have little economic leverage as individuals, especially in relation to the companies that exploit their works. Such persons can only gain strength by acting collectively. That explains why copyright collecting societies were formed. Their function is to negotiate on behalf on their members, to collect royalties for them and to pursue infringers. The essential characteristic of copyright collecting societies is that they are able to negotiate and act without consulting individual members because, as a rule, the copyright owners assign their rights to the society.[368] Copyright collecting societies are in effect trade unions for copyright owners. Like trade unions, their existence is justified and necessary as a means of compensating for the weakness and vulnerability of their individual members. Like trade unions, their collective power can sometimes be so great that they are in a position to act oppressively not only towards the economic forces against which they are supposed to protect their members but also against those very members.[369]

---

[366] Tritton suggests that the dominant undertaking should simply be ordered to 'cease and desist its abusive behaviour'. It could then choose whether to supply spare parts or license the independent repairer: op. cit. (n. 140), at p. 652.

[367] Also known as 'copyright management societies'.

[368] Bently and Sherman, op. cit. (n. 312), at p. 268.

[369] For a critique of copyright collecting societies, see H. Cohen Jehoram, *The Future of Copyright Collecting Societies* [2001] EIPR 134.

It is not surprising therefore that efforts have been made to control the activities of copyright collecting societies, both nationally and at European level. In the United Kingdom the Copyright Tribunal has the power to review licensing schemes operated by collecting societies.[370]

As regards European law, Article 82 is the obvious vehicle for restricting the activities of collecting societies. It is normally taken for granted that copyright collecting societies have a dominant position. The niceties of defining the relevant market are often dispensed with. In fact, a copyright collecting society provides different services to different people. To its members it provides the service of managing their copyrights. To its clients it provides the service of licensing the use of works protected by copyright. On both markets it will in normal circumstances have a near monopoly. There is no room for more than one society in any particular area. So dominance seems inevitable.

The question whether collecting societies abuse their dominance by charging excessive royalties was raised in *Basset v SACEM*[371] and, a few years later, in *Ministère Public v Tournier*[372] and *Lucazeau v SACEM*.[373] All those cases arose out of the activities of SACEM, of which Mr Tournier was the director. SACEM was the French organization that looked after the rights of authors, composers, and publishers. One of the issues was whether SACEM had abused its dominant position by charging excessive royalties in return for allowing discotheques in France to use its repertory of recorded music. SACEM charged discotheques in France a royalty of 8.25 per cent of their gross receipts (of which 1.65 per cent was in respect of a 'supplementary mechanical reproduction right').[374] In 1978 there began 'a determined revolt by a minority of French discotheque owners against the terms required by SACEM for the use of its repertory'.[375] This led to litigation, which culminated in references to the Court of Justice for preliminary rulings. In *Basset v SACEM* the Court of Justice ruled that: 'It is not impossible . . . that the amount of the royalty, or of the combined royalties, charged by the copyright-management society may be such that Article [82] applies.'[376] The Court went on to note that the national court had already decided that the royalties charged by SACEM were not unfair.

In both *Tournier* and *Lucazeau* the Court was asked to rule, *inter alia*, on the question whether a copyright collecting society abused its dominant

---

[370] See ss. 116 *et seq.* of the Copyright, Designs and Patents Act 1988. For further information see Bently and Sherman, op. cit. (n. 312), at pp. 289 *et seq.*

[371] Case 402/85 [1987] ECR 1747. [372] Case 395/87 [1989] ECR 2521.

[373] Joined Cases 100/88, 241/88 and 242/88 [1989] ECR 2811.

[374] This is discussed in Chap. 10 in connection with the *Basset* case.

[375] See para. 13 of the opinion of Advocate General Jacobs in *Tournier* and *Lucazeau*.

[376] At para. 19 of the judgment.

position by charging a royalty that was much higher than the royalty charged by equivalent organizations in other Member States.

The information brought to the Court's attention in those cases suggests that SACEM's royalties were indeed excessive to the point of being abusive. According to a survey carried out by the Commission, a typical French discotheque could expect to pay fifteen times as much in royalties as a similar German discotheque and eight times as much as its equivalent in the United Kingdom.[377] Moreover, a remarkably small proportion of the total revenue raised by SACEM was distributed to the society's members.[378] SACEM's administrative costs appear to have been exceptionally high. This was noted by the Court, which observed pointedly that 'the possibility cannot be ruled out that it is precisely the lack of competition on the market in question that accounts for the heavy burden of administration and hence the high level of royalties'.[379]

The Court ruled as follows:

Article [82] of the Treaty must be interpreted as meaning that a national copyright-management society holding a dominant position in a substantial part of the Common Market imposes unfair trading conditions where the royalties which it charges to discothèques are appreciably higher than those charged in other Member States, the rates being compared on a consistent basis. That would not be the case if the copyright-management society in question were able to justify such a difference by reference to objective and relevant dissimilarities between copyright manage-ment in the Member States concerned and copyright management in the other Member States.

The legitimacy of using a comparison with charges in other Member States cannot be doubted. Since SACEM held an unchallengeable monopoly in France, there was no other point of reference. The only measure of the reasonableness of its charges lay in a comparison with royalties charged by equivalent organizations in other Member States. What is surprising is the choice of the adverb 'appreciably' in the Court's ruling. To hold that a collecting society's royalties are abusive merely because they are *appreciably* higher than those being charged in other Member States is surely going too far. It was certainly going further than necessary in the light of the facts of the cases and the wording of the questions referred to the Court of Justice. In *Tournier* the national court asked whether it was abusive to fix a royalty 'several times greater than' that applied in other Member States. In *Lucazeau* the national court referred to the royalty being 'manifestly higher' than in other countries. If the Court of Justice had inserted one of those expressions into its ruling, the result would have been acceptable. But 'appreciably

---

[377] See para. 61 of the Advocate General's opinion.
[378] See para. 58 of the Advocate General's opinion.
[379] At para. 42 of the judgment in *Tournier* and para. 29 of the judgment in *Lucazeau*.

higher' is the wrong criterion; it appears to impose a *de facto* harmonization of royalties for which there is no legislative basis. The fixing of royalties depends on several factors: notably, the relative bargaining power of the collecting society and the discotheque owners, the differing traditions and practices in the Member States, the different bases of calculation and so forth. It would be astonishing if there were no appreciable differences between the royalties charged in the Member States. Admittedly the Court allows the collecting society whose rates are appreciably higher to rebut the presumption of abuse by showing that there are 'objective and relevant dissimilarities' between copyright management in the Member States concerned. It is difficult to see why any collecting society should be subjected to such a burden simply because its rates are appreciably higher than in other countries. The obligation to justify a disparity should only arise if the disparity is considerable.

As part of their campaign against SACEM, the French discotheque owners had lodged a complaint with the Commission alleging that SACEM was infringing Articles 81 and 82, in particular by charging excessive royalties. The Commission rejected the complaint on the ground that there was no Community interest involved, having regard to the principles of subsidiarity and decentralization, since the contested practices were essentially national and the matter was already before the French courts. The Commission's refusal was upheld by the Court of First Instance[380] and by the Court of Justice.[381] This does not mean that SACEM's activities did not have an appreciable effect on trade between Member States. Not all restrictions and practices that have such an effect have to be investigated by the Commission. The principle laid down in *Automec v Commission* ('*Automec II*')[382] is that the Commission only has to deal with the most important cases.[383]

It appears in any event that, following the judgments in *Thurnier* and *Lucazeau*, the excessive differences in royalties have been reduced, though SACEM's are still higher than those of most of the equivalent organizations in other Member States.[384]

4.3.6 *Discrimination on grounds of nationality*

There are two express Treaty provisions that might be invoked against a dominant undertaking if it practised discrimination on grounds of

---

[380] Case T-114/92 *BENIM v Commission* [1995] ECR II-147.

[381] Case C-91/95 P *Tremblay v Commission* [1996] ECR I-5547.

[382] Case T-24/90 [1992] ECR II-2223.

[383] P. L. C. Torremans and I. A. Stamatoudi, 'Collecting Societies: Sorry, the Community is no longer interested!' (1997) 22 EL Rev. 352, 355.

[384] Ibid., at 357.

nationality: namely, the general prohibition of such discrimination laid down in Article 12 and the specific provisions against 'applying dissimilar conditions to equivalent transactions' in Article 82(2)(c).

Both provisions were cited by the Commission in its *GVL* decision.[385] There the Commission held that a German copyright collection society had abused its dominant position by refusing to manage the rights of performing artists who were nationals of Member States other than Germany unless they were resident in Germany. The Court of Justice upheld the Commission's decision but without indicating expressly whether the discrimination practised by GVL was caught by Article 12 or by Article 82(2)(c).[386]

In an earlier decision[387] the Commission held that another German copyright collecting society (GEMA) had abused its dominant position by refusing to accept the nationals of other Member States as ordinary members.

4.3.7 *Charging a flat-rate royalty regardless of actual use of a service*

In the *Grüne Punkt* case the Commission found that a German company called Der Grüne Punkt – Duales System Deutschland AG (DSD) had abused its dominant position on the market for recovering used sales packaging from consumers in Germany. DSD organizes the recovery and recycling of such packaging. To that end it registered a logo known as 'Der Grüne Punkt' (the green dot) as a collective trade mark. Manufacturers and distributors who wish to take part in the system obtain a licence from DSD to place the logo on their products. Packaging with the logo is collected in special containers close to private households and taken to recycling plants by companies under contract to DSD. Participation in this scheme means that the undertakings concerned are exempted from a statutory requirement, under German law, to take packaging back from consumers, free of charge, at or near the point of sale. The licensing agreement which DSD requires the participating undertakings to sign provides for the payment of a licence fee in respect of all packaging bearing the logo. The fee is calculated on the basis of the weight of the packaging, the type of material used, and the volume and surface area of the packaging. The undertakings are required to use the logo on all registered packaging.

DSD notified the scheme to the Commission with a view to obtaining an exemption or negative clearance. The Commission adopted a decision in which it considered that DSD was abusing its dominant position by requiring undertakings to affix the green dot logo to all registered packaging and

[385] Decision 81/1030/EEC of 29 October 1981 (OJ 1981 L 370, p. 49).
[386] Case 7/82 *GVL v Commission* [1983] ECR 483.
[387] Decision 71/224/EEC of 2 June 1971 (OJ 1971 L 134, p. 15).

by charging the licence fee in respect of all the packaging on which the logo was placed regardless of whether the packaging was collected by DSD or not.[388] The gist of the Commission's argument is that undertakings that participate in the scheme are deterred from using a competing service for part of their packaging because they would in effect be paying twice for the same service. The Commission ordered DSD to bring the infringement to an end immediately. In particular, the Commission required DSD to undertake *vis-à-vis* all parties to the licensing agreement not to charge any licence fee for quantities of sales packaging carrying the green dot logo for which the collection service is not used.[389]

DSD challenged the Commission's decision in the Court of First Instance and applied for suspension of the operation of Article 3 of the decision. The President of the Court of First Instance refused the application for suspension by order of 15 November 2001 on the grounds that the applicant had not proved that there was a danger it would suffer serious and irreparable damage without a suspension and that the balance of interests leaned in favour of not suspending the decision.[390] At the time of writing the action for annulment brought by DSD was still pending.

4.3.8 *Strengthening a dominant position by acquiring intellectual property rights*

In *Tetra Pak Rausing v Commission*[391] the Court of First Instance upheld a Commission decision finding that Tetra Pak had abused its dominant position on the market for packaging milk by buying a company which owned an exclusive licence to exploit a patent for important technology relating to the sterilization of milk cartons. The abuse lay in the fact that Tetra Pak had strengthened its dominant position by acquiring an exclusive right over the new technology, which would alone have enabled another undertaking to compete with Tetra Pak. The fact that the patent licensing agreement was itself exempt from the prohibition laid down in Article 81(1) by virtue of the Patent Licensing Regulation was held to be irrelevant.

4.3.9 *Blocking parallel imports from outside the European Union*

As a result of the principle of EEA-wide exhaustion, the owner of an intellectual property right will not be able to block parallel imports of goods that he has marketed within the EEA. He can, however, rely on his intellectual property rights to prevent the importation into the European

---

[388] Decision 2001/463/EC of 20 April 2001 (OJ 2001 L 166, p. 1).
[389] Art. 3 of the decision.
[390] Case T-151/01 R *Der Grüne Punkt – DSD v Commission* [2001] ECR II-3295.
[391] Case T-51/89 [1990] ECR II-309.

Union of goods that he has marketed outside the EEA.[392] Such a practice does not call in question the unity of the common market.

That does not, however, preclude the application of Article 82 to a dominant undertaking which uses its intellectual property rights to prevent parallel imports of its own goods into Europe. Surprisingly, the Commission seems to have thought otherwise, at least until the judgment of the Court of First Instance in *Micro Leader Business v Commission*.[393] The case arose out of Microsoft's attempts to prevent copies of French-language software that it had marketed in Canada from being imported into France. Microsoft issued a newsletter to its dealers in France stating that certain distributors had been distorting its market by selling Microsoft products in France at markedly lower prices than those generally found. The newsletter added that action had been taken to prevent such 'unfair competition' and to 'stem such illegal imports'.[394] Micro Leader Business had been selling Microsoft products in France which it imported from Canada. As a result of Microsoft's action it was no longer able to do so. Micro Leader Business complained to the Commission, arguing that Microsoft had infringed Articles 81 and 82 of the Treaty. The Commission adopted a decision rejecting the complaint on the ground that no infringement of EC competition law had been committed.

The Commission's decision contains the remarkable understatement: 'It cannot be ruled out that an inquiry conducted by DG IV might be able to establish that Microsoft holds a dominant position on one or more software markets.'[395] The Commission thought that even then Microsoft could not have abused its dominant position because its prohibition of parallel imports was a lawful enforcement of its copyright under Article 4(c) of Council Directive 91/250. The Commission's position seems to have been based on a misunderstanding of the *Silhouette* judgment.[396]

The Court of First Instance annulled the Commission's decision on the ground that, while the enforcement of copyright as a means of preventing the copyright-holder's own goods from entering the European Union was not *per se* contrary to Article 82, it might involve abusive conduct 'in exceptional circumstances'.[397] Interestingly, the Court cited the *Magill* judgment on that point. Although the facts are very different, the principle is perhaps the same: a *prima facie* lawful exercise of copyright may be an abuse of a dominant position in exceptional circumstances.

---

[392] See Chap. 7 on the exhaustion of rights.   [393] Case T-198/98 |1999| ECR II-3989.
[394] See para. 2 of the judgment.
[395] At para. 50. DG IV was the Commission department responsible for competition. It is now called the 'Directorate General for Competition'.
[396] Case C-355/96 *Silhouette v Hartlauer* |1998| ECR I-4799.
[397] At para. 56 of the judgment.

The judgment in *Micro Leader Business* has the potential to mitigate the effects of the *Silhouette* ruling to the effect that a trade mark owner may treat imports into Europe of his own genuine goods as trade mark infringements. If the trade mark owner has a dominant position on the relevant market, such use of trade mark rights to wall off the European market against parallel imports might be treated as abusive.[398] Unfortunately the recourse to the *Magill* case law and the concept of 'exceptional circumstances' means that it will be difficult to say when Article 82 operates as a way of bringing in international exhaustion through the back door.

[398] This possibility was envisaged by Advocate General Jacobs in his opinion in *Silhouette* (at para. 53).

Index